ULTIMATE AMERICAN FARM TRACTOR DATA BOOK
NEBRASKA TEST TRACTORS 1920-1960

LORRY DUNNING

Publishing Company

Dedication

To my wife Beverly,
who has given her support and endurance, tending to family and grandchildren, through
the many long days and nights while this book was in progress. It is greatly appreciated!

First published in 1999 by MBI Publishing Company, 729 Prospect Avenue, PO Box 1, Osceola, WI 54020-0001 USA

© Lorry Dunning, 1999

The information in this book is true and complete to the best of our knowledge. All recommendations are made without any guarantee on the part of the author or Publisher, who also disclaim any liability incurred in connection with the use of this data or specific details.
We recognize that some words, model names and designations, for example, mentioned herein are the property of the trademark holder. We use them for identification purposes only. This is not an official publication.

MBI Publishing Company books are also available at discounts in bulk quantity for industrial or sales-promotional use. For details write to Special Sales Manager at Motorbooks International Wholesalers & Distributors, 729 Prospect Avenue, Osceola, WI 54020-0001 USA.

Library of Congress Cataloging-in-Publication Data Available
ISBN 0-7603-0477-7

On the front cover: Top: International's Farmall 340 Row-Crop Diesel was a tractor ahead of its time. For a majority of farmers, gasoline was the fuel of choice for tractors up to 50 horsepower. The 1961 diesel engine has a 3.6875x3.875-inch bore and stroke and produces 35.48 horsepower on the drawbar and 38.93 horsepower on the PTO. With 10 speeds forward and 2 reverse, it had enough power for the longest day's work. Diesel wasn't the favored form of power at the time, and this tractor is one of four 340 Row-Crop Diesels in existence. *Randy Leffingwell* Bottom: The Waterloo Boy Model N was the first tractor tested at the Nebraska Tractor Test Lab in 1920. The Model N used an engine with a 6.5x7.0-inch bore and stroke, producing 12 horsepower on the drawbar and 25 horsepower on the belt. It featured 2 speeds forward from 2.25 to 3 miles per hour and 1 reverse at 2.25 miles per hour. It sold new for $1,050. *Randy Leffingwell*

On the back cover: Top: The famous handshake in 1938 between Henry Ford and Harry Ferguson initiated the most important innovation in tractor development—the three-point hitch. This 1949 8N has a three-point hitch and a bore and stroke of 3.1875x3.75 inches. This was every small farmers' workhorse, and it was every farm boys' dream to drive one. Farm boy and eventual author Lorry Dunning drove this tractor at age 12 when it was new. *Randy Leffingwell* Bottom: The Massey-Harris Model 333 produced in 1956–1957 had an engine with a 3.675x4.875-inch bore and stroke. It was rated at 29.93 horsepower on the drawbar and 37.10 horsepower on the belt. It featured a 10-speed forward and 2-speed reverse high/low transmission. This gasoline row crop sold for $2,838. *Randy Leffingwell*

Edited by Paul Johnson

Designed by Rebecca Allen

Printed in the United States of America

CONTENTS

ACKNOWLEDGMENTS

It has taken nearly two years of diligent searching and digging for accurate records to complete this book. However, it would have been impossible to complete this research without the assistance of dedicated collectors and those wonderful archivists who preserve the records of our past.

Special thanks to Dr. Leonard L. Bashford, professor of agricultural engineering, and Dave Morgan, Brent Sampson, and Dr. William E. Splinter of the University of Nebraska Tractor Testing Lab. It is the often unappreciated diligence of these individuals, and many others before them, that has accurately tested these tractors. They have provided a service to farming and industry that has resulted in tractor improvements felt around the world.

To John Skarstad, archivist, Department of Special Collections, University Library, University of California, Davis, for his sincere devotion to agricultural history. He simply never stopped helping make this book better.

With much love and gratitude to Gayle Robison, Kevin Dunning, and David Dunning, my children, for the many hours of data entry and computer technical support.

To Jack Krause who was always there with his technical support.

I wish to thank Ed Akin, Placerville, California (Caterpillar); ASAE, St. Joseph, Missouri; Bill Bechthold Sr. and Jr., Lodi, California (Cletrac); Rex Bridgeford, Shelbyville, Iowa (CO-OP); David Brown, Stockton, California (Terratrac); Ed Claessen, Waverly, Minnesota (Best); Dan Crist, Quinter, Kansas (Rumely); Thomas Diehl, Navarre, Ohio (Russell); Sue Dougan, Ostrander, Minnesota (Minneapolis and Twin-City); Dan Ehlerding, Jamestown, Ohio (Aultman & Taylor and Avery); Fred Ertel, Wilmington, Ohio (Avery); Guy Fay, Madison, Wisconsin (Farmall, International, and McCormick-Deering); Don Flegel, Brant, Michigan (Lausen); Tom Graverson, Bremen, Indiana (Case); and Leon Hord, Willard, Ohio (Silver King).

My thanks to Don Huber, Moline, Illinois (Huber); Nan Jones, *Old Allis News*, Bellevue, Minnesota (Allis-Chalmers and Monarch); Wes McKeen, Woodland, California (Caterpillar); Dennis Meloy, Woodland, California (Allis-Chalmers crawlers); Roger Mohr, Vail, Iowa (Minneapolis-Moline and Twin City); Nebraska State Historical Society, Lincoln, Nebraska; Joe Nehl, Vernon Hills, Illinois (International crawlers); Keith Oltrogge, Denver, Iowa (Ferguson, Massey-Ferguson, Massey-Harris, and Wallis); Lewis Pebbles, Akron, Ohio (Lausen); Dennis Powers, Ogden, Iowa (Russell); Brian Rukes, Geary, Oklahoma (*Minneapolis-Moline Registry*); and SAE, Warrendale, Pennsylvania.

My thanks also go to Sherry Schaefer, Smithboro, Illinois (Hart-Parr Oliver Collectors' Association); Earl Scheetz, Clinton, Ohio (Russell); Dan Shima, Eldridge, Iowa (Minneapolis and Twin-City); Dean Simmons, Fredericktown, Ohio (Ford Dexta); Les Stegh, Deere & Co., Moline, Illinois (John Deere); Doug Strawser, Oregon, Illinois (Hart-Parr); Paul Summers, Frederick, Maryland (Cockshutt); Mary Ann Townsend, Floyd County Museum, Charles City, Iowa (Hart-Parr and Oliver); Allan Wallace, Sacramento, California (Terratrac); Don and Diane Winn, Stockton, California (Garden Tractors); and Landis Zimmerman, Ephrata, Pennsylvania (Cletrac and Oliver Crawlers).

I am grateful to my editor Lee Klancher for suggesting the idea and allowing me to do it. To editor Paul Johnson for his assistance in the final design. With great appreciation to Jane Mausser for her diligence in making sure it was correct.

Special thanks to my friend Walter Swann, Woodland, California, who has made most of these tractors run, for his never-ending advice. Without him I would have put the mags on backwards and the carburetors upside down.

And what can I say about Randy Leffingwell? A friend! A confidant! My guiding light in the trials and tribulations of book writing. Thank you is a trivial statement for the appreciation I bestow upon him.

Lorry Dunning
Davis, California

INTRODUCTION

In 1919 the state of Nebraska passed a tractor-testing law intended to fulfill two purposes: The tests would serve as an independent, unbiased, objective evaluation of the performance of all makes of tractors to be sold in the state. The tests would also encourage improvements in the design and manufacture of farm tractors.

Today the results of the Nebraska Tests carry a stamp of considerable authority because of the scientific, accurate, and objective means used to record tractor performance.

Several publications list the test results of the Nebraska Tests in various formats. *Ultimate American Farm Tractor Data Book: Nebraska Test Tractors 1920–1960* is no exception. The reader will find only a small fraction of the actual test results in this publication: maximum brake (belt/PTO) horsepower and maximum drawbar horsepower. This is the portion of the test that best applies to use by the farmer in the field. The intent of this book was to bring together each tractor's specifications to help identify the tractors and their functions for collectors, enthusiasts, and mechanics.

The data presented here is the most accurate that could be found from the available resources. Some models have very little information because very little information was available. In a work of this breadth and depth, mistakes can't be entirely eliminated. Fortunately, there will always be someone who has more experience and knowledge about his or her beloved piece of iron. I hope that if you do find errors or omissions, you share them with me to assist in the production of an accurate and complete database.

To help you understand the data in this book, several types of entries need explanation and clarification:

• Serial Number: The designation "no end" means that the ending serial number is not known. The last number shown is usually the beginning number of the last production year, and tractor production numbers go beyond that number. The designation "end" means that the number shown is the ending serial number for the production of the listed tractor.

• Test Date versus Tractor Manufacture Year: Often the serial number of the test tractor indicates the year of manufacture as the year prior to the test at Nebraska. Production years for the manufacturers vary from July to December. If the tractor was tested in the spring of the year, it was often manufactured in the fall of the previous year. If the tractor was tested during the fall of a given year, it was probably manufactured in the spring of that year.

• Tread Width: The tread width is measured from center to center of tracks on tracklayers and center to center of wheels on wheel tractors. If two or more widths appear for tracklayers, this means that the manufacturer offered a narrow-gauge and wide-gauge track. It required more parts to produce a wide gauge; therefore, the weight is greater. Some wheel tractors have two tread widths, achieved by reversing the dish attachment of the wheels. Others have long axles for adjusting the wheel tread to various crop widths.

• Width: The width of a tracklayer varies depending on the width of the grouser or track shoe. Most companies offered several grouser widths to accommodate the customer's needs. Widths for the wheel tractors are outside to outside of the rear wheels. If the wheel tractor has adjustable rear wheels, the width includes the length of the long axle.

• Height Variance: The height measurement will vary from manufacturer to manufacturer. Some manufacturers measure from the ground to the top of the radiator, others measure to the top of the steering wheel or the top of the cab, and others measure to the top of the exhaust pipe. When measuring, evaluate your tractor, and determine which measurement fits best.

• Weight Variance: Most of the tractor weights presented in this book are shipping weights from the manufacturer. What does this mean? Some tractors are shipped without fluids, meaning no oil or water. Also, various tire sizes create a wide variety of weight differences. In addition, most tractors are shipped without accessories, so the weight of the accessories must be added if you are determining a tractor's total weight. If the weight in this text *is not* in parentheses, it is a shipping weight from tractor data sheets (these can vary). If the tractor weight *is* in parentheses, i.e. (10,000), the weight is a Nebraska Test weight. Most of the tractors tested put on several hundred pounds for ballast to give better traction on the test course. This weight was used in this text if no other weight was available.

• Make and Model: Various names appear in the text. Various data sources listed different names for the same make and model. The name used by the Nebraska Test is referenced in this book and other listings for that tractor from other sources.

• Parentheses: If a listed item is in parentheses ( ), this entry is from the Nebraska Test report. Other information will also be included in the same entry. This usually occurs with carburetors, magnetos, air cleaners, tracklayer grouser size, and weights. The manufacturer could select equipment used during the Nebraska Test. The item listed in the parentheses was not always standard market equipment sold on that tractor. The equipment listed, which is not in parentheses, is the equipment listed in data resources as standard equipment.

- Maximum Brake Horsepower Tests: On some tested tractors, the maximum brake horsepower information is not shown. This is because the test could not be performed on large tracklayers because test equipment was not available to fit the size of the tractors. In other cases the tractor tested did not have a belt pulley or PTO available to perform the test.
- Ignition: Take, for example, this sample entry—Auto-Lite, 12; 2, 6v battery. This entry indicates the ignition system was Auto-Lite on a 12-volt system using two 6-volt batteries in series to produce the 12 volts.

Test reports may be purchased from the Department of Agricultural Engineering, University of Nebraska, Lincoln, Nebraska 68583-0832; telephone (402) 472-6885. The Tractor Test Lab also contains over 40 file cabinets of Tractor Test Archives, which have instruction manuals, some parts manuals, and sales brochures for each tractor tested. Copies may be obtained for a fee.

Photos of the test tractors can be found in the book *Nebraska Tractor Tests Since 1920* by C. H. Wendel, published by MBI Publishing Company in 1985.

POWER TEST TIMELINE

The events featured in this timeline depict some of the major developments leading to the testing and improvements in the tractors we see today.

Human history is attached to the history of agriculture and the production of food—more specifically to the production of wheat. The majority of human food comes from the seeds of less than a dozen plant species. To be of use, these seeds must be harvested by hand or machine. The harvesting tools of antiquity date back to grain and flax threshing in ancient Egypt. As populations grew, so did the demand for more food production, and the methods became more expeditious and cheaper. Devices harnessed the power of animals for plowing, planting, and harvesting of crops.

During American colonial times, the tools a farmer used were not drastically different than those used by farmers in the Roman Empire. From the founding of Jamestown in 1607 until 1790, the basic farm tools were the hoe, plow, and spade for tillage; the hand rake, sickle, and scythe for harvesting and mowing; and the flail and winnowing basket for threshing.

From 1790 through 1865, technological advances brought rapid change in American agriculture. The number of work hours needed to produce 100 bushels of wheat dropped from 373 in 1800 to 233 in 1840. Iron replaced wood, leading to such innovations as John Deere's steel plow (1836), the Nye chilled plow by Silas Nye (1855), the reaper by Cyrus McCormick (1834), and the thresher by Jerome Case (1842). Also during this time period, James Watt, often referred to as the father of the steam engine (because he developed it from 1774 to 1800), introduced the concept of "horsepower" as a means of measuring harnessed power. Joseph Henry developed the electromagnet (1831), which started the development of electric motors, dynamos, and generators. Abraham Gesner, a Canadian geologist, produced an illuminating oil which he named "kerosene" (1845). Edwin Laurencine Drake, the founder of the petroleum industry, drilled the first oil well at Titusville, Pennsylvania (1859). "Carburine," the first true gasoline, was developed in 1859 by Dr. Eugene Carless of Britain while refining burning oils from the coal tar "naphtha" and Scottish shale. To increase illumination power, Carless imported American petroleum in wooden barrels (1866). Horses and mules became a major source of power with 4,896,000 power units in 1850, increasing to 8,270,000 in 1870. As a source of power, a 1,200-pound horse was equivalent to about eight 150-pound farmers. These and many other technological advances opened the door to the industrial revolution.

From the end of the Civil War in 1865 to the end of the nineteenth century, advances in the technology of mechanical power catapulted. Harvesting evolved from the horse sweep to the simple portable steam engine to huge steam-traction engines. This was made possible by the improvements in metallurgy from wrought iron to pig iron to cast iron. With the advances in the blast furnace and the coal-fired furnace, steel was produced to make gears for steam engines, as well as plowshares and hand tools. The Standish steam rotary plow "Mayflower" was built in California in 1868. Steel also advanced rail transportation, and in 1869 the transcontinental railroad was completed. Farm machinery inventors produced suitable gearing for the rear wheels, and chain or belt drives from the engine flywheel of portable steam engines for self propulsion (1870–1880). Case brought out his first steam-traction engine in 1884. The direct-flue-type boiler provided motion, but horses were still needed for steering. Soon after, a steering wheel was attached to a worm gear, and chains pulled the front axle left or right for effective steering. In 1890 some 3,000 steam-traction engines and 2,660 steam threshers were built. Thirty-two hitch-horse and mule teams typically pulled huge grain harvesters in the West. Horse and mule power units increased to 12,170,296 in 1880. The work-hours necessary to produce 100 bushels of wheat decreased to 180.

During this time improved fuels and internal-combustion engines began to take on importance. The four-stroke engine was developed by Nicolaus August Otto (Germany, 1876), and news of his achievements spread around the world. By 1877 the "Otto Silent" engine was used in the United States. In 1884 with improvements to his engine, Otto introduced the low-tension magneto. The Otto "make and break" design was not patented in Germany; therefore, Robert Bosch was able to make improvements on the magneto, which made him famous. Thomas Edison developed the light bulb (1879), which brought more efficient lumination to our cities. Rudolph Diesel, a German inventor, developed a new form of internal-combustion engine known as the diesel engine (1893).

With the introduction of the Otto engine, stationary power became abundant. Local blacksmiths and inventors everywhere began designing their ideas of gas engines from 1/2 to 200 horsepower. It was from these engines that the early gas-traction engines emerged. John Froelich mounted a 20-horsepower Van Duzen 14x14-inch (bore and stroke) gas, single-cylinder engine on a Robinson steam-engine chassis (1892). Others had produced gas-traction engines earlier, but the Froelich was the first with all the essential elements: internal-combustion engine, powertrain, clutch, an engaging forward and reverse gear, manual steering, and drawbar.

While development of the gas engine continued, the use of steam power continued to increase. At the turn of the twentieth century, implement companies were building more than 5,000 steam-traction engines annually. Prior to 1905, practically all power plowing had been done by horses, mules, and steam. Census reports for 1900 list 15,506,000 horses, 2,753,000 mules, and 70,000 steam engines on farms. The work-hours needed to produce 100 bushels of wheat declined to 108. Steam plowing had been in vogue for a number of years, and gargantuan machines developed large farming establishments in the Dakotas, Montana, the Northwest, and Canada. However, these machines required fuel that was too bulky for the amount of power they produced. Also, the constant strain and rough usage necessary for plowing required considerable maintenance and repair. Operators began to demand an easier way of life. With the rapid development of internal combustion, engine manufacturers directed attention to the gas-traction engine. While operators were not satisfied with the steam-traction engines, there were considerable reservations against the gas tractor. Many obstacles stood in the way of converting from horses to steam or gasoline including changing farming methods and the costs of new equipment. The small farmer could not afford the large plowing and threshing outfits. Progress, however, forged ahead. When the first gas-engined units were produced, in order to maintain confidence with the operators, many of these early tractors were built to look much like the steam-traction engines.

By 1908 the gas tractor had generated so much interest throughout the Northwest that manufacturers decided to hold a motor competition in conjunction with the Winnipeg Industrial Exhibition at Winnipeg, Canada. The events featured included plowing, hauling, manipulation, Prony Brake Tests (belt horsepower), and efficiency testing. The early tests were unsatisfactory in less than ideal soil conditions, rules barred certain sizes of tractors, and testing methods varied producing inconsistent results. The competitiveness caused keen rivalry among the manufacturers and led to disagreeable features. The contests were significant because they publicly displayed the weak points of the tractors, which lead to the development of practical motors for small tractors. In 1910 it was estimated that there were 50 firms or individuals making, or attempting to make, tractors. That same year the estimated power units on farms was 72,000 steam engines and 10,000 gas tractors. However, demand for horses and mules continued to rise with 17,474,000 horses and 3,017,000 mules reported. The Winnipeg test results produced many columns of figures unintelligible to the average farmer. The Winnipeg Agricultural Motor Competition ended in 1913.

A surge of interest in the gas tractor occurred from 1913 to 1920. Tractor shows, demonstrations, and expositions appeared as numerous cities across the nation tried to put on demonstrations. Manufacturers took special means to protect themselves from bogus contests. The Fremont, Nebraska, show was inaugurated without any competitive features, which proved successful in attracting buyers with no hard feelings among the manufacturers. The National Tractor and Thresher Manufacturers Association was organized to establish sanctions and limitations governing the demonstrations. Tractor clubs formed in cities and states. The American Society of Agricultural Engineers prepared rules for the exhibition of tractors and equipment. Literally thousands, from the curious to the potential farm customer, attended the shows. Both the public and the exhibitors had grown weary of contests cloaked with accusations of dishonesty and unfairness. The people of Fremont (1913–1917) and the shows without contests were credited and heralded by industry leaders. Not only did these demonstrations educate the public about the advantages of tractor farming, but the economic conditions brought on by World War I made the technology featured at these shows a national necessity.

The war took its toll on horse and mule populations. Horse breeders were still trying to recover from the United States' sale of over 250,000 horses and mules to Great Britain for the Boer War (1899–1902). With the United States now at war, the army required nearly as many horses as men. The life of a horse on the front lines was a mere 7 to 10 days. This country had already supplied over 500,000 horses by 1915 and many more would be needed before the war's end. Because of this, horse prices were high, and population recovery would be slow since it takes a horse 6 years to develop from gestation to maturity. The power of the tractor became more appealing every working day.

The tractor industry had entered a challenging phase of development—standardization. Engineers and development firms were concerned with the manufacture of parts for repair and replacement. Many tractors were produced by backyard developers with no engineering standards. Tractor rating procedures were questionable with the varied performance of some makes. There were two methods of tractor rating: the brake-drawbar method and the number of plows a tractor could pull. Using the brake-drawbar method, a tractor rated at 10-20 was supposed to deliver 10 horsepower on the drawbar and 20 horsepower on the belt pulley. The plow rating was open to question with variations in soil conditions and moisture. Some examples of this measurement are as follows: the Fordson F 10-20 was a 2 plow; the Avery 14-28 was a 3–4 plow; the Oil Pull 16-30 was a 4 plow; the 30-60 Oil Pull was an 8–10 plow; and the Twin City 60-90 was a 12 plow.

As testing methods continued to develop, tractor production was rapidly increasing. In 1915 there were 61 firms producing 21,000 tractors with 25,000 already in use on farms. By 1920 there were 191 firms producing 203,207 tractors. Census figures in 1920 showed 246,000 gas tractors, 17,221,000 horses, and 4,652,000 mules on farms. The number of horses increased until about 1918 then declined rapidly from the death toll of the war and increased tractor use. The number of mules continued to increase until 1925 due to their use in the Cotton Belt, where the change from animal to mechanical power was not as rapid. Meanwhile, the number of work-hours necessary to produce 100 bushels of wheat dropped to 87.

As time passed, the Agricultural College Engineering Professors, the American Society of Agricultural Engineers, the Society of Automobile Engineers, and industry leaders continued to improve testing procedures and test equipment. Professor Leon W. Chase and Oscar W. Sjogren, University of Nebraska, Professor Jay B. Davidson, University of California, and John B. Bartholomew,

Avery Co. were leaders in the development of testing. In addition, several states and the United States Department of Agriculture considered and presented proposals to their respective legislatures. One such proposal came from Wilmot F. Crozier. He had purchased an unreliable Minneapolis Ford, prompting him to investigate other makes such as the Rumely Oil-Pull (which exceeded his expectations). With the assistance of Leon W. Chase, Agricultural Engineering, University of Nebraska, Crozier presented a bill to establish tractor testing to the Nebraska House in 1919.

Official testing began in 1920 at the University of Nebraska with Claude K. Shedd as the engineer in charge. Through the use of the records of the Nebraska Tests, one can follow the development of the tractor through fuels, ignition, carburetion, wheels, frame and body shape, comfort and safety to the operator, and a myriad of other improvements. The dates listed in the timeline of this book are the test dates of the tractor and the listed improvement. This date has no bearing on the date of the invention or the manufacturer who developed the improvement. Oftentimes the tractor tested does represent the manufacturing origin of the development. By studying the events in the testing sequence, you can appreciate the chronology of tractor development.

Year	Event
1784	James Watt, Scottish engineer (January 19, 1736–August 25, 1819) introduced horsepower as a unit of measure. To measure the performance of his steam engine, Watt determined that a draft horse, pulling for 1 minute, could lift 32,400 pounds to a height of 1 foot. He later rounded this off and set the standard unit at 33,000 pounds. One horsepower is equivalent to 550 foot-pounds per second, the scientific standard still used today.
1821	Gaspard de Prony (July 22, 1755–July 29, 1839; Paris, France; engineer, educator, and mathematician) invented the "de Prony Brake" to measure the performance of machines and engines. It was used for determining brake (belt) horsepower on steam-traction engines and gas tractors.
January 1853	Review of the Trials of Horsepowers and Threshing Machines by the committee of New York State Agricultural Society at Geneva and Utica, New York, reported in *The Cultivator*.
1855	Obed Hussey tested his steam plow before the Maryland Agricultural Society.
1861–1865	Civil War
July 10, 1866	Second National Trial of Mowers, Reapers, Horsepowers, and Hay Presses at Auburn, New York, New York State Agricultural Society.

October 1, 1872 First official tractor test in the United States. Professor R. H. Thurston conducted a public trial at South Orange, New Jersey. W. C. Castler, New York agent for Aveling & Porter of England, asked for the trial and furnished the traction engine. Seven trials were conducted for pulling power on various grades, maneuverability, speed on grades, and maximum loads.

January 18, 1904 Organizational meeting of the Society of Automobile Engineers (SAE), Hotel Navarre, New York; held during the 1904 New York Automobile Show. Andrew L. Riker was elected President. SAE can be traced to an idea put forth in 1902 by E. T. Birdsell, a New York consulting engineer, when in conversation with Horace M. Swetland, publisher of *The Automobile* of New York, and Allen H. Whiting of Whiting Motors Co., New York, he mentioned organizing an automobile engineering society. Other prominent industry leaders solicited were H. W. Alden and Hiram P. Maxim of the Electric Vehicle Co., Hartford, Connecticut; Henry Ford, Ford Motor Co., Detroit, Michigan; and Andrew L. Riker of Locomobile Co. First formal meeting of SAE was in New York in January 1905. The name was later changed to Society of Automotive Engineers in 1916.

1906 First tractor school in the United States, Minnesota State Fair grounds, St. Paul, Minnesota. Under direction of D. D. Mayne, School of Agriculture, University of Minnesota, and B. B. Clarke, editor of *American Thresherman*. Instructors were: William Boss and H. B. White, University of Minnesota, and Philip S. Rose, North Dakota Agricultural College. This tractor school prompted similar courses to be taught at other agricultural colleges and by tractor manufacturers.

December 1907 Founding of the American Society of Agricultural Engineers (ASAE) in the Agricultural Engineering Building at the University of Wisconsin, Madison, Wisconsin. Founded by Jay Brownlee Davidson (1880–1957) of Iowa State University; he would become the first president of ASAE.

July 11–17, 1908 Winnipeg Industrial Exhibition, western Canada. First Agricultural Motor Contest ever held in North America. Seven "light" gas tractors were tested and rated on plowing and hauling capabilities for fuel efficiency. The "light tractor" contest rules limited the weight of the tractors to 14,000 pounds to keep out the 10- to 12-ton steam-traction engines. The rule excluded one gas tractor, the Hart-Parr. A. Burness Gregg conceived the idea of a plowing demonstration.

July 7–17, 1909 Second Light Agricultural Motor Competition at the Winnipeg Exhibition; 22 entries—5 steam and 17 gas.

1909 The first tractor demonstration held in the United States was in Omaha, Nebraska, with five tractors exhibited at the Omaha Land Show. It was conducted as an exhibition and not as a competition between machines. Plans to make this exhibition a permanent feature were abandoned for lack of a suitable land site for plowing. Organized by A. E. Hildebrand.

January 1910 SAE Standards Committee organized under the direction of Henry Souther.

July 13–23, 1910 Agricultural Motor Competition at Winnipeg Industrial Exhibition; 18 entries—6 steam and 12 gas. 500 points on the score card: Prony brake test, 150; hauling, 100; plowing, 200; design and construction, 50.

June 1911 SAE Handbook of Standards and Recommended Practices was published to govern development of parts and materials.

July 5–22, 1911 Winnipeg Agricultural Motor Competition; 31 tractors tested.

October 9–14, 1911 Peoria Exposition sponsored by the National Implement & Vehicle Show Co. Inc. at the Mile Race Track; directed by John B. Bartholomew of the Avery Co. The Exposition was the first of its kind ever undertaken. It included tractor displays, engine plowing, and field demonstrations, with no competitive contests.

July 3–20, 1912 Winnipeg Agricultural Motor Competition; 29 tractors tested—4 steam.

September 27–October 5, 1912 The National Implement & Vehicle Show at Peoria, Illinois. This second annual show was under the direction of John B. Bartholomew, president of the Avery Co. [$100,000 Stock and 140-acre land site.] The show featured 18 plowing tractors giving daily exhibitions.

July 1–16, 1913 Winnipeg Agricultural Motor Competition; 19 tractors tested, represented by 3 companies—8 gasoline, 5 kerosene, and 6 steam. First Motor Contest conducted by and under rules of American Society of Agricultural Engineers (ASAE) as established by the Motor Contest Rules Committee at the previous winter meeting in Chicago. Professor Leon W. Chase, University of Nebraska and president of ASAE, were the engineers in charge. Other members were: Professor R. H. Riley, Cornell University, New York; Professor Jay B. Davidson, Iowa State College; Professor Dickinson, University of Illinois; and Professor L. J. Smith, Manitoba Agricultural College. The show was discontinued this year.

September 8–13, 1913 First Tractor Demonstration at Fremont, Nebraska, sponsored by the Commercial Club of Fremont and business interests of Omaha. Five hundred acres were used for demonstration purposes. This show was not a contest but featured educational and training values for the farmer. No measurements were taken of fuel used or acres of ground plowed. The demonstration required a minimum plow depth of 6 inches and no monopoly of field use by any one company. Sixteen companies were represented. Directed by A. E. Hildebrand.

1914–1918 War I: steel quotas, material shortages, and limited railroad transportation except for war goods.

February 19–21, 1914 Tractor demonstrations began in California as gasoline tractors, particularly local manufacturers such as Best, Holt, Samson, and Yuba, gained popularity. Twenty-five tractors demonstrated tractor plowing on Bullard Ranch near Fresno, California, with no contests. Professor Fred L. Peterson, chief of the Division of Farm Mechanics of University of California was head of a three-man committee to judge fairness as to quantity and quality of work performed. Railroad rates to the event were reduced to assist travelers from valley locations.

May 7–9, 1914 Great Tractor Demonstration, West Sacramento, California; 10-acre lots assigned to various machines under supervision of Professor Fred Peterson of University Farm, Davis, California. 800–1,000 in attendance daily. 21 tractors demonstrated from 13 companies.

August 17–22, 1914 Second Fremont, Nebraska, Plowing Demonstration on 100-acre site. 50 entries with more than half in the lightweight division. 25,000 people in attendance with 66 percent being farmers. Holt Mfg. Co. of Stockton and Peoria demonstrated a 60-40 horsepower tracklayer pulling three gangs and a 30-20 horsepower tracklayer pulling two gangs. This is the first demonstration of a Caterpillar disc plow east of the Rocky Mountains. Directed by A. E. Hildebrand.

January 18–February 13, 1915 Tractor school featuring lectures, demonstrations, and practical operation of traction engines and harvesters for all owners and operators handling the machines at the Holt Mfg. Co. factory in Stockton, California. The instructor was Professor Fred L. Peterson, University of California. 83 in attendance at Stockton with 107 in attendance at the same time in Spokane, Washington.

August 9–14, 1915 Third Fremont, Nebraska, Plowing Demonstration; tractor short course for education and entertainment in the operation and maintenance of tractors and equipment; 12,000 people in attendance; no contests; directed by A. E. Hildebrand

1916 Society of Automobile Engineers held its first tractor meeting. Action was initiated to combine the Society of Automobile Engineers, the Society of Aeronautic Engineers, the Society of Tractor Engineers, the standardization and engineering work of the National Association of Engine and Boat Manufacturers, and the National Gas Engine Association into the Society of Automotive Engineers.

1916 Eight national tractor demonstrations; presented under the auspices of the National Tractor and Thresher Manufacturers Association. The Demonstration Committee laid down rules and regulations for the management of the shows—no entry fees were to be charged and no featured contests were to be held. The rules governing the demonstrations were prepared by ASAE. Managers were selected for each show, with A. E. Hildebrand as general manager. Show times: July 17–21, Dallas, Texas; July 24–28, Hutchinson, Kansas; July 31–August 4, St. Louis, Missouri; August 7–11, Fremont, Nebraska; August 14–18, Cedar Rapids, Iowa; August 21–25, Bloomington, Illinois; August 28–September 1, Indianapolis, Indiana; September 4–8, Madison, Wisconsin.

August 6–10, 1917 The National Farm Tractor Demonstration, Fremont, Nebraska. Demonstrations conducted under the auspices of the Tractor Demonstration Committee of the National Implement and Vehicle Association. A. E. Hildebrand of the *Twentieth Century Farmer* was general manager for all National Tractor Demonstrations.

December 1917 SAE Tractor Division meeting in Minneapolis. ASAE representatives in attendance cooperated with the division in the formation of tractor standards. SAE considered tractor standards. The subcommittee recommended rules for consideration.

February 11–16, 1918 Kansas City Tractor Club, Third Annual National Tractor Show. 80,000 attended, including 225 tractor and accessories exhibitors, showing 150 tractor models. Organizer was Guy H. Hall. Most buyers' interest was in the three-plow tractors. All tractors available by companies were projected to be sold by June. Material and transportation shortages posed a problem. Three-thousand freight cars were needed to ship available tractors.

May 15, 1918 The Iowa Recording Traction Dynamometer was one of the most accurate instruments used to test drawbar horsepower. Designed by Professor Jay B. Davidson, engineer, Iowa State College. It was later sold to the Central Science Company.

May 29–31, 1918 Pullman Tractor Show, Pullman, Washington. Dealers from California, Oregon, Idaho, and Washington exhibited, including 25 tractor companies, 4 plow companies, and 4 threshing machine companies. Tests of tractors were conducted by Professor Jay B. Davidson, head of the Department of Agricultural Engineering, University of California.

July 29–August 2, 1918 National Tractor Demonstration at Salina, Kansas, under control of the Tractor and Thresher Department of the National Implement & Vehicle Association. Three tests were conducted on 66 tractors: 1. field tests—fuel, lubricating oil, and water used per acre; 2. drawbar pull—measured by Iowa Integrating Dynamometer under direction of Professor Jay B. Davidson, University Farm, Davis, California, and Hyatt Integrating Dynamometer under direction of L. S. Newman and Harry Wooley, representatives from Hyatt Roller Bearing; 3. brake horsepower—measured by Prony Friction Brake with fuel use measured for fuel used per horsepower. Forty-eight manufacturers showed 232 tractors. Attendance was 75,000. Directed by John B. Bartholomew, president of the Avery Company.

October 7, 21, & 28, 1918 Farm tractor schools in Pacific-coast centers: Madera, Merced, and Saticoy. Only Pacific-coast tractors used: Best, Fageol, Holt, Samson, Union Tool, and Yuba. They were known as "California Free Tractor Training Centers and Scientific Handling of Farm Machinery." Building, repairing, maintaining, and operating farm tractors were topics of instruction.

January 27–31, 1919 Second Annual Farmers Tractor School, Ohio State University, Columbus, Ohio. Tractor test rules established. Tractor brakes tested on the Prony brake. An electric tachometer recorded the instantaneous speed of the motor. Fuel consumption recorded.

February 24–March 1, 1919 Kansas City Tractor Club, Fourth Annual National Tractor Show, Kansas City, Missouri. Under direction of Guy H. Hall.

March 20, 1919 Initial enactment of the Nebraska Tractor Test Law, which became effective, July 15, 1919. Tractor Test Bill submitted to Nebraska Legislature by Representative Wilmot F. Crozier, a farmer from Osceola, Nebraska. Charles Warner sponsored the bill in the Senate.

July 28 & 29, 1919 Ohio Tractor Tests in Columbus; August 1 & 2 in Middleton; August 6 & 7 in Fostoria; August 12 & 13 in Akron. A total of 56 tractors were tested with 26 manufacturers represented, and about 170 acres of land plowed at each of the four demonstrations. Drawbar tests, and plowing and seeding demonstrations were managed by Professor H. C. Ramsower, Agricultural Engineering, Ohio State University, Columbus, Ohio.

September 15, 1919 Nebraska test equipment. The tractor tests under the new Nebraska law were conducted at the University of Nebraska under the direction of Professor Claude K. Shedd of the Agricultural Engineering Department. An electric dynamometer was installed at a cost of $6,000 for testing belt horsepower and a traction dynamometer for $2,000 to test drawbar pull. A dynamometer car was constructed for use on the half-mile cinder track.

October 25, 1919 "The Testing of Farm Tractors" at Purdue University. A paper presented before the Midwest section of the American Society of Mechanical Engineers in Indianapolis, Indiana, by Charles H. Benjamin, dean, Purdue University, Lafayette, Indiana. Test equipment and testing procedures with types of experiments were presented.

November 12, 1919 SAE begins tractor standardization work. A meeting of tractor engine and tractor transmission manufacturers was convened in Chicago by R. S. Burnett, chairman of the Standards Division of the Society of Automotive Engineers. Standards were recommended for tractor engine support, arms, and flywheel housings.

December 2, 1919 National Implement and Vehicle Association meeting in Chicago Illinois. Tractor and Thresher Department committee ruled out holding national or regional tractor demonstrations in 1920.

December 18, 1919 The Federal Tests. A bill was introduced in the House of Representatives entitled "A Bill to create a Bureau of Agricultural Engineering in the Department of Agriculture, to provide for the testing and certification of farm tractors, and for other purposes." The Secretary of Agriculture asked for an annual appropriation of $100,000 for this work.

February 16–21, 1920 Kansas City Tractor Club, Fifth Annual Tractor Show; under direction of Guy Hall. This show was the only official tractor exhibition sanctioned by the National Implement and Vehicle Association in 1920. Rules and regulations were administered by the Association, admitting only the manufacturers who abided by the rules of the committee. One hundred three tractors were exhibited by 66 manufacturers.

Nebraska Tests

March 31–April 9, 1920 Test No. 1; first official tractor tested at Nebraska Test Lab. Waterloo Boy, Model N, Serial No. 19851. Tractor tested using kerosene fuel.

April 9–May 5, 1920 Test No. 6; first three-wheel or tricycle tractor tested. Case 10-20, Serial No. 18849.

June 2–12, 1920 est No. 18; first cast tractor frame used. Fordson, Model F, Serial No. 96100.

June 11–July 3, 1920 Test No. 22; first tractor tested on gasoline fuel. Gray 18-36, Serial No. 8097.

June 14–19, 1920 Test No. 24; first tractor tested with a power take-off (PTO). International 15-30, Serial No. EC 3786.

June 22–July 2, 1920 Test No. 28; first garden tractor tested. Beeman, Model G, Serial No. G 204582.

July 12–August 14, 1920 Test No. 39; first six cylinder tested. Avery, Model C, Serial No. 25904.

July 14–17, 1920 Test No. 33; first general-purpose tractor. Moline Universal, Model D, Serial No. 28268.

July 21–25, 1920 Test No. 40; first motor cultivator tested. Avery Motor Cultivator, Serial No. 2730.

July 29–August 9, 1920 Test No. 45; first tracklayer tested. Cletrac, Model W, Serial No. 19585.

September 27–October 7, 1920 Test No. 66; first mechanical lift of implements with direct engine drive. Square Turn, Model 18-35, Serial No. T 406 A.

June 6–25, 1921 Test No. 78; Russell Giant, 30-60 horsepower, Serial No. X2141. Presently owned by Dennis Powers, Ogden, Iowa. One of 7 known to remain of 214 produced from 1910–1924. Originally sold for $4,800.

April 1–May 10, 1922 Test No. 84; first four-wheel-drive articulated with hydraulic power steering. Rogers, Serial No. 207.

September 14–19, 1925 Test No. 117; first row-crop tractor. Farmall, Serial No. QC 693.

October 18–25, 1926 Test No. 128; first tractor tested on distillate fuel, replacing kerosene. Hart Parr, Serial No. 26145.

April 2–16, 1928 Test No. 148; Lauson 20-35. Effective with the first test of 1928, one carburetor setting was allowed which remained unchanged throughout the test. Prior to 1928 changes were allowed during the test.

April 24–May 10, 1928 Test No. 149; first tractor tested with battery and electric starter. Cletrac 40, Serial No. 150.

October 1–8, 1928 Test No. 152; Twin City FT, 21-32 horsepower, Serial No. X4. Six experimental tractors produced, X1–X6. X1 and X4 are presently owned by Sue Dougan, Ostrander, Minnesota.

January 1, 1930 Improved Test Standards inaugurated by American Society of Agricultural Engineers and Society of Automotive Engineers. Past drawbar and belt horsepower were corrected by calculation to reflect standard operating conditions of 29.92 inches mercury atmospheric pressure (sea level pressure) and 60 degrees Fahrenheit temperature.

March 11–April 8, 1930 Test No. 173; first import tractor tested, from Cork, Ireland. Fordson F, Serial No. 757447.

April 14–24, 1930 Test No. 176; first row crop with adjustable rear wheels on a splined axle. Oliver Hart-Parr, Serial No. 100003.

July 20–27, 1931 Test No. 194; first hard rubber tires. McCormick-Deering Industrial 20, Serial No. IN 16675.

June 14–July 20, 1932 Test No. 208; first diesel-fueled tracklayer tractor. Caterpillar Diesel Sixty-Five, Serial No. 1C 15.

May 2–16, 1934 Test No. 223; first pneumatic tires and a comparative test with steel wheels. Allis-Chalmers WC, Serial No. WC 109.

October 23–November 9, 1934 Test No. 229; last tractor tested using kerosene fuel. McCormick-Deering W-12, Serial No. WS 687.

September 23–27, 1935 Test No. 246; first diesel-fueled wheel tractor. McCormick-Deering WD-40, Serial No. 644.

October 22–November 10, 1936 Test Nos. 274 and 275; the only tractors driven to Nebraska Test from factory in Battle Creek, Michigan. CO-OP No. 2 and CO-OP No. 3., Serial No. 2*198 and 3*140.

August 26–September 2, 1937 Test No. 285; first tractor to feature fuel injection with spark ignition. Allis-Chalmers WK-O Diesel, Serial No. WKO 6989.

April 6–14, 1938 Test No. 296; first hydraulic lift system for implements. Graham-Bradley 503.103, Serial No. 50560.

1939–1945 World War II; steel, rubber, and fuel quotas.

April 9–18, 1940 Test No. 339; first three-point lift hitch with draft control. Ford-Ferguson 9N, Serial No. 9N 12840.

October 15–21, 1940 Test No. 360; first crawler tractor to feature two-cycle diesel engine. Allis-Chalmers HD-7W Diesel, Serial No. HD-7W 176.

October 27–November 3, 1941 Test No. 378; last tractor tested until 1946 due to World War II. Last distillate-fueled tractor tested. John Deere AR, Serial No. 260725.

November 3, 1941–July 22, 1946 World War II: no tractor tests

July 22–August 8, 1946 Test No. 379; first tractor tested after World War II. Ellinwood Bear Cat 3000-1 Garden Tractor, Serial No. 46-3-5814.

May 21–June 3, 1947 Test No. 382; first independent PTO tested. Cockshutt 30, Serial No. 47-30 1318.

July 2–16, 1948 Test No. 397; first torque converter in a tracklayer. Allis-Chalmers, HD-19 Diesel, Serial No. HD-19 H-52.

July 16–30, 1948 Test No. 399; first tractor tested using tractor fuel. Tractor fuel was introduced with an octane rating of 40-45 while gasoline had an octane rating of 74. This tractor also featured power spacing of the rear wheels with spiral bars on the rim. Allis-Chalmers WD, Serial No. WD 21.

May 31–June 8, 1949 Test No. 411; first LPG tractor tested. Minneapolis Moline, Model U, Standard, Serial No. 0124900417.

1950–1953 Korean War

September 11–20, 1950 Test No. 449; smallest tractor tested. Choremaster B, Garden Tractor, Serial No. 38926.

May 27–June 7, 1954 Test No. 521; last use of tractor fuel during a test. Minneapolis Moline U, Serial No. 01212648.

October 19–22, 1954 Test No. 528; first hydraulic power–assist steering. John Deere 70 Diesel, Row Crop, Serial No. 7017500.

1955–1975 Vietnam War

March 28–April 4, 1955 Test No. 532; first torque amplifier, partial power shift transmission. Farmall 400, Serial No. 4164 S.

July 6–18, 1955 Test No. 550; first super-charger used in a crawler. Allis-Chalmers HD-21 AC Diesel, Serial No. HD-21A 7302.

January 1956 Nebraska Tractor Test Code and Society of Automotive Engineers (SAE) Tractor Test Code were consolidated to form the SAE Agricultural Tractor Test Code—SAE-J708. This code serves as a guide and reference for conducting the tests at the Nebraska Test Lab.

July 31–August 4, 1956 Test No. 584; first turbo-charger used in a tracklayer. Largest tractor tested. Caterpillar D9, Diesel, Serial No. 18A 915.

November 12–19, 1956 Test No. 606; last use of distillate fuel during a test. John Deere 720, All-Fuel, Serial No. 7200003.

January 1, 1959 New test procedure introduced to provide better performance information for modern tractors with changing trends in tractor design. Discontinuance of calculating "corrected" horsepower ratings, and only one carburetor adjustment is permitted, selected by the manufacturer. Belt testing is discontinued with engine testing through the power take-off.

February 28–March 16, 1959 Test No. 684; Nebraska Test Lab began testing and reporting PTO horsepower instead of belt horsepower. Fordson Dexta Diesel, Serial No. 1419112.

May 21–June 9, 1959 Test No. 699; first air-cooled diesel engine in a tractor. Porsche L108, Diesel Junior, Serial No. L 546 H.

June 4–10, 1959 Test No. 700; first enclosed cab and air conditioner on four-wheel-drive tractor. Wagner TR-14A Diesel, Serial No. 1980.

September 12–23, 1960 Test No. 759; first hydrostatic power steering. John Deere 4010, Row Crop, Serial No. 21T 1494.

MEASUREMENT CONVERSIONS

Fractions to Decimals

1/16	=	.0625	9/16	=	.5625
1/8	=	.125	5/8	=	.625
3/16	=	.1875	2/3	=	.66
1/4	=	.25	11/16	=	.6875
5/16	=	.3125	3/4	=	.75
1/3	=	.33	13/16	=	.8125
3/8	=	.375	7/8	=	.875
7/16	=	.4375	15/16	=	.9375
1/2	=	.50			

Chapter 1

ALLIS-CHALMERS

Allis-Chalmers 6-12, General Purpose

Manufacturer ....Allis-Chalmers Mfg.
Co., Milwaukee, WI
Nebraska test number 54
Test date ....August 17–26, 1920
Test tractor serial number 10633
Years produced 1919–1926
Number produced ....approximately 1,470
Engine ....Le Roi
Test engine serial number 14053
Cylinders 4
Bore and stroke (in.) ....3.125 x 4.50
Rated rpm 1,200
Displacement (c.i.) 138.1
Fuel ....gasoline
Fuel tank capacity (gal.) 8.50
Carburetor ....Kingston L, 0.875-in.
Air cleaner ....Bennett
Ignition ....Dixie 46 magneto
Cooling capacity (gal.) 3.50
Maximum brake horsepower tests
    PTO/belt horsepower 12.37
    Crankshaft rpm 1,008
    Fuel use (gal./hr.) 1.75
Maximum drawbar horsepower tests
    Drawbar horsepower 6.27
    Pull weight (lb.) 1,142
    Speed (mph) 2.06
    Percent slippage 14.65
SAE drawbar horsepower 6
SAE belt/PTO horsepower 12
Type ....2 drive wheels, 2 rear
carriage wheels
Front wheel (in.) ....steel: 48 x 6 drive
wheel
Rear wheel (in.) ....steel: 28 x 6
Length (in.) 156
Height (in.) 72
Rear width (in.) 54
Weight (lb.) 2,500
Gear/speed (mph) ....forward: 1/2.50;
reverse: 1/na

Allis-Chalmers 18-30

Manufacturer ....Allis-Chalmers Mfg.
Co., Milwaukee, WI
Nebraska test number 55
Test date ....August 23 to
September 6, 1920
Test tractor serial number 5729
Years produced 1918–1921
Serial number range ....5000–6160 end
Serial number location ....metal tag on
transmission case
forward of gear shift
Number produced 1,160
Engine ....Allis-Chalmers vertical,
valve-in-head
Test engine serial number 5729

Cylinders 4
Bore and stroke (in.) ....4.75 x 6.50
Rated rpm 830
Displacement (c.i.) 460.7
Fuel ....kerosene/gasoline
Main tank capacity (gal.) 25
Auxiliary tank capacity (gal.) 7.75
Carburetor ....Kingston Dual, 1.50-in.
Air cleaner ....Bennett
Ignition ....Dixie 46 magneto
Cooling capacity (gal.) 10
Maximum brake horsepower tests
    PTO/belt horsepower 33.41
    Crankshaft rpm 842
    Fuel use (gal./hr.) 4.61
Maximum drawbar horsepower tests
    Gear ....low
    Drawbar horsepower 20.19
    Pull weight (lb.) 3,500
    Speed (mph) 2.18
    Percent slippage 14.80
SAE drawbar horsepower 18
SAE belt/PTO horsepower 30
Type ....4 wheel
Front wheel (in.) ....steel: 36 x 6
Rear wheel (in.) ....steel: 50 x 12
Length (in.) ....wheelbase: 94
Height (in.) 68
Rear width (in.) 66
Weight (lb.) 6,150
Gear/speed (mph) ....forward: 1/2.31,
2/2.82; reverse: 1/2.31

Allis-Chalmers 12-20, L, Became 15-25

Manufacturer ....Allis-Chalmers Mfg.
Co., Milwaukee, WI
Nebraska test number 82
Test date ....September 13–24,
1921
Test tractor serial number 20134
Years produced 1921–1927
Serial number range ....20001–21705 end
Serial number location ....brass plate at center of
rear fuel tank support
Number produced 1,705
Engine ....Midwest vertical,
valve-in-head
Test engine serial number 10998
Cylinders 4
Bore and stroke (in.) ....4.125 x 5.25
Rated rpm 1,100
Displacement (c.i.) 280.6
Fuel ....gasoline
Fuel tank capacity (gal.) 20
Carburetor ....Kingston L, 1.25-in.
Air cleaner ....Taco No. 2
Ignition ....Splitdorf Dixie 46 C
magneto
Cooling capacity (gal.) 6

Maximum brake horsepower tests
PTO/belt horsepower............................33.18
Crankshaft rpm 1,105
Fuel use (gal./hr.)................................3.86
Maximum drawbar horsepower tests
Gear...high
Drawbar horsepower............................21.42
Pull weight (lb.)....................................2,560
Speed (mph) 3.14
Percent slippage..................................11.74
SAE drawbar horsepower..........................12
SAE belt/PTO horsepower..........................20
Type ....4 wheel
Front wheel (in.)..steel: 32 x 6
Rear wheel (in.)..steel: 46 x 12
Length (in.) 135
Height (in.) 62
Rear width (in.) 66
Weight (lb.) 4,400
Gear/speed (mph) ....forward: 1/2.30,
2/3.10; reverse: 1/3.10

Allis-Chalmers 18-30

Manufacturer..Allis-Chalmers Mfg.
Co., Milwaukee, WI
Nebraska test number 83
Test date ....September 15–24,
1921
Test tractor serial number............................5929
Years produced..1918–1921
Serial number range....................................5000–6160 end
Serial number location ....metal tag on
transmission case
forward of gear shift
Number produced 1,161
Engine ....Allis-Chalmers vertical,
valve-in-head
Test engine serial number...........................30450
Cylinders 4
Bore and stroke (in.) ....4.75 x 6.50
Rated rpm 930
Displacement (c.i.) 637.9
Fuel ....gasoline
Fuel tank capacity (gal.) 25
Carburetor..Kingston L, 1.50-in.
Air cleaner..Taco No. 2
Ignition..Eisemann G4 magneto
Cooling capacity (gal.) 10
Maximum brake horsepower tests
PTO/belt horsepower............................43.73
Crankshaft rpm 937
Fuel use (gal./hr.)................................4.72
Maximum drawbar horsepower tests
Gear...high
Drawbar horsepower............................25.45
Pull weight (lb.)....................................3,075
Speed (mph) 3.10
Percent slippage..................................11.70
SAE drawbar horsepower..........................22
SAE belt/PTO horsepower..........................38
Type ....4 wheel
Front wheel (in.)..steel: 36 x 6
Rear wheel (in.)..steel: 50 x 12
Length (in.) 96
Height (in.) 68

Rear width (in.) 66
Weight (lb.) 6,150
Gear/speed (mph) ....forward: 1/2.58,
2/3.16; reverse: 1/2.58

Allis-Chalmers 20-35

Manufacturer..Allis-Chalmers Mfg.
Co., Milwaukee, WI
Nebraska test number 151
Test date ....June 19–26, 1928
Test tractor serial number............................13620
Years produced..1923–1930
Serial number range....................................6161–24185 end
Serial number location ....metal tag on
transmission case
forward of gear shift
Number produced 18,025
Engine ....Allis-Chalmers vertical
I-head, valve-in-head
Test engine serial number...........................36002
Cylinders 4
Bore and stroke (in.) ....4.75 x 6.50
Rated rpm 930
Displacement (c.i.) 460.7
Fuel ....gasoline
Fuel tank capacity (gal.) 30
Carburetor..Kingston L, 1.50-in.
Air cleaner..Donaldson and
Allis-Chalmers
Ignition..Eisemann GS4
magneto
Cooling capacity (gal.) 10
Maximum brake horsepower tests
PTO/belt horsepower............................44.29
Crankshaft rpm 931
Fuel use (gal./hr.)................................5.02
Maximum drawbar horsepower tests
Gear...high
Drawbar horsepower............................33.20
Pull weight (lb.)....................................4,400
Speed (mph) 2.83
Percent slippage..................................9.19
SAE drawbar horsepower..........................20
SAE belt/PTO horsepower..........................35
Type ....4 wheel
Front wheel (in.)..steel: 36 x 6
Rear wheel (in.)..steel: 50 x 12
Length (in.) 152
Height (in.) 65
Rear width (in.) 76
Weight (lb.) 6,000
Gear/speed (mph) ....forward: 1/2.50,
2/3.25; reverse: 1/3.25

Allis-Chalmers U, United

Manufacturer..Allis-Chalmers Mfg.
Co., Milwaukee, WI
Nebraska test number 170
Test date ....October 21 to
November 7, 1929
Test tractor serial number............................U 946
Years produced..1929–1932
Serial number range....................................U 1 to U 7404 end
Serial number location ....stamped on rear axle
housing beside PTO

Number produced 7,404
Engine ....Continental S10
vertical L-head
Test engine serial number.........................3S 101716
Cylinders 4
Bore and stroke (in.) ....4.25 x 5.00
Rated rpm 1,200
Displacement (c.i.) 283.7
Fuel ....gasoline
Fuel tank capacity (gal.) 24
Carburetor ....Kingston (Schebler
HD), 1.25-in.
Air cleaner ....Donaldson or
Allis-Chalmers
Ignition...Eisemann G4 magneto
Cooling capacity (gal.) 5

Maximum brake horsepower tests
    PTO/belt horsepower...........................35.04
    Crankshaft rpm 1,200
    Fuel use (gal./hr.) 4.18
Maximum drawbar horsepower tests
    Gear..3rd
    Drawbar horsepower.............................25.63
    Pull weight (lb.)....................................3,680
    Speed (mph) 2.61
    Percent slippage..................................8.51
Type ....4 wheel
Front wheel (in.).......................................steel: 28 x 6
Rear wheel (in.)..steel: 42 x 11
Length (in.) 118.50
Height (in.)...53.50
Rear width (in.) 63.13
Weight (lb.) 4,125
Gear/speed (mph) ....forward: 1/2.33,
2/3.33, 3/5.00; reverse:
1/2.66

Allis-Chalmers UC, All Crop
Manufacturer...Allis-Chalmers Mfg.
Co., Milwaukee, WI
Nebraska test number 189
Test date ....April 17 to
May 13, 1931
Test tractor serial number.........................UC 217
Years produced 1930–1933
Serial number range..................................UC 1 to UC 1268 end
Serial number location ....stamped on rear axle
housing beside PTO
Number produced 1,268
Engine ....Continental
vertical L-head
Cylinders 4
Bore and stroke (in.) ....4.25 x 5.00
Rated rpm 1,200
Displacement (c.i.) 283.7
Fuel ....gasoline
Fuel tank capacity (gal.) 24
Carburetor ....Kingston (Zenith C5 E),
1.25-in.
Air cleaner ....Vortox (Donaldson)
and Allis-Chalmers
Ignition...Eisemann GL4
magneto
Cooling capacity (gal.) 5

Maximum brake horsepower tests
    PTO/belt horsepower...........................36.09
    Crankshaft rpm 1,198
    Fuel use (gal./hr.) 4.09
Maximum drawbar horsepower tests
    Gear..3rd
    Drawbar horsepower.............................24.98
    Pull weight (lb.)....................................3,763
    Speed (mph) 2.49
    Percent slippage..................................10.15
SAE drawbar horsepower...........................18.21
SAE belt/PTO horsepower 31.34
Type ....4 wheel, tricycle
Front wheel (in.).......................................steel: 24 x 5
Rear wheel (in.)..steel: 42 x 2
Length (in.) 138
Height (in.)...67.63
Rear width (in.) 81
Weight (lb.) 5,815
Gear/speed (mph) ....forward: 1/2.33,
2/3.33, 3/5.00; reverse:
1/2.66

Allis-Chalmers EK, E, and 25-40
Manufacturer...Allis-Chalmers Mfg.
Co., Milwaukee, WI
Nebraska test number 193
Test date ....June 18–25, 1931
Test tractor serial number.........................24559
Years produced 1930–1936
Serial number range..................................24186–25611 end
Serial number location ....on transmission case
forward of gear shift
quadrant
Number produced 2,426
Engine ....Allis-Chalmers
vertical I-head
Test engine serial number.........................15575
Cylinders 4
Bore and stroke (in.) ....5.00 x 6.50
Rated rpm 1,000
Displacement (c.i.) 510.5
Fuel ....distillate/gasoline
Fuel tank capacity (gal.) 30
Auxiliary tank capacity (gal.) 1
Carburetor ....Zenith C6EV, 1.50-in.
Air cleaner ....Vortox (Donaldson)
and Allis-Chalmers
Ignition...Bendix (Eisemann G4)
magneto
Cooling capacity (gal.) 10

Maximum brake horsepower tests
    PTO/belt horsepower...........................47.00
    Crankshaft rpm 999
    Fuel use (gal./hr.) 5.47
Maximum drawbar horsepower tests
    Gear..low
    Drawbar horsepower.............................33.82
    Pull weight (lb.)....................................4,133
    Speed (mph) 3.07
    Percent slippage..................................5.48
SAE drawbar horsepower...........................27.16
SAE belt/PTO horsepower 42.58
Type ....tricycle

Front wheel (in.) ....steel: 36 x 6
Rear wheel (in.) ....steel: 50 x 12
Length (in.) 152
Height (in.) 65
Rear width (in.) 76
Weight (lb.) 7,000
Gear/speed (mph) ....forward: 1/2.50,
2/3.25; reverse: 1/3.25

Allis-Chalmers L

Manufacturer...Allis-Chalmers Mfg.
Co., Springfield, IL
Nebraska test number 200
Test date ....March 17 to
April 11, 1932
Test tractor serial number ....L 69
Years produced 1931–1942
Serial number range................................1–3357 end
Serial number location ....stamped on right rear
shelf to transmission
case or on instrument
panel
Number produced 3,357
Engine ....IHC vertical I-head
Test engine serial number.........................ML 1105
Cylinders 6
Bore and stroke (in.) ....5.25 x 6.50
Rated rpm 1,050
Displacement (c.i.) 844.3
Fuel ....gasoline
Fuel tank capacity (gal.) 75
Carburetor..2 Zenith C6 EV,
1.50-in.
Air cleaner ....Pomona Vortox
Ignition...Eisemann GV-6
magneto
Cooling capacity (gal.) 19
Maximum brake horsepower tests
PTO/belt horsepower...........................91.93
Crankshaft rpm 1,048
Fuel use (gal./hr.) 10.87
Maximum drawbar horsepower tests
Gear...2nd
Drawbar horsepower...........................76.01
Pull weight (lb.)...................................11,826
Speed (mph)..2.41
Percent slippage.................................2.00
SAE drawbar horsepower...........................60.02
SAE belt/PTO horsepower 80.48
Type ....tracklayer
Length (in.) 153
Height (in.) 104
Rear width (in.) 93
Weight (lb.) 22,000
Track length (in.).....................................85.50 on ground,
276 total
Grouser shoe..16
Gear/speed (mph) ....forward: 1/1.94,
2/2.45, 3/3.05, 4/4.10,
5/5.20, 6/6.47; reverse:
1/1.45, 2/3.07

Allis-Chalmers K, Special K

Manufacturer..Allis-Chalmers Mfg.
Co., Springfield, IL

Nebraska test number 215
Test date ....September 21 to
October 4, 1933
Test tractor serial number..........................WK 2848
Years produced 1929–1943
Serial number range................................1–9468 end
Serial number location ....stamped on upper right
corner of rear
transmission case, or
on instrument panel
Number produced 9,468
Engine ....Allis-Chalmers
vertical I-head
Test engine serial number.........................M 7815
Cylinders 4
Bore and stroke (in.) ....5.00 x 6.50
Rated rpm 1,050
Displacement (c.i.) 510.5
Fuel ....gasoline
Fuel tank capacity (gal.) 33
Carburetor..Zenith, 1.50-in.
Air cleaner ....Vortox
Ignition...Scintilla (Eisemann
GL-4) magneto
Cooling capacity (gal.) 11
Maximum brake horsepower tests
PTO/belt horsepower...........................55.24
Crankshaft rpm 1,050
Fuel use (gal./hr.) 5.89
Maximum drawbar horsepower tests
Gear...1st
Drawbar horsepower...........................47.87
Pull weight (lb.)...................................8,865
Speed (mph)..2.03
Percent slippage.................................3.25
SAE drawbar horsepower...........................35.51
SAE belt/PTO horsepower 49.29
Type ....tracklayer
Length (in.) 119
Height (in.) 66
Rear width (in.) 66
Weight (lb.) 11,500
Track length (in.).....................................67 on ground, 221
total
Grouser shoe..34 links; 15, (18)
Gear/speed (mph) ....forward: 1/2.08,
2/3.10, 3/4.50; reverse:
1/2.39

Allis-Chalmers M

Manufacturer..Allis-Chalmers Mfg.
Co., Springfield, IL
Nebraska test number 216
Test date ....September 23 to
October 9, 1933
Test tractor serial number..........................M 255
Years produced 1932–1942
Serial number range................................1–14524 end
Serial number location ....stamped on right side
transmission case
behind master clutch
inspection case
Number produced 14,524
Engine ....Allis-Chalmers
vertical I-head

Allis-Chalmers

Test engine serial number ....UM 393
Cylinders 4
Bore and stroke (in.) ....4.375 x 5.00
Rated rpm 1,200
Displacement (c.i.) 300.7
Fuel ....gasoline
Fuel tank capacity (gal.) 24
Carburetor ....Zenith K-5, 1.25-in.
Air cleaner ....Vortox
Ignition ....Scintilla (Eisemann GL-4) magneto
Cooling capacity (gal.) 6

Maximum brake horsepower tests
  PTO/belt horsepower 35.43
  Crankshaft rpm 1,199
  Fuel use (gal./hr.) 3.58
Maximum drawbar horsepower tests
  Gear 1st
  Drawbar horsepower 29.65
  Pull weight (lb.) 5,166
  Speed (mph) 2.15
  Percent slippage 5.00
SAE drawbar horsepower 21.81
SAE belt/PTO horsepower 31.81
Type ....tracklayer
Length (in.) 101.38
Height (in.) 56.19
Rear width (in.) 57.25
Weight (lb.) 6,200
Track length (in.) ....56.38 on ground, 186 total
Grouser shoe ....31 links; 12 inches wide
Gear/speed (mph) ....forward: 1/2.23, 2/3.20, 3/4.15, 4/5.82; reverse: 1/2.55

Allis-Chalmers WC

Manufacturer ....Allis-Chalmers Mfg. Co., Milwaukee, WI
Nebraska test number 223
Test date ....May 2–16, 1934
Test tractor serial number ....WC 109
Years produced 1933–1948
Serial number range ....WC 1 to WC 178202 end
Serial number location ....stamped on rear of differential housing near oil fill plug
Number produced 178,202
Engine ....Allis-Chalmers vertical I-head
Test engine serial number ....W 110
Cylinders 4
Bore and stroke (in.) ....4.00 x 4.00
Rated rpm 1,300
Displacement (c.i.) 201.1
Fuel ....distillate/gasoline
Main tank capacity (gal.) 15
Auxiliary tank capacity (gal.) 1
Carburetor ....Zenith 124.5, 1.00-in.
Air cleaner ....United
Ignition ....Fairbanks-Morse (Bendix-Scintilla C-4) magneto

Cooling capacity (gal.) 4
Maximum brake horsepower tests
  PTO/belt horsepower 21.48
  Crankshaft rpm 1,300
  Fuel use (gal./hr.) 2.12
Maximum drawbar horsepower tests
  Gear 2nd
  Drawbar horsepower ....steel: 14.36; rubber: 14.19
  Pull weight (lb.) ....steel: 1,430; rubber: 1,735
  Speed (mph) ....steel: 3.77; rubber: 3.07
  Percent slippage ....steel: 10.86; rubber: 15.92
SAE drawbar horsepower 12.14
SAE belt/PTO horsepower 20.77
Type ....4 wheel, tricycle
Front wheel (in.) ....steel: 24 x 5.25; rubber, 5.25 x 17
Rear wheel (in.) ....steel: 40 x 11.25; rubber: 11.25 x 24
Length (in.) 136
Height (in.) 63
Rear width (in.) ....71 and 82
Weight (lb.) ....steel: 2,700; rubber: 3,300
Gear/speed (mph) ....forward: 1/2.50, 2/3.50, 3/4.75, 4/9.25; reverse: 1/2.00

Allis-Chalmers U, 19-30

Manufacturer ....Allis-Chalmers Mfg. Co., Milwaukee, WI
Nebraska test number 237
Test date ....July 15 to August 5, 1935
Test tractor serial number ....U 8263
Years produced 1932–1952
Serial number range ....U 7405 to U 17819; 18022–23056 end
Serial number location ....stamped on rear axle housing beside PTO
Number produced ....approximately 15,450
Engine ....Allis-Chalmers UM vertical I-head
Test engine serial number ....UM 2632
Cylinders 4
Bore and stroke (in.) ....4.375 x 5.00
Rated rpm 1,200
Displacement (c.i.) 300.7
Fuel ....distillate/gasoline
Main tank capacity (gal.) 24
Auxiliary tank capacity (gal.) 1
Carburetor ....Zenith K-5, 1.25-in.
Air cleaner ....Vortox
Ignition ....Bendix-Scintilla C-4 magneto
Cooling capacity (gal.) 6
Maximum brake horsepower tests
  PTO/belt horsepower 34.12
  Crankshaft rpm 1,200
  Fuel use (gal./hr.) 4.06
Maximum drawbar horsepower tests
  Gear ....steel: 2nd; rubber: 2nd
  Drawbar horsepower ....steel: 23.83; rubber: 20.49

Pull weight (lb.)..................................steel: 2,502;
rubber: 2,452
Speed (mph) ....steel: 3.57;
rubber: 3.13
Percent slippage..............................steel: 14.82;
rubber: 15.07
SAE drawbar horsepower..............................19.23
SAE belt/PTO horsepower..............................30.97
Type ....4 wheel
Front wheel (in.).................................steel: 28 x 6;
rubber: 6.00 x 16
Rear wheel (in.)................................steel: 42 x 11.13;
rubber: 12.75 x 24
Length (in.) 118.50
Height (in.)..............................53.50
Rear width (in.)..............................63.13
Weight (lb.)..............................steel: 4,125;
rubber: 4,600
Gear/speed (mph) ....forward: 1/2.33, 2/3.33,
3/5.00, 4/10.00;
reverse: 1/2.67

Allis-Chalmers UC

Manufacturer..............................Allis-Chalmers Mfg.
Co., Milwaukee, WI
Nebraska test number 238
Test date ....July 16 to August 8, 1935
Test tractor serial number..............................UC 1704
Years produced 1933–1951
Serial number range..............................UC 1269 to UC 5037;
5806–5938 end
Serial number location ....stamped on rear axle
housing beside PTO
Number produced ....approximately 3,902
Engine..............................Allis-Chalmers U
vertical I-head
Test engine serial number ....UM 2364
Cylinders 4
Bore and stroke (in.)..............................4.375 x 5.00
Rated rpm 1,200
Displacement (c.i.) 300.7
Fuel ....distillate/gasoline
Main tank capacity (gal.)..............................24
Auxiliary tank capacity (gal.) 1
Carburetor..............................Zenith K-5, 1.25-in.
Air cleaner..............................Vortox
Ignition..............................Bendix-Scintilla
C-4 magneto
Cooling capacity (gal.) 6
Maximum brake horsepower tests
PTO/belt horsepower..............................34.09
Crankshaft rpm 1,199
Fuel use (gal./hr.)..............................4.10
Maximum drawbar horsepower tests
Gear..............................2nd
Drawbar horsepower..............................steel: 23.67;
rubber: 21.14
Pull weight (lb.)..............................steel: 2,297;
rubber: 2,593
Speed (mph) ....steel: 3.86;
rubber: 3.06
Percent slippage..............................steel: 4.07;
rubber: 16.49
SAE drawbar horsepower..............................19.10
SAE belt/PTO horsepower..............................30.86
Type ....4 wheel, tricycle

Front wheel (in.)..............................steel: 24 x 5;
rubber: 6.00 x 16
Rear wheel (in.)..............................steel: 42 x 2;
rubber: 12.75 x 24
Length (in.) 138
Height (in.)..............................67.63
Rear width (in.)..............................81.06
Weight (lb.)..............................steel: 5,335;
rubber: 5,940
Gear/speed (mph) ....forward: 1/2.33,
2/3.33, 3/5.00,
4/10.00; reverse:
1/2.67

Allis-Chalmers M

Manufacturer..............................Allis-Chalmers Mfg.
Co., Springfield, IL
Nebraska test number 239
Test date ....August 1–9, 1935
Test tractor serial number..............................M 3120
Years produced 1932–1942
Serial number range..............................1–14524 end
Serial number location ....stamped on right side
transmission case
behind master clutch
inspection case
Number produced 14,524
Engine..............................Allis-Chalmers
vertical I-head
Test engine serial number ....UM 2602
Cylinders 4
Bore and stroke (in.)..............................4.375 x 5.00
Rated rpm 1,200
Displacement (c.i.) 300.7
Fuel ....distillate/gasoline
Main tank capacity (gal.)..............................24
Auxiliary tank capacity (gal.) 1
Carburetor..............................Zenith K-5, 1.25-in.
Air cleaner..............................Vortox
Ignition..............................Bendix-Scintilla C-4
with 6-v battery
Cooling capacity (gal.) 6
Maximum brake horsepower tests
PTO/belt horsepower..............................35.05
Crankshaft rpm 1,200
Fuel use (gal./hr.)..............................4.16
Maximum drawbar horsepower tests
Gear..............................2nd
Drawbar horsepower..............................28.66
Pull weight (lb.)..............................3,450
Speed (mph)..............................3.12
Percent slippage..............................3.74
SAE drawbar horsepower..............................22.79
SAE belt/PTO horsepower..............................31.64
Type ....tracklayer
Length (in.)..............................101.38
Height (in.)..............................56.19
Rear width (in.)..............................57.25
Weight (lb.)..............................6,200
Track length (in.)..............................56.38 on ground,
186 total
Grouser shoe..............................31 links;
12 inches wide
Gear/speed (mph) ....forward: 1/2.23,
2/3.20, 3/4.15, 4/1.83;
reverse: 1/2.55

Allis-Chalmers

Allis-Chalmers K, WK-O Diesel

Manufacturer	Allis-Chalmers Mfg. Co., Milwaukee, WI
Nebraska test number	285
Test date	August 26 to September 2, 1937
Test tractor serial number	WKO 6989
Years produced	1929–1943
Serial number range	1–9468 end
Serial number location	stamped on rear transmission case, upper right corner, or on instrument panel
Number produced	9,468 total, diesel interspersed
Engine	Allis-Chalmers vertical I-head
Test engine serial number	KO 21154
Cylinders	4
Bore and stroke (in.)	5.25 x 6.50
Rated rpm	1,050
Displacement (c.i.)	562.8
Fuel	diesel
Fuel tank capacity (gal.)	39
Carburetor	Deco Fuel System
Air cleaner	United
Ignition	Mallory MO-90 AT with 6-v battery
Cooling capacity (gal.)	11.50

Maximum brake horsepower tests

PTO/belt horsepower	59.06
Crankshaft rpm	1,050
Fuel use (gal./hr.)	4.62

Maximum drawbar horsepower tests

Gear	2nd
Drawbar horsepower	49.26
Pull weight (lb.)	7,209
Speed (mph)	2.56
Percent slippage	1.86
SAE drawbar horsepower	39.71
SAE belt/PTO horsepower	53.26
Type	tracklayer
Length (in.)	119.56
Height (in.)	64
Rear width (in.)	65.88 or 80.88
Weight (lb.)	11,012/11,425
Track length (in.)	67 on ground, 221 total
Grouser shoe	34 links; 18
Gear/speed (mph)	forward: 1/1.72, 2/2.59, 3/3.26, 4/5.92; reverse: 1/2.10

Allis-Chalmers S-O Diesel

Manufacturer	Allis-Chalmers Mfg. Co., Milwaukee, WI
Nebraska test number	286
Test date	September 16–26, 1937
Test tractor serial number	SO 218
Years produced	1937–1942
Serial number range	3–1227 end, S and S-O
Serial number location	stamped on top right rear of transmission case or on instrument panel
Number produced	1,225 total, diesel interspersed
Engine	Allis-Chalmers vertical I-head
Test engine serial number	SO 10263
Cylinders	4
Bore and stroke (in.)	5.75 x 6.50
Rated rpm	1,050
Displacement (c.i.)	675.1
Fuel	diesel
Fuel tank capacity (gal.)	64
Carburetor	Deco Fuel System
Air cleaner	United
Ignition	Mallory MO 4 with 6-v battery
Cooling capacity (gal.)	12.50

Maximum brake horsepower tests

PTO/belt horsepower	74.82
Crankshaft rpm	1,051
Fuel use (gal./hr.)	6.05

Maximum drawbar horsepower tests

Gear	2nd
Drawbar horsepower	62.39
Pull weight (lb.)	10,218
Speed (mph)	2.29
Percent slippage	1.42
SAE drawbar horsepower	47.73
SAE belt/PTO horsepower	66.01
Type	tracklayer
Length (in.)	146
Height (in.)	74.19
Rear width (in.)	84.63 or 96.63
Weight (lb.)	18,700/19,500
Track length (in.)	77.07 on ground, 249 total
Grouser shoe	32 links; 18
Gear/speed (mph)	forward: 1/1.51, 2/2.32, 3/3.25, 4/4.55, 5/6.37; reverse: 1/1.76

Allis-Chalmers L-O Diesel

Manufacturer	Allis-Chalmers Mfg. Co., Milwaukee, WI
Nebraska test number	287
Test date	September 9–22, 1937
Test tractor serial number	LO 2459
Year produced	1935
Serial number range	L-O 4001 to L-O 4021 end
Serial number location	stamped on right rear shelf to transmission case or on instrument panel
Number produced	21
Engine	Allis-Chalmers vertical I-head
Test engine serial number	LO 15441
Cylinders	6
Bore and stroke (in.)	5.25 x 6.50
Rated rpm	1,050
Displacement (c.i.)	844.3
Fuel	diesel
Fuel tank capacity (gal.)	75
Carburetor	Deco Fuel System
Air cleaner	United

Ignition ....Mallory MO 4,
                                                      6-v battery
Cooling capacity (gal.) 19
Maximum brake horsepower tests
    PTO/belt horsepower............................91.56
    Crankshaft rpm 1,049
    Fuel use (gal./hr.) 7.35
Maximum drawbar horsepower tests
    Gear..2nd
    Drawbar horsepower..........................76.75
    Pull weight (lb.)...............................15,341
    Speed (mph) 1.88
    Percent slippage...............................3.44
SAE drawbar horsepower...........................60.50
SAE belt/PTO horsepower..........................79.70
Type ....tracklayer
Length (in.) 153.25
Height (in.) 81.25
Rear width (in.) 93
Weight (lb.) 23,000
Track length (in.)....................................85.44 on ground,
                                                      273 total
Grouser shoe...35 links; 20
Gear/speed (mph) ....forward: 1/1.48,
                                                      2/1.94, 3/2.68, 4/3.50,
                                                      5/4.90, 6/6.41; reverse:
                                                      1/1.72, 2/2.25

Allis-Chalmers B
Manufacturer...Allis-Chalmers Mfg.
                                                      Co., Milwaukee, WI
Nebraska test number 302
Test date ....May 31 to
                                                      June 8, 1938
Test tractor serial number..........................B 3712
Years produced......................................1937–1957
Serial number range................................1–127186 no end
Serial number location ....stamped on top of
                                                      transmission case in
                                                      front of shift lever
Number produced ....approximately 118,500
Engine ....Allis-Chalmers vertical
                                                      I-head
Test engine serial number..........................BE 3483
Cylinders 4
Bore and stroke (in.) ....3.25 x 3.50
Rated rpm 1,400
Displacement (c.i.) 116.1
Fuel ....distillate/gasoline
Main tank capacity (gal.) 12
Auxiliary tank capacity (gal.) 1
Carburetor..Zenith 61A7, 0.875-in.
Air cleaner ....Donaldson
Ignition..Fairbanks-Morse F.M.
                                                      4B magneto
Cooling capacity (gal.) 2
Maximum brake horsepower tests
    PTO/belt horsepower............................15.68
    Crankshaft rpm 1,400
    Fuel use (gal./hr.) 1.54
Maximum drawbar horsepower tests
    Gear..2nd
    Drawbar horsepower..........................12.97
    Pull weight (lb.)...............................1,473
    Speed (mph) 3.30

    Percent slippage...............................15.23
SAE drawbar horsepower...........................10.16
SAE belt/PTO horsepower..........................13.86
Type ....standard
Front tire (in.) ....5.00 x 15
Rear tire (in.) ....7.00 x 24
Length (in.) 111
Height (in.) 53
Rear width (in.) ....53, 40-52 tread
Weight (lb.) 2,100
Gear/speed (mph) ....forward: 1/2.50,
                                                      2/4.00, 3/7.75; reverse:
                                                      1/2.00

Allis-Chalmers WC,
Manufacturer...Allis-Chalmers Mfg.
                                                      Co., Milwaukee, WI
Nebraska test number 303
Test date ....May 31 to
                                                      June 14, 1938
Test tractor serial number..........................WC 65623
Years produced......................................1933–1948
Serial number range................................WC 1 to WC 178202
                                                      end
Serial number location ....stamped on rear of
                                                      differential housing
                                                      near oil fill plug
Number produced 178,202
Engine ....Allis-Chalmers
                                                      vertical I-head
Test engine serial number..........................W 67859 K
Cylinders 4
Bore and stroke (in.) ....4.00 x 4.00
Rated rpm 1,300
Displacement (c.i.) 201.1
Fuel ....distillate/gasoline
Fuel tank capacity (gal.) 15
Auxiliary tank capacity (gal.) 1
Carburetor..Zenith 124 1/2 TOP,
                                                      1.125-in.
Air cleaner ....United
Ignition..Fairbanks-Morse F.M.
                                                      4B magneto
Cooling capacity (gal.) 4
Maximum brake horsepower tests
    PTO/belt horsepower............................25.45
    Crankshaft rpm 1,300
    Fuel use (gal./hr.) 2.61
Maximum drawbar horsepower tests
    Gear..steel: 2nd; rubber: 3rd
    Drawbar horsepower..........................steel: 18.72;
                                                      rubber: 20.41
    Pull weight (lb.)...............................steel: 1,841;
                                                      rubber: 1,644
    Speed (mph) ....steel: 3.81;
                                                      rubber: 4.65
    Percent slippage...............................steel: 2.02;
                                                      rubber: 5.12
SAE drawbar horsepower...........................14.80
SAE belt/PTO horsepower..........................22.98
Type ....tricycle
Front wheel (in.).....................................steel: 24 x 4;
                                                      rubber: 5.50 x 16
Rear wheel (in.) ....steel: 40 x 6;
                                                      rubber: 11.25 x 24

Allis-Chalmers

Length (in.) 136
Height (in.) 63
Rear width (in.) ....71 and 82
Weight (lb.) ....steel: 2,700;
rubber: 3,300
Gear/speed (mph) ....forward: 1/2.50,
2/3.50, 3/4.75, 4/9.00;
reverse: 1/2.00

Allis-Chalmers WC
Manufacturer ....Allis-Chalmers Mfg.
Co., Milwaukee, WI
Nebraska test number 304
Test date ....June 2–16, 1938
Test tractor serial number ....WC 65625
Years produced 1933–1948
Serial number range ....WC 1 to WC 178202
end
Serial number location ....stamped on rear of
differential housing
near oil fill plug
Number produced 178,202
Engine ....Allis-Chalmers
vertical I-head
Test engine serial number ....W 67860 HA
Cylinders 4
Bore and stroke (in.) ....4.00 x 4.00
Rated rpm 1,300
Compression ratio 5.00:1
Displacement (c.i.) 201.1
Fuel ....gasoline
Fuel tank capacity (gal.) 15
Carburetor ....Zenith 124 1/2 TOP,
1.125-in.
Air cleaner ....United
Ignition ....Fairbanks-Morse
F.M. 4B magneto
Cooling capacity (gal.) 4
Maximum brake horsepower tests
PTO/belt horsepower 29.93
Crankshaft rpm 1,300
Fuel use (gal./hr.) 2.86
Maximum drawbar horsepower tests
Gear ....steel: 2nd; rubber: 3rd
Drawbar horsepower ....steel: 22.29;
rubber: 24.16
Pull weight (lb.) ....steel: 2,198;
rubber: 2,017
Speed (mph) ....steel: 3.80;
rubber: 4.49
Percent slippage ....steel: 4.94;
rubber: 8.12
SAE drawbar horsepower 17.69
SAE belt/PTO horsepower 26.72
Type ....tricycle
Front wheel (in.) ....steel: 24 x 4;
rubber: 5.50 x 16
Rear wheel (in.) ....steel: 40 x 6;
rubber: 11.25 x 24
Length (in.) 136
Height (in.) 63
Rear width (in.) ....71 and 82
Weight (lb.) ....steel: 2,700;
rubber: 3,300

Gear/speed (mph) ....forward: 1/2.50,
2/3.50, 3/4.75, 4/9.00;
reverse: 1/2.00

Allis-Chalmers RC,
Manufacturer ....Allis-Chalmers Mfg.
Co., Milwaukee, WI
Nebraska test number 316
Test date ....April 19–24, 1939
Test tractor serial number ....RC 3004
Years produced 1939–1941
Serial number range ....4–5504 end
Serial number location ....stamped on rear of
differential housing
near oil fill plug
Number produced 5,504
Engine ....Allis-Chalmers
vertical I-head
Test engine serial number ....R 3060 K
Cylinders 4
Bore and stroke (in.) ....3.375 x 3.50
Rated rpm 1,500
Displacement (c.i.) 125.2
Fuel ....distillate/gasoline
Main tank capacity (gal.) 13
Auxiliary tank capacity (gal.) 1
Carburetor ....Zenith 61- AJ-7,
0.875-in.
Air cleaner ....Donaldson
Ignition ....Fairbanks-Morse
magneto
Cooling capacity (gal.) 2.25
Maximum brake horsepower tests
PTO/belt horsepower 18.21
Crankshaft rpm 1,500
Fuel use (gal./hr.) 1.51
Maximum drawbar horsepower tests
Gear ....rubber: 3rd
Drawbar horsepower 15.25
Pull weight (lb.) 1,551
Speed (mph) 3.69
Percent slippage 5.12
SAE drawbar horsepower 12.09
SAE belt/PTO horsepower 16.16
Type ....tricycle
Front wheel (in.) ....steel: 24 x 4;
(rubber: 4.75 x 15)
Rear wheel (in.) ....steel: 40 x 6;
(rubber: 10.00 x 28)
Length (in.) 126
Height (in.) 66
Rear width (in.) 76–87
Weight (lb.) ....steel: 2,495;
rubber: 3,204
Gear/speed (mph) ....forward: 1/2.00,
2/2.80, 3/3.75, 4/7.50;
reverse: 1/1.75

Allis-Chalmers K, WK, Wide
Manufacturer ....Allis-Chalmers Mfg.
Co., Milwaukee, WI
Nebraska test number 336
Test date ....November 21–27,
1939
Test tractor serial number ....WK 8276

Years produced 1929–1943
Serial number range.............................1–9468 end
Serial number location ....stamped on rear transmission case, upper right corner, or on instrument panel
Number produced 9,468
Engine ....Allis-Chalmers vertical I-head
Test engine serial number......................12078 G
Cylinders 4
Bore and stroke (in.) ....5.00 x 6.50
Rated rpm 1,050
Displacement (c.i.) 510.5
Fuel ....gasoline
Fuel tank capacity (gal.) 39
Carburetor ....Zenith 62AJ12, 1.50-in.
Air cleaner ....Vortox
Ignition ....Fairbanks-Morse FMO4B magneto
Cooling capacity (gal.) 11.50

Maximum brake horsepower tests
    PTO/belt horsepower...........................62.22
    Crankshaft rpm 1,050
    Fuel use (gal./hr.)..............................6.16

Maximum drawbar horsepower tests
    Gear...2nd
    Drawbar horsepower...........................53.60
    Pull weight (lb.) 7,813
    Speed (mph) 2.57
    Percent slippage..............................1.63
SAE drawbar horsepower.......................41.24
SAE belt/PTO horsepower......................54.37
Type ....tracklayer
Length (in.) 119
Height (in.)..64
Rear width (in.)...................................65.88 or 80.88
Tread width (in.).................................48 or 63
Weight (lb.) ....(13,165)
Track length (in.).................................67 on ground, 221 total
Grouser shoe......................................34 links; 15, (18)
Gear/speed (mph) ....forward: 1/1.72, 2/2.59, 3/3.26, 4/5.92; reverse: 1/2.10

Allis-Chalmers S, WS, Wide
Manufacturer.......................................Allis-Chalmers Mfg. Co., Milwaukee, WI
Nebraska test number 337
Test date ....November 18–24, 1939
Test tractor serial number......................WS 901
Years produced 1937–1942
Serial number range.............................3–1227 end
Serial number location..........................stamped on top right rear of tran smission case or on instrument panel
Number produced 1,225
Engine ....Allis-Chalmers vertical I-head
Test engine serial number......................269 G
Cylinders 4
Bore and stroke (in.) ....5.75 x 6.50
Rated rpm 1,050

Displacement (c.i.) 675.1
Fuel ....gasoline
Fuel tank capacity (gal.) 64
Carburetor ....Zenith 62A-12, 1.50-in.
Air cleaner ....United
Ignition ....Delco-Remy 1111510 9F5, with 12-v battery
Cooling capacity (gal.) 12.50

Maximum brake horsepower tests
    PTO/belt horsepower...........................84.34
    Crankshaft rpm 1,050
    Fuel use (gal./hr.)..............................8.21

Maximum drawbar horsepower tests
    Gear...2nd
    Drawbar horsepower...........................68.86
    Pull weight (lb.) 11,367
    Speed (mph) 2.27
    Percent slippage..............................2.67
SAE drawbar horsepower.......................52.83
SAE belt/PTO horsepower......................72.90
Type ....tracklayer
Length (in.) 146
Height (in.)...74.19
Rear width (in.)...................................84.63 or 96.63
Tread width (in.).................................62 or 74
Weight (lb.) ....(20,155)
Track length (in.).................................77.13 on ground, 252 total
Grouser shoe......................................32 links; 18
Gear/speed (mph) ....forward: 1/1.52, 2/2.32, 3/3.25, 4/4.55, 5/6.37; reverse: 1/1.76

Allis-Chalmers L
Manufacturer.......................................Allis-Chalmers Mfg. Co., Milwaukee, WI
Nebraska test number 338
Test date ....November 23–28, 1939
Test tractor serial number......................L 3133
Years produced 1931–1942
Serial number range.............................1–3357 end
Serial number location ....stamped on right rear shelf to transmission case or on instrument panel
Number produced 3,357
Engine ....Allis-Chalmers vertical I-head
Test engine serial number......................ML 3634 A
Cylinders 6
Bore and stroke (in.) ....5.25 x 6.50
Rated rpm 1,050
Displacement (c.i.) 844.3
Fuel ....gasoline
Fuel tank capacity (gal.) 75
Carburetor ....Zenith 62AX-J10, 1.25-in.
Air cleaner ....Vortox
Ignition ....Fairbanks-Morse RV-6B magneto
Cooling capacity (gal.) 19

Maximum brake horsepower tests
    PTO/belt horsepower...........................108.84
    Crankshaft rpm 1,050
    Fuel use (gal./hr.)..............................10.54

Allis-Chalmers

Maximum drawbar horsepower tests

Gear 2nd
Drawbar horsepower 91.99
Pull weight (lb.) 18,410
Speed (mph) 1.87
Percent slippage 3.44
SAE drawbar horsepower 68.65
SAE belt/PTO horsepower 93.63
Type .... tracklayer
Length (in.) 153.25
Height (in.) 81.25
Rear width (in.) 93
Tread width (in.) 68
Weight (lb.) .... (25,930)
Track length (in.) .... 85.44 on ground,
273 total
Grouser shoe .... 35 links; 20
Gear/speed (mph) .... forward: 1/1.48,
2/1.94, 3/2.68, 4/3.50,
5/4.90, 6/6.41; reverse:
1/1.72, 2/2.25

Allis-Chalmers HD-7W Diesel

Manufacturer .... Allis-Chalmers Mfg.
Co., Milwaukee, WI
Nebraska test number 360
Test date .... October 15–21, 1940
Test tractor serial number HD-7W-176
Years produced 1940–1950
Serial number range .... 3–18505 end, includes
HD-7, HD-7W, HD-7
Military
Serial number location .... stamped on rear of
transmission case
upper right corner or
on plate on cowl facing
operator
Number produced 1,803
Engine .... General Motors (GM)
"71" 2-cycle vertical
I-head
Test engine serial number 3711064
Cylinders 3
Bore and stroke (in.) .... 4.25 x 5.00
Rated rpm 1,500
Compression ratio 16.0:1
Displacement (c.i.) 213
Fuel .... diesel
Fuel tank capacity (gal.) 31
Air cleaner .... United
Ignition .... 12-v; with 2,
6-v battery
Cooling capacity (gal.) 5.75

Maximum brake horsepower tests

PTO/belt horsepower 68.68
Crankshaft rpm 1,499
Fuel use (gal./hr.) 4.84

Maximum drawbar horsepower tests

Gear 2nd
Drawbar horsepower 57.29
Pull weight (lb.) 8,570
Speed (mph) 2.51
Percent slippage 1.86
SAE drawbar horsepower 45.08
SAE belt/PTO horsepower 60.42

Type .... tracklayer
Length (in.) 128
Height (in.) 69.13
Rear width (in.) .... 70.81 or 81
Tread width (in.) .... 52 or (63)
Weight (lb.) .... (14,000)
Track length (in.) .... 67 on ground,
221 total
Grouser shoe .... 34 links; 16, (18)
Gear/speed (mph) .... forward: 1/1.84, 2/2.55,
3/3.45, 4/5.82; reverse:
1/2.19

Allis-Chalmers HD-10W Diesel

Manufacturer .... Allis-Chalmers Mfg.
Co., Milwaukee, WI
Nebraska test number 361
Test date .... October 15–25, 1940
Test tractor serial number HD-10W-201
Years produced 1942–1950
Serial number range .... 1446–10198 end
Serial number location .... stamped on rear of
transmission case
upper right corner or
on plate on dash
Number produced .... approximately 8,753
Engine .... GM "71" 2-cycle
vertical I-head
Test engine serial number 471877
Cylinders 4
Bore and stroke (in.) .... 4.25 x 5.00
Rated rpm 1,600
Compression ratio 16.0:1
Displacement (c.i.) 284
Fuel .... diesel
Fuel tank capacity (gal.) 44
Air cleaner .... United
Ignition .... 12-v; with 2, 6-v battery
Cooling capacity (gal.) 9.75

Maximum brake horsepower tests

PTO/belt horsepower 98.47
Crankshaft rpm 1,600
Fuel use (gal./hr.) 6.83

Maximum drawbar horsepower tests

Gear 2nd
Drawbar horsepower 82.19
Pull weight (lb.) 15,507
Speed (mph) 1.99
Percent slippage 3.68
SAE drawbar horsepower 64.97
SAE belt/PTO horsepower 86.38
Type .... tracklayer
Length (in.) 150
Height (in.) 77.75
Rear width (in.) .... 82.50 or (94.25)
Tread width (in.) .... 62 or (74)
Weight (lb.) .... (21,455)
Track length (in.) .... 77.13 on ground,
252 total
Grouser shoe .... 32 links; 18, (20)
Gear/speed (mph) .... forward: 1/1.69,
2/2.06, 3/2.68, 4/3.78,
5/4.62, 6/6.03; reverse:
1/1.86, 2/4.17

Allis-Chalmers HD-14 Diesel

Manufacturer	Allis-Chalmers Mfg. Co., Milwaukee, WI
Nebraska test number	362
Test date	October 15 to November 5, 1940
Test tractor serial number	HD-14-265
Years produced	1939–1947
Serial number range	18–6422 end, includes 14C
Serial number location	stamped on right side shelf to rear of transmission case
Number produced	6,405
Engine	GM "71" 2-cycle vertical, I-head
Test engine serial number	6711079
Cylinders	6
Bore and stroke (in.)	4.25 x 5.00
Rated rpm	1,500
Compression ratio	16.0:1
Displacement (c.i.)	425
Fuel	diesel
Fuel tank capacity (gal.)	68
Air cleaner	United
Ignition	12-v; with 2, 6-v battery
Cooling capacity (gal.)	12

Maximum brake horsepower tests

PTO/belt horsepower	145.39
Crankshaft rpm	1,501
Fuel use (gal./hr.)	9.58

Maximum drawbar horsepower tests

Gear	2nd
Drawbar horsepower	126.98
Pull weight (lb.)	22,699
Speed (mph)	2.10
Percent slippage	4.14
SAE drawbar horsepower	27.66
SAE belt/PTO horsepower	36.07
Type	tracklayer
Length (in.)	165
Height (in.)	80
Rear width (in.)	91.75
Tread width (in.)	68
Weight (lb.)	(28,575)
Track length (in.)	85.44 on ground, 274 total
Grouser shoe	35 links; 22
Gear/speed (mph)	forward: 1/1.72, 2/2.18, 3/2.76, 4/3.50, 5/4.36, 6/7.00; reverse: 1/2.00, 2/3.20

Allis-Chalmers C,

Manufacturer	Allis-Chalmers Mfg. Co., Milwaukee, WI
Nebraska test number	363
Test date	October 28 to November 6, 1940
Test tractor serial number	C 78
Years produced	1940–1950
Serial number range	1–84030 end
Serial number location	stamped on top of transmission case in front of shift lever
Number produced	84,030, all types
Engine	Allis-Chalmers vertical I-head
Test engine serial number	CE 79K
Cylinders	4
Bore and stroke (in.)	3.375 x 3.50
Rated rpm	1,500
Displacement (c.i.)	125
Fuel	distillate/gasoline
Fuel tank capacity (gal.)	13
Carburetor	Zenith 61-AJ-7, 0.875-in.
Air cleaner	Donaldson
Ignition	Fairbanks-Morse FM-J4B magneto
Cooling capacity (gal.)	2

Maximum brake horsepower tests

PTO/belt horsepower	19.40
Crankshaft rpm	1,500
Fuel use (gal./hr.)	1.63

Maximum drawbar horsepower tests

Gear	2nd
Drawbar horsepower	15.96
Pull weight (lb.)	1,878
Speed (mph)	3.19
Percent slippage	13.15
SAE drawbar horsepower	12.57
SAE belt/PTO horsepower	17.17
Type	tricycle
Front tire (in.)	4.00 x 15
Rear tire (in.)	9.00 x 24
Length (in.)	114
Height (in.)	62.75
Rear width (in.)	68.50–89.50
Tread width (in.)	52–80
Weight (lb.)	(3,030)
Gear/speed (mph)	forward: 1/2.50, 2/3.75, 3/7.50; reverse: 1/2.75

Allis-Chalmers C

Manufacturer	Allis-Chalmers Mfg. Co., Milwaukee, WI
Nebraska test number	364
Test date	October 28 to November 7, 1940
Test tractor serial number	C 81
Years produced	1940–1950
Serial number range	1–84030 end
Serial number location	stamped on top of transmission case in front of shift lever
Number produced	84,030, all types
Engine	Allis-Chalmers vertical I-head
Test engine serial number	CE 93G
Cylinders	4
Bore and stroke (in.)	3.375 x 3.50
Rated rpm	1,500
Compression ratio	5.75:1
Displacement (c.i.)	125
Fuel	gasoline
Fuel tank capacity (gal.)	13
Carburetor	Zenith 61-AJ-7, 0.875-in.

119231

Air cleaner ....Donaldson
Ignition...Fairbanks-Morse
FM-J4B magneto
Cooling capacity (gal.) 2

Maximum brake horsepower tests
PTO/belt horsepower............................23.30
Crankshaft rpm 1,499
Fuel use (gal./hr.)................................2.03

Maximum drawbar horsepower tests
Gear..2nd
Drawbar horsepower...........................18.43
Pull weight (lb.)..................................2,206
Speed (mph).......................................3.13
Percent slippage................................15.95
SAE drawbar horsepower......................14.06
SAE belt/PTO horsepower 20.24
Type ....tricycle
Front tire (in.)....................................4.00 x 15
Rear tire (in.).....................................9.00 x 24
Length (in.) 114
Height (in.)..62.75
Rear width (in.)..................................68.50–89.50
Tread width (in.)................................52–80
Weight (lb.) ....(3,030)
Gear/speed (mph) ....forward: 1/2.50,
2/3.75, 3/7.50;
reverse: 1/2.75

Allis-Chalmers HD-5B Diesel

Manufacturer......................................Allis-Chalmers Mfg.
Co., Milwaukee, WI
Nebraska test number 396
Test date ....July 1–16, 1948
Test tractor serial number.....................HD-5B 2104
Years produced 1946–1955
Serial number range...........................1–29255 end
Serial number location ....stamped on rear steering
clutch housing upper
right corner or on plate
on cowl facing operator
Number produced 29,255
Engine ....GM 2-71, 2-cycle
vertical I-head
Test engine serial number....................2-71 14439
Cylinders 4
Bore and stroke (in.) ....4.25 x 5.00
Rated rpm 1,800
Compression ratio.............................16.0:1
Displacement (c.i.) 142
Fuel ....diesel
Fuel tank capacity (gal.) 37
Air cleaner.......................................United
Ignition..Delco-Remy, 12-v;
with 2, 6-v battery
Cooling capacity (gal.) 3.75

Maximum brake horsepower tests
PTO/belt horsepower............................47.85
Crankshaft rpm 1,801
Fuel use (gal./hr.)................................3.77

Maximum drawbar horsepower tests
Gear..2nd
Drawbar horsepower...........................38.24
Pull weight (lb.)..................................5,969
Speed (mph).......................................2.40
Percent slippage................................2.40

SAE drawbar horsepower......................30.20
SAE belt/PTO horsepower 42.71
Type ....tracklayer
Length (in.) 124.88
Height (in.)..60.38
Rear width (in.)..................................73
Tread width (in.)................................60
Weight (lb.) 11,250
Track length (in.)................................226 total
Grouser shoe.....................................33 links; 13, (16)
Gear/speed (mph) ....forward: 1/1.46,
2/2.44, 3/3.30, 4/3.96,
5/5.47; reverse: 1/2.00

Allis-Chalmers HD-19 Diesel

Manufacturer......................................Allis-Chalmers Mfg.
Co., Milwaukee, WI
Nebraska test number 397
Test date ....July 2–16, 1948
Test tractor serial number.....................HD-19 H-452
Years produced 1947–1950
Serial number range...........................4–2640 end
Serial number location ....stamped on rear steering
clutch housing upper
right corner or plate on
cowl facing operator
Number produced 2,650
Engine ....GM 6-71, 2-cycle
vertical I-head
Test engine serial number....................671 157821
Cylinders 6
Bore and stroke (in.) ....4.25 x 5.00
Rated rpm 1,750
Displacement (c.i.) 426
Fuel ....diesel
Fuel tank capacity (gal.) 109
Carburetor..GM injector pump
Air cleaner.......................................United
Ignition..Delco-Remy, 12-v;
with 2, 6-v battery
Cooling capacity (gal.) 11

Maximum brake horsepower tests
PTO/belt horsepower............................129.08
Crankshaft rpm 1,727
Fuel use (gal./hr.)................................11.72

Maximum drawbar horsepower tests
Gear..2nd, low range
Drawbar horsepower...........................110.73
Pull weight (lb.)..................................24,791
Speed (mph).......................................1.68
Percent slippage................................2.40

SAE drawbar horsepower......................110.73
SAE belt/PTO horsepower 129.08
Type ....tracklayer
Length (in.) 190.75
Height (in.)..89.44
Rear width (in.)..................................109.25
Tread width (in.)................................84
Weight (lb.) ....(40,220)
Track length (in.)................................106.63 on ground,
332 total
Grouser shoe.....................................24
Gear/speed (mph) ....forward: high/0–7.00,
low/0–3.00; reverse:
low/0–5.50

Allis-Chalmers G

Manufacturer	Allis-Chalmers Mfg. Co., Milwaukee, WI
Nebraska test number	398
Test date	July 16–30, 1948
Test tractor serial number	G-42
Years produced	1948–1955
Serial number range	6–29976 end
Serial number location	stamped on top of transmission case to rear of shift lever
Number produced	approximately 29,971
Engine	Continental N-62, vertical L-head
Test engine serial number	AN 62 1407
Cylinders	4
Bore and stroke (in.)	2.375 x 3.50
Rated rpm	1,800
Compression ratio	5.4:1
Displacement (c.i.)	62
Fuel	gasoline
Fuel tank capacity (gal.)	5
Carburetor	Marvel-Schebler TSV-13, 0.625-in.
Air cleaner	Donaldson
Ignition	Delco-Remy, 6-v battery
Cooling capacity (gal.)	1.63

Maximum brake horsepower tests

PTO/belt horsepower	10.33
Crankshaft rpm	1,798
Fuel use (gal./hr.)	1.17

Maximum drawbar horsepower tests

Gear	2nd
Drawbar horsepower	9.04
Pull weight (lb.)	1,096
Speed (mph)	3.09
Percent slippage	11.00
SAE drawbar horsepower	7.19
SAE belt/PTO horsepower	9.27
Type	standard
Front tire (in.)	4.00 x 12
Rear tire (in.)	6.00 x 30
Length (in.)	114.50
Height (in.)	55.69
Tread width (in.)	36–64
Weight (lb.)	1,285
Gear/speed (mph)	forward: 1/2.25, 2/3.50, 3/7.00, sp. low/1.60; reverse: 1/2.00

Allis-Chalmers WD

Manufacturer	Allis-Chalmers Mfg. Co., Milwaukee, WI
Nebraska test number	399
Test date	July 16–30, 1948
Test tractor serial number	WD 21
Years produced	1948–1954
Serial number range	7–146606 end
Serial number location	stamped on rear face of transmission
Number produced	146,575
Engine	Allis-Chalmers W vertical I-head
Test engine serial number	WD 196529K

Cylinders	4
Bore and stroke (in.)	4.00 x 4.00
Rated rpm	1,400
Compression ratio	5.50:1
Displacement (c.i.)	201
Fuel	tractor fuel
Fuel tank capacity (gal.)	15
Carburetor	Marvel-Schebler TSX-159, 1.00-in.
Air cleaner	United
Ignition	Fairbanks-Morse FMI 4B3 magneto or 6-v battery
Cooling capacity (gal.)	3.50

Maximum brake horsepower tests

PTO/belt horsepower	26.14
Crankshaft rpm	1,404
Fuel use (gal./hr.)	2.66

Maximum drawbar horsepower tests

Gear	2nd
Drawbar horsepower	24.31
Pull weight (lb.)	2,536
Speed (mph)	3.59
Percent slippage	6.87
SAE drawbar horsepower	19.19
SAE belt/PTO horsepower	23.46
Type	tricycle
Front tire (in.)	5.50 x 16
Rear tire (in.)	11.00 x 28
Length (in.)	127.10
Height (in.)	81.50
Tread width (in.)	56–90
Weight (lb.)	3,975
Gear/speed (mph)	forward: 1/2.50, 2/3.75, 3/5.00, 4/9.75; reverse: 1/2.25

Allis-Chalmers B

Manufacturer	Allis-Chalmers Mfg. Co., Milwaukee, WI
Nebraska test number	439
Test date	May 17–24, 1950
Test tractor serial number	B 73430
Years produced	1937–1957
Serial number range	1–127186, no end
Serial number location	stamped on top of transmission case in front of shift lever
Number produced	approximately 118,500
Engine	Allis-Chalmers C vertical I-head
Test engine serial number	CE128908G
Cylinders	4
Bore and stroke (in.)	3.375 x 3.50
Rated rpm	1,500
Compression ratio	5.75:1
Displacement (c.i.)	125
Fuel	gasoline
Fuel tank capacity (gal.)	13
Carburetor	Marvel-Schebler TSX-154, 0.875-in.
Air cleaner	Donaldson
Ignition	Fairbanks-Morse magneto or 6-v battery
Cooling capacity (gal.)	2

Allis-Chalmers

Maximum brake horsepower tests
- PTO/belt horsepower............................22.25
- Crankshaft rpm 1,500
- Fuel use (gal./hr.)................................2.09

Maximum drawbar horsepower tests
- Gear...2nd
- Drawbar horsepower............................19.51
- Pull weight (lb.)...................................1,742
- Speed (mph)......................................4.20
- Percent slippage................................7.01

SAE drawbar horsepower........................15.45
SAE belt/PTO horsepower.......................19.44
Type ....standard
Front tire (in.)....................................4.00 x 15
Rear tire (in.)....................................10.00 x 24
Length (in.) 110.25
Height (in.)...62.75
Tread width (in.).................................40–52
Weight (lb.)..2,060
Gear/speed (mph) ....forward: 1/2.50,
2/4.00, 3/7.50;
reverse: 1/3.00

Allis-Chalmers WD

Manufacturer...............................Allis-Chalmers Mfg.
Co., Milwaukee, WI
Nebraska test number 440
Test date ....May 17 to
June 1, 1950
Test tractor serial number...................WD 48595
Years produced 1948–1954
Serial number range...........................7–146606 end
Serial number location ....stamped on rear face
of transmission
Number produced 146,575
Engine ....Allis-Chalmers W
vertical I-head
Test engine serial number.................WD 247330
Cylinders 4
Bore and stroke (in.) ....4.00 x 4.00
Rated rpm 1,400
Compression ratio............................5.75:1
Displacement (c.i.) 201
Fuel ....gasoline
Fuel tank capacity (gal.) 15
Carburetor.......................................Marvel-Schebler
TSX-159, 1.00-in.
Air cleaner ....United
Ignition..Fairbanks-Morse
magneto or 6-v battery
Cooling capacity (gal.) 3.50

Maximum brake horsepower tests
- PTO/belt horsepower............................34.63
- Crankshaft rpm 1,400
- Fuel use (gal./hr.)................................3.22

Maximum drawbar horsepower tests
- Gear...3rd
- Drawbar horsepower............................30.23
- Pull weight (lb.)...................................2,369
- Speed (mph)......................................4.79
- Percent slippage................................5.90

SAE drawbar horsepower........................23.76
SAE belt/PTO horsepower.......................30.43
Type ....tricycle
Front tire (in.)....................................5.50 x 16

Rear tire (in.)....................................11.00 x 28
Length (in.)...127.13
Height (in.)...81.50
Tread width (in.).................................56–90
Weight (lb.)...3,975
Gear/speed (mph) ....forward: 1/2.50,
2/3.75, 3/5.00, 4/9.75;
reverse: 1/2.25

Allis-Chalmers CA

Manufacturer...................................The Allis-Chalmers
Mfg. Co., Milwaukee,
WI
Nebraska test number 453
Test date ....October 31 to
November 9, 1950
Test tractor serial number...................CA 12
Years produced 1950–1957
Serial number range...........................12–38618 no end
Serial number location ....stamped on top of
transmission case in
front of shift lever
Number produced ....approximately 38,606
Engine ....Allis-Chalmers CE
vertical I-head
Test engine serial number.................CE 138073 GA
Cylinders 4
Bore and stroke (in.) ....3.375 x 3.50
Rated rpm 1,650
Compression ratio............................6.25:1
Displacement (c.i.) 125
Fuel ....gasoline
Fuel tank capacity (gal.) 13
Carburetor.......................................Zenith 161AJ7,
0.875-in.
Air cleaner ....MRI
Ignition..Fairbanks-Morse
magneto
Cooling capacity (gal.) 2

Maximum brake horsepower tests
- PTO/belt horsepower............................25.96
- Crankshaft rpm 1,650
- Fuel use (gal./hr.)................................2.37

Maximum drawbar horsepower tests
- Gear...2nd
- Drawbar horsepower............................22.97
- Pull weight (lb.)...................................2,735
- Speed (mph)......................................3.15
- Percent slippage................................8.82

SAE drawbar horsepower........................17.66
SAE belt/PTO horsepower.......................22.63
Type ....tricycle
Front tire (in.)....................................4.00 x 15
Rear tire (in.)....................................10.00 x 24
Length (in.) 124.63
Height (in.)...73.38
Tread width (in.).................................52–80
Weight (lb.)...2,835
Gear/speed (mph) ....forward: 1/2.00, 2/3.50,
3/4.50, 4/11.25;
reverse: 1/3.50

Allis-Chalmers HD-9 Diesel

Manufacturer...................................Allis-Chalmers Mfg.
Co., Milwaukee, WI

Nebraska test number 463
Test date ....July 17–28, 1951
Test tractor serial number HD-9B 196
Years produced 1951–1955
Serial number range ....1–5850 end
Serial number location ....stamped on rear steering clutch housing upper right corner or on plate on cowl facing operator
Number produced 5,850
Engine ....GM 4-71, 2-cycle vertical I-head
Test engine serial number 4A 13663
Cylinders 4
Bore and stroke (in.) ....4.25 x 5.00
Rated rpm 1,600
Compression ratio 16:1
Displacement (c.i.) 284
Fuel ....diesel
Fuel tank capacity (gal.) 55
Carburetor ....GM injector pump
Air cleaner ....United
Ignition ....Delco-Remy, 12-v; with 2, 6-v battery
Cooling capacity (gal.) 7.25
Maximum brake horsepower tests
  PTO/belt horsepower 79.10
  Crankshaft rpm 1,602
  Fuel use (gal./hr.) 5.86
Maximum drawbar horsepower tests
  Gear 2nd
  Drawbar horsepower 67.39
  Pull weight (lb.) 12,239
  Speed (mph) 2.06
  Percent slippage 1.71
SAE drawbar horsepower 54.37
SAE belt/PTO horsepower 71.88
Type ....tracklayer
Length (in.) 150
Height (in.) 72.75
Tread width (in.) 74
Weight (lb.) 18,800
Track length (in.) 265.50
Grouser shoe ....38 links; 16, (20)
Gear/speed (mph) ....forward: 1/1.39, 2/2.10, 3/2.93, 4/3.77, 5/4.41, 6/5.68; reverse: 1/1.56, 2/3.45, 3/4.43

Allis-Chalmers HD-15 Diesel
Manufacturer ....Allis-Chalmers Mfg. Co., Milwaukee, WI
Nebraska test number 464
Test date ....July 17 to August 2, 1951
Test tractor serial number HD-15A 90
Years produced 1951–1955
Serial number range ....1–3909 end
Serial number location ....stamped on rear steering clutch housing upper right corner or on plate on dash
Number produced 3,909
Engine ....GM 6-71, 2-cycle vertical I-head

Test engine serial number 6A 12358
Cylinders 6
Bore and stroke (in.) ....4.25 x 5.00
Rated rpm 1,600
Compression ratio 16:1
Displacement (c.i.) 426
Fuel ....diesel
Fuel tank capacity (gal.) 91.50
Carburetor ....GM injector pump
Air cleaner ....United
Ignition ....Delco-Remy, 12-v; with 2, 6-v battery
Cooling capacity (gal.) 11.75
Maximum brake horsepower tests
  PTO/belt horsepower 117.68
  Crankshaft rpm 1,600
  Fuel use (gal./hr.) 8.56
Maximum drawbar horsepower tests
  Gear 2nd
  Drawbar horsepower 104.37
  Pull weight (lb.) 19,081
  Speed (mph) 2.05
  Percent slippage 2.25
SAE drawbar horsepower 81.76
SAE belt/PTO horsepower 105.30
Type ....tracklayer
Length (in.) 190.75
Height (in.) 95.25
Tread width (in.) 84
Weight (lb.) 27,850
Track length (in.) 297
Grouser shoe ....38 links; 18, 20, 22, (24)
Gear/speed (mph) ....forward: 1/1.39, 2/2.09, 3/2.97, 4/3.87, 5/4.45, 6/5.80; reverse: 1/1.54, 2/3.47, 3/4.51

Allis-Chalmers HD-20 Diesel
Manufacturer ....Allis-Chalmers Mfg. Co., Milwaukee, WI
Nebraska test number 465
Test date ....July 20 to August 3, 1951
Test tractor serial number HD-20H 3275
Years produced 1951–1954
Serial number range ....3001–6100 end
Serial number location ....stamped on rear steering clutch housing upper right corner or on plate on cowl facing operator
Number produced 3,100
Engine ....GM 6-110, vertical I-head
Test engine serial number 6B 847
Cylinders 6
Bore and stroke (in.) ....5.00 x 5.60
Rated rpm 1,700
Compression ratio 18.0:1
Displacement (c.i.) 660
Fuel ....diesel
Fuel tank capacity (gal.) 120
Carburetor ....GM injector pump
Air cleaner ....United

Ignition ....Delco-Remy, 24-v;
with 2, 12-v battery
Cooling capacity (gal.) 15
Maximum drawbar horsepower tests
    Gear ....2nd, low range
    Drawbar horsepower............................116.69
    Pull weight (lb.)..............................30,464
    Speed (mph) 1.44
    Percent slippage..............................3.01
SAE drawbar horsepower............................116.69
Type ....tracklayer
Length (in.) 190.75
Height (in.) 95.25
Tread width (in.)....................................84
Weight (lb.) 41,000
Track length (in.) 332.50
Grouser shoe..37 links; 22, 24, 26, (28)
Gear/speed (mph) ....forward: high/0–7.00,
low/0–3.00; reverse:
low/0–5.50

Allis-Chalmers WD-45

Manufacturer..Allis-Chalmers Mfg.
Co., Milwaukee, WI
Nebraska test number 499
Test date ....July 29 to
August 10, 1953
Test tractor serial number..........................WD 147753
Years produced 1953–1957
Serial number range................................146607–236958 end
Serial number location ....stamped on rear face
of transmission
Number produced ....90,352, all types
Engine ....Allis-Chalmers W-45
vertical I-head
Test engine serial number..........................45 3600 G
Cylinders 4
Bore and stroke (in.) ....4.00 x 4.50
Rated rpm 1,400
Compression ratio..................................6.45:1
Displacement (c.i.) 226
Fuel ....gasoline
Fuel tank capacity (gal.) 15
Carburetor ....Marvel-Schebler
TSX-464, 1.00-in.
Air cleaner ....United
Ignition..Delco-Remy with
6-v battery
Cooling capacity (gal.) 3.50
Maximum brake horsepower tests
    PTO/belt horsepower..........................43.21
    Crankshaft rpm 1,400
    Fuel use (gal./hr.)...........................3.80
Maximum drawbar horsepower tests
    Gear 3rd
    Drawbar horsepower............................37.84
    Pull weight (lb.)..............................2,856
    Speed (mph) 4.97
    Percent slippage..............................6.27
SAE drawbar horsepower............................30.01
SAE belt/PTO horsepower...........................38.48
Type ....tricycle
Front wheel (in.) ....5.50 x 16
Rear wheel (in.) ....13.00 x 28
Length (in.) 127.25

Height (in.) 81.50
Tread width (in.) 56–90
Weight (lb.) 3,780
Gear/speed (mph) ....forward: 1/2.50,
2/3.75, 3/5.00,
4/11.25; reverse:
1/3.25

Allis-Chalmers WD-45

Manufacturer..Allis-Chalmers Mfg.
Co., Milwaukee, WI
Nebraska test number 511
Test date ....October 26–31, 1953
Test tractor serial number..........................WD 149901
Years produced 1953–1957
Serial number range................................146607–236958 end
Serial number location ....stamped on rear face
of transmission
Number produced ....90,352, all types
Engine ....Allis-Chalmers
vertical I-head
Test engine serial number..........................45 5449K
Cylinders 4
Bore and stroke (in.) ....4.00 x 4.50
Rated rpm 1,400
Compression ratio..................................4.75:1
Displacement (c.i.) 226
Fuel ....tractor fuel
Fuel tank capacity (gal.) 15
Carburetor ....Marvel Schebler
TSX-561, 1.00-in.
Air cleaner ....United
Ignition..Delco-Remy with
6-v battery
Cooling capacity (gal.) 3.50
Maximum brake horsepower tests
    PTO/belt horsepower..........................33.01
    Crankshaft rpm 1,401
    Fuel use (gal./hr.)...........................3.29
Maximum drawbar horsepower tests
    Gear 3rd
    Drawbar horsepower............................29.49
    Pull weight (lb.)..............................2,204
    Speed (mph) 5.02
    Percent slippage..............................4.52
SAE drawbar horsepower............................22.94
SAE belt/PTO horsepower...........................28.85
Type ....tricycle
Front wheel (in.) ....5.50 x 16
Rear wheel (in.) ....13.00 x 28
Length (in.) 127.13
Height (in.) 81.50
Tread width (in.) 56–90
Weight (lb.) 3,780
Gear/speed (mph) ....forward: 1/2.50,
2/3.75, 3/5.00,
4/11.25; reverse:
1/3.25

Allis-Chalmers WD-45 LP, LPG

Manufacturer..Allis-Chalmers Mfg.
Co., Milwaukee, WI
Nebraska test number 512
Test date ....October 26 to
November 4, 1953

Test tractor serial number............WD 150743
Years produced............1953–1957
Serial number range............146607–236958 end
Serial number location ....stamped on rear face
of transmission
Number produced ....90,352, all types, LPG
interspersed
Engine ....Allis-Chalmers
vertical I-head
Test engine serial number............45 4519-G
Cylinders............4
Bore and stroke (in.)............4.00 x 4.50
Rated rpm............1,400
Compression ratio............7.2:1
Displacement (c.i.)............226
Fuel............LPG
Carburetor............Ensign Kgnl, 1.00-in.
Air cleaner............United
Ignition............Delco-Remy with
6-v battery
Cooling capacity (gal.) 3.50
Maximum brake horsepower tests
PTO/belt horsepower............44.13
Crankshaft rpm 1,401
Fuel use (gal./hr.)............4.97
Maximum drawbar horsepower tests
Gear............3rd
Drawbar horsepower............38.53
Pull weight (lb.)............2,891
Speed (mph)............5.00
Percent slippage............5.08
SAE drawbar horsepower............30.08
SAE belt/PTO horsepower............38.44
Type............tricycle
Front wheel (in.)............5.50 x 16
Rear wheel (in.)............13.00 x 28
Length (in.)............127.13
Height (in.)............81.50
Tread width (in.)............56–90
Weight (lb.)............3,974
Gear/speed (mph)............forward: 1/2.50,
2/3.75, 3/5.00,
4/11.25; reverse:
1/3.25

Allis-Chalmers HD-21 AC Diesel
Manufacturer............Allis-Chalmers Mfg.
Co., Springfield, IL
Nebraska test number............550
Test date ....July 6–18, 1955
Test tractor serial number............HD-21A 7302
Years produced............1954–1965
Serial number range............7001–13737 no end
Serial number location ....stamped on rear
steering clutch housing
upper right corner or
on plate on cowl facing
operator
Engine ....Allis-Chalmers HDS844
vertical I-head
Test engine serial number............1643
Cylinders............6
Bore and stroke (in.)............5.25 x 6.50
Rated rpm 1,800

Compression ratio............13.3:1
Displacement (c.i.)............844
Fuel............diesel
Fuel tank capacity (gal.)............135
Carburetor............Bosch injector pump
Air cleaner............United
Ignition............Delco-Remy, 24-v;
with 2, 12-v battery
Cooling capacity (gal.)............20
Maximum drawbar horsepower tests
Gear............2nd, low range
Drawbar horsepower............135.12
Pull weight (lb.)............29,067
Speed (mph)............1.74
Percent slippage............2.77
SAE drawbar horsepower............135.12
Type............tracklayer
Length (in.)............197.75
Height (in.)............98.88
Tread width (in.)............84
Weight (lb.)............44,000
Track length (in.)............331.50
Grouser shoe............37 links; 24, (28)
Gear/speed (mph)............forward: 1 low
range/0–3.00, 2 high
range/0–7.50; reverse:
1/0–5.50

Allis-Chalmers HD-16 AC Diesel
Manufacturer............Allis-Chalmers Mfg.
Co., Springfield, IL
Nebraska test number............551
Test date............July 6–18, 1955
Test tractor serial number............HD-16 AC 280
Years produced............1955–1965
Serial number range............101–6965 no end
Serial number location ....stamped on rear
steering clutch housing
upper right corner or
on plate on cowl facing
operator
Engine............Allis-Chalmers HD844
vertical I-head
Test engine serial number............4901
Cylinders............6
Bore and stroke (in.)............5.25 x 6.50
Rated rpm 1,800
Compression ratio............14.15:1
Displacement (c.i.)............844
Fuel............diesel
Fuel tank capacity (gal.)............100
Carburetor............Bosch injector pump
Air cleaner............United
Ignition............Delco-Remy, 24-v;
with 2, 12-v battery
Cooling capacity (gal.) 15.75
Maximum drawbar horsepower tests
Gear............2nd, middle range
Drawbar horsepower............101.33
Pull weight (lb.)............15,117
Speed (mph) 2.51
Percent slippage............1.12
SAE drawbar horsepower............101.33
Type ....tracklayer

Length (in.) 178
Height (in.) 89.88
Tread width (in.) 74
Weight (lb.) 31,500
Track length (in.) 297
Grouser shoe .... 38 links; 20, (22)
Gear/speed (mph) .... forward: 1 low
range/0–2.50, 2 middle
range/0–4.30, 3 high
range/0–7.20; reverse:
1/0–5.50

Allis-Chalmers HD-16 A Diesel

Manufacturer .... Allis-Chalmers Mfg.
Co., Springfield, IL
Nebraska test number 552
Test date .... July 6–18, 1955
Test tractor serial number HD-16A 282
Years produced 1955–1965
Serial number range .... 101–6965 no end
Serial number location .... stamped on rear steering
clutch housing upper
right corner or on plate
on cowl facing operator
Engine .... Allis-Chalmers HD844
vertical, I-head
Test engine serial number 6320
Cylinders 6
Bore and stroke (in.) .... 5.25 x 6.50
Rated rpm 1,600
Compression ratio 14.15:1
Displacement (c.i.) 844
Fuel .... diesel
Fuel tank capacity (gal.) 100
Carburetor .... Bosch injector pump
Air cleaner .... United
Ignition .... Delco-Remy, 24-v;
with 2, 12-v battery
Cooling capacity (gal.) 15.75
Maximum brake horsepower tests
PTO/belt horsepower 133.83
Crankshaft rpm 1,600
Fuel use (gal./hr.) 9.09
Maximum drawbar horsepower tests
Gear 2nd
Drawbar horsepower 118.69
Pull weight (lb.) 21,735
Speed (mph) 2.05
Percent slippage 2.93
SAE drawbar horsepower 93.59
SAE belt/PTO horsepower 119.94
Type .... tracklayer
Length (in.) 178
Height (in.) 89.88
Tread width (in.) 74
Weight (lb.) 31,500
Track length (in.) 297
Grouser shoe .... 38 links; 20, (22)
Gear/speed (mph) .... forward: 1/1.40,
2/2.10, 3/3.00, 4/3.90,
5/4.50, 6/5.80; reverse:
1/1.50, 2/3.50, 3/4.50

Allis-Chalmers WD-45 Diesel

Manufacturer .... Allis-Chalmers Mfg.
Co., Milwaukee, WI

Nebraska test number 563
Test date .... October 4–11, 1955
Test tractor serial number .... WD 199022 D
Years produced 1953–1957
Serial number range .... 146607–236958 end
Serial number location .... stamped on left brake
cover or left rear
transmission housing
Number produced .... 90,352, all types,
diesel interspersed
Engine .... Allis-Chalmers vertical
I-head
Test engine serial number 73928
Cylinders 6
Bore and stroke (in.) .... 3.4375 x 4.125
Rated rpm 1,625
Compression ratio 15.5:1
Displacement (c.i.) 230
Fuel .... diesel
Fuel tank capacity (gal.) 15
Carburetor .... Bosch injector pump
Air cleaner .... United
Ignition .... Delco-Remy, 12-v;
with 2, 6-v battery
Cooling capacity (gal.) 4.25
Maximum brake horsepower tests
PTO/belt horsepower 43.29
Crankshaft rpm 1,625
Fuel use (gal./hr.) 3.08
Maximum drawbar horsepower tests
Gear 3rd
Drawbar horsepower 39.50
Pull weight (lb.) 3,045
Speed (mph) 4.87
Percent slippage 6.40
SAE drawbar horsepower 30.32
SAE belt/PTO horsepower 38.61
Type .... tricycle
Front wheel (in.) .... 5.50 x 16
Rear wheel (in.) .... 13.00 x 28
Length (in.) 128.44
Height (in.) 69.88
Tread width (in.) 56–90
Weight (lb.) 4,730
Gear/speed (mph) .... forward: 1/2.50,
2/4.00, 3/5.50,
4/12.00; reverse:
1/3.50

Allis-Chalmers HD-6B Diesel

Manufacturer .... Allis-Chalmers Mfg.
Co., Springfield, IL
Nebraska test number 580
Test date .... July 7–14, 1956
Test tractor serial number HD-6B 2851
Years produced 1955–1965
Serial number range .... 101–18189 no end
Serial number location .... stamped on rear
steering clutch housing
upper right corner or
on plate on cowl facing
operator
Engine .... Allis-Chalmers HD-344
vertical I-head
Test engine serial number 88973
Cylinders 4

Bore and stroke (in.) ....4.4375 x 5.5625
Rated rpm 1,800
Compression ratio 15:1
Displacement (c.i.) 344
Fuel ....diesel
Fuel tank capacity (gal.) 37
Carburetor ....GM injector pump
Air cleaner ....United
Ignition ....Delco-Remy, 24-v;
    with 2, 12-v battery
Cooling capacity (gal.) 3.75
Maximum brake horsepower tests
    PTO/belt horsepower.............................60.51
    Crankshaft rpm 1,800
    Fuel use (gal./hr.) 5.27
Maximum drawbar horsepower tests
    Gear...2nd
    Drawbar horsepower 49.95
    Pull weight (lb.) 7,928
    Speed (mph) 2.36
    Percent slippage...................................3.32
SAE drawbar horsepower...............................39.06
SAE belt/PTO horsepower..............................54.38
Type ....tracklayer
Length (in.) 127
Height (in.) 65.62
Tread width (in.)..60
Weight (lb.) 13,400
Track length (in.) 221
Grouser shoe...34 links; 13, (16)
Gear/speed (mph) ....forward: 1/1.46,
    2/2.44, 3/3.30, 4/3.96,
    5/5.47; reverse: 1/1.99

Allis-Chalmers HD-11B Diesel

Manufacturer..Allis-Chalmers Mfg.
    Co., Springfield, IL
Nebraska test number 581
Test date ....July 9–13, 1956
Test tractor serial number HD-11B 1675
Years produced..1955–1965
Serial number range.....................................101–10533 no end
Serial number location..................................stamped on rear steering
    clutch housing upper
    right corner or on plate
    on cowl facing operator
Engine ....Allis-Chalmers HD-516
    vertical I-head
Test engine serial number 89087
Cylinders 6
Bore and stroke (in.) ....4.4375 x 5.5625
Rated rpm 1,800
Compression ratio..15:1
Displacement (c.i.) 516
Fuel ....diesel/gasoline
Fuel tank capacity (gal.) 60
Carburetor..Bosch injector pump
Air cleaner ....United
Ignition ....Delco-Remy, 24-v;
    with 2, 12-v battery
Cooling capacity (gal.) 10
Maximum brake horsepower tests
    PTO/belt horsepower..............................89.75
    Crankshaft rpm 1,800
    Fuel use (gal./hr.) 6.93

Maximum drawbar horsepower tests
    Gear...2nd
    Drawbar horsepower..............................73.80
    Pull weight (lb.)....................................13,410
    Speed (mph) 2.06
    Percent slippage...................................1.89
SAE drawbar horsepower...............................58.25
SAE belt/PTO horsepower..............................80.29
Type ....tracklayer
Length (in.) 154
Height (in.) 84
Tread width (in.) 74
Weight (lb.) 22,200
Track length (in.) 266
Grouser shoe...38 links; 16, (20)
Gear/speed (mph) ....forward: 1/1.39,
    2/2.10, 3/2.93, 4/3.77,
    5/4.41, 6/5.68; reverse:
    1/1.56, 2/3.45, 3/4.43

Allis-Chalmers D-14

Manufacturer...Allis-Chalmers Mfg.
    Co., Milwaukee, WI
Nebraska test number 623
Test date ....June 1–7, 1957
Test tractor serial number ....D 14 1093
Years produced 1957–1960
Serial number range.....................................1001–24050 end
Serial number location ....left front of torque
    housing
Number produced ....approximately 23,050
Engine ....Allis-Chalmers 149
    vertical I-head
Test engine serial number ....149 1481 B
Cylinders 4
Bore and stroke (in.) ....3.50 x 3.875
Rated rpm 1,650
Compression ratio..7.5:1
Displacement (c.i.) 149
Fuel ....gasoline
Fuel tank capacity (gal.) 14
Carburetor ....Marvel-Schebler
    TSX-670, 0.875-in.
Air cleaner ....Donaldson
Ignition..Delco-Remy with
    6-v battery
Cooling capacity (gal.) 2.25
Maximum brake horsepower tests
    PTO/belt horsepower.............................34.08
    Crankshaft rpm 1,650
    Fuel use (gal./hr.)................................3.04
Maximum drawbar horsepower tests
    Gear...3rd, high range
    Drawbar horsepower..............................30.91
    Pull weight (lb.).....................................2,396
    Speed (mph) 4.84
    Percent slippage...................................6.42
SAE drawbar horsepower...............................24.14
SAE belt/PTO horsepower..............................30.30
Type ....tricycle
Front wheel (in.) ....5.50 x 16
Rear wheel (in.) ....12.00 x 26
Height (in.) 79.56
Tread width (in.)..54–80
Weight (lb.) 4,000

Gear/speed (mph)..............forward: 1 high range/2.20, 1 low range/1.50, 2 high range/3.75, 2 low range/2.60, 3 high range/4.75, 3 low range/3.70, 4 high range/12.00, 4 low range/8.50; reverse: 1 high/3.75, 1 low/2.60

Allis-Chalmers D-17

Manufacturer..Allis-Chalmers Mfg. Co., Milwaukee, WI
Nebraska test number 635
Test date ....November 14–25, 1957
Test tractor serial number............D-17 1128
Years produced 1958–1967
Serial number range..................4300–89213 end
Serial number location ....left front of torque housing
Number produced ....approximately 84,914
Engine ....Allis-Chalmers vertical I-head
Test engine serial number................17 1071M
Cylinders 4
Bore and stroke (in.) ....4.00 x 4.50
Rated rpm 1,650
Compression ratio..............................7.25:1
Displacement (c.i.) 226
Fuel ....gasoline
Fuel tank capacity (gal.) 19
Carburetor.........................Zenith 267-8, 1.00-in.
Air cleaner ....United
Ignition................................Delco-Remy with 12-v battery
Cooling capacity (gal.) 3.63
Maximum brake horsepower tests
    PTO/belt horsepower............................52.70
    Crankshaft rpm 1,650
    Fuel use (gal./hr.)............................4.54
Maximum drawbar horsepower tests
    Gear..3rd, high range
    Drawbar horsepower..........................48.64
    Pull weight (lb.)..............................3,457
    Speed (mph) 5.28
    Percent slippage..............................5.78
SAE drawbar horsepower............................36.11
SAE belt/PTO horsepower 46.27
Type ....tricycle
Front wheel (in.)................................6.00 x 16
Rear wheel (in.)................................14.00 x 28
Height (in.)..81
Tread width (in.)..............................58–92
Weight (lb.) 5,540
Gear/speed (mph)..............forward: 1 high range/2.60, 1 Power Director/1.80, 2 high range/4.00, 2 Power Director/3.00, 3 high range/5.50, 3 Power Director/4.00, 4 high range/12.00, 4 Power Director/8.50; reverse: 1 high range/3.50, 1 Power Director/2.40

Allis-Chalmers D-17 Diesel

Manufacturer..Allis-Chalmers Mfg. Co., Milwaukee, WI
Nebraska test number 636
Test date ....November 14–26, 1957

Test tractor serial number............D-17 1001D
Years produced 1958–1967
Serial number range..................4300–89213 end
Serial number location ....left front of torque housing
Number produced ....approximately 84,914 total, diesel interspersed
Engine ....Allis-Chalmers vertical I-head
Test engine serial number................100274
Cylinders 6
Bore and stroke (in.) ....3.5625 x 4.375
Rated rpm 1,650
Compression ratio..............................15.7:1
Displacement (c.i.) 262
Fuel ....diesel
Fuel tank capacity (gal.) 19
Carburetor.........................Roosa injector pump
Air cleaner ....United
Ignition................................Delco-Remy, 12-v; with 2, 6-v battery
Cooling capacity (gal.) 3.63
Maximum brake horsepower tests
    PTO/belt horsepower............................51.14
    Crankshaft rpm 4,650
    Fuel use (gal./hr.)............................3.72
Maximum drawbar horsepower tests
    Gear..3rd, high range
    Drawbar horsepower..........................46.20
    Pull weight (lb.)..............................3,287
    Speed (mph) 5.27
    Percent slippage..............................5.04
SAE drawbar horsepower............................35.30
SAE belt/PTO horsepower 45.42
Type ....tricycle
Front wheel (in.)................................6.00 x 16
Rear wheel (in.)................................14.00 x 28
Height (in.)..81
Tread width (in.)..............................58–92
Weight (lb.) 5,540
Gear/speed (mph)..............forward: 1 high range/2.60, 1 Power Director/1.80, 2 high range/4.00, 2 Power Director/3.00, 3 high range/5.50, 3 Power Director/4.00, 4 high range/12.00, 4 Power Director/8.50; reverse: 1 high range/3.50, 1 Power Director/2.40

Allis-Chalmers D-17 LPG

Manufacturer..Allis-Chalmers Mfg. Co., Milwaukee, WI
Nebraska test number 644
Test date ....April 1–12, 1958
Test tractor serial number............D-17 5773
Years produced 1958–1967
Serial number range..................4300–89213 end
Serial number location ....left front of torque housing
Number produced ....approximately 84,914 total, LPG interspersed
Engine ....Allis-Chalmers vertical I-head
Test engine serial number............17 5217V
Cylinders 4

Bore and stroke (in.) ....4.00 x 4.50
Rated rpm 1,650
Compression ratio.............................8.25:1
Displacement (c.i.) 226
Fuel ....LPG
Fuel tank capacity (gal.) 22.30
Carburetor ....Ensign 1MG1,
1.00-in.
Air cleaner ....United
Ignition..Delco-Remy with
12-v battery
Cooling capacity (gal.) 3.63
Maximum brake horsepower tests
  PTO/belt horsepower...........................50.79
  Crankshaft rpm 1,650
  Fuel use (gal./hr.)...............................5.45
Maximum drawbar horsepower tests
  Gear...3rd, high range
  Drawbar horsepower.............................46.23
  Pull weight (lb.).....................................3,311
  Speed (mph) 5.24
  Percent slippage...................................5.67
SAE drawbar horsepower.........................35.43
SAE belt/PTO horsepower 45.05
Type ....tricycle
Front wheel (in.)......................................6.00 x 16
Rear wheel (in.)..14.00 x 28
Height (in.) 81
Tread width (in.).......................................58.25–92.75
Weight (lb.) 5,440
Gear/speed (mph)..............forward: 1 high/2.60, 1 Power
Director/1.80, 2 high/4.00, 2 Power
Director/3.00, 3 high/5.50, 3 Power
Director/3.80, 4 high/12.00, 4 Power
Director/8.50; reverse: 1 high/3.50, 1
Power Director/2.40

Allis-Chalmers D-14 LPG

Manufacturer...Allis-Chalmers Mfg.
Co., Milwaukee, WI
Nebraska test number 645
Test date ....April 1–12, 1958
Test tractor serial number.............................D-14 9643
Years produced 1957–1960
Serial number range......................................1001–24050 end
Serial number location ....left front of torque
housing
Number produced ....approximately 23,050
total, LPG interspersed
Engine ....Allis-Chalmers 149
vertical I-head
Test engine serial number.............................149 10033T
Cylinders 4
Bore and stroke (in.) ....3.50 x 3.875
Rated rpm 1,650
Compression ratio.......................................8.5:1
Displacement (c.i.) 149
Fuel ....LPG
Fuel tank capacity (gal.) 22.30
Carburetor ....Ensign 1MG1,
1.00-in.
Air cleaner ....Donaldson
Ignition..Delco-Remy,
6-v battery
Cooling capacity (gal.) 2.25

Maximum brake horsepower tests
  PTO/belt horsepower...........................31.86
  Crankshaft rpm 1,650
  Fuel use (gal./hr.)................................3.67
Maximum drawbar horsepower tests
  Gear...3rd, high range
  Drawbar horsepower.............................28.67
  Pull weight (lb.).....................................2,204
  Speed (mph) 4.88
  Percent slippage....................................4.68
SAE drawbar horsepower..........................22.21
SAE belt/PTO horsepower 28.25
Type ....tricycle
Front wheel (in.).......................................5.50 x 16
Rear wheel (in.)..12.00 x 26
Height (in.)...79.56
Tread width (in.).......................................54–80
Weight (lb.) 4,060
Gear/speed (mph)............forward: 1 high/2.20, 1 Power
Director/1.50, 2 high/3.75, 2 Power
Director/2.60, 3 high/4.75, 3 Power
Director/3.75, 4 high/12.00, 4 Power
Director/8.50; reverse: 1 high/3.75, 1
Power Director/2.60

Allis-Chalmers HD-21A Diesel

Manufacturer...Allis-Chalmers Mfg.
Co., Springfield, IL
Nebraska test number 664
Test date ....August 26 to
September 3, 1958
Test tractor serial number.............................HD-21A 10002
Years produced 1954–1965
Serial number range......................................7001–13737 no end
Serial number location ....stamped on rear
steering clutch housing
upper right corner or
on plate on cowl facing
operator
Engine ....Allis-Chalmers HDS844
vertical I-head
Test engine serial number.............................21 2474
Cylinders 6
Bore and stroke (in.) ....5.25 x 6.50
Rated rpm 1,825
Compression ratio.......................................14.5:1
Displacement (c.i.) 844.3
Fuel ....diesel
Fuel tank capacity (gal.) 135
Carburetor ....Bosch injector pump
Air cleaner ....United
Ignition..Delco-Remy, 24-v;
with 2, 12-v battery
Cooling capacity (gal.) 20
Maximum drawbar horsepower tests
  Gear...low range
  Drawbar horsepower.............................147.19
  Pull weight (lb.).....................................36,140
  Speed (mph) 1.53
  Percent slippage....................................3.08
SAE drawbar horsepower..........................147.18
Type ....tracklayer
Tread width (in.).......................................84
Weight (lb.) 47,280
Track length (in.)......................................360

Allis-Chalmers

Grouser shoe................................40 links; 24, (26)
Gear/speed (mph) ....forward: 1 low
range/0–3.10, 2 high
range/0–8.00; reverse:
1/0–6.00

Allis-Chalmers D-12
Manufacturer...............................Allis-Chalmers Mfg.
Co., Milwaukee, WI
Nebraska test number 723
Test date ....October 13–20, 1959
Test tractor serial number............D-12 1123
Years produced 1959–1967
Serial number range.....................1001–9830 no end
Serial number location ....left front of torque
housing
Engine..Allis-Chalmers 10
vertical L-head
Test engine serial number............10 1251 S
Cylinders 4
Bore and stroke (in.) ....3.375 x 3.875
Rated rpm 1,650
Compression ratio.......................7.75:1
Displacement (c.i.) 138.7
Fuel ....gasoline
Fuel tank capacity (gal.) 15.75
Carburetor ....Zenith 161J7, 0.875-in.
Air cleaner ....Donaldson
Ignition.......................................Fairbanks-Morse
FMJ4B4A magneto
or Delco-Remy,
6-v battery
Cooling capacity (gal.) 2.25
Maximum brake horsepower tests
PTO/belt horsepower...........28.56
Crankshaft rpm 1,650
Fuel use (gal./hr.) 2.34
Maximum drawbar horsepower tests
Gear....................................3rd
Drawbar horsepower.............23.56
Pull weight (lb.)....................2,057
Speed (mph) 4.29
Percent slippage...................6.18
SAE drawbar horsepower.......24.86
SAE belt/PTO horsepower 28.56
Type ....standard
Front wheel (in.)..........................5.00 x 15
Rear wheel (in.)...........................11.00 x 24
Height (in.) 76.50
Tread width (in.)...........................52–79.25
Weight (lb.) 2,800
Gear/speed (mph) ....forward: 1/2.00,
2/3.50, 3/4.50,
4/11.40; reverse:
1/3.50

Allis-Chalmers D-10
Manufacturer...............................Allis-Chalmers Mfg.
Co., Milwaukee, WI
Nebraska test number 724
Test date ....October 13–20, 1959
Test tractor serial number............D-10 1164
Years produced 1959–1967
Serial number range.....................1001–10100 end
Serial number location ....left front of torque
housing
Number produced ....approximately 9,100
Engine..Allis-Chalmers 10
vertical L-head
Test engine serial number............10 1227 S
Cylinders 4
Bore and stroke (in.) ....3.375 x 3.875
Rated rpm 1,650
Compression ratio.......................7.75:1
Displacement (c.i.) 138.7
Fuel ....gasoline
Fuel tank capacity (gal.) 15.75
Carburetor ....Zenith 161J7, 0.875-in.
Air cleaner ....Donaldson
Ignition.......................................Fairbanks-Morse
FMJ4B4A magneto
or Delco-Remy,
6-v battery
Cooling capacity (gal.) 2.25
Maximum brake horsepower tests
PTO/belt horsepower...........28.51
Crankshaft rpm 1,650
Fuel use (gal./hr.) 2.23
Maximum drawbar horsepower tests
Gear....................................3rd
Drawbar horsepower.............25.73
Pull weight (lb.)....................2,409
Speed (mph) 4.01
Percent slippage...................8.55
SAE drawbar horsepower 25.84
SAE belt/PTO horsepower 28.51
Type ....standard
Front wheel (in.)..........................5.00 x 15
Rear wheel (in.)...........................10.00 x 24
Height (in.) 76
Tread width (in.)...........................42–72
Weight (lb.) 2,700
Gear/speed (mph) ....forward: 1/2.00,
2/3.50, 3/4.50,
4/11.40; reverse:
1/3.50

Chapter 2

ALLWORK

Allwork 14-28

Manufacturer	Electric Wheel Co., Quincy, IL
Nebraska test number	53
Test date	August 16 to September 14, 1920
Test tractor serial number	5043
Years produced	1918–1923
Engine	Electric Wheel Co. vertical L-head
Test engine serial number	5043
Cylinders	4
Bore and stroke (in.)	5.00 x 6.00
Rated rpm	900
Displacement (c.i.)	471.3
Fuel	kerosene/gasoline
Fuel tank capacity (gal.)	25
Auxiliary tank capacity (gal.)	5
Carburetor	Kingston E
Air cleaner	Bennett
Ignition	Kingston L magneto
Cooling capacity (gal.)	13

Maximum brake horsepower tests	
PTO/belt horsepower	28.86
Crankshaft rpm	915
Fuel use (gal./hr.)	4.95
Maximum drawbar horsepower tests	
Gear	low
Drawbar horsepower	19.69
Pull weight (lb.)	3,950
Speed (mph)	1.87
Percent slippage	15.10
SAE drawbar horsepower	14
SAE belt/PTO horsepower	28
Type	4 wheel
Front wheel (in.)	steel: 32 x 6
Rear wheel (in.)	steel: 48 x 12
Length (in.)	125
Height (in.)	69
Rear width (in.)	79
Weight (lb.)	5,000
Gear/speed (mph)	forward: 1/1.75, 2/2.50; reverse: 1/1.75

Chapter 3

AULTMAN & TAYLOR

Aultman & Taylor 30-60

Manufacturer	Aultman & Taylor Machinery Co., Mansfield, OH
Nebraska test number	30
Test date	June 30 to July 20, 1920
Test tractor serial number	3455
Years produced	1911–1924
Engine	Aultman & Taylor horizontal, valve-in-head
Test engine serial number	3455
Cylinders	4
Bore and stroke (in.)	7.00 x 9.00
Rated rpm	500–550
Displacement (c.i.)	1,385.4
Fuel	kerosene/gasoline
Fuel tank capacity (gal.)	60
Auxiliary tank capacity (gal.)	20
Carburetor	Kingston E, 2.50-in.

Ignition	Eisemann G4 magneto
Cooling capacity (gal.)	120
Maximum brake horsepower tests	
PTO/belt horsepower	80.10
Crankshaft rpm	556
Fuel use (gal./hr.)	9.10 (gasoline)
Maximum drawbar horsepower tests	
Drawbar horsepower	58.05
Pull weight (lb.)	9,160
Speed (mph)	2.38
Percent slippage	4.30
SAE drawbar horsepower	30
SAE belt/PTO horsepower	60
Type	4 wheel
Front wheel (in.)	steel: 44 x 12
Rear wheel (in.)	steel: 90 x 24
Length (in.)	wheelbase: 136; total: 218
Height (in.)	136
Rear width (in.)	131

Weight (lb.) 25,000
Gear/speed (mph) ....forward: 1/2.42;
reverse: 1/2.89

Aultman & Taylor 15-30
Manufacturer..Aultman & Taylor
Machinery Co.,
Mansfield, OH
Nebraska test number 31
Test date ....July 1–8, 1920
Test tractor serial number.....................3317
Years produced 1919–1923
Serial number location ....cast-iron tag on left
frame rail next to
engine
Number produced ....approximately 500
Engine...Climax vertical L-head
Test engine serial number.....................2622
Cylinders 4
Bore and stroke (in.) ....5.00 x 6.50
Rated rpm 900
Displacement (c.i.) 510.5
Fuel ....kerosene/gasoline
Main tank capacity (gal.).......................16
Auxiliary tank capacity (gal.) 6
Carburetor..Kingston L, 1.50-in.
Air cleaner ....Bennett
Ignition...Eisemann G4 magneto
Cooling capacity (gal.) 5
Maximum brake horsepower tests
PTO/belt horsepower...........................34.37
Crankshaft rpm 898
Fuel use (gal./hr.) 5.79
Maximum drawbar horsepower tests
Drawbar horsepower............................21.19
Pull weight (lb.)....................................2,838
Speed (mph) 2.80
Percent slippage..................................5.90
SAE drawbar horsepower.......................15
SAE belt/PTO horsepower......................30
Type ....4 wheel
Front wheel (in.).....................................steel: 36 x 5
Rear wheel (in.)......................................steel: 70 x 12
Length (in.) ....98.50 wheel, 176 total
Height (in.)..104
Rear width (in.).......................................80
Weight (lb.) 7,800
Gear/speed (mph) ....forward: 1/2.49;
reverse: 1/1.52

Aultman & Taylor 22-45
Manufacturer..Aultman & Taylor
Machinery Co.,
Mansfield, OH
Nebraska test number 32
Test date ....July 1–19, 1920
Test tractor serial number.....................3356
Years produced 1919–1923
Serial number location ....cast iron tag on front
cross-member under
radiator/stamped outer
rim of flywheel, left
side
Number produced ....approximately 1,200
Engine...Aultman & Taylor
horizontal
valve-in-head
Test engine serial number.....................3356
Cylinders 4
Bore and stroke (in.) ....5.50 x 8.00
Rated rpm 600
Displacement (c.i.) 760.3
Fuel ....kerosene/gasoline
Main tank capacity (gal.).......................35
Auxiliary tank capacity (gal.) 20
Carburetor..Kingston E, 2.00-in.
Ignition...Eisemann G4 magneto
Cooling capacity (gal.) 85
Maximum brake horsepower tests
PTO/belt horsepower...........................46.66
Crankshaft rpm 607
Fuel use (gal./hr.) 6.23
Maximum drawbar horsepower tests
Gear...low
Drawbar horsepower............................28.10
Pull weight (lb.)....................................4,986
Speed (mph) 2.11
Percent slippage..................................3.80
SAE drawbar horsepower.......................22
SAE belt/PTO horsepower......................45
Type ....4 wheel
Front wheel (in.).....................................steel: 38 x 10
Rear wheel (in.)......................................steel: 70 x 20
Length (in.) ....102 wheel, 166 total
Height (in.)..125
Rear width (in.).......................................89.75
Weight (lb.) 12,800
Gear/speed (mph) ....forward: 1/2.13,
2/2.93; reverse: 1/2.08

Chapter 4

AVERY

Avery C, 6-cylinder
Manufacturer...Avery Co., Peoria, IL
Nebraska test number...............................39
Test date ....July 21 to August 4, 1920
Test tractor serial number.........................25904
Years produced..1920–1922
Serial number range.................................001–28561 Last known number, consecutive
Serial number location ....stamped right side frame in front of radiator/brass plate middle rear frame
Number produced ....all models interspersed
Engine ....Avery type vertical L-head
Test engine serial number.........................GL 2121
Cylinders 6
Bore and stroke (in.) ....3.00 x 4.00
Rated rpm 1,250
Displacement (c.i.) 169.6
Fuel ....gasoline
Fuel tank capacity (gal.) 10
Carburetor..Kingston L, 0.75-in.
Air cleaner ....Bennett
Ignition...K-W, T magneto
Maximum brake horsepower tests
    PTO/belt horsepower..........................14.63
    Crankshaft rpm 1,246
    Fuel use (gal./hr.) 2.39
Maximum drawbar horsepower tests
    Gear...low
    Drawbar horsepower............................8.65
    Pull weight (lb.)..................................1,862
    Speed (mph)......................................1.74
    Percent slippage.................................18.80
SAE drawbar horsepower...........................None
SAE belt/PTO horsepower ....None
Type ....4 wheel
Front wheel (in.).......................................steel: 28 x 5.
Rear wheel (in.)..steel: 38 x 10
Length (in.) ....90 wheel, 136 total
Rear width (in.) 50
Weight (lb.) 3,150
Gear/speed (mph) ....forward: 1/1.63, 2/2.25, 3/4.50; reverse: 1/1.625

Avery Motor Cultivator/Planter 5-10
Manufacturer...Avery Co., Peoria, IL
Nebraska test number...............................40
Test date ....July 21–28, 1920
Test tractor serial number.........................2730
Years produced..1916–1920
Serial number range.................................001–28561 Last known number, consecutive
Serial number location ....stamped right side frame in front of radiator/brass plate middle rear frame

Number produced ....all models interspersed
Engine ....Avery vertical L-head
Test engine serial number.........................GL 2186
Cylinders 6
Bore and stroke (in.) ....3.00 x 4.00
Rated rpm 1,250
Displacement (c.i.) 169.6
Fuel ....gasoline
Fuel tank capacity (gal.) 10
Carburetor..Kingston L, 0.75-in.
Air cleaner ....Bennett
Ignition...K-W, T magneto
Maximum brake horsepower tests
    PTO/belt horsepower..........................15.77
    Crankshaft rpm 1,240
    Fuel use (gal./hr.) 2.54
Maximum drawbar horsepower tests
    Gear...low
    Drawbar horsepower............................8.99
    Pull weight (lb.)..................................1,674
    Speed (mph)......................................2.01
    Percent slippage.................................13.80
SAE drawbar horsepower...........................5
SAE belt/PTO horsepower 10
Type ....2 rear drive wheels, 1 front guide
Front wheel (in.).......................................steel: 28 x 5
Rear wheel (in.)..steel: 42 x 6
Length (in.) 184
Height (in.) 65
Rear width (in.) 112
Weight (lb.) 3,450
Gear/speed (mph) ....forward: 1/2.00, 2/2.50, 3/5.33; reverse: 1/2.00

Avery 12-20
Manufacturer...Avery Co., Peoria, IL
Nebraska test number...............................41
Test date ....July 22 to August 2, 1920
Test tractor serial number.........................21196
Years produced..1920–1922
Serial number range.................................001–28561 Last known number, consecutive
Serial number location ....stamped right side frame in front of radiator/brass plate middle rear frame
Number produced ....all models interspersed
Engine ....Avery horizontal opposed, valve-in-head
Test engine serial number.........................2
Cylinders 4
Bore and stroke (in.) ....4.375 x 6.00
Rated rpm 800
Displacement (c.i.) 360.8
Fuel ....kerosene/gasoline
Main tank capacity (gal.)...........................16
Auxiliary tank capacity (gal.) 6

Carburetor .... Kingston E dual, 1.25-in.
Ignition .... K-W, TK magneto
Cooling capacity (gal.) 11
Maximum brake horsepower tests
    PTO/belt horsepower 24.26
    Crankshaft rpm 800
    Fuel use (gal./hr.) 3.80
Maximum drawbar horsepower tests
    Gear .... low
    Drawbar horsepower 17.58
    Pull weight (lb.) 2,608
    Speed (mph) 2.53
    Percent slippage 14.25
SAE drawbar horsepower 12
SAE belt/PTO horsepower 20
Type .... 4 wheel
Front wheel (in.) .... steel: 32 x 5
Rear wheel (in.) .... steel: 52 x 14
Length (in.) 130
Height (in.) 78
Rear width (in.) 56
Weight (lb.) 5,500
Gear/speed (mph) .... forward: 1/2.38, 2/3.50; reverse: 1/na

Avery 14-28

Manufacturer .... Avery Co., Peoria, IL
Nebraska test number 42
Test date .... July 23 to August 2, 1920
Test tractor serial number 26030
Years produced 1919–1922
Serial number range .... 001–28561 Last known number, consecutive
Serial number location .... stamped right side frame in front of radiator/brass plate middle rear frame
Number produced .... all models interspersed
Engine .... Avery horizontal opposed, valve-in-head
Test engine serial number .... A 1568
Cylinders 4
Bore and stroke (in.) .... 4.625 x 7.00
Rated rpm 700–900
Displacement (c.i.) 470.4
Fuel .... kerosene/gasoline
Main tank capacity (gal.) 20
Auxiliary tank capacity (gal.) 3.25
Carburetor .... Kingston E dual, 1.25-in.
Ignition .... K-W, T magneto
Cooling capacity (gal.) 30
Maximum brake horsepower tests
    PTO/belt horsepower 31.83
    Crankshaft rpm 898
    Fuel use (gal./hr.) 4.17
Maximum drawbar horsepower tests
    Gear .... low
    Drawbar horsepower 21.52
    Pull weight (lb.) 3,049
    Speed (mph) 2.65
    Percent slippage 8.30

SAE drawbar horsepower 14
SAE belt/PTO horsepower 28
Type .... 4 wheel
Front wheel (in.) .... steel: 36 x 6
Rear wheel (in.) .... steel: 60 x 16
Length (in.) 152
Height (in.) 104
Rear width (in.) 68
Weight (lb.) 6,800
Gear/speed (mph) .... forward: 1/2.33, 2/3.50; reverse: 1/na

Avery 25-50

Manufacturer .... Avery Co., Peoria, IL
Nebraska test number 43
Test date .... July 26–30, 1920
Test tractor serial number 26005
Years produced 1914–1922/Improved 1922–1932
Serial number range .... 001–28561 Last known number, consecutive
Serial number location .... stamped right side frame in front of radiator/brass plate middle rear frame
Number produced .... all models interspersed
Engine .... Avery horizontal opposed, valve-in-head
Test engine serial number .... TB 1
Cylinders 4
Bore and stroke (in.) .... 6.50 x 8.00
Rated rpm 700
Displacement (c.i.) 1061.9
Fuel .... kerosene/gasoline
Main tank capacity (gal.) 50
Auxiliary tank capacity (gal.) 5
Carburetor .... Kingston, dual, 2.00-in.
Ignition .... K-W, HK magneto
Cooling capacity (gal.) 55
Maximum brake horsepower tests
    PTO/belt horsepower 56.68
    Crankshaft rpm 712
    Fuel use (gal./hr.) 7.04
Maximum drawbar horsepower tests
    Gear .... high
    Drawbar horsepower 32.62
    Pull weight (lb.) 3,225
    Speed (mph) 3.79
    Percent slippage 1.40
SAE drawbar horsepower 25
SAE belt/PTO horsepower 50
Type .... 4 wheel
Front wheel (in.) .... steel: 38 x 10
Rear wheel (in.) .... steel: 69 x 20
Length (in.) 176
Height (in.) 108
Rear width (in.) 90.50
Weight (lb.) 12,500
Gear/speed (mph) .... forward: 1/2.00, 2/3.00; reverse: 1/na

Avery 40-80

Manufacturer .... Avery Co., Peoria, IL
Nebraska test number 44

Test date .... July 26 to August 3, 1920
Test tractor serial number 25259
Years produced 1913–1920
Serial number range .... 001–28561 Last known number, consecutive
Serial number location .... stamped right side frame in front of radiator/brass plate middle rear frame
Number produced .... all models interspersed
Engine .... Avery horizontal opposed, valve-in-head
Test engine serial number .... ZB 1073
Cylinders 4
Bore and stroke (in.) .... 7.75 x 8.00
Rated rpm 500–600
Displacement (c.i.) 1509.5
Fuel .... kerosene/gasoline
Main tank capacity (gal.) 44
Auxiliary tank capacity (gal.) 6.75
Carburetor .... Kingston, dual, 2.00-in.
Ignition .... K-W, HK magneto
Cooling capacity (gal.) 90
Maximum brake horsepower tests
    PTO/belt horsepower 69.23
    Crankshaft rpm 597
    Fuel use (gal./hr.) 8.23
Maximum drawbar horsepower tests
    Gear .... low
    Drawbar horsepower 49.97
    Pull weight (lb.) 8,475
    Speed (mph) 2.21
    Percent slippage 7.29
SAE drawbar horsepower 40
SAE belt/PTO horsepower 80
Type .... 4 wheel
Front wheel (in.) .... steel: 42 x 16
Rear wheel (in.) .... steel: 87.50 x 24
Length (in.) 215
Height (in.) 121
Rear width (in.) 111.50
Weight (lb.) 22,000
Gear/speed (mph) .... forward: 1/2.00, 2/3.00; reverse: 1/na

Avery 5-10, 1-Row Cultivator
Manufacturer .... Avery Co., Peoria, IL
Nebraska test number 57
Test date .... August 25 to September 8, 1920
Test tractor serial number 2681
Years produced 1920–1922
Serial number range .... 001–28561 Last known number, consecutive
Serial number location .... stamped right side frame in front of radiator/brass plate middle rear frame
Number produced .... all models interspersed
Engine .... Avery vertical L-head
Test engine serial number .... GK - 818
Cylinders 4
Bore and stroke (in.) .... 3.00 x 4.00

Rated rpm 1,200
Displacement (c.i.) 113.1
Fuel .... gasoline
Fuel tank capacity (gal.) 10
Carburetor .... Kingston L, .75-in.
Air cleaner .... Bennett
Ignition .... K-W, TK magneto
Cooling capacity (gal.) 4.50
Maximum brake horsepower tests
    PTO/belt horsepower 11.14
    Crankshaft rpm 1,228
    Fuel use (gal./hr.) 1.86
Maximum drawbar horsepower tests
    Gear .... low
    Drawbar horsepower 5.42
    Pull weight (lb.) 1,116
    Speed (mph) 1.82
    Percent slippage 8.10
SAE drawbar horsepower 5
SAE belt/PTO horsepower 10
Type .... 4 wheel
Front wheel (in.) .... steel: 28 x 4
Rear wheel (in.) .... steel: 42 x 5
Length (in.) 118
Rear width (in.) 51
Weight (lb.) 2,650
Gear/speed (mph) .... forward: 1/1.50, 2/2.12, 3/4.25; reverse: 1/2.00

Avery 18-36
Manufacturer .... Avery Co., Peoria, IL
Nebraska test number 58
Test date .... August 25 to September 9, 1920
Test tractor serial number 26456
Years produced 1916–1921
Serial number range .... 001–28561 Last known number, consecutive
Serial number location .... stamped right side frame in front of radiator/brass plate middle rear frame
Number produced .... all models interspersed
Engine .... Avery horizontal valve-in-head
Test engine serial number .... ZD 2
Cylinders 4
Bore and stroke (in.) .... 5.50 x 6.00
Rated rpm 800
Displacement (c.i.) 570.2
Fuel .... kerosene/gasoline
Main tank capacity (gal.) 27
Auxiliary tank capacity (gal.) 6
Carburetor .... Kingston dual, 1.50-in.
Ignition .... K-W, TK magneto
Cooling capacity (gal.) 33
Maximum brake horsepower tests
    PTO/belt horsepower 44.50
    Crankshaft rpm 812
    Fuel use (gal./hr.) 6.84
Maximum drawbar horsepower tests
    Gear .... low
    Drawbar horsepower 27.50

Pull weight (lb.) 4,590
Speed (mph) 2.25
Percent slippage................................14.93
SAE drawbar horsepower...........................18
SAE belt/PTO horsepower 36
Type ....4 wheel
Front wheel (in.) ....steel: 35 x 8
Rear wheel (in.) ....steel: 65 x 20
Length (in.) 152
Height (in.) 105
Rear width (in.) 84
Weight (lb.) 9,250
Gear/speed (mph) ....forward: 1/2.75,
2/4.00; reverse: 1/2.00

Avery 12-25

Manufacturer......................................Avery Co., Peoria, IL
Nebraska test number 71
Test date ....March 25 to June 13,
1921
Test tractor serial number 27189
Years produced 1912–1922
Serial number range................................001–28561 Last known
number, consecutive
Serial number location ....stamped right side
frame in front of
radiator/brass plate
middle rear frame
Number produced ....all models interspersed
Engine ....Avery horizontal
valve-in-head
Test engine serial number ....WB - 6445
Cylinders 2
Bore and stroke (in.) ....6.50 x 7.00
Rated rpm 700
Displacement (c.i.) 464.6
Fuel ....gasoline
Fuel tank capacity (gal.) 14
Carburetor ....Kingston E, 1.50-in.
Ignition...K-W, Number 155369
TK magneto
Cooling capacity (gal.) 17.50
Maximum brake horsepower tests
PTO/belt horsepower........................25.08
Crankshaft rpm 703
Fuel use (gal./hr.) 3.46
Maximum drawbar horsepower tests
Gear...low
Drawbar horsepower.........................13.46
Pull weight (lb.)............................2,500
Speed (mph) 2.02
Percent slippage............................12.10
SAE drawbar horsepower...........................12
SAE belt/PTO horsepower 25
Type ....4 wheel
Front wheel (in.) ....steel: 30 x 8
Rear wheel (in.) ....steel: 56 x 20
Length (in.) 164
Height (in.) 105
Rear width (in.) 80
Weight (lb.) 7,500
Gear/speed (mph) ....forward: 1/2.06,
2/3.33; reverse: 1/2.00

Avery 8-16

Manufacturer......................................Avery Co., Peoria, IL
Nebraska test number 72
Test date ....March 28 to May 31,
1921
Test tractor serial number 26690
Years produced 1916–1922
Serial number range................................001–28561 Last known
number, consecutive
Serial number location ....stamped right side
frame in front of
radiator/brass plate
middle rear frame
Number produced ....all models interspersed
Engine ....Avery horizontal
opposed, valve-in-head
Test engine serial number ....LB 3630
Cylinders 2
Bore and stroke (in.) ....5.50 x 6.00
Rated rpm 750
Displacement (c.i.) 285.1
Fuel ....gasoline
Fuel tank capacity (gal.) 12
Carburetor ....Kingston E, 1.25-in.
Ignition...K-W, Number 151742
TK magneto
Cooling capacity (gal.) 12.50
Maximum brake horsepower tests
PTO/belt horsepower........................16.76
Crankshaft rpm 753
Fuel use (gal./hr.) 2.29
Maximum drawbar horsepower tests
Gear...low
Drawbar horsepower.........................9.99
Pull weight (lb.)............................1,690
Speed (mph) 2.22
Percent slippage............................9.40
SAE drawbar horsepower...........................8
SAE belt/PTO horsepower 16
Type ....4 wheel
Front wheel (in.) ....steel: 30 x 5
Rear wheel (in.) ....steel: 50 x 12
Length (in.) 130
Height (in.) 72
Rear width (in.) 56
Weight (lb.) 4,900
Gear/speed (mph) ....forward: 1/2.25,
2/3.50; reverse: 1/1.75,
2/2.25

Avery Track-Runner, 15-25

Manufacturer......................................Avery Co., Peoria, IL
Nebraska test number 89
Test date ....March 16 to April 12,
1923
Test tractor serial number 35534
Years produced 1922–1925
Serial number range................................001–28561 Last known
number, consecutive
Serial number location ....stamped right side
frame in front of
radiator/brass plate
middle rear frame

Number produced ....all models interspersed
Engine ....Avery vertical,
                                                            valve-in-head
Test engine serial number ............................T.R.S. 534
Cylinders 4
Bore and stroke (in.) ....4.00 x 5.50
Rated rpm 1,125
Displacement (c.i.) 276.5
Fuel ....gasoline
Fuel tank capacity (gal.) 33
Carburetor ....Kingston L, 1.25-in.
Air cleaner ....Avery
Ignition..Splitdorf (K-W, T.K.,
                                                            Number 0133488)
                                                            magneto

Maximum brake horsepower tests
    PTO/belt horsepower...........................30.60
    Crankshaft rpm 1,121
    Fuel use (gal./hr.) 4.68
Maximum drawbar horsepower tests
    Gear...low
    Drawbar horsepower.............................20.13
    Pull weight (lb.)..................................3,280
    Speed (mph) 2.30
    Percent slippage..................................2.44
SAE drawbar horsepower............................15
SAE belt/PTO horsepower 25
Type ....half-track; 2 wheels,
                                                            2 tracks
Front wheel (in.)...steel: 26 x 3
Rear wheel (in.)..Tracks
Length (in.) 108
Height (in.) 58
Rear width (in.) 48
Weight (lb.) 5,000
Grouser shoe..10
Gear/speed (mph) ....forward: 1/2.43,
                                                            2/2.93, 3/3.90; reverse:
                                                            1/na

Avery 20-35
Manufacturer..Avery Co., Peoria, IL
Nebraska test number 96
Test date ....June 24 to July 2, 1923
Test tractor serial number 28110

Years produced 1923–1927
Serial number range.....................................001–28561 Last known
                                                            number, consecutive
Serial number location ....stamped right side
                                                            frame in front of
                                                            radiator/brass plate
                                                            middle rear frame
Number produced ....all models interspersed
Engine ....Avery horizontal
                                                            opposed, valve-in
Test engine serial number ............................A.M. 149
Cylinders 4
Bore and stroke (in.) ....4.875 x 7.00
Rated rpm 900
Displacement (c.i.) 522.6
Fuel ....kerosene/gasoline
Main tank capacity (gal.) 30
Auxiliary tank capacity (gal.) 3.50
Carburetor ....Kingston E double,
                                                            1.50-in.
Air cleaner ....Avery
Ignition..K-W, TK, Number
                                                            0104283 magneto
Cooling capacity (gal.) 30
Maximum brake horsepower tests
    PTO/belt horsepower...........................37.33
    Crankshaft rpm 893
    Fuel use (gal./hr.) 6.70
Maximum drawbar horsepower tests
    Gear...low
    Drawbar horsepower.............................22.62
    Pull weight (lb.)..................................3,080
    Speed (mph) 2.75
    Percent slippage..................................11.64
SAE drawbar horsepower............................20
SAE belt/PTO horsepower 35
Type ....4 wheel
Front wheel (in.)...steel: 36 x 6
Rear wheel (in.)..steel: 60 x 16
Length (in.) 152
Height (in.) 80
Rear width (in.) 68
Weight (lb.) 7,500
Gear/speed (mph) ....forward: 1/3.00,
                                                            2/4.00; reverse: 1/na

Chapter 5

BAKER

Baker 43-67 (Was 25-50)

Manufacturer .... A.D. Baker Co., Swanton, OH
Nebraska test number 161
Test date .... May 16–24, 1929
Test tractor serial number .... G 29140
Years produced 1927–1937
Engine .... Le Roi vertical I, valve-in-head
Test engine serial number 1176-3
Cylinders 4
Bore and stroke (in.) .... 5.50 x 7.00
Rated rpm 1,100
Displacement (c.i.) 665.2
Fuel .... gasoline
Fuel tank capacity (gal.) 40
Carburetor .... Stromberg M4, 1.75-in.
Air cleaner .... Pomona Vortox
Ignition .... American Bosch (Eisemann G4) magneto
Cooling capacity (gal.) 12

Maximum brake horsepower tests
    PTO/belt horsepower 75.88
    Crankshaft rpm 1,101
    Fuel use (gal./hr.) 8.27
Maximum drawbar horsepower tests
    Gear .... high
    Drawbar horsepower 55.72
    Pull weight (lb.) 7,840
    Speed (mph) 2.67
    Percent slippage 9.26
SAE drawbar horsepower 43
SAE belt/PTO horsepower 67
Type .... 4 wheel
Front wheel (in.) .... steel: 39 x 8
Rear wheel (in.) .... steel: 61 x 20–24
Length (in.) 159
Height (in.) 79
Rear width (in.) 78
Weight (lb.) 9,200
Gear/speed (mph) .... forward: 1/2.00–2.50, 2/3.00–3.50; reverse: 1/2.50

Chapter 6

BATES STEEL MULE

Bates Steel Mule 15-22, Model D

Manufacturer .... Bates Machine & Tractor Co., Joliet, IL
Nebraska test number 60
Test date .... August 30 to September 7, 1920
Test tractor serial number 4300
Serial number location .... cast brass plate on front frame under crank handle
Engine .... Erd vertical, valve-in-head
Test engine serial number 10783
Cylinders 4
Bore and stroke (in.) .... 4.25 x 6.00
Rated rpm 1,100
Displacement (c.i.) 340.5
Fuel .... kerosene/gasoline
Main tank capacity (gal.) 12
Auxiliary tank capacity (gal.) 3
Carburetor .... Bennett J, 1.50-in.
Air cleaner .... Bennett

Ignition .... Splitdorf, Dixie Aero magneto
Cooling capacity (gal.) 8
Maximum brake horsepower tests
    PTO/belt horsepower 24.84
    Crankshaft rpm 1,116
    Fuel use (gal./hr.) 3.76
Maximum drawbar horsepower tests
    Gear .... low
    Drawbar horsepower 20.66
    Pull weight (lb.) 2,996
    Speed (mph) 2.59
    Percent slippage 3.70
SAE drawbar horsepower 15
SAE belt/PTO horsepower 22
Type .... tracklayer: 2 wheels, 2 tracks
Front wheel (in.) .... steel: 30 x 5
Length (in.) 105
Height (in.) 58
Rear width (in.) 62
Weight (lb.) 4,600

Track length (in.)....................................51 on ground
Grouser shoe..10
Gear/speed (mph) ....forward: 1/3.00,
2/4.50; reverse: 1/2.00

Bates Steel Mule 15-22, Model F
Manufacturer...Bates Machine &
Tractor Co., Joliet, IL
Nebraska test number 68
Test date ....October 12–18, 1920
Test tractor serial number......................5100
Years produced 1919–1920
Serial number location ....cast brass plate under
crank handle
Engine ....Midwest HD 402
vertical, valve-in-head
Test engine serial number.......................10048
Cylinders 4
Bore and stroke (in.) ....4.125 x 5.25
Rated rpm 1,100
Displacement (c.i.) 280.6
Fuel ....gasoline
Fuel tank capacity (gal.) 18
Carburetor...Bennett J, 1.25-in.
Air cleaner...Bennett (R-W)
Ignition..Splitdorf, Dixie Aero
D magneto
Cooling capacity (gal.) 6
Maximum brake horsepower tests
PTO/belt horsepower...........................29.78
Crankshaft rpm 1,108
Fuel use (gal./hr.) 3.59
Maximum drawbar horsepower tests
Gear...low
Drawbar horsepower............................23.19
Pull weight (lb.)...................................3,100
Speed (mph) 2.81
Percent slippage..................................8.28
SAE drawbar horsepower.........................15
SAE belt/PTO horsepower 22
Type ....tracklayer; 2 wheels,
2 tracks
Front wheel (in.)....................................steel: 30 x 5
Rear wheel (in.).....................................tracks
Length (in.) 105
Height (in.) 58
Rear width (in.) 62
Weight (lb.) 4,600
Track length (in.)....................................51 on ground
Grouser shoe..10
Gear/speed (mph) ....forward: 1/3.00,
2/4.50; reverse: 1/2.00

Bates Steel Mule 35, 35-45
Manufacturer...Foote Bros. Gear &
Machine Co., Chicago,
IL
Nebraska test number 186
Test date ....April 6–18, 1931
Test tractor serial number......................356001
Engine ....Waukesha 6MZ vertical
L-head
Test engine serial number.......................275697
Cylinders 6

Bore and stroke (in.) ....4.25 x 4.75
Rated rpm 1,500
Displacement (c.i.) 404.3
Fuel ....gasoline
Fuel tank capacity (gal.) 35
Carburetor...Schebler HDX, 1.50-in.
Air cleaner...Vortox
Ignition..American Bosch U6
magneto
Cooling capacity (gal.) 6
Maximum brake horsepower tests
PTO/belt horsepower...........................52.58
Crankshaft rpm 1,498
Fuel use (gal./hr.) 6.40
Maximum drawbar horsepower tests
Gear...low
Drawbar horsepower............................43.73
Pull weight (lb.)...................................8,375
Speed (mph) 1.96
Percent slippage..................................4.43
SAE drawbar horsepower.........................32.91
SAE belt/PTO horsepower 46.90
Type ....tracklayer
Length (in.) 120
Height (in.) 70
Rear width (in.) 72
Weight (lb.) 10,750
Track length (in.)....................................70 on ground, 216
total
Grouser shoe..36 links; 12
Gear/speed (mph) ....forward: 1/1.90, 2/2.85,
3/3.80; reverse: 1/2.65

Bates Steel Mule 45, 45-55
Manufacturer...Foote Bros. Gear &
Machine Co., Chicago,
IL
Nebraska test number 187
Test date ....April 8–28, 1931
Test tractor serial number......................456001
Engine ....Waukesha 6SRK
vertical L-head
Test engine serial number.......................273044
Cylinders 6
Bore and stroke (in.) ....4.625 x 5.125
Rated rpm 1,500
Displacement (c.i.) 516.6
Fuel ....gasoline
Fuel tank capacity (gal.) 45
Carburetor...Schebler HDX, 1.50-in.
Air cleaner...Vortox
Ignition..American Bosch
U6 magneto
Cooling capacity (gal.) 10
Maximum brake horsepower tests
PTO/belt horsepower...........................66.53
Crankshaft rpm 1,501
Fuel use (gal./hr.) 7.82
Maximum drawbar horsepower tests
Gear...low
Drawbar horsepower............................54.43
Pull weight (lb.)...................................10,312
Speed (mph) 1.98
Percent slippage..................................3.68

SAE drawbar horsepower 40.07
SAE belt/PTO horsepower 60.38
Type .... tracklayer
Length (in.) 128
Height (in.) 72
Rear width (in.) 74
Weight (lb.) 14,000

Track length (in.) .... 82 on ground,
245 total
Grouser shoe .... 41 links; 14
Gear/speed (mph) .... forward: 1/1.92,
2/2.92, 3/3.87; reverse:
1/1.40

Chapter 7

BEAR

Bear B, 25-35

Manufacturer .... Bear Tractors Inc., New
York City, NY
Nebraska test number 100
Test date .... October 4–18, 1923
Test tractor serial number 10048
Years produced 1923–1925
Engine .... Stearns vertical, valve-
in-head
Test engine serial number .... AR 424
Cylinders 4
Bore and stroke (in.) .... 4.75 x 6.50
Rated rpm 1,190
Displacement (c.i.) 460.7
Fuel .... gasoline
Fuel tank capacity (gal.) 42
Carburetor .... Schebler A, 1.75-in.
Air cleaner .... Pomona Vortox
Ignition .... Bosch AT4-16V2
magneto

Maximum brake horsepower tests
PTO/belt horsepower 49.99
Crankshaft rpm 1,195
Fuel use (gal./hr.) 7.09
Maximum drawbar horsepower tests
Gear 2nd
Drawbar horsepower 35.68
Pull weight (lb.) 4,323
Speed (mph) 3.10
Percent slippage 11.23
SAE drawbar horsepower 25
SAE belt/PTO horsepower 35
Type .... tracklayer
Length (in.) 125.25
Height (in.) 54
Rear width (in.) 62.50
Weight (lb.) 6,000
Track length (in.) .... 64 on ground
Grouser shoe 12
Gear/speed (mph) .... forward: 1/2.17,
2/3.50, 3/5.67;
reverse: 1/2.00

Bear B, 25-35

Manufacturer .... Bear Tractors Inc.,
New York City, NY
Nebraska test number 101
Test date .... April 1–8, 1924
Test tractor serial number 10143
Years produced 1923–1925
Engine .... Stearns vertical,
valve-in-head
Test engine serial number 719
Cylinders 4
Bore and stroke (in.) .... 4.75 x 6.50
Rated rpm 1,290
Displacement (c.i.) 460.7
Fuel .... gasoline
Fuel tank capacity (gal.) 42
Carburetor .... Wheeler Schebler A,
1.75-in.
Air cleaner .... Pomona Vortox
Ignition .... Bosch AT41CV2
Number 3453161
magneto

Maximum brake horsepower tests
PTO/belt horsepower 55.56
Crankshaft rpm 1,295
Fuel use (gal./hr.) 8.43
Maximum drawbar horsepower tests
Gear 2nd
Drawbar horsepower 44.64
Pull weight (lb.) 4,863
Speed (mph) 3.44
Percent slippage 9.13
SAE drawbar horsepower 25
SAE belt/PTO horsepower 35
Type .... tracklayer
Length (in.) 125.25
Height (in.) 54
Rear width (in.) 62.50
Weight (lb.) 6,000
Track length (in.) .... 64 on ground
Grouser shoe 12
Gear/speed (mph) .... forward: 1/2.35, 2/3.80,
3/6.15; reverse: 1/2.00

Chapter 8

BEEMAN GARDEN TRACTOR

Beeman Garden Tractor G, 2-4, Garden

Manufacturer..Beeman Tractor Co., Minneapolis, MN
Nebraska test number..............................28
Test date...June 22 to July 2, 1920
Test tractor serial number......................G 204582
Years produced...1918–1926
Engine...Beeman vertical L-head
Test engine serial number......................G 204582
Cylinders..1
Bore and stroke (in.)................................3.50 x 4.50
Rated rpm..230–1,500
Displacement (c.i.)...................................43.3
Fuel...gasoline
Fuel tank capacity (gal.)..........................1
Carburetor...Kingston Y, 0.75-in.
Air cleaner...Donaldson
Ignition..Heinze AW-1 magneto
Cooling capacity (gal.).............................2.50

Maximum brake horsepower tests
  PTO/belt horsepower.............................2.37
  Crankshaft rpm.......................................1,023
  Fuel use (gal./hr.)...................................0.42
Maximum drawbar horsepower tests
  Drawbar horsepower..............................0.78
  Pull weight (lb.).......................................186.7
  Speed (mph)..1.56
  Percent slippage.....................................29.20
SAE drawbar horsepower........................2
SAE belt/PTO horsepower.......................4
Type...garden (2 drive wheels, 2 castor)
Front wheel (in.)..steel: 25 x 3.50
Length (in.)..86
Height (in.)..40
Rear width (in.)...17.25
Weight (lb.)..550
Gear/speed (mph)....................................forward: 1/.75, 2/2.50; reverse: none

Chapter 9

BEST

Best 60, Sixty, 35-55

Manufacturer..C.L. Best Tractor Co., San Leandro, CA
Nebraska test number..............................76
Test date...May 6–24, 1921
Test tractor serial number......................845 A
Years produced...1919–1925
Serial number range.................................101 A–2546 A end
Serial number location.............................brass plate left side front frame
Number produced.....................................2,446
Engine...Best vertical, valve-in-head
Test engine serial number......................2577
Cylinders..4
Bore and stroke (in.)................................6.50 x 8.50
Rated rpm..650
Displacement (c.i.)...................................1128.2
Fuel...gasoline
Fuel tank capacity (gal.)..........................50
Carburetor...Ensign G, 2.00-in.
Air cleaner...Pomona
Ignition..Bosch ZR41S, Number 3215582 magneto

Cooling capacity (gal.).............................18
Maximum brake horsepower tests
  PTO/belt horsepower.............................56.33
  Crankshaft rpm.......................................655
  Fuel use (gal./hr.)...................................6.90
Maximum drawbar horsepower tests
  Gear...low
  Drawbar horsepower..............................50.20
  Pull weight (lb.).......................................11,000
  Speed (mph)..1.71
  Percent slippage.....................................6.85
SAE drawbar horsepower........................35
SAE belt/PTO horsepower.......................55
Type...tracklayer
Length (in.)..140
Height (in.)..76.50
Rear width (in.)...90
Tread width (in.).......................................72
Weight (lb.)..17,500
Track length (in.).......................................88 on ground
Grouser shoe...16, 18, 20
Gear/speed (mph)....................................forward: 1/1.88, 2/2.63; reverse: 1/1.25

Best 30, Thirty, 18-30

Manufacturer................................C.L. Best Tractor Co., San Leandro, CA
Nebraska test number 77
Test date ....May 9–20, 1921
Test tractor serial number............1140
Years produced 1921–1925
Serial number range......................S 999–approximately S 3400
Serial number location ....brass plate, right side transmission housing above grease cup
Number produced ....approximately 2,400
Engine ....Best vertical, valve-in-head
Test engine serial number ....S 2846
Cylinders 4
Bore and stroke (in.) ....4.75 x 6.50
Rated rpm 800
Displacement (c.i.) 460.7
Fuel ....gasoline
Fuel tank capacity (gal.) 28
Carburetor ....Ensign G, 1.50-in.
Air cleaner ....Pomona
Ignition..Bosch (Berling EQ41, Number 207650) magneto
Cooling capacity (gal.) 12
Maximum brake horsepower tests
    PTO/belt horsepower.................30.43
    Crankshaft rpm 806
    Fuel use (gal./hr.)......................4.31
Maximum drawbar horsepower tests
    Gear...low
    Drawbar horsepower..................24.53
    Pull weight (lb.)........................4,343
    Speed (mph)............................2.12
    Percent slippage......................2.37
SAE drawbar horsepower..............18
SAE belt/PTO horsepower 30
Type..tracklayer
Length (in.) 112
Height (in.) 59
Rear width (in.) 53.25
Tread width (in.)...........................41.75
Weight (lb.) 7,400
Track length (in.)..........................68 on ground
Grouser shoe.................................11.50
Gear/speed (mph) ....forward: 1/2.00, 2/3.06; reverse: 1/2.50

Best 60, Sixty, 40-60

Manufacturer................................C.L. Best Tractor Co., San Leandro, CA
Nebraska test number 98
Test date ....September 10–14, 1923
Test tractor serial number............1429 A
Years produced 1919–1925
Serial number range......................101 A–2546 A end
Serial number location ....brass plate left side front frame
Number produced 2,446
Engine ....Best vertical, valve-in-head

Test engine serial number............3635
Cylinders 4
Bore and stroke (in.) ....6.50 x 8.50
Rated rpm 650
Displacement (c.i.) 1128.2
Fuel ....gasoline
Fuel tank capacity (gal.) 56
Carburetor ....Ensign (Stromberg M4, Number 1951417) 2.00-in.
Air cleaner ....Pomona
Ignition..Bosch ZR4, Number 3449020 magneto
Cooling capacity (gal.) 18
Maximum brake horsepower tests
    PTO/belt horsepower.................65.87
    Crankshaft rpm 652
    Fuel use (gal./hr.)......................8.93
Maximum drawbar horsepower tests
    Gear...2nd
    Drawbar horsepower..................54.85
    Pull weight (lb.)........................8,430
    Speed (mph)............................2.44
    Percent slippage......................1.50
SAE drawbar horsepower..............40
SAE belt/PTO horsepower 60
Type..tracklayer
Length (in.) 156
Height (in.) 78
Rear width (in.) 92
Tread width (in.)...........................72
Weight (lb.) 18,580
Track length (in.)..........................89 on ground
Grouser shoe.................................16, 18, 20
Gear/speed (mph) ....forward: 1/1.88, 2/2.63, 3/3.60; reverse: 1/na

Best 30, Thirty, 20-30

Manufacturer................................C.L. Best Tractor Co., San Leandro, CA
Nebraska test number 99
Test date ....September 11–24, 1923
Test tractor serial number............S 1800
Years produced 1921–1925
Serial number range......................S 999–approximately S 3400
Serial number location ....brass plate, right side transmission housing above grease cup
Number produced ....approximately 2,400
Engine ....Best vertical, valve-in-head
Test engine serial number............3888
Cylinders 4
Bore and stroke (in.) ....4.75 x 6.50
Rated rpm 800
Displacement (c.i.) 460.7
Fuel ....gasoline
Fuel tank capacity (gal.) 28
Carburetor ....Ensign GT, 1.50-in.
Air cleaner ....Pomona
Ignition..Bosch ZR4, Number 3506081 magneto

Cooling capacity (gal.) 12
Maximum brake horsepower tests
    PTO/belt horsepower............................32.55
    Crankshaft rpm 802
    Fuel use (gal./hr.)................................5.07
Maximum drawbar horsepower tests
    Gear..low
    Drawbar horsepower............................25.96
    Pull weight (lb.)..................................4,930
    Speed (mph) 1.98
    Percent slippage.................................2.63
SAE drawbar horsepower............................20
SAE belt/PTO horsepower 30
Type ....tracklayer
Length (in.) 129
Height (in.) 59
Rear width (in.).......................................55.25
Tread width (in.).......................................42
Weight (lb.)...8,100
Track length (in.)......................................68 on ground
Grouser shoe...11.50, 17
Gear/speed (mph) ....forward: 1/2.03,
    2/3.10; reverse: 1/2.50

Best 30, S, Thirty, 25-30

Manufacturer...C.L. Best Tractor Co.,
    San Leandro, CA
Nebraska test number 104
Test date ....September
    15–22, 1924
Test tractor serial number.........................2460
Years produced 1921–1925
Serial number range.................................S 999–approximately
    S 3400
Serial number location ....brass plate, right side
    transmission housing
    to rear of grease cup
Number produced ....approximately 2,400
Engine ....Best vertical,
    valve-in-head
Test engine serial number.........................4,335
Cylinders 4
Bore and stroke (in.) ....4.75 x 6.50
Rated rpm 850
Displacement (c.i.) 460.7
Fuel ....gasoline
Fuel tank capacity (gal.) 28
Carburetor..Ensign Gte (Stromberg
    MP3) 1.50-in.
Air cleaner ....Pomona
Ignition..Bosch ZR4 magneto
Cooling capacity (gal.) 12
Maximum brake horsepower tests
    PTO/belt horsepower............................37.83
    Crankshaft rpm 850
    Fuel use (gal./hr.)................................4.91
Maximum drawbar horsepower tests
    Gear..2nd
    Drawbar horsepower............................33.21
    Pull weight (lb.)..................................4,823
    Speed (mph) 2.58
    Percent slippage.................................1.96
SAE drawbar horsepower............................25

SAE belt/PTO horsepower 30
Type ....tracklayer
Length (in.) 129
Height (in.) 58.75
Rear width (in.).......................................58.38
Tread width (in.).......................................42
Weight (lb.)...8,700
Track length (in.)......................................68 on ground
Grouser shoe...13
Gear/speed (mph) ....forward: 1/1.75,
    2/2.63, 3/3.63;
    reverse: 1/2.00

Best 60, A, Sixty, 50-60

Manufacturer...C.L. Best Tractor Co.,
    San Leandro, CA
Nebraska test number 105
Test date ....September 15–29,
    1924
Test tractor serial number.........................1965 A
Years produced 1919–1925
Serial number range.................................101 A-2546 A end
Serial number location ....brass plate left side
    front frame
Number produced 2,446
Engine ....Best vertical,
    valve-in-head
Test engine serial number.........................1965 A
Cylinders 4
Bore and stroke (in.) ....6.50 x 8.50
Rated rpm 650
Displacement (c.i.) 1128.2
Fuel ....gasoline
Fuel tank capacity (gal.) 56
Carburetor..Ensign (Stromberg
    M4 Special) 2.00-in.
Air cleaner ....Pomona
Ignition..Bosch ZR4 Ed. 18
    magneto
Cooling capacity (gal.) 18
Maximum brake horsepower tests
    PTO/belt horsepower............................72.51
    Crankshaft rpm 653
    Fuel use (gal./hr.)................................11.36
Maximum drawbar horsepower tests
    Gear..low
    Drawbar horsepower............................61.33
    Pull weight (lb.)..................................12,360
    Speed (mph) 1.86
    Percent slippage.................................3.36
SAE drawbar horsepower............................50
SAE belt/PTO horsepower 50
Type ....tracklayer
Length (in.) 156
Height (in.) 78
Rear width (in.).......................................95
Tread width (in.).......................................72
Weight (lb.)...19,095
Track length (in.)......................................89 on ground
Grouser shoe...16, 18, 20
Gear/speed (mph) ....forward: 1/1.88,
    2/2.63, 3/3.63;
    reverse: 1/1.35

Chapter 10
BOLENS

Bolens 12BB, Garden Tractor

Manufacturer .... Bolens Products Div., Food Mach., Port Washington, WI
Nebraska test number 473
Test date .... June 9–14, 1952
Engine .... Briggs & Stratton vertical L-head
Test engine serial number 199540
Cylinders 1
Bore and stroke (in.) .... 2.25 x 2.00
Rated rpm 3,600
Compression ratio 5.4:1
Displacement (c.i.) 7.95
Fuel .... gasoline
Fuel tank capacity (gal.) 2
Carburetor .... 0.50-in.
Ignition .... magneto
Cooling .... air

Maximum brake horsepower tests
　PTO/belt horsepower 1.95
　Crankshaft rpm 3,600
　Fuel use (gal./hr.) 0.30
Maximum drawbar horsepower tests
　Gear 1st
　Drawbar horsepower 1.63
　Pull weight (lb.) 205
　Speed (mph) 2.99
　Percent slippage 11.30
SAE drawbar horsepower 1.30
SAE belt/PTO horsepower 1.76
Type .... garden, 4 wheel
Front wheel (in.) .... 5.00 x 12
Length (in.) 67
Height (in.) 40
Tread width (in.) 17.25–23
Weight (lb.) 364
Gear/speed (mph) .... forward: 1/1.25 to 3.25

Chapter 11
CASE

Case Serial Number Designations

1912–1928　Consecutive numbers for all models from 100 to 69803.
1928　Case introduced 6 digit serial number, consecutive for all models. Formula for detrmining year of manufacture: subtract 3 from the 1st and 4th digits of the serial number.
1938　Case introduced 7 digit serial number, consecutive for all models. Formula for determining year of manufacture: subtract 4 from the first 2 digits of the serial number.
1952　After the 5600000 series, 7 digit serial numbers were assigned in blocks of numbers for a specific year of manufacture to model series tractors. They begin with a 6, 8 or 9. The production year for Case started in October of each year.

Case 10-18

Manufacturer .... J.I. Case Threshing Machine Co., Racine, WI
Nebraska test number 3
Test date .... April 7,8,9,15, 1920
Test tractor serial number 26541
Years produced 1918–1922
Serial number range .... 13285–45280 end; all models interspersed

Serial number location .... brass oval plate right side front frame
Number produced 7,367
Engine .... Case vertical, valve-in-head
Cylinders 4
Bore and stroke (in.) .... 3.875 x 5.00
Rated rpm 1,050
Displacement (c.i.) 235.9
Fuel .... kerosene/gasoline
Main tank capacity (gal.) 10.50
Auxiliary tank capacity (gal.) 2.00
Carburetor .... Kingston L, 1.125-in.
Air cleaner .... Case
Ignition .... Bosch (Kingston) magneto
Cooling capacity (gal.) 9
Maximum brake horsepower tests
　PTO/belt horsepower 18.14
　Crankshaft rpm 1,043
　Fuel use (gal./hr.) 2.75
Maximum drawbar horsepower tests
　Gear .... low
　Drawbar horsepower 11.24
　Pull weight (lb.) 1,730
　Speed (mph) 2.41
　Percent slippage 11.40

SAE drawbar horsepower 10
SAE belt/PTO horsepower 18
Type ....4 wheel
Front wheel (in.) ....steel: 30 x 6
Rear wheel (in.) ....steel: 42 x 9
Length (in.) ....65 wheel, 101.50 total
Height (in.) 54.50
Rear width (in.) 56
Weight (lb.) 3,500
Gear/speed (mph) ....forward: 1/2.25,
2/3.50; reverse: 1/1.62

Case 15-27
Manufacturer ....J.I. Case Threshing
Machine Co.,
Racine, WI
Nebraska test number 4
Test date ....April 2–30, 1920
Test tractor serial number 34503
Years produced 1919–1924
Serial number range ....22223–51677 end; all
models interspersed
Serial number location ....brass oval plate right
side front frame
Number produced 17,629
Engine ....Case vertical,
valve-in-head
Cylinders 4
Bore and stroke (in.) ....4.50 x 6.00
Rated rpm 900
Displacement (c.i.) 381.7
Fuel ....kerosene/gasoline
Main tank capacity (gal.) 20
Auxiliary tank capacity (gal.) 2.75
Carburetor ....Kingston L, 2.00-in.
Air cleaner ....Case
Ignition..Berling EQ41 magneto
Cooling capacity (gal.) 11
Maximum brake horsepower tests
    PTO/belt horsepower...........................31.23
    Crankshaft rpm 924.4
    Fuel use (gal./hr.) 3.16
Maximum drawbar horsepower tests
    Gear...high
    Drawbar horsepower............................21.81
    Pull weight (lb.) 2,840
    Speed (mph) 2.88
    Percent slippage................................15.80
SAE drawbar horsepower 15
SAE belt/PTO horsepower 27
Type ....4 wheel
Front wheel (in.) ....steel: 32 x 6
Rear wheel (in.) ....steel: 52 x 14
Length (in.) ....76.50 wheel, 127 total
Height (in.) 68
Rear width (in.) 72
Weight (lb.) 5,700
Gear/speed (mph) ....forward: 1/2.25,
2/3.00; reverse: 1/1.66

Case 22-40
Manufacturer ....J.I. Case Threshing
Machine Co.,
Racine, WI

Nebraska test number 5
Test date ....April 7 to May 6, 1920
Test tractor serial number 32929
Years produced 1919–1925
Serial number range ....22223-55918 end; all
models interspersed
Serial number location ....brass oval plate right
side front frame
Number produced 1,757
Engine ....Case vertical,
valve-in-head
Cylinders 4
Bore and stroke (in.) ....5.50 x 6.75
Rated rpm 850
Displacement (c.i.) 641.5
Fuel ....kerosene/gasoline
Main tank capacity (gal.) 26.50
Auxiliary tank capacity (gal.) 3.75
Carburetor ....Kingston E, 2.00-in.
Air cleaner ....Case
Ignition..Bosch ZR4 magneto
Cooling capacity (gal.) 15.50
Maximum brake horsepower tests
    PTO/belt horsepower...........................49.97
    Crankshaft rpm 867
    Fuel use (gal./hr.) 6.90
Maximum drawbar horsepower tests
    Gear...high
    Drawbar horsepower............................31.27
    Pull weight (lb.) 3,780
    Speed (mph) 3.10
    Percent slippage................................12.86
SAE drawbar horsepower 22
SAE belt/PTO horsepower 40
Type ....4 wheel
Front wheel (in.) ....steel: 40 x 8
Rear wheel (in.) ....steel: 56 x 16
Length (in.) ....96 wheel, 153 total
Height (in.) 79.50
Rear width (in.) 82.50
Weight (lb.) 10,200
Gear/speed (mph) ....forward: 1/2.20,
2/3.20; reverse: 1/1.40

Case 10-20
Manufacturer ....J.I. Case Threshing
Machine Co.,
Racine, WI

Nebraska test number 6
Test date ....April 9 to May 5, 1920
Test tractor serial number 18849
Years produced 1915–1918
Serial number range ....2842-22222 end; all
models interspersed
Serial number location ....brass oval plate on
rear frame
Number produced 4,875
Engine ....Case vertical,
valve-in-head
Cylinders 4
Bore and stroke (in.) ....4.25 x 6.00
Rated rpm 900
Displacement (c.i.) 340.5
Fuel ....kerosene/gasoline

Fuel tank capacity (gal.) 20
Carburetor ....Kingston L
Air cleaner ....Case
Ignition..Bosch (Kingston H.T.)
                                                                    magneto
Cooling capacity (gal.) 10
Maximum brake horsepower tests
    PTO/belt horsepower...........................22.81
    Crankshaft rpm 895
    Fuel use (gal./hr.)...............................2.61
Maximum drawbar horsepower tests
    Drawbar horsepower..........................15.28
    Pull weight (lb.)..................................2,631
    Speed (mph) 2.18
    Percent slippage................................17.83
SAE drawbar horsepower.......................10
SAE belt/PTO horsepower 20
Type ....3 wheel
Front wheel (in.)...................................1, steel
Rear wheel (in.).....................................2 steel: 52 x 22 & 10
Length (in.) 150
Height (in.) 60
Rear width (in.) 67
Weight (lb.) 4,900
Gear/speed (mph) ....forward: 1/2.25;
                                                                    reverse: 1/na

Case 20-40
Manufacturer..J.I. Case Threshing
                                                                    Machine Co., Racine,
                                                                    WI
Nebraska test number 7
Test date ....April 10 to
                                                                    May 7, 1920
Test tractor serial number......................22518
Years produced 1912–1919
Serial number range...............................100–32840 end; all
                                                                    models interspersed
Serial number location ....brass oval plate, left
                                                                    side front frame
Number produced 4,303
Engine ....Case horizontal
                                                                    opposed
Cylinders 2
Bore and stroke (in.) ....8.75 x 9.00
Rated rpm 475
Displacement (c.i.) 1082.4
Fuel ....kerosene/gasoline
Main tank capacity (gal.).......................26
Auxiliary tank capacity (gal.) 11
Carburetor ....Kingston E, 2.50-in.
Ignition..K-W, HK magneto
Cooling capacity (gal.) 28
Maximum brake horsepower tests
    PTO/belt horsepower...........................42.80
    Crankshaft rpm 473
    Fuel use (gal./hr.)...............................7.68
Maximum drawbar horsepower tests
    Gear..low
    Drawbar horsepower..........................24.66
    Pull weight (lb.)..................................5,537
    Speed (mph) 1.67
    Percent slippage................................10.13
SAE drawbar horsepower.......................20
SAE belt/PTO horsepower 40

Type ....4 wheel
Front wheel (in.)...................................steel: 40 x 10
Rear wheel (in.).....................................steel: 66 x 20
Length (in.) ....114 wheel, 177 total
Height (in.) 107
Rear width (in.) 100
Weight (lb.) 14,000
Gear/speed (mph) ....forward: 1/2.00,
                                                                    2/3.00; reverse: 1/2.00

Case 12-20
Manufacturer..J.I. Case Threshing
                                                                    Machine Co.,
                                                                    Racine, WI
Nebraska test number 88
Test date ....August 14–17, 1922
Test tractor serial number......................44381
Years produced 1921–1927
Serial number range...............................42256–68403 end; all
                                                                    models interspersed
Serial number location ....brass oval plate right
                                                                    side front frame
Number produced 9,237
Engine ....Case vertical,
                                                                    valve-in-head
Test engine serial number......................44381
Cylinders 4
Bore and stroke (in.) ....4.125 x 5.00
Rated rpm 1,050
Displacement (c.i.) 267.3
Fuel ....kerosene/gasoline
Main tank capacity (gal.).......................17.50
Auxiliary tank capacity (gal.) 2.25
Carburetor ....Kingston L, 1.25-in.
Air cleaner ....Case
Ignition..Bosch (Berling F41)
                                                                    magneto
Cooling capacity (gal.) 10
Maximum brake horsepower tests
    PTO/belt horsepower...........................22.51
    Crankshaft rpm 1,061
    Fuel use (gal./hr.)...............................4.08
Maximum drawbar horsepower tests
    Gear..high
    Drawbar horsepower..........................13.85
    Pull weight (lb.)..................................1,900
    Speed (mph) 2.73
    Percent slippage................................18.65
SAE drawbar horsepower.......................12
SAE belt/PTO horsepower 20
Type ....4 wheel
Front wheel (in.)...................................steel: 30 x 6
Rear wheel (in.).....................................steel: 42 x 12
Length (in.) 109
Height (in.) 55.50
Rear width (in.) 61
Weight (lb.) 4,232
Gear/speed (mph) ....forward: 1/2.20,
                                                                    2/3.00; reverse: 1/na

Case 40-72
Manufacturer..J.I. Case Threshing
                                                                    Machine Co.,
                                                                    Racine, WI
Nebraska test number 90

Test date ...... April 6–29, 1923
Test tractor serial number 44361
Years produced 1921–1923
Serial number range ...... 42256–48412 end; all models interspersed
Serial number location ...... brass oval plate right side front frame
Number produced 42
Engine ...... Case vertical, valve-in-head
Test engine serial number 44361
Cylinders 4
Bore and stroke (in.) ...... 7.00 x 8.00
Rated rpm 800
Displacement (c.i.) 1231.5
Fuel ...... kerosene/gasoline
Main tank capacity (gal.) 52
Auxiliary tank capacity (gal.) 9
Carburetor ...... Kingston L, 2.50-in.
Air cleaner ...... Case
Ignition ...... Bosch ZR4 ISed 18, Number 3428259 magneto

Maximum brake horsepower tests
    PTO/belt horsepower 91.42
    Crankshaft rpm 801
    Fuel use (gal./hr.) 11.37
Maximum drawbar horsepower tests
    Gear ...... high
    Drawbar horsepower 55.14
    Pull weight (lb.) 7,400
    Speed (mph) 2.79
    Percent slippage 7.37
SAE drawbar horsepower 40
SAE belt/PTO horsepower 72
Type ...... 4 wheel
Front wheel (in.) ...... steel: 48 x 10
Rear wheel (in.) ...... steel: 72 x 20
Length (in.) 200
Height (in.) 110
Rear width (in.) 105
Weight (lb.) 21,200
Gear/speed (mph) ...... forward: 1/2.22, 2/3.18; reverse: 1/na

Case 12-20
Manufacturer ...... J.I. Case Threshing Machine Co., Racine, WI
Nebraska test number 91
Test date ...... April 6–17, 1923
Test tractor serial number 44551
Years produced 1921–1927
Serial number range ...... 42256–68403 end; all models interspersed
Serial number location ...... brass oval plate right side front frame
Number produced 9,237
Engine ...... Case vertical, valve-in-head
Test engine serial number 44551
Cylinders 4
Bore and stroke (in.) ...... 4.125 x 5.00
Rated rpm 1,050
Displacement (c.i.) 267.3

Fuel ...... kerosene/gasoline
Main tank capacity (gal.) 17.50
Auxiliary tank capacity (gal.) 2.25
Carburetor ...... Kingston L - 3, 1.25-in.
Air cleaner ...... Case
Ignition ...... Bosch AT4 ED1 magneto
Cooling capacity (gal.) 10
Maximum brake horsepower tests
    PTO/belt horsepower 25.54
    Crankshaft rpm 1,055
    Fuel use (gal./hr.) 3.60
Maximum drawbar horsepower tests
    Gear ...... low
    Drawbar horsepower 17.52
    Pull weight (lb.) 3,150
    Speed (mph) 2.09
    Percent slippage 14.51
SAE drawbar horsepower 12
SAE belt/PTO horsepower 20
Type ...... 4 wheel
Front wheel (in.) ...... steel: 30 x 6
Rear wheel (in.) ...... steel: 42 x 12
Length (in.) 109
Height (in.) 55.50
Rear width (in.) 61
Weight (lb.) 4,232
Gear/speed (mph) ...... forward: 1/2.02, 2/3.00; reverse: 1/na

Case 18-32
Manufacturer ...... J.I. Case Threshing Machine Co., Racine, WI
Nebraska test number 109
Test date ...... October 27 to November 4, 1924
Test tractor serial number 51320
Years produced 1925–1927
Serial number range ...... 51678–68403 end; all models interspersed
Serial number location ...... brass oval plate right side front frame
Number produced 9,890
Engine ...... Case vertical, valve-in-head
Test engine serial number 51321
Cylinders 4
Bore and stroke (in.) ...... 4.50 x 6.00
Rated rpm 1,000
Displacement (c.i.) 381.7
Fuel ...... kerosene/gasoline
Main tank capacity (gal.) 20
Auxiliary tank capacity (gal.) 2.75
Carburetor ...... Kingston L, 1.375-in.
Air cleaner ...... Case (Donaldson, Simplex)
Ignition ...... Bosch AT4, IVC3 magneto
Cooling capacity (gal.) 11
Maximum brake horsepower tests
    PTO/belt horsepower 36.73
    Crankshaft rpm 1,002
    Fuel use (gal./hr.) 3.98

Case

Maximum drawbar horsepower tests

Gear	2nd
Drawbar horsepower	24.52
Pull weight (lb.)	2,883
Speed (mph)	3.19
Percent slippage	11.91
SAE drawbar horsepower	18
SAE belt/PTO horsepower	32
Type	4 wheel
Front wheel (in.)	steel: 32 x 6
Rear wheel (in.)	steel: 52 x 14
Length (in.)	127
Height (in.)	68
Rear width (in.)	72
Weight (lb.)	6,500
Gear/speed (mph)	forward: 1/2.46, 2/3.28; reverse: 1/1.80

Case 25-45

Manufacturer	J.I. Case Threshing Machine Co., Racine, WI
Nebraska test number	110
Test date	October 28 to November 9, 1924
Test tractor serial number	51577
Years produced	1924–1927
Serial number range	48413–68403 end; all models interspersed
Serial number location	brass oval plate right side front frame
Number produced	1,184
Engine	Case vertical, valve-in-head
Test engine serial number	51577
Cylinders	4
Bore and stroke (in.)	5.50 x 6.75
Rated rpm	850
Displacement (c.i.)	641.5
Fuel	kerosene/gasoline
Main tank capacity (gal.)	26.50
Auxiliary tank capacity (gal.)	3.70
Carburetor	Kingston L, 2.00-in.
Air cleaner	Case (Donaldson, Simplex)
Ignition	Bosch ZR4 magneto
Cooling capacity (gal.)	15.50

Maximum brake horsepower tests

PTO/belt horsepower	52.59
Crankshaft rpm	852
Fuel use (gal./hr.)	5.75

Maximum drawbar horsepower tests

Gear	2nd
Drawbar horsepower	34.65
Pull weight (lb.)	3,969
Speed (mph)	3.28
Percent slippage	6.61
SAE drawbar horsepower	25
SAE belt/PTO horsepower	45
Type	4 wheel
Front wheel (in.)	steel: 40 x 8
Rear wheel (in.)	steel: 56 x 16
Length (in.)	153
Height (in.)	90
Rear width (in.)	82.50

Weight (lb.)	10,065
Gear/speed (mph)	forward: 1/2.20, 2/3.20; reverse: 1/1.40

Case L, 26-40

Manufacturer	J.I. Case Threshing Machine Co., Racine, WI
Nebraska test number	155
Test date	March 16–27, 1929
Test tractor serial number	300202
Years produced	1929–1940
Serial number range	300201-301001, 6 digit; 4200001-4400001, 7 digit; all models
Serial number location	metal plate on instrument panel
Number produced	31,871
Engine	Case vertical I-head, valve-in-head
Test engine serial number	300202
Cylinders	4
Bore and stroke (in.)	4.625 x 6.00
Rated rpm	1,100
Compression ratio	5.75:1
Displacement (c.i.)	403.2
Fuel	kerosene/gasoline
Main tank capacity (gal.)	26
Auxiliary tank capacity (gal.)	3.50
Carburetor	Kingston L3, 1.50-in.
Air cleaner	Case
Ignition	Robert Bosch FU4 magneto
Cooling capacity (gal.)	12.50

Maximum brake horsepower tests

PTO/belt horsepower	44.01
Crankshaft rpm	1,099
Fuel use (gal./hr.)	4.46

Maximum drawbar horsepower tests

Gear	2nd
Drawbar horsepower	30.08
Pull weight (lb.)	2,645
Speed (mph)	4.26
Percent slippage	11.05
SAE drawbar horsepower	26
SAE belt/PTO horsepower	40
Type	4 wheel
Front wheel (in.)	steel: 30 x 6
Rear wheel (in.)	steel: 48 x 12
Length (in.)	130
Height (in.)	57
Rear width (in.)	67
Weight (lb.)	5,157
Gear/speed (mph)	forward: 1/2.50, 2/3.25, 3/4.00; reverse: 1/2.75

Case C, 17-27

Manufacturer	J.I. Case Co., Racine, WI
Nebraska test number	167
Test date	August 12–19, 1929
Test tractor serial number	C 300219

Years produced 1929–1939
Serial number range.............................300201–301001,
6 digit;
4200001–4300001,
7 digit; all models
Serial number location ....metal plate on
instrument panel
Number produced 20,478
Engine ....Case vertical I-head,
valve-in-head
Test engine serial number........................C 300219
Cylinders 4
Bore and stroke (in.) ....3.875 x 5.50
Rated rpm 1,100
Compression ratio...................................4.88:1
Displacement (c.i.) 259.5
Fuel ....kerosene/gasoline
Main tank capacity (gal.)..........................18
Auxiliary tank capacity (gal.) 2
Carburetor ....Kingston L3, 1.25-in.
Air cleaner ....Case
Ignition..Robert Bosch FU4 ARS
magneto
Cooling capacity (gal.) 5
Maximum brake horsepower tests
PTO/belt horsepower...........................29.81
Crankshaft rpm 1,102
Fuel use (gal./hr.)...............................2.62
Maximum drawbar horsepower tests
Gear...low
Drawbar horsepower.............................21.41
Pull weight (lb.)...................................2,358
Speed (mph) 3.40
Percent slippage..................................14.38
SAE drawbar horsepower..........................17
SAE belt/PTO horsepower 27
Type ....4 wheel
Front wheel (in.).....................................steel: 28 x 6
Rear wheel (in.)......................................steel: 42 x 12
Length (in.) 114.50
Height (in.) 53.25
Rear width (in.).......................................61.50
Weight (lb.) 4,105
Gear/speed (mph) ....forward: 1/2.30,
2/3.28, 3/4.50;
reverse: 1/2.59

Case CC 3

Manufacturer...J.I. Case Co.,
Racine, WI
Nebraska test number 169
Test date ....September 10–18,
1929
Test tractor serial number.........................300219
Years produced 1929–1939
Serial number range.................................300201–301001,
6 digit;
4200001–4300001,
7 digit; all models
Serial number location ....metal plate on
instrument panel
Number produced 28,656
Engine ....Case vertical, I-head,
valve-in-head

Test engine serial number.........................300219
Cylinders 4
Bore and stroke (in.) ....3.875 x 5.50
Rated rpm 1,100
Compression ratio...................................4.88:1
Displacement (c.i.) 259.5
Fuel ....kerosene/gasoline
Main tank capacity (gal.)..........................18
Auxiliary tank capacity (gal.) 2
Carburetor ....Kingston L3V, 1.25-in.
Air cleaner ....Case
Ignition..Robert Bosch
FU4 magneto
Cooling capacity (gal.) 5
Maximum brake horsepower tests
PTO/belt horsepower...........................28.97
Crankshaft rpm 1,101
Fuel use (gal./hr.)...............................2.88
Maximum drawbar horsepower tests
Gear...3rd
Drawbar horsepower.............................22.70
Pull weight (lb.)...................................2,950
Speed (mph) 2.88
Percent slippage..................................6.30
SAE drawbar horsepower..........................None
SAE belt/PTO horsepower ....None
Type ....4 wheel; tricycle
Front wheel (in.).....................................steel: 25 x 4
Rear wheel (in.)......................................steel: 48 x 8
Length (in.) 137
Height (in.) 56.50
Rear width (in.) ....Variable 48–84
Weight (lb.) 4,090
Gear/speed (mph) ....forward: 1/2.60,
2/3.72, 3/5.14; reverse:
1/2.95

Case RC

Manufacturer...J.I. Case Co., Racine,
WI
Nebraska test number 251
Test date ....April 7–16, 1936
Test tractor serial number.........................RC 300875
Years produced 1935–1940
Serial number range.................................300801–301001,
6 digit;
4200001–4400001,
7 digit; all models
Serial number location ....metal plate on
instrument panel
Number produced ....15,948 All Types
Engine ....Waukesha FWJ
vertical L-head
Test engine serial number.........................RC 300875
Cylinders 4
Bore and stroke (in.) ....3.25 x 4.00
Rated rpm 1,425
Displacement (c.i.) 132.7
Fuel ....gasoline
Fuel tank capacity (gal.) 15
Carburetor ....Zenith, 193.5, .875-in.
Air cleaner ....United
Ignition..American Bosch,
MJB4A108 magneto

55

Case

Cooling capacity (gal.) 4.50
Maximum brake horsepower tests
    PTO/belt horsepower............................19.80
    Crankshaft rpm 1,428
    Fuel use (gal./hr.) 2.33
Maximum drawbar horsepower tests
    Gear 2nd
    Drawbar horsepower............................14.21
    Pull weight (lb.) 1,519
    Speed (mph) 3.51
    Percent slippage................................4.51
SAE drawbar horsepower...........................11.27
SAE belt/PTO horsepower..........................17.44
Type ....3 wheel; tricycle
Front wheel (in.)......................................(steel: 20.50 x 6)
    rubber: 7.50 x 10
Rear wheel (in.)..(steel: 48 x 2.50)
    rubber: 8.25 x 36
Length (in.) 124.50
Height (in.) 63
Rear width (in.) 44-80
Gear/speed (mph) ....forward: 1/2.33,
    2/3.33, 3/4.50;
    reverse: 1/2.50

Case R

Manufacturer...J.I. Case Co.,
    Racine, WI
Nebraska test number 308
Test date ....October 10–20, 1938
Test tractor serial number..........................4230270
Years produced 1935–1940
Serial number range..................................300801–301001,
    6 digit;
    4200001–4400001,
    7 digit; all models
Serial number location ....metal plate on
    instrument panel
Number produced ....15,948 All Types
Engine ....Waukesha
    vertical L-head
Test engine serial number..........................433794
Cylinders 4
Bore and stroke (in.) ....3.25 x 4.00
Rated rpm 1,425
Displacement (c.i.) 133
Fuel ....gasoline
Fuel tank capacity (gal.) 15
Carburetor..Zenith, 193 1/2,
    .875-in.
Air cleaner ....United
Ignition..Amer. Bosch,
    MJB4A108 magneto
Cooling capacity (gal.) 4.25
Maximum brake horsepower tests
    PTO/belt horsepower............................20.52
    Crankshaft rpm 1,425
    Fuel use (gal./hr.) 2.17
Maximum drawbar horsepower tests
    Gear 2nd
    Drawbar horsepower............................18.23
    Pull weight (lb.) 1,979
    Speed (mph) 3.45
    Percent slippage................................6.45

SAE drawbar horsepower...........................14.17
SAE belt/PTO horsepower..........................18.30
Type ....Standard
Front wheel (in.).......................................steel: 25 x 2.50;
    (rubber: 5.00 x
Rear wheel (in.)..steel: 42 x 8;
    (rubber: 11.25 x 24)
Length (in.) 104
Height (in.) 49.50
Rear width (in.) 55
Weight (lb.) ....St 3,700 (Ru 3,965)
Gear/speed (mph) ....forward: 1/2.33,
    2/3.33, 3/4.50;
    reverse: 1/2.50

Case L

Manufacturer...J.I. Case Co.,
    Racine, WI
Nebraska test number 309
Test date ....October 10–24, 1938
Test tractor serial number..........................4210443
Years produced 1929–1940
Serial number range..................................300201–301001,
    6 digit;
    4200001–4400001,
    7 digit; all models
Serial number location ....metal plate on
    instrument panel
Number produced 31,871
Engine ....Case vertical I-head,
    valve-in-head
Test engine serial number..........................L 4210443
Cylinders 4
Bore and stroke (in.) ....4.625 x 6.00
Rated rpm 1,100
Compression ratio....................................5.75:1
Displacement (c.i.) 403.4
Fuel ....distillate/gasoline
Main tank capacity (gal.) 26
Auxiliary tank capacity (gal.) 3.50
Carburetor..Zenith, K-6-A, 1.50-in.
Air cleaner ....Case
Ignition..Case, magneto
Cooling capacity (gal.) 12.50
Maximum brake horsepower tests
    PTO/belt horsepower............................47.04
    Crankshaft rpm 1,101
    Fuel use (gal./hr.) 4.46
Maximum drawbar horsepower tests
    Gear...St 2nd, Ru 2nd
    Drawbar horsepower............................St 31.94, Ru 40.80
    Pull weight (lb.)................................St 3,394, Ru 3,635
    Speed (mph)......................................St 3.53, Ru 4.21
    Percent slippage................................St 6.68, Ru 8.79
SAE drawbar horsepower...........................32.04
SAE belt/PTO horsepower..........................42.02
Type ....Standard
Front wheel (in.).......................................(steel: 30 x 6;
    rubber: 7.50 x 20)
Rear wheel (in.)..(steel: 48 x 12;
    rubber: 13.50 x 28)
Length (in.) 132
Height (in.) 57
Rear width (in.) 67

Weight (lb.) ....(St 5,125, Ru 7,850)
Gear/speed (mph) ....forward: 1 On
rubber/3.52, 2/4.48,
3/5.58; reverse: 1/3.78

Case DC 3
Manufacturer...J.I. Case Co.,
Racine, WI
Nebraska test number 340
Test date ....April 18 to
May 4, 1940
Test tractor serial number........................D 4302471
Years produced 1939–1953
Serial number range..................................4300001–5700001,
8023171, 7 digit; all
models interspersed
Serial number location ....metal plate on
instrument panel
Number produced 54,925
Engine ....Case vertical I-head
Test engine serial number........................D 4302471
Cylinders 4
Bore and stroke (in.) ....3.875 x 5.50
Rated rpm 1,100
Compression ratio.....................................5.58:1
Displacement (c.i.) 259.5
Fuel ....gasoline
Fuel tank capacity (gal.) 17
Carburetor ....Zenith, 62AXJ9,
1.25-in.
Air cleaner ....Case
Ignition ....Case, 10334 magneto
Cooling capacity (gal.) 6.50
Maximum brake horsepower tests
PTO/belt horsepower...........................37.28
Crankshaft rpm 1,100
Fuel use (gal./hr.) 3.40
Maximum drawbar horsepower tests
Gear...2nd
Drawbar horsepower...........................33.06
Pull weight (lb.)...................................3,616
Speed (mph) 3.43
Percent slippage.................................8.58
SAE drawbar horsepower..........................25.56
SAE belt/PTO horsepower 32.83
Type ....tricycle
Front wheel (in.)..steel: 25 x 4;
(rubber: 5.50 x 16)
Rear wheel (in.)...steel: 48 x 2.50;
(rubber: 11.25 x 36)
Length (in.) 132
Height (in.)...56.50
Rear width (in.) 48-84
Weight (lb.)..(6,835)
Gear/speed (mph) ....forward: 1/2.50,
2/3.50, 3/5.00,
4/10.00; reverse:
1/2.75

Case VC
Manufacturer...J.I. Case Co.,
Racine, WI
Nebraska test number 348
Test date ....June 18–25, 1940
Test tractor serial number........................VC 4415115

Years produced 1940–1942
Serial number range..................................4400001–4600001,
7 digit; all models
interspersed
Serial number location ....metal plate on
instrument panel
Number produced 12,462
Engine ....Continental
vertical L-head
Test engine serial number........................CFA 124 4934
Cylinders 4
Bore and stroke (in.) ....3.00 x 4.375
Rated rpm 1,650
Displacement (c.i.) 123.7
Fuel ....gasoline
Fuel tank capacity (gal.) 10
Carburetor ....Schebler, TSX 43,
1.00-in.
Air cleaner ....United
Ignition ....Edison-Splitdorf, RM
03139 magneto
Cooling capacity (gal.) 3
Maximum brake horsepower tests
PTO/belt horsepower...........................24.48
Crankshaft rpm 1,650
Fuel use (gal./hr.) 2.21
Maximum drawbar horsepower tests
Gear...2nd
Drawbar horsepower...........................18.55
Pull weight (lb.)...................................2,034
Speed (mph) 3.42
Percent slippage.................................7.05
SAE drawbar horsepower..........................15.00
SAE belt/PTO horsepower 22.06
Type ....tricycle
Front wheel (in.)..tire, 5.00 x 15
Rear wheel (in.)...tire, 9.00 x 32
Length (in.) 116
Height (in.)...55
Weight (lb.)..(4,115)
Gear/speed (mph) ....forward: 1/2.65,
2/3.64, 3/4.67,
4/10.03; reverse:
1/2.25

Case D
Manufacturer...J.I. Case Co.,
Racine, WI
Nebraska test number 349
Test date ....June 18–27, 1940
Test tractor serial number........................D 4401035
Years produced 1939–1953
Serial number range..................................4300001–5700001,
8020001, 7 digit; all
models interspersed
Serial number location ....metal plate on
instrument panel
Number produced 14,396
Engine ....Case vertical I-head
Test engine serial number........................D 4401035
Cylinders 4
Bore and stroke (in.) ....3.875 x 5.50
Rated rpm 1,200
Compression ratio.....................................4.88:1
Displacement (c.i.) 259.5

Case

Fuel ....distillate/gasoline
Main tank capacity (gal.) 17
Auxiliary tank capacity (gal.) 2
Carburetor ....Zenith, 62AXJ9,
                                                    1.25-in.
Air cleaner ....Case
Ignition ....Case, X4498 magneto
Cooling capacity (gal.) 6.50
Maximum brake horsepower tests
    PTO/belt horsepower 35.36
    Crankshaft rpm 1,200
    Fuel use (gal./hr.) 3.31
Maximum drawbar horsepower tests
    Gear 2nd
    Drawbar horsepower 30.67
    Pull weight (lb.) 3,091
    Speed (mph) 3.72
    Percent slippage..............................6.84
SAE drawbar horsepower..........................24.77
SAE belt/PTO horsepower 31.83
Type ....Standard
Front wheel (in.) ....steel: 28 x 5;
                                                    (rubber: 7.50 x 16)
Rear wheel (in.) ....steel: 42 x 12;
                                                    (rubber: 12.75 x 24)
Length (in.) 114
Height (in.) 48
Rear width (in.) 61.50
Tread width (in.)...................................48
Weight (lb.) ....(6,830)
Gear/speed (mph) ....forward: 1/2.75,
                                                    2/4.00, 3/5.50,
                                                    4/11.00; reverse:
                                                    1/3.08

Case SC
Manufacturer...J.I. Case Co.,
                                                    Racine, WI
Nebraska test number 367
Test date ....April 29 to May 16,
                                                    1941
Test tractor serial number.........................SC 4500637
Years produced 1941–1954
Serial number range................................4500001–5600001,
                                                    8027115, 7 digit; all
                                                    models interspersed
Serial number location ....metal plate on
                                                    instrument panel
Number produced 58,991
Engine ....Case vertical I-head
Test engine serial number.........................SC 4500637
Cylinders 4
Bore and stroke (in.) ....3.50 x 4.00
Rated rpm 1,550
Displacement (c.i.) 153.9
Fuel ....distillate/gasoline
Main tank capacity (gal.) 14
Auxiliary tank capacity (gal.) 1.25
Carburetor...Zenith, 161AXJ7,
                                                    1.00-in.
Air cleaner ....United
Ignition...Edison-Splitdorf,
                                                    W15587, RM03189
                                                    magneto
Cooling capacity (gal.) 4

Maximum brake horsepower tests
    PTO/belt horsepower............................22.29
    Crankshaft rpm 1,550
    Fuel use (gal./hr.) 2.29
Maximum drawbar horsepower tests
    Gear ....Ru 2nd
    Drawbar horsepower 19.44
    Pull weight (lb.) 2,177
    Speed (mph) 3.35
    Percent slippage..............................5.86
SAE drawbar horsepower..........................15.82
SAE belt/PTO horsepower 20.16
Type ....tricycle
Front wheel (in.) ....steel: 24.75 x 4;
                                                    (rubber: 5.00 x
Rear wheel (in.) ....steel: 48 x 2.50;
                                                    (rubber: 10.00 x 38)
Length (in.) 126.25
Height (in.) 67.88
Rear width (in.) 74.50
Tread width (in.) 44–80
Weight (lb.) 4,025
Gear/speed (mph) ....forward: 1/2.50,
                                                    2/3.50, 3/4.75, 4/9.66;
                                                    reverse: 1/2.75

Case VAC
Manufacturer...J.I. Case Co.,
                                                    Racine, WI
Nebraska test number 430
Test date ....October 15–26, 1949
Test tractor serial number.........................VAC 5258734
Years produced 1942–1953
Serial number range................................4600001–5700001,
                                                    7 digit; all models
                                                    interspersed
Serial number location ....metal plate on
                                                    instrument panel
Number produced 94,267
Engine ....Case, VA vertical
                                                    I-head
Test engine serial number.........................74B07313
Cylinders 4
Bore and stroke (in.) ....3.25 x 3.75
Rated rpm 1,425
Compression ratio................................5.01:1
Displacement (c.i.) 124
Fuel ....tractor fuel
Fuel tank capacity (gal.) 9.25
Carburetor...Marvel-Schebler,
                                                    TSX-253, .875-in.
Air cleaner ....Vortox
Ignition...Auto-Lite, 6-v battery
Cooling capacity (gal.) 3.25
Maximum brake horsepower tests
    PTO/belt horsepower............................17.92
    Crankshaft rpm 1,425
    Fuel use (gal./hr.) 1.72
Maximum drawbar horsepower tests
    Gear 3rd
    Drawbar horsepower 15.63
    Pull weight (lb.) 1,493
    Speed (mph) 3.93
    Percent slippage..............................5.96
SAE drawbar horsepower..........................12.40

SAE belt/PTO horsepower 15.89
Type ....tricycle
Front wheel (in.) ....tire: 5.50 x 15
Rear wheel (in.) ....tire: 10.00 x 28
Length (in.) 119.50
Height (in.) 56.25
Tread width (in.) ....48–80 or 88
Weight (lb.) 3,024
Gear/speed (mph) ....forward: 1/2.32,
2/3.08, 3/4.00, 4/8.40;
reverse: 1/3.20

Case VAC

Manufacturer..J.I. Case Co.,
Racine, WI
Nebraska test number 431
Test date ....October 17–26, 1949
Test tractor serial number ....VAC 5258733
Years produced 1942–1953
Serial number range.................................4600001–5700001,
7 digit; all models
interspersed
Serial number location ....metal plate on
instrument panel
Number produced 94,267
Engine ....Case vertical I-head
Test engine serial number 72D073112
Cylinders 4
Bore and stroke (in.) ....3.25 x 3.75
Rated rpm 1,425
Compression ratio....................................5.99:1
Displacement (c.i.) 124
Fuel ....gasoline
Fuel tank capacity (gal.) 9.25
Carburetor ....Marvel-Schebler,
TSX-114, .875-in.
Air cleaner ....Vortox
Ignition..Auto-Lite, 6-v battery
Cooling capacity (gal.) 3.25
Maximum brake horsepower tests
    PTO/belt horsepower...........................21.33
    Crankshaft rpm 1,425
    Fuel use (gal./hr.) 2.06
Maximum drawbar horsepower tests
    Gear..3rd
    Drawbar horsepower...........................19.10
    Pull weight (lb.)...................................1,828
    Speed (mph).......................................3.92
    Percent slippage.................................5.06
SAE drawbar horsepower...........................14.93
SAE belt/PTO horsepower.........................18.96
Type ....tricycle
Front wheel (in.) ....tire: 5.50 x 15
Rear wheel (in.) ....tire: 10.00 x 28
Length (in.) 119.50
Height (in.) 56.25
Tread width (in.) ....48–80 or 88
Weight (lb.) 3,024
Gear/speed (mph) ....forward: 1/2.32,
2/3.08, 3/4.00, 4/8.40;
reverse: 1/3.20

Case LA

Manufacturer..J.I. Case Co., Racine, WI
Nebraska test number 480

Test date ....August 15–28, 1952
Test tractor serial number ....5523277 LA
Years produced 1940–1952
Serial number range.................................4400001–5600001,
7 digit; all models
interspersed
Serial number location ....metal plate on
instrument panel
Number produced 35,493
Engine ....J.I. Case vertical I-head
Test engine serial number ....5523277 LA
Cylinders 4
Bore and stroke (in.) ....4.625 x 6.00
Rated rpm 1,150
Compression ratio....................................5.75:1
Displacement (c.i.) 403.4
Fuel ....gasoline
Fuel tank capacity (gal.) 30
Carburetor ....Zenith K6A, 1.50-in.
Air cleaner ....Case
Ignition..Case 4CMA Mag/
6-v battery
Cooling capacity (gal.) 15.25
Maximum brake horsepower tests
    PTO/belt horsepower...........................58.53
    Crankshaft rpm 1,150
    Fuel use (gal./hr.) 5.78
Maximum drawbar horsepower tests
    Gear..3rd
    Drawbar horsepower...........................51.68
    Pull weight (lb.)...................................4,187
    Speed (mph).......................................4.63
    Percent slippage.................................5.93
SAE drawbar horsepower...........................41.30
SAE belt/PTO horsepower.........................52.50
Type ....Standard
Front wheel (in.) ....7.50 x 18
Rear wheel (in.) ....15.00 x 30
Length (in.) 140
Height (in.) 61.44
Tread width (in.) 59.75
Weight (lb.) 6,516
Gear/speed (mph) ....forward: 1/2.50,
2/3.33, 3/4.33,
4/10.00; reverse:
1/2.75

Case LA

Manufacturer..J.I. Case Co.,
Racine, WI
Nebraska test number 481
Test date ....August 18–29, 1952
Test tractor serial number ....5523273 LA
Years produced 1940–1952
Serial number range.................................4400001–5600001,
7 digit; all models
interspersed
Serial number location ....metal plate on
instrument panel
Number produced 35,493
Engine ....J.I. Case vertical I-head
Test engine serial number ....5523273 LA
Cylinders 4
Bore and stroke (in.) ....4.625 x 6.00
Rated rpm 1,150

Case

Compression ratio 4.55:1
Displacement (c.i.) 403.2
Fuel .... tractor fuel
Fuel tank capacity (gal.) 30
Carburetor .... Zenith K6A, 1.50-in.
Air cleaner .... Case
Ignition .... Case 4CMA Mag/6-v battery
Cooling capacity (gal.) 15.25

Maximum brake horsepower tests
    PTO/belt horsepower 48.86
    Crankshaft rpm 1,150
    Fuel use (gal./hr.) 5.04

Maximum drawbar horsepower tests
    Gear 3rd
    Drawbar horsepower 44.51
    Pull weight (lb.) 3,563
    Speed (mph) 4.68
    Percent slippage 4.91
SAE drawbar horsepower 34.82
SAE belt/PTO horsepower 42.95
Type .... Standard
Front wheel (in.) .... 7.50 x 18
Rear wheel (in.) .... 15.00 x 30
Length (in.) 140
Height (in.) 61.44
Tread width (in.) 59.75
Weight (lb.) 6,516
Gear/speed (mph) .... forward: 1/2.50, 2/3.33, 3/4.33, 4/10.00; reverse: 1/2.75

Case LA, LPG

Manufacturer .... J.I. Case Co., Racine, WI
Nebraska test number 482
Test date .... August 21 to September 6, 1952
Test tractor serial number .... 5522054 LA
Years produced 1940–1952
Serial number range .... 4400001–5600001, 7 digit; all models interspersed
Serial number location .... metal plate on instrument panel
Number produced 35,493
Engine .... J.I. Case vertical I-head
Test engine serial number .... 5522054 LA
Cylinders 4
Bore and stroke (in.) .... 4.625 x 6.00
Rated rpm 1,150
Compression ratio 7.58:1
Displacement (c.i.) 403.2
Fuel .... LPG
Carburetor .... Ensign, 1.50-in.
Air cleaner .... Case
Ignition .... Case 4CMA Mag/6-v battery
Cooling capacity (gal.) 15.25

Maximum brake horsepower tests
    PTO/belt horsepower 59.60
    Crankshaft rpm 1,150
    Fuel use (gal./hr.) 6.67

Maximum drawbar horsepower tests
    Gear 3rd
    Drawbar horsepower 51.73
    Pull weight (lb.) 4,181
    Speed (mph) 4.64
    Percent slippage 5.39
SAE drawbar horsepower 40.91
SAE belt/PTO horsepower 52.62
Type .... Standard
Front wheel (in.) .... 7.50 x 18
Rear wheel (in.) .... 15.00 x 30
Length (in.) 140
Height (in.) 61.44
Tread width (in.) 59.75
Weight (lb.) 6,516
Gear/speed (mph) .... forward: 1/2.50, 2/3.33, 3/4.33, 4/10.00; reverse: 1/2.75

Case SC

Manufacturer .... J.I. Case Co., Racine, WI
Nebraska test number 496
Test date .... June 15–20, 1953
Test tractor serial number .... SC 8032498
Years produced 1941–1954
Serial number range .... 4500001–5600001, 8027115, 7 digit; all models interspersed
Serial number location .... metal plate on instrument panel
Number produced 58,991
Engine .... J.I. Case S vertical I-head
Test engine serial number .... SC 8032498
Cylinders 4
Bore and stroke (in.) .... 3.875 x 4.00
Rated rpm 1,600
Compression ratio 6.25:1
Displacement (c.i.) 165.1
Fuel .... gasoline
Fuel tank capacity (gal.) 14
Carburetor .... Zenith 161JX7, 1.1875-in.
Air cleaner .... United
Ignition .... Case 41 magneto/Auto-Lite, 6-v battery
Cooling capacity (gal.) 4

Maximum brake horsepower tests
    PTO/belt horsepower 31.71
    Crankshaft rpm 1,600
    Fuel use (gal./hr.) 2.97

Maximum drawbar horsepower tests
    Gear 2nd
    Drawbar horsepower 27.68
    Pull weight (lb.) 2,919
    Speed (mph) 3.56
    Percent slippage 6.34
SAE drawbar horsepower 22.36
SAE belt/PTO horsepower 28.13
Type .... tricycle
Front wheel (in.) .... 5.50 x 16
Rear wheel (in.) .... 11.00 x 38

Length (in.) 133
Height (in.) 55.50
Tread width (in.)..44–80
Weight (lb.) 4,790
Gear/speed (mph) ....forward: 1/2.50,
2/3.66, 3/5.00,
4/10.33; reverse:
1/3.00

Case SC
Manufacturer..J.I. Case Co.,
Racine, WI
Nebraska test number 497
Test date ....June 16–26, 1953
Test tractor serial number.........................SC 8032497
Years produced 1941–1954
Serial number range....................................4500001–5600001,
8027115, 7 digit; all
models interspersed
Serial number location ....metal plate on
instrument panel
Number produced 58,991
Engine ....J.I. Case S
vertical I-head
Test engine serial number ....SC 8032497
Cylinders 4
Bore and stroke (in.) ....3.625 x 4.00
Rated rpm 1,600
Compression ratio.......................................4.8:1
Displacement (c.i.).......................................165.1
Fuel ....tractor fuel
Fuel tank capacity (gal.) 14
Carburetor ....Zenith 161JX7,
1.1875-in.
Air cleaner ....United
Ignition...Case 41 magneto/
Auto-Lite, 6-v battery
Cooling capacity (gal.) 4
Maximum brake horsepower tests
PTO/belt horsepower...........................24.97
Crankshaft rpm 1,600
Fuel use (gal./hr.) 2.86
Maximum drawbar horsepower tests
Gear...2nd
Drawbar horsepower.............................23.25
Pull weight (lb.).....................................2,423
Speed (mph) 3.60
Percent slippage...................................5.38
SAE drawbar horsepower............................18.31
SAE belt/PTO horsepower...........................22.24
Type ....tricycle
Front wheel (in.)..5.50 x 16
Rear wheel (in.)...11.00 x 38
Length (in.) 133
Height (in.) 56.50
Tread width (in.)..44–80
Weight (lb.) 4,790
Gear/speed (mph) ....forward: 1/2.50, 2/3.66,
3/5.00, 4/10.33;
reverse: 1/3.00

Case 500 Diesel
Manufacturer..J.I. Case Co.,
Racine, WI
Nebraska test number 508

Test date ....October 5–10, 1953
Test tractor serial number.........................8032765
Years produced 1953–1956
Serial number range....................................5700001, 8032499,
8060001, 8080001, no
end, 7 digit; all models
Serial number location ....metal plate near
instrument panel
Engine ....J.I. Case vertical I-head
Test engine serial number 8032765
Cylinders 6
Bore and stroke (in.) ....4.00 x 5.00
Rated rpm 1,350
Compression ratio.......................................15.0:1
Displacement (c.i.).......................................377
Fuel ....diesel
Fuel tank capacity (gal.) 30
Carburetor ....Injector Pump; Bosch
Air cleaner ....Donaldson
Ignition...Auto-Lite, 12-v; with 2,
6-v battery
Cooling capacity (gal.) 14
Maximum brake horsepower tests
PTO/belt horsepower...........................63.81
Crankshaft rpm 1,350
Fuel use (gal./hr.) 4.04
Maximum drawbar horsepower tests
Gear...3rd
Drawbar horsepower.............................56.32
Pull weight (lb.).....................................4,252
Speed (mph) 4.98
Percent slippage...................................5.17
SAE drawbar horsepower............................43.91
SAE belt/PTO horsepower...........................55.09
Type ....Standard
Front wheel (in.)..7.50 x 18
Rear wheel (in.)...15.00 x 30
Length (in.) 144.25
Height (in.) 61.44
Tread width (in.)..60.75
Weight (lb.) 7,953
Gear/speed (mph) ....forward: 1/2.69,
2/3.70, 3/4.91,
4/10.10; reverse:
1/2.94

Case 401 Diesel
Manufacturer..J.I. Case Co., Racine,
WI
Nebraska test number 565
Test date ....October 17–25, 1955
Test tractor serial number.........................8067411
Years produced 1955–1957
Serial number range....................................8060001-8100001 no
end; all models
interspersed
Serial number location ....metal plate on
instrument panel
Engine ....J.I. Case vertical I-head
Test engine serial number 8067411
Cylinders 4
Bore and stroke (in.) ....4.00 x 5.00
Rated rpm 1,500
Compression ratio.......................................15:1
Displacement (c.i.).......................................251

Fuel ....diesel
Fuel tank capacity (gal.) 21
Carburetor..Injector Pump, Bosch
Air cleaner..Donaldson
Ignition..Auto-Lite, 12-v; with 2,
6-v battery
Cooling capacity (gal.) 7.40
Maximum brake horsepower tests
PTO/belt horsepower..........................49.40
Crankshaft rpm 1,501
Fuel use (gal./hr.) 3.09
Maximum drawbar horsepower tests
Gear...5th
Drawbar horsepower..........................43.82
Pull weight (lb.) 3,439
Speed (mph) 4.78
Percent slippage................................5.65
SAE drawbar horsepower........................33.63
SAE belt/PTO horsepower........................43.27
Type ....tricycle
Front wheel (in.).....................................6.00 x 16
Rear wheel (in.)......................................13.00 x 38
Length (in.)..142.63
Height (in.)...93.50
Tread width (in.)......................................52–88
Weight (lb.) 6,407
Gear/speed (mph) ....forward: 1/1.36,
2/1.94, 3/2.66, 4/3.85, 5/4.84, 6/6.89, 7/9.44, 8/13.66;
reverse: 1/1.75, 2/6.22

Case 411

Manufacturer..J.I. Case Co., Racine, WI
Nebraska test number 566
Test date ....October 17–26, 1955
Test tractor serial number.......................8067066
Years produced 1955–1957
Serial number range................................8060001–8100001
no end; all models
interspersed
Serial number location ....metal plate on
instrument panel
Engine ....J.I. Case vertical I-head
Test engine serial number..........................8067066
Cylinders 4
Bore and stroke (in.) ....4.00 x 5.00
Rated rpm 1,500
Compression ratio...................................6.5:1
Displacement (c.i.) 251
Fuel ....gasoline
Fuel tank capacity (gal.) 21
Carburetor..Marvel-Schebler
TSX616, 1.25-in.
Air cleaner..Donaldson
Ignition..Auto-Lite, 6-v battery
Cooling capacity (gal.) 7.40
Maximum brake horsepower tests
PTO/belt horsepower..........................53.25
Crankshaft rpm 1,499
Fuel use (gal./hr.) 4.49
Maximum drawbar horsepower tests
Gear...5th
Drawbar horsepower..........................44.89
Pull weight (lb.) 3,489
Speed (mph) 4.83
Percent slippage................................5.30

SAE drawbar horsepower........................35.41
SAE belt/PTO horsepower........................46.53
Type ....tricycle
Front wheel (in.).....................................6.00 x 16
Rear wheel (in.)......................................13.00 x 38
Length (in.)..142.63
Height (in.)...93.50
Tread width (in.)......................................52–88
Weight (lb.) 6,144
Gear/speed (mph) ....forward: 1/1.36,
2/1.94, 3/2.66, 4/3.85, 5/4.84, 6/6.89, 7/9.44, 8/13.66;
reverse: 1/1.75, 2/6.22

Case 311

Manufacturer..J.I. Case Co.,
Racine, WI
Nebraska test number 613
Test date ....April 15–23, 1957
Test tractor serial number.......................6075363
Years produced 1956–1957
Serial number range................................6050301–6075001
no end; all models
interspersed
Serial number location ....metal plate on dash
Engine ....Case, G148
vertical I-head
Test engine serial number.......................110N 00114
Cylinders 4
Bore and stroke (in.) ....3.375 x 4.125
Rated rpm 1,750
Compression ratio...................................7.1:1
Displacement (c.i.) 148
Fuel ....gasoline
Fuel tank capacity (gal.) 13
Carburetor..Marvel-Schebler
TSX635, .875-in.
Air cleaner..Donaldson
Ignition..Case, 41
magneto/Auto-Lite,
6-v battery
Cooling capacity (gal.) 3
Maximum brake horsepower tests
PTO/belt horsepower..........................33.00
Crankshaft rpm 1,750
Fuel use (gal./hr.) 3.01
Maximum drawbar horsepower tests
Gear...3rd
Drawbar horsepower..........................29.29
Pull weight (lb.) 2,183
Speed (mph) 5.03
Percent slippage................................4.39
SAE drawbar horsepower........................23.19
SAE belt/PTO horsepower........................29.24
Type ....tricycle
Front wheel (in.).....................................5.50 x 16
Rear wheel (in.)......................................12.00 x 28
Tread width (in.)......................................48–88
Weight (lb.) 4,017
Gear/speed (mph) ....forward: 1/2.68, 2/3.94,
3/5.18, 4/12.80;
reverse: 1/3.19

Case 301 Diesel

Manufacturer..J.I. Case Co., Racine, WI
Nebraska test number 614

Test date ....April 15–23, 1957
Test tractor serial number...........................6075362
Years produced 1956–1957
Serial number range....................................6050301–6075001 no end; 7 digit; all models interspersed
Serial number location ....metal plate on dash
Engine ....Continental, GD157 vertical I-head
Test engine serial number..........................4114
Cylinders 4
Bore and stroke (in.) ....3.375 x 4.375
Rated rpm 1,750
Compression ratio......................................15.54:1
Displacement (c.i.) 157
Fuel ....diesel
Fuel tank capacity (gal.) 13
Carburetor ....injector pump, Bosch
Air cleaner ....Donaldson
Ignition..Auto-Lite, 12-v; with 2, 6-v battery
Cooling capacity (gal.) 3

Maximum brake horsepower tests
    PTO/belt horsepower..........................30.80
    Crankshaft rpm 1,750
    Fuel use (gal./hr.)..............................2.23

Maximum drawbar horsepower tests
    Gear...3rd
    Drawbar horsepower 28.73
    Pull weight (lb.)................................2,151
    Speed (mph) 5.01
    Percent slippage...............................4.31
SAE drawbar horsepower............................22.05
SAE belt/PTO horsepower 27.11
Type ....tricycle
Front wheel (in.)...5.50 x 16
Rear wheel (in.)..12.00 x 28
Tread width (in.)...48-88
Weight (lb.) 4,017
Gear/speed (mph)......................................forward: 1/2.68, 2/3.94, 3/5.18, 4/12.80; reverse: 1/3.19

Case 511-B
Manufacturer..J.I. Case Co., Racine, WI
Nebraska test number 646
Test date ....April 14–18, 1958
Test tractor serial number...........................6096141
Years produced 1958–1959
Serial number range....................................6095001–6120001 no end; all models interspersed
Serial number location ....metal plate on instrument panel
Engine ....Case G164 vertical I-head
Test engine serial number..........................171PO1970
Cylinders 4
Bore and stroke (in.) ....3.5625 x 4.125
Rated rpm 2,000
Compression ratio......................................7.26:1
Displacement (c.i.) 164.5
Fuel ....gasoline
Fuel tank capacity (gal.) 13.8

Carburetor ....Marvel-Schebler TSX749, 1.25-in.
Air cleaner ....Donaldson
Ignition..Case 41 magneto/Auto-Lite, 12-v battery
Cooling capacity (gal.) 3

Maximum brake horsepower tests
    PTO/belt horsepower..........................45.10
    Crankshaft rpm 1,999
    Fuel use (gal./hr.)..............................4.07

Maximum drawbar horsepower tests
    Gear...5th
    Drawbar horsepower 39.05
    Pull weight (lb.)................................3,859
    Speed (mph) 3.79
    Percent slippage...............................7.69
SAE drawbar horsepower............................30.86
SAE belt/PTO horsepower 40.02
Type ....tricycle
Front wheel (in.)...6.00 x 16
Rear wheel (in.)..13.90 x 36
Height (in.)...84
Tread width (in.)...52-88
Weight (lb.) 4,546
Gear/speed (mph) ....forward: 1/1.60, 10/8.80, 11/13.00, 12/21.70, 2/2.40, 3/2.70, 4/3.20, 5/4.00, 6/4.50, 7/5.30, 8/6.70, 9/7.80; reverse: 1/1.90, 2/3.20, 3/5.40

Case 711-B
Manufacturer...J.I. Case Co., Racine, WI
Nebraska test number 678
Test date ....October 27 to November 13, 1958
Test tractor serial number...........................8123458
Years produced 1958–1959
Serial number range....................................8120001–8140001 no end; all models interspersed
Serial number location ....metal plate on instrument panel
Engine ....Case, A251S vertical I-head
Test engine serial number..........................8123458
Cylinders 4
Bore and stroke (in.) ....4.00 x 5.00
Rated rpm 1,500
Compression ratio......................................6.5:1
Displacement (c.i.) 251
Fuel ....gasoline
Fuel tank capacity (gal.) 22
Carburetor ....Marvel-Schebler TSX, 1.25-in.
Air cleaner ....Donaldson
Ignition..Case 41 magneto/Delco-Remy, 12-v battery
Cooling capacity (gal.) 7.40

Maximum brake horsepower tests
    PTO/belt horsepower..........................52.19
    Crankshaft rpm 1,500
    Fuel use (gal./hr.)..............................4.45

Case

Maximum drawbar horsepower tests
- Gear...5th
- Drawbar horsepower......................46.64
- Pull weight (lb.)............................3,693
- Speed (mph)................................4.74
- Percent slippage..........................4.47

SAE drawbar horsepower............................35.95
SAE belt/PTO horsepower...........................45.73
Type ....tricycle
Front wheel (in.)....................................6.00 x 16
Rear wheel (in.)....................................15.50 x 38
Height (in.)...93.50
Tread width (in.)....................................52–88
Weight (lb.)...6,181
Gear/speed (mph)................................forward: 1/1.40, 2/1.90, 3/2.70, 4/3.80, 5/4.80, 6/6.90, 7/9.40, 8/13.70; reverse: 1/1.70, 2/6.20

Case 811-B

Manufacturer....................................J.I. Case Co., Racine, WI
Nebraska test number 679
Test date ....October 27 to November 17, 1958
Test tractor serial number..............8124770
Years produced 1958–1959
Serial number range.......................8120001–8140001 no end; all models interspersed
Serial number location ....metal plate on instrument panel
Engine ....Case, A251S vertical I-head
Test engine serial number..............8124770
Cylinders 4
Bore and stroke (in.)......................4.00 x 5.00
Rated rpm 1,800
Compression ratio..........................6.5:1
Displacement (c.i.)........................251
Fuel ....gasoline
Fuel tank capacity (gal.)................22
Carburetor.....................................Marvel-Schebler TSX, 1.25-in.
Air cleaner ....Donaldson
Ignition..Wico, DB4 magneto/Delco-Remy, 12-v battery
Cooling capacity (gal.) 7.50

Maximum brake horsepower tests
- PTO/belt horsepower......................53.90
- Crankshaft rpm 1,800
- Fuel use (gal./hr.)..........................5.15

Maximum drawbar horsepower tests
- Gear...4th
- Drawbar horsepower......................49.29
- Pull weight (lb.)............................4,293
- Speed (mph)................................4.31
- Percent slippage..........................5.94

SAE drawbar horsepower............................37.66
SAE belt/PTO horsepower...........................47.31
Type ....tricycle
Front wheel (in.)....................................6.00 x 16
Rear wheel (in.)....................................15.50 x 38
Height (in.)...93.50
Tread width (in.)....................................52–88

Weight (lb.) 6,532
Gear/ speed ....1/1.60, 1 Torque Converter/0–1.90, 2/2.29, 2 Torque Converter/0–2.10, 3/3.13, 3 Torque Converter/0–2.90, 4/4.53, 4 Torque Converter/0–4.10, 5/5.89, 5 Torque Converter/0–5.40, 6/8.40, 6 Torque Converter/0–7.70, 7/11.51, 7 Torque Converter/0–9.00, 8/16.64, 8 Torque Converter/0–14.00; reverse: 1/2.06, 1 Torque Converter/0–1.90, 2/7.58, 2 Torque Converter/0–7.00

Case 801-B Diesel

Manufacturer....................................J.I. Case Co., Racine, WI
Nebraska test number 680
Test date ....October 27 to November 14, 1958
Test tractor serial number..............8124603
Years produced 1958–1959
Serial number range.......................8120001–8140001 no end; all models interspersed
Serial number location ....metal plate on instrument panel
Engine ....Case, A267D vertical I-head
Test engine serial number..............8124603
Cylinders 4
Bore and stroke (in.)......................4.125 x 5.00
Rated rpm 1,800
Compression ratio..........................15:1
Displacement (c.i.)........................267
Fuel ....diesel
Fuel tank capacity (gal.)................22
Carburetor.....................................Injector Pump, Robert Bosch
Air cleaner ....Donaldson
Ignition..Case 41 magneto/Delco-Remy, 12-v; with 2, 6-v battery
Cooling capacity (gal.) 7.50

Maximum brake horsepower tests
- PTO/belt horsepower......................54.42
- Crankshaft rpm 1,801
- Fuel use (gal./hr.)..........................4.02

Maximum drawbar horsepower tests
- Gear...4th
- Drawbar horsepower......................50.14
- Pull weight (lb.)............................4,352
- Speed (mph)................................4.32
- Percent slippage..........................5.51

SAE drawbar horsepower............................39.49
SAE belt/PTO horsepower...........................48.14
Type ....tricycle
Front wheel (in.)....................................6.00 x 16
Rear wheel (in.)....................................15.50 x 38
Height (in.)...93.50
Tread width (in.)....................................52–88
Weight (lb.)...6,745
Gear/speed ....1/1.60, 1 Torque Converter/0–1.50, 2/2.29, 2 Torque Converter/0–2.10, 3/3.13, 3 Torque Converter/0–2.90, 4/4.53, 4 Torque Converter/0–4.10, 5/5.89, 5 Torque Converter/0–5.40,

Gear/speed (cont.)............6/8.40, 6 Torque Converter/0–7.70, 7/11.51, 7 Torque Converter/0–9.00, 8/16.64, 8 Torque Converter/0–14.00; reverse: 1/2.06, 1 Torque Converter/0–1.90, 2/7.58, 2 Torque Converter/0–7.00

Case 611-B

Manufacturer	J.I. Case Co., Racine, WI
Nebraska test number	687
Test date	March 19 to April 16, 1959
Test tractor serial number	6122894
Years produced	1958–1959
Serial number range	6095001–6120001 no end, 7 digit; all models interspersed
Serial number location	metal plate on instrument panel
Engine	Case, G164 vertical L-head
Test engine serial number	6122894
Cylinders	4
Bore and stroke (in.)	3.5625 x 4.125
Rated rpm	2,250
Compression ratio	7.26:1
Displacement (c.i.)	164.5
Fuel	gasoline
Fuel tank capacity (gal.)	13.8
Carburetor	Marvel-Schebler TSX749, or Zenith 62AJ10
Air cleaner	Donaldson
Ignition	Auto-Lite or Delco-Remy, 12-v battery
Cooling capacity (gal.)	3

Maximum brake horsepower tests

PTO/belt horsepower	44.56
Crankshaft rpm	2,250
Fuel use (gal./hr.)	4.56

Maximum drawbar horsepower tests

Gear	5th
Drawbar horsepower	37.04
Pull weight (lb.)	3,233
Speed (mph)	4.30
Percent slippage	5.86
SAE drawbar horsepower	37.50
SAE belt/PTO horsepower	44.56
Type	tricycle
Front wheel (in.)	6.00 x 16
Rear wheel (in.)	13.90 x 36
Height (in.)	84
Tread width (in.)	54–88
Weight (lb.)	4,447
Gear/Speed	1/1.50, 1 Torque Converter/0-1.50, 2/2.20, 2 Torque Converter/0–2.20, 3/2.50, 3 Torque Converter/0–2.50, 4/2.90, 4 Torque Converter/0–2.90, 5/3.60, 5 Torque Converter/0–3.60, 6/4.70, 6 Torque Converter/0–4.70, 7/7.00, 7 Torque Converter/0–7.00, 8/11.20, 8 Torque Converter/0–11.20; reverse: 1/1.80, 1 Torque Converter/0–1.80, 2/2.90, 2 Torque Converter/0–2.90

Case 211-B

Manufacturer	J.I. Case Co., Racine, WI
Nebraska test number	688
Test date	March 19–25, 1959
Test tractor serial number	6122893
Years produced	1958–1959
Serial number range	6095001–6120001 no end; 7 digit; all models interspersed
Serial number location	metal plate on dash
Engine	Case, G126 vertical L-head
Test engine serial number	136P0 9838
Cylinders	4
Bore and stroke (in.)	3.125 x 4.125
Rated rpm	1,900
Compression ratio	7.4:1
Displacement (c.i.)	126.5
Fuel	gasoline
Fuel tank capacity (gal.)	13
Carburetor	Marvel-Schebler TSX635, .875-in.
Air cleaner	Donaldson
Ignition	Auto-Lite or Delco-Remy, 6-v battery
Cooling capacity (gal.)	3

Maximum brake horsepower tests

PTO/belt horsepower	30.84
Crankshaft rpm	1,900
Fuel use (gal./hr.)	2.76

Maximum drawbar horsepower tests

Gear	3rd
Drawbar horsepower	24.84
Pull weight (lb.)	1,742
Speed (mph)	5.35
Percent slippage	4.46
SAE drawbar horsepower	25.46
SAE belt/PTO horsepower	30.84
Type	tricycle
Front wheel (in.)	5.00 x 15
Rear wheel (in.)	11.00 x 28
Height (in.)	79
Tread width (in.)	48–88
Weight (lb.)	3,164
Gear/speed (mph)	forward: 1/2.80, 2/4.10, 3/5.40, 4/13.40; reverse: 1/3.00

Case 411-B

Manufacturer	J.I. Case Co., Racine, WI
Nebraska test number	689
Test date	March 20 to April 16, 1959
Test tractor serial number	6122895
Years produced	1958–1959
Serial number range	6095001–6120001 no end; all models interspersed
Serial number location	metal plate on instrument panel
Engine	Case, G148 vertical L-head
Test engine serial number	152R 098
Cylinders	4
Bore and stroke (in.)	3.375 x 4.125
Rated rpm	2,000

Compression ratio 7.1:1
Displacement (c.i.) 148
Fuel .... gasoline
Fuel tank capacity (gal.) 13
Carburetor .... Marvel-Schebler TSX749 or Zenith 62AJ10
Air cleaner .... Donaldson
Ignition .... Auto-Lite or Delco Remy, 12-v battery
Cooling capacity (gal.) 3

Maximum brake horsepower tests
    PTO/belt horsepower 37.12
    Crankshaft rpm 2,000
    Fuel use (gal./hr.) 3.47

Maximum drawbar horsepower tests
    Gear 5th
    Drawbar horsepower 29.72
    Pull weight (lb.) 2,374
    Speed (mph) 4.69
    Percent slippage 4.30
SAE drawbar horsepower 30.67
SAE belt/PTO horsepower 37.12
Type .... tricycle
Front wheel (in.) .... 5.50 x 16
Rear wheel (in.) .... 13.00 x 28
Height (in.) 79
Tread width (in.) 48–88
Weight (lb.) 3,902
Gear/Speed .... 1/1.57, 1 Torque Converter/0-1.57, 2/2.30, 2 Torque Converter/0–2.30, 3/2.52, 3 Torque Converter/0–2.52, 4/3.02, 4 Torque Converter/0–3.02, 5/3.71, 5 Torque Converter/0–3.71, 6/4.88, 6 Torque Converter/0–4.88, 7/7.18, 7 Torque Converter/0–7.18, 8/11.60, 8 Torque Converter/0–11.60; reverse: 1/2.24, 1 Torque Converter/0–2.24, 2/3.00, 2 Torque Converter/0–3.00

Case 900-B Diesel

Manufacturer .... J.I. Case Co., Racine, WI
Nebraska test number 692
Test date .... April 20–29, 1959
Test tractor serial number 8123655
Years produced 1957–1959
Serial number range .... 8100001–8140001 no end; all models interspersed
Serial number location .... metal plate near instrument panel
Engine .... Case, A377D vertical L-head
Test engine serial number 8123655
Cylinders 6
Bore and stroke (in.) .... 4.00 x 5.00
Rated rpm 1,500
Compression ratio 15:1
Displacement (c.i.) 377
Fuel .... diesel
Fuel tank capacity (gal.) 30
Carburetor .... Injector Pump, Robert Bosch

Air cleaner .... Donaldson
Ignition .... Case 601 magneto/Delco-Remy, 12-v; with 2, 6-v battery
Cooling capacity (gal.) 14

Maximum brake horsepower tests
    PTO/belt horsepower 70.24
    Crankshaft rpm 1,500
    Fuel use (gal./hr.) 4.79

Maximum drawbar horsepower tests
    Gear 3rd
    Drawbar horsepower 66.21
    Pull weight (lb.) 5,527
    Speed (mph) 4.49
    Percent slippage 4.44
SAE drawbar horsepower 65.59
SAE belt/PTO horsepower 70.24
Type .... Standard
Front wheel (in.) .... 7.50 x 18
Rear wheel (in.) .... 18.00 x 26
Height (in.) 93.50
Tread width (in.) 67.50
Weight (lb.) 7,882
Gear/speed (mph) .... forward: 1/2.7, 2/3.8, 3/4.8, 4/5.8, 5/7.1, 6/13.9; reverse: 1/3.20

Case 701-B Diesel

Manufacturer .... J.I. Case Co., Racine, WI
Nebraska test number 693
Test date .... April 20–29, 1959
Test tractor serial number 8125663
Years produced 1958–1959
Serial number range .... 8120001–8140001 no end; all models interspersed
Serial number location .... metal plate on instrument panel
Engine .... Case, A267D vertical L-head
Test engine serial number 8125663
Cylinders 4
Bore and stroke (in.) .... 4.125 x 5.00
Rated rpm 1,500
Compression ratio 15.0:1
Displacement (c.i.) 267
Fuel .... diesel
Fuel tank capacity (gal.) 22
Carburetor .... Injecter Pump, Robert Bosch
Air cleaner .... Donaldson
Ignition .... Case 41 magneto/Delco-Remy, 12-v; with 2, 6-v battery
Cooling capacity (gal.) 7.40

Maximum brake horsepower tests
    PTO/belt horsepower 51.20
    Crankshaft rpm 1,500
    Fuel use (gal./hr.) 3.39

Maximum drawbar horsepower tests
    Gear 5th
    Drawbar horsepower 46.44

Pull weight (lb.)..................................3,624
Speed (mph) 4.81
Percent slippage................................5.02
SAE drawbar horsepower......................47.24
SAE belt/PTO horsepower 51.20
Type ....tricycle
Front wheel (in.)..................................6.00 x 16
Rear wheel (in.).................................15.50 x 38
Height (in.) 93.50
Tread width (in.)..................................52–88
Weight (lb.) 6,394
Gear/speed (mph) ....forward: 1/1.4, 2/1.9,
3/2.7, 4/3.8, 5/4.8,
6/6.9, 7/9.4, 8/13.7;
reverse: 1/1.70, 2/6.20

Case 711-B LPG
Manufacturer....................................J.I. Case Co.,
Racine, WI
Nebraska test number 694
Test date ....April 22 to
May 15, 1959
Test tractor serial number................8131213
Years produced 1958–1959
Serial number range.........................8120001–8140001
no end; all models
interspersed
Serial number location ....metal plate on
instrument panel
Engine ....Case, A251S
vertical L-head
Test engine serial number................8131213
Cylinders 4
Bore and stroke (in.) ....4.00 x 5.00
Rated rpm 1,500
Compression ratio...........................7.46:1
Displacement (c.i.) 251
Fuel ....LPG
Carburetor.......................................Ensign XG, 1.25-in.
Air cleaner ....Donaldson
Ignition..Case 41
magneto/Delco-Remy,
12-v battery
Cooling capacity (gal.) 7.40
Maximum brake horsepower tests
PTO/belt horsepower....................53.31
Crankshaft rpm 1,500
Fuel use (gal./hr.)........................5.44
Maximum drawbar horsepower tests
Gear...5th
Drawbar horsepower....................47.96
Pull weight (lb.)...........................3,800
Speed (mph) 4.73
Percent slippage..........................5.19
SAE drawbar horsepower..................48.34
SAE belt/PTO horsepower 53.31
Type ....tricycle
Front wheel (in.)..............................6.00 x 16
Rear wheel (in.).............................15.50 x 38
Height (in.) 93.50
Tread width (in.)..............................52–88
Weight (lb.) 6,181
Gear/speed (mph) ....forward: 1/1.4, 2/1.9,
3/2.7, 4/3.8, 5/4.8,
6/6.9, 7/9.4, 8/13.7;
reverse: 1/1.70, 2/6.20

Case 811-B LPG
Manufacturer....................................J.I. Case Co.,
Racine, WI
Nebraska test number 695
Test date ....April 27 to
May 16, 1959
Test tractor serial number................8130940
Years produced 1958–1959
Serial number range.........................8120001–8140001
no end; all models
interspersed
Serial number location ....metal plate on
instrument panel
Engine ....Case, A251S
vertical L-head
Test engine serial number................8130940
Cylinders 4
Bore and stroke (in.) ....4.00 x 5.00
Rated rpm 1,800
Compression ratio...........................8.0:1
Displacement (c.i.) 251
Fuel ....LPG
Carburetor.......................................Ensign XG, 1.25-in.
Air cleaner ....Donaldson
Ignition..Case 41
magneto/Delco-Remy,
12-v battery
Cooling capacity (gal.) 7.50
Maximum brake horsepower tests
PTO/belt horsepower....................55.58
Crankshaft rpm 1,800
Fuel use (gal./hr.)........................6.19
Maximum drawbar horsepower tests
Gear...4th
Drawbar horsepower....................50.62
Pull weight (lb.)...........................4,309
Speed (mph) 4.41
Percent slippage..........................5.11
SAE drawbar horsepower..................50.81
SAE belt/PTO horsepower 55.58
Type ....tricycle
Front wheel (in.)..............................6.00 x 16
Rear wheel (in.).............................15.50 x 38
Height (in.) 93.50
Tread width (in.)..............................57–88
Weight (lb.) 6,532
Gear/Speed......................1/1.60, 1 Torque Converter/0–1.90,
2/2.29, 2 Torque Converter/0–2.10,
3/3.13, 3 Torque Converter/0–2.90,
4/4.53, 4 Torque Converter/0–4.10,
5/5.89, 5 Torque Converter/0–5.40,
6/8.40, 6 Torque Converter/0–7.70,
7/11.51, 7 Torque Converter/0–9.00,
8/16.64, 8 Torque Converter/0–14.00;
reverse: 1/2.06, 1 Torque
Converter/0–1.90, 2/7.58, 2 Torque
Converter/0–7.00

Case 910-B LPG
Manufacturer....................................J.I. Case Co, Racine, WI
Nebraska test number 696
Test date ....April 29 to May 15,
1959
Test tractor serial number................8124550
Years produced 1957–1959

Serial number range................................8100001–8140001 no end; all models interspersed

Serial number location ....metal plate near instrument panel

Engine ....Case, A377S vertical L-head

Test engine serial number..........................8124550

Cylinders 6

Bore and stroke (in.) ....4.00 x 5.00

Rated rpm 1,350

Compression ratio..................................8.0:1

Displacement (c.i.) 377

Fuel ....LPG

Fuel tank capacity (gal.) 33

Carburetor ....Ensign Kgl, 1.50-in.

Air cleaner ....Donaldson

Ignition ....Case 601 magneto/Delco-Remy, 12-v; with 2, 6-v battery

Cooling capacity (gal.) 10.50

Maximum brake horsepower tests

    PTO/belt horsepower...........................71.05

    Crankshaft rpm 1,350

    Fuel use (gal./hr.) 7.11

Maximum drawbar horsepower tests

    Gear...3rd

    Drawbar horsepower.............................62.14

    Pull weight (lb.)................................5,747

    Speed (mph) 4.05

    Percent slippage................................4.46

SAE drawbar horsepower............................62.07

SAE belt/PTO horsepower...........................71.05

Type ....Standard

Front wheel (in.) ....7.50 x 18

Rear wheel (in.) ....18.00 x 26

Height (in.) 93.50

Tread width (in.) 67.50

Weight (lb.) 7,920

Gear/speed (mph) ....forward: 1/2.5, 2/3.4, 3/4.3, 4/5.2, 5/6.4, 6/12.5; reverse: 1/2.90

Case 310-C

Manufacturer.......................................J.I. Case Co., Racine, WI

Nebraska test number 709

Test date ....July 14–31, 1959

Test tractor serial number..........................3008915

Years produced 1956–1958

Serial number range................................6050301, 6075001, 6095001 no end, all models interspersed

Serial number location ....metal plate on dash

Engine ....Case G148B vertical L-head

Test engine serial number...........................199R 06533

Cylinders 4

Bore and stroke (in.) ....3.375 x 4.125

Rated rpm 1,850

Compression ratio..................................7.1:1

Displacement (c.i.) 148

Fuel ....gasoline

Fuel tank capacity (gal.) 13

Carburetor ....Marvel-Schebler TSX635, .875-in.

Air cleaner ....Donaldson

Ignition ....Auto-Lite, 12-v battery

Cooling capacity (gal.) 3

Maximum brake horsepower tests

    PTO/belt horsepower...........................33.32

    Crankshaft rpm 1,850

    Fuel use (gal./hr.) 2.90

Maximum drawbar horsepower tests

    Gear...2nd

    Drawbar horsepower.............................26.75

    Pull weight (lb.)................................3,706

    Speed (mph) 2.71

    Percent slippage................................3.33

SAE drawbar horsepower............................27.74

SAE belt/PTO horsepower...........................33.32

Type ....tracklayer

Height (in.) 69

Tread width (in.).....................................48.25

Weight (lb.) 5,375

Track length (in.) ....na on ground, 210 total

Grouser shoe..30 links; 12

Gear/speed (mph) ....forward: 1/1.74, 2/2.75, 3/4.52; reverse: 1/2.01

Case 1010-C Terratrac Diesel

Manufacturer.......................................J.I. Case Co., Racine, WI

Nebraska test number 712

Test date ....August 14–28, 1959

Test tractor serial number..........................7101713

Years produced 1957–1960

Serial number range................................7100001–7101000 end, consecutive; Models 1000 and 1010

Serial number location ....metal plate on instrument panel

Number produced 1,000

Engine ....Continental JD382 vertical L-head

Test engine serial number..........................15537

Cylinders 4

Bore and stroke (in.) ....4.50 x 6.00

Rated rpm 2,250

Compression ratio..................................15.0:1

Displacement (c.i.) 382

Fuel ....diesel

Fuel tank capacity (gal.) 40

Carburetor ....Injector Pump, Roosa

Ignition ....Auto-Lite, 24v; with 4, 6-v battery

Cooling capacity (gal.) 8.50

Maximum brake horsepower tests

    PTO/belt horsepower...........................None

Maximum drawbar horsepower tests

    Gear...2nd

    Drawbar horsepower.............................52.91

    Pull weight (lb.)................................7,546

    Speed (mph) 2.63

    Percent slippage................................1.56

SAE drawbar horsepower............................55.51

SAE belt/PTO horsepower ....None
Type ....tracklayer
Height (in.) 92.75
Tread width (in.) 60
Weight (lb.) 15,550
Track length (in.) ....na on ground,
    243 total
Grouser shoe ....39 links; 16
Gear/speed (mph) ....forward: 1/0–1.60,
    2/0–2.90, 3/0–3.30,
    4/0–6.00; reverse:
    1/0–1.90, 2/0–3.50,
    3/0–4.00, 4/0–7.20

Case 810-C Terratrac Diesel
Manufacturer ....J.I. Case Co., Racine, WI
Nebraska test number 713
Test date ....August 14–28, 1959
Test tractor serial number 7081503
Years produced 1957–1961
Serial number range 7080001–7082001
    end, consecutive;
    Models 800 and 810
Serial number location ....metal plate on
    instrument panel
Number produced 2,001
Engine ....Continental HD277
    vertical L-head
Test engine serial number 5824
Cylinders 4
Bore and stroke (in.) ....4.00 x 5.50
Rated rpm 2,250
Compression ratio 15.9:1
Displacement (c.i.) 277
Fuel ....diesel
Fuel tank capacity (gal.) 40
Carburetor ....Injector Pump,
    Robert Bosch
Air cleaner ....Donaldson
Ignition ....Delco-Remy, 24v;
    with 4, 6-v battery
Cooling capacity (gal.) 7.50
Maximum brake horsepower tests
    PTO/belt horsepower ....None
Maximum drawbar horsepower tests
    Gear 2nd
    Drawbar horsepower 38.57
    Pull weight (lb.) 7,240
    Speed (mph) 2.00
    Percent slippage 1.69
SAE drawbar horsepower 40.00
SAE belt/PTO horsepower ....None
Type ....tracklayer
Height (in.) 90.50
Tread width (in.) 54
Weight (lb.) 13,510
Track length (in.) ....na on ground, 231 total
Grouser shoe ....37 links; 15
Gear/speed (mph) ....forward: 1/0–1.60,
    2/0–2.90, 3/0–3.30,
    4/0–6.00; reverse:
    1/0–1.90, 2/0–3.50,
    3/0–4.00, 4/0–7.20

Case 610 Terratrac Diesel
Manufacturer ....J.I. Case Co.,
    Racine, WI
Nebraska test number 714
Test date ....August 19–28, 1959
Test tractor serial number 7061472
Years produced 1957–1960
Serial number range 7060001–7061616
    end, consecutive;
    Models 600 and 610
Serial number location ....metal plate on
    instrument panel
Number produced 1,616
Engine ....Continental ED208
    vertical L-head
Test engine serial number 3437
Cylinders 4
Bore and stroke (in.) ....3.6875 x 4.875
Rated rpm 2,250
Compression ratio 16.0:1
Displacement (c.i.) 208
Fuel ....diesel
Fuel tank capacity (gal.) 25
Carburetor ....Injector Pump, Roosa
Ignition ....Auto-Lite, 12-v; with 2,
    6-v battery
Cooling capacity (gal.) 4.50
Maximum brake horsepower tests
    PTO/belt horsepower 38.58
    Crankshaft rpm 2,100
    Fuel use (gal./hr.) 4.15
Maximum drawbar horsepower tests
    Gear 2nd
    Drawbar horsepower 32.40
    Pull weight (lb.) 4,277
    Speed (mph) 2.84
    Percent slippage 1.84
SAE drawbar horsepower 32.95
SAE belt/PTO horsepower 38.56
Type ....tracklayer
Height (in.) 73.75
Tread width (in.) 49
Weight (lb.) 8,401
Track length (in.) ....na on ground,
    198 total
Grouser shoe ....34 links; 14
Gear/speed (mph) ....forward: 1/0–1.67,
    2/0–3.22, 3/0–3.40,
    4/0–6.56; reverse:
    1/0–1.83, 2/0–3.51,
    3/0–3.74, 4/0–7.20

Case 83-C Diesel
Manufacturer ....J.I. Case Co., Racine, WI
Nebraska test number 736
Test date ....April 5–19, 1960
Test tractor serial number 8161055
Years produced 1960–1969
Serial number range 8160001–8356251
    no end; all models
    interspersed
Serial number location ....metal plate near
    instrument panel

Engine ....Case A301D
vertical L-head
Test engine serial number............................8161055
Cylinders 4
Bore and stroke (in.) ....4.375 x 5.00
Rated rpm 1,900
Compression ratio................................15.3:1
Displacement (c.i.) 301
Fuel ....diesel
Carburetor ....Injector Pump,
Robert Bosch
Air cleaner ....Donaldson
Ignition ....Case 41
magneto/Delco-Remy,
12-v; with 2, 6-v battery
Cooling capacity (gal.) 7.50
Maximum brake horsepower tests
PTO/belt horsepower........................63.74
Crankshaft rpm 1,900
Fuel use (gal./hr.) 4.56
Maximum drawbar horsepower tests
Gear..4th
Drawbar horsepower........................58.30
Pull weight (lb.)........................4,721
Speed (mph)........................4.63
Percent slippage........................5.47
SAE drawbar horsepower........................58.48
SAE belt/PTO horsepower........................63.74
Type ....Standard
Front wheel (in.)........................6.00 x 16
Rear wheel (in.)........................15.50 x 38
Height (in.)........................93.88
Tread width (in.)........................52–88
Weight (lb.)........................6,526
Gear/Speed ....1/1.70, 1 Torque Converter/0–1.40,
2/2.40, 2 Torque Converter/0–2.00,
3/3.30, 3 Torque Converter/0–2.70,
4/4.80, 4 Torque Converter/0–4.00,
5/6.20, 5 Torque Converter/0–5.10,
6/8.90, 6 Torque Converter/0–7.40,
7/12.10, 7 Torque Converter/0–10.00,
8/17.60, 8 Torque Converter/0–14.60;
reverse: 1/2.20, 1 Torque Converter/
0–1.80, 2/8.00, 2 Torque Converter/0–6.60

Case 831 Diesel

Manufacturer................................J.I. Case Co., Racine, WI
Nebraska test number........................737
Test date ....April 5–23, 1960
Test tractor serial number........................8161054
Years produced 1960–1969
Serial number range................................8160001–8356251
no end; all models
interspersed
Serial number location ....metal plate near
instrument panel
Engine ....Case A301D vertical
L-head
Test engine serial number........................8161054
Cylinders 4
Bore and stroke (in.)........................5.375 x 5.00
Rated rpm 1,700
Compression ratio........................15.3:1
Displacement (c.i.)........................301
Fuel ....diesel

Carburetor ....Injector Pump,
Robert Bosch
Air cleaner ....Donaldson
Ignition ....Case 41
magneto/Delco-Remy,
12-v; with2, 6-v battery
Cooling capacity (gal.) 7.50
Maximum brake horsepower tests
PTO/belt horsepower........................63.76
Crankshaft rpm 1,700
Fuel use (gal./hr.)........................4.26
Maximum drawbar horsepower tests
Gear..4th
Drawbar horsepower........................54.27
Pull weight (lb.)........................4,997
Speed (mph)........................4.07
Percent slippage........................6.93
SAE drawbar horsepower........................55.46
SAE belt/PTO horsepower........................63.76
Type ....Standard
Front wheel (in.)........................6.00 x 16
Rear wheel (in.)........................15.50 x 38
Height (in.)........................93.88
Tread width (in.)........................52–88
Weight (lb.)........................6,462
Gear/speed (mph)............forward: 1/1.50, 2/2.10, 3/2.90, 4/4.30,
5/5.60, 6/8.00, 7/10.70, 8/15.70;
reverse: 1/2.00, 2/7.20

Case 841

Manufacturer................................J.I. Case Co.,
Racine, WI
Nebraska test number 738
Test date ....April 5–23, 1960
Test tractor serial number........................8161056
Years produced 1960–1969
Serial number range................................8160001–8356251
no end; all models
interspersed
Serial number location ....metal plate near
instrument panel
Engine ....Case A284S
vertical L-head
Test engine serial number........................8161056
Cylinders 4
Bore and stroke (in.) ....4.25 x 5.00
Rated rpm 1,700
Compression ratio................................7.4:1
Displacement (c.i.)........................284
Fuel ....gasoline
Carburetor ....Marvel-Schebler
TSX785, 1.25-in.
Air cleaner ....Donaldson
Ignition ....Delco-Remy, 12-v
battery
Maximum brake horsepower tests
PTO/belt horsepower........................64.57
Crankshaft rpm 1,700
Fuel use (gal./hr.)........................5.07
Maximum drawbar horsepower tests
Gear..4th
Drawbar horsepower........................53.34
Pull weight (lb.)........................4,902
Speed (mph)........................4.08
Percent slippage........................6.49

SAE drawbar horsepower..................................53.68
SAE belt/PTO horsepower 64.57
Type ....Standard
Front wheel (in.)..6.00 x 16
Rear wheel (in.) ....15.50 x 38
Height (in.) 93.88
Tread width (in.)...52–88
Weight (lb.) 6,462
Gear/speed (mph)..............forward: 1/1.50, 2/2.10, 3/2.90, 4/4.30,
                5/5.60, 6/8.00, 7/10.70, 8/15.70;
                reverse: 1/2.00, 2/7.20

Case 940 LPG

Manufacturer..J.I. Case Co., Racine, WI
Nebraska test number 739
Test date..April 5–23, 1960
Test tractor serial number...............................8161061
Years produced 1960–1969
Serial number range..8060001–8356251
                no end; models
                interspersed
Serial number location ....metal plate near
                instrument panel
Engine..Case A377S
                vertical L-head
Test engine serial number...............................8161061
Cylinders 6
Bore and stroke (in.) ....4.00 x 5.00
Rated rpm 1,600
Compression ratio...8.0:1
Displacement (c.i.)...377
Fuel ....LPG
Carburetor ....Ensign Kgl, 1.50-in.
Air cleaner ....Donaldson
Ignition...Delco-Remy, 12-v
                battery
Cooling capacity (gal.) 10.50
Maximum brake horsepower tests
   PTO/belt horsepower...............................79.64
   Crankshaft rpm 1,600
   Fuel use (gal./hr.) 8.71
Maximum drawbar horsepower tests
   Gear...3rd
   Drawbar horsepower...............................69.99
   Pull weight (lb.).......................................5,552
   Speed (mph) 4.73
   Percent slippage.....................................4.38
SAE drawbar horsepower.................................71.16
SAE belt/PTO horsepower 79.64
Type ....Standard
Front wheel (in.)..7.50 x 18
Rear wheel (in.) ....18.00 x 26
Height (in.) 91.38
Tread width (in.)...67.50
Weight (lb.) 8,399
Gear/speed (mph) ....forward: 1/2.50,
                2/3.70, 3/4.70, 4/5.70,
                5/7.00, 6/13.60;
                reverse: 1/3.10

Case 841 LPG

Manufacturer..J.I. Case Co., Racine, WI
Nebraska test number 740
Test date ....April 11–23, 1960
Test tractor serial number...............................8161058

Years produced 1960–1969
Serial number range..8160001–8356251
                no end; all models
                interspersed
Serial number location ....metal plate near
                instrument panel
Engine..Case A284S vertical
                L-head
Test engine serial number...............................8161058
Cylinders 4
Bore and stroke (in.) ....4.25 x 5.00
Rated rpm 1,700
Compression ratio...8.4:1
Displacement (c.i.)...284
Fuel ....LPG
Carburetor ....Ensign XG, 1.25-in.
Air cleaner ....Donaldson
Ignition...Delco-Remy, 12-v
                battery
Cooling capacity (gal.) 7.50
Maximum brake horsepower tests
   PTO/belt horsepower...............................63.38
   Crankshaft rpm 1,700
   Fuel use (gal./hr.) 6.52
Maximum drawbar horsepower tests
   Gear...4th
   Drawbar horsepower...............................52.99
   Pull weight (lb.).......................................4,876
   Speed (mph) 4.08
   Percent slippage.....................................6.63
SAE drawbar horsepower.................................54.01
SAE belt/PTO horsepower 63.38
Type ....Standard
Front wheel (in.)..6.00 x 16
Rear wheel (in.) ....15.50 x 38
Height (in.) 93.88
Tread width (in.)...52–88
Weight (lb.) 6,462
Gear/speed (mph)..............forward: 1/1.50, 2/2.10, 3/2.90, 4/4.30,
                5/5.60, 6/8.00, 7/10.70, 8/15.70;
                reverse: 1/2.00, 2/7.20

Case 930 Diesel

Manufacturer..J.I. Case Co., Racine, WI
Nebraska test number 741
Test date ....April 14 to May 5,
                1960
Test tractor serial number...............................8161060
Years produced 1960–1969
Serial number range..8160001–8356251
                no end; all models
                interspersed
Serial number location ....metal plate near
                instrument panel
Engine..Case A401D
                vertical L-head
Test engine serial number...............................8161060
Cylinders 6
Bore and stroke (in.) ....4.125 x 5.00
Rated rpm 1,600
Compression ratio...15.2:1
Displacement (c.i.) 401
Fuel ....diesel
Carburetor ....Injector Pump,
                Robert Bosch

Case

Air cleaner ....Donaldson
Ignition ....Case X12154
magneto/Delco-Remy,
12-v; with 2, 6-v battery
Cooling capacity (gal.) 10
Maximum brake horsepower tests
    PTO/belt horsepower............................80.65
    Crankshaft rpm 1,600
    Fuel use (gal./hr.)................................5.31
Maximum drawbar horsepower tests
    Gear...3rd
    Drawbar horsepower...........................70.93
    Pull weight (lb.)..................................5,670
    Speed (mph) 4.69
    Percent slippage.................................4.43
SAE drawbar horsepower..................................71.11
SAE belt/PTO horsepower 80.65
Type ....Standard
Front wheel (in.)..7.50 x 18
Rear wheel (in.)...18.00 x 26
Height (in.) 91.38
Tread width (in.) 67.50
Weight (lb.) 8,399
Gear/speed (mph) ....forward: 1/2.50,
2/3.70, 3/4.70, 4/5.70,
5/7.00, 6/13.60;
reverse: 1/3.10

Case 731-C Diesel
Manufacturer...J.I. Case Co., Racine, WI
Nebraska test number 742
Test date ....April 19 to
May 6, 1960
Test tractor serial number...............................8161049
Years produced 1960–1969
Serial number range.......................................8160001–8356251
no end; all models
interspersed
Serial number location ....metal plate near
instrument panel
Engine ....Case A267D
vertical L-head
Test engine serial number...............................8161049
Cylinders 4
Bore and stroke (in.) ....4.125 x 5.00
Rated rpm 1,900
Compression ratio...15.2:1
Displacement (c.i.) 267
Fuel ....diesel/gasoline
Carburetor..Injector Pump,
Robert Bosch
Air cleaner ....Donaldson
Ignition..Case 41
magneto/Delco-Remy,
12-v; with2, 6-v battery
Cooling capacity (gal.) 7.50
Maximum brake horsepower tests
    PTO/belt horsepower............................56.50
    Crankshaft rpm 1,900
    Fuel use (gal./hr.)................................4.28
Maximum drawbar horsepower tests
    Gear...4th
    Drawbar horsepower...........................48.31
    Pull weight (lb.)..................................3,901
    Speed (mph) 4.64
    Percent slippage.................................4.21

SAE drawbar horsepower..................................50.64
SAE belt/PTO horsepower 56.50
Type ....Standard
Front wheel (in.)..6.00 x 16
Rear wheel (in.)...15.50 x 38
Height (in.) 93.88
Tread width (in.) 52–88
Weight (lb.) 6,337
Gear 1/1.70, 1 Torque Converter/0-1.40, 2/2.40, 2 Torque
Converter/0-2.00, 3/3.30, 3 Torque
Converter/0-2.70, 4/4.80, 4 Torque
Converter/0-4.00, 5/6.20, 5 Torque
Converter/0-5.10, 6/8.90, 6 Torque
Converter/0-7.40, 7/12.10, 7 Torque
Converter/0-10.00, 8/17.60, 8 Torque
Converter/0-14.60; reverse: 1/2.20, 1
Torque Converter/0-1.80, 2/8.00, 2
Torque Converter/0-6.60

Case 731 Diesel
Manufacturer...J.I. Case Co., Racine, WI
Nebraska test number 743
Test date ....April 21 to
May 6, 1960
Test tractor serial number...............................8161048
Years produced 1960–1969
Serial number range.......................................8160001–8356251
no end; all models
interspersed
Serial number location ....metal plate near
instrument panel
Engine ....Case A267D vertical
L-head
Test engine serial number...............................8161048
Cylinders 4
Bore and stroke (in.) ....4.125 x 5.00
Rated rpm 1,700
Compression ratio...15.2:1
Displacement (c.i.) 267
Fuel ....diesel
Carburetor..Injector Pump,
Robert Bosch
Air cleaner ....Donaldson
Ignition..Case X12154
magneto/Delco-Remy,
12-v; with2, 6-v battery
Cooling capacity (gal.) 7.50
Maximum brake horsepower tests
    PTO/belt horsepower............................56.43
    Crankshaft rpm 1,700
    Fuel use (gal./hr.)................................3.79
Maximum drawbar horsepower tests
    Gear...4th
    Drawbar horsepower...........................48.33
    Pull weight (lb.)..................................4,459
    Speed (mph) 4.06
    Percent slippage.................................6.37
SAE drawbar horsepower..................................48.69
SAE belt/PTO horsepower 56.43
Type ....Standard
Front wheel (in.)..6.00 x 16
Rear wheel (in.)...15.50 x 38
Height (in.) 93.88
Tread width (in.) 52–88
Weight (lb.) 6,240

Gear/speed (mph) ....forward: 1/1.50, 2/2.10, 3/2.90, 4/4.30, 5/5.60, 6/8.00, 7/10.70, 8/15.70; reverse: 1/2.00, 2/7.20

Case 541-C
Manufacturer...............................J.I. Case Co., Racine, WI
Nebraska test number 769
Test date ....October 11–22, 1960
Test tractor serial number............6150864
Years produced 1960–1969
Serial number range.....................614001–6162601, 8190001-8356251 no end, 7 digit; all models
Serial number location ....metal plate on instrument panel
Engine ....Case G159 vertical L-head
Test engine serial number 291S 01281
Cylinders 4
Bore and stroke (in.) ....3.50 x 4.125
Rated rpm 2,100
Compression ratio.......................7.42:1
Displacement (c.i.) 158.7
Fuel ....gasoline
Carburetor ....Zenith 12509, 1.25-in.
Air cleaner ....Donaldson
Ignition......................................Auto-Lite, 12-v battery
Cooling capacity (gal.) 3.50
Maximum brake horsepower tests
    PTO/belt horsepower...........41.26
    Crankshaft rpm 2,100
    Fuel use (gal./hr.) 3.74
Maximum drawbar horsepower tests
    Gear....................................5th
    Drawbar horsepower..............36.37
    Pull weight (lb.).....................2,819
    Speed (mph) 4.84
    Percent slippage...................3.54
SAE drawbar horsepower.............37.14
SAE belt/PTO horsepower 41.26
Type ....tricycle
Front wheel (in.) ....5.50 x 16
Rear wheel (in.)..........................14.90 x 28
Height (in.) 61
Tread width (in.).........................48–88
Weight (lb.) 4,150
Gear/speed (mph)............forward: 1/1.87, 1 Torque Converter/, 2/2.64, 2 Torque Converter/, 3/3.11, 3 Torque Converter/, 4/3.61, 4 Torque Converter/, 5/4.57, 5 Torque Converter/, 6/6.01, 6 Torque Converter/, 7/8.91, 7 Torque Converter/, 8/14.84, 8 Torque Converter/; reverse: 1/2.21, 1 Torque Converter/, 2/3.70, 2 Torque Converter/

Case 640-C
Manufacturer...............................J.I. Case Co., Racine, WI
Nebraska test number 770
Test date ....October 11–22, 1960
Test tractor serial number............6153130
Years produced 1960–1963

Serial number range.....................6144001–8208001 no end; all models interspersed
Serial number location ....metal plate on instrument panel
Engine ....Case G188B vertical L-head
Test engine serial number ....322 SO 4249
Cylinders 4
Bore and stroke (in.) ....3.8125 x 4.125
Rated rpm 2,250
Compression ratio.......................7.34:1
Displacement (c.i.) 188.4
Fuel ....gasoline
Carburetor ....Zenith 12534, 1.25-in.
Air cleaner ....Donaldson
Ignition......................................Auto-Lite, 12-v battery
Cooling capacity (gal.) 4.1
Maximum brake horsepower tests
    PTO/belt horsepower...........49.72
    Crankshaft rpm 2,250
    Fuel use (gal./hr.) 4.36
Maximum drawbar horsepower tests
    Gear....................................5th
    Drawbar horsepower..............43.25
    Pull weight (lb.).....................3,560
    Speed (mph) 4.56
    Percent slippage...................4.71
SAE drawbar horsepower.............43.26
SAE belt/PTO horsepower 49.72
Type ....Standard
Front wheel (in.) ....7.50 x 16
Rear wheel (in.)..........................16.90 x 28
Height (in.) 60
Tread width (in.).........................48–76
Weight (lb.) 4,177
Gear/speed (mph)............forward: 1/1.77, 1 Torque Converter/, 2/2.60, 2 Torque Converter/, 3/2.86, 3 Torque Converter/, 4/3.43, 4 Torque Converter/, 5/4.20, 5 Torque Converter/, 6/5.52, 6 Torque Converter/, 7/8.46, 7 Torque Converter/, 8/13.64, 8 Torque Converter/; reverse: 1/2.04, 1 Torque Converter/, 2/3.40, 2 Torque Converter/

Case 541
Manufacturer...............................J.I. Case Co., Racine, WI
Nebraska test number 771
Test date ....October 11–27, 1960
Test tractor serial number............6150796
Years produced 1960–1969
Serial number range.....................6144001–6162601, 8190001–8356251, no end, 7 digit; all models
Serial number location ....metal plate on instrument panel
Engine ....Case G159 vertical L-head
Test engine serial number ....362 SO 1345
Cylinders 4
Bore and stroke (in.) ....3.50 x 4.125
Rated rpm 1,900
Compression ratio.......................7.42:1
Displacement (c.i.) 158.7
Fuel ....gasoline

Carburetor ....Zenith 12509, 1.25-in.
Air cleaner ....Donaldson
Ignition ....Auto-Lite, 12-v battery
Cooling capacity (gal.) 3.50
Maximum brake horsepower tests
    PTO/belt horsepower............................39.50
    Crankshaft rpm 1,900
    Fuel use (gal./hr.) 3.33
Maximum drawbar horsepower tests
    Gear...5th
    Drawbar horsepower............................32.85
    Pull weight (lb.)...................................2,825
    Speed (mph)..4.36
    Percent slippage.................................4.57
SAE drawbar horsepower.........................33.85
SAE belt/PTO horsepower 39.50
Type ....tricycle
Front wheel (in.).......................................5.50 x 16
Rear wheel (in.)..14.90 x 28
Height (in.) 61
Tread width (in.).......................................48–88
Weight (lb.) 3,456
Gear/speed (mph)............forward: 1/1.60, 10/9.07, 11/13.43, 12/22.38, 2/2.48, 3/2.81, 4/3.26, 5/4.13, 6/4.69, 7/5.44, 8/6.89, 9/8.06; reverse: 1/2.01, 2/3.35

Case 531 Diesel

Manufacturer...J.I. Case Co., Racine, WI
Nebraska test number 772
Test date ....October 12–27, 1960
Test tractor serial number.........................6153312
Years produced 1960–1969
Serial number range.................................6144004–6162601, 8190001–8356251, no end, 7 digit; all models interspersed
Serial number location ....metal plate on right side of of engine hood
Engine ....Case G188D vertical L-head
Test engine serial number.........................517 SO 4331
Cylinders 4
Bore and stroke (in.) ....3.8125 x 4.125
Rated rpm 1,900
Compression ratio....................................17.5:1
Displacement (c.i.) 188.4
Fuel ....diesel
Carburetor ....Injector Pump, Roosa
Air cleaner ....Donaldson
Ignition ....Delco-Remy, 12-v; with 2, 6-v battery
Cooling capacity (gal.) 4.1
Maximum brake horsepower tests
    PTO/belt horsepower............................41.27
    Crankshaft rpm 1,900
    Fuel use (gal./hr.) 2.52
Maximum drawbar horsepower tests
    Gear...5th
    Drawbar horsepower............................37.03
    Pull weight (lb.)...................................3,205
    Speed (mph)..4.33
    Percent slippage.................................5.01
SAE drawbar horsepower.........................37.20
SAE belt/PTO horsepower 41.27
Type ....tricycle

Front wheel (in.).......................................5.50 x 16
Rear wheel (in.)..14.90 x 28
Height (in.) 61
Tread width (in.).......................................48–88
Weight (lb.) 3,600
Gear/speed (mph)............forward: 1/1.60, 10/9.07, 11/13.43, 12/22.38, 2/2.48, 3/2.81, 4/3.26, 5/4.13, 6/4.69, 7/5.44, 8/6.89, 9/8.06; reverse: 1/2.01, 2/3.35

Case 640

Manufacturer...J.I. Case Co., Racine, WI
Nebraska test number 773
Test date ....October 13–27, 1960
Test tractor serial number.........................6153368
Years produced 1960–1963
Serial number range.................................6144001–8208001 no end; all models interspersed
Serial number location ....metal plate on instrument panel
Engine ....Case G188B vertical L-head
Test engine serial number.........................303 SO 4600
Cylinders 4
Bore and stroke (in.) ....3.8125 x 4.125
Rated rpm 2,000
Compression ratio....................................7.34:1
Displacement (c.i.) 188.4
Fuel ....gasoline
Carburetor ....Zenith 12534, 1.25-in.
Air cleaner ....Donaldson
Ignition ....Auto-Lite, 12-v battery
Cooling capacity (gal.) 4.1
Maximum brake horsepower tests
    PTO/belt horsepower............................50.61
    Crankshaft rpm 2,001
    Fuel use (gal./hr.) 4.19
Maximum drawbar horsepower tests
    Gear...7th
    Drawbar horsepower............................41.93
    Pull weight (lb.)...................................2,911
    Speed (mph)..5.40
    Percent slippage.................................4.07
SAE drawbar horsepower.........................l42.69
SAE belt/PTO horsepower 50.61
Type ....Standard
Front wheel (in.).......................................7.50 x 16
Rear wheel (in.)..16.90 x 28
Height (in.) 60
Tread width (in.).......................................48–76
Weight (lb.) 3,993
Gear/speed (mph)............forward: 1/1.52, 10/8.18, 11/12.12, 12/20.20, 2/2.24, 3/2.54, 4/2.94, 5/3.73, 6/4.23, 7/4.91, 8/6.22, 9/7.28; reverse: 1/1.81, 2/3.02

Case 441

Manufacturer...J.I. Case Co., Racine, WI
Nebraska test number 774
Test date ....October 13–27, 1960
Test tractor serial number.........................6150846
Years produced 1960–1969

Serial number range..................6144001, 6162601,
8190001–8356251 no
end, all models
Serial number location ....metal plate on
instrument panel
Engine ....Case G148B vertical
L-head
Test engine serial number..........278 SO 1323
Cylinders 4
Bore and stroke (in.) ....3.375 x 4.125
Rated rpm 1,750
Compression ratio 7.1:1
Displacement (c.i.) 148
Fuel ....gasoline
Carburetor ....Marvel-Schebler TSX,
1.00-in.
Air cleaner ....Donaldson
Ignition ....Auto-Lite, 12-v battery
Cooling capacity (gal.)l.............3.50
Maximum brake horsepower tests
PTO/belt horsepower...........33.11
Crankshaft rpm 1,750
Fuel use (gal./hr.)..............2.79
Maximum drawbar horsepower tests
Gear...................................3rd
Drawbar horsepower............29.15
Pull weight (lb.)..................2,170
Speed (mph) 5.04
Percent slippage................4.13
SAE drawbar horsepower.............29.39
SAE belt/PTO horsepower 33.11
Type ....tricycle
Front wheel (in.) ....5.00 x 15
Rear wheel (in.) ....13.60 x 28
Height (in.) 49.50
Tread width (in.) 48–88
Weight (lb.) 3,456
Gear/speed (mph) ....forward: 1/2.49, 2/3.66,
3/4.81, 4/11.88;
reverse: 1/2.96

Case 841-C
Manufacturer............................J.I. Case Co.,
Racine, WI
Nebraska test number 777
Test date ....November 2–12, 1960
Test tractor serial number.........8161057
Years produced 1960–1969
Serial number range.................8160001–8356251
no end; all models
interspersed
Serial number location ....metal plate near
instrument panel
Engine ....Case A284S vertical
L-head
Test engine serial number.........8161057
Cylinders 4
Bore and stroke (in.) ....4.25 x 5.00
Rated rpm 1,900
Compression ratio...................7.4:1
Displacement (c.i.) 284
Fuel ....gasoline
Carburetor ....Marvel-Schebler
TSX785, 1.25-in.
Air cleaner ....Donaldson

Ignition ....Delco-Remy,
12-v battery
Cooling capacity (gal.) 7.50
Maximum brake horsepower tests
PTO/belt horsepower...........65.64
Crankshaft rpm 1,900
Fuel use (gal./hr.)..............5.82
Maximum drawbar horsepower tests
Gear...................................4th
Drawbar horsepower............58.41
Pull weight (lb.)..................4,716
Speed (mph) 4.64
Percent slippage................4.48
SAE drawbar horsepower.............59.81
SAE belt/PTO horsepower 65.64
Type ....Standard
Front wheel (in.) ....6.00 x 16
Rear wheel (in.) ....15.50 x 38
Height (in.) 93.88
Tread width (in.) 52–88
Weight (lb.) 6,526
Gear/speed (mph)............forward: 1/1.70, 2/2.40, 3/3.30, 4/4.80,
5/6.20, 6/8.90, 7/12.10, 8/17.60;
reverse: 1/2.20, 2/8.00

Case 741-C
Manufacturer............................J.I. Case Co., Racine, WI
Nebraska test number 778
Test date ....November 2–12, 1960
Test tractor serial number.........8161051
Years produced 1960–1969
Serial number range.................8160001–8356251
no end; all models
interspersed
Serial number location ....metal plate near
instrument panel
Engine ....Case A252S vertical
L-head
Test engine serial number.........8161051
Cylinders 4
Bore and stroke (in.) ....4.00 x 5.00
Rated rpm 1,900
Compression ratio....................6.88:1
Displacement (c.i.) 251
Fuel ....gasoline
Carburetor ....Marvel-Schebler
TSX785, 1.25-in.
Air cleaner ....Donaldson
Ignition...................................Delco-Remy,
12-v battery
Cooling capacity (gal.) 7.50
Maximum brake horsepower tests
PTO/belt horsepower...........57.88
Crankshaft rpm 1,900
Fuel use (gal./hr.)..............5.08
Maximum drawbar horsepower tests
Gear...................................4th
Drawbar horsepower............50.58
Pull weight (lb.)..................4,083
Speed (mph) 4.65
Percent slippage................4.35
SAE drawbar horsepower.............50.38
SAE belt/PTO horsepower 57.88
Type ....Standard
Front wheel (in.) ....6.00 x 16

Rear wheel (in.)..15.50 x 38
Height (in.)..93.88
Tread width (in.)...52–88
Weight (lb.)...6,526
Gear/speed (mph).............forward: 1/1.70, 2/2.40, 3/3.30,
4/4.80, 5/6.20, 6/8.90, 7/12.10,
8/17.60; reverse: 1/2.20, 2/8.00

Case 741
Manufacturer..J.I. Case Co., Racine, WI
Nebraska test number..............................779
Test date..November 3–12, 1960
Test tractor serial number.......................8161050
Years produced..1960–1969
Serial number range.................................8160001–8356251
no end; all models
interspersed
Serial number location.............................metal plate near
instrument panel
Engine...Case A251S vertical
L-head
Test engine serial number........................8161050
Cylinders..4
Bore and stroke (in.)................................4.00 x 5.00
Rated rpm...1,700
Compression ratio....................................6.88:1
Displacement (c.i.)...................................251
Fuel..gasoline
Carburetor..Marvel-Schebler
TSX785, 1.25-in.
Air cleaner..Donaldson
Ignition...Delco-Remy, 12-v battery
Cooling capacity (gal.)..............................7.50
Maximum brake horsepower tests
PTO/belt horsepower.........................57.79
Crankshaft rpm..................................1,700
Fuel use (gal./hr.).............................4.91
Maximum drawbar horsepower tests
Gear...4th
Drawbar horsepower..........................51.45
Pull weight (lb.)................................4,733
Speed (mph)......................................4.08
Percent slippage...............................6.03
SAE drawbar horsepower..........................51.39
SAE belt/PTO horsepower........................57.79
Type...Standard
Front wheel (in.)......................................6.00 x 16
Rear wheel (in.).......................................15.50 x 38
Height (in.)...93.88
Tread width (in.)......................................52–88
Weight (lb.)..6,240
Gear/speed (mph)....................................forward: 1/1.50,
2/2.10, 3/2.90, 4/4.30,
5/5.60, 6/8.00,
7/10.70, 8/15.70;
reverse: 1/2.00, 2/7.20

Case 841-C LPG
Manufacturer..J.I. Case Co., Racine, WI
Nebraska test number..............................780
Test date..November 4–19, 1960
Test tractor serial number.......................8161059
Years produced..1960–1969
Serial number range.................................8160001–8356251 no
end; all models
interspersed

Serial number location.............................metal plate near
instrument panel
Engine...Case A284S vertical
L-head
Test engine serial number........................8161059
Cylinders..4
Bore and stroke (in.)................................4.25 x 5.00
Rated rpm...1,900
Compression ratio....................................8.37:1
Displacement (c.i.)...................................284
Fuel..LPG
Carburetor..Ensign XG, 1.25-in.
Air cleaner..Donaldson
Ignition...Delco-Remy,
12-v battery
Cooling capacity (gal.)..............................7.50
Maximum brake horsepower tests
PTO/belt horsepower.........................65.96
Crankshaft rpm..................................1,900
Fuel use (gal./hr.).............................7.14
Maximum drawbar horsepower tests
Gear...4th
Drawbar horsepower..........................57.46
Pull weight (lb.)................................4,645
Speed (mph)......................................4.64
Percent slippage...............................4.63
SAE drawbar horsepower..........................57.31
SAE belt/PTO horsepower........................65.96
Type...Standard
Front wheel (in.)......................................6.00 x 16
Rear wheel (in.).......................................15.50 x 38
Height (in.)...93.88
Tread width (in.)......................................52–88
Weight (lb.)..6,526
Gear/speed (mph)....................................forward: 1/1.70, 2/2.40, 3/3.30, 4/4.80,
5/6.20, 6/8.90, 7/12.10, 8/17.60;
reverse: 1/2.20, 2/8.00

Case 741-C LPG
Manufacturer..J.I. Case Co.,
Racine, WI
Nebraska test number..............................781
Test date..November
4–19, 1960
Test tractor serial number.......................8161053
Years produced..1960–1969
Serial number range.................................8160001–8356251
no end; all models
interspersed
Serial number location.............................metal plate near
instrument panel
Engine...Case A251S vertical
L-head
Test engine serial number........................8161053
Cylinders..4
Bore and stroke (in.)................................4.00 x 5.00
Rated rpm...1,900
Compression ratio....................................8.0:1
Displacement (c.i.)...................................251
Fuel..LPG
Carburetor..Ensign XG, 1.25-in.
Air cleaner..Donaldson
Ignition...Delco-Remy,
12-v battery
Cooling capacity (gal.)..............................7.50

Maximum brake horsepower tests
    PTO/belt horsepower............................57.19
    Crankshaft rpm 1,900
    Fuel use (gal./hr.)..............................7.22
Maximum drawbar horsepower tests
    Gear...4th
    Drawbar horsepower...........................51.98
    Pull weight (lb.)..................................4,241
    Speed (mph)......................................4.60
    Percent slippage................................4.83
SAE drawbar horsepower............................52.45
SAE belt/PTO horsepower 57.19
Type ....Standard
Front wheel (in.).......................................6.00 x 16
Rear wheel (in.)..15.50 x 38
Height (in.)...93.88
Tread width (in.).......................................52–88
Weight (lb.)..6,526
Gear/speed (mph) ....forward: 1/1.70,
    2/2.40, 3/3.30, 4/4.80,
    5/6.20, 6/8.90,
    7/12.10, 8/17.60;
    reverse: 1/2.20, 2/8.00

Case 741 LPG
Manufacturer...J.I. Case Co., Racine, WI
Nebraska test number 782
Test date ....November 7–19, 1960
Test tractor serial number..........................8161052
Years produced 1960–1969
Serial number range..................................8160001–8356251
    no end; all models
    interspersed
Serial number location ....metal plate near
    instrument panel

Engine ....Case A251S vertical
    L-head
Test engine serial number..........................8161052
Cylinders 4
Bore and stroke (in.).................................4.00 x 5.00
Rated rpm 1,700
Compression ratio....................................8.0:1
Displacement (c.i.) 251
Fuel ....LPG
Carburetor ....Ensign XG, 1.25-in.
Air cleaner ....Donaldson
Ignition ....Delco-Remy, 12-v
    battery
Cooling capacity (gal.) 7.50
Maximum brake horsepower tests
    PTO/belt horsepower............................57.92
    Crankshaft rpm 1,700
    Fuel use (gal./hr.)..............................6.18
Maximum drawbar horsepower tests
    Gear...4th
    Drawbar horsepower...........................52.51
    Pull weight (lb.)..................................4,795
    Speed (mph)......................................4.11
    Percent slippage................................5.13
SAE drawbar horsepower............................51.91
SAE belt/PTO horsepower 57.92
Type ....Standard
Front wheel (in.).......................................6.00 x 16
Rear wheel (in.)..15.50 x 38
Height (in.)...93.88
Tread width (in.).......................................52–88
Weight (lb.)..6,240
Gear/speed (mph).............forward: 1/1.50, 2/2.10, 3/2.90, 4/4.30,
    5/5.60, 6/8.00, 7/10.70, 8/15.70;
    reverse: 1/2.00, 2/7.20

Chapter 12

CATERPILLAR

Caterpillar 20, Twenty, 20-25
Manufacturer...Caterpillar Tractor Co.,
    San Leandro, CA
Nebraska test number 150
Test date ....May 17–29, 1928
Test tractor serial number..........................L 436
Years produced ....L, 1927–1931; PL,
    1928–1931
Serial number range..................................L 1–L 1970, San
    Leandro; PL 1–PL
    6319, Peoria
Serial number location ....brass plate, upper right
    rear transmission
    boss/left front upper
    crankcase to rear of oil fill
Number produced ....Model L, 1,970; Model
    PL, 6,319

Engine ....Caterpillar vertical
    I-head, valve-in-head
Test engine serial number..........................L 436
Cylinders 4
Bore and stroke (in.).................................4.00 x 5.50
Rated rpm 1,100
Displacement (c.i.) 276.5
Fuel ....gasoline
Fuel tank capacity (gal.) 25
Carburetor ....Ensign AE, 1.25-in.
Air cleaner ....Pomona
Ignition ....Eisemann G4 magneto
Cooling capacity (gal.) 5
Maximum brake horsepower tests
    PTO/belt horsepower............................29.49
    Crankshaft rpm 1,102
    Fuel use (gal./hr.)..............................3.33

Maximum drawbar horsepower tests

Gear	2nd
Drawbar horsepower	26.32
Pull weight (lb.)	5,721
Speed (mph)	1.73
Percent slippage	4.37
SAE drawbar horsepower	20
SAE belt/PTO horsepower	25
Type	tracklayer
Length (in.)	115.50
Height (in.)	60.50
Rear width (in.)	61
Tread width (in.)	42 or 55
Weight (lb.)	7,000
Track length (in.)	63 on ground, 195 total
Grouser shoe	29 links; 11-in.
Gear/speed (mph)	forward: 1/1.79, 2/3.07, 3/4.67; reverse: 1/2.35

Caterpillar 15, Fifteen, 15-20

Manufacturer	Caterpillar Tractor Co., San Leandro, CA
Nebraska test number	159
Test date	May 9–14, 1929
Test tractor serial number	PV 14
Years produced	1929–1932
Serial number range	PV 1–PV 7559 end
Serial number location	stamped on boss next to lower left shift lever plate/left top front engine block boss/brass patent and instruction plate on rear seat back
Number produced	7,559
Engine	Caterpillar vertical L-head
Test engine serial number	PV 14
Cylinders	4
Bore and stroke (in.)	3.75 x 5.00
Rated rpm	1,250
Displacement (c.i.)	220.9
Fuel	gasoline
Fuel tank capacity (gal.)	23
Carburetor	Ensign BeV, 1.00-in.
Air cleaner	Pomona Vortox
Ignition	Eisemann G4 magneto
Cooling capacity (gal.)	4.75

Maximum brake horsepower tests

PTO/belt horsepower	24.77
Crankshaft rpm	1,249
Fuel use (gal./hr.)	3.01

Maximum drawbar horsepower tests

Gear	low
Drawbar horsepower	21.79
Pull weight (lb.)	3,175
Speed (mph)	2.57
Percent slippage	1.60
SAE drawbar horsepower	15
SAE belt/PTO horsepower	20
Type	tracklayer
Length (in.)	104.13
Height (in.)	58
Rear width (in.)	57.75
Tread width (in.)	40 or 50
Weight (lb.)	5,700
Track length (in.)	54.50 on ground, 183 total
Grouser shoe	30 links; 10-in.
Gear/speed (mph)	forward: 1/1.99, 2/2.58, 3/3.57; reverse: 1/2.06

Caterpillar 10, Ten, 10-15

Manufacturer	Caterpillar Tractor Co., San Leandro, CA
Nebraska test number	160
Test date	May 6–21, 1929
Test tractor serial number	PT 341
Years produced	1928–1932
Serial number range	PT 1–PT 4929 end
Serial number location	stamped on boss next to lower left shift lever plate/left top front engine block boss/brass patent and instruction plate on rear seat back
Number produced	4,929
Engine	Caterpillar vertical L-head
Test engine serial number	PT 341
Cylinders	4
Bore and stroke (in.)	3.375 x 4.00
Rated rpm	1,500
Displacement (c.i.)	143.1
Fuel	gasoline
Fuel tank capacity (gal.)	17
Carburetor	Ensign BeT, 1.00-in.
Air cleaner	Pomona Vortox
Ignition	Eisemann G4 magneto
Cooling capacity (gal.)	4

Maximum brake horsepower tests

PTO/belt horsepower	18.10
Crankshaft rpm	1,501
Fuel use (gal./hr.)	2.11

Maximum drawbar horsepower tests

Gear	2nd
Drawbar horsepower	14.89
Pull weight (lb.)	2,816
Speed (mph)	1.98
Percent slippage	1.82
SAE drawbar horsepower	10
SAE belt/PTO horsepower	15
Type	tracklayer
Length (in.)	99.75
Height (in.)	51.43
Rear width (in.)	45.75 or 52.75
Tread width (in.)	37 or 44
Weight (lb.)	4,420
Track length (in.)	51 on ground, 165 total
Grouser shoe	29 links; 8-in.
Gear/speed (mph)	forward: 1/2.02, 2/2.59, 3/3.50; reverse: 1/2.07

Caterpillar 25, Twenty-Five

Manufacturer..Caterpillar Tractor Co.,
Peoria, IL
Nebraska test number.................................203
Test date..May 16–23, 1932
Test tractor serial number...........................3C 2
Years produced..1931–1933
Serial number range.....................................3C 1–3C 638 end
Serial number location.................................brass plate, upper right
rear transmission
boss/left front engine
block under oil fill
Number produced...638
Engine...Caterpillar vertical
I-head, valve-in-head
Test engine serial number............................3 C 2
Cylinders..4
Bore and stroke (in.)....................................4.00 x 5.50
Rated rpm...1,100
Displacement (c.i.)..276.5
Fuel...gasoline
Fuel tank capacity (gal.)...............................25
Carburetor..Ensign A e L c, 1.25-in.
Air cleaner..Caterpillar-Vortox
Ignition...Eisemann GV-4
magneto
Cooling capacity (gal.).................................5.50
Maximum brake horsepower tests
PTO/belt horsepower............................32.97
Crankshaft rpm.....................................1,100
Fuel use (gal./hr.)..................................3.42
Maximum drawbar horsepower tests
Gear..2nd
Drawbar horsepower.............................27.11
Pull weight (lb.).....................................4,068
Speed (mph)...2.50
Percent slippage...................................3.57
SAE drawbar horsepower............................22.07
SAE belt/PTO horsepower...........................29.94
Type..tracklayer
Length (in.)...115.50
Height (in.)...60.50
Rear width (in.)..61.50
Tread width (in.)..42 or 55
Weight (lb.)...7,670
Track length (in.)...56.50 on ground,
196.50 total
Grouser shoe..29 links; 11-in.
Gear/speed (mph)..forward: 1/1.80,
2/2.60, 3/3.60;
reverse: 1/2.00

Caterpillar 50, Fifty

Manufacturer..Caterpillar Tractor Co.,
Peoria, IL
Nebraska test number.................................204
Test date..May 18 to June 11,
1932
Test tractor serial number...........................5A 98
Years produced..1931–1937
Serial number range.....................................5A 1–5A 536; 5A
645-5A 1808 end
Serial number location.................................brass plate left rear
transmission case/left
center crankcase
between inspection
plates below carburetor
Number produced...1,700
Engine...Caterpillar vertical
I-head, valve-in-head
Test engine serial number............................5 A 98
Cylinders..4
Bore and stroke (in.)....................................5.50 x 6.50
Rated rpm...850
Displacement (c.i.)..617.7
Fuel...gasoline
Fuel tank capacity (gal.)...............................65
Carburetor..Ensign, K 0, 1.50-in.
Air cleaner..Caterpillar-Vortox
Ignition...Eisemann GV-4
magneto
Cooling capacity (gal.).................................11.50
Maximum brake horsepower tests
PTO/belt horsepower............................56.14
Crankshaft rpm.....................................850
Fuel use (gal./hr.)..................................6.71
Maximum drawbar horsepower tests
Gear..1st
Drawbar horsepower.............................49.30
Pull weight (lb.).....................................12,061
Speed (mph)...1.53
Percent slippage...................................2.86
SAE drawbar horsepower............................38.96
SAE belt/PTO horsepower...........................51.64
Type..tracklayer
Length (in.)...146.25
Height (in.)...75.75
Rear width (in.)..79
Tread width (in.)..60 or 74
Weight (lb.)...17,190
Track length (in.)...82 on ground,
264 total
Grouser shoe..35 links; 15-in.
Gear/speed (mph)..forward: 1/1.60,
2/2.40, 3/3.40, 4/4.70;
reverse: 1/1.90

Caterpillar 20, Twenty

Manufacturer..Caterpillar Tractor Co.,
Peoria, IL
Nebraska test number.................................205
Test date..May 20 to
June 22, 1932
Test tractor serial number...........................8C 1
Serial number range.....................................brass plate upper right
rear drawbar bracket
boss/left front upper
engine block above
carburetor elbow
Years produced..1932–1934
Serial number range.....................................8C 1–8C 652 end
Number produced...652
Engine...Caterpillar
vertical L-head
Test engine serial number............................8 C 1

Cylinders 4
Bore and stroke (in.) ....3.75 x 5.00
Rated rpm 1,250
Displacement (c.i.) 220.9
Fuel ....gasoline
Fuel tank capacity (gal.) 25
Carburetor ....Ensign BeV, 1.00-in.
Air cleaner ....Caterpillar-Vortox
Ignition ....Eisemann GV-4
                                                               magneto
Cooling capacity (gal.) 4.75

Maximum brake horsepower tests
    PTO/belt horsepower............................27.43
    Crankshaft rpm 1,251
    Fuel use (gal./hr.)...............................2.89

Maximum drawbar horsepower tests
    Gear..2nd
    Drawbar horsepower.............................22.18
    Pull weight (lb.)...................................3,267
    Speed (mph) 2.55
    Percent slippage..................................1.81
SAE drawbar horsepower......................17.96
SAE belt/PTO horsepower.....................24.60
Type ....tracklayer
Length (in.) 104
Height (in.) 58
Rear width (in.) 57.75
Tread width (in.)...................................40 or 50
Weight (lb.) 5,900
Track length (in.) ....54.50 on ground,
                                                               184 total
Grouser shoe..30 links; 10-in.
Gear/speed (mph) ....forward: 1/2.00,
                                                               2/2.60, 3/3.60; reverse:
                                                               1/2.10

Caterpillar 35, Thirty-Five

Manufacturer...Caterpillar Tractor Co.,
                                                               Peoria, IL
Nebraska test number 206
Test date ....June 6–24, 1932
Test tractor serial number....................5C 107
Years produced 1932–1934
Serial number range..............................5C 1–5C 1728 end
Serial number location ....brass plate left rear
                                                               transmission case/left
                                                               side crankcase
Number produced 1,728
Engine ....Caterpillar vertical
                                                               l-head, valve-in-head
Test engine serial number.....................5 C 107
Cylinders 4
Bore and stroke (in.) ....4.875 x 6.50
Rated rpm 850
Displacement (c.i.) 485.3
Fuel ....gasoline
Fuel tank capacity (gal.) 50
Carburetor ....Ensign, A e S c, 1.50in.
Air cleaner ....Donaldson or Vortox
Ignition ....Eisemann GV-4
                                                               magneto
Cooling capacity (gal.) 9.25

Maximum brake horsepower tests
    PTO/belt horsepower............................43.80
    Crankshaft rpm 850
    Fuel use (gal./hr.)...............................4.92

Maximum drawbar horsepower tests
    Gear..2nd
    Drawbar horsepower.............................36.22
    Pull weight (lb.)...................................5,542
    Speed (mph) 2.45
    Percent slippage..................................1.21
SAE drawbar horsepower......................29.15
SAE belt/PTO horsepower.....................39.58
Type ....tracklayer
Length (in.) 139.38
Height (in.) 69.25
Rear width (in.) 72.13
Tread width (in.)...................................53 or 74
Weight (lb.) 12,280
Track length (in.) ....71 on ground,
                                                               230 total
Grouser shoe..34 links; 14-in.
Gear/speed (mph) ....forward: 1/1.70,
                                                               2/2.50, 3/3.20, 4/4.60;
                                                               reverse: 1/1.90

Caterpillar 15, Fifteen

Manufacturer...Caterpillar Tractor Co.,
                                                               Peoria, IL
Nebraska test number 207
Test date ....June 7–29, 1932
Test tractor serial number....................7C 1
Years produced 1932–1933
Serial number range..............................7C 1–7C 307 end
Serial number location ....stamped on boss next
                                                               to lower left shift lever
                                                               plate/left top front
                                                               engine block
                                                               boss/brass patent and
                                                               instruction plate rear
                                                               seat back
Number produced 307
Engine ....Caterpillar
                                                               vertical L-head
Test engine serial number.....................7 C 1
Cylinders 4
Bore and stroke (in.) ....3.375 x 4.00
Rated rpm 1,500
Displacement (c.i.) 143.1
Fuel ....gasoline
Fuel tank capacity (gal.) 19.40
Carburetor ....Ensign, B o T, 1.00-in.
Air cleaner ....Caterpillar-Vortox
Ignition ....Eisemann GV-4
                                                               magneto
Cooling capacity (gal.) 4

Maximum brake horsepower tests
    PTO/belt horsepower............................20.39
    Crankshaft rpm 1,501
    Fuel use (gal./hr.)...............................2.24

Maximum drawbar horsepower tests
    Gear..2nd
    Drawbar horsepower.............................16.99
    Pull weight (lb.)...................................2,507
    Speed (mph) 2.54
    Percent slippage..................................2.11
SAE drawbar horsepower......................13.46
SAE belt/PTO horsepower.....................18.45
Type ....tracklayer
Length (in.) 99.75
Height (in.) 52.25

Rear width (in.) ....45.75 or 52.75
Tread width (in.)......................................37 or 44
Weight (lb.) 4,467
Track length (in.).....................................51 on ground,
165 total
Grouser shoe...29 links; 8-in.
Gear/speed (mph) ....forward: 1/2.00,
2/2.60, 3/3.50;
reverse: 1/2.10

Caterpillar Diesel Sixty-Five
Manufacturer...Caterpillar Tractor Co.,
Peoria, IL
Nebraska test number 208
Test date ....June 14 to
July 20, 1932
Test tractor serial number 1C 15
Years produced 1931–1932
Serial number range....................................1C 1–1C 157 end
Serial number location ....brass plate, upper left
rear transmission
case/left side front
engine block
Number produced 157
Engine ....Caterpillar vertical
I-head, valve-in-head
Test engine serial number 1C 15
Cylinders 4
Bore and stroke (in.) ....6.125 x 9.25
Rated rpm 700
Displacement (c.i.) 1090.2
Fuel ....diesel/gasoline
Main tank capacity (gal.) 75
Auxiliary tank capacity (gal.) 2
Carburetor ....start; Ensign
Air cleaner ....Caterpillar-Vortox
Ignition ....start; Eisemann RC-20
magneto
Cooling capacity (gal.) 32
Maximum brake horsepower tests
PTO/belt horsepower............................77.08
Crankshaft rpm 700
Fuel use (gal./hr.) 5.98
Maximum drawbar horsepower tests
Gear...1st
Drawbar horsepower.............................65.11
Pull weight (lb.)..............................11,991
Speed (mph)....................................2.04
Percent slippage...............................1.22
SAE drawbar horsepower.................................54.00
SAE belt/PTO horsepower................................73.85
Type ....tracklayer
Length (in.) 161.25
Height (in.) 86.63
Rear width (in.) 101
Weight (lb.) 24,390
Track length (in.).....................................83.50 on ground,
271 total
Grouser shoe...34 links; 16-in.
Gear/speed (mph) ....forward: 1/2.10, 2/2.80,
3/4.70; reverse: 1/1.50

Caterpillar 65, Sixty-Five
Manufacturer...Caterpillar Tractor Co.,
Peoria, IL

Nebraska test number 209
Test date ....July 5–22, 1932
Test tractor serial number 2D 148
Years produced 1932–1933
Serial number range....................................2D 1–2D 521 end
Serial number location ....brass plate, right
rear transmission
hitch brace/left
center engine block
between inspection
plates
Number produced 521
Engine ....Caterpillar vertical
I-head, valve-in-head
Test engine serial number 2D 148
Cylinders 4
Bore and stroke (in.) ....7.00 x 8.50
Rated rpm 650
Displacement (c.i.) 1308.5
Fuel ....gasoline
Fuel tank capacity (gal.) 90
Carburetor ....Ensign, K, 1.75-in.
Air cleaner ....Caterpillar-Vortox
Ignition ....Eisemann GV-4
magneto
Cooling capacity (gal.) 28.50
Maximum brake horsepower tests
PTO/belt horsepower............................78.41
Crankshaft rpm 650
Fuel use (gal./hr.) 9.47
Maximum drawbar horsepower tests
Gear...1st
Drawbar horsepower.............................67.86
Pull weight (lb.)..............................13,597
Speed (mph)....................................1.87
Percent slippage...............................2.19
SAE drawbar horsepower.................................54.15
SAE belt/PTO horsepower................................72.02
Type ....tracklayer
Length (in.) 158.87
Height (in.) 87.50
Rear width (in.) 101.25
Tread width (in.)......................................72
Weight (lb.) 23,007
Track length (in.).....................................83.50 on ground,
271 total
Grouser shoe...34 links; 16, (20)-in.
Gear/speed (mph) ....forward: 1/1.90,
2/2.60, 3/4.40;
reverse: 1/1.40

Caterpillar 70, Seventy
Manufacturer...Caterpillar Tractor Co.,
Peoria, IL
Nebraska test number 213
Test date ....May 15 to June 6,
1933
Test tractor serial number 8D 39
Years produced 1933–1937
Serial number range....................................8D 1–8D 266 end
Serial number location ....brass plate, left rear
transmission case/left
center engine block
between inspection
plates below air cleaner

Caterpillar

Number produced 266
Engine ....Caterpillar vertical
I-head, valve-in-head
Test engine serial number 8D 39
Cylinders 4
Bore and stroke (in.) ....7.00 x 8.50
Rated rpm 700
Displacement (c.i.) 1308.5
Fuel ....gasoline
Fuel tank capacity (gal.) 90
Carburetor ....Ensign, K e B, 1.75-in.
Air cleaner ....Caterpillar-Vortox
Ignition ....Eisemann GV-4
magneto
Cooling capacity (gal.) 30
Maximum brake horsepower tests
    PTO/belt horsepower 82.40
    Crankshaft rpm 700
    Fuel use (gal./hr.) 9.70
Maximum drawbar horsepower tests
    Gear 1st
    Drawbar horsepower 72.73
    Pull weight (lb.) 16,796
    Speed (mph) 1.62
    Percent slippage 2.17
SAE drawbar horsepower 58.28
SAE belt/PTO horsepower 77.44
Type ....tracklayer
Length (in.) 175
Height (in.) 88.88
Rear width (in.) 103.75
Tread width (in.) 78
Weight (lb.) 31,070
Track length (in.) ....97.63 on ground,
303 total
Grouser shoe ....38 links; (18), 20-in.
Gear/speed (mph) ....forward: 1/1.70,
2/2.30, 3/2.70, 4/3.10,
5/3.70, 6/5.00; reverse:
1/1.70, 2/2.70

Caterpillar Diesel Fifty
Manufacturer ....Caterpillar Tractor Co.,
Peoria, IL
Nebraska test number 214
Test date ....May 17 to June 2,
1933
Test tractor serial number 1E 50
Years produced 1933–1935
Serial number range 1E 1–1E 2065
Serial number location ....brass plate, left rear
transmission case/left
front lower engine
block under water
pump
Number produced 2,065
Engine ....Caterpillar vertical
I-head, valve-in-head
Test engine serial number 1E 50
Cylinders 4
Bore and stroke (in.) ....5.25 x 8.00
Rated rpm 850
Displacement (c.i.) 692.7
Fuel ....diesel/gasoline

Main tank capacity (gal.) 60
Auxiliary tank capacity (gal.) 2
Carburetor ....start; Ensign
Air cleaner ....Caterpillar-Vortox
Ignition ....start; Eisemann
RC-20 magneto
Cooling capacity (gal.) 18.50
Maximum brake horsepower tests
    PTO/belt horsepower 61.26
    Crankshaft rpm 851
    Fuel use (gal./hr.) 4.57
Maximum drawbar horsepower tests
    Gear 1st
    Drawbar horsepower 52.61
    Pull weight (lb.) 12,765
    Speed (mph) 1.55
    Percent slippage 2.42
SAE drawbar horsepower 40.12
SAE belt/PTO horsepower 55.74
Type ....tracklayer
Length (in.) 150.25
Height (in.) 81.63
Rear width (in.) 81.63
Tread width (in.) 60
Weight (lb.) 20,250
Track length (in.) ....81.88 on ground,
264 total
Grouser shoe ....35 links; 18-in.
Gear/speed (mph) ....forward: 1/1.60,
2/2.40, 3/3.40, 4/4.70;
reverse: 1/1.90

Caterpillar Diesel Thirty Five
Manufacturer ....Caterpillar Tractor Co.,
Peoria, IL
Nebraska test number 217
Test date ....October 10–25, 1933
Test tractor serial number 6E 234
Years produced 1933–1934
Serial number range ....6E1–6E1999 end
Serial number location ....brass plate, left rear
transmission case/left
front lower engine
block under water
pump
Number produced 1,999
Engine ....Caterpillar vertical
I-head, valve-in-head
Test engine serial number 6E 234
Cylinders 3
Bore and stroke (in.) ....5.25 x 8.00
Rated rpm 850
Displacement (c.i.) 519.5
Fuel ....diesel/gasoline
Main tank capacity (gal.) 45
Auxiliary tank capacity (gal.) 2
Carburetor ....start; Ensign
Air cleaner ....Donaldson (Vortox)
Ignition ....start; Wico magneto
Cooling capacity (gal.) 16
Maximum brake horsepower tests
    PTO/belt horsepower 44.72
    Crankshaft rpm 850
    Fuel use (gal./hr.) 3.25

Maximum drawbar horsepower tests
Gear...1st
Drawbar horsepower............................39.53
Pull weight (lb.)..............................9,135
Speed (mph) 1.62
Percent slippage..............................4.07
SAE drawbar horsepower...........................29.98
SAE belt/PTO horsepower 39.29
Type ....tracklayer
Length (in.) 139.38
Height (in.)...................................69.25
Rear width (in.)...............................72.50
Tread width (in.)..............................53
Weight (lb.)..................................12,597
Track length (in.).............................71.38 on ground,
230 total
Grouser shoe..................................34 links; 16-in.
Gear/speed (mph) ....forward: 1/1.70,
2/2.50, 3/3.20, 4/4.60;
reverse: 1/1.90

Caterpillar Diesel Seventy Five
Manufacturer.................................Caterpillar Tractor Co.,
Peoria, IL
Nebraska test number 218
Test date ....October 10–31, 1933
Test tractor serial number.....................2E 111
Years produced................................1933–1935
Serial number range...........................2E 1–2E 1078 end
Serial number location ....brass plate, upper left
rear transmission
case/left side front
engine block
Number produced 1,078
Engine ....Caterpillar vertical
I-head, valve-in-head
Test engine serial number.....................2E 111
Cylinders 6
Bore and stroke (in.) ....5.25 x 8.00
Rated rpm 820
Displacement (c.i.)............................1039.1
Fuel ....diesel/gasoline
Main tank capacity (gal.)......................69
Auxiliary tank capacity (gal.) 2
Carburetor ....start; Ensign
Air cleaner ....Donaldson (Vortox)
Ignition......................................start; Eisemann
RC-20 magneto
Cooling capacity (gal.) 28
Maximum brake horsepower tests
PTO/belt horsepower...........................92.85
Crankshaft rpm 820
Fuel use (gal./hr.) 6.51
Maximum drawbar horsepower tests
Gear...2nd
Drawbar horsepower...........................80.57
Pull weight (lb.).............................13,334
Speed (mph) 2.27
Percent slippage.............................1.87
SAE drawbar horsepower.........................62.18
SAE belt/PTO horsepower 83.22
Type ....tracklayer
Length (in.) 183
Height (in.)..................................84.13
Rear width (in.)..............................103.75
Tread width (in.).............................78

Weight (lb.) 32,534
Track length (in.)............................97.63 on ground,
303 total
Grouser shoe.................................38 links; (18), 20-in.
Gear/speed (mph) ....forward: 1/1.70,
2/2.30, 3/2.70, 4/3.10,
5/3.70, 6/5.00; reverse:
1/1.70, 2/2.70

Caterpillar R5
Manufacturer................................Caterpillar Tractor Co.,
Peoria, IL
Nebraska test number 224
Test date ....July 12–20, 1934
Test tractor serial number....................5E 3001
Years produced...............................1934–1940
Serial number range..........................5E 3001-5E 3500;
4H 501-4H 1500;
3R 1-3R 49 end
Serial number location ....brass plate upper left
rear transmission
case/upper left front
crankcase
Number produced ....Model 5E, 500; Model
4H, 1,000; Model 3R,
49
Engine ....Caterpillar vertical
I-head, valve-in-head
Test engine serial number....................5E 3001
Cylinders 4
Bore and stroke (in.) ....5.50 x 6.50
Rated rpm 950
Displacement (c.i.)...........................617.7
Fuel ....gasoline
Fuel tank capacity (gal.).....................50
Carburetor ....Zenith (Ensign, K e d)
1.50-in.
Air cleaner ....Donaldson
(Caterpillar-Vortox)
Ignition.....................................Eisemann GT-4
magneto
Cooling capacity (gal.) 9.25
Maximum brake horsepower tests
PTO/belt horsepower..........................58.89
Crankshaft rpm 950
Fuel use (gal./hr.) 6.11
Maximum drawbar horsepower tests
Gear..2nd
Drawbar horsepower..........................49.44
Pull weight (lb.)............................6,778
Speed (mph) 2.74
Percent slippage............................1.73
SAE drawbar horsepower........................41.24
SAE belt/PTO horsepower 54.64
Type ....tracklayer
Length (in.) 139.38
Height (in.).................................72.19
Rear width (in.).............................75 or 93
Tread width (in.)............................58 or 77
Weight (lb.)................................13,260 or 13,970
Track length (in.)...........................74.75 on ground,
230 total
Grouser shoe................................34 links; 16, (18)-in.
Gear/speed (mph) ....forward: 1/1.90,
2/2.80, 3/3.60, 4/5.10;
reverse: 1/2.10

Caterpillar

Caterpillar R2

Manufacturer	Caterpillar Tractor Co., Peoria, IL
Nebraska test number	225
Test date	September 24 to October 16, 1934
Test tractor serial number	5E 3502
Years produced	1934–1937
Serial number range	5E 3501–5E 3583 end
Serial number location	brass Patent plate on right outside seat side
Number produced	83
Engine	Caterpillar vertical I-head, valve-in-head
Test engine serial number	5E 3502
Cylinders	4
Bore and stroke (in.)	4.00 x 5.00
Rated rpm	1,250
Displacement (c.i.)	251.3
Fuel	gasoline
Fuel tank capacity (gal.)	20
Carburetor	Zenith, K 5 A, 1.25-in.
Air cleaner	Donaldson (Caterpillar-Vortox)
Ignition	Eisemann CT-4 magneto
Cooling capacity (gal.)	7.75

Maximum brake horsepower tests

PTO/belt horsepower	32.47
Crankshaft rpm	1,249
Fuel use (gal./hr.)	3.70

Maximum drawbar horsepower tests

Gear	1st
Drawbar horsepower	27.15
Pull weight (lb.)	5,274
Speed (mph)	1.93
Percent slippage	3.70
SAE drawbar horsepower	21.48
SAE belt/PTO horsepower	29.11
Type	tracklayer
Length (in.)	110
Height (in.)	57.69
Rear width (in.)	65.75
Tread width (in.)	50
Weight (lb.)	6,120 or 6,250
Track length (in.)	54.50 on ground, 184 total
Grouser shoe	30 links; 12, (13)-in.
Gear/speed (mph)	forward: 1/2.00, 2/2.60, 3/3.60; reverse: 1/2.10

Caterpillar 22, Twenty-Two

Manufacturer	Caterpillar Tractor Co., Peoria, IL
Nebraska test number	226
Test date	September 25 to October 9, 1934
Test tractor serial number	2F 1117
Years produced	1934–1939
Serial number range	2F 1–2F 9999; 1J 1–1J 5157 end
Serial number location	brass plate, left front engine block above oil fill/right upper rear transmission housing on flat boss
Number produced	Model 2F, 9,999; Model 1J, 5,157
Engine	Caterpillar vertical I-head, valve-in-head
Test engine serial number	2 F 1117
Cylinders	4
Bore and stroke (in.)	4.00 x 5.00
Rated rpm	1,250
Displacement (c.i.)	251.3
Fuel	distillate/gasoline
Main tank capacity (gal.)	22
Auxiliary tank capacity (gal.)	2
Carburetor	Ensign (Zenith, K 5 A) 1.25-in.
Air cleaner	Caterpillar-Vortox
Ignition	Eisemann CT-4 magneto
Cooling capacity (gal.)	5

Maximum brake horsepower tests

PTO/belt horsepower	29.36
Crankshaft rpm	1,252
Fuel use (gal./hr.)	2.97

Maximum drawbar horsepower tests

Gear	1st
Drawbar horsepower	23.43
Pull weight (lb.)	4,534
Speed (mph)	1.94
Percent slippage	2.84
SAE drawbar horsepower	18.86
SAE belt/PTO horsepower	26.75
Type	tracklayer
Length (in.)	106.50
Height (in.)	56.50
Rear width (in.)	57.75
Tread width (in.)	40 or 55
Weight (lb.)	6,150
Track length (in.)	54.50 on ground, 184 total
Grouser shoe	30 links; 10-in.
Gear/speed (mph)	forward: 1/2.00, 2/2.60, 3/3.60; reverse: 1/2.10

Caterpillar R3

Manufacturer	Caterpillar Tractor Co., Peoria, IL
Nebraska test number	227
Test date	September 26 to October 15, 1934
Test tractor serial number	5E 2527
Years produced	1934–1935
Serial number range	5E 2501–5E 2560 end
Serial number location	brass Patent plate on right outside seat side
Number produced	60
Engine	Caterpillar vertical I-head
Test engine serial number	5 E 2527
Cylinders	4
Bore and stroke (in.)	4.50 x 5.50
Rated rpm	1,100
Displacement (c.i.)	349.9
Fuel	gasoline
Carburetor	Ensign, Ko, 1.25-in.
Air cleaner	Caterpillar-Vortox

Ignition ....Eisemann CT-4 magneto

Maximum brake horsepower tests
    PTO/belt horsepower............................41.99
    Crankshaft rpm 1,101
    Fuel use (gal./hr.).................................4.93

Maximum drawbar horsepower tests
    Gear..2nd
    Drawbar horsepower............................34.44
    Pull weight (lb.).....................................5,131
    Speed (mph) 2.52
    Percent slippage.................................3.21
SAE drawbar horsepower............................27.47
SAE belt/PTO horsepower............................37.33
Type ....tracklayer
Rear width (in.)..71
Tread width (in.)...55
Weight (lb.) 10,116
Track length (in.)..na on ground, 196 total
Grouser shoe...29 links; 16-in.
Gear/speed (mph) ....forward: 1/1.80, 2/2.60, 3/3.60; reverse: 1/2.00

Caterpillar 22, Twenty-Two

Manufacturer..Caterpillar Tractor Co., Peoria, IL
Nebraska test number 228
Test date ....October 17–30, 1934
Test tractor serial number............................2F 1117
Years produced 1934–1939
Serial number range......................................2F 1–2F 9999; 1J 1-1J 5157 end
Serial number location ....brass plate, left front engine block above oil fill/right upper rear transmission housing on flat boss
Number produced ....Model 2F, 9,999; Model 1J, 5,157
Engine ....Caterpillar vertical I-head, valve-in-head
Test engine serial number.............................2F 1117
Cylinders 4
Bore and stroke (in.) ....4.00 x 5.00
Rated rpm 1,250
Displacement (c.i.) 251.3
Fuel ....gasoline
Fuel tank capacity (gal.) 22
Carburetor..Ensign (Zenith K 5 A) 1.25-in.
Air cleaner ....Caterpillar-Vortox
Ignition ....Eisemann CT-4 magneto
Cooling capacity (gal.) 5

Maximum brake horsepower tests
    PTO/belt horsepower............................30.71
    Crankshaft rpm 1,250
    Fuel use (gal./hr.).................................3.35

Maximum drawbar horsepower tests
    Gear..1st
    Drawbar horsepower............................25.26
    Pull weight (lb.).....................................4,900
    Speed (mph) 1.93
    Percent slippage.................................3.29

SAE drawbar horsepower............................19.34
SAE belt/PTO horsepower............................27.17
Type ....tracklayer
Length (in.) 106.50
Height (in.) 56.50
Rear width (in.) 57.75
Tread width (in.)...40 or 55
Weight (lb.) 6,150
Track length (in.) ....54.50 on ground, 184 total
Grouser shoe...30 links; 10-in.
Gear/speed (mph) ....forward: 1/2.00, 2/2.60, 3/3.60; reverse: 1/2.10

Caterpillar Diesel Fifty

Manufacturer..Caterpillar Tractor Co., Peoria, IL
Nebraska test number ....240. Test numbers 240 and 241: these tests indicate that the tractor is a Caterpillar Diesel 50. The serial number for the tractor chassis and engine tested is 5E 7522 which is the serial number series for the RD-7. Caterpillar Diesel 50 number series is 1E. The serial number and the data presented fit an RD-7. No explanation has been found to explain the differences.
Test date ....August 19–29, 1935
Test tractor serial number............................5E 7522
Year produced..1935
Serial number range......................................5E 7501–5E 7524 end
Serial number location ....brass plate, upper left rear transmission case/left front lower engine block under water pump
Number produced 24
Engine ....Caterpillar, D8800 vertical I-head, valve-in-head
Test engine serial number............................5E 7522
Cylinders 4
Bore and stroke (in.) ....5.75 x 8.00
Rated rpm 850
Displacement (c.i.) 831
Fuel ....diesel/gasoline
Main tank capacity (gal.) 60
Auxiliary tank capacity (gal.) 2
Carburetor..start; Zenith
Air cleaner ....Donaldson
Ignition ....start; Eisemann RC-20 magneto
Cooling capacity (gal.) 18.50

Maximum brake horsepower tests
    PTO/belt horsepower............................61.04
    Crankshaft rpm 850
    Fuel use (gal./hr.).................................4.14

Maximum drawbar horsepower tests
    Gear..2nd
    Drawbar horsepower............................52.99
    Pull weight (lb.).....................................8,268
    Speed (mph) 2.40
    Percent slippage.................................1.92
SAE drawbar horsepower............................42.21

SAE belt/PTO horsepower 53.65
Type ....tracklayer
Length (in.) 150.25
Height (in.) 81.63
Rear width (in.) ....95.63 or 81.63
Tread width (in.) 56
Weight (lb.) 21,130/20,410
Track length (in.) ....81.88 on ground, 261 total
Grouser shoe..35 links; 18-in.
Gear/speed (mph) ....forward: 1/1.60, 2/2.40, 3/3.40, 4/4.70; reverse: 1/1.90

Caterpillar Diesel Fifty

Manufacturer...Caterpillar Tractor Co., Peoria, IL
Nebraska test number.......241. Test numbers 240 and 241: these tests indicate that the tractor is a Caterpillar Diesel 50. The serial number for the tractor chassis and engine tested is 5E 7522 which is the serial number series for the RD-7. Caterpillar Diesel 50 number series is 1E. The serial number and the data presented fit an RD-7. No explanation has been found to explain the differences.
Test date ....August 29 to September 16, 1935
Test tractor serial number.........................5E 7522
Year produced..1935
Serial number range.................................5E 7501–5E 7524 end
Serial number location ....brass plate, upper left rear transmission case/left front lower engine block under water pump
Number produced 24
Engine ....Caterpillar, D8800 vertical I-head, valve-in-head
Test engine serial number.........................5E7522
Cylinders 4
Bore and stroke (in.) ....5.75 x 8.00
Rated rpm ....(1,000) 850
Displacement (c.i.) 831
Fuel ....diesel/gasoline
Main tank capacity (gal.).........................60
Auxiliary tank capacity (gal.) 2
Carburetor...start; Zenith
Air cleaner ....Donaldson
Ignition...start; Eisemann RC-20 magneto
Cooling capacity (gal.) 18.50
Maximum brake horsepower tests
    PTO/belt horsepower............................71.81
    Crankshaft rpm 1,002
    Fuel use (gal./hr.)...............................5.11
Maximum drawbar horsepower tests
    Gear...2nd
    Drawbar horsepower...........................60.62
    Pull weight (lb.)..................................7,976
    Speed (mph) 2.85
    Percent slippage.................................1.26
SAE drawbar horsepower..........................48.29

SAE belt/PTO horsepower 64.82
Type ....tracklayer
Length (in.) 150.25
Height (in.) 81.63
Rear width (in.) ....95.63 or 81.63
Tread width (in.).....................................56
Weight (lb.) 21,130/20,410
Track length (in.) ....81.88 on ground, 261 total
Grouser shoe..35 links; 18-in.
Gear/speed (mph) ....forward: 1/1.80, 2/2.90, 3/4.00, 4/5.50; reverse: 1/2.20

Caterpillar Diesel Forty

Manufacturer...Caterpillar Tractor Co., Peoria, IL
Nebraska test number ....242. Test numbers 242 and 243: these tests indicate that the tractor is a Caterpillar Diesel 40. The serial number for the tractor chassis and engine tested is 5E 8501 which is the serial number for the RD-6. Caterpillar Diesel 40 number series is 3G. The serial number and the data presented fit an RD-6. No explanation has been found to explain the differences.
Test date ....August 19 to September 9, 1935
Test tractor serial number.........................5E 8501
Years produced.......................................5E, 1935; 2H, 1935–1937
Serial number range.................................5E 8501–5E 8505; 2H 1–2H 4060 end
Serial number location ....brass plate, left rear transmission case/left front lower engine block under water pump
Number produced ....Model 5E, 5; Model 2H, 4,060
Engine ....Caterpillar vertical I-head, valve-in-head
Test engine serial number.........................5E 8501
Cylinders 3
Bore and stroke (in.) ....5.75 x 8.00
Rated rpm ....(1,000) 850
Displacement (c.i.) 623.2
Fuel ....diesel/gasoline
Main tank capacity (gal.).........................45
Auxiliary tank capacity (gal.) 2
Carburetor...start; Zenith
Air cleaner ....Donaldson
Ignition...start; Eisemann RC-20 magneto
Cooling capacity (gal.) 16
Maximum brake horsepower tests
    PTO/belt horsepower............................56.05
    Crankshaft rpm 1,000
    Fuel use (gal./hr.)...............................4.09
Maximum drawbar horsepower tests
    Gear...2nd
    Drawbar horsepower...........................50.44
    Pull weight (lb.)..................................6,716
    Speed (mph) 2.82
    Percent slippage.................................3.74

SAE drawbar horsepower..............................39.46
SAE belt/PTO horsepower...........................50.12
Type ....tracklayer
Length (in.) 138.38
Height (in.)...72.06
Rear width (in.) ....75 or 93
Tread width (in.)...60 or 78
Weight (lb.) 14,820/15,560
Track length (in.)..74.75 on ground,
236 total
Grouser shoe..35 links; 16-in.
Gear/speed (mph) ....forward: 1/2.00,
2/2.90, 3/3.80, 4/5.40;
reverse: 1/2.20

Caterpillar Diesel Forty

Manufacturer...Caterpillar Tractor Co.,
Peoria, IL
Nebraska test number ....243. Test numbers 242 and 243: these
tests indicate that the tractor is a
Caterpillar Diesel 40. The serial number for
the tractor chassis and engine tested is 5E
8501 which is the serial number for the
RD-6. Caterpillar Diesel 40 number series
is 3G. The serial number and the data
presented fit an RD-6. No explanation has
been found to explain the differences.
Test date ....September 10–12,
1935
Test tractor serial number..........................5E 8501
Years produced 5E, 1935; 2H,
1935–1937
Serial number range....................................5E 8501–5E 8505;
2H 1–2H 4060 end
Serial number location ....brass plate, left rear
transmission case/left
front lower engine
block under water
pump
Number produced ....Model 5E, 5; Model
2H, 4,060
Engine ....Caterpillar vertical
I-head, valve-in-head
Test engine serial number...........................5E 8501
Cylinders 3
Bore and stroke (in.) ....5.75 x 8.00
Rated rpm 850
Displacement (c.i.)......................................623.2
Fuel ....diesel/gasoline
Main tank capacity (gal.).............................45
Auxiliary tank capacity (gal.) 2
Carburetor...start; Zenith
Air cleaner ....Donaldson
Ignition...start; Eisemann
RC-20 magneto
Cooling capacity (gal.) 16
Maximum brake horsepower tests
PTO/belt horsepower...........................48.60
Crankshaft rpm 850
Fuel use (gal./hr.)................................3.38
Maximum drawbar horsepower tests
Gear..2nd
Drawbar horsepower............................42.78
Pull weight (lb.)...................................6,524
Speed (mph) 2.46

Percent slippage...................................0.97
SAE drawbar horsepower..............................33.56
SAE belt/PTO horsepower...........................44.08
Type ....tracklayer
Length (in.) 138.38
Height (in.)...72.06
Rear width (in.) ....75 or 93
Weight (lb.) 14,820/15,560
Track length (in.)..74.75 on ground,
236 total
Grouser shoe..35 links; 16-in.
Gear/speed (mph) ....forward: 1/1.70,
2/2.50, 3/3.20, 4/4.60;
reverse: 1/1.90

Caterpillar 40, Forty

Manufacturer...Caterpillar Tractor Co.,
Peoria, IL
Nebraska test number 244
Test date ....September 16–20,
1935
Test tractor serial number..........................5G 278
Years produced 1934–1936
Serial number range....................................5G 1–5G 584 end
Serial number location ....brass plate, left rear
transmission case/left
center crankcase
between inspection
plates below carburetor
Number produced 584
Engine ....Caterpillar vertical
I-head, valve-in-head
Test engine serial number...........................5G278
Cylinders 4
Bore and stroke (in.) ....5.125 x 6.50
Rated rpm 850
Displacement (c.i.)......................................536.4
Fuel ....gasoline
Fuel tank capacity (gal.) 50
Carburetor...Zenith (Ensign K-3)
1.25-in.
Air cleaner ....Donaldson or Vortox
Ignition...Eisemann CT-4
magneto
Cooling capacity (gal.) 9.25
Maximum brake horsepower tests
PTO/belt horsepower...........................48.57
Crankshaft rpm 850
Fuel use (gal./hr.)................................5.94
Maximum drawbar horsepower tests
Gear..2nd
Drawbar horsepower............................41.78
Pull weight (lb.)...................................6,486
Speed (mph) 2.41
Percent slippage..................................2.57
SAE drawbar horsepower............................33.14
SAE belt/PTO horsepower...........................43.80
Type ....tracklayer
Length (in.) 139.38
Height (in.)...70
Rear width (in.) ....75 or 93
Tread width (in.)...56 or 74
Weight (lb.) 13,310/13,910
Track length (in.)..74.75 on ground,
235 total

Caterpillar

Grouser shoe..35 links; 16-in.
Gear/speed (mph) ....forward: 1/1.70,
2/2.50, 3/3.20, 4/4.60;
reverse: 1/1.90

Caterpillar 40, Forty
Manufacturer..Caterpillar Tractor Co.,
Peoria, IL
Nebraska test number 245
Test date ....September 18–23,
1935
Test tractor serial number.....................5G 271
Years produced 1934–1936
Serial number range..............................5G 1–5G 584 end
Serial number location ....brass plate, left rear
transmission case/left
center crankcase
between inspection
plates below carburetor
Number produced 584
Engine ....Caterpillar vertical
I-head, valve-in-head
Test engine serial number.....................5G271
Cylinders 4
Bore and stroke (in.) ....5.125 x 6.50
Rated rpm 1,000
Displacement (c.i.) 536.4
Fuel ....gasoline
Fuel tank capacity (gal.) 50
Carburetor..Zenith, K-6-A, 1.25-in.
Air cleaner ....Donaldson or Vortox
Ignition..Eisemann CT-4
magneto
Cooling capacity (gal.) 9.25
Maximum brake horsepower tests
    PTO/belt horsepower.........................56.42
    Crankshaft rpm 999
    Fuel use (gal./hr.) 6.93
Maximum drawbar horsepower tests
    Gear..2nd
    Drawbar horsepower..........................48.91
    Pull weight (lb.) 6,436
    Speed (mph) 2.85
    Percent slippage.................................2.29
SAE drawbar horsepower.......................38.12
SAE belt/PTO horsepower......................50.41
Type ....tracklayer
Length (in.) 139.38
Height (in.) 70
Rear width (in.).......................................75 or 93
Tread width (in.)......................................56 or 74
Weight (lb.) 13,310/13,910
Track length (in.).....................................74.75 on ground,
235 total
Grouser shoe...35 links; 16-in.
Gear/speed (mph) ....forward: 1/2.00,
2/2.90, 3/3.80, 4/5.40;
reverse: 1/2.20

Caterpillar RD-7, Diesel, 61 H.P.
Manufacturer..Caterpillar Tractor Co.,
Peoria, IL
Nebraska test number 253
Test date ....May 5–15, 1936

Test tractor serial number.....................9G 687
Year produced 1936
Serial number range..............................9G 1–9G 2777 end
Serial number location ....brass plate, left rear
transmission case/left
front lower engine block
under water pump
Number produced 2,777
Engine ....Caterpillar, D8800
vertical I-head,
valve-in-head
Test engine serial number.....................9G 687
Cylinders 4
Bore and stroke (in.) ....5.75 x 8.00
Rated rpm 850
Displacement (c.i.) 830.9
Fuel ....diesel/gasoline
Main tank capacity (gal.) 60
Auxiliary tank capacity (gal.) 2
Carburetor..start; Zenith
Air cleaner ....Donaldson
Ignition..start; Eisemann
GV-2Q/Wico magneto
Cooling capacity (gal.) 18.50
Maximum brake horsepower tests
    PTO/belt horsepower.........................68.24
    Crankshaft rpm 851
    Fuel use (gal./hr.) 4.69
Maximum drawbar horsepower tests
    Gear..2nd
    Drawbar horsepower..........................59.89
    Pull weight (lb.) 9,248
    Speed (mph) 2.43
    Percent slippage.................................1.03
SAE drawbar horsepower.......................52.06
SAE belt/PTO horsepower......................69.73
Type ....tracklayer
Length (in.) 150.25
Height (in.) 81.63
Rear width (in.).......................................81.63 or 95.63
Tread width (in.)......................................60 or 74
Weight (lb.) 20,410/21,130
Track length (in.).....................................81.88 on ground,
262 total
Grouser shoe...35 links; 18-in.
Gear/speed (mph) ....forward: 1/1.60,
2/2.40, 3/3.40, 4/4.70;
reverse: 1/1.90

Caterpillar RD-7, Diesel
Manufacturer..Caterpillar Tractor Co.,
Peoria, IL
Nebraska test number 254
Test date ....May 16–20, 1936
Test tractor serial number.....................9G 687
Year produced 1936
Serial number range..............................9G 1–9G 2777 end
Serial number location ....brass plate, left rear
transmission case/left
front lower engine block
under water pump
Number produced 2,777
Engine ....Caterpillar, D8800
vertical I-head,
valve-in-head

Test engine serial number..........................9G 687
Cylinders 4
Bore and stroke (in.) ....5.75 x 8.00
Rated rpm 850
Displacement (c.i.) 830.9
Fuel ....diesel/gasoline
Main tank capacity (gal.) 60
Auxiliary tank capacity (gal.) 2
Carburetor ....start; Zenith
Air cleaner ....Donaldson
Ignition ....start; Eisemann
GV-2Q/Wico magneto
Cooling capacity (gal.) 18.50
Maximum brake horsepower tests
PTO/belt horsepower..........................77.47
Crankshaft rpm 850
Fuel use (gal./hr.) 5.29
Maximum drawbar horsepower tests
Gear..2nd
Drawbar horsepower..........................65.73
Pull weight (lb.) 10,236
Speed (mph) 2.41
Percent slippage................................1.81
SAE drawbar horsepower..........................52.34
SAE belt/PTO horsepower 69.96
Type ....tracklayer
Length (in.) 150.25
Height (in.) 81.63
Rear width (in.) ....81.63 or 95.63
Tread width (in.)......................................60 or 74
Weight (lb.) 20,845
Track length (in.)....................................81.88 on ground, 262 total
Grouser shoe..35 links; 18-in.
Gear/speed (mph) ....forward: 1/1.60,
2/2.40, 3/3.40, 4/4.70;
reverse: 1/1.90

Caterpillar RD-7, Diesel
Manufacturer..Caterpillar Tractor Co.,
Peoria, IL
Nebraska test number 255
Test date ....May 21–25, 1936
Test tractor serial number........................9G 687
Years produced 1935–1937
Serial number range................................9G 1–9G 2777 end
Serial number location..............................brass plate, left rear
transmission case/left
front lower engine block
under water pump
Number produced 2,777
Engine ....Caterpillar, D8800
vertical I-head,
valve-in-head
Test engine serial number........................9G 687
Cylinders 4
Bore and stroke (in.) ....5.75 x 8.00
Rated rpm ....(1,000) 850
Displacement (c.i.) 830.9
Fuel ....diesel/gasoline
Main tank capacity (gal.) 60
Auxiliary tank capacity (gal.) 2
Carburetor ....start; Zenith
Air cleaner ....Donaldson
Ignition..start; Eisemann
GV-2Q/Wico magneto

Cooling capacity (gal.) 18.50
Maximum brake horsepower tests
PTO/belt horsepower..........................95.97
Crankshaft rpm 1,000
Fuel use (gal./hr.) 8.95
Maximum drawbar horsepower tests
Gear..2nd
Drawbar horsepower..........................78.35
Pull weight (lb.) 10,376
Speed (mph) 2.83
Percent slippage................................1.92
SAE drawbar horsepower..........................61.94
SAE belt/PTO horsepower 85.82
Type ....tracklayer
Length (in.) 150.25
Height (in.) 81.63
Rear width (in.) ....81.63 or 95.63
Tread width (in.)......................................60 or 74
Weight (lb.) 20,410/21,130
Track length (in.) ....81.88 on ground,
262 total
Grouser shoe..35 links; 18-in.
Gear/speed (mph) ....forward: 1/1.80,
2/2.90, 3/4.00, 4/5.50;
reverse: 1/2.20

Caterpillar RD-8, Diesel
Manufacturer..Caterpillar Tractor Co.,
Peoria, IL
Nebraska test number 256
Test date ....May 7–19, 1936
Test tractor serial number........................1H 425
Years produced 1936–1937
Serial number range................................1H 1–1H 2408 end
Serial number location ....brass plate, left rear
transmission case/left
front lower engine block
under water pump
Number produced 2,408
Engine ....Caterpillar, D13000
vertical I-head,
valve-in-head
Test engine serial number........................1H 425
Cylinders 6
Bore and stroke (in.) ....5.75 x 8.00
Rated rpm 850
Displacement (c.i.) 1246.4
Fuel ....diesel/gasoline
Main tank capacity (gal.) 69
Auxiliary tank capacity (gal.) 2
Carburetor..start; Zenith
Air cleaner ....Donaldson
Ignition ....start; Eisemann
GV-2Q/Wico magneto
Cooling capacity (gal.) 28
Maximum brake horsepower tests
PTO/belt horsepower..........................103.21
Crankshaft rpm 849
Fuel use (gal./hr.) 7.28
Maximum drawbar horsepower tests
Gear..2nd
Drawbar horsepower..........................91.36
Pull weight (lb.) 14,529
Speed (mph) 2.36
Percent slippage................................1.86

Caterpillar

SAE drawbar horsepower.............................71.88
SAE belt/PTO horsepower.............................92.11
Type ....tracklayer
Length (in.) 183
Height (in.) 90
Rear width (in.)......................................103.75
Tread width (in.).....................................78
Weight (lb.) 32,790
Track length (in.).....................................97.63 on ground,
                                                          304 total
Grouser shoe..38 links; 20-in.
Gear/speed (mph) ....forward: 1/1.70,
                                                          2/2.40, 3/2.80, 4/3.20,
                                                          5/3.90, 6/5.30; reverse:
                                                          1/1.70, 2/2.80

Caterpillar RD-8, Diesel

Manufacturer...Caterpillar Tractor Co.,
                                                          Peoria, IL
Nebraska test number 257
Test date ....May 19–25, 1936
Test tractor serial number.........................1H 425
Years produced......................................1936–1937
Serial number range................................1H 1–1H 2408 end
Serial number location ....brass plate, left rear
                                                          transmission case/left
                                                          front lower engine block
                                                          under water pump
Number produced 2,408
Engine ....Caterpillar, D13000
                                                          vertical I-head,
                                                          valve-in-head
Test engine serial number.........................1H 425
Cylinders 6
Bore and stroke (in.) ....5.75 x 8.00
Rated rpm ....(1,000) 850
Displacement (c.i.) 1246.4
Fuel ....diesel/gasoline
Main tank capacity (gal.)..........................69
Auxiliary tank capacity (gal.) 2
Carburetor..start; Zenith
Air cleaner ....Donaldson
Ignition..start; Eisemann
                                                          GV-2Q/Wico magneto
Cooling capacity (gal.) 28
Maximum brake horsepower tests
     PTO/belt horsepower...........................118.29
     Crankshaft rpm 1,000
     Fuel use (gal./hr.)..........................8.57
Maximum drawbar horsepower tests
     Gear...2nd
     Drawbar horsepower...........................101.89
     Pull weight (lb.)............................13,786
     Speed (mph) 2.77
     Percent slippage............................2.08
SAE drawbar horsepower.............................79.94
SAE belt/PTO horsepower............................107.19
Type ....tracklayer
Length (in.) 183
Height (in.) 90
Rear width (in.)......................................103.75
Tread width (in.).....................................78
Weight (lb.) 32,790

Track length (in.)......................................97.63 on ground, 304
                                                          total
Grouser shoe..38 links; 20-in.
Gear/speed (mph) ....forward: 1/2.00,
                                                          2/2.80, 3/3.30, 4/3.80,
                                                          5/4.60, 6/6.20; reverse:
                                                          1/2.00, 2/3.30

Caterpillar 30, Thirty

Manufacturer...Caterpillar Tractor Co.,
                                                          Peoria, IL
Nebraska test number 271
Test date ....October 13–24, 1936
Test tractor serial number.........................6G 427 W
Years produced......................................6G, 1935–1937; R4,
                                                          1937–1944
Serial number range................................6G 1–6G 875 became
                                                          R4, 6G 876–6G
                                                          5383 end
Serial number location ....brass plate, left rear
                                                          transmission case/left
                                                          rear upper engine
                                                          block above electric
                                                          starter
Number produced 6G, 875; R4, 4,508
Engine ....Caterpillar vertical
                                                          I-head, valve-in-head
Test engine serial number.........................6G 427 W
Cylinders 4
Bore and stroke (in.) ....4.25 x 5.50
Rated rpm 1,400
Displacement (c.i.) 312.1
Fuel ....distillate/gasoline
Carburetor..Zenith, K5A, 1.25-in.
Air cleaner ....Donaldson
Ignition..Eisemann CM-4
                                                          magneto
Cooling capacity (gal.) 12
Maximum brake horsepower tests
     PTO/belt horsepower...........................36.37
     Crankshaft rpm 1,400
     Fuel use (gal./hr.)..........................4.45
Maximum drawbar horsepower tests
     Gear...2nd
     Drawbar horsepower...........................30.88
     Pull weight (lb.)............................5,032
     Speed (mph) 2.30
     Percent slippage............................2.67
SAE drawbar horsepower.............................24.29
SAE belt/PTO horsepower............................32.27
Type ....tracklayer
Length (in.) 129
Height (in.) 60.63
Rear width (in.)......................................67
Tread width (in.).....................................44 or 60
Weight (lb.) ....9,010 or 9,280
Track length (in.)......................................61.13 on ground,
                                                          209 total
Grouser shoe..31 links; 13-in.
Gear/speed (mph) ....forward: 1/1.70,
                                                          2/2.40, 3/3.00, 4/3.70,
                                                          5/5.40; reverse: 1/1.90

Caterpillar 30, Thirty

Manufacturer	Caterpillar Tractor Co., Peoria, IL
Nebraska test number	272
Test date	October 13–23, 1936
Test tractor serial number	6G 413 WSP
Years produced	6G, 1935–1937; R4, 1937–1944
Serial number range	6G 1–6G 875 became R4, 6G 876–6G 5383 end
Serial number location	brass plate, left rear transmission case/left rear upper engine block above electric starter
Number produced	6G, 875; R4, 4,508
Engine	Caterpillar vertical I-head, valve-in-head
Test engine serial number	6G 413 WSP
Cylinders	4
Bore and stroke (in.)	4.25 x 5.50
Rated rpm	1,400
Displacement (c.i.)	312.1
Fuel	gasoline
Carburetor	Zenith, K5A, 1.25-in.
Air cleaner	Donaldson
Ignition	Eisemann CM-4 magneto
Cooling capacity (gal.)	12

Maximum brake horsepower tests

PTO/belt horsepower	39.15
Crankshaft rpm	1,400
Fuel use (gal./hr.)	4.78

Maximum drawbar horsepower tests

Gear	2nd
Drawbar horsepower	35.05
Pull weight (lb.)	5,775
Speed (mph)	2.28
Percent slippage	3.44
SAE drawbar horsepower	26.50
SAE belt/PTO horsepower	34.71
Type	tracklayer
Length (in.)	129
Height (in.)	60.63
Rear width (in.)	67
Tread width (in.)	44 or 60
Weight (lb.)	9,775
Track length (in.)	61.13 on ground, 209 total
Grouser shoe	31 links; 13-in.
Gear/speed (mph)	forward: 1/1.70, 2/2.40, 3/3.00, 4/3.70, 5/5.40; reverse: 1/1.90

Caterpillar RD-4, Diesel

Manufacturer	Caterpillar Tractor Co., Peoria, IL
Nebraska test number	273
Test date	October 14–28, 1936
Test tractor serial number	4G 2233 W
Years produced	1936–1938
Serial number range	4G 1–4G 9999 end
Serial number location	brass plate, left rear transmission case/left rear top of engine block behind start lever

Number produced	9,999
Engine	Caterpillar, D4400 vertical I-head, valve-in-head
Test engine serial number	4G 2233 W
Cylinders	4
Bore and stroke (in.)	4.25 x 5.50
Rated rpm	1,400
Displacement (c.i.)	312.1
Fuel	diesel/gasoline
Main tank capacity (gal.)	25
Auxiliary tank capacity (gal.)	2
Carburetor	start; ?
Air cleaner	Donaldson
Ignition	start; Eisemann GV-2Q magneto
Cooling capacity (gal.)	11

Maximum brake horsepower tests

PTO/belt horsepower	39.82
Crankshaft rpm	1,400
Fuel use (gal./hr.)	2.89

Maximum drawbar horsepower tests

Gear	2nd
Drawbar horsepower	35.36
Pull weight (lb.)	5,811
Speed (mph)	2.28
Percent slippage	3.27
SAE drawbar horsepower	26.76
SAE belt/PTO horsepower	34.99
Type	tracklayer
Length (in.)	121.56
Height (in.)	60.63
Rear width (in.)	62 or 78
Tread width (in.)	44 or 60
Weight (lb.)	9,370 or 9,740
Track length (in.)	61.13 on ground, 208 total
Grouser shoe	31 links; 13-in.
Gear/speed (mph)	forward: 1/1.70, 2/2.40, 3/3.00, 4/3.70, 5/5.40; reverse: 1/1.90

Caterpillar D-8, Diesel

Manufacturer	Caterpillar Tractor Co., Peoria, IL
Nebraska test number	314
Test date	November 28–30, 1938
Test tractor serial number	1H 3765 SP
Years produced	1937–1941
Serial number range	1H 2409–1H 9999 end
Serial number location	brass plate, left rear transmission case/left rear upper engine block behind start engine lever
Number produced	7,591
Engine	Caterpillar, D13000 vertical I-head, valve-in-head
Test engine serial number	1H 3765 SP
Cylinders	6
Bore and stroke (in.)	5.75 x 8.00
Rated rpm	850
Compression ratio	15.7:1
Displacement (c.i.)	1,246

Caterpillar

Fuel ....diesel/gasoline
Main tank capacity (gal.) 68.50
Auxiliary tank capacity (gal.) ....4.50 qt
Carburetor ....start Engine; Zenith
Air cleaner ....Donaldson
Ignition ....start Engine;
Wico magneto
Cooling capacity (gal.) 30
Maximum brake horsepower tests
    PTO/belt horsepower...........................109.64
    Crankshaft rpm 850
    Fuel use (gal./hr.) 7.03
Maximum drawbar horsepower tests
    Gear..2nd
    Drawbar horsepower.............................96.37
    Pull weight (lb.)....................................18,740
    Speed (mph) 1.93
    Percent slippage...................................2.59
SAE drawbar horsepower.............................73.43
SAE belt/PTO horsepower.............................95.99
Type ....tracklayer
Length (in.) 183
Height (in.) 90
Rear width (in.) 103.75
Tread width (in.)..78
Weight (lb.) 33,110
Track length (in.)...97.63 on ground,
304 total
Grouser shoe..38 links; 20-in.
Gear/speed (mph) ....forward: 1/1.40,
2/2.00, 3/2.30,
4/2.70, 5/3.20, 6/4.40;
reverse: 1/1.40, 2/2.30

Caterpillar R-2

Manufacturer..Caterpillar Tractor Co.,
Peoria, IL
Nebraska test number 320
Test date ....July 17 to August 3, 1939
Test tractor serial number............................6J 203
Years produced 1938–1942
Serial number range.....................................4J 1–4J 1185; 6J 1–6J
1150 end
Serial number location ....brass patent plate on
right outside seat side
Number produced ....Model 4J, 1,185;
Model 6J, 1,150
Engine ....Caterpillar, R2
vertical I-head,
valve-in-head
Test engine serial number.............................6J 203
Cylinders 4
Bore and stroke (in.) ....3.75 x 5.00
Rated rpm 1,525
Displacement (c.i.) 220.9
Fuel ....gasoline
Fuel tank capacity (gal.) 20
Carburetor ....Zenith, K-5A, 1.25-in.
Air cleaner ....Donaldson
Ignition..Eisemann CM-4
magneto
Cooling capacity (gal.) 7.75
Maximum brake horsepower tests
    PTO/belt horsepower...........................29.31
    Crankshaft rpm 1,525
    Fuel use (gal./hr.) 3.56

Maximum drawbar horsepower tests
    Gear..2nd
    Drawbar horsepower.............................23.46
    Pull weight (lb.)....................................3,655
    Speed (mph) 2.41
    Percent slippage...................................3.23
SAE drawbar horsepower.............................18.80
SAE belt/PTO horsepower.............................26.41
Type ....tracklayer
Length (in.) 110
Height (in.) 57.69
Rear width (in.) ....55.75 or 65.75
Tread width (in.)..40 or 50
Weight (lb.) ....6,120 or 6,250
Track length (in.)...54.50 on ground,
184 total
Grouser shoe..30 links; 12-in.
Gear/speed (mph) ....forward: 1/1.70,
2/2.50, 3/3.00, 4/3.60,
5/5.10; reverse: 1/2.10

Caterpillar R-2

Manufacturer..Caterpillar Tractor Co.,
Peoria, IL
Nebraska test number 321
Test date ....July 24 to
August 3, 1939
Test tractor serial number............................6J 254 SP
Years produced 1938–1942
Serial number range.....................................4J 1–4J 1185; 6J 1–6J
1150 end
Serial number location ....brass Patent plate on
right outside seat side
Number produced ....Model 4J, 1,185;
Model 6J, 1,150
Engine ....Caterpillar, R2 vertical
I-head, valve-in-head
Test engine serial number.............................6J 254 SP
Cylinders 4
Bore and stroke (in.) ....3.75 x 5.00
Rated rpm 1,525
Displacement (c.i.) 220.9
Fuel ....distillate/gasoline
Main tank capacity (gal.) 20
Auxiliary tank capacity (gal.) 2
Carburetor ....Zenith, K-5A, 1.25-in.
Air cleaner ....Donaldson
Ignition..Eisemann CM-4
magneto
Cooling capacity (gal.) 7.75
Maximum brake horsepower tests
    PTO/belt horsepower...........................28.56
    Crankshaft rpm 1,526
    Fuel use (gal./hr.) 3.68
Maximum drawbar horsepower tests
    Gear..2nd
    Drawbar horsepower.............................22.98
    Pull weight (lb.)....................................3,596
    Speed (mph) 2.40
    Percent slippage...................................3.53
SAE drawbar horsepower.............................18.50
SAE belt/PTO horsepower.............................26.20
Type ....tracklayer
Length (in.) 110
Height (in.) 57.69
Rear width (in.) ....55.75 or 65.75

Caterpillar

Tread width (in.)............................40 or 50
Weight (lb.) ....6,120 or 6,250
Track length (in.).........................54.50 on ground,
                                        184 total
Grouser shoe..............................30 links; 12-in.
Gear/speed (mph) ....forward: 1/1.70,
                                        2/2.50, 3/3.00, 4/3.60,
                                        5/5.10; reverse: 1/2.10

Caterpillar D-2, Diesel
Manufacturer...............................Caterpillar Tractor Co.,
                                        Peoria, IL
Nebraska test number 322
Test date ....July 24 to
                                        August 4, 1939
Test tractor serial number.............5J 1509
Years produced 1938–1947
Serial number range......................5J 1–5J 10561 end
Serial number location ....brass plate, left upper
                                        rear transmission
                                        case/left rear upper
                                        engine block behind
                                        start lever
Number produced 10,561
Engine ....Caterpillar, D3110
                                        vertical I-head,
                                        valve-in-head
Test engine serial number..............5J 1509
Cylinders 4
Bore and stroke (in.) ....3.75 x 5.00
Rated rpm 1,525
Displacement (c.i.) 221
Fuel ....diesel/gasoline
Main tank capacity (gal.)................20
Auxiliary tank capacity (gal.) 2
Carburetor.................................start; Zenith, TU4C
Air cleaner ....Donaldson
Ignition.....................................start; Eisemann
                                        magneto
Cooling capacity (gal.) 7.75
Maximum brake horsepower tests
    PTO/belt horsepower.................29.98
    Crankshaft rpm 1,526
    Fuel use (gal./hr.)..................2.26
Maximum drawbar horsepower tests
    Gear....................................2nd
    Drawbar horsepower.................24.12
    Pull weight (lb.)......................3,798
    Speed (mph) 2.38
    Percent slippage.....................4.65
SAE drawbar horsepower...............19.40
SAE belt/PTO horsepower 27.19
Type ....tracklayer
Length (in.) 105.56
Height (in.) 57.69
Rear width (in.) ....55.75 or 65.75
Tread width (in.)..........................40 or 50
Weight (lb.) ....6,520 or 6,650
Track length (in.).........................54.50 on ground,
                                        184 total
Grouser shoe..............................30 links; 10, 12,
                                        (16)-in.
Gear/speed (mph) ....forward: 1/1.70,
                                        2/2.50, 3/3.00, 4/3.60,
                                        5/5.10; reverse: 1/2.10

Caterpillar D-8, Diesel
Manufacturer...............................Caterpillar Tractor Co.,
                                        Peoria, IL
Nebraska test number 357
Test date ....October 11–16, 1940
Test tractor serial number.............1H 6852
Years produced 1937–1941
Serial number range......................1H 2409–1H 9999 end
Serial number location ....brass plate, left rear
                                        transmission case/left
                                        rear upper engine
                                        block behind start
                                        engine lever
Number produced 7,591
Engine ....Caterpillar, D13000
                                        vertical I-head
Test engine serial number..............617
Cylinders 6
Bore and stroke (in.) ....5.75 x 8.00
Rated rpm 950
Compression ratio 15.7:1
Displacement (c.i.) 1246
Fuel ....diesel/gasoline
Main tank capacity (gal.)................68.50
Auxiliary tank capacity (gal.) ....4.50 qt
Carburetor.................................start Engine; Zenith
Air cleaner ....Donaldson
Ignition.....................................start Engine;
                                        Wico magneto
Cooling capacity (gal.) 30
Maximum brake horsepower tests
    PTO/belt horsepower.................127.93
    Crankshaft rpm 950
    Fuel use (gal./hr.)..................8.61
Maximum drawbar horsepower tests
    Gear....................................2nd
    Drawbar horsepower.................110.06
    Pull weight (lb.).....................19,537
    Speed (mph) 2.11
    Percent slippage.....................4.25
SAE drawbar horsepower...............84.86
SAE belt/PTO horsepower 111.35
Type ....tracklayer
Length (in.) 183
Height (in.) 90
Rear width (in.) 103.75
Tread width (in.)..........................78
Weight (lb.) ....(34,825)
Track length (in.).........................97.63 on ground,
                                        303 total
Grouser shoe..............................38 links; 20, (24)-in.
Gear/speed (mph) ....forward: 1/1.60,
                                        2/2.20, 3/2.60, 4/3.00,
                                        5/3.60, 6/4.90; reverse:
                                        1/1.60, 2/2.60

Caterpillar D-7, Diesel
Manufacturer...............................Caterpillar Tractor Co.,
                                        Peoria, IL
Nebraska test number 358
Test date ....October 2–11, 1940
Test tractor serial number.............7M 715 SP
Years produced 1940–1945
Serial number range......................7M 1–7M 9999 end

Caterpillar

Serial number location ....brass plate, upper left rear transmission case/lower left rear engine block
Number produced 9,999
Engine ....Caterpillar, D8800 vertical I-head
Test engine serial number............................729
Cylinders 4
Bore and stroke (in.) ....5.75 x 8.00
Rated rpm 1,000
Compression ratio............................15.7:1
Displacement (c.i.) 831
Fuel ....diesel
Main tank capacity (gal.)............................65
Auxiliary tank capacity (gal.) 2
Carburetor ....start Engine; Zenith 22 AX8
Air cleaner ....Donaldson
Ignition............................start Engine; Bosch MJK magneto
Cooling capacity (gal.) 18

Maximum brake horsepower tests
    PTO/belt horsepower............................89.10
    Crankshaft rpm 1,000
    Fuel use (gal./hr.)............................5.99

Maximum drawbar horsepower tests
    Gear............................2nd
    Drawbar horsepower............................78.48
    Pull weight (lb.)............................13,454
    Speed (mph)............................2.19
    Percent slippage............................1.98
SAE drawbar horsepower............................60.33
SAE belt/PTO horsepower............................78.91
Type ....tracklayer
Length (in.) 162.25
Height (in.)............................80
Rear width (in.)............................78 or (97)
Tread width (in.)............................60 or (74)
Weight (lb.)............................(24,615)
Track length (in.)............................93.25 on ground, 288 total
Grouser shoe............................36 links; 18, (24)-in.
Gear/speed (mph) ....forward: 1/1.40, 2/2.20, 3/3.20, 4/4.60, 5/6.00; reverse: 1/1.60, 2/2.60, 3/3.80, 4/5.40

Caterpillar D-6, Diesel

Manufacturer............................Caterpillar Tractor Co., Peoria, IL
Nebraska test number............................374
Test date ....September 6–13, 1941
Test tractor serial number............................4R 196
Years produced............................1941–1947
Serial number range............................4R 1–4R 3633; 5R 1-5R 5515 end
Serial number location ....brass plate, left rear transmission case/left front side crankcase
Number produced ....Model 4R, 3,633; Model 5R, 5,515
Engine ....Caterpillar, D6600 vertical I-head
Test engine serial number............................4R 196
Cylinders 6
Bore and stroke (in.) ....4.25 x 5.50

Rated rpm 1,400
Displacement (c.i.) 468
Fuel ....diesel/gasoline
Main tank capacity (gal.)............................48
Auxiliary tank capacity (gal.) 2
Carburetor ....start Engine; Zenith
Air cleaner ....Donaldson
Ignition............................start Engine; Amer. Bosch magneto
Cooling capacity (gal.) 12.25

Maximum brake horsepower tests
    PTO/belt horsepower............................78.03
    Crankshaft rpm 1,400
    Fuel use (gal./hr.)............................5.69

Maximum drawbar horsepower tests
    Gear............................2nd
    Drawbar horsepower............................63.34
    Pull weight (lb.)............................10,747
    Speed (mph)............................2.21
    Percent slippage............................2.74
SAE drawbar horsepower............................49.93
SAE belt/PTO horsepower............................68.51
Type ....tracklayer
Length (in.) 149
Height (in.)............................72.50
Rear width (in.)............................80.25 or (94.25)
Tread width (in.)............................60 or (74)
Weight (lb.)............................(17,575)
Track length (in.)............................85.63 on ground, 262 total
Grouser shoe............................39 links; 16, (18)-in.
Gear/speed (mph) ....forward: 1/1.40, 2/2.30, 3/3.20, 4/4.40, 5/5.80; reverse: 1/1.80, 2/2.80, 3/3.90, 4/5.40

Caterpillar D-8, Diesel

Manufacturer............................Caterpillar Tractor Co., Peoria, IL
Nebraska test number............................415
Test date ....July 11–19, 1949
Test tractor serial number............................2U 7266
Years produced............................1946–1953
Serial number range............................2U 1–2U 23537 end
Serial number location ....brass plate, left rear main frame/left rear crankcase behind start engine clutch handle
Number produced 23,537
Engine ....Caterpillar, D13000 vertical I-head
Test engine serial number............................2U 7266
Cylinders 6
Bore and stroke (in.) ....5.75 x 8.00
Rated rpm 1,000
Compression ratio............................15.7:1
Displacement (c.i.) 1246
Fuel ....diesel/gasoline
Main tank capacity (gal.)............................68.50
Auxiliary tank capacity (gal.) ....4.50 qt
Carburetor ....start Engine; Zenith, 22AX8
Air cleaner ....Donaldson
Ignition............................start Engine; Bosch MJK magneto

Cooling capacity (gal.) 30
Maximum brake horsepower tests
    PTO/belt horsepower......None
Maximum drawbar horsepower tests
    Gear......2nd
    Drawbar horsepower......123.89
    Pull weight (lb.)......20,880
    Speed (mph)......2.23
    Percent slippage......1.60
SAE drawbar horsepower......98.40
SAE belt/PTO horsepower......None
Type......tracklayer
Length (in.)......189.25
Height (in.)......90
Rear width (in.)......103.75
Tread width (in.)......78
Weight (lb.)......35,950
Track length (in.)......na on ground, 309 total
Grouser shoe......39 links; 22, (24)-in.
Gear/speed (mph) ......forward: 1/1.70,
2/2.30, 3/2.80, 4/3.70,
5/4.80; reverse: 1/2.20,
2/3.00, 3/3.70

Caterpillar D-6, Diesel
Manufacturer......Caterpillar Tractor Co., Peoria, IL
Nebraska test number......416
Test date......July 11–23, 1949
Test tractor serial number......9U 2914
Years produced......1947–1959
Serial number range......8U 1–8U 11045; 9U 1–9U 29764 end
Serial number location......brass plate, left rear transmission case/left side rear crankcase behind start engine
Number produced......Model 8U, 11,045; Model 9U, 29,764
Engine......Caterpillar, D318 vertical I-head
Test engine serial number......9U 2914
Cylinders......6
Bore and stroke (in.)......4.50 x 5.50
Rated rpm......1,400
Compression ratio......17.3:1
Displacement (c.i.)......525
Fuel......diesel/gasoline
Main tank capacity (gal.)......51.50
Auxiliary tank capacity (gal.)......5.50 qt
Carburetor......start engine; Zenith, TU4C
Air cleaner......Donaldson
Ignition......start engine; Bosch MJK magneto
Cooling capacity (gal.)......14.50
Maximum brake horsepower tests
    PTO/belt horsepower......76.90
    Crankshaft rpm......1,400
    Fuel use (gal./hr.)......5.54
Maximum drawbar horsepower tests
    Gear......2nd
    Drawbar horsepower......61.76
    Pull weight (lb.)......10,399
    Speed (mph)......2.23
    Percent slippage......2.00

SAE drawbar horsepower......49.23
SAE belt/PTO horsepower......68.77
Type......tracklayer
Length (in.)......147.06
Height (in.)......73.25
Rear width (in.)......76 or (92)
Tread width (in.)......60 or (74)
Weight (lb.)......16,725
Track length (in.)......na on ground, 269 total
Grouser shoe......40 links; 16, (18)-in.
Gear/speed (mph)......forward: 1/1.40, 2/2.30, 3/3.20, 4/4.40, 5/5.80; reverse: 1/1.80, 2/2.80, 3/3.90, 4/5.40

Caterpillar D-4, Diesel
Manufacturer......Caterpillar Tractor Co., Peoria, IL
Nebraska test number......417
Test date......July 11–26, 1949
Test tractor serial number......7U 5294
Years produced......1947–1959
Serial number range......7U 1–7U 44307 end
Serial number location......brass plate, left rear transmission case/left front side crankcase
Number produced......44,307
Engine......Caterpillar, D315 vertical I-head
Test engine serial number......7U 5294
Cylinders......4
Bore and stroke (in.)......4.50 x 5.50
Rated rpm......1,400
Compression ratio......17.3:1
Displacement (c.i.)......350
Fuel......diesel/gasoline
Main tank capacity (gal.)......25
Auxiliary tank capacity (gal.)......2
Carburetor......start engine; Zenith, TU4C
Air cleaner......Donaldson
Ignition......start engine; Bosch MJK magneto
Cooling capacity (gal.)......11
Maximum brake horsepower tests
    PTO/belt horsepower......51.81
    Crankshaft rpm......1,400
    Fuel use (gal./hr.)......3.70
Maximum drawbar horsepower tests
    Gear......2nd
    Drawbar horsepower......41.65
    Pull weight (lb.)......6,851
    Speed (mph)......2.28
    Percent slippage......3.33
SAE drawbar horsepower......33.01
SAE belt/PTO horsepower......46.42
Type......tracklayer
Length (in.)......124.25
Height (in.)......69.38
Rear width (in.)......62 or (78)
Tread width (in.)......44 or (60)
Weight (lb.)......10,065
Track length (in.)......na on ground, 396 total
Grouser shoe......32 links; 13, (16)-in.
Gear/speed (mph)......forward: 1/1.70, 2/2.40, 3/3.00, 4/3.70, 5/5.40; reverse: 1/1.90

Caterpillar

Caterpillar D-2, Diesel

Manufacturer...Caterpillar Tractor Co., Peoria, IL
Nebraska test number..................................418
Test date ....July 11–26, 1949
Test tractor serial number...........................5U 2826
Years produced..1947–1957
Serial number range.....................................5U 1–5U 18894 end
Serial number location ....brass plate, left upper rear transmission case/left upper rear engine block behind start lever
Number produced 18,894
Engine ....Caterpillar D311 vertical I-head
Test engine serial number............................5U 2826
Cylinders 4
Bore and stroke (in.)....................................4.00 x 5.00
Rated rpm 1,525
Compression ratio..19.0:1
Displacement (c.i.) 252
Fuel ....diesel/gasoline
Main tank capacity (gal.)..............................20
Auxiliary tank capacity (gal.) 2
Carburetor..start engine; Zenith TU4C
Air cleaner ....Donaldson
Ignition..start engine; Bosch MJK magneto
Cooling capacity (gal.) 7.75
Maximum brake horsepower tests
    PTO/belt horsepower.............................36.02
    Crankshaft rpm 1,526
    Fuel use (gal./hr.)..................................2.64
Maximum drawbar horsepower tests
    Gear...2nd
    Drawbar horsepower..............................30.31
    Pull weight (lb.).....................................4,786
    Speed (mph) 2.37
    Percent slippage....................................4.24
SAE drawbar horsepower.............................24.05
SAE belt/PTO horsepower............................32.73
Type ....tracklayer
Length (in.)...107.88
Height (in.)...61.88
Rear width (in.)..65.75
Tread width (in.)..50
Weight (lb.) 6,710
Track length (in.)..na on ground, 189 total
Grouser shoe..31 links; 12-in.
Gear/speed (mph) ....forward: 1/1.70, 2/2.50, 3/3.00, 4/3.60, 5/5.10; reverse: 1/2.10

Caterpillar D-2, Diesel

Manufacturer...Caterpillar Tractor Co., Peoria, IL
Nebraska test number..................................553
Test date ....July 25–30, 1955
Test tractor serial number...........................5U 15427
Years produced..1947–1957
Serial number range.....................................5U 1–5U 18894 end
Serial number location ....brass plate, upper left rear transmission case/left upper rear engine block behind start lever
Number produced 18,894
Engine ....Caterpillar D311 vertical I-head
Test engine serial number............................5U15427
Cylinders 4
Bore and stroke (in.)....................................4.00 x 5.00
Rated rpm 1,650
Compression ratio..18.5:1
Displacement (c.i.) 252
Fuel ....diesel/gasoline
Main tank capacity (gal.)..............................26
Auxiliary tank capacity (gal.) 2
Carburetor..start engine; Zenith TU4C
Air cleaner ....Donaldson
Ignition..start engine; Bosch MJK magneto
Cooling capacity (gal.) 7.50
Maximum brake horsepower tests
    PTO/belt horsepower.............................41.86
    Crankshaft rpm 1,650
    Fuel use (gal./hr.)..................................3.40
Maximum drawbar horsepower tests
    Gear...2nd
    Drawbar horsepower..............................36.62
    Pull weight (lb.).....................................5,205
    Speed (mph) 2.64
    Percent slippage....................................2.81
SAE drawbar horsepower.............................29.06
SAE belt/PTO horsepower............................38.62
Type ....tracklayer
Length (in.)...107.88
Height (in.)...61.88
Rear width (in.)..65.75
Tread width (in.)..50
Weight (lb.) 7,175
Track length (in.)..na on ground, 189 total
Grouser shoe..32 links; 12-in.
Gear/speed (mph) ....forward: 1/1.80, 2/2.70, 3/3.20, 4/3.90, 5/5.50; reverse: 1/2.20

Caterpillar D-4, Diesel

Manufacturer...Caterpillar Tractor Co., Peoria, IL
Nebraska test number..................................554
Test date ....July 25 to August 10, 1955
Test tractor serial number...........................7U 32017
Years produced..1947–1959
Serial number range.....................................7U 1–7U 44307 end
Serial number location ....brass plate, left rear transmission case/left front side crankcase
Number produced 44,307
Engine ....Caterpillar D315 vertical I-head
Test engine serial number............................7U 32017
Cylinders 4

Bore and stroke (in.) ....4.50 x 5.50
Rated rpm 1,600
Compression ratio..18:1
Displacement (c.i.) 350
Fuel ....diesel/gasoline
Main tank capacity (gal.) 30
Auxiliary tank capacity (gal.) 2
Carburetor ....start engine;
Zenith TR4C
Air cleaner ....Donaldson
Ignition..start engine; Bosch
MJK magneto
Cooling capacity (gal.) 11
Maximum brake horsepower tests
PTO/belt horsepower...........................58.88
Crankshaft rpm 1,601
Fuel use (gal./hr.) 4.42
Maximum drawbar horsepower tests
Gear..2nd
Drawbar horsepower............................48.72
Pull weight (lb.)...................................6,930
Speed (mph) 2.64
Percent slippage..................................2.38
SAE drawbar horsepower.............................39.14
SAE belt/PTO horsepower 53.01
Type ....tracklayer
Length (in.) 124.25
Height (in.) 69.38
Rear width (in.)..62 or (78)
Tread width (in.)...44 or (60)
Weight (lb.) 10,375
Track length (in.)..na on ground,
209 total
Grouser shoe..31 links; 13, (20)-in.
Gear/speed (mph) ....forward: 1/1.90,
2/2.70, 3/3.40, 4/4.20,
5/6.10; reverse: 1/2.20

Caterpillar D-6, Diesel
Manufacturer..Caterpillar Tractor Co.,
Peoria, IL
Nebraska test number 555
Test date ....July 25 to
August 12, 1955
Test tractor serial number...........................9U 19169
Years produced...1947–1959
Serial number range......................................8U 1–8U 11045; 9U
1–9U 29764 end
Serial number location ....brass plate, left rear
transmission case/left
side rear crankcase
behind start engine
Number produced ....Model 8U, 11,045;
Model 9U, 29,764
Engine ....Caterpillar, D318
Type ....vertical, I-head
Test engine serial number............................9U 19169
Cylinders 6
Bore and stroke (in.) ....4.50 x 5.50
Rated rpm 1,600
Compression ratio..18:1
Displacement (c.i.) 525
Fuel ....diesel/gasoline
Main tank capacity (gal.) 48

Auxiliary tank capacity (gal.) ....5.50 qt
Carburetor ....start engine;
Zenith TU4C
Air cleaner ....Donaldson
Ignition..start engine; Bosch
MJK magneto
Cooling capacity (gal.) 14.50
Maximum brake horsepower tests
PTO/belt horsepower...........................92.52
Crankshaft rpm 1,600
Fuel use (gal./hr.) 6.73
Maximum drawbar horsepower tests
Gear..2nd
Drawbar horsepower............................73.34
Pull weight (lb.)...................................10,907
Speed (mph) 2.52
Percent slippage..................................2.70
SAE drawbar horsepower.............................58.44
SAE belt/PTO horsepower 81.91
Type ....tracklayer
Length (in.) 147.06
Height (in.) 73.25
Rear width (in.)..76 or (92)
Tread width (in.)...60 or (74)
Weight (lb.) 17,195
Track length (in.)..na on ground,
286 total
Grouser shoe..39 links; 16, (24)-in.
Gear/speed (mph) ....forward: 1/1.70,
2/2.60, 3/3.60, 4/5.00,
5/6.60; reverse: 1/2.00,
2/3.20, 3/4.50, 4/6.20

Caterpillar D-7, Diesel
Manufacturer..Caterpillar Tractor Co.,
Peoria, IL
Nebraska test number 582
Test date ....July 23 to August 6, 1956
Test tractor serial number............................17A 3337
Years produced...1954–1962
Serial number range......................................17A 1–17A 19442 end
Serial number location ....brass plate, upper left
rear transmission
case/lower left rear
engine block
Number produced 19,442
Engine ....Caterpillar D339/D
339T vertical I-head
Test engine serial number............................17A 3337
Cylinders 4
Bore and stroke (in.) ....5.75 x 8.00
Rated rpm 1,200
Compression ratio..15.7:1
Displacement (c.i.) 831
Fuel ....diesel/gasoline
Main tank capacity (gal.) 70
Auxiliary tank capacity (gal.) ....3.75 qt
Carburetor ....start engine;
Zenith, 22AX8
Air cleaner ....Donaldson
Ignition..start engine; Bosch
MJK magneto/Delco-
Remy, 6-v battery
Cooling capacity (gal.) 17

Maximum brake horsepower tests
 PTO/belt horsepower............................121.70
 Crankshaft rpm 1,200
 Fuel use (gal./hr.)..............................9.75
Maximum drawbar horsepower tests
 Gear..2nd
 Drawbar horsepower............................103.65
 Pull weight (lb.)..................................17,834
 Speed (mph) 2.18
 Percent slippage................................2.08
SAE drawbar horsepower..............................81.69
SAE belt/PTO horsepower..............................109.90
Type ....tracklayer
Length (in.)..167.62
Height (in.)..81.25
Rear width (in.)...97
Tread width (in.)..74
Weight (lb.)...25,970
Track length (in.)...na on ground,
             296 total
Grouser shoe...37 links; 18 (20), 22,
             24-in.
Gear/speed (mph) ....forward: 1/1.50,
             2/2.20, 3/3.20, 4/4.60,
             5/5.90; reverse: 1/1.80,
             2/2.60, 3/3.80, 4/5.40

Caterpillar D-8, Diesel
Manufacturer...Caterpillar Tractor Co.,
             Peoria, IL
Nebraska test number 583
Test date ....July 27–30, 1956
Test tractor serial number 14A 3047
Years produced 1954–1958
Serial number range.....................................14A 1–14A 9692 end
Serial number location ....brass plate, lower left
             transmission case/lower
             left rear engine block
             behind start lever
Number produced 9,692
Engine ....Caterpillar D13000
             vertical I-head
Test engine serial number...........................14A 3047
Cylinders 6
Bore and stroke (in.) ....5.75 x 8.00
Rated rpm 1,200
Compression ratio.......................................15.7:1
Displacement (c.i.) 1,246
Fuel ....diesel/gasoline
Main tank capacity (gal.) 69
Auxiliary tank capacity (gal.) ....4.50 qt
Carburetor...start engine;
             Zenith 22AX8
Air cleaner..Donaldson
Ignition...start engine; Bosch
             MJK magneto/Delco-
             Remy, 6-v battery
Cooling capacity (gal.) 25
Maximum brake horsepower tests
 PTO/belt horsepower............................None
Maximum drawbar horsepower tests
 Gear..2nd
 Drawbar horsepower............................157.58
 Pull weight (lb.)..................................31,064

Speed (mph) 1.90
 Percent slippage................................1.37
SAE drawbar horsepower..............................125.18
SAE belt/PTO horsepower..............................None
Type ....tracklayer
Length (in.)..192.13
Height (in.)..89.13
Rear width (in.)...103.75
Tread width (in.)..78
Weight (lb.)...40,144
Track length (in.)...na on ground,
             336 total
Grouser shoe...42 links; 22-in.
Gear/speed (mph) ....forward: 1/1.50,
             2/1.90, 3/2.70, 4/3.90,
             5/5.20; reverse: 1/2.00,
             2/2.70, 3/3.80

Caterpillar D-9, Diesel
Manufacturer...Caterpillar Tractor Co.,
             Peoria, IL
Nebraska test number 584
Test date ....July 31 to August 4,
             1956
Test tractor serial number 18A 915
Years produced 1954–1959
Serial number range.....................................18A 1–18A 2505 end
Serial number location ....brass plate, upper left
             rear transmission
             case/lower left rear
             engine block below
             starting engine
Number produced 2,505
Engine ....Caterpillar D353 Turbo
             vertical I-head
Test engine serial number...........................18A 915
Cylinders 6
Bore and stroke (in.) ....6.25 x 8.00
Rated rpm 1,240
Compression ratio.......................................15.5:1
Displacement (c.i.) 1,473
Fuel ....diesel/gasoline
Main tank capacity (gal.) 157
Auxiliary tank capacity (gal.) ....4.50 qt
Carburetor...start engine; Zenith 7H7
Air cleaner..Donaldson
Ignition...start engine; Bosch
             MJK magneto/Delco-
             Remy, 6-v battery
Cooling capacity (gal.) 35
Maximum brake horsepower tests
 PTO/belt horsepower............................None
Maximum drawbar horsepower tests
 Gear..2nd
 Drawbar horsepower............................252.33
 Pull weight (lb.)..................................44,817
 Speed (mph) 2.11
 Percent slippage................................2.54
SAE drawbar horsepower..............................202.63
SAE belt/PTO horsepower..............................None
Type ....tracklayer
Length (in.)..214.75
Height (in.)..105
Rear width (in.)...119.25

Tread width (in.)..................................90
Weight (lb.)......................................57,286
Track length (in.)................................na on ground,
387 total
Grouser shoe.....................................43 links; 27-in.
Gear/speed (mph) ....forward: 1/1.70,
2/2.20, 3/3.00, 4/3.90,
5/5.00, 6/7.00; reverse:
1/1.70, 2/2.20, 3/3.00,
4/3.90, 5/5.00, 6/7.00

Caterpillar D-7, Diesel
Manufacturer...................................Caterpillar Tractor Co.,
Peoria, IL
Nebraska test number 710
Test date ....August 3–11, 1959
Test tractor serial number...............17A 12730
Years produced 1954–1962
Serial number range........................17A 1–17A 19442 end
Serial number location ....brass plate, upper left
rear transmission
case/lower left rear
engine block
Number produced 19,442
Engine ....Caterpillar D 339/D
339T vertical L-head
Test engine serial number................17A 12730
Cylinders 4
Bore and stroke (in.) ....5.75 x 8.00
Rated rpm 1,200
Compression ratio...........................15.7:1
Displacement (c.i.) 831
Fuel ....diesel/gasoline
Main tank capacity (gal.)..................85
Auxiliary tank capacity (gal.) ....3.75 qt
Carburetor......................................start engine;
Zenith 261-8
Air cleaner ....Donaldson
Ignition..start engine; Wico
5M2850
magneto/Delco-Remy,
12-v battery
Cooling capacity (gal.) 17
Maximum brake horsepower tests
PTO/belt horsepower.........................None
Maximum drawbar horsepower tests
Gear..2nd
Drawbar horsepower..........................109.79
Pull weight (lb.)................................18,959
Speed (mph) 2.17
Percent slippage...............................2.60
SAE drawbar horsepower...................114.60
SAE belt/PTO horsepower..................None
Type ....tracklayer
Length (in.) 167.62
Height (in.)......................................81.25
Rear width (in.) 97
Tread width (in.)..............................74
Weight (lb.).....................................26,555
Track length (in.)..............................na on ground,
295 total
Grouser shoe....................................37 links; 18 (20), 22,
24-in.

Gear/speed (mph) ....forward: 1/1.50,
2/2.20, 3/3.20, 4/4.60,
5/5.90; reverse: 1/1.80,
2/2.60, 3/3.80, 4/5.40

Caterpillar D-8, Diesel
Manufacturer...................................Caterpillar Tractor Co.,
Peoria, IL
Nebraska test number 711
Test date ....August 3–12, 1959
Test tractor serial number...............36A 1207
Years produced 1958–1974
Serial number range........................36A 1–36A 5601
number end
Serial number location ....brass plate, left rear
main frame/left rear
crankcase behind start
engine clutch lever
Engine ....Caterpillar D342T
vertical L-head
Test engine serial number................36A 1207
Cylinders 6
Bore and stroke (in.) ....5.75 x 8.00
Rated rpm 1,200
Compression ratio...........................15.7:1
Displacement (c.i.) 1,246
Fuel ....diesel/gasoline
Main tank capacity (gal.)..................134
Auxiliary tank capacity (gal.) ....5 qt
Carburetor......................................start engine;
Zenith 261-8
Air cleaner ....Donaldson
Ignition..start engine; Wico
5M2850
magneto/Delco-Remy,
12-v battery
Cooling capacity (gal.) 27
Maximum brake horsepower tests
PTO/belt horsepower.........................None
Maximum drawbar horsepower tests
Gear..2nd
Drawbar horsepower..........................168.38
Pull weight (lb.)................................33,452
Speed (mph) 1.89
Percent slippage...............................2.70
SAE drawbar horsepower...................177.44
SAE belt/PTO horsepower..................None
Type ....tracklayer
Length (in.) 204.75
Height (in.)......................................94
Rear width (in.) 108.50
Tread width (in.)..............................84
Weight (lb.).....................................46,462
Track length (in.)..............................na on ground, 351
total
Grouser shoe....................................39 links; 20, 22, (24),
26-in.
Gear/speed (mph) ....forward: 1/1.50,
2/1.90, 3/2.70, 4/3.50,
5/4.60, 6/6.30; reverse:
1/1.50, 2/2.00, 3/2.70,
4/3.60, 5/4.60, 6/6.40

Caterpillar

Caterpillar D-4, Diesel

Manufacturer	Caterpillar Tractor Co., Peoria, IL
Nebraska test number	746
Test date	June 14–29, 1960
Test tractor serial number	40A 796
Years produced	1959–1963
Serial number range	40A 1–40A 5001 number end
Serial number location	brass plate, left rear transmission case/left front side crankcase
Engine	Caterpillar D330 vertical L-head
Test engine serial number	40A 796
Cylinders	4
Bore and stroke (in.)	4.50 x 5.50
Rated rpm	1,600
Compression ratio	18:1
Displacement (c.i.)	350
Fuel	diesel/gasoline
Main tank capacity (gal.)	42
Auxiliary tank capacity (gal.)	3 qt
Carburetor	start engine; Zenith
Air cleaner	Donaldson
Ignition	start engine; Bosch magneto/Delco-Remy, 12-v battery
Cooling capacity (gal.)	10

Maximum brake horsepower tests

PTO/belt horsepower	56.54
Crankshaft rpm	1,600
Fuel use (gal./hr.)	4.31

Maximum drawbar horsepower tests

Gear	2nd
Drawbar horsepower	49.31
Pull weight (lb.)	8,072
Speed (mph)	2.29
Percent slippage	2.46
SAE drawbar horsepower	50.18
SAE belt/PTO horsepower	56.54
Type	tracklayer
Length (in.)	120.25
Height (in.)	69.88
Rear width (in.)	57 or (78)
Tread width (in.)	44 or (60)
Weight (lb.)	11,440
Track length (in.)	na on ground, 235 total
Grouser shoe	35 links; 13-in.
Gear/speed (mph)	forward: 1/1.60, 2/2.30, 3/3.20, 4/4.20, 5/5.50; reverse: 1/1.90, 2/2.70, 3/3.80, 4/4.90

Caterpillar D-6, Diesel

Manufacturer	Caterpillar Tractor Co., Peoria, IL
Nebraska test number	747
Test date	June 14–29, 1960
Test tractor serial number	44A 1018
Years produced	1959–1967
Serial number range	37A 1–37A 2201; 44A 1–44A 12166 number end
Serial number location	brass plate, left rear transmission case/left front side crankcase
Engine	Caterpillar D333 vertical L-head
Test engine serial number	44A 1018
Cylinders	6
Bore and stroke (in.)	4.50 x 5.50
Rated rpm	1,600
Compression ratio	18:1
Displacement (c.i.)	525
Fuel	diesel/gasoline
Main tank capacity (gal.)	65
Auxiliary tank capacity (gal.)	3.75 qt
Carburetor	start engine; Zenith
Air cleaner	Donaldson
Ignition	start engine; Bosch magneto/Delco-Remy, 12-v battery
Cooling capacity (gal.)	11

Maximum brake horsepower tests

PTO/belt horsepower	None

Maximum drawbar horsepower tests

Gear	2nd
Drawbar horsepower	74.82
Pull weight (lb.)	10,925
Speed (mph)	2.57
Percent slippage	1.26
SAE drawbar horsepower	75.14
SAE belt/PTO horsepower	74.82
Type	tracklayer
Length (in.)	151.75
Height (in.)	75
Rear width (in.)	79.50 or (93.50)
Tread width (in.)	60 or (74)
Weight (lb.)	17,780
Track length (in.)	na on ground, 268.50 total
Grouser shoe	40 links; 16-in.
Gear/speed (mph)	forward: 1/1.70, 2/2.60, 3/3.60, 4/5.00, 5/6.60; reverse: 1/2.00, 2/3.20, 3/4.40, 4/6.20

Chapter 13
CENTAUR

Centaur KV 48

Manufacturer	The LeRoi Co., Centaur Division, Greenwich, OH
Nebraska test number	402
Test date	September 27 to October 6, 1948
Test tractor serial number	4482355
Engine	LeRoi vertical I-head
Test engine serial number	19 x 1513
Cylinders	4
Bore and stroke (in.)	3.50 x 3.625
Rated rpm	1,500
Displacement (c.i.)	139.5
Fuel	gasoline
Carburetor	Zenith 161 x 7, 0.875-in.
Air cleaner	Vortox
Ignition	Auto-Lite with 6-v battery

Maximum brake horsepower tests

PTO/belt horsepower	24.00
Crankshaft rpm	1,502
Fuel use (gal./hr.)	2.57

Maximum drawbar horsepower tests

Gear	2nd
Drawbar horsepower	20.28
Pull weight (lb.)	2,035
Speed (mph)	3.74
Percent slippage	10.59
SAE drawbar horsepower	16.04
SAE belt/PTO horsepower	21.28
Type	standard
Front tire (in.)	5.00 x 15
Rear tire (in.)	9.00 x 24
Tread width (in.)	48–59
Weight (lb.)	2,649
Gear/speed (mph)	forward: 1/2.40, 2/4.50, 3/7.40, 4/15.90; reverse: 1/1.90

Chapter 14
CHOREMASTER

Choremaster B, Garden Tractor

Manufacturer	The Lidge & Shipley Co., Cincinnati, OH
Nebraska test number	449
Test date	September 11–20, 1950
Test tractor serial number	38926
Engine	Clinton Model B 700 vertical L-head
Test engine serial number	48730
Cylinders	1
Bore and stroke (in.)	2.00 x 1.875
Rated rpm	3,600
Compression ratio	5.65:1
Displacement (c.i.)	5.89
Fuel	gasoline
Fuel tank capacity (gal.)	2
Carburetor	na, 0.625-in.
Ignition	magneto, rope-pull start

Cooling	air

Maximum brake horsepower tests

PTO/belt horsepower	1.47
Crankshaft rpm	3,601
Fuel use (gal./hr.)	0.26

Maximum drawbar horsepower tests

Gear	1st
Drawbar horsepower	0.77
Pull weight (lb.)	119
Speed (mph)	2.43
Percent slippage	11.92
SAE drawbar horsepower	0.61
SAE belt/PTO horsepower	1.31
Type	garden, 1 wheel
Rear tire (in.)	4.50 x 6.00
Length (in.)	58
Height (in.)	36
Weight (lb.)	116
Gear/speed (mph)	forward: 1/1.75, 2/2.66

Chapter 15

CLETRAC

Cletrac W, 12-20

Manufacturer	Cleveland Tractor Co., Cleveland, OH
Nebraska test number	45
Test date	July 29 to August 9, 1920
Test tractor serial number	19585
Years produced	1919–1932
Serial number range	13756–30971 end
Serial number location	steel plate on top of transmission
Number produced	17,216
Engine	Weidley vertical overhead-valve
Test engine serial number	48468
Cylinders	4
Bore and stroke (in.)	4.00 x 5.50
Rated rpm	1,265
Displacement (c.i.)	276.5
Fuel	kerosene/gasoline
Main tank capacity (gal.)	2
Auxiliary tank capacity (gal.)	1
Carburetor	Kingston L, 1.125-in.
Air cleaner	Cletrac
Ignition	Teagle 66-S magneto
Cooling capacity (gal.)	5

Maximum brake horsepower tests

PTO/belt horsepower	24.94
Crankshaft rpm	1,321
Fuel use (gal./hr.)	2.90

Maximum drawbar horsepower tests

Drawbar horsepower	15.52
Pull weight (lb.)	1,734
Speed (mph)	3.36
Percent slippage	8.80
SAE drawbar horsepower	12
SAE belt/PTO horsepower	20
Type	tracklayer
Length (in.)	96
Height (in.)	52
Rear width (in.)	50
Tread width (in.)	38
Weight (lb.)	3,482
Track length (in.)	50 on ground
Grouser shoe	38 links; 8-in.
Gear/speed (mph)	forward: 1/1.00–4.00; reverse: 1/2.00

Cletrac F, 9-16

Manufacturer	Cleveland Tractor Co., Cleveland, OH
Nebraska test number	85
Test date	April 14–20, 1922
Test tractor serial number	725-36
Years produced	1920–1922
Serial number range	1–3000 end
Serial number location	steel plate on top of transmission
Number produced	3,000
Engine	Cletrac vertical L-head
Test engine serial number	727
Cylinders	4
Bore and stroke (in.)	3.25 x 4.50
Rated rpm	1,600
Displacement (c.i.)	149.3
Fuel	kerosene/gasoline
Main tank capacity (gal.)	6
Auxiliary tank capacity (gal.)	0.25
Carburetor	Tillotson C.D. 1A, 1.00-in.
Air cleaner	Cletrac
Ignition	Eisemann GS 4 No. 610947 magneto
Cooling capacity (gal.)	3.66

Maximum brake horsepower tests

PTO/belt horsepower	19.61
Crankshaft rpm	1,620
Fuel use (gal./hr.)	1.26

Maximum drawbar horsepower tests

Drawbar horsepower	13.15
Pull weight (lb.)	1,780
Speed (mph)	2.77
Percent slippage	10.11
SAE drawbar horsepower	9
SAE belt/PTO horsepower	16
Type	tracklayer
Length (in.)	80
Height (in.)	50
Rear width (in.)	43
Tread width (in.)	25 or 36
Weight (lb.)	1,865
Track length (in.)	48 on ground
Grouser shoe	33 links on low/34 on high; 5.50-in.
Gear/speed (mph)	forward: 1/1.00–3.00; reverse: 1/1.00–3.00

Cletrac K, 20, 15-25

Manufacturer	Cleveland Tractor Co., Cleveland, OH
Nebraska test number	119
Test date	April 22 to May 5, 1926
Test tractor serial number	K 890
Years produced	1925–1932
Serial number range	101–10207 end
Serial number location	steel plate on top of transmission
Number produced	10,106
Engine	Cletrac vertical, valve-in-head
Test engine serial number	K 800 S
Cylinders	4
Bore and stroke (in.)	4.00 x 5.50
Rated rpm	1,375
Displacement (c.i.)	276.5

Fuel ....kerosene/gasoline
Main tank capacity (gal.) 13
Auxiliary tank capacity (gal.) 0.75
Carburetor ....Tillotson R2, 1.125-in.
Air cleaner ....Pomona
Ignition ....Eisemann GS4
                                          magneto
Cooling capacity (gal.) 5
Maximum brake horsepower tests
    PTO/belt horsepower.................28.44
    Crankshaft rpm 1,378
    Fuel use (gal./hr.).................3.10
Maximum drawbar horsepower tests
    Gear................................low
    Drawbar horsepower.................23.42
    Pull weight (lb.)..................4,375
    Speed (mph) 2.01
    Percent slippage...................7.14
SAE drawbar horsepower.......................15
SAE belt/PTO horsepower......................25
Type ....tracklayer
Length (in.) 105
Height (in.) 54
Rear width (in.) 48.50
Tread width (in.)...........................39
Weight (lb.)................................4,838
Track length (in.)..........................60 on ground
Grouser shoe................................22 links; (9.50), 12-in.
Gear/speed (mph) ....forward: 1/2.25,
                                          2/4.50; reverse: 1/2.25

Cletrac K, 20, 15-25
Manufacturer................................Cleveland Tractor Co.,
                                          Cleveland, OH
Nebraska test number 120
Test date ....April 30 to May 5,
                                          1926
Test tractor serial number..................K 890
Years produced 1925–1932
Serial number range.........................101–10207 end
Serial number location ....steel plate on top of
                                          transmission
Number produced 10,106
Engine ....Cletrac vertical,
                                          valve-in-head
Test engine serial number...................K 800 S
Cylinders 4
Bore and stroke (in.) ....4.00 x 5.50
Rated rpm 1,375
Displacement (c.i.) 276.5
Fuel ....gasoline
Fuel tank capacity (gal.) 13
Carburetor..................................Tillotson R2, 1.125-in.
Air cleaner.................................Pomona
Ignition....................................Eisemann GS4
                                          magneto
Cooling capacity (gal.) 6
Maximum brake horsepower tests
    PTO/belt horsepower.................30.15
    Crankshaft rpm 1,380
    Fuel use (gal./hr.).................4.27
Maximum drawbar horsepower tests
    Gear................................low
    Drawbar horsepower.................24.53

Pull weight (lb.)...........................4,590
    Speed (mph) 2.01
    Percent slippage...................7.00
SAE drawbar horsepower......................15
SAE belt/PTO horsepower.....................25
Type ....tracklayer
Length (in.) 105
Height (in.) 54
Rear width (in.) 48.50
Tread width (in.) 39
Weight (lb.) 4,838
Track length (in.)..........................60 on ground
Grouser shoe................................22 links; (9.50), 12-in.
Gear/speed (mph) ....forward: 1/2.25,
                                          2/4.50; reverse: 1/2.25

Cletrac 30 A, A, 30-45
Manufacturer................................Cleveland Tractor Co.,
                                          Cleveland, OH
Nebraska test number 125
Test date ....August 27 to
                                          September 7, 1926
Test tractor serial number..................18
Years produced 1926–1929
Serial number range.........................6–1421 end
Serial number location ....steel plate on rear of
                                          firewall
Number produced 1,415
Engine ....Wisconsin H vertical,
                                          valve-in-head
Test engine serial number...................1216
Cylinders 6
Bore and stroke (in.) ....4.00 x 5.00
Rated rpm 1,577
Displacement (c.i.) 377
Fuel ....gasoline
Fuel tank capacity (gal.) 20
Carburetor..................................Tillotson ST3A,
                                          1.50-in.
Air cleaner.................................Pomona Vortox
Ignition....................................Eisemann GS6
                                          magneto
Cooling capacity (gal.) 5
Maximum brake horsepower tests
    PTO/belt horsepower.................48.62
    Crankshaft rpm 1,575
    Fuel use (gal./hr.).................5.93
Maximum drawbar horsepower tests
    Gear................................low
    Drawbar horsepower.................38.58
    Pull weight (lb.)..................6,170
    Speed (mph) 2.35
    Percent slippage...................5.41
SAE drawbar horsepower......................30
SAE belt/PTO horsepower.....................45
Type ....tracklayer
Length (in.) 108.50
Height (in.) 57
Rear width (in.) 57
Tread width (in.)...........................44
Weight (lb.)................................7,000
Track length (in.)..........................75 on ground
Grouser shoe................................25 links; 12-in.
Gear/speed (mph) ....forward: 1/2.40,
                                          2/4.75; reverse: 1/1.80

Cletrac 40

Manufacturer	Cleveland Tractor Co., Cleveland, OH
Nebraska test number	149
Test date	April 24 to May 10, 1928
Test tractor serial number	150
Years produced	1928–1935
Serial number range	40: 101–1833; 55-40: 1835–1889; 55: 1890–3852 end
Serial number location	steel plate on side of battery cover
Number produced	40: 1,733; 55-40: 55; 55: 1,963
Engine	Wisconsin Z in 40; ZT in 55-40 and 55 vertical I-head, valve-in-head
Test engine serial number	1393
Cylinders	6
Bore and stroke (in.)	4.50 x 5.00
Rated rpm	1,575
Displacement (c.i.)	477.1
Fuel	gasoline
Fuel tank capacity (gal.)	40
Carburetor	Wheeler-Schebler AT, 1.75-in.
Air cleaner	Pomona
Ignition	Eisemann magneto or Delco-Remy with 6-v battery
Cooling capacity (gal.)	7

Maximum brake horsepower tests

PTO/belt horsepower	63.00
Crankshaft rpm	1,579
Fuel use (gal./hr.)	8.45

Maximum drawbar horsepower tests

Gear	2nd
Drawbar horsepower	55.51
Pull weight (lb.)	9,725
Speed (mph)	2.14
Percent slippage	2.03
SAE drawbar horsepower	40
SAE belt/PTO horsepower	55
Type	tracklayer
Length (in.)	132
Height (in.)	63
Rear width (in.)	69
Tread width (in.)	48
Weight (lb.)	12,000
Track length (in.)	80 on ground, 240 total
Grouser shoe	24 links; (14), 17-in.
Gear/speed (mph)	forward: 1/2.00, 2/3.50, 3/5.50; reverse: 1/3.00

Cletrac 80-60

Manufacturer	Cleveland Tractor Co., Cleveland, OH
Nebraska test number	182
Test date	October 2–23, 1930
Test tractor serial number	199
Years produced	1930–1932
Serial number range	113–409 end
Serial number location	steel plate on left side of fuel tank or dash
Number produced	297
Engine	Wisconsin (DT3) DT4 vertical I-head, valve-in-head
Test engine serial number	1050
Cylinders	6
Bore and stroke (in.)	DT3: 5.50 x 6.50, DT4: 5.75 x 6.50
Rated rpm	1,050
Displacement (c.i.)	DT3 926.6/DT4 1012.7
Fuel	gasoline
Fuel tank capacity (gal.)	70
Carburetor	2 Schebler HDX12, 1.50-in.
Air cleaner	Pomona Vortox
Ignition	Delco-Remy with 6-v battery
Cooling capacity (gal.)	19

Maximum brake horsepower tests

PTO/belt horsepower	90.23
Crankshaft rpm	1,047
Fuel use (gal./hr.)	12.08

Maximum drawbar horsepower tests

Gear	3rd
Drawbar horsepower	83.53
Pull weight (lb.)	18,551
Speed (mph)	1.74
Percent slippage	6.68
SAE drawbar horsepower	59.96
SAE belt/PTO horsepower	81.91
Type	tracklayer
Length (in.)	156
Height (in.)	82
Rear width (in.)	96
Tread width (in.)	67
Weight (lb.)	20,250
Track length (in.)	97 on ground, 226 total
Grouser shoe	22 links; (17), 20-in.
Gear/speed (mph)	forward: 1/1.75, 2/2.50, 3/3.60; reverse: 1/2.10

Cletrac 40-30

Manufacturer	Cleveland Tractor Co., Cleveland, OH
Nebraska test number	195
Test date	July 28 to August 17, 1931
Test tractor serial number	205
Years produced	1930–1935
Serial number range	40-30: 76–381 end, consecutive numbers; 35: 400–2834 end, even numbers
Serial number location	steel plate on right side of fuel tank
Number produced	40-30: 306; 35: 1,218
Engine	Hercules WXT vertical L-head
Test engine serial number	600329
Cylinders	6

Bore and stroke (in.) ....4.25 x 4.50
Rated rpm 1,450
Displacement (c.i.) 383.0
Fuel ....gasoline
Fuel tank capacity (gal.) 30
Carburetor ....Tillotson Y7A, 1.50-in.
Air cleaner ....Pomona Vortox
Ignition ....Eisemann magneto or
Delco-Remy with 6-v
battery
Cooling capacity (gal.) 7
Maximum brake horsepower tests
PTO/belt horsepower...........................45.64
Crankshaft rpm 1,449
Fuel use (gal./hr.) 5.59
Maximum drawbar horsepower tests
Gear..3rd
Drawbar horsepower............................40.66
Pull weight (lb.) 7,580
Speed (mph) 2.01
Percent slippage..................................3.62
SAE drawbar horsepower.............................31.17
SAE belt/PTO horsepower 42.44
Type ....tracklayer
Length (in.) 117
Height (in.) 63
Rear width (in.) 61.50
Tread width (in.)...48 or 61
Weight (lb.) 10,022
Track length (in.)..68 on ground,
217 total
Grouser shoe..30 links; 13, (14), 16,
18, 24-in.
Gear/speed (mph) ....forward: 1/2.06,
2/3.05, 3/4.42; reverse:
1/2.28

Cletrac 15 and 15-22
Manufacturer...Cleveland Tractor Co.,
Cleveland, OH
Nebraska test number 196
Test date ....July 28 to August 13,
1931
Test tractor serial number.............................305
Years produced 1931–1933
Serial number range.....................................76–1360 end, even
numbers
Serial number location ....steel plate on right
rear corner on hood
Number produced 643
Engine ....Hercules OOC
vertical L-head
Test engine serial number............................224447
Cylinders 4
Bore and stroke (in.) ....4.00 x 4.50
Rated rpm 1,250
Displacement (c.i.) 226.2
Fuel ....gasoline
Fuel tank capacity (gal.) 20
Carburetor ....Tillotson P1A,
1.125-in.
Air cleaner ....Pomona Vortox
Ignition ....Eisemann GL4
magneto

Cooling capacity (gal.) 4
Maximum brake horsepower tests
PTO/belt horsepower...........................25.83
Crankshaft rpm 1,249
Fuel use (gal./hr.) 3.03
Maximum drawbar horsepower tests
Gear..low
Drawbar horsepower............................18.69
Pull weight (lb.) 3,927
Speed (mph) 1.79
Percent slippage..................................8.39
SAE drawbar horsepower.............................14.80
SAE belt/PTO horsepower 23.59
Type ....tracklayer
Length (in.) 93.50
Height (in.) 52.50
Rear width (in.) 50.50
Tread width (in.)...40
Weight (lb.) 5,170
Track length (in.)..53 on ground,
171 total
Grouser shoe..26 links; (9), 10, 11-in.
Gear/speed (mph) ....forward: 1/1.95,
2/3.05, 3/4.37;
reverse: 1/2.20

Cletrac 25
Manufacturer...Cleveland Tractor Co.,
Cleveland, OH
Nebraska test number 201
Test date ....April 9–30, 1932
Test tractor serial number.............................370
Years produced 1931–1935
Serial number range.....................................76–1372 end, even
numbers
Serial number location ....steel plate on right side
of fuel tank
Number produced 649
Engine ....Hercules JXC vertical
L-head
Test engine serial number............................504164
Cylinders 6
Bore and stroke (in.) ....3.75 x 4.25
Rated rpm 1,250
Displacement (c.i.) 281.6
Fuel ....gasoline
Fuel tank capacity (gal.) 23
Carburetor ....Tillotson Y8A, 1.25-in.
Air cleaner ....Vortox
Ignition ....Delco-Remy 643 V
with 6-v battery or
Eisemann magneto
Cooling capacity (gal.) 5
Maximum brake horsepower tests
PTO/belt horsepower...........................33.11
Crankshaft rpm 1,250
Fuel use (gal./hr.) 3.72
Maximum drawbar horsepower tests
Gear..2nd
Drawbar horsepower............................26.79
Pull weight (lb.) 3,613
Speed (mph) 2.78
Percent slippage..................................1.57
SAE drawbar horsepower.............................21.52

SAE belt/PTO horsepower 30.35
Type ....tracklayer
Length (in.) 105
Height (in.) 55.25
Rear width (in.) 57.50
Tread width (in.) ....42 or 52
Weight (lb.) 7,000
Track length (in.) ....62 on ground,
193 total
Grouser shoe ....29 links; (12), 13-in.
Gear/speed (mph) ....forward: 1/1.95, 2/2.80,
3/4.00; reverse: 1/1.83

Cletrac 15

Manufacturer..Cleveland Tractor Co.,
Cleveland, OH
Nebraska test number 202
Test date ....April 9 to May 4, 1932
Test tractor serial number 1138
Years produced 1931–1933
Serial number range................................76–1360 end, even
numbers
Serial number location ....steel plate on right
rear corner on hood
Number produced 643
Engine ....Hercules OOC
vertical L-head
Test engine serial number 227158
Cylinders 4
Bore and stroke (in.) ....4.00 x 4.50
Rated rpm 1,250
Displacement (c.i.) 226.2
Fuel ....gasoline
Fuel tank capacity (gal.) 20
Carburetor..Tillotson P1B,
1.125-in.
Air cleaner ....Vortox
Ignition..Eisemann GL4
magneto
Cooling capacity (gal.) 4
Maximum brake horsepower tests
    PTO/belt horsepower...........................26.94
    Crankshaft rpm 1,250
    Fuel use (gal./hr.) 3.06
Maximum drawbar horsepower tests
    Gear..2nd
    Drawbar horsepower.............................22.14
    Pull weight (lb.)...................................3,008
    Speed (mph) 2.76
    Percent slippage...................................2.23
SAE drawbar horsepower 17.75
SAE belt/PTO horsepower 24.44
Type ....tracklayer
Length (in.) 93.50
Height (in.) 52.50
Rear width (in.) 53.50
Tread width (in.).......................................40
Weight (lb.) 5,800
Track length (in.) ....56 on ground, 180 total
Grouser shoe...26/27 links; 9, 10, (11)-in.
Gear/speed (mph) ....forward: 1/1.95,
2/2.80, 3/4.00; reverse:
1/1.83

Cletrac 40 D, 46-60, Diesel

Manufacturer..Cleveland Tractor Co.,
Cleveland, OH

Nebraska test number 235
Test date ....June 13–24, 1935
Test tractor serial number 10438
Years produced 1934–1936
Serial number range..................................35 D: 10000–10217,
consecutive; 40 D:
10218–10830, even,
end
Serial number location ....steel plate on right side
of fuel tank
Number produced ....35 D: 217; 40 D: 307
Engine ....Hercules DRXH vertical
I-head, valve-in-head
Test engine serial number.........................L 380274
Cylinders 6
Bore and stroke (in.) ....4.375 x 5.25
Rated rpm 1,200
Displacement (c.i.) 473.5
Fuel ....diesel
Fuel tank capacity (gal.) 30
Carburetor..American Bosch
APE6B70 fuel system
Air cleaner ....Vortox
Ignition..Leece-Neville start
system
Cooling capacity (gal.) 7.50
Maximum brake horsepower tests
    PTO/belt horsepower............................63.64
    Crankshaft rpm 1,199
    Fuel use (gal./hr.) 4.85
Maximum drawbar horsepower tests
    Gear..2nd
    Drawbar horsepower.............................57.94
    Pull weight (lb.)...................................7,451
    Speed (mph) 2.92
    Percent slippage...................................1.73
SAE drawbar horsepower 45.89
SAE belt/PTO horsepower 57.55
Type ....tracklayer
Length (in.) 132
Height (in.) 64.75
Rear width (in.) 65.50
Tread width (in.) ....48 or 61
Weight (lb.) 11,500
Track length (in.).....................................75 on ground, 224 total
Grouser shoe...31 links; 15, (16), 18,
24-in.
Gear/speed (mph) ....forward: 1/1.80,
2/3.00, 3/4.30;
reverse: 1/2.20

Cletrac CG

Manufacturer..Cleveland Tractor Co.,
Cleveland, OH
Nebraska test number 258
Test date ....June 16–24, 1936
Test tractor serial number 2926
Years produced 1936–1942
Serial number range..................................2836–4999;
5M000–5M608 end,
even numbers
Serial number location ....1936–1937: steel plate
on right side of dash;
1937-up: front of
firewall
Number produced 1,387

Engine ....Hercules WXTP vertical L-head
Test engine serial number 601601
Cylinders 6
Bore and stroke (in.) ....4.25 x 4.50
Rated rpm 1,450
Displacement (c.i.) 383.0
Fuel ....gasoline
Fuel tank capacity (gal.) 30
Carburetor ....Tillotson Y-7-B, 1.50-in.
Air cleaner ....Vortox
Ignition ....Bosch MJB6A101 magneto or Delco-Remy with 6-v battery
Cooling capacity (gal.) 5.50

Maximum brake horsepower tests
   PTO/belt horsepower...............51.13
   Crankshaft rpm 1,449
   Fuel use (gal./hr.) 6.78
Maximum drawbar horsepower tests
   Gear.................................2nd
   Drawbar horsepower................39.82
   Pull weight (lb.).....................4,901
   Speed (mph) 3.05
   Percent slippage...................1.07
SAE drawbar horsepower...............32.17
SAE belt/PTO horsepower 45.68
Type ....tracklayer
Length (in.) 127
Height (in.) 63.88
Rear width (in.) ....67.25 or 80.25
Tread width (in.) ....48 or 61
Weight (lb.) 11,500
Track length (in.) ....74.75 on ground, 224 total
Grouser shoe............................31 links; 14, (15), 16-in.
Gear/speed (mph) ....forward: 1/1.87, 2/3.05, 3/4.44; reverse: 1/2.28

Cletrac BG
Manufacturer...........................Cleveland Tractor Co., Cleveland, OH
Nebraska test number 259
Test date ....June 16 to July 10, 1936
Test tractor serial number............4C 36
Years produced 1936–1944
Serial number range...................2C80–4C858 end, even numbers
Serial number location ....1936: steel plate on right side of dash; 1937-up: front of firewall
Number produced 1,600
Engine ....Hercules JXC vertical L-head
Test engine serial number...........563217
Cylinders 6
Bore and stroke (in.) ....3.75 x 4.25
Rated rpm 1,400
Displacement (c.i.) 281.6
Fuel ....gasoline
Fuel tank capacity (gal.) 23

Carburetor...............................Tillotson Y-8-C, 1.25-in.
Air cleaner ....Vortox
Ignition ....(Delco-Remy 645 H, 6-v battery) Bosch magneto
Cooling capacity (gal.) 5
Maximum brake horsepower tests
   PTO/belt horsepower...............39.07
   Crankshaft rpm 1,401
   Fuel use (gal./hr.) 4.64
Maximum drawbar horsepower tests
   Gear................................2nd
   Drawbar horsepower................28.27
   Pull weight (lb.).....................4,088
   Speed (mph) 2.59
   Percent slippage...................2.46
SAE drawbar horsepower...............22.90
SAE belt/PTO horsepower 34.81
Type ....tracklayer
Length (in.) 116.50
Height (in.) 59
Rear width (in.) ....60.13 or 68.13
Tread width (in.) ....44 or 52
Weight (lb.) 8,350
Track length (in.) ....63 on ground, 199 total
Grouser shoe............................30 links; (14), 15, 16, 18, 20-in.
Gear/speed (mph) ....forward: 1/1.80, 2/2.63, 3/3.50; reverse: 1/1.38

Cletrac AG
Manufacturer............................Cleveland Tractor Co., Cleveland, OH
Nebraska test number 260
Test date ....June 16–26, 1936
Test tractor serial number............14982
Years produced 1936–1943
Serial number range...................14552–20200; 2 x 0202–2 x 3548 end, even numbers
Serial number location ....1936: steel plate on right side of dash; 1936-up: front of firewall
Number produced 4,449
Engine ....Hercules OOC vertical L-head
Test engine serial number...........235266
Cylinders 4
Bore and stroke (in.) ....4.00 x 4.50
Rated rpm 1,400
Displacement (c.i.) 226.2
Fuel ....gasoline
Fuel tank capacity (gal.) 18
Carburetor...............................Tillotson P-1-B, 1.13-in.
Air cleaner ....Vortox
Ignition ....American Bosch MJB4A-101 magneto
Cooling capacity (gal.) 4
Maximum brake horsepower tests
   PTO/belt horsepower...............30.25
   Crankshaft rpm 1,398
   Fuel use (gal./hr.) 3.46

Maximum drawbar horsepower tests
- Gear 2nd
- Drawbar horsepower 24.44
- Pull weight (lb.) 3,584
- Speed (mph) 2.56
- Percent slippage 3.12

SAE drawbar horsepower 19.28
SAE belt/PTO horsepower 27.72
Type .... tracklayer
Length (in.) 106
Height (in.) 55
Rear width (in.) 57.25
Tread width (in.) .... 42 or 50
Weight (lb.) 6,800
Track length (in.) .... 62 on ground, 193 total
Grouser shoe .... 29 links; (12), 14, 17, 20-in.
Gear/speed (mph) .... forward: 1/1.75, 2/2.63, 3/3.75; reverse: 1/1.38

Cletrac E, Not Streamlined

Manufacturer .... Cleveland Tractor Co., Cleveland, OH
Nebraska test number 261
Test date .... June 16 to July 9, 1936
Test tractor serial number 1A 110
Years produced 1934–1936
Serial number range .... 1A00 to 7A21; 1A000–1A408 end, even numbers
Serial number location .... steel plate on right side of dash
Number produced 566
Engine .... Hercules OOC vertical L-head
Test engine serial number 235102
Cylinders 4
Bore and stroke (in.) .... 4.00 x 4.50
Rated rpm 1,300
Displacement (c.i.) 226.2
Fuel .... gasoline
Fuel tank capacity (gal.) 18
Carburetor .... Tillotson P-1-B, 1.13-in.
Air cleaner .... Vortox
Ignition .... American Bosch MJB4A-101 or Wico magneto
Cooling capacity (gal.) 4

Maximum brake horsepower tests
- PTO/belt horsepower 28.76
- Crankshaft rpm 1,300
- Fuel use (gal./hr.) 3.27

Maximum drawbar horsepower tests
- Gear 2nd
- Drawbar horsepower 20.47
- Pull weight (lb.) 2,940
- Speed (mph) 2.61
- Percent slippage 6.61

SAE drawbar horsepower 16.58

SAE belt/PTO horsepower 25.93
Type .... tracklayer
Length (in.) 105.50
Height (in.) 55.50
Rear width (in.) 75.50, 80.50, 89.50
Tread width (in.) .... 31, 38, 42, 62, 68, or 72
Weight (lb.) 5,075
Track length (in.) .... 59.50 on ground, 184 total
Grouser shoe .... 29 links; 8, 10, 12, (13), 15-in.
Gear/speed (mph) .... forward: 1/2.13, 2/2.75, 3/4.00; reverse: 1/1.63

Cletrac FG

Manufacturer .... Cleveland Tractor Co., Cleveland, OH
Nebraska test number 262
Test date .... June 16 to July 16, 1936
Test tractor serial number 882
Years produced 1936–1943
Serial number range .... 850 to 1C880 end, even numbers
Serial number location .... 1936–1938: steel plate on right side of dash; 1938-up: front of firewall
Number produced 297
Engine .... Hercules HXE vertical L-head
Test engine serial number 320821
Cylinders 6
Bore and stroke (in.) .... 5.75 x 6.00
Rated rpm 1,120
Displacement (c.i.) 934.8
Fuel .... gasoline
Fuel tank capacity (gal.) 72
Carburetor .... Tillotson YX1BX, 2.00-in.
Air cleaner .... Vortox
Ignition .... American Bosch MJA6B-102 magneto
Cooling capacity (gal.) 14

Maximum brake horsepower tests
- PTO/belt horsepower 104.16
- Crankshaft rpm 1,120
- Fuel use (gal./hr.) 11.98

Maximum drawbar horsepower tests
- Gear 2nd
- Drawbar horsepower 87.85
- Pull weight (lb.) 13,094
- Speed (mph) 2.52
- Percent slippage 2.34

SAE drawbar horsepower 70.50
SAE belt/PTO horsepower 94.29
Type .... tracklayer
Length (in.) 173
Height (in.) 84
Rear width (in.) 94.25
Tread width (in.) 67

Weight (lb.) 25,000
Track length (in.).............................96 on ground, 277 total
Grouser shoe..................................28 links; 20-in.
Gear/speed (mph) ....forward: 1/1.75, 2/2.50, 3/4.30; reverse: 1/2.10

Cletrac FD, Diesel

Manufacturer.................................Cleveland Tractor, Co., Cleveland, OH
Nebraska test number 263
Test date ....June 15 to July 17, 1936
Test tractor serial number...............6364
Years produced 1936–1944
Serial number range........................6322–6698; 8Y000 to 9Y228 end, even numbers
Serial number location ....1936–1938: steel plate on right side of dash; 1938-up: front of firewall
Number produced 3-speed: 189; 4-speed: 615
Engine ....Hercules DHX vertical I-head, valve-in-head
Test engine serial number...............H 360340
Cylinders 6
Bore and stroke (in.) ....5.00 x 6.00
Rated rpm 1,300
Displacement (c.i.) 706.9
Fuel ....diesel
Fuel tank capacity (gal.) 62
Air cleaner ....Vortox
Ignition..start system; Leece-Neville 12-v; with 2, 6-v battery
Cooling capacity (gal.) 14
Maximum brake horsepower tests
 PTO/belt horsepower.............100.58
 Crankshaft rpm 1,298
 Fuel use (gal./hr.) 7.40
Maximum drawbar horsepower tests
 Gear......................................2nd
 Drawbar horsepower..............83.75
 Pull weight (lb.).....................11,435
 Speed (mph) 2.75
 Percent slippage....................1.03
SAE drawbar horsepower................68.28
SAE belt/PTO horsepower 91.39
Type ....tracklayer
Length (in.) 173
Height (in.)....................................84
Rear width (in.)..............................94.50
Tread width (in.)............................67
Weight (lb.)....................................25,800
Track length (in.)............................96 on ground, 277 total
Grouser shoe..................................28 links; 20-in.
Gear/speed (mph) ....forward: 1/1.75, 2/2.75, 3/4.25; reverse: 1/2.13

Cletrac BD, Diesel

Manufacturer..................................Cleveland Tractor Co., Cleveland, OH

Nebraska test number 288
Test date ....September 16 to October 2, 1937
Test tractor serial number...............2D 644
Years produced 1935–1956
Serial number range........................1D00 to 20D387 end, even numbers to 1951 then consecutive
Serial number location ....1935–1936: steel plate on right side of dash; 1936-up: front of firewall
Number produced ....10,653 to 1953; 1953–1954 all models interspersed
Engine ....Hercules DJXB vertical L-head
Test engine serial number...............F 802526
Cylinders 6
Bore and stroke (in.) ....3.50 x 4.50
Rated rpm 1,530
Compression ratio..........................15.50:1
Displacement (c.i.) 260
Fuel ....diesel
Fuel tank capacity (gal.) 23
Carburetor.....................................Bosch fuel system
Air cleaner ....Vortox
Ignition..Leece-Neville, 12-v; with 2, 6-v battery
Cooling capacity (gal.) 5
Maximum brake horsepower tests
 PTO/belt horsepower.............41.97
 Crankshaft rpm 1,531
 Fuel use (gal./hr.) 3.45
Maximum drawbar horsepower tests
 Gear......................................2nd
 Drawbar horsepower..............34.48
 Pull weight (lb.).....................4,964
 Speed (mph) 2.60
 Percent slippage....................2.13
SAE drawbar horsepower................26.92
SAE belt/PTO horsepower 37.35
Type ....tracklayer
Length (in.) 116.50
Height (in.)....................................59
Rear width (in.)..............................60.13 or 68.13
Tread width (in.)............................44 or 52
Weight (lb.)....................................8,800
Track length (in.)............................63 on ground, 199 total
Grouser shoe..................................30 links; (14), 15, 16, 18, 20-in.
Gear/speed (mph) ....forward: 1/1.80, 2/2.63, 3/3.50; reverse: 1/1.33

Cletrac CG

Manufacturer..................................Cleveland Tractor Co., Cleveland, OH
Nebraska test number 289
Test date ....September 16 to October 4, 1937
Test tractor serial number...............5M 110
Years produced 1936–1942

Serial number range 2836–4999;
5M000–5M608 end,
even numbers
Serial number location ....1936–1937: steel plate
on right side of dash;
1937-up: front of firewall
Number produced 1,387
Engine ....Hercules WXTP
vertical L-head
Test engine serial number 601791
Cylinders 6
Bore and stroke (in.) ....4.25 x 4.50
Rated rpm 1,565
Displacement (c.i.) 383
Fuel ....gasoline
Fuel tank capacity (gal.) 30
Carburetor ....Tillotson Y-7-B,
1.50-in.
Air cleaner ....Vortox
Ignition ....Delco-Remy 642W,
6-v battery
Cooling capacity (gal.) 5.50
Maximum brake horsepower tests
PTO/belt horsepower 52.60
Crankshaft rpm 1,565
Fuel use (gal./hr.) 6.56
Maximum drawbar horsepower tests
Gear 2nd
Drawbar horsepower 43.23
Pull weight (lb.) 5,367
Speed (mph) 3.02
Percent slippage 1.42
SAE drawbar horsepower 34.01
SAE belt/PTO horsepower 47.08
Type ....tracklayer
Length (in.) 127
Height (in.) 63.88
Rear width (in.) ....67.25 or 80.25
Tread width (in.) ....48 or 61
Weight (lb.) 11,500
Track length (in.) ....74.75 on ground,
224 total
Grouser shoe ....31 links; 14, (15),
16-in.
Gear/speed (mph) ....forward: 1/1.87, 2/3.05,
3/4.44; reverse: 1/2.28

Cletrac General GG

Manufacturer ....Cleveland Tractor Co.,
Cleveland, OH
Nebraska test number 323
Test date ....August 10–30, 1939
Test tractor serial number 2FA 970
Years produced 1939–1942
Serial number range ....1FA000 to 9FA998;
1FA0000–1FA0164;
1FA1000–1FA6886
end, even numbers
Serial number location ....steel plate on right
frame rail in front of axle
Number produced 7,527
Engine ....Hercules IXA3
vertical L-head
Test engine serial number 667995
Cylinders 4

Bore and stroke (in.) ....3.00 x 4.00
Rated rpm 1,400
Displacement (c.i.) 113.1
Fuel ....gasoline
Fuel tank capacity (gal.) 12
Carburetor ....Tillotson YC2A,
0.875-in.
Air cleaner ....Vortox
Ignition ....Wico C-1113B
magneto
Cooling capacity (gal.) 3
Maximum brake horsepower tests
PTO/belt horsepower 19.29
Crankshaft rpm 1,700
Fuel use (gal./hr.) 2.19
Maximum drawbar horsepower tests
Gear 2nd
Drawbar horsepower 13.29
Pull weight (lb.) 1,661
Speed (mph) 3.00
Percent slippage 18.09
SAE drawbar horsepower 10.46
SAE belt/PTO horsepower 17.42
Type ....tricycle
Front tire (in.) ....5.50 x 16
Rear tire (in.) ....9.00 x 24
Length (in.) 80
Height (in.) 55
Rear width (in.) 46–85
Weight (lb.) 2,105
Gear/speed (mph) ....forward: 1/2.25,
2/3.50, 3/6.00;
reverse: 1/2.50

Cletrac HG

Manufacturer ....Cleveland Tractor Co.,
Cleveland, OH
Nebraska test number 324
Test date ....August 12–30, 1939
Test tractor serial number 1GA 276
Years produced 1939–1951
Serial number range ....1GA000–59GA858 end,
even numbers
Serial number location ....steel plate on right rail
frame to No. 47GA838;
47GA840-up, right side
of bell housing
Number produced 29,930
Engine ....Hercules IXA3
vertical L-head
Test engine serial number 668182
Cylinders 4
Bore and stroke (in.) ....3.00 x 4.00
Rated rpm 1,400
Displacement (c.i.) 113.1
Fuel ....gasoline
Fuel tank capacity (gal.) 12
Carburetor ....Tillotson YC2A, 0.875-in.
Air cleaner ....Vortox
Ignition ....Wico C-1113B magneto
Cooling capacity (gal.) 3
Maximum brake horsepower tests
PTO/belt horsepower 19.36
Crankshaft rpm 1,700
Fuel use (gal./hr.) 2.19

Maximum drawbar horsepower tests

Gear	2nd
Drawbar horsepower	14.01
Pull weight (lb.)	1,748
Speed (mph)	3.00
Percent slippage	2.74
SAE drawbar horsepower	11.09
SAE belt/PTO horsepower	17.49
Type	tracklayer
Length (in.)	91
Height (in.)	50
Rear width (in.)	52.50 or 78.25
Tread width (in.)	42 or 68
Weight (lb.)	2,950
Track length (in.)	51 on ground, 176 total
Grouser shoe	30 links; 6, 8, (10)-in.
Gear/speed (mph)	forward: 1/2.00, 2/3.00, 3/5.00; reverse: 1/2.25

Cletrac BD, Diesel

Manufacturer	Cleveland Tractor Co., Cleveland, OH
Nebraska test number	325
Test date	August 10–30, 1939
Test tractor serial number	3D 876
Years produced	1935–1956
Serial number range	1D00 to 20D387 end, even numbers to 1951 then consecutive
Serial number location	1935–1936: metal plate on right side of dash; 1936-up: front of firewall
Number produced	10,653 to 1953; 1953–1954 all models interspersed
Engine	Hercules DJXC vertical overhead-valve
Test engine serial number	K 803736
Cylinders	6
Bore and stroke (in.)	3.75 x 4.50
Rated rpm	1,400
Displacement (c.i.)	298.2
Fuel	diesel
Fuel tank capacity (gal.)	23
Air cleaner	Vortox
Ignition	Leece-Neville, 12-v; with 2, 6-v battery
Cooling capacity (gal.)	5

Maximum brake horsepower tests

PTO/belt horsepower	45.37
Crankshaft rpm	1,400
Fuel use (gal./hr.)	3.46

Maximum drawbar horsepower tests

Gear	2nd
Drawbar horsepower	36.07
Pull weight (lb.)	5,295
Speed (mph)	2.55
Percent slippage	4.23
SAE drawbar horsepower	28.54
SAE belt/PTO horsepower	40.88
Type	tracklayer
Length (in.)	116

Height (in.)	57.38
Rear width (in.)	60.13 or 68.13
Tread width (in.)	44 or 52
Weight (lb.)	8,800
Track length (in.)	63 on ground, 199 total
Grouser shoe	30 links; (14), 15, 16, 18, 20-in.
Gear/speed (mph)	forward: 1/1.81, 2/2.64, 3/3.46; reverse: 1/1.38

Cletrac FD, Diesel

Manufacturer	Cleveland Tractor Co., Cleveland, OH
Nebraska test number	326
Test date	August 17–30, 1939
Test tractor serial number	8Y 270
Years produced	1936–1944
Serial number range	6322 to 9Y228 end, even numbers
Serial number location	1936–1938: steel plate on right side of dash; 1938-up
Number produced	804
Engine	Hercules DHXB vertical I-head, valve-in-head
Test engine serial number	P 360835
Cylinders	6
Bore and stroke (in.)	5.00 x 6.00
Rated rpm	1,300
Displacement (c.i.)	707
Fuel	diesel
Fuel tank capacity (gal.)	60
Air cleaner	Vortox
Ignition	Leece-Neville, 6-v battery
Cooling capacity (gal.)	14

Maximum brake horsepower tests

PTO/belt horsepower	107.25
Crankshaft rpm	1,300
Fuel use (gal./hr.)	7.66

Maximum drawbar horsepower tests

Gear	low
Drawbar horsepower	91.16
Pull weight (lb.)	21,831
Speed (mph)	1.57
Percent slippage	2.93
SAE drawbar horsepower	71.58
SAE belt/PTO horsepower	96.54
Type	tracklayer
Length (in.)	180
Height (in.)	88
Rear width (in.)	100
Tread width (in.)	69
Weight (lb.)	28,000
Track length (in.)	96 on ground, 286 total
Grouser shoe	34 links; (20), 22-in.
Gear/speed (mph)	forward: 1/1.61, 2/2.75, 3/3.66, 4/5.00; reverse: 1/1.58, 2/2.82

Chapter 16

CO-OP

CO-OP No. 3

Manufacturer	Duplex Machinery Co., Battle Creek, MI
Nebraska test number	274
Test date	October 22 to November 5, 1936
Test tractor serial number	3*140
Years produced	1936–1942
Serial number range	3*100 to 3*3603 (last known number)
Serial number location	stamped on left side of frame rail near distributor; casting date left side of transmission
Engine	Chrysler Industrial vertical L-head
Test engine serial number	301
Cylinders	6
Bore and stroke (in.)	3.375 x 4.50
Rated rpm	1,600
Displacement (c.i.)	241.5
Fuel	gasoline
Fuel tank capacity (gal.)	28
Carburetor	Zenith 124.50 EX, 1.25-in.
Air cleaner	Donaldson
Ignition	Auto-Lite GAR4608-C-5 with 6-v battery
Cooling capacity (gal.)	5

Maximum brake horsepower tests

PTO/belt horsepower	42.29
Crankshaft rpm	1,600
Fuel use (gal./hr.)	4.02

Maximum drawbar horsepower tests

Gear	3rd
Drawbar horsepower	37.50
Pull weight (lb.)	2,308
Speed (mph)	6.09
Percent slippage	9.67
SAE drawbar horsepower	28.97
SAE belt/PTO horsepower	37.09
Type	4 wheel
Front tire (in.)	7.50 x 16
Rear tire (in.)	12.75 x 28
Length (in.)	132.25
Height (in.)	62
Rear width (in.)	76.50
Weight (lb.)	5,000
Gear/speed (mph)	forward: 1/2.70, 2/4.60, 3/6.60, 4/13.00, 5/20.00; reverse: 1/3.30

CO-OP No. 2

Manufacturer	Duplex Machinery Co., Battle Creek, MI
Nebraska test number	275
Test date	October 22 to November 10, 1936
Test tractor serial number	2*198
Years produced	1936–1942
Serial number range	2*100 to 2*1290 (last known number)
Serial number location	stamped on left side of frame rail near distributor; casting date left side of transmission
Engine	Chrysler Industrial vertical L-head
Test engine serial number	766
Cylinders	6
Bore and stroke (in.)	3.125 x 4.375
Rated rpm	1,500
Displacement (c.i.)	201.3
Fuel	gasoline
Fuel tank capacity (gal.)	22
Carburetor	Zenith 124.50 E, 1.00-in.
Air cleaner	Donaldson
Ignition	Auto-Lite GAR4608- C-5 with 6-v battery
Cooling capacity (gal.)	4.50

Maximum brake horsepower tests

PTO/belt horsepower	33.17
Crankshaft rpm	1,500
Fuel use (gal./hr.)	3.52

Maximum drawbar horsepower tests

Gear	3rd
Drawbar horsepower	29.67
Pull weight (lb.)	1,839
Speed (mph)	6.05
Percent slippage	9.57
SAE drawbar horsepower	22.70
SAE belt/PTO horsepower	29.44
Type	4 wheel
Front tire (in.)	6.00 x 16
Rear tire (in.)	11.25 x 28
Length (in.)	124.75
Height (in.)	57.50
Rear width (in.)	76.50
Weight (lb.)	4,050
Gear/speed (mph)	forward: 1/2.70, 2/4.70, 3/6.80, 4/14.20, 5/21.30; reverse: 1/3.50

Chapter 17
COCKSHUTT

Cockshutt 30, CO-OP E-3, Gamble's Farmcrest 30

Manufacturer ....Cockshutt Plow Co., Ltd., Brantford, Ontario, Canada
Nebraska test number 382
Test date ....May 21 to June 3, 1947
Test tractor serial number 47-30 1318
Years produced 1946–1958
Serial number range....................................1–50259 end
Serial number location ....stamped on right cast frame forward of transmission
Number produced 37,328
Engine ....Buda 4B 153 vertical I-head
Test engine serial number 291504
Cylinders 4
Bore and stroke (in.) ....3.4375 x 4.125
Rated rpm 1,650
Compression ratio.......................................6.00:1
Displacement (c.i.) 153
Fuel ....gasoline
Fuel tank capacity (gal.) 15
Carburetor...Marvel-Schebler, 0.875-in.
Air cleaner...Donaldson
Ignition..Auto-Lite with 6-v Exide SS 151 battery
Cooling capacity (gal.) 4.50
Maximum brake horsepower tests
    PTO/belt horsepower..........................31.88
    Crankshaft rpm 1,651
    Fuel use (gal./hr.) 3.01
Maximum drawbar horsepower tests
    Gear...2nd
    Drawbar horsepower...........................27.25
    Pull weight (lb.)..................................2,747
    Speed (mph) 3.72
    Percent slippage.................................9.30
SAE drawbar horsepower............................21.32
SAE belt/PTO horsepower 28.01
Type ....tricycle
Front tire (in.)..5.50 x 16
Rear tire (in.)...11.00 x 38
Length (in.) 132
Height (in.) 60
Rear width (in.)..74.50–98
Tread width (in.)..56–84
Weight (lb.) 3,434
Gear/speed (mph) ....forward: 1/2.50, 2/3.60, 3/5.00, 4/10.00; reverse: 1/3.20

Cockshutt 40, CO-OP E4

Manufacturer..Cockshutt Plow Co., Ltd., Brantford, Ontario, Canada
Nebraska test number 442

Test date ....June 12–17, 1950
Test tractor serial number 40 1042
Years produced 1949–1958
Serial number range....................................101–50372 end
Serial number location ....stamped on right cast frame forward of transmission
Number produced 14,929
Engine ....Buda 6B 230 vertical I-head
Test engine serial number 332620
Cylinders 6
Bore and stroke (in.) ....3.4375 x 4.125
Rated rpm 1,650
Compression ratio.......................................6.18:1
Displacement (c.i.) 230
Fuel ....gasoline
Fuel tank capacity (gal.) 21
Carburetor...Zenith 162J9
Air cleaner...Donaldson
Ignition..Auto-Lite with 6-v battery
Cooling capacity (gal.) 4.75
Maximum brake horsepower tests
    PTO/belt horsepower..........................43.30
    Crankshaft rpm 1,650
    Fuel use (gal./hr.) 4.54
Maximum drawbar horsepower tests
    Gear...4th
    Drawbar horsepower...........................37.85
    Pull weight (lb.)..................................2,748
    Speed (mph) 5.16
    Percent slippage.................................4.55
SAE drawbar horsepower............................30.05
SAE belt/PTO horsepower 38.75
Type ....standard
Front tire (in.)..7.50 x 16
Rear tire (in.)...13.00 x 38
Length (in.) 132
Height (in.) 79.50
Tread width (in.)..61.75–78.75
Weight (lb.) 4,600
Gear/speed (mph) ....forward: 1/1.60, 2/2.70, 3/3.70, 4/5.25, 5/6.25, 6/12.00; reverse: 1/2.20

Cockshutt 20, CO-OP E2

Manufacturer..Cockshutt Farm Equipment Co. Ltd., Brantford, Ontario, Canada
Nebraska test number 474
Test date ....June 16–24, 1952
Test tractor serial number 20 294
Years produced 1952–1958
Serial number range....................................101–40115 end
Serial number location ....stamped on right cast frame forward of transmission

Cockshutt

Number produced 4,000
Engine ....Continental F124/F140 vertical L-head
Test engine serial number 23285
Cylinders 4
Bore and stroke (in.) ....3.1875 x 4.375
Rated rpm 1,800
Compression ratio 6.75:1
Displacement (c.i.) 140
Fuel ....gasoline
Fuel tank capacity (gal.) 12.50
Carburetor ....Marvel-Schebler TSX480, 1.00-in.
Air cleaner ....Donaldson
Ignition ....Auto-Lite with 6-v battery
Cooling capacity (gal.) 3.10
Maximum brake horsepower tests
    PTO/belt horsepower 28.94
    Crankshaft rpm 1,800
    Fuel use (gal./hr.) 2.89
Maximum drawbar horsepower tests
    Gear 3rd
    Drawbar horsepower 25.47
    Pull weight (lb.) 1,866
    Speed (mph) 5.12
    Percent slippage 6.35
SAE drawbar horsepower 20.06
SAE belt/PTO horsepower 25.88
Type ....standard
Front wheel (in.) ....5.00 x 15
Rear wheel (in.) ....11.00 x 24
Length (in.) 115
Height (in.) 76
Tread width (in.) 48–76
Weight (lb.) 2,080
Gear/speed (mph) ....forward: 1/2.50, 2/3.75, 3/5.25, 4/13.25; reverse: 1/3.00

Cockshutt D50, CO-OP E5, Diesel

Manufacturer ....Cockshutt Farm Equipment Co., Ltd., Brantford, Ontario, Canada
Nebraska test number 487
Test date ....October 29 to November 6, 1952
Test tractor serial number 50 D126
Years produced 1952–1958
Serial number range ....101–40257 end
Serial number location ....stamped on right cast frame forward of transmission
Number produced 3,974
Engine ....Buda 6DA 273 vertical I-head
Test engine serial number 60018
Cylinders 6
Bore and stroke (in.) ....3.75 x 4.125
Rated rpm 1,650
Compression ratio 14.3:1
Displacement (c.i.) 273
Fuel ....diesel

Fuel tank capacity (gal.) 21
Carburetor ....Bosch injector pump
Air cleaner ....Donaldson
Ignition ....Auto-Lite with 12-v; with 2, 6-v battery
Cooling capacity (gal.) 4.75
Maximum brake horsepower tests
    PTO/belt horsepower 51.05
    Crankshaft rpm 1,650
    Fuel use (gal./hr.) 3.51
Maximum drawbar horsepower tests
    Gear 4th
    Drawbar horsepower 46.22
    Pull weight (lb.) 4,029
    Speed (mph) 4.30
    Percent slippage 10.02
SAE drawbar horsepower 35.37
SAE belt/PTO horsepower 45.26
Type ....standard
Front wheel (in.) ....7.50 x 16
Rear wheel (in.) ....14.00 x 34
Length (in.) 132
Height (in.) 79.50
Tread width (in.) 60–80
Weight (lb.) 5,900
Gear/speed (mph) ....forward: 1/1.52, 2/2.57, 3/3.53, 4/4.32, 5/5.95, 6/9.85; reverse: 1/2.10, 2/4.75

Cockshutt 50, CO-OP E5

Manufacturer ....Cockshutt Farm Equipment Co., Ltd., Brantford, Ontario, Canada
Nebraska test number 488
Test date ....October 29 to November 6, 1952
Test tractor serial number 50 142
Years produced 1952–1958
Serial number range ....101–40257 end
Serial number location ....stamped on right cast frame forward of transmission
Number produced 3,974
Engine ....Buda 6B 273 vertical I-head
Test engine serial number 355263
Cylinders 6
Bore and stroke (in.) ....3.75 x 4.125
Rated rpm 1,650
Compression ratio 6.6:1
Displacement (c.i.) 273
Fuel ....gasoline
Fuel tank capacity (gal.) 21
Carburetor ....Zenith 162J9, 1.125-in.
Air cleaner ....Donaldson
Ignition ....Auto-Lite with 6-v battery
Cooling capacity (gal.) 4.75
Maximum brake horsepower tests
    PTO/belt horsepower 55.56
    Crankshaft rpm 1,650
    Fuel use (gal./hr.) 5.00

Maximum drawbar horsepower tests
- Gear..4th
- Drawbar horsepower..........................51.59
- Pull weight (lb.)................................4,399
- Speed (mph)......................................4.40
- Percent slippage...............................7.96
- SAE drawbar horsepower.......................38.63
- SAE belt/PTO horsepower.......................49.14
- Type...standard
- Front wheel (in.)..................................7.50 x 16
- Rear wheel (in.)..................................14.00 x 34
- Length (in.)...132
- Height (in.)...79.50
- Tread width (in.).................................60–80
- Weight (lb.)...5,900
- Gear/speed (mph)..............................forward: 1/1.52, 2/2.57, 3/3.53, 4/4.32, 5/5.95, 6/9.85; reverse: 1/2.10, 2/4.75

Cockshutt 550 Diesel

- Manufacturer...................................Cockshutt Farm Equipment Ltd., Brantford, Ontario, Canada
- Nebraska test number.................................681
- Test date..November 12–26, 1958
- Test tractor serial number...........................BM 1699 D
- Years produced................................1958–1962
- Serial number range..........................BM1001 to BR1001 no end
- Serial number location ....stamped on right cast frame forward of transmission
- Number produced 2,930
- Engine...Hercules DD 198 vertical I-head
- Test engine serial number.........................3200 268
- Cylinders 4
- Bore and stroke (in.)...........................3.75 x 4.50
- Rated rpm 1,650
- Compression ratio................................17.8:1
- Displacement (c.i.)...............................198
- Fuel ....diesel
- Fuel tank capacity (gal.)........................19.25
- Carburetor...Bosch injector pump
- Air cleaner..Donaldson
- Ignition..Delco-Remy 12-v; with 2, 6-v battery
- Cooling capacity (gal.) 4.50

Maximum brake horsepower tests
- PTO/belt horsepower..........................38.45
- Crankshaft rpm 1,650
- Fuel use (gal./hr.).............................2.54

Maximum drawbar horsepower tests
- Gear..3rd
- Drawbar horsepower..........................34.97
- Pull weight (lb.)................................3,711
- Speed (mph)......................................3.53
- Percent slippage...............................6.15
- SAE drawbar horsepower.......................26.33
- SAE belt/PTO horsepower.......................34.15
- Type...standard

- Front wheel (in.)..................................6.00 x 16
- Rear wheel (in.)..................................13.00 x 38
- Height (in.)...85
- Tread width (in.).................................60
- Weight (lb.)...4,520
- Gear/speed (mph)..............................forward: 1/1.88, 2/2.50, 3/3.50, 4/4.88, 5/7.00, 6/13.50; reverse: 1/3.25, 2/6.25

Cockshutt 560 Diesel

- Manufacturer...................................Cockshutt Farm Equipment Ltd., Brantford, Ontario, Canada
- Nebraska test number.................................682
- Test date..November 10–26, 1958
- Test tractor serial number...........................CN 5121 D
- Years produced................................1958–1961
- Serial number range..........................CM1001 to CP1001 no end
- Serial number location ....stamped on right cast frame forward of transmission
- Number produced 2,910
- Engine...Perkins 270 D vertical I-head
- Test engine serial number.........................6072
- Cylinders 4
- Bore and stroke (in.)...........................4.25 x 4.75
- Rated rpm 1,650
- Compression ratio................................16:1
- Displacement (c.i.)...............................269.5
- Fuel ....diesel
- Fuel tank capacity (gal.)........................30
- Carburetor...C.A.V. injector pump
- Air cleaner..Donaldson
- Ignition..Delco-Remy 12-v; with 2, 6-v
- Cooling capacity (gal.) 3.80

Maximum brake horsepower tests
- PTO/belt horsepower..........................48.52
- Crankshaft rpm 1,651
- Fuel use (gal./hr.).............................2.74

Maximum drawbar horsepower tests
- Gear..3rd
- Drawbar horsepower..........................45.61
- Pull weight (lb.)................................5,228
- Speed (mph)......................................3.27
- Percent slippage...............................7.40
- SAE drawbar horsepower.......................34.99
- SAE belt/PTO horsepower.......................42.90
- Type...standard
- Front wheel (in.)..................................7.50 x 18
- Rear wheel (in.)..................................15.00 x 34
- Height (in.)...82
- Tread width (in.).................................64
- Weight (lb.)...5,122
- Gear/speed (mph)..............................forward: 1/1.81, 2/2.50, 3/3.45, 4/4.67, 5/6.94, 6/13.20; reverse: 1/3.19, 2/6.08

Cockshutt 570 Diesel

Manufacturer....................................Cockshutt Farm Equipment Ltd., Brantford, Ontario, Canada
Nebraska test number...............................683
Test date ....November 12–27, 1958
Test tractor serial number.........................DM 20920
Years produced 1958–1960
Serial number range................................DM1001 to DO7001 no end
Serial number location ....stamped on right cast frame forward of transmission
Number produced 3,100
Engine ....Hercules DD 298 vertical I-head
Test engine serial number..........................3401019
Cylinders 6
Bore and stroke (in.) ....3.75 x 4.50
Rated rpm 1,650
Compression ratio..................................17.8:1
Displacement (c.i.) 298
Fuel ....diesel
Fuel tank capacity (gal.) 30
Carburetor ....Bosch injector pump

Air cleaner ....Donaldson
Ignition...Delco-Remy 12-v; with 2, 6-v battery
Cooling capacity (gal.) 4.80

Maximum brake horsepower tests
    PTO/belt horsepower............................60.84
    Crankshaft rpm 1,650
    Fuel use (gal./hr.)............................4.05

Maximum drawbar horsepower tests
    Gear...4th
    Drawbar horsepower.............................52.25
    Pull weight (lb.)..............................4,266
    Speed (mph)....................................4.59
    Percent slippage...............................5.54
SAE drawbar horsepower.............................39.73
SAE belt/PTO horsepower............................54.11
Type ....standard
Front wheel (in.)..................................7.50 x 18
Rear wheel (in.)...................................15.00 x 34
Height (in.).......................................82
Tread width (in.)..................................64
Weight (lb.).......................................6,320
Gear/speed (mph) ....forward: 1/1.81, 2/2.50, 3/3.45, 4/4.67, 5/6.94, 6/13.20; reverse: 1/3.19, 2/6.08

Chapter 18

COLEMAN

Coleman B, 16-30

Manufacturer....................................Coleman Tractor Corp., Kansas City, MO
Nebraska test number 35
Test date ....July 16–21, 1920
Test tractor serial number.........................1182
Years produced 1919–1921
Engine ....Climax vertical L-head
Test engine serial number..........................2586
Cylinders 4
Bore and stroke (in.) ....5.00 x 6.50
Rated rpm 800–900
Displacement (c.i.) 510.5
Fuel ....kerosene/gasoline
Main tank capacity (gal.) 14
Auxiliary tank capacity (gal.) 4
Carburetor ....Bennett (Stromberg) 1.75-in.
Air cleaner ....Bennett
Ignition...Berling (Splitdorf 448 Aero) magneto
Cooling capacity (gal.) 10

Maximum brake horsepower tests
    PTO/belt horsepower............................30.41
    Crankshaft rpm 907
    Fuel use (gal./hr.)............................5.72

Maximum drawbar horsepower tests
    Gear...high
    Drawbar horsepower.............................15.87
    Pull weight (lb.)..............................1,802
    Speed (mph)....................................3.30
    Percent slippage...............................5.40
SAE drawbar horsepower.............................16
SAE belt/PTO horsepower............................30
Type ....4 wheel
Front wheel (in.)..................................steel: 34 x 4
Rear wheel (in.)...................................steel: 44 x 10
Length (in.) ....wheelbase: 86; total: 106
Height (in.).......................................66
Rear width (in.)...................................66
Weight (lb.).......................................5,100
Gear/speed (mph) ....forward: 1/2.00, 2/3.00; reverse: 1/1.50

Chapter 19
CONTINENTAL CULTOR

Continental Cultor 32

Manufacturer .... Continental Cultor Co., Springfield, OH
Nebraska test number 138
Test date .... August 6–17, 1927
Test tractor serial number 5099
Years produced 1927–1928
Engine .... Ford Model T vertical L-head
Test engine serial number 14688337
Cylinders 4
Bore and stroke (in.) .... 3.75 x 4.00
Rated rpm 1,050

Displacement (c.i.) 176.7
Fuel .... gasoline
Carburetor .... Holley-Ford
Ignition .... Ford Model T magneto
Maximum drawbar horsepower tests
    Drawbar horsepower 8.41
    Pull weight (lb.) 1,050
    Speed (mph) 3.01
    Percent slippage 11.70
Type .... 2 wheel
Weight (lb.) 1,690
Gear/speed (mph) .... forward: 1/3.00

Chapter 20
CORBITT

Corbitt G 50

Manufacturer .... The Corbitt Co., Henderson, NC
Nebraska test number 422
Test date .... August 29 to September 3, 1949
Test tractor serial number 5047
Years produced 1949–1952
Engine .... LeRoi D176 vertical I-head
Test engine serial number .... 25 x 4256
Cylinders 4
Bore and stroke (in.) .... 3.75 x 4.00
Rated rpm 1,800
Compression ratio 5.44:1
Displacement (c.i.) 176
Fuel .... gasoline
Fuel tank capacity (gal.) 12
Carburetor .... Zenith 62AJ9, 1.00-in.
Air cleaner .... United
Ignition .... Delco-Remy, 6-v battery
Cooling capacity (gal.) 16

Maximum brake horsepower tests
    PTO/belt horsepower 34.63
    Crankshaft rpm 1,799
    Fuel use (gal./hr.) 3.68
Maximum drawbar horsepower tests
    Gear 2nd
    Drawbar horsepower 30.74
    Pull weight (lb.) 2,766
    Speed (mph) 4.17
    Percent slippage 6.31
SAE drawbar horsepower 24.18
SAE belt/PTO horsepower 30.79
Type .... tricycle
Front tire (in.) .... 6.00 x 16
Rear tire (in.) .... 11.00 x 38
Length (in.) 128
Height (in.) 69.50
Tread width (in.) 56–84
Weight (lb.) 3,400
Gear/speed (mph) .... forward: 1/2.50, 2/3.60, 3/5.00, 4/10.00; reverse: 1/3.20

Chapter 21
DAVID BRADLEY

David Bradley General Purpose

Manufacturer...Bradley Tractor Co.,
Chicago, IL
Nebraska test number 192
Test date ....June 10–18, 1931
Test tractor serial number.........................281
Engine ....Waukesha XAK
vertical L-head
Test engine serial number.........................284570
Cylinders 4
Bore and stroke (in.) ....3.75 x 4.75
Rated rpm 1,250
Displacement (c.i.) 209.8
Fuel ....gasoline
Carburetor..Kingston Z, 1.00-in.
Air cleaner ....Pomona Vortox
Ignition...American Bosch U4
Ed4V3 magneto

Maximum brake horsepower tests
    PTO/belt horsepower............................24.96
    Crankshaft rpm 1,250
    Fuel use (gal./hr.) 2.71
Maximum drawbar horsepower tests
    Gear..2nd
    Drawbar horsepower............................20.05
    Pull weight (lb.).....................................2,728
    Speed (mph) 2.76
    Percent slippage..................................8.14
SAE drawbar horsepower...........................15.89
SAE belt/PTO horsepower..........................22.93
Type ....4 wheel, tricycle
Front wheel (in.) ....steel
Rear wheel (in.)...steel: 42 x 7
Weight (lb.) 4,000
Gear/speed (mph) ....forward: 1/1.75,
2/2.50, 3/3.00, 4/4.50;
reverse: 1/1.50, 2/2.00

David Bradley Garden Tractor

Manufacturer...David Bradley Mfg.
Works, Bradley, IL
Nebraska test number 456
Test date ....May 7–18, 1951
Test tractor serial number.........................276
Engine ....Briggs and Stratton
vertical L-head
Test engine serial number.........................1255927
Cylinders 1
Bore and stroke (in.) ....2.00 x 2.00
Rated rpm 3,200
Compression ratio.....................................5.86:1
Displacement (c.i.) 6.28
Fuel ....gasoline
Carburetor..0.50-in.
Ignition...magneto
Cooling...air

Maximum brake horsepower tests
    PTO/belt horsepower............................1.56
    Crankshaft rpm 3,201
    Fuel use (gal./hr.) 0.23
Maximum drawbar horsepower tests
    Gear..2nd
    Drawbar horsepower............................1.29
    Pull weight (lb.).....................................207
    Speed (mph) 2.33
    Percent slippage..................................2.63
SAE drawbar horsepower...........................1.01
SAE belt/PTO horsepower..........................1.40
Type ....garden, 2 wheel
Rear tire (in.)...6.00 x 16
Weight (lb.) 311
Gear/speed (mph) ....forward: 1/2.10, 2/2.40

David Bradley Super Power, Garden Tractor

Manufacturer...David Bradley Mfg.
Works, Bradley, IL
Nebraska test number 515
Test date ....November 16–20,
1953
Test tractor serial number.........................367912
Engine ....Briggs & Stratton
vertical L-head
Test engine serial number.........................367912
Cylinders 1
Bore and stroke (in.) ....2.25 x 2.00
Rated rpm 3,200
Compression ratio.....................................5.7:1
Displacement (c.i.) 7.95
Fuel ....gasoline
Fuel tank capacity (gal.) 2
Carburetor..0.50-in.
Ignition...magneto
Cooling...air

Maximum brake horsepower tests
    PTO/belt horsepower............................2.01
    Crankshaft rpm 3,204
    Fuel use (gal./hr.) 0.30
Maximum drawbar horsepower tests
    Gear..1st
    Drawbar horsepower............................1.64
    Pull weight (lb.).....................................268
    Speed (mph) 2.29
    Percent slippage..................................4.89
SAE drawbar horsepower...........................1.29
SAE belt/PTO horsepower..........................1.73
Type ....garden, 2 wheel
Front wheel (in.) ....6.00 x 16
Weight (lb.) 493
Gear/speed (mph) ....forward: 1/2.40

David Bradley Suburban, Garden Tractor

Manufacturer...David Bradley Mfg.
Works, Bradley, IL

Nebraska test number 729
Test date ....November 17 to
December 7, 1959
Test tractor serial number 4985
Engine ....Briggs & Stratton
vertical
Test engine serial number 48741
Cylinders 1
Bore and stroke (in.) ....2.75 x 2.375
Rated rpm 3,600
Compression ratio 5.6:1
Displacement (c.i.) 14.1
Fuel ....gasoline
Fuel tank capacity (gal.) 2
Carburetor ....0.75-in.
Ignition ....12-v battery
Cooling ....air
Maximum brake horsepower tests
    PTO/belt horsepower 3.90
    Crankshaft rpm 3,599
    Fuel use (gal./hr.) 0.62
Maximum drawbar horsepower tests
    Drawbar horsepower 2.80
    Pull weight (lb.) 431
    Speed (mph) 2.43
    Percent slippage...................................8.40
SAE drawbar horsepower...........................2.84
SAE belt/PTO horsepower 3.90
Type ....garden, 4 wheel
Front wheel (in.) ....4.80 or 4.00 x 8
Rear wheel (in.) ....6.00 x 12
Tread width (in.)..24–28
Weight (lb.) 450
Gear/speed (mph) ....forward: 1/2.10 to 4.60

David Bradley Super 575, Garden Tractor
Manufacturer...David Bradley Mfg.
Works, Bradley, IL
Nebraska test number 730
Test date ....November 19–28,
1959
Test tractor serial number 53796
Engine ....Briggs & Stratton
vertical
Test engine serial number 48743
Cylinders 1
Bore and stroke (in.) ....2.75 x 2.375
Rated rpm 3,600
Compression ratio 5.6:1
Displacement (c.i.) 14.1
Fuel ....gasoline
Fuel tank capacity (gal.) 2
Carburetor ....0.75-in.
Ignition ....magneto
Cooling ....air
Maximum brake horsepower tests
    PTO/belt horsepower 3.88
    Crankshaft rpm 3,600
    Fuel use (gal./hr.) 0.59
Maximum drawbar horsepower tests
    Drawbar horsepower 3.13
    Pull weight (lb.) 292
    Speed (mph) 4.02
    Percent slippage...................................4.34

SAE drawbar horsepower...........................2.57
SAE belt/PTO horsepower 3.88
Type ....garden, 2 wheel
Front wheel (in.) ....6.70 x 15
Tread width (in.)..20–27
Weight (lb.) 375
Gear/speed (mph) ....forward: 1/2.50 to 4.75

David Bradley Super 300, Garden Tractor
Manufacturer...David Bradley Mfg.
Works, Bradley, IL
Nebraska test number 731
Test date ....November 19 to
December 7, 1959
Test tractor serial number 55126
Engine ....Briggs & Stratton
vertical
Test engine serial number 5910190
Cylinders 1
Bore and stroke (in.) ....2.375 x 1.75
Rated rpm 3,600
Compression ratio 6.2:1
Displacement (c.i.) 7.75
Fuel ....gasoline
Fuel tank capacity (gal.) 2
Carburetor ....0.50-in.
Ignition ....magneto
Cooling ....air
Maximum brake horsepower tests
    PTO/belt horsepower 1.77
    Crankshaft rpm 3,600
    Fuel use (gal./hr.) 0.38
Maximum drawbar horsepower tests
    Drawbar horsepower 1.65
    Pull weight (lb.) 241
    Speed (mph) 2.57
    Percent slippage...................................3.23
SAE drawbar horsepower...........................1.75
SAE belt/PTO horsepower 1.77
Type ....garden, 2 wheel
Front wheel (in.) ....6.70 x 15
Tread width (in.)..20–27
Weight (lb.) 334
Gear/speed (mph) ....forward: 1/2.70

David Bradley Handiman, Garden Tractor
Manufacturer...David Bradley Mfg.
Works, Bradley, IL
Nebraska test number 732
Test date ....November 30 to
December 9, 1959
Test tractor serial number 26553
Engine ....Briggs & Stratton
vertical
Test engine serial number 910200
Cylinders 1
Bore and stroke (in.) ....2.375 x 1.75
Rated rpm 3,600
Compression ratio 6.2:1
Displacement (c.i.) 7.75
Fuel ....gasoline
Fuel tank capacity (gal.) 1
Carburetor ....0.50-in.
Ignition ....magneto

Cooling..air
Maximum brake horsepower tests
    PTO/belt horsepower..........................2.19
    Crankshaft rpm 3,600
    Fuel use (gal./hr.)............................0.32
Maximum drawbar horsepower tests
    Drawbar horsepower............................0.69
    Pull weight (lb.)..................................115
    Speed (mph) 2.24
    Percent slippage..............................14.18

SAE drawbar horsepower...........................0.65
SAE belt/PTO horsepower 2.19
Type ....garden, 2 wheel
Front wheel (in.)....................................3.00 x 12
Tread width (in.)....................................15.50
Weight (lb.) 152
Gear/speed (mph) ....forward: 1/0.60, 2/2.50;
    reverse: 1/0.30, 2/1.40

Chapter 22
DAVID BROWN

David Brown 25
Manufacturer..David Brown Tractors Ltd., Meltham, Huddersfield, England
Nebraska test number 530
Test date ....November 1–6, 1954
Test tractor serial number P25 15803
Years produced 1958
Serial number location ....stamped on top right side front bolster
Engine ....David Brown vertical I-head
Test engine serial number...........................AG4/3/3.5/7617
Cylinders 4
Bore and stroke (in.) ....3.50 x 4.00
Rated rpm 2,000
Compression ratio....................................7.0:1
Displacement (c.i.) 154
Fuel ....gasoline
Carburetor..30 mm
Ignition..12-v battery
Maximum brake horsepower tests
    PTO/belt horsepower..........................34.89
    Crankshaft rpm 2,000
    Fuel use (gal./hr.)............................3.28
Maximum drawbar horsepower tests
    Gear...3rd
    Drawbar horsepower............................25.91
    Pull weight (lb.)..................................2,868
    Speed (mph) 3.39
    Percent slippage..............................12.43
SAE drawbar horsepower...........................20.02
SAE belt/PTO horsepower 30.47
Type ....Standard
Front wheel (in.)......................................tire, 6.00 x 19
Rear wheel (in.).......................................tire, 11.00 x 28
Weight (lb.) 3,556

Gear/speed (mph) ....forward: 1/1.53, 2/2.84, 3/3.77, 4/5.64, 5/7.00, 6/13.90; reverse: 1/2.46, 2/6.08

David Brown 950 Diesel
Manufacturer..David Brown Ind. Ltd., Yorkshire, England
Nebraska test number 691
Test date ....March 10–18, 1959
Test tractor serial number T950D 57529
Years produced 1959
Serial number location ....stamped on top right side front bolster
Engine ....David Brown AD4/40T vertical L-head
Test engine serial number...........................AD 4/40T 489
Cylinders 4
Bore and stroke (in.) ....3.625 x 4.00
Rated rpm 2,200
Compression ratio....................................17:1
Displacement (c.i.) 165
Fuel ....diesel
Carburetor..injector pump, C.A.V.
Air cleaner ....AC
Ignition..Lucas, 12-v; with 2, 6-v battery
Maximum brake horsepower tests
    PTO/belt horsepower..........................39.85
    Crankshaft rpm 2,200
    Fuel use (gal./hr.)............................2.79
Maximum drawbar horsepower tests
    Gear...4th
    Drawbar horsepower............................35.28
    Pull weight (lb.)..................................2,624
    Speed (mph) 5.04
    Percent slippage..............................6.92

SAE drawbar horsepower............................36.26
SAE belt/PTO horsepower 39.85
Type ....Standard
Front wheel (in.).....................................6.00 x 16
Rear wheel (in.)......................................13.00 x 28
Height (in.)...78.50
Tread width (in.).......................................52–76
Weight (lb.)..4,230
Gear/speed (mph) ....forward: 1/1.58,
2/2.69, 3/3.53, 4/4.79,
5/6.01, 6/10.70;
reverse: 1/2.65, 2/5.93

David Brown 850 Diesel
Manufacturer...David Brown Ind. Ltd.,
Yorkshire, England
Nebraska test number 734
Test date ....March 12–26, 1960
Test tractor serial number.........................2A 850L
Years produced 1960
Serial number location ....stamped on top right
side front bolster
Engine ....David Brown AD-4/36A
vertical L-head
Test engine serial number.........................AD4/36A 106
Cylinders 4
Bore and stroke (in.) ....3.50 x 4.00
Rated rpm 2,000
Compression ratio....................................17:1
Displacement (c.i.) 154
Fuel ....diesel
Carburetor ....injector pump, C.A.V.
Air cleaner ....AC
Ignition...Lucas, 12-v; with 2,
6-v battery

Maximum brake horsepower tests
 PTO/belt horsepower............................33.56
 Crankshaft rpm 2,000
 Fuel use (gal./hr.) 2.16
Maximum drawbar horsepower tests
 Gear...3rd
 Drawbar horsepower.............................30.93
 Pull weight (lb.)...................................2,536
 Speed (mph) 4.57
 Percent slippage..................................7.57
SAE drawbar horsepower...........................31.84
SAE belt/PTO horsepower 33.56
Type ....Standard
Front wheel (in.).....................................5.50 x 16
Rear wheel (in.)......................................11.00 x 28
Height (in.)...81.44

Tread width (in.).......................................52–76
Weight (lb.)..3,650
Gear/speed (mph) ....forward: 1/2.17,
2/3.60, 3/4.86, 4/6.58,
5/8.06, 6/14.70;
reverse: 1/3.58, 2/8.00

David Brown 850
Manufacturer...David Brown Ind. Ltd.,
Yorkshire, England
Nebraska test number 735
Test date ....March 14 to April 2,
1960
Test tractor serial number.........................2A 850
Years produced 1960
Serial number location ....stamped on top right
side front bolster
Engine ....David Brown UAG-
4/36A vertical L-head
Test engine serial number.........................UAG/36A 106
Cylinders 4
Bore and stroke (in.) ....3.50 x 4.00
Rated rpm 2,000
Compression ratio....................................6.25:1
Displacement (c.i.) 154
Fuel ....gasoline
Carburetor ....Solex 30F.V., 30 mm
Air cleaner ....AC
Ignition...Lucas, 12-v battery
Maximum brake horsepower tests
 PTO/belt horsepower............................32.00
 Crankshaft rpm 2,000
 Fuel use (gal./hr.) 3.00
Maximum drawbar horsepower tests
 Gear...3rd
 Drawbar horsepower.............................27.64
 Pull weight (lb.)...................................2,253
 Speed (mph) 4.60
 Percent slippage..................................5.78
SAE drawbar horsepower...........................28.90
SAE belt/PTO horsepower 32.00
Type ....Standard
Front wheel (in.).....................................5.50 x 16
Rear wheel (in.)......................................11.00 x 28
Height (in.)...81.44
Tread width (in.).......................................52–76
Weight (lb.)..3,550
Gear/speed (mph) ....forward: 1/2.17,
2/3.60, 3/4.86, 4/6.58,
5/8.06, 6/14.70;
reverse: 1/3.58, 2/8.00

Chapter 23

DODGE POWER WAGON

Dodge Power Wagon T137

Manufacturer	Chrysler Corp., Detroit, MI
Nebraska test number	454
Test date	November 13–21, 1950
Test tractor serial number	83920188
Engine	Chrysler, Ind. 6A vertical L-head
Test engine serial number	T137 20265
Cylinders	6
Bore and stroke (in.)	3.25 x 4.625
Rated rpm	1,700
Compression ratio	6.7:1
Displacement (c.i.)	230.2
Fuel	gasoline
Carburetor	na, 1.50-in.
Ignition	na, 6-v battery

Maximum brake horsepower tests

PTO/belt horsepower	42.40
Crankshaft rpm	1,701
Fuel use (gal./hr.)	4.91

Maximum drawbar horsepower tests

Gear	3rd
Drawbar horsepower	40.02
Pull weight (lb.)	3,267
Speed (mph)	4.59
Percent slippage	4.40
SAE drawbar horsepower	30.41
SAE belt/PTO horsepower	36.77
Type	4 wheel drive
Front wheel (in.)	tire, 9.00 x 16
Rear wheel (in.)	tire, 9.00 x 16
Weight (lb.)	5,634
Gear/speed (mph)	forward: 1/4.00, 2/8.00, 3/9.00, 4/18.00, 5/16.00, 6/32.00, 7/28.00, 8/54.00; reverse: 1/4.00, 2/7.00

Chapter 24

EAGLE

Eagle 16-30, H

Manufacturer	Eagle Manufacturing Co., Appleton, WI
Nebraska test number	80
Test date	August 17–25, 1921
Test tractor serial number	1037
Years produced	1916–1932
Engine	Eagle horizontal, valve-in-head
Test engine serial number	1037
Cylinders	2
Bore and stroke (in.)	8.00 x 8.00
Rated rpm	500
Displacement (c.i.)	804.2
Fuel	kerosene/gasoline
Main tank capacity (gal.)	18
Auxiliary tank capacity (gal.)	5
Carburetor	Schebler A, 1.75-in.
Air cleaner	Eagle
Ignition	Splitdorf Dixie 462 magneto
Cooling capacity (gal.)	15

Maximum brake horsepower tests

PTO/belt horsepower	31.80
Crankshaft rpm	503
Fuel use (gal./hr.)	4.24

Maximum drawbar horsepower tests

Gear	low
Drawbar horsepower	19.97
Pull weight (lb.)	3,615
Speed (mph)	2.07
Percent slippage	6.78
SAE drawbar horsepower	16
SAE belt/PTO horsepower	30
Type	4 wheel
Front wheel (in.)	steel: 32 x 8
Rear wheel (in.)	steel: 52 x 12
Length (in.)	141
Height (in.)	78
Rear width (in.)	70
Weight (lb.)	7,100
Gear/speed (mph)	forward: 1/2.00, 2/3.00; reverse: 1/1.75

Eagle 12-22, F

Manufacturer ....Eagle Manufacturing
Co., Appleton, WI
Nebraska test number 81
Test date ....August 18 to
September 21, 1921
Test tractor serial number 1023
Years produced 1918–1924
Engine ....Eagle horizontal,
valve-in-head
Test engine serial number 1023
Cylinders 2
Bore and stroke (in.) ....7.00 x 8.00
Rated rpm 500
Displacement (c.i.) 615.8
Fuel ....kerosene/gasoline
Main tank capacity (gal.) 12
Auxiliary tank capacity (gal.) 4
Carburetor ....Schebler A, 1.50-in.
Air cleaner ....Eagle
Ignition ....Splitdorf, Dixie 462
magneto
Cooling capacity (gal.) 12
Maximum brake horsepower tests
PTO/belt horsepower 23.35
Crankshaft rpm 503
Fuel use (gal./hr.) 3.18
Maximum drawbar horsepower tests
Gear ....low
Drawbar horsepower 14.75
Pull weight (lb.) 2,715
Speed (mph) 2.04
Percent slippage 7.30
SAE drawbar horsepower 12
SAE belt/PTO horsepower 22
Type ....4 wheel
Front wheel (in.) ....steel: 28 x 6
Rear wheel (in.) ....steel: 48 x 12
Length (in.) 132
Height (in.) 76
Rear width (in.) 65
Weight (lb.) 5,850
Gear/speed (mph) ....forward: 1/2.00,
2/3.00; reverse: 1/1.75

Eagle 6A

Manufacturer ....Eagle Manufacturing
Co., Appleton, WI
Nebraska test number 184
Test date ....October 21 to
November 1, 1939
Test tractor serial number 2216
Years produced 1930–1938
Serial number range ....1987–2457 no end
Engine ....Hercules WXC vertical
L-head
Test engine serial number 162415
Cylinders 6
Bore and stroke (in.) ....4.00 x 4.50
Rated rpm 1,416
Displacement (c.i.) 339.3
Fuel ....gasoline
Fuel tank capacity (gal.) 30
Carburetor ....Zenith 96ATO, 1.50-in.
Air cleaner ....Vortox
Ignition ....Splitdorf (American
Bosch U6) magneto
Cooling capacity (gal.) 8.50
Maximum brake horsepower tests
PTO/belt horsepower 40.36
Crankshaft rpm 1,417
Fuel use (gal./hr.) 4.30
Maximum drawbar horsepower tests
Gear 2nd
Drawbar horsepower 29.52
Pull weight (lb.) 3,282
Speed (mph) 3.37
Percent slippage 11.38
SAE drawbar horsepower 22.17
SAE belt/PTO horsepower 37.09
Type ....4 wheel
Front wheel (in.) ....steel: 30 x 6
Rear wheel (in.) ....steel: 48 x 12
Length (in.) 134
Height (in.) 61
Rear width (in.) 70
Weight (lb.) 5,000
Gear/speed (mph) ....forward: 1/2.50, 2/3.33,
3/4.50; reverse: 1/2.50

Chapter 25
ECONOMY SPECIAL

Economy Special, Garden Tractor

Manufacturer .... Engineering Products Co., Waukesha, WI
Nebraska test number 483
Test date .... September 20–27, 1952
Engine .... Briggs & Stratton 23FB vertical L-head
Test engine serial number 138957
Cylinders 1
Bore and stroke (in.) .... 3.00 x 3.25
Rated rpm 3,200
Compression ratio 5.40:1
Displacement (c.i.) 22.97
Fuel .... gasoline
Fuel tank capacity (gal.) 2
Carburetor .... 23/32-in.
Ignition .... magneto
Cooling .... air

Maximum brake horsepower tests
  PTO/belt horsepower 6.23
  Crankshaft rpm 3,201
  Fuel use (gal./hr.) 0.84

Maximum drawbar horsepower tests
  Gear 2nd
  Drawbar horsepower 5.70
  Pull weight (lb.) 491
  Speed (mph) 4.35
  Percent slippage 4.82
SAE drawbar horsepower 4.43
SAE belt/PTO horsepower 5.54
Type .... garden, 4 wheel
Front wheel (in.) .... 3.00 x 12
Rear wheel (in.) .... 7.00 x 24
Length (in.) 83
Height (in.) 43
Rear width (in.) 40
Tread width (in.) 33–45
Weight (lb.) 770
Gear/speed (mph) .... forward: 1/2.25, 2/4.50, 3/8.00; reverse: 1/2.25

Chapter 26
EIMCO

Eimco 105

Manufacturer .... The Eimco Corp., Salt Lake City, UT
Nebraska test number 628
Test date .... July 26 to August 2, 1957
Test tractor serial number 1050590
Years produced 1953–1961
Serial number range .... 1050001–1051279 no end
Number produced .... approximately 1,279
Engine .... GM 4-71 vertical I-head
Test engine serial number 4A 64401
Cylinders 4
Bore and stroke (in.) .... 4.25 x 5.00
Rated rpm 2,000
Compression ratio 17:1
Displacement (c.i.) 283.7
Fuel .... diesel
Fuel tank capacity (gal.) 60
Air cleaner .... Vortox

Ignition .... Delco-Remy, 12-v battery
Cooling capacity (gal.) 7.50

Maximum drawbar horsepower tests
  Gear .... 2nd, low range
  Drawbar horsepower 72.29
  Pull weight (lb.) 12,146
  Speed (mph) 2.23
  Percent slippage 1.93
SAE drawbar horsepower 72.29
Type .... tracklayer
Height (in.) 114
Tread width (in.) 74
Weight (lb.) 28,000
Track length (in.) 302
Grouser shoe .... 40 links; 20-in.
Gear/speed (mph) .... forward: high range/0–5.45, low range/0–2.27; reverse: high range/0–5.45, low range/0–2.27

Chapter 27
ELLINWOOD

Ellinwood Bear Cat, 3000-1, Garden Tractor

Manufacturer	Ellinwood Industries, Los Angeles, CA
Nebraska test number	379
Test date	July 22 to August 8, 1946
Test tractor serial number	46-3-5814
Engine	Lauson vertical L-head
Test engine serial number	533097
Cylinders	1
Bore and stroke (in.)	2.25 x 2.25
Rated rpm	3,300
Displacement (c.i.)	8.9
Fuel	gasoline
Fuel tank capacity (gal.)	2
Carburetor	(Tillotson Ms-74J, 0.50-in.) Lausen, 0.75
Air cleaner	United
Ignition	(Eisemann 71-R); Lausen magneto
Cooling	air

Maximum brake horsepower tests

PTO/belt horsepower	2.19
Crankshaft rpm	3,299
Fuel use (gal./hr.)	0.32

Maximum drawbar horsepower tests

Gear	1st
Drawbar horsepower	1.77
Pull weight (lb.)	350
Speed (mph)	1.90
Percent slippage	6.31
SAE drawbar horsepower	1.42
SAE belt/PTO horsepower	1.96
Type	garden, 2 wheel
Front tire (in.)	5.50 x 16
Weight (lb.)	316
Gear/speed (mph)	forward: 1/.50–3.00

Ellinwood Tiger Cat, Garden Tractor

Manufacturer	Ellinwood Industries, Los Angeles, CA
Nebraska test number	390
Test date	November 11 to December 1, 1947
Test tractor serial number	47-T-1092
Engine	Ellinwood
Type	45-degree angle, L-head
Test engine serial number	6210
Cylinders	1
Bore and stroke (in.)	2.625 x 2.625
Rated rpm	3,200
Displacement (c.i.)	14.2
Fuel	gasoline
Fuel tank capacity (gal.)	2
Carburetor	Bendix Stromberg 427078, 0.625-in.
Air cleaner	Air Maze
Ignition	Bendix-Scintilla K 1-7 magneto

Maximum brake horsepower tests

PTO/belt horsepower	4.30
Crankshaft rpm	3,198
Fuel use (gal./hr.)	0.54

Maximum drawbar horsepower tests

Gear	1st
Drawbar horsepower	2.63
Pull weight (lb.)	397
Speed (mph)	2.48
Percent slippage	6.35
SAE drawbar horsepower	2.04
SAE belt/PTO horsepower	3.80
Type	garden, 2 wheel
Rear tire (in.)	5.50 x 16
Weight (lb.)	378
Gear/speed (mph)	forward: 1/2.50

Chapter 28

EMERSON-BRANTINGHAM

Emerson-Brantingham E-B, 12-20 AA

Manufacturer..Emerson-Brantingham Implement Co., Rockford, IL
Nebraska test number...................................20
Test date..August 27 to September 3, 1920
Test tractor serial number...........................33815-D
Years produced..1917–1928
Engine..Emerson-Brantingham vertical L-head
Test engine serial number...........................59835
Cylinders...4
Bore and stroke (in.).....................................4.75 x 5.00
Rated rpm..900
Displacement (c.i.)..354.4
Fuel..kerosene/gasoline
Main tank capacity (gal.)..............................20
Auxiliary tank capacity (gal.).......................4
Carburetor..Bennett (Stromberg M3), 1.50-in.
Air cleaner..Bennett
Ignition..K-W TK magneto
Cooling capacity (gal.)..................................10

Maximum brake horsepower tests
    PTO/belt horsepower.............................25.90
    Crankshaft rpm 915.5
    Fuel use (gal./hr.)..................................3.53
Maximum drawbar horsepower tests
    Gear..low
    Drawbar horsepower..............................17.55
    Pull weight (lb.)....................................3,022
    Speed (mph)...2.18
    Percent slippage...................................10.40
SAE drawbar horsepower..............................12
SAE belt/PTO horsepower.............................20
Type...4 wheel
Front wheel (in.)...steel: 36 x 6
Rear wheel (in.)..steel: 54 x 12
Length (in.)..wheelbase: 87; total: 132
Height (in.)...75.25
Rear width (in.)..61
Weight (lb.)..4,365
Gear/speed (mph)...forward: 1/2.10, 2/2.77; reverse: 1/2.01

Chapter 29

FARMASTER

Farmaster FD 33

Manufacturer..Farmaster Corp., Clifton, NJ
Nebraska test number...................................419
Test date..August 3–15, 1949
Years produced..1949–1951
Engine..Buda 4BD-153 vertical I-head
Test engine serial number...........................45438
Cylinders...4
Bore and stroke (in.).....................................3.4375 x 4.125
Rated rpm..1,650
Compression ratio..15:1
Displacement (c.i.)..153
Fuel..diesel
Fuel tank capacity (gal.)...............................15
Carburetor..Bosch injector pump
Air cleaner..Donaldson
Ignition..Auto-Lite with 12-v; with 2, 6-v battery

Cooling capacity (gal.)..................................3.50
Maximum brake horsepower tests
    PTO/belt horsepower.............................23.59
    Crankshaft rpm 1,650
    Fuel use (gal./hr.)..................................1.92
Maximum drawbar horsepower tests
    Gear..2nd
    Drawbar horsepower..............................21.93
    Pull weight (lb.)....................................2,130
    Speed (mph)...3.86
    Percent slippage...................................5.78
SAE drawbar horsepower..............................17.42
SAE belt/PTO horsepower.............................21.45
Type...tricycle
Front tire (in.)...5.50 x 16
Rear tire (in.)..11.00 x 38
Length (in.)..132
Height (in.)...60
Tread width (in.)...56–84
Weight (lb.)..3,350

Gear/speed (mph) ....forward: 1/2.75,
2/4.00, 3/5.50,
4/11.00; reverse:
1/3.50

Farmaster FG 33

Manufacturer...Farmaster Corp.,
Clifton, NJ
Nebraska test number 421
Test date ....August 3–23, 1949
Years produced 1949–1951
Engine ....Buda 4B153
vertical I-head
Test engine serial number 318238
Cylinders 4
Bore and stroke (in.) ....3.4375 x 4.125
Rated rpm 1,650
Compression ratio..6.18:1
Displacement (c.i.) 153
Fuel ....gasoline
Fuel tank capacity (gal.) 15
Carburetor ....Zenith 162J9, 1.00-in.
Air cleaner ....Donaldson
Ignition..Delco-Remy,
6-v battery

Cooling capacity (gal.) 3.50
Maximum brake horsepower tests
PTO/belt horsepower.............................28.36
Crankshaft rpm 1,650
Fuel use (gal./hr.)..................................2.91
Maximum drawbar horsepower tests
Gear..2nd
Drawbar horsepower..............................25.26
Pull weight (lb.)......................................2,519
Speed (mph) 3.76
Percent slippage....................................7.88
SAE drawbar horsepower............................19.83
SAE belt/PTO horsepower...........................25.44
Type ....tricycle
Front tire (in.)..5.50 x 16
Rear tire (in.)..11.00 x 38
Length (in.) 132
Height (in.) 60
Tread width (in.)..56–84
Weight (lb.) 3,200
Gear/speed (mph) ....forward: 1/2.75,
2/4.00, 3/5.50,
4/11.00; reverse:
1/3.50

Chapter 30

FERGUSON

Ferguson TE-20

Manufacturer...Harry Ferguson Ltd.,
Coventry, England
Nebraska test number 392
Test date ....April 26 to May 10,
1948
Test tractor serial number ....TE 20817
Years produced 1947–1951
Serial number range.....................................316–172500 end
Serial number location ....stamped on instrument
panel nameplate
Number produced 172,185
Engine ....Continental Z 120
vertical I-head
Test engine serial number Z120 16627
Cylinders 4
Bore and stroke (in.) ....3.1875 x 3.75
Rated rpm 1,750
Displacement (c.i.) 119.7
Fuel ....gasoline
Fuel tank capacity (gal.) 10
Carburetor ....Marvel-Schebler TXC-
312, 0.875-in.
Air cleaner ....Donaldson or Vortox
Ignition..Delco-Remy,
6-v battery
Cooling capacity (gal.) 2.50

Maximum brake horsepower tests
PTO/belt horsepower.............................25.41
Crankshaft rpm 1,998
Fuel use (gal./hr.)..................................2.53
Maximum drawbar horsepower tests
Gear..2nd
Drawbar horsepower..............................20.70
Pull weight (lb.)......................................2,146
Speed (mph) 3.62
Percent slippage....................................6.35
SAE drawbar horsepower............................16.33
SAE belt/PTO horsepower...........................22.53
Type ....standard
Front tire (in.)..4.00 x 19
Rear tire (in.)..10.00 x 28
Length (in.) 115
Height (in.) 51.75
Rear width (in.) 63.50
Tread width (in.)..48–80
Weight (lb.) 2,585
Gear/speed (mph) ....forward: 1/2.90, 2/3.99,
3/5.50, 4/11.49; reverse:
1/3.35

Ferguson TO-30

Manufacturer...Harry Ferguson, Inc.,
Detroit, MI

Nebraska test number 466
Test date ....October 5–11, 1951
Test tractor serial number ....TO 60540
Years produced 1951–1954
Serial number range ....60001–140000 end
Serial number location ....stamped on instrument panel nameplate
Number produced 80,000
Engine ....Continental Z129 vertical I-head
Test engine serial number Z129 300004
Cylinders 4
Bore and stroke (in.) ....3.25 x 3.875
Rated rpm 1,750
Compression ratio 6.5:1
Displacement (c.i.) 129
Fuel ....gasoline
Fuel tank capacity (gal.) 10
Carburetor ....Marvel-Schebler TSX-458, 0.875-in.
Air cleaner ....Donaldson or Vortox
Ignition ....Delco-Remy with 6-v battery
Cooling capacity (gal.) 2.50
Maximum brake horsepower tests
    PTO/belt horsepower 29.32
    Crankshaft rpm 2,001
    Fuel use (gal./hr.) 2.70
Maximum drawbar horsepower tests
    Gear 2nd
    Drawbar horsepower 24.37
    Pull weight (lb.) 2,371
    Speed (mph) 3.85
    Percent slippage 8.86
SAE drawbar horsepower 18.93
SAE belt/PTO horsepower 25.73
Type ....standard
Front tire (in.) ....6.00 x 16
Rear tire (in.) ....11.00 x 28
Length (in.) 115
Height (in.) 51.75
Tread width (in.) 48–76
Weight (lb.) 2,480
Gear/speed (mph) ....forward: 1/2.90, 2/4.00, 3/5.50, 4/11.48; reverse: 1/3.35

Ferguson TO-35

Manufacturer ....Massey-Harris-Ferguson Inc., Detroit, MI
Nebraska test number 564
Test date ....October 10–17, 1955
Test tractor serial number ....TO 157535
Years produced 1954–1959
Serial number range ....TO 140001 to TO 201273 end
Serial number location ....stamped on instrument panel nameplate
Number produced ....61,273, all types interspersed
Engine ....Continental Z134 vertical I-head
Test engine serial number Z134 600323

Cylinders 4
Bore and stroke (in.) ....3.3125 x 3.875
Rated rpm 2,000
Compression ratio 6.6:1
Displacement (c.i.) 134
Fuel ....gasoline
Fuel tank capacity (gal.) 13.90
Carburetor ....Marvel Schebler TSX-605, 0.875-in.
Air cleaner ....Donaldson
Ignition ....Delco-Remy with 6-v battery
Cooling capacity (gal.) 2.25
Maximum brake horsepower tests
    PTO/belt horsepower 33.24
    Crankshaft rpm 2,001
    Fuel use (gal./hr.) 3.09
Maximum drawbar horsepower tests
    Gear 4th
    Drawbar horsepower 30.51
    Pull weight (lb.) 2,516
    Speed (mph) 4.55
    Percent slippage 7.49
SAE drawbar horsepower 23.76
SAE belt/PTO horsepower 29.33
Type ....standard
Front wheel (in.) ....6.00 x 16
Rear wheel (in.) ....11.00 x 28
Length (in.) 116.75
Height (in.) 54.25
Tread width (in.) 48–76
Weight (lb.) 2,792
Gear/speed (mph) ....forward: 1/1.23, 2/1.84, 3/3.37, 4/4.90, 5/7.36, 6/13.49; reverse: 1/1.64, 2/6.55

Ferguson 40, F-40

Manufacturer ....Massey-Harris-Ferguson Inc., Detroit, MI
Nebraska test number 596
Test date ....September 27 to October 2, 1956
Test tractor serial number ....SGM 401451
Years produced 1956–1957
Serial number range ....400001–409097 end
Serial number location ....stamped on instrument panel nameplate
Number produced 9,097
Engine ....Continental Z-134 vertical I-head
Test engine serial number Z134 640289
Cylinders 4
Bore and stroke (in.) ....3.3125 x 3.875
Rated rpm 2,000
Compression ratio 6.6:1
Displacement (c.i.) 134
Fuel ....gasoline
Fuel tank capacity (gal.) 13.90
Carburetor ....Marvel-Schebler TSX-605, 0.875-in.
Air cleaner ....Donaldson
Ignition ....Delco-Remy with 12-v battery
Cooling capacity (gal.) 2.25

Maximum brake horsepower tests
PTO/belt horsepower............................32.80
Crankshaft rpm 2,000
Fuel use (gal./hr.) 3.10
Maximum drawbar horsepower tests
Gear...4th
Drawbar horsepower............................30.84
Pull weight (lb.)...................................2,290
Speed (mph) 5.05
Percent slippage.................................6.08
SAE drawbar horsepower........................23.75
SAE belt/PTO horsepower........................29.09
Type ....standard
Front wheel (in.).....................................6.00 x 16
Rear wheel (in.).......................................11.00 x 28
Height (in.)...57
Tread width (in.).......................................48–76
Weight (lb.) 3,282
Gear/speed (mph) ....forward: 1/1.33,
2/1.99, 3/3.65, 4/5.30,
5/7.96, 6/14.59;
reverse: 1/1.77, 2/7.09

Ferguson TO-35 Diesel
Manufacturer...Massey-Ferguson Inc.,
Detroit, MI
Nebraska test number 690
Test date ....April 3–13, 1959
Test tractor serial number.........................SDM 183757
Years produced 1958–1959
Serial number range.................................TO 180742 to TO
201273 end
Serial number location ....stamped on instrument
panel nameplate
Number produced 20,532
Engine ....standard motor 23-C
vertical L-head

Test engine serial number......................SJ 70122 E
Cylinders 4
Bore and stroke (in.) ....3.3125 x 4.00
Rated rpm 2,000
Compression ratio....................................20.0:1
Displacement (c.i.) 137.8
Fuel ....diesel/gasoline
Fuel tank capacity (gal.) 10.8
Carburetor...C.A.V. injector pump
Air cleaner ....Donaldson
Ignition..Delco-Remy with 12-v;
with 2, 6-v battery
Cooling capacity (gal.) 2.63
Maximum brake horsepower tests
PTO/belt horsepower............................32.93
Crankshaft rpm 2,000
Fuel use (gal./hr.) 2.25
Maximum drawbar horsepower tests
Gear...4th
Drawbar horsepower............................30.49
Pull weight (lb.)...................................2,282
Speed (mph) 5.01
Percent slippage.................................6.44
SAE drawbar horsepower........................30.49
SAE belt/PTO horsepower........................32.93
Type ....standard
Front wheel (in.).....................................6.00 x 16
Rear wheel (in.).......................................11.00 x 28
Height (in.)...57
Tread width (in.).......................................48–76
Weight (lb.) 3,200
Gear/speed (mph) ....forward: 1/1.33,
2/1.99, 3/3.64, 4/5.32,
5/7.96, 6/14.57;
reverse: 1/1.77, 2/7.09

Chapter 31
FIAT

Fiat 411-R, Diesel
Manufacturer...Fiat S.P.A., Turin, Italy
Nebraska test number 707
Test date ....June 29 to
July 13, 1959
Test tractor serial number.........................402137
Years produced 1959–1963
Serial number range.................................401980–430155 no
end
Number produced ....approximately 30,000
Engine ....Fiat 615.000 vertical
L-head
Test engine serial number.........................002996
Cylinders 4
Bore and stroke (in.) ....3.35 x 3.94
Rated rpm 2,300

Compression ratio....................................21.5:1
Displacement (c.i.) 138.5
Fuel ....diesel
Ignition..24-v; with 2,
12-v battery
Maximum brake horsepower tests
PTO/belt horsepower............................36.75
Crankshaft rpm 2,300
Fuel use (gal./hr.) 2.86
Maximum drawbar horsepower tests
Gear...4th
Drawbar horsepower............................32.37
Pull weight (lb.)...................................2,596
Speed (mph) 4.68
Percent slippage.................................3.66
SAE drawbar horsepower........................33.24

SAE belt/PTO horsepower 36.75
Type .... standard
Front wheel (in.) .... 6.00 x 16
Rear wheel (in.) .... 11.00 x 28
Height (in.) 54
Tread width (in.) 47.25–74.88
Weight (lb.) 3,040
Gear/speed (mph) .... forward: 1/1.4, 2/2.5, 3/3.9, 4/5.0, 5/9.0, 6/14.2; reverse: 1/2.00, 2/7.30

Fiat 411-C, Diesel

Manufacturer .... Fiat S.P.A., Turin, Italy
Nebraska test number 708
Test date .... June 30 to July 13, 1959
Test tractor serial number 000696
Years produced 1958–1965
Serial number range .... 1–16906 no end
Engine .... Fiat 615.010 vertical L-head
Test engine serial number 002526
Cylinders 4
Bore and stroke (in.) .... 3.35 x 3.94
Rated rpm 2,300
Compression ratio 21.5:1
Displacement (c.i.) 138.5
Fuel .... diesel
Ignition .... 24-v; with 2, 12-v battery

Maximum brake horsepower tests
   PTO/belt horsepower 37.33
   Crankshaft rpm 2,300
   Fuel use (gal./hr.) 2.85
Maximum drawbar horsepower tests
   Gear 4th
   Drawbar horsepower 28.34
   Pull weight (lb.) 3,230
   Speed (mph) 3.29
   Percent slippage 3.42
SAE drawbar horsepower 29.38
SAE belt/PTO horsepower 37.33
Type .... tracklayer
Height (in.) 62.63
Tread width (in.) 43.33
Weight (lb.) 5,020
Track length (in.) 175.75
Grouser shoe .... 32 links; 10.25-in.
Gear/speed (mph) .... forward: 1/0.98, 2/1.78, 3/2.30, 4/3.38, 5/4.21, 6/6.18; reverse: 1/1.83, 2/3.36

Chapter 32
FLOUR CITY

Flour City 18-35, 20-35

Manufacturer .... Kinnard & Sons Mfg. Co., Minneapolis, MN
Nebraska test number 50
Test date .... August 9–25, 1920
Test tractor serial number 2016
Years produced 1911–1927
Engine .... Kinnard & Sons vertical overhead-valve
Test engine serial number 2016
Cylinders 4
Bore and stroke (in.) .... 5.50 x 6.00
Rated rpm 800
Displacement (c.i.) 570.2
Fuel .... kerosene/gasoline
Main tank capacity (gal.) 25
Auxiliary tank capacity (gal.) 3
Carburetor .... Schebler A
Ignition .... K-W TK magneto
Maximum brake horsepower tests
   PTO/belt horsepower 35.46
   Crankshaft rpm 807
   Fuel use (gal./hr.) 4.68
Maximum drawbar horsepower tests
   Gear .... high
   Drawbar horsepower 19.51
   Pull weight (lb.) 2,964
   Speed (mph) 2.47
   Percent slippage 12.05
SAE drawbar horsepower 18
SAE belt/PTO horsepower 35
Type .... 4 wheel
Front wheel (in.) .... steel: 42 x 6
Rear wheel (in.) .... steel: 72 x 18
Weight (lb.) 10,000
Gear/speed (mph) .... forward: 1/2.25, 2/3.00; reverse: 1/2.25

Flour City 40-70

Manufacturer .... Kinnard & Sons Mfg. Co., Minneapolis, MN
Nebraska test number 52
Test date .... August 13–24, 1920
Test tractor serial number 1992
Years produced 1910–1927
Engine .... Kinnard & Sons vertical overhead-valve

Test engine serial number.............................1992
Cylinders 4
Bore and stroke (in.) ....7.50 x 9.00
Rated rpm 575
Displacement (c.i.) 1,590.4
Fuel ....kerosene/gasoline
Main tank capacity (gal.)............................48
Auxiliary tank capacity (gal.) 5
Carburetor ....Schebler A
Ignition...K-W HK magneto
Maximum brake horsepower tests
    PTO/belt horsepower...........................72.52
    Crankshaft rpm 563
    Fuel use (gal./hr.) 9.62

Maximum drawbar horsepower tests
    Drawbar horsepower............................52.84
    Pull weight (lb.)...................................8,404
    Speed (mph).......................................2.37
    Percent slippage.................................15.10
SAE drawbar horsepower.............................40
SAE belt/PTO horsepower.............................70
Type ....4 wheel
Front wheel (in.)...steel: 48 x 10
Rear wheel (in.)..steel: 96 x 24
Weight (lb.) 21,000
Gear/speed (mph) ....forward: 1/2.00,
    2/2.50; reverse: 1/2.50

Chapter 33
FORD

Fordson F
Manufacturer..Ford Motor Co.,
    Detroit, MI
Nebraska test number 18
Test date ....June 2–12, 1920
Test tractor serial number...........................96100
Years produced 1917–1928
Serial number range....................................U.S.: 1–747681;
    Ireland:
    63001–253552, end
Serial number location ....stamped on engine
    block top right front
    above exhaust
    manifold
Number produced ....U.S.: 674,476;
    Ireland: 7,595
Engine ....Ford vertical L-head
Test engine serial number............................96100
Cylinders 4
Bore and stroke (in.) ....4.00 x 5.00
Rated rpm 1,000
Displacement (c.i.) 251.3
Fuel ....kerosene/gasoline
Main tank capacity (gal.)..............................21
Auxiliary tank capacity (gal.) 1
Carburetor ....Holley Fordson,
    1.25-in.
Air cleaner ....Ford
Ignition..Fordson magneto
Cooling capacity (gal.) 12
Maximum brake horsepower tests
    PTO/belt horsepower...........................19.15
    Crankshaft rpm 1,014
    Fuel use (gal./hr.) 3.00
Maximum drawbar horsepower tests
    Gear...low
    Drawbar horsepower............................9.34

    Pull weight (lb.)...................................2,187
    Speed (mph) 1.60
    Percent slippage..................................36.10
SAE drawbar horsepower.............................18
Type ....4 wheel
Front wheel (in.)...steel: 28 x 5
Rear wheel (in.)..steel: 42 x 12
Length (in.) ....wheelbase: 63;
    total: 102
Height (in.) 54.75
Rear width (in.) 62
Weight (lb.) 2,710
Gear/speed (mph) ....forward: 1/1.34,
    2/2.70, 3/6.83;
    reverse: 1/2.61

Fordson F
Manufacturer..Ford Motor Co.,
    Detroit, MI
Nebraska test number 124
Test date ....June 21–28, 1926
Test tractor serial number...........................609748
Years produced 1917–1928
Serial number range....................................U.S.: 1–74781; Ireland:
    63001–253552, end
Serial number location ....stamped on engine
    block top right front
    above exhaust
    manifold
Number produced ....U.S.: 674,476;
    Ireland: 7,595
Engine ....Ford vertical L-head
Test engine serial number............................609748
Cylinders 4
Bore and stroke (in.) ....4.00 x 5.00
Rated rpm 1,000
Displacement (c.i.) 251.3

Fuel .... kerosene/gasoline
Main tank capacity (gal.) 21
Auxiliary tank capacity (gal.) 0.60
Carburetor .... Holley Special 235,
1.25-in.
Air cleaner .... Ford
Ignition .... Fordson Special
magneto
Cooling capacity (gal.) 12

Maximum brake horsepower tests
    PTO/belt horsepower 22.28
    Crankshaft rpm 1,006
    Fuel use (gal./hr.) 2.49

Maximum drawbar horsepower tests
    Gear 2nd
    Drawbar horsepower 12.33
    Pull weight (lb.) 2,142
    Speed (mph) 2.16
    Percent slippage 14.74
Type .... 4 wheel
Front wheel (in.) .... steel: 28 x 5
Rear wheel (in.) .... steel: 42 x 12
Length (in.) 102
Height (in.) 54.75
Rear width (in.) 61.38
Weight (lb.) 2,710
Gear/speed (mph) .... forward: 1/1.58,
2/2.24, 3/7.05;
reverse: 1/2.14

Fordson N, 11-21

Manufacturer .... Ford Motor Co.,
Dearborn, MI
Nebraska test number 173
Test date .... March 11 to
April 8, 1930
Test tractor serial number 757447
Years produced 1929–1945
Serial number range .... 747682–980519 end
Serial number location .... stamped on engine
block top right front
above exhaust
manifold
Number produced 245,789
Engine .... Ford vertical L-head
Test engine serial number 757447
Cylinders 4
Bore and stroke (in.) .... 4.125 x 5.00
Rated rpm 1,100
Displacement (c.i.) 267.3
Fuel .... kerosene/gasoline
Main tank capacity (gal.) 20
Auxiliary tank capacity (qt.) 5
Carburetor .... Zenith (Kingston MD2),
1.25-in.
Air cleaner .... Ford
Ignition .... Robert Bosch FU4B
RS29 magneto
Cooling capacity (gal.) 11.50

Maximum brake horsepower tests
    PTO/belt horsepower 23.24
    Crankshaft rpm 1,104
    Fuel use (gal./hr.) 3.29

Maximum drawbar horsepower tests
    Gear 3rd
    Drawbar horsepower 13.60
    Pull weight (lb.) 3,289
    Speed (mph) 1.55
    Percent slippage 19.85
SAE drawbar horsepower 11.03
SAE belt/PTO horsepower 21.58
Type .... 4 wheel
Front wheel (in.) .... steel: 30 x 5
Rear wheel (in.) .... steel: 42 x 12
Length (in.) 102
Height (in.) 55
Rear width (in.) 61.50
Weight (lb.) 3,670
Gear/speed (mph) .... forward: 1/1.75,
2/3.13, 3/7.75;
reverse: 1/3.00

Fordson N, 14-26

Manufacturer .... Ford Motor Co.,
Dearborn, MI
Nebraska test number 174
Test date .... March 20 to
April 10, 1930
Test tractor serial number 758223
Years produced 1929–1945
Serial number range .... 747682–980519 end
Serial number location .... stamped on engine
block top right front
above exhaust
manifold
Number produced 245,789
Engine .... Ford vertical L-head
Test engine serial number 758223
Cylinders 4
Bore and stroke (in.) .... 4.125 x 5.00
Rated rpm 1,100
Displacement (c.i.) 267.3
Fuel .... gasoline
Fuel tank capacity (gal.) 20
Carburetor .... Zenith IN5F, 1.25-in.
Air cleaner .... Ford
Ignition .... Robert Bosch FU4B
RS29 magneto
Cooling capacity (gal.) 11.50

Maximum brake horsepower tests
    PTO/belt horsepower 29.09
    Crankshaft rpm 1,100
    Fuel use (gal./hr.) 3.06

Maximum drawbar horsepower tests
    Gear 2nd
    Drawbar horsepower 18.30
    Pull weight (lb.) 2,226
    Speed (mph) 3.08
    Percent slippage 13.61
SAE drawbar horsepower 14.92
SAE belt/PTO horsepower 26.01
Type .... 4 wheel
Front wheel (in.) .... steel: 30 x 5
Rear wheel (in.) .... steel: 42 x 12
Length (in.) 102
Height (in.) 55

Rear width (in.) 62.50
Weight (lb.) 3,770
Gear/speed (mph) .... forward: 1/2.13, 2/3.13, 3/7.75; reverse: 1/3.00

Fordson All-Around, N

Manufacturer .... Ford Motor Co., Ltd., Dagenham, Essex, England
Nebraska test number 282
Test date .... May 17 to June 10, 1937
Test tractor serial number 810062
Years produced 1937–1940
Serial number range .... approximately 807581–874913 end
Serial number location .... stamped on engine block top right front above exhaust manifold
Number produced .... na, interspersed
Engine .... Ford vertical L-head
Test engine serial number 810062
Cylinders 4
Bore and stroke (in.) .... 4.125 x 5.00
Rated rpm 1,100
Displacement (c.i.) 267
Fuel .... distillate/gasoline
Main tank capacity (gal.) 20
Auxiliary tank capacity (qt.) 5
Carburetor .... Kingston, 1.25-in.
Air cleaner .... Handy
Ignition .... American Bosch U4ED3VI magneto
Cooling capacity (gal.) 12
Maximum brake horsepower tests
PTO/belt horsepower 22.44
Crankshaft rpm 1,100
Fuel use (gal./hr.) 3.35
Maximum drawbar horsepower tests
Gear .... steel: 2nd; rubber: 2nd
Drawbar horsepower .... steel: 14.84; rubber: 18.33
Pull weight (lb.) .... steel: 1,784; rubber: 2,425
Speed (mph) .... steel: 3.12; rubber: 2.83
Percent slippage .... steel: 7.18; rubber: 6.63
SAE drawbar horsepower 11.84
SAE belt/PTO horsepower 20.16
Type .... tricycle
Front wheel (in.) .... (steel: 24 x 4; rubber: 5.50 x 16)
Rear wheel (in.) .... (steel: 50 x 2; rubber: 9.00 x 36)
Length (in.) 130
Height (in.) 63
Rear width (in.) 62
Weight (lb.) 3,700
Gear/speed (mph) .... forward: 1/1.92, 2/2.91, 3/5.13; reverse: 1/1.65

Fordson All-Around, N

Manufacturer .... Ford Motor Co., Ltd., Dagenham, Essex, England
Nebraska test number 299
Test date .... May 9–20, 1938
Test tractor serial number 810062
Years produced 1937–1940
Serial number range .... approximately 807581–874913 end
Serial number location .... stamped on engine block top right front above exhaust manifold
Number produced .... na, interspersed
Engine .... Ford vertical L-head
Test engine serial number 810062
Cylinders 4
Bore and stroke (in.) .... 4.125 x 5.00
Rated rpm 1,100
Displacement (c.i.) 267
Fuel .... gasoline
Fuel tank capacity (gal.) 20
Carburetor .... Zenith 1N5T, 1.25-in.
Air cleaner .... Handy
Ignition .... Robert Bosch FU4B RS29-T magneto
Cooling capacity (gal.) 12
Maximum brake horsepower tests
PTO/belt horsepower 28.44
Crankshaft rpm 1,100
Fuel use (gal./hr.) 3.50
Maximum drawbar horsepower tests
Gear .... steel: 2nd; rubber: 3rd
Drawbar horsepower .... steel: 19.25; rubber: 21.09
Pull weight (lb.) .... steel: 2,307; rubber: 1,532
Speed (mph) .... steel: 3.13; rubber: 5.16
Percent slippage .... steel: 2.74; rubber: 6.19
SAE drawbar horsepower 15.06
SAE belt/PTO horsepower 25.41
Type .... tricycle
Front wheel (in.) .... (steel: 24 x 4; rubber: 5.50 x 16)
Rear wheel (in.) .... (steel: 50 x 2; rubber: 9.00 x 36)
Length (in.) 130
Height (in.) 63
Rear width (in.) 62
Weight (lb.) .... steel: 3,790; (rubber: 4,795)
Gear/speed (mph) .... forward: 1/1.92, 2/2.91, 3/5.13; reverse: 1/1.61

Ford 9N, Ford-Ferguson System

Manufacturer .... Ferguson-Sherman Mfg. Corp., Dearborn, MI
Nebraska test number 339
Test date .... April 9–18, 1940

Ford

Test tractor serial number 9N 12840
Years produced 1939–1942
Serial number range....................................1–99002 end
Serial number location ....stamped on left side
of engine block
Number produced 99,002
Engine ....Ford vertical L-head
Test engine serial number 9N 12840
Cylinders 4
Bore and stroke (in.) ....3.1875 x 3.75
Rated rpm 2,000
Displacement (c.i.) 119.7
Fuel ....gasoline
Fuel tank capacity (gal.) 10
Carburetor ....Marvel-Schebler
TSX-33, 0.875-in.
Air cleaner ....United
Ignition ....Ford 9N distributor
with 6-v battery
Cooling capacity (gal.) 3.50
Maximum brake horsepower tests
    PTO/belt horsepower...........................23.56
    Crankshaft rpm 2,000
    Fuel use (gal./hr.) 2.43
Maximum drawbar horsepower tests
    Gear...2nd
    Drawbar horsepower............................16.31
    Pull weight (lb.)...................................2,146
    Speed (mph) 2.85
    Percent slippage..................................13.55
SAE drawbar horsepower.............................12.68
SAE belt/PTO horsepower............................20.29
Type ....standard
Front tire (in.) ....4.00 x 19
Rear tire (in.)...8.00 x 32
Length (in.) 115
Height (in.) 52
Rear width (in.) 64
Tread width (in.)..48–76
Weight (lb.) 2,340
Gear/speed (mph) ....forward: 1/2.51, 2/3.23,
3/7.48; reverse: 1/2.69

Ford 8N

Manufacturer...Ford Motor Co.,
Detroit, MI
Nebraska test number 385
Test date ....September 8–19, 1947
Test tractor serial number 8N 1777
Years produced 1947–1952
Serial number range....................................1–524076 end
Serial number location ....stamped on left side
of engine block
Number produced 524,076
Engine ....Ford vertical L-head
Test engine serial number 8N 1777
Cylinders 4
Bore and stroke (in.) ....3.1875 x 3.75
Rated rpm 1,500
Compression ratio.......................................6.37:1
Displacement (c.i.) 119.7
Fuel ....gasoline
Fuel tank capacity (gal.) 10
Carburetor ....Marvel-Schebler
TSX-33, 0.875-in.

Air cleaner ....Oakes-United
Ignition ....Ford with 6-v battery,
positive ground
Cooling capacity (gal.) 3
Maximum brake horsepower tests
    PTO/belt horsepower...........................21.06
    Crankshaft rpm 2,000
    Fuel use (gal./hr.) 2.70
Maximum drawbar horsepower tests
    Gear...2nd
    Drawbar horsepower............................17.06
    Pull weight (lb.)...................................1,993
    Speed (mph) 3.21
    Percent slippage..................................7.49
SAE drawbar horsepower.............................13.47
SAE belt/PTO horsepower............................18.31
Type ....standard
Front tire (in.) ....4.00 x 19
Rear tire (in.) ....10.00 x 28
Length (in.) 115
Height (in.) 54.50
Rear width (in.) 64.75
Tread width (in.) 48–76
Weight (lb.) 2,540
Gear/speed (mph) ....forward: 1/2.75,
2/3.54, 3/4.87,
4/10.16; reverse:
1/4.52

Ford 8N

Manufacturer..Ford Motor Co.,
Dearborn, MI
Nebraska test number 393
Test date ....May 11–18, 1948
Test tractor serial number 8N 49380
Years produced 1947–1952
Serial number range....................................1–524076 end
Serial number location ....stamped on left side
of engine block
Number produced 524,076
Engine ....Ford vertical L-head
Test engine serial number 8N 49380
Cylinders 4
Bore and stroke (in.) ....3.1875 x 3.75
Rated rpm 1,750
Compression ratio.......................................6.37:1
Displacement (c.i.) 119.7
Fuel ....gasoline
Fuel tank capacity (gal.) 10
Carburetor ....Marvel-Schebler
TSX-33, .87-in.
Air cleaner ....Oakes
Ignition ....Ford with 6-v battery,
positive ground
Cooling capacity (gal.) 3
Maximum brake horsepower tests
    PTO/belt horsepower...........................25.77
    Crankshaft rpm 2,003
    Fuel use (gal./hr.) 2.38
Maximum drawbar horsepower tests
    Gear...2nd
    Drawbar horsepower............................21.72
    Pull weight (lb.)...................................2,229
    Speed (mph) 3.65
    Percent slippage..................................8.65

SAE drawbar horsepower..................17.07
SAE belt/PTO horsepower..............22.46
Type ....standard
Front tire (in.).............................4.00 x 19
Rear tire (in.)............................10.00 x 28
Length (in.) 115
Height (in.) 54.50
Tread width (in.)..............................48–76
Weight (lb.) 2,410
Gear/speed (mph) ....forward: 1/2.97, 2/3.83,
3/5.27, 4/10.97;
reverse: 1/4.89

Ford 8N

Manufacturer...............................Ford Motor Co.,
Detroit, MI
Nebraska test number 443
Test date ....June 16–27, 1950
Test tractor serial number............8N 273570
Years produced 1947–1952
Serial number range......................1–524076 end
Serial number location ....stamped on left side
of engine block
Number produced 524,076
Engine ....Ford vertical L-head
Test engine serial number............8N 273570
Cylinders 4
Bore and stroke (in.) ....3.1875 x 3.75
Rated rpm 2,000
Compression ratio.......................6.5:1
Displacement (c.i.)......................119.7
Fuel ....gasoline
Fuel tank capacity (gal.) 10
Carburetor ....Marvel-Schebler
TSX-241, 0.875-in.
Ignition.......................................Ford with 6-v battery,
positive ground
Cooling capacity (gal.) 3
Maximum brake horsepower tests
PTO/belt horsepower..................26.19
Crankshaft rpm 1,999
Fuel use (gal./hr.) 2.35
Maximum drawbar horsepower tests
Gear...2nd
Drawbar horsepower...................21.95
Pull weight (lb.)..........................2,236
Speed (mph) 3.68
Percent slippage........................7.78
SAE drawbar horsepower.............17.37
SAE belt/PTO horsepower............23.22
Type ....standard
Front tire (in.).............................4.00 x 19
Rear tire (in.)............................10.00 x 28
Length (in.) 115
Height (in.) 54.50
Tread width (in.)..............................48–76
Weight (lb.) 2,410
Gear/speed (mph) ....forward: 1/3.23,
2/4.16, 3/5.72,
4/11.92; reverse:
1/5.31

Ford 8NAN

Manufacturer...............................Ford Motor Co.,
Detroit, MI
Nebraska test number 444

Test date ....June 22–29, 1950
Test tractor serial number............8N 273571
Years produced 1947–1952
Serial number range......................1–524076 end
Serial number location ....stamped on left side
of engine block
Number produced ....na, interspersed
Engine ....Ford vertical L-head
Test engine serial number............8N 273571
Cylinders 4
Bore and stroke (in.) ....3.1875 x 3.75
Rated rpm 2,000
Compression ratio.......................4.75:1
Displacement (c.i.)......................119.7
Fuel ....tractor fuel
Fuel tank capacity (gal.) 10
Carburetor ....Marvel-Schebler
TSX-241, 0.875-in.
Ignition.......................................Ford, 6-v battery,
positive ground
Cooling capacity (gal.) 3
Maximum brake horsepower tests
PTO/belt horsepower..................21.87
Crankshaft rpm 2,000
Fuel use (gal./hr.) 2.36
Maximum drawbar horsepower tests
Gear...2nd
Drawbar horsepower...................18.79
Pull weight (lb.)..........................1,895
Speed (mph) 3.72
Percent slippage........................6.42
SAE drawbar horsepower.............14.83
SAE belt/PTO horsepower............19.51
Type ....standard
Front tire (in.).............................4.00 x 19
Rear tire (in.)............................10.00 x 28
Length (in.) 115
Height (in.) 54.50
Tread width (in.)..............................48–76
Weight (lb.) 2,410
Gear/speed (mph) ....forward: 1/3.23,
2/4.16, 3/5.72,
4/11.92; reverse:
1/5.31

Ford NAA, Golden Jubliee

Manufacturer...............................Ford Motor Co.,
Dearborn, MI
Nebraska test number 494
Test date ....May 22 to June 1,
1953
Test tractor serial number............NAA 37790
Years produced 1953–1954
Serial number range......................NAA 1 to NAA77475
no end
Serial number location ....stamped on left side
of engine block
Engine ....Ford "Red Tiger"
vertical I-head
Test engine serial number............NAA 37790
Cylinders 4
Bore and stroke (in.) ....3.4375 x 3.60
Rated rpm 2,000
Compression ratio.......................6.6:1
Displacement (c.i.) 134

Ford

Fuel ....gasoline
Fuel tank capacity (gal.) 11
Carburetor ....Marvel-Schebler
TSX, 0.875-in.
Air cleaner ....Houdaille-Hershey
Ignition ....Ford with 6-v battery
Cooling capacity (gal.) 3.75
Maximum brake horsepower tests
    PTO/belt horsepower..........................31.14
    Crankshaft rpm 2,000
    Fuel use (gal./hr.) 2.87
Maximum drawbar horsepower tests
    Gear...2nd
    Drawbar horsepower...........................25.30
    Pull weight (lb.)............................2,632
    Speed (mph).................................3.60
    Percent slippage............................8.34
SAE drawbar horsepower..............................20.12
SAE belt/PTO horsepower.............................27.55
Type ....standard
Front wheel (in.) ....5.50 x 16
Rear wheel (in.) ....10.00 x 28
Length (in.) 188.81
Height (in.) 57.50
Tread width (in.)...................................48–76
Weight (lb.) 2,600
Gear/speed (mph) ....forward: 1/3.13,
2/4.02, 3/5.54,
4/11.55; reverse:
1/3.64

Ford New Fordson Major Diesel, FMD

Manufacturer.......................................Ford Motor Co., Ltd.,
Dagenham, Essex,
England
Nebraska test number 500
Test date ....August 17–27, 1953
Test tractor serial number.........................1260402
Years produced 1953–1958
Serial number range................................1247381–1458381
no end
Serial number location ....stamped on left flywheel
housing or right side
of engine block
Engine ....Ford E1ADDN
vertical I-head
Test engine serial number..........................1260402
Cylinders 4
Bore and stroke (in.) ....3.9375 x 4.524
Rated rpm 1,600
Compression ratio..................................16.0:1
Displacement (c.i.)................................220.4
Fuel ....diesel
Fuel tank capacity (gal.) 15
Carburetor...Simms injector pump
Air cleaner..AC/Burgess
Ignition...Lucas with 12-v battery
Cooling capacity (gal.) 3.60
Maximum brake horsepower tests
    PTO/belt horsepower..........................38.49
    Crankshaft rpm 1,600
    Fuel use (gal./hr.) 2.48
Maximum drawbar horsepower tests
    Gear...3rd
    Drawbar horsepower...........................34.17

Pull weight (lb.)..................................3,703
    Speed (mph) 3.46
    Percent slippage............................8.47
SAE drawbar horsepower.............................27.22
SAE belt/PTO horsepower............................34.49
Type ....standard
Front wheel (in.) ....7.50 x 16
Rear wheel (in.) ....14.00 x 30
Length (in.) 130.50
Height (in.) 63
Tread width (in.)..................................52–72
Weight (lb.) 5,250
Gear/speed (mph) ....forward: 1/2.07,
2/2.92, 3/3.73, 4/5.25,
5/7.32, 6/13.16;
reverse: 1/2.80, 2/5.03

New Fordson Major

Manufacturer.......................................Ford Motor Co., Ltd.,
Dagenham, Essex,
England
Nebraska test number 501
Test date ....August 17–26, 1953
Test tractor serial number.........................1260403
Years produced 1953–1958
Serial number range................................1247381–1458381
no end
Serial number location ....stamped on left
flywheel housing or
right side of engine
block
Engine ....Ford E1ADDN
vertical I-head
Test engine serial number..........................1260403
Cylinders 4
Bore and stroke (in.) ....3.74 x 4.524
Rated rpm 1,600
Compression ratio..................................5.5:1
Displacement (c.i.) 199
Fuel ....gasoline
Fuel tank capacity (gal.) 15
Carburetor...Zenith Downdraft
(Europe), 29/32-in.
Air cleaner..AC/Burgess
Ignition...Lucas with 12-v battery
Cooling capacity (gal.) 3.60
Maximum brake horsepower tests
    PTO/belt horsepower..........................33.56
    Crankshaft rpm 1,600
    Fuel use (gal./hr.) 3.34
Maximum drawbar horsepower tests
    Gear...3rd
    Drawbar horsepower...........................29.88
    Pull weight (lb.)............................3,178
    Speed (mph).................................3.53
    Percent slippage............................7.64
SAE drawbar horsepower.............................23.54
SAE belt/PTO horsepower............................29.44
Type ....standard
Front wheel (in.) ....7.50 x 16
Rear wheel (in.)...................................14.00 x 30
Length (in.) 130.50
Height (in.) 63
Tread width (in.)..................................52–72
Weight (lb.) 5,250

Gear/speed (mph) ....forward: 1/2.07, 2/2.92, 3/3.73, 4/5.25, 5/7.32, 6/13.16; reverse: 1/2.80, 2/5.03

Ford 640
Manufacturer ....Ford Motor Co., Birmingham, MI
Nebraska test number 560
Test date ....September 19 to October 4, 1955
Test tractor serial number 24262
Years produced 1954–1957
Serial number range................................1–116368 no end
Serial number location ....stamped number on left of transmission case
Number produced ....na, models interspersed
Engine ....Ford, EAE vertical I-head
Test engine serial number 24262
Cylinders 4
Bore and stroke (in.) ....3.4375 x 3.60
Rated rpm 2,000
Compression ratio................................6.6:1
Displacement (c.i.) 134
Fuel ....gasoline
Fuel tank capacity (gal.) 11
Carburetor ....Marvel-Schebler TSX, 0.875-in.
Air cleaner ....Houdaille-Hershey
Ignition...Ford with 6-v battery
Cooling capacity (gal.) 3.75
Maximum brake horsepower tests
    PTO/belt horsepower.......................31.01
    Crankshaft rpm 2,000
    Fuel use (gal./hr.) 2.91
Maximum drawbar horsepower tests
    Gear...2nd
    Drawbar horsepower.........................28.59
    Pull weight (lb.) 2,437
    Speed (mph) 4.40
    Percent slippage................................9.79
SAE drawbar horsepower........................22.02
SAE belt/PTO horsepower 27.58
Type ....standard
Front wheel (in.)......................................5.50 x 16
Rear wheel (in.).......................................11.00 x 28
Length (in.) 120.88
Height (in.) 56.94
Tread width (in.).......................................52–76
Weight (lb.) 2,800
Gear/speed (mph) ....forward: 1/3.13, 2/4.02, 3/5.54, 4/11.55; reverse: 1/3.64

Ford 660
Manufacturer ....Ford Motor Co., Birmingham, MI
Nebraska test number 561
Test date ....September 21 to October 7, 1955
Test tractor serial number 24432

Years produced 1954–1957
Serial number range................................1–116368 no end
Serial number location ....stamped number on left of transmission case
Number produced ....na, models interspersed
Engine ....Ford EAE vertical I-head
Test engine serial number 24432
Cylinders 4
Bore and stroke (in.) ....3.4375 x 3.60
Rated rpm 2,200
Compression ratio................................6.6:1
Displacement (c.i.) 134
Fuel ....gasoline
Fuel tank capacity (gal.) 11
Carburetor ....Marvel-Schebler TSX, 0.875-in.
Air cleaner ....Houdaille-Hershey
Ignition...Ford with 6-v battery
Cooling capacity (gal.) 3.75
Maximum brake horsepower tests
    PTO/belt horsepower.......................34.25
    Crankshaft rpm 2,201
    Fuel use (gal./hr.) 3.17
Maximum drawbar horsepower tests
    Gear...3rd
    Drawbar horsepower.........................28.23
    Pull weight (lb.) 2,277
    Speed (mph) 4.65
    Percent slippage................................6.32
SAE drawbar horsepower........................22.31
SAE belt/PTO horsepower 29.92
Type ....standard
Front wheel (in.)......................................5.50 x 16
Rear wheel (in.).......................................11.00 x 28
Length (in.) 120.88
Height (in.) 56.94
Tread width (in.).......................................52–76
Weight (lb.) 2,800
Gear/speed (mph) ....forward: 1/2.22, 2/3.52, 3/4.72, 4/6.48, 5/11.75; reverse: 1/3.80

Ford 860
Manufacturer...Ford Motor Co., Birmingham, MI
Nebraska test number 562
Test date ....September 21 to October 6, 1955
Test tractor serial number 33812
Years produced 1954–1957
Serial number range................................1–116368 no end
Serial number location ....stamped number on left of transmission case
Number produced ....na, models interspersed
Engine ....Ford EAF vertical I-head
Test engine serial number 33812
Cylinders 4
Bore and stroke (in.) ....3.90 x 3.60

Rated rpm 2,200
Compression ratio..6.75:1
Displacement (c.i.) 172
Fuel ....gasoline
Fuel tank capacity (gal.) 14
Carburetor ....Marvel-Schebler
TSX, 1.00-in.
Air cleaner ....Houdaille-Hershey
Ignition..Ford with 6-v battery
Cooling capacity (gal.) 3.75
Maximum brake horsepower tests
PTO/belt horsepower...........................45.41
Crankshaft rpm 2,200
Fuel use (gal./hr.)................................4.05
Maximum drawbar horsepower tests
Gear..3rd
Drawbar horsepower............................39.00
Pull weight (lb.)...................................3,330
Speed (mph) 4.39
Percent slippage.................................8.60
SAE drawbar horsepower................................30.14
SAE belt/PTO horsepower 39.86
Type ....standard
Front wheel (in.)..6.00 x 16
Rear wheel (in.)...12.00 x 28
Length (in.) 120.88
Height (in.) 57.38
Tread width (in.)...52–76
Weight (lb.) 2,960
Gear/speed (mph) ....forward: 1/2.22,
2/3.52, 3/4.72, 4/6.48,
5/11.75; reverse:
1/3.80

Ford 960
Manufacturer..Ford Motor Co.,
Birmingham, MI
Nebraska test number 569
Test date ....November 7–15, 1955
Test tractor serial number..............................56214
Years produced 1954–1957
Serial number range.......................................1–116368 no end
Serial number location ....stamped number on
left of transmission
case
Number produced ....na, models
interspersed
Engine ....Ford EAF
vertical I-head
Test engine serial number..............................56214
Cylinders 4
Bore and stroke (in.) ....3.90 x 3.60
Rated rpm 2,200
Compression ratio..6.75:1
Displacement (c.i.) 172
Fuel ....gasoline
Fuel tank capacity (gal.) 14
Carburetor ....Marvel-Schebler
TSX, 1.00-in.
Air cleaner ....Houdaille-Hershey
Ignition..Ford with 6-v battery
Cooling capacity (gal.) 3.75
Maximum brake horsepower tests
PTO/belt horsepower...........................46.27

Crankshaft rpm 2,200
Fuel use (gal./hr.) 4.10
Maximum drawbar horsepower tests
Gear..3rd
Drawbar horsepower............................38.40
Pull weight (lb.)...................................3,250
Speed (mph) 4.43
Percent slippage.................................7.66
SAE drawbar horsepower................................30.47
SAE belt/PTO horsepower 39.75
Type ....tricycle
Front wheel (in.)..6.00 x 16
Rear wheel (in.)...12.00 x 28
Length (in.) 132.63
Height (in.) 65.88
Tread width (in.)...56–80
Weight (lb.) 3,280
Gear/speed (mph) ....forward: 1/2.22,
2/3.52, 3/4.75, 4/6.48,
5/11.75; reverse:
1/3.80

Ford 740
Manufacturer..Ford Motor Co.,
Birmingham, MI
Nebraska test number 570
Test date ....November 7–15, 1955
Test tractor serial number..............................56683
Years produced 1954–1957
Serial number range.......................................1–116368 no end
Serial number location ....stamped number on
left of transmission
case
Number produced ....na, models
interspersed
Engine ....Ford EAE
vertical I-head
Test engine serial number..............................56683
Cylinders 4
Bore and stroke (in.) ....3.4375 x 3.60
Rated rpm 2,000
Compression ratio..6.6:1
Displacement (c.i.) 134
Fuel ....gasoline
Fuel tank capacity (gal.) 11
Carburetor ....Marvel-Schebler
TSX, 0.875-in.
Air cleaner ....Houdaille-Hershey
Ignition..Ford with 6-v battery
Cooling capacity (gal.) 3.75
Maximum brake horsepower tests
PTO/belt horsepower...........................31.62
Crankshaft rpm 2,001
Fuel use (gal./hr.)................................2.99
Maximum drawbar horsepower tests
Gear..2nd
Drawbar horsepower............................28.32
Pull weight (lb.)...................................2,615
Speed (mph) 4.06
Percent slippage.................................9.27
SAE drawbar horsepower................................21.92
SAE belt/PTO horsepower 27.91
Type ....tricycle
Front wheel (in.)..5.50 x 16
Rear wheel (in.)...11.00 x 28

Length (in.) 132.13
Height (in.) 65
Tread width (in.)....................................56–80
Weight (lb.) 3,079
Gear/speed (mph) ....forward: 1/3.50, 2/4.5, 3/6.25, 4/13.0; reverse: 1/4.00

Ford 850 L, LPG
Manufacturer...Ford Motor Co., Birmingham, MI
Nebraska test number 626
Test date ....June 24 to July 12, 1957
Test tractor serial number ....850 L 127727
Years produced 1954–1957
Serial number range..............................1–116368 no end
Serial number location ....stamped number on left of transmission case
Number produced ....na, models interspersed
Engine ....Ford EAF vertical I-head
Test engine serial number 850-L 127727
Cylinders 4
Bore and stroke (in.) ....3.90 x 3.60
Rated rpm 2,200
Compression ratio.................................8.0:1
Displacement (c.i.) 172
Fuel ....LPG
Carburetor ....Marvel-Schebler TSX-593, 1.00-in.
Air cleaner ....Houdaille-Hershey
Ignition ....Ford with 6-v battery
Cooling capacity (gal.) 3.75
Maximum brake horsepower tests
    PTO/belt horsepower..........................39.55
    Crankshaft rpm 2,200
    Fuel use (gal./hr.) 5.01
Maximum drawbar horsepower tests
    Gear...3rd
    Drawbar horsepower..........................35.16
    Pull weight (lb.)..................................2,947
    Speed (mph) 4.47
    Percent slippage................................6.44
SAE drawbar horsepower........................28.03
SAE belt/PTO horsepower 35.46
Type ....standard
Front wheel (in.).....................................6.00 x 16
Rear wheel (in.)......................................12.00 x 28
Height (in.)...57.38
Tread width (in.)......................................52–76
Weight (lb.) 2,991
Gear/speed (mph) ....forward: 1/2.30, 2/3.66, 3/4.87, 4/6.72, 5/11.96; reverse: 1/3.93

Ford 640-L, LPG
Manufacturer...Ford Motor Co., Birmingham, MI
Nebraska test number 627
Test date ....June 24 to July 12, 1957

Test tractor serial number.......................640-L 129026
Years produced.....................................1954–1957
Serial number range...............................1–116368 no end
Serial number location ....stamped number on left of transmission case
Number produced ....na, models interspersed
Engine ....Ford EAE vertical I-head
Test engine serial number.......................640-L 129026
Cylinders 4
Bore and stroke (in.) ....3.4375 x 3.60
Rated rpm 2,000
Compression ratio.................................6.6:1
Displacement (c.i.) 134
Fuel ....LPG
Carburetor ....Marvel-Schebler TSX-580, 1.00-in.
Air cleaner ....Houdaille-Hershey
Ignition ....Ford with 6-v battery
Cooling capacity (gal.) 3.75
Maximum brake horsepower tests
    PTO/belt horsepower..........................28.45
    Crankshaft rpm 2,000
    Fuel use (gal./hr.) 3.92
Maximum drawbar horsepower tests
    Gear...2nd
    Drawbar horsepower..........................27.11
    Pull weight (lb.)..................................2,276
    Speed (mph) 4.47
    Percent slippage................................8.58
SAE drawbar horsepower........................21.41
SAE belt/PTO horsepower 25.46
Type ....standard
Front wheel (in.).....................................5.50 x 16
Rear wheel (in.)......................................11.00 x 28
Height (in.)...56.94
Tread width (in.)......................................52–76
Weight (lb.) 2,855
Gear/speed (mph) ....forward: 1/3.81, 2/4.89, 3/6.73, 4/14.05; reverse: 1/4.17

Ford 841 L, LPG
Manufacturer...Ford Motor Co., Birmingham, MI
Nebraska test number 639
Test date ....March 12–31, 1958
Test tractor serial number.......................841 12911
Years produced.....................................1957–1961
Serial number range...............................1001–131427 no end
Serial number location ....stamped number on left of transmission case
Number produced ....na, models interspersed
Engine ....Ford EAF vertical I-head
Test engine serial number.......................841 12911
Cylinders 4
Bore and stroke (in.) ....3.90 x 3.60
Rated rpm 2,000
Compression ratio.................................8.65:1

Ford

Displacement (c.i.) 172
Fuel ....LPG
Fuel tank capacity (gal.) 19.25
Carburetor ....Zenith, 1.00-in.
Air cleaner ....Donaldson
Ignition ....Ford with 6-v battery
Cooling capacity (gal.) 3.75
Maximum brake horsepower tests
    PTO/belt horsepower...........................41.97
    Crankshaft rpm 2,000
    Fuel use (gal./hr.) 4.98
Maximum drawbar horsepower tests
    Gear...5th
    Drawbar horsepower............................40.32
    Pull weight (lb.)...................................3,726
    Speed (mph) 4.06
    Percent slippage..................................7.81
SAE drawbar horsepower...............................30.36
SAE belt/PTO horsepower...............................36.98
Type ....standard
Front wheel (in.) ....6.00 x 16
Rear wheel (in.) ....12.00 x 28
Height (in.) 56
Tread width (in.) 52–76
Weight (lb.) 3,180
Gear/speed (mph) ....forward: 1/2.46,
    2/2.99, 3/3.67, 4/4.32,
    5/4.46, 6/5.57, 7/6.50,
    8/6.79, 9/9.06,
    10/9.83, 11/13.56,
    12/15.47; reverse:
    1/2.57, 2/3.85, 3/5.84

Ford 851

Manufacturer..Ford Motor Co.,
    Birmingham, MI
Nebraska test number 640
Test date ....March 12–31, 1958
Test tractor serial number.............................851 7731
Years produced 1957–1961
Serial number range......................................1001–131427 no end
Serial number location ....stamped number on
    left of transmission
    case
Number produced ....na, models
    interspersed
Engine ....Ford EAF
    vertical I-head
Test engine serial number.............................851 7731
Cylinders 4
Bore and stroke (in.) ....3.90 x 3.60
Rated rpm 2,200
Compression ratio...7.5:1
Displacement (c.i.).......................................172
Fuel ....gasoline
Fuel tank capacity (gal.) 17
Carburetor ....Marvel-Schebler
    TSX-662, 1.00-in.
Air cleaner ....Donaldson
Ignition..Ford with 6-v battery
Cooling capacity (gal.) 3.75
Maximum brake horsepower tests
    PTO/belt horsepower...........................48.37
    Crankshaft rpm 2,200
    Fuel use (gal./hr.) 4.55

Maximum drawbar horsepower tests
    Gear...3rd
    Drawbar horsepower............................41.54
    Pull weight (lb.)...................................3,499
    Speed (mph) 4.45
    Percent slippage..................................7.13
SAE drawbar horsepower...............................32.46
SAE belt/PTO horsepower...............................42.67
Type ....standard
Front wheel (in.) ....6.00 x 16
Rear wheel (in.) ....13.60 x 28
Height (in.) 56
Tread width (in.) 52–76
Weight (lb.) 3,180
Gear/speed (mph) ....forward: 1/2.30,
    2/3.66, 3/4.87, 4/6.72,
    5/11.96; reverse:
    1/3.93

Ford 841

Manufacturer..Ford Motor Co.,
    Birmingham, MI
Nebraska test number 641
Test date ....March 14–31, 1958
Test tractor serial number.............................841 S 9682
Years produced 1957–1961
Serial number range......................................1001–131427 no end
Serial number location ....stamped number on
    left of transmission
    case
Number produced ....na, models
    interspersed
Engine ....Ford EAF
    vertical I-head
Test engine serial number.............................841-S 9682
Cylinders 4
Bore and stroke (in.) ....3.90 x 3.60
Rated rpm 2,000
Compression ratio...7.5:1
Displacement (c.i.).......................................172
Fuel ....gasoline
Fuel tank capacity (gal.) 17
Carburetor ....Marvel-Schebler
    TSX-662, 1.00-in.
Air cleaner ....Donaldson
Ignition..Ford with 6-v battery
Cooling capacity (gal.) 3.75
Maximum brake horsepower tests
    PTO/belt horsepower...........................44.71
    Crankshaft rpm 2,000
    Fuel use (gal./hr.) 4.19
Maximum drawbar horsepower tests
    Gear...5th
    Drawbar horsepower............................41.44
    Pull weight (lb.)...................................3,851
    Speed (mph) 4.04
    Percent slippage..................................8.65
SAE drawbar horsepower...............................31.59
SAE belt/PTO horsepower...............................39.55
Type ....standard
Front wheel (in.) ....6.00 x 16
Rear wheel (in.) ....13.60 x 28
Height (in.) 56
Tread width (in.) 52–76
Weight (lb.) 3,180

Gear/speed (mph) ....forward: 1/2.46, 2/2.99, 3/3.67, 4/4.32, 5/4.46, 6/5.57, 7/6.50, 8/6.79, 9/9.06, 10/9.83, 11/13.56, 12/15.47; reverse: 1/2.57, 2/3.85, 3/5.84

Ford 641

Manufacturer ....Ford Motor Co., Birmingham, MI
Nebraska test number 642
Test date ....March 20– 31, 1958
Test tractor serial number 641S 8635
Years produced 1957–1961
Serial number range..................1001–131427 no end
Serial number location ....stamped number on left of transmission case
Number produced ....na, models interspersed
Engine ....Ford EAE vertical I-head
Test engine serial number..........641S 8635
Cylinders 4
Bore and stroke (in.) ....3.4375 x 3.60
Rated rpm 2,000
Compression ratio....................7.5:1
Displacement (c.i.) 134
Fuel ....gasoline
Fuel tank capacity (gal.) 13
Carburetor...............................Marvel-Schebler TSX-692, 1.00-in.
Air cleaner ....Donaldson
Ignition...................................Ford with 6-v battery
Cooling capacity (gal.) 3.75
Maximum brake horsepower tests
    PTO/belt horsepower............33.65
    Crankshaft rpm 2,000
    Fuel use (gal./hr.) 3.38
Maximum drawbar horsepower tests
    Gear.....................................5th
    Drawbar horsepower..............29.82
    Pull weight (lb.)....................2,606
    Speed (mph) 4.29
    Percent slippage....................6.26
SAE drawbar horsepower...........23.05
SAE belt/PTO horsepower 29.96
Type ....standard
Front wheel (in.).......................5.50 x 16
Rear wheel (in.)........................12.40 x 28
Height (in.)..............................56
Tread width (in.).......................52–76
Weight (lb.)..............................2,825
Gear/speed (mph) ....forward: 1/2.54, 2/3.09, 3/3.80, 4/4.47, 5/4.61, 6/5.77, 7/6.72, 8/7.03, 9/9.38, 10/10.18, 11/14.04, 12/16.01; reverse: 1/2.65, 2/3.98, 3/6.04

Ford 651

Manufacturer ....Ford Motor Co., Birmingham, MI

Nebraska test number 643
Test date ....March 21–29, 1958
Test tractor serial number 651 8813
Years produced 1957–1961
Serial number range..................1001–131427 no end
Serial number location ....stamped number on left of transmission case
Number produced ....na, models interspersed
Engine ....Ford EAE vertical I-head
Test engine serial number 651 8813
Cylinders 4
Bore and stroke (in.) ....3.44 x 3.60
Rated rpm 2,200
Compression ratio....................7.5:1
Displacement (c.i.) 134
Fuel ....gasoline
Fuel tank capacity (gal.) 13
Carburetor...............................Marvel-Schebler TSX-692, 1.00-in.
Air cleaner ....Donaldson
Ignition...................................Ford with 6-v battery
Cooling capacity (gal.) 3.75
Maximum brake horsepower tests
    PTO/belt horsepower............35.79
    Crankshaft rpm 2,200
    Fuel use (gal./hr.) 3.27
Maximum drawbar horsepower tests
    Gear.....................................3rd
    Drawbar horsepower..............29.49
    Pull weight (lb.)....................2,375
    Speed (mph) 4.66
    Percent slippage....................6.58
SAE drawbar horsepower...........22.60
SAE belt/PTO horsepower 31.78
Type ....standard
Front wheel (in.).......................5.50 x 16
Rear wheel (in.)........................12.40 x 28
Height (in.)..............................56
Tread width (in.).......................52–76
Weight (lb.)..............................2,825
Gear/speed (mph) ....forward: 1/2.39, 2/3.79, 3/5.04, 4/6.96, 5/12.38; reverse: 1/4.07

Ford 841 Diesel

Manufacturer ....Ford Motor Co., Birmingham, MI
Nebraska test number 653
Test date ....June 2–10, 1958
Test tractor serial number ....841 DS 24161
Years produced 1957–1961
Serial number range..................1001–131427 no end
Serial number location ....stamped number on left of transmission case
Number produced ....na, models interspersed
Engine ....Ford EAF 172 vertical I-head
Test engine serial number..........841DS 24161
Cylinders 4

Ford

Bore and stroke (in.) ....3.90 x 3.60
Rated rpm 2,000
Compression ratio..16.8:1
Displacement (c.i.) 172
Fuel ....diesel
Fuel tank capacity (gal.) 17
Carburetor...Roosa injector pump
Air cleaner...Donaldson
Ignition..Ford with 12-v battery
Cooling capacity (gal.) 3.75
Maximum brake horsepower tests
    PTO/belt horsepower...........................39.88
    Crankshaft rpm 2,000
    Fuel use (gal./hr.) 2.81
Maximum drawbar horsepower tests
    Gear..5th
    Drawbar horsepower............................36.77
    Pull weight (lb.)...................................3,408
    Speed (mph) 4.05
    Percent slippage..................................8.33
SAE drawbar horsepower.................................28.31
SAE belt/PTO horsepower................................35.30
Type ....standard
Front wheel (in.)..6.00 x 16
Rear wheel (in.)...13.60 x 28
Height (in.) 77
Tread width (in.) 52–76
Weight (lb.) 3,180
Gear/speed (mph) ....forward: 1/2.46,
2/2.99, 3/3.67, 4/4.32,
5/4.46, 6/5.57, 7/6.50,
8/6.79, 9/9.06,
10/9.83, 11/13.56,
12/15.47; reverse:
1/2.57, 2/3.85, 3/5.84

Ford 851 Diesel

Manufacturer..Ford Motor Co.,
Birmingham, MI
Nebraska test number 654
Test date ....June 2–11, 1958
Test tractor serial number...............................851D 24214
Years produced 1957–1961
Serial number range..1001–131427 no end
Serial number location ....stamped number on
left of transmission
case
Number produced ....na, models
interspersed
Engine ....Ford EAF 172
vertical I-head
Test engine serial number...............................851D 24214
Cylinders 4
Bore and stroke (in.) ....3.90 x 3.60
Rated rpm 2,200
Compression ratio..16.8:1
Displacement (c.i.) 172
Fuel ....diesel
Fuel tank capacity (gal.) 17
Carburetor..Roosa injector pump
Air cleaner..Donaldson
Ignition...Ford with 12-v battery
Cooling capacity (gal.) 3.75

Maximum brake horsepower tests
    PTO/belt horsepower...........................41.98
    Crankshaft rpm 2,200
    Fuel use (gal./hr.) 2.98
Maximum drawbar horsepower tests
    Gear..3rd
    Drawbar horsepower............................36.66
    Pull weight (lb.)...................................3,069
    Speed (mph) 4.48
    Percent slippage..................................7.24
SAE drawbar horsepower.................................29.18
SAE belt/PTO horsepower................................37.83
Type ....standard
Front wheel (in.)..6.00 x 16
Rear wheel (in.)...13.60 x 28
Height (in.) 77
Tread width (in.) 52–76
Weight (lb.) 3,180
Gear/speed (mph) ....forward: 1/2.30,
2/3.66, 3/4.87, 4/6.72,
5/11.96; reverse:
1/3.93

Fordson Dexta

Manufacturer..Ford Motor Co., Ltd.,
Dagenham, Essex,
England
Nebraska test number 684
Test date ....February 28 to March
16, 1959
Test tractor serial number...............................1419112
Years produced 1958–1964
Serial number range..144–928248 no end
Serial number location ....stamped on left side of
clutch housing flange
Number produced ....na, Dexta and Super
Dexta
Engine ....Perkins P3 vertical
Test engine serial number...............................1419112
Cylinders 3
Bore and stroke (in.) ....3.50 x 5.00
Rated rpm 2,000
Compression ratio..16.5:1
Displacement (c.i.) 144
Fuel ....No. 2 diesel
Fuel tank capacity (gal.) 7
Carburetor..Simms injector pump
Air cleaner..AC/Delco
Ignition...Lucas with 12-v battery
Cooling capacity (gal.) 2.25
Maximum brake horsepower tests
    PTO/belt horsepower...........................31.41
    Crankshaft rpm 2,000
    Fuel use (gal./hr.) 2.03
Maximum drawbar horsepower tests
    Gear..3rd
    Drawbar horsepower............................27.03
    Pull weight (lb.)...................................2,144
    Speed (mph) 4.73
    Percent slippage..................................4.45
SAE drawbar horsepower.................................27.57
SAE belt/PTO horsepower................................31.41
Type ....standard

Front wheel (in.) ....5.50 x 16
Rear wheel (in.) ....12.40 x 28
Height (in.) 54
Tread width (in.) 48–76
Weight (lb.) 2,994
Gear/speed (mph) ....forward: 1/1.56,
2/3.64, 3/4.80, 4/6.14,
5/10.49, 6/17.33;
reverse: 1/2.54, 2/7.51

Fordson Power Major Diesel, FPM
Manufacturer.......................................Ford Motor Co., Ltd.,
Dagenham, Essex,
England
Nebraska test number 685
Test date ....February 27 to March
16, 1959
Test tractor serial number.........................1484654
Years produced 1958–1961
Serial number range..................................1481091–1583906
no end
Serial number location ....stamped on left
flywheel housing or
right side of engine
block
Engine ....Ford EIADDN vertical
L-head
Test engine serial number.........................1484654
Cylinders 4
Bore and stroke (in.) ....3.9375 x 4.524
Rated rpm 1,700
Compression ratio.....................................16:1
Displacement (c.i.) 220
Fuel ....No. 2 diesel
Fuel tank capacity (gal.) 18
Carburetor...Simms injector pump
Air cleaner ....Burgess or AS
Ignition..Lucas with 12-v battery
Cooling capacity (gal.) 5.40
Maximum brake horsepower tests
    PTO/belt horsepower...........................47.65
    Crankshaft rpm 1,700
    Fuel use (gal./hr.) 3.18
Maximum drawbar horsepower tests
    Gear..3rd
    Drawbar horsepower............................42.63
    Pull weight (lb.).....................................4,341
    Speed (mph) 3.68
    Percent slippage..................................6.44
SAE drawbar horsepower...........................42.59
SAE belt/PTO horsepower 47.65
Type ....standard
Front wheel (in.) ....7.50 x 16
Rear wheel (in.) ....14.00 x 30
Height (in.) 62.50
Tread width (in.) 58–62
Weight (lb.) 5,461
Gear/speed (mph) ....forward: 1/1.91,
2/2.83, 3/3.76, 4/5.40,
5/7.62, 6/13.84;
reverse: 1/2.74, 2/5.12

Ford 641-D, Diesel
Manufacturer...Ford Motor Co.,
Birmingham, MI

Nebraska test number 686
Test date ....March 11–18, 1959
Test tractor serial number............................641 DS 53448
Years produced 1957–1961
Serial number range.....................................1001–131427 no end
Serial number location ....stamped number on
left of transmission
case
Number produced ....na, models
interspersed
Engine ....Ford 144D
vertical L-head
Test engine serial number............................641 DS 53448
Cylinders 4
Bore and stroke (in.) ....3.5625 x 3.60
Rated rpm 2,000
Compression ratio.......................................16.8:1
Displacement (c.i.) 144
Fuel ....No. 2 diesel
Fuel tank capacity (gal.) 13
Carburetor...Roosa injector pump
Air cleaner ....Donaldson
Ignition..Ford with 12-v battery
Cooling capacity (gal.) 3.75
Maximum brake horsepower tests
    PTO/belt horsepower...........................31.78
    Crankshaft rpm 2,000
    Fuel use (gal./hr.) 2.20
Maximum drawbar horsepower tests
    Gear..5th
    Drawbar horsepower............................29.33
    Pull weight (lb.).....................................2,572
    Speed (mph) 4.28
    Percent slippage..................................5.64
SAE drawbar horsepower.............................28.47
SAE belt/PTO horsepower 31.78
Type ....standard
Front wheel (in.) ....5.50 x 16
Rear wheel (in.) ....12.40 x 28
Height (in.) 57
Tread width (in.) 52–76
Weight (lb.) 3,000
Gear/speed (mph) ....forward: 1/2.54,
2/3.09, 3/3.80, 4/4.47,
5/4.61, 6/5.77, 7/6.72,
8/7.03, 9/9.38,
10/10.18, 11/14.04,
12/16.01; reverse:
1/2.65, 2/3.98, 3/6.04

Ford 881
Manufacturer...Ford Motor Co.,
Birmingham, MI
Nebraska test number 701
Test date ....June 6–17, 1959
Test tractor serial number............................66892
Years produced 1957–1961
Serial number range.....................................1001–131427 no end
Serial number location ....stamped number on
left of transmission
case
Number produced ....na, models
interspersed
Engine ....Ford 172 vertical
L-head

Ford

Test engine serial number 66892
Cylinders 4
Bore and stroke (in.) ....3.90 x 3.60
Rated rpm 2,200
Compression ratio....................................7.5:1
Displacement (c.i.) 172
Fuel ....gasoline
Fuel tank capacity (gal.) 17
Carburetor ....Marvel-Schebler
TSX-769, 1.0-in.
Air cleaner ....Donaldson
Ignition..Ford with 6-v battery
Cooling capacity (gal.) 3.75
Maximum brake horsepower tests
    PTO/belt horsepower....................46.16
    Crankshaft rpm 2,200
    Fuel use (gal./hr.)..........................3.82
Maximum drawbar horsepower tests
    Gear..6th
    Drawbar horsepower......................37.02
    Pull weight (lb.)............................3,347
    Speed (mph) 4.15
    Percent slippage............................8.26
SAE drawbar horsepower............................37.07
SAE belt/PTO horsepower............................46.14
Type ....standard
Front wheel (in.) ....6.00 x 16
Rear wheel (in.)..13.60 x 28
Height (in.) 57.38
Tread width (in.)..52–76
Weight (lb.) 3,333
Gear/speed (mph) ....forward: 1/1.06,
2/1.51, 3/1.58, 4/2.25,
5/3.58, 6/4.61, 7/5.30,
8/6.81, 9/11.04,
10/16.36; reverse:
1/3.16, 2/4.67

Ford 681
Manufacturer..Ford Motor Co.,
Birmingham, MI
Nebraska test number 702
Test date ....June 11–20, 1959
Test tractor serial number........................71094
Years produced..1957–1961
Serial number range..................................1001–131427 no end
Serial number location ....stamped number on
left of transmission
case
Number produced ....na, models
interspersed
Engine ....Ford 134
vertical L-head
Test engine serial number..........................71094
Cylinders 4
Bore and stroke (in.) ....3.44 x 3.60
Rated rpm 2,200
Compression ratio....................................7.5:1
Displacement (c.i.) 134
Fuel ....gasoline
Fuel tank capacity (gal.) 13
Carburetor..Marvel-Schebler
TSX-765, 1.0-in.
Air cleaner ....Donaldson
Ignition..Ford with 6-v battery

Cooling capacity (gal.) 3.75
Maximum brake horsepower tests
    PTO/belt horsepower....................34.33
    Crankshaft rpm 2,200
    Fuel use (gal./hr.)..........................3.13
Maximum drawbar horsepower tests
    Gear..6th
    Drawbar horsepower......................26.81
    Pull weight (lb.)............................2,274
    Speed (mph) 4.42
    Percent slippage............................6.15
SAE drawbar horsepower............................27.04
SAE belt/PTO horsepower............................34.33
Type ....standard
Front wheel (in.) ....5.50 x 16
Rear wheel (in.)..12.40 x 28
Height (in.) 56.94
Tread width (in.)..52–76
Weight (lb.) 3,136
Gear/speed (mph) ....forward: 1/1.01,
2/1.57, 3/1.63, 4/2.32,
5/3.70, 6/4.77, 7/5.49,
8/7.06, 9/11.43,
10/16.94; reverse:
1/3.27, 2/4.84

Ford 881 L, LPG
Manufacturer..Ford Motor Co.,
Birmingham, MI
Nebraska test number 703
Test date ....June 16–24, 1959
Test tractor serial number........................68250
Years produced..1957–1961
Serial number range..................................1001–131427 no end
Serial number location ....stamped number on
left of transmission
case
Number produced ....na, models
interspersed
Engine ....Ford 172
vertical L-head
Test engine serial number..........................68250
Cylinders 4
Bore and stroke (in.) ....3.90 x 3.60
Rated rpm 2,200
Compression ratio....................................8.65:1
Displacement (c.i.) 172
Fuel ....LPG
Fuel tank capacity (gal.) 19.25
Carburetor..Zenith, 1.0-in.
Air cleaner ....Donaldson
Ignition..Ford with 6-v battery
Cooling capacity (gal.) 3.75
Maximum brake horsepower tests
    PTO/belt horsepower....................43.61
    Crankshaft rpm 2,200
    Fuel use (gal./hr.)..........................5.00
Maximum drawbar horsepower tests
    Gear..6th
    Drawbar horsepower......................34.28
    Pull weight (lb.)............................3,076
    Speed (mph) 4.18
    Percent slippage............................7.89
SAE drawbar horsepower............................34.97
SAE belt/PTO horsepower............................43.61

Type ....standard
Front wheel (in.) ....6.00 x 16
Rear wheel (in.) ....13.60 x 28
Height (in.) 57.38
Tread width (in.) 52–76
Weight (lb.) 3,333
Gear/speed (mph) ....forward: 1/1.06,
2/1.51, 3/1.58, 4/2.25,
5/3.58, 6/4.61, 7/5.30,
8/6.81, 9/11.04,
10/16.36; reverse:
1/3.16, 2/4.67

Ford 681-L, LPG
Manufacturer ....Ford Motor Co.,
Birmingham, MI
Nebraska test number 704
Test date ....June 18–25, 1959
Test tractor serial number 71105
Years produced 1957–1961
Serial number range..............................1001–131427 no end
Serial number location ....stamped number on
left of transmission
case
Number produced ....na, models
interspersed
Engine ....Ford 134
vertical L-head
Test engine serial number 71105
Cylinders 4
Bore and stroke (in.) ....3.4375 x 3.60
Rated rpm 2,200
Compression ratio.................................7.5:1
Displacement (c.i.) 134
Fuel ....LPG
Fuel tank capacity (gal.) 19.25
Carburetor...Zenith, 1.0-in.
Air cleaner ....Donaldson
Ignition ....Ford with 6-v battery
Cooling capacity (gal.) 3.75
Maximum brake horsepower tests
PTO/belt horsepower.........................32.57
Crankshaft rpm 2,200
Fuel use (gal./hr.) 4.04
Maximum drawbar horsepower tests
Gear..6th
Drawbar horsepower.........................25.52
Pull weight (lb.)................................2,162
Speed (mph) 4.43
Percent slippage...............................19.95
SAE drawbar horsepower......................26.14
SAE belt/PTO horsepower 32.57
Type ....standard
Front wheel (in.) ....5.50 x 16
Rear wheel (in.) ....12.40 x 28
Height (in.) 56.94
Tread width (in.)....................................52–76
Weight (lb.) 3,136
Gear/speed (mph) ....forward: 1/1.01,
2/1.57, 3/1.63, 4/2.32,
5/3.70, 6/4.77, 7/5.49,
8/7.06, 9/11.43,
10/16.94; reverse:
1/3.27, 2/4.84

Ford 881 D, Diesel
Manufacturer...Ford Motor Co.,
Birmingham, MI
Nebraska test number 705
Test date ....June 28 to
July 2, 1959
Test tractor serial number 52919
Years produced 1957–1961
Serial number range...................................1001–131427 no end
Serial number location ....stamped number
on left of
transmission case
Number produced ....na, models
interspersed
Engine ....Ford 172
vertical L-head
Test engine serial number 52919
Cylinders 4
Bore and stroke (in.) ....3.90 x 3.60
Rated rpm 2,200
Compression ratio.......................................16.8:1
Displacement (c.i.) 172
Fuel ....diesel
Fuel tank capacity (gal.) 17
Carburetor..Roosa injector pump
Air cleaner...Donaldson
Ignition ....Ford with 12-v battery
Cooling capacity (gal.) 3.75
Maximum brake horsepower tests
PTO/belt horsepower............................41.36
Crankshaft rpm 2,200
Fuel use (gal./hr.) 2.98
Maximum drawbar horsepower tests
Gear...6th
Drawbar horsepower.............................33.60
Pull weight (lb.)....................................3,005
Speed (mph) 4.19
Percent slippage...................................6.37
SAE drawbar horsepower..........................33.91
SAE belt/PTO horsepower 41.36
Type ....standard
Front wheel (in.) ....6.00 x 16
Rear wheel (in.) ....13.60 x 17
Height (in.) 57.38
Tread width (in.)...52–76
Weight (lb.) 3,333
Gear/speed (mph) ....forward: 1/1.06, 2/1.51,
3/1.58, 4/2.25, 5/3.58,
6/4.61, 7/5.30, 8/6.81,
9/11.05, 10/16.36;
reverse: 1/3.16, 2/4.67

Ford 681-D, Diesel
Manufacturer...Ford Motor Co.,
Birmingham, MI
Nebraska test number 706
Test date ....June 20–26, 1959
Test tractor serial number 70858
Years produced 1957–1961
Serial number range...................................1001–131427 no end
Serial number location ....stamped number on left
of transmission case
Number produced ....na, models
interspersed

Engine ....Ford 144
vertical L-head
Test engine serial number.......................70858
Cylinders 4
Bore and stroke (in.) ....3.562 x 3.600
Rated rpm 2,200
Compression ratio...................................16.8:1
Displacement (c.i.) 144
Fuel ....diesel
Fuel tank capacity (gal.) 13
Carburetor ....Roosa injector pump
Air cleaner ....Donaldson
Ignition..Ford with 12-v battery
Cooling capacity (gal.) 3.75

Maximum brake horsepower tests
    PTO/belt horsepower.........................31.56
    Crankshaft rpm 2,200
    Fuel use (gal./hr.)..............................2.37

Maximum drawbar horsepower tests
    Gear..6th
    Drawbar horsepower...........................25.52
    Pull weight (lb.).................................2,162
    Speed (mph) 4.43
    Percent slippage................................5.28
SAE drawbar horsepower...............................25.61
SAE belt/PTO horsepower 31.56
Type ....standard
Front wheel (in.)...5.50 x 16
Rear wheel (in.)..12.40 x 28
Height (in.)...56.94
Tread width (in.)...52–76
Weight (lb.)...3,187
Gear/speed (mph) ....forward: 1/1.01,
2/1.57, 3/1.63, 4/2.32,
5/3.70, 6/4.77, 7/5.49,
8/7.06, 9/11.43,
10/16.94; reverse:
1/3.27, 2/4.84

Chapter 34
FOUR DRIVE

Four Drive E, 15-25, Cat 15-30

Manufacturer...Four Drive Tractor Co.,
Big Rapids, MI
Nebraska test number 165
Test date ....July 1–17, 1929
Test tractor serial number..........................3017
Year produced..1929
Engine ....Waukesha CR
vertical L-head
Test engine serial number..........................169770
Cylinders 4
Bore and stroke (in.) ....4.375 x 5.75
Rated rpm 1,100
Displacement (c.i.) 345.8
Fuel ....kerosene/gasoline
Main tank capacity (gal.)............................25
Auxiliary tank capacity (gal.) 23
Carburetor...Kingston L3, 1.25-in.
Air cleaner ....Donaldson
Ignition...Eisemann (American
Bosch U4 Ed1)
magneto
Cooling capacity (gal.) 7

Maximum brake horsepower tests
    PTO/belt horsepower.........................28.42
    Crankshaft rpm 1,100
    Fuel use (gal./hr.)..............................3.95

Maximum drawbar horsepower tests
    Gear..2nd
    Drawbar horsepower...........................18.97
    Pull weight (lb.).................................3,023
    Speed (mph) 2.35
    Percent slippage................................6.74
SAE drawbar horsepower...............................15
SAE belt/PTO horsepower 25
Type ....4 wheel drive
Front wheel (in.)...steel: 40 x 12
Rear wheel (in.)..steel: 40 x 12
Length (in.) 106
Height (in.) 61
Rear width (in.) 70
Weight (lb.)...5,800
Gear/speed (mph) ....forward: 1/2.10,
2/3.10, 3/6.00;
reverse: 1/3.90

Chapter 35
FRICK

Frick C, 15-28

Manufacturer .... Frick Co., Inc.,
Waynesboro, PA
Nebraska test number 46
Test date .... August 2–6, 1920
Test tractor serial number 1277
Years produced 1921–1924
Engine .... Beaver vertical,
valve-in-head
Test engine serial number 184 58
Cylinders 4
Bore and stroke (in.) .... 4.75 x 6.00
Rated rpm 900
Displacement (c.i.) 425.3
Fuel .... kerosene/gasoline
Main tank capacity (gal.) 20
Auxiliary tank capacity (gal.) 3
Carburetor .... Bennett J
Air cleaner .... Bennett
Ignition .... Splitdorf Dixie
46 magneto

Maximum brake horsepower tests
PTO/belt horsepower 29.72
Crankshaft rpm 917
Fuel use (gal./hr.) 5.21
Maximum drawbar horsepower tests
Gear .... low
Drawbar horsepower 19.48
Pull weight (lb.) 3,264
Speed (mph) 2.24
Percent slippage 12.20
SAE drawbar horsepower 15
SAE belt/PTO horsepower 28
Type .... 4 wheel
Front wheel (in.) .... steel: 46 x 5
Rear wheel (in.) .... steel: 60 x 12
Length (in.) 158.50
Height (in.) 66
Rear width (in.) 81.50
Weight (lb.) 6,100
Gear/speed (mph) .... forward: 1/2.30,
2/3.80; reverse: 1/2.00

Frick A, 12-20

Manufacturer .... Frick Co., Inc.,
Waynesboro, PA
Nebraska test number 47
Test date .... August 3–10, 1920
Test tractor serial number 1010
Years produced 1921–1924
Engine .... Erd vertical,
valve-in-head
Test engine serial number .... T 8299
Cylinders 4
Bore and stroke (in.) .... 4.00 x 6.00
Rated rpm 900
Displacement (c.i.) 301.6
Fuel .... kerosene/gasoline
Main tank capacity (gal.) 20
Auxiliary tank capacity (gal.) 3
Carburetor .... Kingston L, 1.25-in.
Air cleaner .... Bennett
Ignition .... Kingston L magneto
Maximum brake horsepower tests
PTO/belt horsepower 22.31
Crankshaft rpm 903
Fuel use (gal./hr.) 3.39
Maximum drawbar horsepower tests
Gear .... low
Drawbar horsepower 14.37
Pull weight (lb.) 2,340
Speed (mph) 2.30
Percent slippage 7.35
SAE drawbar horsepower 12
SAE belt/PTO horsepower 20
Type .... 4 wheel
Front wheel (in.) .... steel: 46 x 4
Rear wheel (in.) .... steel: 60 x 10
Length (in.) 158.50
Height (in.) 66
Rear width (in.) 77.50
Weight (lb.) 5,800
Gear/speed (mph) .... forward: 1/2.30,
2/3.80; reverse: 1/2.00

Chapter 36
GIBSON

Gibson H

Manufacturer	The Gibson Mfg. Corp., Longmont, CO
Nebraska test number	407
Test date	May 2–7, 1949
Test tractor serial number	2423987
Years produced	1949–1953
Engine	Hercules IXB3 vertical L-head
Test engine serial number	IXB3
Cylinders	4
Bore and stroke (in.)	3.25 x 4.00
Rated rpm	1,800
Compression ratio	6.24:1
Displacement (c.i.)	133
Fuel	gasoline
Fuel tank capacity (gal.)	17
Carburetor	Marvel-Schebler TSX-388, 0.875-in.
Air cleaner	Vortox
Ignition	Delco-Remy with 6-v battery
Cooling capacity (gal.)	3.50

Maximum brake horsepower tests

PTO/belt horsepower	24.54
Crankshaft rpm	1,801
Fuel use (gal./hr.)	2.55

Maximum drawbar horsepower tests

Gear	3rd
Drawbar horsepower	22.77
Pull weight (lb.)	2,029
Speed (mph)	4.21
Percent slippage	5.72
SAE drawbar horsepower	18.15
SAE belt/PTO horsepower	22.09
Type	tricycle
Front tire (in.)	5.50 x 15
Rear tire (in.)	11.00 x 38
Length (in.)	127.25
Height (in.)	67
Tread width (in.)	47–85
Weight (lb.)	3,650
Gear/speed (mph)	forward: 1/2.00, 2/3.50, 3/5.10, 4/14.70; reverse: 1/2.30

Gibson I

Manufacturer	The Gibson Mfg. Corp., Longmont, CO
Nebraska test number	408
Test date	May 8–12, 1949
Test tractor serial number	776167
Years produced	1949–1953
Engine	Hercules QXLD vertical L-head
Test engine serial number	776167
Cylinders	6
Bore and stroke (in.)	3.4375 x 4.125
Rated rpm	1,800
Compression ratio	6.71:1
Displacement (c.i.)	236.7
Fuel	gasoline
Fuel tank capacity (gal.)	20
Carburetor	Marvel-Schebler TSX-389, 1.25-in.
Air cleaner	Vortox
Ignition	Delco-Remy with 6-v battery
Cooling capacity (gal.)	4

Maximum brake horsepower tests

PTO/belt horsepower	41.03
Crankshaft rpm	1,798
Fuel use (gal./hr.)	4.21

Maximum drawbar horsepower tests

Gear	3rd
Drawbar horsepower	36.73
Pull weight (lb.)	3,458
Speed (mph)	3.98
Percent slippage	7.02
SAE drawbar horsepower	28.59
SAE belt/PTO horsepower	36.59
Type	tricycle
Front tire (in.)	5.50 x 16
Rear tire (in.)	12.00 x 38
Length (in.)	127.25
Height (in.)	67
Tread width (in.)	49–90
Weight (lb.)	4,020
Gear/speed (mph)	forward: 1/2.00, 2/3.50, 3/5.10, 4/14.70; reverse: 1/2.30

Chapter 37

GRAHAM-BRADLEY

Graham-Bradley 503.103, 32 HP

Manufacturer	Graham-Paige Motors Corp., Detroit, MI
Nebraska test number	296
Test date	April 6–14, 1938
Test tractor serial number	50560
Years produced	1938–1939
Engine	Graham-Paige vertical L-head
Test engine serial number	300600
Cylinders	6
Bore and stroke (in.)	3.25 x 4.375
Rated rpm	1,500
Displacement (c.i.)	217.8
Fuel	gasoline
Fuel tank capacity (gal.)	16
Carburetor	Schebler TRX-15, 1.00-in.
Air cleaner	Donaldson
Ignition	Delco-Remy, 1110503
Cooling capacity (gal.)	4

Maximum brake horsepower tests

PTO/belt horsepower	30.38
Crankshaft rpm	1,502
Fuel use (gal./hr.)	3.08

Maximum drawbar horsepower tests

Gear	2nd
Drawbar horsepower	25.20
Pull weight (lb.)	2,283
Speed (mph)	4.14
Percent slippage	9.29
SAE drawbar horsepower	19.87
SAE belt/PTO horsepower	26.99
Type	tricycle
Front tire (in.)	5.50 x 16
Rear tire (in.)	9.00 x 36
Length (in.)	132
Height (in.)	69
Rear width (in.)	74
Weight (lb.)	3,550
Gear/speed (mph)	forward: 1/2.77, 2/4.42, 3/5.67, 4/19.80; reverse: 1/2.03

Chapter 38

GRAY

Gray 18-36

Manufacturer	Gray Tractor Co., Inc., Minneapolis, MN
Nebraska test number	22
Test date	June 11 to July 3, 1920
Test tractor serial number	8097
Years produced	1918–1921
Engine	Waukesha vertical L-head
Test engine serial number	16882
Cylinders	4
Bore and stroke (in.)	4.75 x 6.75
Rated rpm	950
Displacement (c.i.)	478.5
Fuel	gasoline
Fuel tank capacity (gal.)	34
Carburetor	Bennett (Stromberg M3), 1.50-in.
Air cleaner	Bennett
Ignition	Bosch DU4 magneto
Cooling capacity (gal.)	9

Maximum brake horsepower tests

PTO/belt horsepower	32.20
Crankshaft rpm	958
Fuel use (gal./hr.)	4.83

Maximum drawbar horsepower tests

Gear	low
Drawbar horsepower	19.15
Pull weight (lb.)	3,390
Speed (mph)	2.12
Percent slippage	25.21
SAE drawbar horsepower	18
SAE belt/PTO horsepower	36
Type	drum drive, 2 guide wheels
Front wheel (in.)	steel: 40 x 8
Rear wheel (in.)	1 steel: 54 x 54
Length (in.)	wheelbase: 104; total: 173
Height (in.)	62
Rear width (in.)	80
Weight (lb.)	6,185
Gear/speed (mph)	forward: 1/2.25, 2/2.75; reverse: 1/2.00

Harris PH53, Power Horse, F8W, F8WC

Manufacturer .... Harris Mfg. Co.,
Stockton, CA
Nebraska test number 479
Test date .... July 27 to
August 9, 1952
Test tractor serial number .... PH 43461
Years produced 1952–1956
Engine .... Chrysler Ind. 8A
vertical L-head
Test engine serial number 60625
Cylinders 6
Bore and stroke (in.) .... 3.4375 x 4.50
Rated rpm 2,000
Compression ratio 6.6:1
Displacement (c.i.) 250.6
Fuel .... gasoline
Fuel tank capacity (gal.) 29
Carburetor .... Carter E7T2, 1.50-in.
Air cleaner .... Donaldson
Ignition .... Auto-Lite with 6-v battery
Cooling capacity (gal.) 3.75
Maximum drawbar horsepower tests
    Gear 3rd
    Drawbar horsepower 50.11
    Pull weight (lb.) 3,816
    Speed (mph) 4.92
    Percent slippage 7.63
SAE drawbar horsepower 39.05
Type .... 4 wheel drive
Front wheel (in.) .... 13.00 x 24
Rear wheel (in.) .... 13.00 x 24
Length (in.) 99.50
Height (in.) 65
Tread width (in.) 48–76
Weight (lb.) 4,860
Gear/speed (mph) .... forward: 1/2.40, 2/3.79,
3/5.33, 4/15.40; reverse:
1/1.97

Harris FDW-C Diesel, Power Horse

Manufacturer .... Harris Mfg. Co.,
Stockton, CA
Nebraska test number 519
Test date .... May 18–22, 1954
Test tractor serial number .... PH 431194
Years produced 1954–1955
Engine .... GM 2-71, 2-cycle
vertical I-head
Test engine serial number 2A 19724
Cylinders 2
Bore and stroke (in.) .... 4.25 x 5.00
Rated rpm 1,800
Compression ratio 16:1
Displacement (c.i.) 142
Fuel .... diesel
Fuel tank capacity (gal.) 29
Carburetor .... GM injector pump
Air cleaner .... Donaldson
Ignition .... Delco-Remy 12-v;
with 2, 6-v battery
Cooling capacity (gal.) 3.75
Maximum drawbar horsepower tests
    Gear 3rd
    Drawbar horsepower 43.63
    Pull weight (lb.) 3,542
    Speed (mph) 4.62
    Percent slippage 5.16
SAE drawbar horsepower 34.25
Type .... 4 wheel drive
Front tire (in.) .... 13.00 x 24
Rear tire (in.) .... 13.00 x 24
Length (in.) 99.50
Height (in.) 66
Tread width (in.) 48–76
Weight (lb.) 5,200
Gear/speed (mph) .... forward: 1/2.16, 2/3.41,
3/4.79, 4/13.86;
reverse: 1/1.77

Harris FDW-C Diesel, Power Horse

Manufacturer .... Harris Mfg. Co.,
Stockton, CA
Nebraska test number 523
Test date .... August 2–16, 1954
Years produced 1954–1955
Engine .... Continental HD 260
vertical I-head
Test engine serial number HD260 1637
Cylinders 4
Bore and stroke (in.) .... 3.875 x 5.50
Rated rpm 1,800
Compression ratio 15:1
Displacement (c.i.) 260
Fuel .... diesel
Fuel tank capacity (gal.) 29
Carburetor .... injector pump
Air cleaner .... Donaldson
Ignition .... Delco-Remy 12-v;
with 2, 6-v battery
Cooling capacity (gal.) 3.75
Maximum drawbar horsepower tests
    Gear 3rd
    Drawbar horsepower 42.52
    Pull weight (lb.) 3,529
    Speed (mph) 4.52
    Percent slippage 4.65
SAE drawbar horsepower 33.49
Type .... 4 wheel drive
Front tire (in.) .... 13.00 x 24
Rear tire (in.) .... 13.00 x 24
Length (in.) 99.50
Height (in.) 66
Tread width (in.) 48–76
Weight (lb.) 5,200
Gear/speed (mph) .... forward: 1/2.16, 2/3.41,
3/4.79, 4/13.86; reverse:
1/1.77

Chapter 40
HART-PARR

Hart-Parr 30, 15-30 A was tested, 15-30 C
Manufacturer...Hart-Parr Co.,
Charles City, IA
Nebraska test number...............................26
Test date ....June 17–22, 1920
Test tractor serial number.......................16563
Years produced ....A: 1918–1922; C:
1922–1924
Serial number range.................................A: 8401–19125; C:
21001–22300 end
Serial number location ....brass plate on right
side of block
Number produced ....A: 9,175; C: 1,300
Engine ....Hart-Parr horizontal
opposed, valve-in-head
Test engine serial number........................16563
Cylinders 2
Bore and stroke (in.) ....6.50 x 7.00
Rated rpm 750
Displacement (c.i.) 464.5
Fuel ....kerosene/gasoline
Main tank capacity (gal.) 23
Auxiliary tank capacity (gal.) 1
Carburetor ....Schebler D
Ignition...Splitdorf Dixie 246
magneto
Cooling capacity (gal.) 10
Maximum brake horsepower tests
PTO/belt horsepower...........................31.37
Crankshaft rpm 756
Fuel use (gal./hr.)...............................4.74
Maximum drawbar horsepower tests
Gear...high
Drawbar horsepower...........................19.65
Pull weight (lb.)...................................2,788
Speed (mph)..2.64
Percent slippage.................................17.81
SAE drawbar horsepower.........................30
Type ....4 wheel
Front wheel (in.).......................................steel: 28 x 5
Rear wheel (in.)..steel: 52 x 10
Length (in.) ....wheelbase: 90;
total: 141
Height (in.)...61
Rear width (in.)..76
Weight (lb.)..5,570
Gear/speed (mph) ....forward: 1/1.98,
2/2.88; reverse: 1/1.50

Hart-Parr 20, 10-20 B
Manufacturer...Hart-Parr Co.,
Charles City, IA
Nebraska test number...............................79
Test date ....June 11–17, 1921
Test tractor serial number........................35144
Years produced 1920–1922
Serial number range.................................35001–35319
Serial number location ....brass plate on front of
governor housing

Number produced 319
Engine ....Hart-Parr horizontal,
valve-in-head
Test engine serial number........................35144
Cylinders 2
Bore and stroke (in.) ....5.25 x 6.50
Rated rpm 800
Displacement (c.i.) 281.4
Fuel ....kerosene/gasoline
Main tank capacity (gal.) 14
Auxiliary tank capacity (gal.) 1
Carburetor ....Schebler (Stromberg
MB3), 1.50-in.
Air cleaner ....Hart-Parr
Ignition...K-W TK No. 0154521
magneto
Maximum brake horsepower tests
PTO/belt horsepower...........................23.01
Crankshaft rpm 811
Fuel use (gal./hr.)...............................2.56
Maximum drawbar horsepower tests
Gear...low
Drawbar horsepower...........................14.08
Pull weight (lb.)...................................2,500
Speed (mph)..2.11
Percent slippage.................................16.53
SAE drawbar horsepower.........................20
Type ....4 wheel
Front wheel (in.).......................................steel: 28 x 5
Rear wheel (in.)..steel: 46 x 10
Length (in.) 116
Height (in.)...56
Rear width (in.)..66
Weight (lb.)..3,800
Gear/speed (mph) ....forward: 1/2.00,
2/3.00; reverse: 1/1.50

Hart-Parr 40, 22-40
Manufacturer...Hart-Parr Co.,
Charles City, IA
Nebraska test number...............................97
Test date ....July 10–19, 1923
Test tractor serial number........................70006
Years produced 1923–1927
Serial number range.................................70001–70500
Serial number location ....brass plate on front of
governor housing
Number produced 500
Engine ....Hart-Parr horizontal,
valve-in-head
Test engine serial number........................70006
Cylinders 4
Bore and stroke (in.) ....5.50 x 6.50
Rated rpm 800
Displacement (c.i.) 617.7
Fuel ....kerosene/gasoline
Main tank capacity (gal.) 29
Auxiliary tank capacity (gal.) 1
Carburetor ....Schebler D, 1.50-in.

Air cleaner ....United
Ignition ....K-W TK No. 0172406
magneto
Cooling capacity (gal.) 15
Maximum brake horsepower tests
    PTO/belt horsepower............................46.40
    Crankshaft rpm 798
    Fuel use (gal./hr.) 7.42
Maximum drawbar horsepower tests
    Gear...high
    Drawbar horsepower............................28.23
    Pull weight (lb.)..................................3,750
    Speed (mph) 2.82
    Percent slippage................................14.93
SAE drawbar horsepower.........................40
SAE belt/PTO horsepower ....na
Type ....4 wheel
Front wheel (in.).....................................steel: 28 x 5
Rear wheel (in.).......................................steel: 53 x 13
Length (in.) 140
Height (in.) 67
Rear width (in.).......................................96
Weight (lb.) 7,500
Gear/speed (mph) ....forward: 1/2.14,
2/3.12; reverse: 1/1.50

Hart-Parr 16-30, E and F
Manufacturer...Hart-Parr Co.,
Charles City, IA
Nebraska test number 106
Test date ....October 14–23, 1924
Test tractor serial number.........................22509
Years produced 1924–1926
Serial number range.................................22501–26000
Serial number location ....brass plate on front
of governor housing
Number produced 3,500
Engine ....Hart-Parr horizontal,
valve-in-head
Test engine serial number.........................22509
Cylinders 2
Bore and stroke (in.) ....6.50 x 7.00
Rated rpm 750
Displacement (c.i.) 464.6
Fuel ....kerosene/gasoline
Main tank capacity (gal.).........................23
Auxiliary tank capacity (gal.) 1
Carburetor...Schebler (Stromberg
MB3), 1.50-in.
Air cleaner ....Simplex (United)
Ignition..Bosch (K-W T) magneto
Cooling capacity (gal.) 11
Maximum brake horsepower tests
    PTO/belt horsepower............................37.03
    Crankshaft rpm 751
    Fuel use (gal./hr.) 4.60
Maximum drawbar horsepower tests
    Gear...high
    Drawbar horsepower............................24.79
    Pull weight (lb.)..................................3,320
    Speed (mph) 2.80
    Percent slippage................................14.74
SAE drawbar horsepower.........................16
SAE belt/PTO horsepower 30

Type ....4 wheel
Front wheel (in.).....................................steel: 28 x 5
Rear wheel (in.).......................................steel: 52 x 10
Length (in.) 132
Height (in.) 67
Rear width (in.).......................................74
Weight (lb.) 5,050
Gear/speed (mph) ....forward: 1/2.00,
2/3.00; reverse: 1/1.50

Hart-Parr 12-24 E
Manufacturer...Hart-Parr Co.,
Charles City, IA
Nebraska test number 107
Test date ....October 14–23, 1924
Test tractor serial number.........................36010
Years produced 1924–1926
Serial number range.................................36001–37100 end
Serial number location ....brass plate on front of
governor housing
Number produced 1,100
Engine ....Hart-Parr horizontal,
valve-in-head
Test engine serial number.........................36010
Cylinders 2
Bore and stroke (in.) ....5.50 x 6.50
Rated rpm 800
Displacement (c.i.) 308.9
Fuel ....kerosene/gasoline
Main tank capacity (gal.).........................14
Auxiliary tank capacity (gal.) 1
Carburetor...Schebler (Stromberg
MB3), 1.50-in.
Air cleaner ....Simplex (United)
Ignition..Bosch (K-W T)
magneto
Cooling capacity (gal.) 7.75
Maximum brake horsepower tests
    PTO/belt horsepower............................26.97
    Crankshaft rpm 799
    Fuel use (gal./hr.) 3.14
Maximum drawbar horsepower tests
    Gear...high
    Drawbar horsepower............................17.54
    Pull weight (lb.)..................................2,080
    Speed (mph) 3.16
    Percent slippage................................14.03
SAE drawbar horsepower.........................12
SAE belt/PTO horsepower 24
Type ....4 wheel
Front wheel (in.).....................................steel: 28 x 5
Rear wheel (in.).......................................steel: 46 x 10
Length (in.) 116
Height (in.) 56
Rear width (in.).......................................66
Weight (lb.) 4,250
Gear/speed (mph) ....forward: 1/2.25,
2/3.50; reverse: 1/1.50

Hart-Parr 18-36 G was tested, H & I
Manufacturer...Hart-Parr Co., Charles
City, IA
Nebraska test number 128
Test date ....October 18–25, 1926

Test tractor serial number 26145
Years produced ....G: 1926–1927;
H: 1927–1928;
I: 1928–1930
Serial number range ....G: 26001–28850;
H: 28851–33752;
I: 33753–35000,
85001–90698
Serial number location ....brass plate on front of
governor housing
Number produced ....G: 2,850; H: 4,902;
I: 6,946
Engine ....Hart-Parr valve-in-head
Test engine serial number 26145
Cylinders 2
Bore and stroke (in.) ....6.75 x 7.00
Rated rpm 800
Displacement (c.i.) 501
Fuel ....distillate/gasoline
Main tank capacity (gal.) 24
Auxiliary tank capacity (gal.) 1
Carburetor ....Schebler (Stromberg
MB3), 1.50-in.
Air cleaner ....Donaldson
Ignition ....Robert Bosch
ZU4/2 magneto
Cooling capacity (gal.) 12
Maximum brake horsepower tests
PTO/belt horsepower 42.85
Crankshaft rpm 795
Fuel use (gal./hr.) 5.03
Maximum drawbar horsepower tests
Gear ....high
Drawbar horsepower 32.26
Pull weight (lb.) 4,075
Speed (mph) 2.97
Percent slippage 8.58
SAE drawbar horsepower 16
SAE belt/PTO horsepower 36
Type ....4 wheel
Front wheel (in.) ....steel: 28 x 5
Rear wheel (in.) ....steel: 52.25 x 12
Length (in.) 126
Height (in.) 61
Rear width (in.) 73
Weight (lb.) 6,250
Gear/speed (mph) ....forward: 1/2.00,
2/3.00; reverse: 1/2.50

Hart-Parr 12-24 G was tested, H

Manufacturer ....Hart-Parr Co.,
Charles City, IA
Nebraska test number 129
Test date ....October 18–28, 1926
Test tractor serial number 37102
Years produced ....G: 1926–1927;
H: 1927–1930
Serial number range ....G: 37101–37900;
H: 37901–43253 end
Serial number location ....brass plate on front
of governor housing
Number produced ....G: 800; H: 5,352
Engine ....Hart-Parr horizontal,
valve-in-head

Test engine serial number 37102
Cylinders 2
Bore and stroke (in.) ....5.75 x 6.50
Rated rpm 850
Displacement (c.i.) 337.6
Fuel ....distillate/gasoline
Main tank capacity (gal.) 14.50
Auxiliary tank capacity (gal.) 1
Carburetor ....Stromberg MB3, 1.50-in.
Air cleaner ....Donaldson
Ignition ....Robert Bosch
ZU4/2 magneto
Cooling capacity (gal.) 7.75
Maximum brake horsepower tests
PTO/belt horsepower 31.99
Crankshaft rpm 856
Fuel use (gal./hr.) 3.90
Maximum drawbar horsepower tests
Gear ....low
Drawbar horsepower 21.78
Pull weight (lb.) 2,950
Speed (mph) 2.77
Percent slippage 9.93
SAE drawbar horsepower 12
SAE belt/PTO horsepower 24
Type ....4 wheel
Front wheel (in.) ....steel: 28 x 5
Rear wheel (in.) ....steel: 43.19 x 10
Length (in.) 116
Height (in.) 56
Rear width (in.) 66
Weight (lb.) 4,444
Gear/speed (mph) ....forward: 1/2.66,
2/3.33; reverse: 1/2.25

Hart-Parr 28-50

Manufacturer ....Hart-Parr Co.,
Charles City, IA
Nebraska test number 140
Test date ....August 17–31, 1927
Test tractor serial number 70618
Years produced 1927–1930
Serial number range 70501–71701
Serial number location ....brass plate on front of
governor housing
Number produced 1,201
Engine ....Hart-Parr horizontal,
valve-in-head
Test engine serial number 70618
Cylinders 4
Bore and stroke (in.) ....5.75 x 6.50
Rated rpm 850
Displacement (c.i.) 675.1
Fuel ....distillate/gasoline
Main tank capacity (gal.) 40
Auxiliary tank capacity (gal.) 1
Carburetor ....Schebler D, 1.50-in.
Air cleaner ....Donaldson
Ignition ....Robert Bosch ZU4
magneto
Cooling capacity (gal.) 13
Maximum brake horsepower tests
PTO/belt horsepower 64.56
Crankshaft rpm 851
Fuel use (gal./hr.) 7.94

Maximum drawbar horsepower tests
    Gear...high
    Drawbar horsepower...........................46.03
    Pull weight (lb.)................................4,940
    Speed (mph)...................................3.49
    Percent slippage.............................4.49
SAE drawbar horsepower...........................28
SAE belt/PTO horsepower..........................50
Type ....4 wheel

Front wheel (in.)................................steel: 28 x 7
Rear wheel (in.)................................steel: 51 x 14
Length (in.) 135
Height (in.) 64.50
Rear width (in.) 88
Weight (lb.) 8,322
Gear/speed (mph) ....forward: 1/2.25,
    2/3.25; reverse: 1/2.75

Chapter 41
HEIDER

Heider C, 12-20
Manufacturer..Rock Island Plow Co.,
    Rock Island, IL
Nebraska test number 16
Test date ....May 28–8, 1920
Test tractor serial number...........................C 8024
Years produced 1916–1927
Engine ....Waukesha
    vertical L-head
Test engine serial number...........................50872
Cylinders 4
Bore and stroke (in.) ....4.50 x 6.75
Rated rpm 900
Displacement (c.i.) 429.4
Fuel ....kerosene/gasoline
Main tank capacity (gal.)...........................14
Auxiliary tank capacity (gal.) 7
Carburetor..Kingston L3, 1.25-in.
Air cleaner ....Bennett
Ignition..Splitdorf Dixie 46
    magneto
Cooling capacity (gal.) 9.33
Maximum brake horsepower tests
    PTO/belt horsepower..........................24.24
    Crankshaft rpm 902
    Fuel use (gal./hr.) 4.34
Maximum drawbar horsepower tests
    Drawbar horsepower...........................13.43
    Pull weight (lb.)................................2,223
    Speed (mph) 2.26
    Percent slippage.............................13.00
SAE drawbar horsepower...........................12
SAE belt/PTO horsepower..........................20
Type ....4 wheel
Front wheel (in.)..steel: 30 x 5
Rear wheel (in.)..steel: 57 x 10
Length (in.) ....wheelbase: 96;
    total: 144
Height (in.) 96

Rear width (in.) 74
Weight (lb.) 6,000
Gear/speed (mph) ....forward: 1/2.25,
    2/2.50, 3/2.75, 4/3.00,
    5/3.25, 6/3.50, 7/3.75,
    8/4.00; reverse: 1/2.25,
    2/2.50, 3/2.75, 4/3.00,
    5/3.25, 6/3.50, 7/3.75

Heider D, 9-16
Manufacturer..Rock Island Plow Co.,
    Rock Island, IL
Nebraska test number 17
Test date ....June 1–9, 1920
Test tractor serial number...........................12531
Years produced 1916–1929
Engine ....Waukesha CSR
    vertical L-head
Test engine serial number...........................44962
Cylinders 4
Bore and stroke (in.) ....4.25 x 5.75
Rated rpm 1,000
Displacement (c.i.) 326.3
Fuel ....kerosene/gasoline
Main tank capacity (gal.)...........................14
Auxiliary tank capacity (gal.) 7
Carburetor..Kingston L3, 1.00-in.
Air cleaner ....Bennett
Ignition..Splitdorf, Dixie 46
    magneto
Cooling capacity (gal.) 8
Maximum brake horsepower tests
    PTO/belt horsepower..........................19.54
    Crankshaft rpm 1,003
    Fuel use (gal./hr.) 2.89
Maximum drawbar horsepower tests
    Drawbar horsepower...........................11.76
    Pull weight (lb.)................................1,900
    Speed (mph) 2.32
    Percent slippage.............................13.90

SAE drawbar horsepower...........................9
SAE belt/PTO horsepower 16
Type ....4 wheel
Front wheel (in.)....................................steel: 30 x 4
Rear wheel (in.).....................................steel: 54 x 8
Length (in.) ....wheelbase: 90;
                                                                total: 130
Height (in.)..60
Rear width (in.) 68
Weight (lb.) 4,000
Gear/speed (mph) ....forward: 1/2.50,
                                                                2/2.75, 3/3.00, 4/3.25,
                                                                5/3.50, 6/3.75, 7/4.00;
                                                                reverse: 1/2.50, 2/2.75,
                                                                3/3.00, 4/3.25, 5/3.50,
                                                                6/3.75, 7/4.00

Heider 15-27

Manufacturer...Rock Island Plow Co.,
                                                                Rock Island, IL
Nebraska test number 114
Test date ....May 7–13, 1925
Test tractor serial number.........................8621
Years produced 1925–1927
Engine ....Waukesha
                                                                vertical L-head
Test engine serial number.........................51405 P
Cylinders 4
Bore and stroke (in.) ....4.75 x 6.75
Rated rpm 900

Displacement (c.i.) 478.5
Fuel ....kerosene/gasoline
Main tank capacity (gal.).............................14
Auxiliary tank capacity (gal.) 7
Carburetor ....Kingston L, 1.50-in.
Air cleaner ....United
Ignition..Splitdorf Dixie
                                                                46 magneto
Cooling capacity (gal.) 9.36
Maximum brake horsepower tests
    PTO/belt horsepower......................30.00
    Crankshaft rpm 906
    Fuel use (gal./hr.)..........................4.61
Maximum drawbar horsepower tests
    Gear...low
    Drawbar horsepower.......................21.54
    Pull weight (lb.)..............................3,302
    Speed (mph)..................................2.45
    Percent slippage............................12.43
SAE drawbar horsepower............................15
SAE belt/PTO horsepower 27
Type ....4 wheel
Front wheel (in.)..steel: 30 x 5
Rear wheel (in.)...steel: 57 x 10
Length (in.) 144
Height (in.) 96
Rear width (in.) 74
Weight (lb.) 6,000
Gear/speed (mph) ....forward: 1/1.00–4.00;
                                                                reverse: 1/1.00–4.00

Chapter 42

HOLT

Holt T-11, 5 Ton, 25-40

Manufacturer...Holt Mfg. Co.,
                                                                Peoria, IL
Nebraska test number 59
Test date ....August 30 to
                                                                September 17, 1920
Test tractor serial number.........................40195
Years produced 1919–1924
Serial number range..................................19001–19151,
                                                                40001–42412,
                                                                43001–44500, Peoria;
                                                                50000–50212,
Serial number location ....brass Patent plate;
                                                                front main frame then
                                                                moved to left side seat
Number produced ....4,063 Peoria; 213
                                                                Stockton
Engine ....Holt vertical,
                                                                valve-in-head
Test engine serial number.........................50195
Cylinders 4
Bore and stroke (in.) ....4.75 x 6.00

Rated rpm 1,050
Displacement (c.i.) 425.3
Fuel ....gasoline
Fuel tank capacity (gal.) 32
Carburetor ....Schebler A special,
                                                                1.50-in.
Air cleaner ....Donaldson
Ignition..Eisemann G4 magneto
Cooling capacity (gal.) 7.50
Maximum brake horsepower tests
    PTO/belt horsepower......................35.52
    Crankshaft rpm 1,066
    Fuel use (gal./hr.)..........................4.38
Maximum drawbar horsepower tests
    Gear...2nd
    Drawbar horsepower.......................33.34
    Pull weight (lb.)..............................3,546
    Speed (mph)..................................3.53
    Percent slippage............................2.00
SAE drawbar horsepower............................25
SAE belt/PTO horsepower 40
Type ....tracklayer

Length (in.) 124
Height (in.) 64
Rear width (in.) 63
Weight (lb.) 9,400
Track length (in.) ....91 on ground
Grouser shoe ....11-in.
Gear/speed (mph) ....forward: 1/1.50,
2/3.00, 3/5.70;
reverse: 1/1.10

Holt T-16, 10 Ton, 40-60
Manufacturer ....Holt Mfg. Co.,
Peoria, IL
Nebraska test number 61
Test date ....September 2–20, 1920
Test tractor serial number 17872
Years produced 1918–1926
Serial number range 15001–18999,
34001–35586, Peoria;
22001–22154
Stockton end
Serial number location ....brass Patent plate,
left front main frame
Number produced ....5,585 Peoria; 149
Stockton
Engine ....Holt vertical,
valve-in-head
Test engine serial number 28118
Cylinders 4
Bore and stroke (in.) ....6.50 x 7.00
Rated rpm 750
Displacement (c.i.) 929.1
Fuel ....gasoline
Fuel tank capacity (gal.) 46
Carburetor ....Kingston E, 2.00-in.
Air cleaner ....Donaldson
Ignition ....K-W, HK magneto
Cooling capacity (gal.) 13.50
Maximum brake horsepower tests
  PTO/belt horsepower 57.21
  Crankshaft rpm 772
  Fuel use (gal./hr.) 8.94
Maximum drawbar horsepower tests
  Gear 2nd
  Drawbar horsepower 51.59
  Pull weight (lb.) 5,250
  Speed (mph) 3.69
  Percent slippage 1.31
SAE drawbar horsepower 40
SAE belt/PTO horsepower 60
Type ....tracklayer
Length (in.) 146
Height (in.) 81
Rear width (in.) 80
Tread width (in.) 62
Weight (lb.) 18,600
Track length (in.) ....105 on ground

Grouser shoe ....15-in.
Gear/speed (mph) ....forward: 1/1.77,
2/3.21, 3/5.13;
reverse: 1/1.00

Holt T-35, 2 Ton, 15-25
Manufacturer ....Holt Mfg. Co.,
Stockton, CA
Nebraska test number 86
Test date ....July 19–26, 1922
Test tractor serial number ....S 25218
Years produced 1921–1924
Serial number range 25003–26352
Stockton;
70001–78989
Peoria end
Serial number location ....brass Patent plate,
right side transmission
case below seat
Number produced ....1,350 Stockton; 8,989
Peoria
Engine ....Hallscott MS 35
vertical, valve-in-head
Test engine serial number 30150
Cylinders 4
Bore and stroke (in.) ....4.00 x 5.50
Rated rpm 1,000
Displacement (c.i.) 276.5
Fuel ....gasoline
Fuel tank capacity (gal.) 30
Carburetor ....Kingston L, 1.50-in.
Air cleaner ....Pomona
Ignition ....Eisemann G4 magneto
Cooling capacity (gal.) 5.50
Maximum brake horsepower tests
  PTO/belt horsepower 25.48
  Crankshaft rpm 1,003
  Fuel use (gal./hr.) 2.70
Maximum drawbar horsepower tests
  Gear 2nd
  Drawbar horsepower 18.17
  Pull weight (lb.) 2,397
  Speed (mph) 2.84
  Percent slippage 7.39
SAE drawbar horsepower 15
SAE belt/PTO horsepower 25
Type ....tracklayer
Length (in.) 103
Height (in.) 52
Rear width (in.) 48
Weight (lb.) 4,000
Track length (in.) ....51 on ground
Grouser shoe ....10-in.
Gear/speed (mph) ....forward: 1/2.18,
2/3.04, 3/5.23;
reverse: 1/2.36

Chapter 43
HUBER

Huber Light Four, 12-25

Manufacturer	Huber Mfg. Co., Marchion, Ohio
Nebraska test number	12
Test date	May 18 to June 3, 1920
Test tractor serial number	39654
Years produced	1916–1928
Serial number location	metal tag on left side frame behind front wheels
Number produced	approximately 6,500
Engine	Waukesha vertical L-head
Cylinders	4
Bore and stroke (in.)	4.00 x 5.75
Rated rpm	1,000
Displacement (c.i.)	289.0
Fuel	kerosene/gasoline
Main tank capacity (gal.)	21.33
Auxiliary tank capacity (gal.)	3
Carburetor	Kingston L, 1.25-in.
Air cleaner	Bennett
Ignition	Kingston magneto

Maximum brake horsepower tests

PTO/belt horsepower	25.70
Crankshaft rpm	1,005
Fuel use (gal./hr.)	4.45

Maximum drawbar horsepower tests

Gear	low
Drawbar horsepower	16.70
Pull weight (lb.)	2,505
Speed (mph)	2.50
Percent slippage	11.60
SAE drawbar horsepower	12
SAE belt/PTO horsepower	25
Type	4 wheel
Front wheel (in.)	steel: 46 x 4
Rear wheel (in.)	steel: 60 x 10
Length (in.)	91 wheel, 150 total
Height (in.)	70
Rear width (in.)	80
Weight (lb.)	5,000
Gear/speed (mph)	forward: 1/2.70, 2/4.15; reverse: 1/1.88

Huber Super 4, 15-30

Manufacturer	Huber Mfg. Co., Marchion, Ohio
Nebraska test number	74
Test date	April 11–20, 1921
Test tractor serial number	6714
Years produced	1920–1925
Serial number location	metal tag on left frame behind front wheels
Number produced	approximately 1,100
Engine	Midwest vertical, valve-in-head

Test engine serial number	1102
Cylinders	4
Bore and stroke (in.)	4.50 x 6.00
Rated rpm	1,000
Displacement (c.i.)	381.7
Fuel	gasoline
Fuel tank capacity (gal.)	24
Carburetor	Kingston L, 1.25-in.
Air cleaner	R-W
Ignition	Eisemann (Kingston LD4) magneto
Cooling capacity (gal.)	9

Maximum brake horsepower tests

PTO/belt horsepower	44.68
Crankshaft rpm	1,216
Fuel use (gal./hr.)	5.18

Maximum drawbar horsepower tests

Gear	low
Drawbar horsepower	26.85
Pull weight (lb.)	3,645
Speed (mph)	2.76
Percent slippage	10.50
SAE drawbar horsepower	15
SAE belt/PTO horsepower	30
Type	4 wheel
Front wheel (in.)	steel: 46 x 4
Rear wheel (in.)	steel: 60 x 10
Length (in.)	150
Height (in.)	69
Rear width (in.)	82.50
Weight (lb.)	5,800
Gear/speed (mph)	forward: 1/2.70, 2/4.15; reverse: 1/2.25

Huber 18-36, Super 4, 21-39

Manufacturer	Huber Mfg. Co., Marchion, Ohio
Nebraska test number	123
Test date	June 7–12, 1926
Test tractor serial number	8110
Years produced	1926–1929
Serial number location	metal tag on steering column support brace
Number produced	approximately 600
Engine	Stearns vertical, valve-in-head
Test engine serial number	266078
Cylinders	4
Bore and stroke (in.)	4.75 x 6.50
Rated rpm	1,000
Displacement (c.i.)	460.7
Fuel	gasoline
Fuel tank capacity (gal.)	42
Carburetor	Ensign (Kingston L3), 1.50-in.
Air cleaner	Pomona Vortox
Ignition	Eisemann GS4 magneto

Cooling capacity (gal.) 12
Maximum brake horsepower tests
    PTO/belt horsepower...........................43.15
    Crankshaft rpm 998
    Fuel use (gal./hr.)...............................5.86
Maximum drawbar horsepower tests
    Gear..high
    Drawbar horsepower..........................30.35
    Pull weight (lb.).................................2,997
    Speed (mph)......................................3.80
    Percent slippage...............................10.35
SAE drawbar horsepower..........................18
SAE belt/PTO horsepower..........................36
Type ....4 wheel
Front wheel (in.)....................................steel: 40 x 6
Rear wheel (in.).....................................steel: 56 x 14
Length (in.) 158
Height (in.)...62
Rear width (in.)...76
Weight (lb.)...7,200
Gear/speed (mph) ....forward: 1/2.20,
    2/3.80; reverse: 1/na

Huber 20-40, Super 4, 32-45

Manufacturer..Huber Mfg. Co.,
    Marchion, Ohio
Nebraska test number 126
Test date ....September 7–16, 1926
Test tractor serial number...........................8282
Years produced...1926–1928
Serial number location ....metal tag on steering
    column support brace
Number produced ....approximately 360
Engine..Stearns, valve-in-head
Test engine serial number.........................263027
Cylinders 4
Bore and stroke (in.) ....5.125 x 6.50
Rated rpm 1,100
Displacement (c.i.) 536.4
Fuel ....gasoline
Fuel tank capacity (gal.) 42
Carburetor ....Ensign (Kingston L 3),
    1.50-in.
Air cleaner ....Pomona Vortox
Ignition...Eisemann GS4
    magneto
Cooling capacity (gal.) 14
Maximum brake horsepower tests
    PTO/belt horsepower...........................50.05
    Crankshaft rpm 1,104
    Fuel use (gal./hr.)...............................7.08
Maximum drawbar horsepower tests
    Gear..low
    Drawbar horsepower..........................40.79
    Pull weight (lb.).................................5,933
    Speed (mph)......................................2.58
    Percent slippage...............................6.31
SAE drawbar horsepower..........................20
SAE belt/PTO horsepower..........................40
Type ....4 wheel
Front wheel (in.)....................................steel: 40 x 7
Rear wheel (in.).....................................steel: 56 x 18
Length (in.) 160
Height (in.)...62
Rear width (in.)...84

Weight (lb.) 8,900
Gear/speed (mph) ....forward: 1/2.47,
    2/3.48; reverse: 1/1.94

Huber Super Four, 40-62, 25-50

Manufacturer..Huber Mfg. Co.,
    Marchion, Ohio
Nebraska test number 135
Test date ....May 17 to June 24,
    1927
Test tractor serial number...........................8568
Years produced...1927–1939
Serial number location ....metal tag on steering
    column brace
Number produced ....approximately 200
Engine..Stearns vertical,
    valve-in-head
Test engine serial number.........................273508
Cylinders 4
Bore and stroke (in.) ....5.50 x 6.50
Rated rpm 1,100
Displacement (c.i.) 617.7
Fuel ....gasoline
Fuel tank capacity (gal.) 55
Carburetor ....Ensign A, 1.75-in.
Air cleaner ....Pomona
Ignition...Eisemann G4 magneto
Cooling capacity (gal.) 15
Maximum brake horsepower tests
    PTO/belt horsepower...........................69.76
    Crankshaft rpm 1,100
    Fuel use (gal./hr.)...............................8.66
Maximum drawbar horsepower tests
    Gear..high
    Drawbar horsepower..........................50.03
    Pull weight (lb.).................................5,355
    Speed (mph)......................................3.51
    Percent slippage...............................7.81
SAE drawbar horsepower..........................40
SAE belt/PTO horsepower..........................62
Type ....4 wheel
Front wheel (in.)....................................steel: 40 x 7
Rear wheel (in.).....................................steel: 56 x 20
Length (in.) 160
Height (in.)...62
Rear width (in.)...88
Weight (lb.)...9,200
Gear/speed (mph) ....forward: 1/2.00-2.50,
    2/3.00-3.50; reverse:
    1/1.75-2.25

Huber Light Four, 20-36

Manufacturer..Huber Mfg. Co.,
    Marchion, Ohio
Nebraska test number 168
Test date ....August 19–24, 1929
Test tractor serial number...........................9699
Years produced...1929–1935
Serial number location ....metal tag on inside left
    fender
Number produced ....approximately 1,000
Engine..Waukesha DKR vertical
    L-head
Test engine serial number.........................192002
Cylinders 4

Bore and stroke (in.) ....4.75 x 6.25
Rated rpm 1,150
Displacement (c.i.) 443
Fuel ....gasoline
Fuel tank capacity (gal.) 32
Carburetor ....Zenith (Stromberg M3) 1.50-in.
Air cleaner ....Donaldson
Ignition ....Amer. Bosch (Eisemann GV 4) magneto
Cooling capacity (gal.) 8

Maximum brake horsepower tests
PTO/belt horsepower...........................42.26
Crankshaft rpm 1,152
Fuel use (gal./hr.) 5.21

Maximum drawbar horsepower tests
Gear..low
Drawbar horsepower............................29.18
Pull weight (lb.).................................3,298
Speed (mph) 3.32
Percent slippage................................11.76
SAE drawbar horsepower..............................20
SAE belt/PTO horsepower.............................36
Type ....4 wheel
Front wheel (in.)..steel: 34 x 6
Rear wheel (in.)...steel: 50 x 12
Length (in.) 136
Height (in.) 86
Rear width (in.) 73.50
Weight (lb.) 5,700
Gear/speed (mph) ....forward: 1/2.32, 2/3.08; reverse: 1/1.83

Huber LC

Manufacturer..Huber Mfg. Co., Marchion, Ohio
Nebraska test number 291
Test date ....October 11–28, 1937
Test tractor serial number........................11915
Years produced..1935–1940
Serial number location ....metal tag on frame, either side, behind front wheels
Number produced ....approximately 650
Engine ....Waukesha VIL vertical overhead-valve
Test engine serial number........................398467
Cylinders 4
Bore and stroke (in.) ....4.50 x 5.25
Rated rpm 1,200
Displacement (c.i.) 334.0
Fuel ....distillate/gasoline
Main tank capacity (gal.)..............................20
Auxiliary tank capacity (gal.) 2
Carburetor ....Zenith 455, 1.25-in.
Air cleaner ....Donaldson
Ignition ....Amer. Bosch, MJB4A-112 magneto
Cooling capacity (gal.) 5

Maximum brake horsepower tests
PTO/belt horsepower...........................43.24
Crankshaft rpm 1,199
Fuel use (gal./hr.) 4.02

Maximum drawbar horsepower tests
Gear..St 2nd, Ru 3rd
Drawbar horsepower............................St 30.47, Ru 31.35
Pull weight (lb.).................................St 2,823, Ru 2,824
Speed (mph) ....St 4.05, Ru 4.16
Percent slippage................................St 5.98, Ru 14.34
SAE drawbar horsepower..............................23.22
SAE belt/PTO horsepower.............................37.42
Type ....tricycle
Front wheel (in.).......................................(steel: 25 x 4.50; rubber: 6.00 x 16
Rear wheel (in.)..(steel: 43 x 10; rubber: 11.25 x 24)
Length (in.) 130
Height (in.) 57
Rear width (in.) 81.50
Weight (lb.) 3,900
Gear/speed (mph) ....forward: 1/2.40, 2/3.50, 3/4.50; reverse: 1/1.80

Huber B

Manufacturer..Huber Mfg. Co., Marchion, Ohio
Nebraska test number 292
Test date ....October 13 to November 8, 1937
Test tractor serial number........................12585
Years produced..1936–1943
Serial number range...................................Unknown–14297 end
Serial number location ....metal tag on frame, either side, behind front wheels
Number produced ....approximately 1,100
Engine ....Buda vertical L-head
Test engine serial number........................230317
Cylinders 4
Bore and stroke (in.) ....3.8125 x 4.50
Rated rpm 1,300
Displacement (c.i.) 205.5
Fuel ....gasoline
Fuel tank capacity (gal.) 16
Carburetor ....Zenith, TU4VP, 1.00-in.
Air cleaner ....Donaldson
Ignition ....American Bosch, MJC4A-102 magneto
Cooling capacity (gal.) 3.25

Maximum brake horsepower tests
PTO/belt horsepower...........................27.50
Crankshaft rpm 1,300
Fuel use (gal./hr.) 3.02

Maximum drawbar horsepower tests
Gear..St 2nd, Ru 4th
Drawbar horsepower............................St 20.72, Ru 22.94
Pull weight (lb.).................................St 2,164, Ru 1,039
Speed (mph) ....St 3.59, Ru 8.28
Percent slippage................................St 2.13, Ru 2.95
SAE drawbar horsepower..............................16.28
SAE belt/PTO horsepower.............................24.00
Type ....tricycle
Front wheel (in.).......................................(steel: 25 x 4.50; rubber: 5.50 x 16
Rear wheel (in.)..(steel: 50 x 8; rubber: 9.00 x 36)

Length (in.) 127.50
Height (in.) 54.63
Rear width (in.) 50–76
Tread width (in.)..St 51–74; Ru 52–73
Weight (lb.) ....St 3,320, Ru 4,040
Gear/speed (mph) ....forward: 1/2.20,
2/3.20, 3/4.30,
4/10.00; reverse:
1/1.80

Huber B, Global

Manufacturer...Huber Mfg. Co.,
Marchion, Ohio
Nebraska test number 433
Test date ....November 1–7, 1949
Test tractor serial number..........................None
Years produced 1949–1950
Serial number location ....metal tag on right side
of frame
Number produced 8
Engine ....Continental, H260
vertical I-head
Test engine serial number..........................HB 2602044
Cylinders 4
Bore and stroke (in.) ....3.875 x 5.50
Rated rpm 1,475
Compression ratio......................................15.0:1
Displacement (c.i.) 259.4
Fuel ....diesel

Fuel tank capacity (gal.) 16
Carburetor..Bosch PSP injector
pump
Air cleaner ....Donaldson
Ignition...Auto-Lite, 12-v; with 2,
6-v battery

Maximum brake horsepower tests
PTO/belt horsepower...........................42.81
Crankshaft rpm 1,475
Fuel use (gal./hr.)................................2.86
Maximum drawbar horsepower tests
Gear...3rd
Drawbar horsepower............................37.67
Pull weight (lb.)....................................2,844
Speed (mph) 4.97
Percent slippage..................................6.77
SAE drawbar horsepower............................29.16
SAE belt/PTO horsepower 38.13
Type ....Standard
Front wheel (in.)...tire, 6.00 x 16
Rear wheel (in.)..tire, 11.00 x 38
Length (in.) 151
Height (in.) 74
Rear width (in.) ....73.5 or 93.86
Tread width (in.)...57 or 77
Weight (lb.) 4,809
Gear/speed (mph) ....forward: 1/1.70, 2/2.90,
3/5.20, 4/10.70,
5/14.00; reverse: 1/2.70

Chapter 44

INDIANA

Indiana 5-10

Manufacturer...Indiana Silo & Tractor
Co., Des Moines, IA
Nebraska test number 62
Test date ....September 13–17,
1920
Test tractor serial number...........................2118
Years produced 1919–1924
Engine ....Le Roi vertical L-head
Test engine serial number..........................21475
Cylinders 4
Bore and stroke (in.) ....3.125 x 4.50
Rated rpm 1,000
Displacement (c.i.) 138
Fuel ....gasoline
Fuel tank capacity (gal.) 12
Carburetor..Kingston L, 0.875-in.
Air cleaner ....Bennett
Ignition...Atwater-Kent K-3
magneto
Cooling capacity (gal.) 4.50

Maximum brake horsepower tests
PTO/belt horsepower...........................11.34
Crankshaft rpm 1,023
Fuel use (gal./hr.)................................2.21
Maximum drawbar horsepower tests
Drawbar horsepower............................5.66
Pull weight (lb.)....................................1,189
Speed (mph) 1.79
Percent slippage..................................24.65
SAE drawbar horsepower............................5
SAE belt/PTO horsepower 10
Type ....2 wheel with rear truck
Front wheel (in.)...steel: 36 x 4
Rear wheel (in.)..steel: 50 x 12
Length (in.) 108
Height (in.) 62
Rear width (in.) 54
Weight (lb.) 2,000
Gear/speed (mph) ....forward: 1/1.00–4.00;
reverse: 1/1.00–4.00

Chapter 45
INTERCONTINENTAL

Intercontinental C-26

Manufacturer.................................Intercontinental Mfg.
Co., Inc., Dallas, TX
Nebraska test number...............................400
Test date ....August 28 to
September 9, 1948
Test tractor serial number......................752
Years produced 1948–1956
Engine ....Continental F-162
vertical L-head
Test engine serial number.........................F 162 91340
Cylinders 4
Bore and stroke (in.) ....3.4375 x 4.375
Rated rpm 1,650
Compression ratio....................................6.1:1
Displacement (c.i.) 162.4
Fuel ....gasoline
Fuel tank capacity (gal.) 15
Carburetor..Marvel-Schebler
TSX-338, 1.00-in.
Air cleaner..Donaldson
Ignition..Auto-Lite, 6-v battery
Cooling capacity (gal.) 2.75
Maximum brake horsepower tests
  PTO/belt horsepower.........................29.65
  Crankshaft rpm 1,649
  Fuel use (gal./hr.).............................2.88
Maximum drawbar horsepower tests
  Gear..2nd
  Drawbar horsepower.........................25.48
  Pull weight (lb.)..............................2,557
  Speed (mph) 3.74
  Percent slippage..............................6.02
SAE drawbar horsepower......................20.26
SAE belt/PTO horsepower 26.55
Type ....tricycle
Front tire (in.).....................................5.50 x 16
Rear tire (in.).......................................11.00 x 38
Length (in.) 130
Height (in.) 73.50
Tread width (in.)..................................56–84
Weight (lb.) 3,100
Gear/speed (mph) ....forward: 1/2.70,
2/3.80, 3/5.30,
4/10.70; reverse: 1/3.4

Intercontinental D-26, DE Diesel

Manufacturer.................................Intercontinental Mfg.
Co., Inc., Dallas, TX
Nebraska test number...............................420
Test date ....August 4–13, 1949
Years produced 1950–1956
Engine ....Buda 4BD153 vertical
I-head
Test engine serial number.........................45989
Cylinders 4
Bore and stroke (in.) ....3.4375 x 4.125
Rated rpm 1,800

Compression ratio....................................15:1
Displacement (c.i.) 153
Fuel ....diesel
Fuel tank capacity (gal.) 17
Carburetor..Bosch injector pump
Air cleaner..United
Ignition..Auto-Lite, 12-v; with 2,
6-v battery
Cooling capacity (gal.) 2.75
Maximum brake horsepower tests
  PTO/belt horsepower.........................28.86
  Crankshaft rpm 1,799
  Fuel use (gal./hr.).............................2.63
Maximum drawbar horsepower tests
  Gear..2nd
  Drawbar horsepower.........................26.11
  Pull weight (lb.)..............................2,349
  Speed (mph) 4.17
  Percent slippage..............................5.50
SAE drawbar horsepower......................20.70
SAE belt/PTO horsepower 26.13
Type ....tricycle
Front tire (in.).....................................5.50 x 16
Rear tire (in.).......................................11.00 x 38
Length (in.) 122
Height (in.) 85.50
Tread width (in.)..................................56–84
Weight (lb.) 3,250
Gear/speed (mph) ....forward: 1/2.50,
2/3.50, 3/4.90, 4/9.80;
reverse: 1/3.10

Intercontinental DF Diesel

Manufacturer.................................Intercontinental Mfg.
Co., Inc., Garland, TX
Nebraska test number...............................498
Test date ....July 24–29, 1953
Years produced 1950–1956
Engine ....Buda 4BD182 vertical
I-head
Test engine serial number.........................53402
Cylinders 4
Bore and stroke (in.) ....3.75 x 4.125
Rated rpm 1,800
Compression ratio....................................15:1
Displacement (c.i.) 182
Fuel ....diesel
Fuel tank capacity (gal.) 17
Carburetor..Bosch injector pump
Air cleaner..Donaldson
Ignition..Auto-Lite, 12-v; with 2,
6-v battery
Cooling capacity (gal.) 2.75
Maximum brake horsepower tests
  PTO/belt horsepower.........................33.84
  Crankshaft rpm 1,800
  Fuel use (gal./hr.).............................2.60

Maximum drawbar horsepower tests
- Gear..2nd
- Drawbar horsepower............................31.38
- Pull weight (lb.)................................2,755
- Speed (mph) 4.27
- Percent slippage...............................5.35

SAE drawbar horsepower....................24.83
SAE belt/PTO horsepower 30.54
Type ....tricycle
Front wheel (in.)............................5.50 x 16

Rear wheel (in.)............................11.00 x 38
Length (in.) 122
Height (in.) 85.50
Tread width (in.)..............................56–84
Weight (lb.) 3,350
Gear/speed (mph) ....forward: 1/3.08, 2/4.45, 3/6.19, 4/12.27; reverse: 1/3.83

Chapter 46

INTERNATIONAL

Titan 10-20

Manufacturer...............................International Harvester Co., Chicago, IL
Nebraska test number 23
Test date ....June 14–19, 1920
Test tractor serial number ....TY 60909
Years produced 1917–1922
Serial number range........................TV116–TV50235; TY50236–TY78464
Serial number location ....stamped front end of right channel
Number produced ....approximately 783,249
Engine ....IHC horizontal, valve-in-head
Test engine serial number.................TY 60909
Cylinders 2
Bore and stroke (in.) ....6.50 x 8.00
Rated rpm 575
Displacement (c.i.) 530.9
Fuel ....kerosene/gasoline
Fuel tank capacity (gal.) 16
Carburetor ....IHC
Air cleaner......................................IHC
Ignition..K-W TK magneto
Cooling capacity (gal.) 40

Maximum brake horsepower tests
- PTO/belt horsepower..........................28.15
- Crankshaft rpm 580
- Fuel use (gal./hr.) 4.64

Maximum drawbar horsepower tests
- Gear...high
- Drawbar horsepower............................15.65
- Pull weight (lb.)................................1,850
- Speed (mph) 3.17
- Percent slippage................................4.80

SAE drawbar horsepower....................10
SAE belt/PTO horsepower 20
Type ....4 wheel
Front wheel (in.)...............................steel: 36 x 6
Rear wheel (in.)................................steel: 54 x 10
Length (in.) ....wheelbase: 91; total: 147

Height (in.) 66.75
Rear width (in.) 60
Weight (lb.) 5,710
Gear/speed (mph) ....forward: 1/2.15, 2/2.90; reverse: 1/2.50

International 15-30, Titan

Manufacturer...............................International Harvester Co., Chicago, IL
Nebraska test number 24
Test date ....June 14–19, 1920
Test tractor serial number ....EC 3786
Years produced 1915–1922
Serial number range........................TS101–TS918; TW101–TW896; EC501–EC4910
Number produced 6,024
Engine ....IHC horizontal, valve-in-head
Test engine serial number.................EC-3786
Cylinders 4
Bore and stroke (in.) ....5.25 x 8.00
Rated rpm 575
Displacement (c.i.) 692.7
Fuel ....kerosene/gasoline
Fuel tank capacity (gal.) 24
Carburetor ....IHC
Air cleaner......................................IHC
Ignition..K-W T magneto
Cooling capacity (gal.) 40

Maximum brake horsepower tests
- PTO/belt horsepower..........................36.98
- Crankshaft rpm 577
- Fuel use (gal./hr.) 7.29

Maximum drawbar horsepower tests
- Gear...high
- Drawbar horsepower............................25.91
- Pull weight (lb.)................................4,210
- Speed (mph) 2.31
- Percent slippage................................11.50

SAE drawbar horsepower....................15
SAE belt/PTO horsepower 30

Type	4 wheel
Front wheel (in.)	steel: 40 x 7
Rear wheel (in.)	steel: 66 x 14
Length (in.)	160
Height (in.)	118
Rear width (in.)	80
Weight (lb.)	8,700
Gear/speed (mph)	forward: 1/1.85, 2/2.48; reverse: 1/1.80

International 8-16

Manufacturer	International Harvester Co., Chicago, IL
Nebraska test number	25
Test date	June 16–21, 1920
Test tractor serial number	IC 503
Years produced	1917–1922
Serial number range	VB501–VB5748; HC501–HC11871; IC501–IC17023
Serial number location	stamped under magneto bracket
Number produced	approximately 33,142
Engine	IHC vertical, valve-in-head
Test engine serial number	IC 503
Cylinders	4
Bore and stroke (in.)	4.25 x 5.00
Rated rpm	1,000
Displacement (c.i.)	283.7
Fuel	kerosene/gasoline
Main tank capacity (gal.)	11
Auxiliary tank capacity (gal.)	1.50
Carburetor	Ensign
Air cleaner	IHC
Ignition	Splitdorf Dixie 46 magneto

Maximum brake horsepower tests

PTO/belt horsepower	18.52
Crankshaft rpm	1,007
Fuel use (gal./hr.)	3.24

Maximum drawbar horsepower tests

Gear	low
Drawbar horsepower	11.00
Pull weight (lb.)	2,588
Speed (mph)	1.59
Percent slippage	18.20
SAE drawbar horsepower	8
SAE belt/PTO horsepower	16
Type	4 wheel
Front wheel (in.)	steel: 32 x 4
Rear wheel (in.)	steel: 40 x 10
Length (in.)	wheelbase: 85; total: 132
Height (in.)	65
Rear width (in.)	54
Weight (lb.)	3,300
Gear/speed (mph)	forward: 1/1.81, 2/2.81, 3/4.10

McCormick-Deering 15-30

Manufacturer	International Harvester Co., Chicago, IL
Nebraska test number	87
Test date	August 9–14, 1922

Test tractor serial number	T.G. 591
Years produced	1921–1929
Serial number range	112–99925 end, through 1928, no data available for 1929
Serial number location	plate on fender and fuel tank support
Number produced	128,125 through 1929
Engine	IHC vertical, valve-in-head
Test engine serial number	1966
Cylinders	4
Bore and stroke (in.)	4.50 x 6.00
Rated rpm	1,000
Displacement (c.i.)	381.7
Fuel	kerosene/gasoline
Main tank capacity (gal.)	18.50
Auxiliary tank capacity (gal.)	1
Carburetor	Ensign J.T.W, 1.50-in.
Air cleaner	International
Ignition	Dixie 46 C Aero magneto
Cooling capacity (gal.)	12

Maximum brake horsepower tests

PTO/belt horsepower	32.86
Crankshaft rpm	1,018
Fuel use (gal./hr.)	3.37

Maximum drawbar horsepower tests

Gear	low
Drawbar horsepower	20.05
Pull weight (lb.)	3,700
Speed (mph)	2.03
Percent slippage	18.18
SAE drawbar horsepower	15
SAE belt/PTO horsepower	30
Type	4 wheel
Front wheel (in.)	steel: 34 x 6
Rear wheel (in.)	steel: 50 x 12
Length (in.)	133
Height (in.)	61
Rear width (in.)	65
Weight (lb.)	5,750
Gear/speed (mph)	forward: 1/2.30, 2/2.93, 3/4.46; reverse: 1/2.75

McCormick-Deering 10-20

Manufacturer	International Harvester Co., Chicago, IL
Nebraska test number	95
Test date	September 25 to October 3, 1923
Test tractor serial number	KC 1356
Years produced	1923–1939
Serial number range	501–215973 end
Serial number location	plate on forward fuel tank support
Number produced	158,203 through 1929
Engine	IHC vertical, valve-in-head
Test engine serial number	KC 1356
Cylinders	4
Bore and stroke (in.)	4.25 x 5.00
Rated rpm	1,000
Displacement (c.i.)	283.7

Fuel .... kerosene/gasoline
Main tank capacity (gal.) 14.50
Auxiliary tank capacity (gal.) 0.75
Carburetor .... Ensign JH, 1.25-in.
Air cleaner .... Pomona (International)
Ignition .... Dixie 46 C Aero, No.
883311 magneto
Cooling capacity (gal.) 9

Maximum brake horsepower tests
    PTO/belt horsepower 21.84
    Crankshaft rpm 1,000
    Fuel use (gal./hr.) 2.27

Maximum drawbar horsepower tests
    Gear .... low
    Drawbar horsepower 15.54
    Pull weight (lb.) 2,640
    Speed (mph) 2.21
    Percent slippage 14.84
SAE drawbar horsepower 10
SAE belt/PTO horsepower 20
Type .... 4 wheel
Front wheel (in.) .... steel: 30 x 4.50
Rear wheel (in.) .... steel: 42 x 12
Length (in.) 123
Height (in.) 62
Rear width (in.) 60
Weight (lb.) 3,700
Gear/speed (mph) .... forward: 1/2.17,
2/3.21, 3/4.25;
reverse: 1/2.75

Farmall Regular, McCormick-Deering

Manufacturer .... International Harvester
Co., Chicago, IL
Nebraska test number 117
Test date .... September 14–19,
1925
Test tractor serial number .... QC 693
Years produced 1924–1932
Serial number range .... 501–134954 end,
includes QC, T, and IT
Types
Serial number location .... plate on toolbox under
fuel tank
Number produced .... approximately 134,650
Engine .... IHC vertical, valve-in-
head
Test engine serial number .... QC 693
Cylinders 4
Bore and stroke (in.) .... 3.75 x 5.00
Rated rpm 1,200
Displacement (c.i.) 220.9
Fuel .... kerosene/gasoline
Main tank capacity (gal.) 13
Auxiliary tank capacity (gal.) 0.86
Carburetor .... Ensign 3DA600F,
1.25-in.
Air cleaner .... Pomona 118
Ignition .... International (Dixie
Aero) magneto
Cooling capacity (gal.) 9

Maximum brake horsepower tests
    PTO/belt horsepower 20.05
    Crankshaft rpm 1,201
    Fuel use (gal./hr.) 2.14

Maximum drawbar horsepower tests
    Gear 2nd
    Drawbar horsepower 13.27
    Pull weight (lb.) 1,625
    Speed (mph) 3.06
    Percent slippage 11.86
Type .... 4 wheel, tricycle
Front wheel (in.) .... steel: 25 x 4
Rear wheel (in.) .... steel: 40 x 6
Length (in.) 123
Height (in.) 67
Rear width (in.) 86
Tread width (in.) 74
Weight (lb.) 3,650
Gear/speed (mph) .... forward: 1/2.00,
2/3.00, 3/4.00; reverse:
1/2.75

McCormick-Deering 15-30

Manufacturer .... International Harvester
Co., Chicago, IL
Nebraska test number 130
Test date .... October 26 to
November 2, 1926
Test tractor serial number .... TG 46953
Years produced 1923–1929
Serial number range .... 112–99925 end,
through 1928, no data
available for 1929
Serial number location .... plate on fuel tank
support
Number produced .... 128,125 through 1929
Engine .... IHC vertical,
valve-in-head
Test engine serial number 6982
Cylinders 4
Bore and stroke (in.) .... 4.50 x 6.00
Rated rpm 1,050
Displacement (c.i.) 381.7
Fuel .... kerosene/gasoline
Main tank capacity (gal.) 18.50
Auxiliary tank capacity (gal.) 1
Carburetor .... Ensign RW, 1.50-in.
Air cleaner .... Pomona Vortox
Ignition .... IHC E4A magneto
Cooling capacity (gal.) 12

Maximum brake horsepower tests
    PTO/belt horsepower 34.91
    Crankshaft rpm 1,054
    Fuel use (gal./hr.) 3.71

Maximum drawbar horsepower tests
    Gear .... low
    Drawbar horsepower 26.67
    Pull weight (lb.) 4,190
    Speed (mph) 2.39
    Percent slippage 9.17
SAE drawbar horsepower 15
SAE belt/PTO horsepower 30
Type .... 4 wheel
Front wheel (in.) .... steel: 34 x 6
Rear wheel (in.) .... steel: 50 x 12
Length (in.) 137
Height (in.) 70
Rear width (in.) 65
Weight (lb.) 5,970

Gear/speed (mph) ....forward: 1/2.00,
2/3.00, 3/4.00; reverse:
1/2.50

McCormick-Deering 10-20
Manufacturer.................................International Harvester
Co., Chicago, IL
Nebraska test number 142
Test date ....October 3–6, 1927
Test tractor serial number ....KC 82367
Years produced 1923–1939
Serial number range.......................501–215973 end
Serial number location ....plate on forward fuel
tank support
Number produced ....158,203 through 1929
Engine ....IHC vertical, valve-in-
head
Test engine serial number ....KC 82367
Cylinders 4
Bore and stroke (in.) ....4.25 x 5.00
Rated rpm 1,025
Displacement (c.i.) 283.7
Fuel ....kerosene/gasoline
Main tank capacity (gal.) 14.50
Auxiliary tank capacity (gal.) 0.75
Carburetor....................................Ensign R, 1.25-in.
Air cleaner....................................Pomona Vortox 118
Ignition...IHC E4A magneto
Cooling capacity (gal.) 9
Maximum brake horsepower tests
PTO/belt horsepower.................24.81
Crankshaft rpm 1,023
Fuel use (gal./hr.) 2.72
Maximum drawbar horsepower tests
Gear...low
Drawbar horsepower.................19.60
Pull weight (lb.).........................2,955
Speed (mph) 2.49
Percent slippage.......................2.25
SAE drawbar horsepower...............10
SAE belt/PTO horsepower..............20
Type ....4 wheel
Front wheel (in.) ....steel: 30 x 4.50
Rear wheel (in.).............................steel: 42 x 12
Length (in.) 123
Height (in.) 62
Rear width (in.) 60
Weight (lb.) 3,920
Gear/speed (mph) ....forward: 1/2.00,
2/3.00, 3/4.00; reverse:
1/2.75

McCormick-Deering 15-30, Later 22-36
Manufacturer.................................International Harvester
Co., Chicago, IL
Nebraska test number 156
Test date ....March 30 to April 9,
1929
Test tractor serial number ....TG 102912 M
Years produced 1929–1934
Serial number range.......................99926–157477 end
Serial number location ....plate on center of rear
hood sheet
Number produced ....approximately 57,464

Engine ....IHC vertical I,
valve-in-head
Test engine serial number ....TG 102912 M
Cylinders 4
Bore and stroke (in.) ....4.75 x 6.00
Rated rpm 1,050
Displacement (c.i.) 425.3
Fuel ....kerosene/gasoline
Main tank capacity (gal.) 19
Auxiliary tank capacity (gal.) 0.75
Carburetor....................................IHC (Ensign RW),
1.50-in.
Air cleaner....................................Pomona Vortox
Ignition...IHC E4A magneto
Cooling capacity (gal.) 11.50
Maximum brake horsepower tests
PTO/belt horsepower.................40.66
Crankshaft rpm 1,050
Fuel use (gal./hr.) 4.07
Maximum drawbar horsepower tests
Gear...3rd
Drawbar horsepower.................30.07
Pull weight (lb.).........................3,913
Speed (mph) 2.88
Percent slippage.......................6.63
SAE drawbar horsepower...............21
SAE belt/PTO horsepower..............36
Type ....4 wheel
Front wheel (in.) ....steel: 34 x 6
Rear wheel (in.).............................steel: 50 x 12
Length (in.) 137
Height (in.) 70
Rear width (in.) 65
Tread width (in.)............................53
Weight (lb.) 6,485
Gear/speed (mph) ....forward: 1/2.50,
2/3.25, 3/3.75; reverse:
1/2.25

McCormick-Deering Industrial 20; I 20
Manufacturer.................................International Harvester
Co., Chicago, IL
Nebraska test number 194
Test date ....July 20–27, 1931
Test tractor serial number ....IN 16675
Years produced 1923–1940
Serial number range.......................501–24999,
32605–45075;
1053–18896 end
Serial number location ....plate on center rear
hood sheet
Number produced ....11,179 through 1929
Engine ....IHC vertical I-head,
valve-in-head
Test engine serial number ....IN 16675
Cylinders 4
Bore and stroke (in.) ....4.25 x 5.00
Rated rpm 1,150
Displacement (c.i.) 283.7
Fuel ....gasoline
Fuel tank capacity (gal.) 24
Carburetor....................................Zenith C5 FE, 1.25-in.
Air cleaner....................................IHC
Ignition...IHC E4A magneto

Cooling capacity (gal.) 10
Maximum brake horsepower tests
    PTO/belt horsepower...........................29.87
    Crankshaft rpm 1,150
    Fuel use (gal./hr.)...............................3.29
Maximum drawbar horsepower tests
    Gear...3rd
    Drawbar horsepower.......................23.01
    Pull weight (lb.)...............................3,144
    Speed (mph) 2.74
    Percent slippage..............................11.39
SAE drawbar horsepower.........................17.27
SAE belt/PTO horsepower.........................27.51
Type ....4 wheel
Front wheel (in.)....................hard rubber, 29 x 5
Rear wheel (in.)...................hard rubber, 40 x 10;
    (42 x 12)
Length (in.) 118
Height (in.) 62
Rear width (in.) 64.50
Tread width (in.) 62
Weight (lb.) 4,740
Gear/speed (mph) ....forward: 1/2.50,
    2/3.50, 3/5.00; reverse:
    1/3.00

Farmall F-30, McCormick-Deering

Manufacturer...................................International Harvester
    Co., Chicago, IL
Nebraska test number 198
Test date ....October 9–23, 1931
Test tractor serial number.......................FB 517
Years produced 1931–1939
Serial number range................................501–30026 end
Serial number location ....plate on toolbox under
    fuel tank
Number produced ....approximately 28,902
Engine ....IHC vertical I-head,
    valve-in-head
Test engine serial number........................AA 518
Cylinders 4
Bore and stroke (in.) ....4.25 x 5.00
Rated rpm 1,150
Displacement (c.i.) 283.7
Fuel ....kerosene/gasoline
Main tank capacity (gal.).........................21
Auxiliary tank capacity (gal.) 1
Carburetor..Zenith K5, 1.25-in.
Air cleaner ....IHC
Ignition..IHC E4A magneto
Cooling capacity (gal.) 9
Maximum brake horsepower tests
    PTO/belt horsepower...........................32.80
    Crankshaft rpm 1,150
    Fuel use (gal./hr.)...............................3.41
Maximum drawbar horsepower tests
    Gear...low
    Drawbar horsepower...........................24.85
    Pull weight (lb.)...............................4,157
    Speed (mph) 2.24
    Percent slippage..............................9.70
SAE drawbar horsepower.........................20.27
SAE belt/PTO horsepower.........................30.29
Type ....4 wheel, tricycle
Front wheel (in.)....................................steel: 25 x 4

Rear wheel (in.)......................................steel: 42 x 12
Length (in.)...147
Height (in.)...81
Rear width (in.) ....89.25 or 97
Tread width (in.)......................................77–85
Weight (lb.)..5,300
Gear/speed (mph) ....forward: 1/2.00,
    2/2.75, 3/3.25, 4/3.75;
    reverse: 1/2.50

McCormick-Deering T-20 TracTracTor

Manufacturer...International Harvester
    Co., Chicago, IL
Nebraska test number 199
Test date ....October 10–26, 1931
Test tractor serial number........................ST 526
Years produced 1931–1939
Serial number range................................501–15699 end
Serial number location ....metal plate on right
    seat side sheet
Number produced 15,199
Engine ....IHC vertical I-head,
    valve-in-head
Test engine serial number........................FM 526
Cylinders 4
Bore and stroke (in.) ....3.75 x 5.00
Rated rpm 1,250
Displacement (c.i.) 220.9
Fuel ....kerosene/gasoline
Main tank capacity (gal.).........................22
Auxiliary tank capacity (gal.) 1
Carburetor..Zenith K5, 1.25-in.
Air cleaner ....IHC
Ignition..IHC E4A magneto
Cooling capacity (gal.) 7
Maximum brake horsepower tests
    PTO/belt horsepower...........................26.59
    Crankshaft rpm 1,248
    Fuel use (gal./hr.)...............................2.65
Maximum drawbar horsepower tests
    Gear...low
    Drawbar horsepower...........................23.33
    Pull weight (lb.)...............................5,156
    Speed (mph) 1.70
    Percent slippage..............................3.12
SAE drawbar horsepower.........................18.33
SAE belt/PTO horsepower.........................25.31
Type ....tracklayer
Length (in.)...112.50
Height (in.)...55.50
Rear width (in.) 54.75
Weight (lb.)..6,250
Track length (in.)....................................52.50 on ground, 181
    total
Grouser shoe...30 links; 10-in.
Gear/speed (mph) ....forward: 1/1.75,
    2/2.75, 3/3.75; reverse:
    1/2.00

McCormick-Deering W 30

Manufacturer...International Harvester
    Co., Chicago, IL
Nebraska test number 210
Test date ....July 26 to August 10,
    1932

Test tractor serial number .... WB 511
Years produced 1932–1940
Serial number range .... 501–33041 end
Serial number location .... plate on rear fuel tank support
Number produced .... approximately 32,541
Engine .... IHC vertical I-head
Test engine serial number .... XC 561
Cylinders 4
Bore and stroke (in.) .... 4.25 x 5.00
Rated rpm 1,160
Displacement (c.i.) 283.7
Fuel .... kerosene/gasoline
Main tank capacity (gal.) 24
Auxiliary tank capacity (gal.) 1
Carburetor .... Zenith K 5, 1.25-in.
Air cleaner .... IHC
Ignition .... IHC E4A magneto
Cooling capacity (gal.) 11

Maximum brake horsepower tests
   PTO/belt horsepower 33.26
   Crankshaft rpm 1,160
   Fuel use (gal./hr.) 3.27

Maximum drawbar horsepower tests
   Gear .... low
   Drawbar horsepower 24.29
   Pull weight (lb.) 3,118
   Speed (mph) 2.92
   Percent slippage 6.58
SAE drawbar horsepower 19.69
SAE belt/PTO horsepower 31.31
Type .... 4 wheel
Front wheel (in.) .... steel: 30 x 4.50
Rear wheel (in.) .... steel: 36 x 12
Length (in.) 121.75
Height (in.) 60
Rear width (in.) 66.25
Weight (lb.) 4,820
Gear/speed (mph) .... forward: 1/2.50, 2/3.25, 3/3.75; reverse: 1/2.75

McCormick-Deering T-40 TracTracTor

Manufacturer .... International Harvester Co., Chicago, IL
Nebraska test number 211
Test date .... October 11–20, 1932
Test tractor serial number .... TAC 522
Years produced 1932–1934
Serial number range .... 501–1813 end
Serial number location .... metal plate on right seat side sheet
Number produced 1,313
Engine .... IHC vertical I-head
Test engine serial number .... FTM 508
Cylinders 6
Bore and stroke (in.) .... 3.625 x 4.50
Rated rpm 1,600
Displacement (c.i.) 278.7
Fuel .... gasoline
Fuel tank capacity (gal.) 42
Carburetor .... Zenith K-5-S, 1.25-in.
Air cleaner .... IHC
Ignition .... IHC (Robert Bosch) magneto

Cooling capacity (gal.) 12
Maximum brake horsepower tests
   PTO/belt horsepower 46.48
   Crankshaft rpm 1,602
   Fuel use (gal./hr.) 5.16
Maximum drawbar horsepower tests
   Gear 2nd
   Drawbar horsepower 42.72
   Pull weight (lb.) 7,490
   Speed (mph) 2.14
Percent slippage 2.44
SAE drawbar horsepower 33.24
SAE belt/PTO horsepower 43.53
Type .... tracklayer
Length (in.) 141
Height (in.) 62.50
Rear width (in.) 61.75
Weight (lb.) 10,600
Track length (in.) .... 70.50 on ground, 226 total
Grouser shoe .... 38 links; 16-in.
Gear/speed (mph) .... forward: 1/1.75, 2/2.25, 3/2.75, 4/3.25, 5/4.00; reverse: 1/2.25

Farmall F-12, McCormick-Deering

Manufacturer .... International Harvester Co., Chicago, IL
Nebraska test number 212
Test date .... May 1–10, 1933
Test tractor serial number .... FS 533
Years produced 1932–1938
Serial number range .... 501–123942 end
Serial number location .... plate on front fuel tank support
Number produced .... approximately 123,442
Engine .... IHC vertical I-head, valve-in-head
Test engine serial number .... FS 609
Cylinders 4
Bore and stroke (in.) .... 3.00 x 4.00
Rated rpm 1,400
Displacement (c.i.) 113.1
Fuel .... gasoline
Fuel tank capacity (gal.) 13
Carburetor .... IHC A-10, 1.00-in.
Air cleaner .... IHC
Ignition .... IHC E4A magneto
Cooling capacity (gal.) 3.50
Maximum brake horsepower tests
   PTO/belt horsepower 16.20
   Crankshaft rpm 1,399
   Fuel use (gal./hr.) 1.70
Maximum drawbar horsepower tests
   Gear 2nd
   Drawbar horsepower 12.31
   Pull weight (lb.) 1,442
   Speed (mph) 3.20
   Percent slippage 0.70
SAE drawbar horsepower 9.74
SAE belt/PTO horsepower 14.68
Type .... 3 wheel, tricycle
Front wheel (in.) .... steel: 23 x 6
Rear wheel (in.) .... steel: 54 x 6
Length (in.) 125.50

Height (in.) 62.50
Rear width (in.) 74.25
Tread width (in.) 44–79
Weight (lb.) 2,700
Gear/speed (mph) ....forward: 1/2.25, 2/3.00, 3/3.75; reverse: 1/2.25

Farmall F-12, McCormick-Deering

Manufacturer ....International Harvester Co., Chicago, IL
Nebraska test number 220
Test date ....November 1–16, 1933
Test tractor serial number ....FS 3098
Years produced 1932–1938
Serial number range ....501–123942 end
Serial number location ....plate on front fuel tank support
Number produced ....approximately 123,442
Engine ....IHC vertical I-head, valve-in-head
Test engine serial number ....FS 3098
Cylinders 4
Bore and stroke (in.) ....3.00 x 4.00
Rated rpm 1,400
Displacement (c.i.) 113.1
Fuel ....kerosene/gasoline
Main tank capacity (gal.) 13
Auxiliary tank capacity (gal.) 0.75
Carburetor ....IHC A 10, 1.00-in.
Air cleaner ....IHC
Ignition ....IHC F-4 magneto
Cooling capacity (gal.) 3.50
Maximum brake horsepower tests
    PTO/belt horsepower 14.59
    Crankshaft rpm 1,399
    Fuel use (gal./hr.) 1.46
Maximum drawbar horsepower tests
    Gear..1st
    Drawbar horsepower 11.81
    Pull weight (lb.) 1,814
    Speed (mph) 2.44
    Percent slippage..............................3.75
SAE drawbar horsepower 9.44
SAE belt/PTO horsepower 13.45
Type ....3 wheel, tricycle
Front wheel (in.) ....steel: 23 x 6
Rear wheel (in.) ....steel: 54 x 6
Length (in.) 125.50
Height (in.) 62.50
Rear width (in.) 74.25
Tread width (in.) 44–79
Weight (lb.) 2,500
Gear/speed (mph) ....forward: 1/2.25, 2/3.00, 3/3.75; reverse: 1/2.25

Farmall F-20, McCormick-Deering

Manufacturer ....International Harvester Co., Chicago, IL
Nebraska test number 221
Test date ....April 3–16, 1934
Test tractor serial number ....FA 832
Years produced 1932–1939
Serial number range................................501–148810 end
Serial number location ....plate on front fuel tank support
Number produced 154,398
Engine ....IHC vertical I-head
Test engine serial number ....FA 832
Cylinders 4
Bore and stroke (in.) ....3.75 x 5.00
Rated rpm 1,200
Displacement (c.i.) 220.9
Fuel ....kerosene/gasoline
Main tank capacity (gal.) 13
Auxiliary tank capacity (gal.) 0.88
Carburetor ....Zenith K 5, 1.25-in.
Air cleaner ....IHC
Ignition ....IHC E4A magneto
Cooling capacity (gal.) 10
Maximum brake horsepower tests
    PTO/belt horsepower........................23.11
    Crankshaft rpm 1,200
    Fuel use (gal./hr.) 2.22
Maximum drawbar horsepower tests
    Gear..2nd
    Drawbar horsepower........................15.39
    Pull weight (lb.) 1,924
    Speed (mph) 3.00
    Percent slippage..............................5.82
SAE drawbar horsepower........................12.68
SAE belt/PTO horsepower 21.93
Type ....4 wheel, tricycle
Front wheel (in.) ....steel: 25 x 4
Rear wheel (in.) ....steel: 40 x 6
Length (in.) 140
Height (in.) 76
Rear width (in.) 86.75–95
Tread width (in.) 74.38, 83
Weight (lb.) 3,950
Gear/speed (mph) ....forward: 1/2.25, 2/2.75, 3/3.25, 4/3.75; reverse: 1/2.75

McCormick-Deering W-12

Manufacturer..International Harvester Co., Chicago, IL
Nebraska test number 229
Test date ....October 23 to November 9, 1934
Test tractor serial number ....WS 687
Years produced 1934–1938
Serial number range................................503–4133 end
Serial number location ....plate on front fuel tank support
Number produced 3,633
Engine ....IHC vertical I-head
Test engine serial number ....WS 637
Cylinders 4
Bore and stroke (in.) ....3.00 x 4.00
Rated rpm 1,700
Displacement (c.i.) 113.1
Fuel ....kerosene/gasoline
Main tank capacity (gal.) 11
Auxiliary tank capacity (gal.) 0.75
Carburetor ....IHC A-10, 1.00-in.
Air cleaner ....IHC
Ignition ....IHC F-4 magneto
Cooling capacity (gal.) 3.50

Maximum brake horsepower tests
- PTO/belt horsepower..........................15.28
- Crankshaft rpm 1,702
- Fuel use (gal./hr.)...........................1.51

Maximum drawbar horsepower tests
- Gear..1st
- Drawbar horsepower...........................12.56
- Pull weight (lb.).............................1,998
- Speed (mph)...................................2.36
- Percent slippage.............................5.43

SAE drawbar horsepower.............................9.55
SAE belt/PTO horsepower 13.88
Type ....4 wheel
Front wheel (in.).................................steel: 22.50 x 3.50
Rear wheel (in.).................................steel: 42 x 8
Length (in.) 103
Height (in.) 55
Rear width (in.) 50
Tread width (in.).................................42.25
Weight (lb.)......................................2,900
Gear/speed (mph) ....forward: 1/2.25, 2/2.75, 3/3.75; reverse: 1/2.25

McCormick-Deering T-40 TracTracTor

Manufacturer......................................International Harvester Co., Chicago, IL
Nebraska test number 230
Test date ....October 25 to November 13, 1934
Test tractor serial number........................TCC 2660
Years produced 1934–1939
Serial number range...............................2501–9565 end
Serial number location ....metal plate on right seat side sheet
Number produced 7,065
Engine ....IHC vertical I-head
Test engine serial number ....TCC 2660
Cylinders 4
Bore and stroke (in.) ....4.75 x 6.50
Rated rpm 1,100
Displacement (c.i.) 460.7
Fuel ....diesel/gasoline
Main tank capacity (gal.).........................14
Auxiliary tank capacity (gal.) 1.25
Carburetor..start; IHC R, 1.25-in.
Air cleaner ....IHC
Ignition..start; IHC E4A magneto
Cooling capacity (gal.) 14

Maximum brake horsepower tests
- PTO/belt horsepower..........................48.26
- Crankshaft rpm 1,096
- Fuel use (gal./hr.)..........................3.19

Maximum drawbar horsepower tests
- Gear...3rd
- Drawbar horsepower...........................43.25
- Pull weight (lb.)............................5,987
- Speed (mph)..................................2.71
- Percent slippage............................1.38

SAE drawbar horsepower.............................33.51
SAE belt/PTO horsepower 43.12
Type ....tracklayer
Length (in.) 140
Height (in.) 65.50
Rear width (in.) 63.75
Weight (lb.)......................................12,000

Track length (in.)................................70 on ground, 228 total
Grouser shoe......................................38 links; 16-in.
Gear/speed (mph) ....forward: 1/1.75, 2/2.25, 3/2.75, 4/3.25, 5/4.00; reverse: 1/2.25

McCormick-Deering W-12

Manufacturer......................................International Harvester Co., Chicago, IL
Nebraska test number 231
Test date ....November 13–16, 1934
Test tractor serial number........................WS 687
Years produced 1934–1938
Serial number range...............................503–4133 end
Serial number location ....plate on front fuel tank support
Number produced 3,633
Engine ....IHC vertical I-head
Test engine serial number ....WS 637
Cylinders 4
Bore and stroke (in.) ....3.00 x 4.00
Rated rpm 1,700
Displacement (c.i.) 113.1
Fuel ....gasoline
Fuel tank capacity (gal.).........................11
Carburetor..IHC A-10, 1.00-in.
Air cleaner ....IHC
Ignition..IHC F-4 magneto
Cooling capacity (gal.) 3.50

Maximum brake horsepower tests
- PTO/belt horsepower..........................17.65
- Crankshaft rpm 1,700
- Fuel use (gal./hr.)..........................1.75

Maximum drawbar horsepower tests
- Gear...1st
- Drawbar horsepower...........................13.52
- Pull weight (lb.)............................2,140
- Speed (mph)..................................2.37
- Percent slippage............................3.53

SAE drawbar horsepower.............................10.46
SAE belt/PTO horsepower 16.07
Type ....4 wheel
Front wheel (in.).................................steel: 22.50 x 3.50
Rear wheel (in.).................................steel: 42 x 8
Length (in.) 103
Height (in.) 55
Rear width (in.) 50
Tread width (in.).................................42.25
Weight (lb.)......................................2,900
Gear/speed (mph) ....forward: 1/2.25, 2/2.75, 3/3.75; reverse: 1/2.25

McCormick-Deering WD-40 Diesel

Manufacturer......................................International Harvester Co., Chicago, IL
Nebraska test number 246
Test date ....September 23–27, 1935
Test tractor serial number........................644
Years produced 1935–1940
Serial number range...............................501–10599 end
Serial number location ....plate on rear hood sheet

Number produced ....na, interspersed with W-40
Engine ....IHC vertical I-head
Test engine serial number..........W.D.C 677
Cylinders 4
Bore and stroke (in.) ....4.75 x 6.50
Rated rpm 1,100
Compression ratio..........................17:1
Displacement (c.i.) 460.7
Fuel ....diesel/gasoline
Main tank capacity (gal.) 31
Auxiliary tank capacity (gal.) 1.25
Carburetor ....starting engine; IHC R, 1.25-in.
Air cleaner ....Donaldson
Ignition..start; IHC F-4 magneto
Cooling capacity (gal.) 14

Maximum brake horsepower tests
    PTO/belt horsepower............................48.79
    Crankshaft rpm 1,100
    Fuel use (gal./hr.).................................3.35
Maximum drawbar horsepower tests
    Gear...2nd
    Drawbar horsepower.............................36.52
    Pull weight (lb.)....................................3,731
    Speed (mph) 3.67
    Percent slippage...................................6.94
SAE drawbar horsepower................27.99
SAE belt/PTO horsepower...............44.04
Type ....4 wheel
Front wheel (in.).............................steel: 34 x 6
Rear wheel (in.)..............................steel: 50 x 12
Length (in.) 141.50
Height (in.).......................................66.75
Rear width (in.) 65.50
Tread width (in.).............................53
Weight (lb.) 7,550
Gear/speed (mph) ....forward: 1/2.60, 2/3.40, 3/3.90; reverse: 1/2.40

Farmall F-20, McCormick-Deering

Manufacturer...................................International Harvester Co., Chicago, IL
Nebraska test number 264
Test date ....July 20–29, 1936
Test tractor serial number............FA 59794
Years produced 1932–1939
Serial number range.......................501–148810 end
Serial number location ....plate on front fuel tank support
Number produced 154,398
Engine ....IHC vertical I-head
Test engine serial number.............FA 59794
Cylinders 4
Bore and stroke (in.) ....3.75 x 5.00
Rated rpm 1,200
Displacement (c.i.) 220.9
Fuel ....distillate/gasoline
Main tank capacity (gal.)................13
Auxiliary tank capacity (gal.) 0.88
Carburetor ....Zenith K-5, 1.25-in.
Air cleaner ....IHC
Ignition..IHC F-4 magneto
Cooling capacity (gal.) 7.25

Maximum brake horsepower tests
    PTO/belt horsepower............................27.97
    Crankshaft rpm 1,200
    Fuel use (gal./hr.).................................3.11
Maximum drawbar horsepower tests
    Gear...3rd
    Drawbar horsepower.............................20.47
    Pull weight (lb.)....................................2,052
    Speed (mph) 3.74
    Percent slippage...................................5.57
SAE drawbar horsepower................16.52
SAE belt/PTO horsepower...............25.63
Type ....4 wheel, tricycle
Front wheel (in.).............................steel: 25 x 4
Rear wheel (in.)..............................steel: (42 x 12), 40 x 6
Length (in.) 140
Height (in.).......................................76
Rear width (in.) 86.75–95
Tread width (in.).............................74.38, 83
Weight (lb.) 3,950
Gear/speed (mph) ....forward: 1/2.25, 2/2.75, 3/3.25, 4/3.75; reverse: 1/2.75

McCormick-Deering WK-40

Manufacturer...................................International Harvester Co., Chicago, IL
Nebraska test number 268
Test date ....August 25 to September 3, 1936
Test tractor serial number............WKC 1690
Years produced 1935–1940
Serial number range.......................501–10599 end, interspersed with W-40
Serial number location ....plate on rear hood sheet
Number produced ....10,099 total, including W-40, WA-40, WK-40
Engine ....IHC vertical I-head
Test engine serial number.............WTM 566 K
Cylinders 6
Bore and stroke (in.) ....3.75 x 4.50
Rated rpm 1,600
Displacement (c.i.) 298.2
Fuel ....distillate/gasoline
Main tank capacity (gal.)................31
Auxiliary tank capacity (gal.) 1.25
Carburetor ....Zenith 50-AY12, 1.25-in.
Air cleaner ....IHC
Ignition..IHC F-6 magneto
Cooling capacity (gal.) 12

Maximum brake horsepower tests
    PTO/belt horsepower............................45.69
    Crankshaft rpm 1,599
    Fuel use (gal./hr.).................................5.40
Maximum drawbar horsepower tests
    Gear...2nd
    Drawbar horsepower.............................31.79
    Pull weight (lb.)....................................3,465
    Speed (mph) 3.44
    Percent slippage...................................6.07
SAE drawbar horsepower................25.85
SAE belt/PTO horsepower...............40.86
Type ....4 wheel

Front wheel (in.)................................steel: 34 x 6
Rear wheel (in.)................................steel: 50 x 12
Length (in.) 141.50
Height (in.) 66.75
Rear width (in.) 65.25
Tread width (in.)...............................53
Weight (lb.) 6,100
Gear/speed (mph) ....forward: 1/2.40,
2/3.10, 3/3.60; reverse:
1/2.20

McCormick-Deering WK-40
Manufacturer.....................................International Harvester
Co., Chicago, IL
Nebraska test number 269
Test date ....September 3–15, 1936
Test tractor serial number................WKC 4625
Years produced.................................1935–1940
Serial number range..........................501–10599 end,
interspersed with W-40
Serial number location ....plate on rear hood
sheet
Number produced ....10,099 total, including
W-40, WA-40, WK-40
Engine ....IHC vertical I-head
Test engine serial number................WKE 1979
Cylinders 6
Bore and stroke (in.) ....3.75 x 4.50
Rated rpm 1,750
Displacement (c.i.) 298.2
Fuel ....distillate/gasoline
Main tank capacity (gal.)...................31
Auxiliary tank capacity (gal.) 1.25
Carburetor..Zenith 50-AY12, 1.50-in.
Air cleaner ....IHC
Ignition...IHC F-6 magneto
Cooling capacity (gal.) 12
Maximum brake horsepower tests
PTO/belt horsepower...........................49.76
Crankshaft rpm 1,749
Fuel use (gal./hr.)................................5.55
Maximum drawbar horsepower tests
Gear...2nd
Drawbar horsepower............................35.22
Pull weight (lb.)....................................3,873
Speed (mph)..3.41
Percent slippage..................................6.72
SAE drawbar horsepower..................28.34
SAE belt/PTO horsepower 44.80
Type ....4 wheel
Front wheel (in.)................................steel: 34 x 6
Rear wheel (in.).................................steel: 50 x 12
Length (in.) 141.50
Height (in.) 66.75
Rear width (in.) 65.25
Tread width (in.)...............................53
Weight (lb.) 6,100
Gear/speed (mph) ....forward: 1/2.38, 2/3.13,
3/3.63; reverse: 1/2.25

Farmall F-20, McCormick-Deering
Manufacturer.....................................International Harvester
Co., Chicago, IL
Nebraska test number 276
Test date ....November 5–12, 1936

Test tractor serial number................FA 46451
Years produced.................................1932–1939
Serial number range..........................501–148810 end
Serial number location ....plate on front fuel tank
support
Number produced 154,398
Engine ....IHC vertical I-head
Test engine serial number................FA 46451
Cylinders 4
Bore and stroke (in.) ....3.75 x 5.00
Rated rpm 1,200
Displacement (c.i.) 220.9
Fuel ....distillate/gasoline
Main tank capacity (gal.)...................13
Auxiliary tank capacity (gal.) 0.75
Carburetor..Zenith K-5, 1.25-in.
Air cleaner ....IHC
Ignition...IHC F-4 magneto
Cooling capacity (gal.) 7.25
Maximum brake horsepower tests
PTO/belt horsepower...........................27.84
Crankshaft rpm 1,201
Fuel use (gal./hr.)................................2.78
Maximum drawbar horsepower tests
Gear...3rd
Drawbar horsepower............................20.66
Pull weight (lb.)....................................2,089
Speed (mph)..3.71
Percent slippage..................................6.89
SAE drawbar horsepower..................15.98
SAE belt/PTO horsepower 23.80
Type ....4 wheel, tricycle
Front wheel (in.)................................(steel: 25 x 4);
rubber: 6.00 x 16
Rear wheel (in.).................................(steel: 42 x 12);
rubber: 9.00 x 36
Length (in.) 140
Height (in.) 76
Rear width (in.) 86.75–95
Tread width (in.)...............................74.38 or 83
Weight (lb.) 3,950
Gear/speed (mph) ....forward: 1/2.25,
2/2.75, 3/3.25, 4/3.75;
reverse: 1/2.75

McCormick-Deering TD-35 Diesel TracTracTor
Manufacturer.....................................International Harvester
Co., Chicago, IL
Nebraska test number 277
Test date ....April 5–27, 1937
Test tractor serial number................TDBB 569
Years produced.................................1937–1939
Serial number range..........................507–6092 end
Serial number location ....metal plate on right
seat side sheet
Number produced ....na, interspersed with
T-35
Engine ....IHC vertical I-head
Test engine serial number................TDB 505
Cylinders 4
Bore and stroke (in.) ....4.50 x 6.50
Rated rpm 1,100
Displacement (c.i.) 413.5
Fuel ....diesel/gasoline
Main tank capacity (gal.)...................40

Auxiliary tank capacity (gal.) 1.25
Carburetor ....start: IHC C-12, 1.25-in.
Air cleaner ....Donaldson
Ignition...start: IHC F-4 magneto
Cooling capacity (gal.) 14
Maximum brake horsepower tests
    PTO/belt horsepower..........................42.20
    Crankshaft rpm 1,100
    Fuel use (gal./hr.)..........................2.85
Maximum drawbar horsepower tests
    Gear...3rd
    Drawbar horsepower...........................35.24
    Pull weight (lb.)............................4,855
    Speed (mph).................................2.72
    Percent slippage............................1.59
SAE drawbar horsepower................................27.02
SAE belt/PTO horsepower...............................36.95
Type ....tracklayer
Length (in.) 132.50
Rear width (in.) 59.50
Weight (lb.) 10,550
Track length (in.)....................................64.38 on ground,
    216 total
Grouser shoe..36 links; 13-in.
Gear/speed (mph) ....forward: 1/1.75,
    2/2.25, 3/2.75, 4/3.25,
    5/4.00; reverse: 1/2.25

McCormick-Deering T-35 TracTracTor

Manufacturer..International Harvester
    Co., Chicago, IL
Nebraska test number 278
Test date ....April 19 to May 10,
    1937
Test tractor serial number............................TKBB 604
Years produced 1937–1939
Serial number range...................................507–6092 end
Serial number location ....metal plate on right
    seat side sheet
Number produced 5,586
Engine ....IHC vertical I-head
Test engine serial number.............................FTM 2306
Cylinders 6
Bore and stroke (in.) ....3.625 x 4.50
Rated rpm 1,750
Displacement (c.i.) 278.7
Fuel ....distillate/gasoline
Main tank capacity (gal.) 40
Auxiliary tank capacity (gal.) 1.25
Carburetor..Zenith K-5-0.50 S,
    1.38-in.
Air cleaner...(Donaldson) or IHC
Ignition..IHC F-6 magneto
Cooling capacity (gal.) 12
Maximum brake horsepower tests
    PTO/belt horsepower..........................42.17
    Crankshaft rpm 1,750
    Fuel use (gal./hr.)..........................4.72
Maximum drawbar horsepower tests
    Gear...3rd
    Drawbar horsepower...........................35.04
    Pull weight (lb.)............................4,721
    Speed (mph).................................2.78
    Percent slippage............................1.48

SAE drawbar horsepower................................27.89
SAE belt/PTO horsepower...............................37.06
Type ....tracklayer
Weight (lb.) 10,050
Track length (in.)....................................64.38 on ground,
    217 total
Grouser shoe..36 links; 13-in.
Gear/speed (mph) ....forward: 1/1.75,
    2/2.25, 3/2.75, 4/3.25,
    5/4.00; reverse: 1/2.25

McCormick-Deering T-35 TracTracTor

Manufacturer..International Harvester
    Co., Chicago, IL
Nebraska test number 279
Test date ....May 14 to June 4,
    1937
Test tractor serial number............................TKBB 604
Years produced 1937–1939
Serial number range...................................507–6092 end
Serial number location ....metal plate on right
    seat side sheet
Number produced 5,586
Engine ....IHC vertical I-head
Test engine serial number.............................FTM 2306
Cylinders 6
Bore and stroke (in.) ....3.625 x 4.50
Rated rpm 1,750
Displacement (c.i.) 278.7
Fuel ....gasoline
Fuel tank capacity (gal.) 40
Carburetor..Zenith K-5-0.50 S,
    1.38-in.
Air cleaner...(Donaldson) IHC
Ignition..IHC F-6 magneto
Cooling capacity (gal.) 12
Maximum brake horsepower tests
    PTO/belt horsepower 44.44
    Crankshaft rpm 1,749
    Fuel use (gal./hr.)..........................5.15
Maximum drawbar horsepower tests
    Gear...3rd
    Drawbar horsepower...........................35.91
    Pull weight (lb.)............................4,883
    Speed (mph).................................2.76
    Percent slippage............................1.92
SAE drawbar horsepower................................29.01
SAE belt/PTO horsepower 39.29
Type ....tracklayer
Weight (lb.) 10,050
Track length (in.)....................................64.38 on ground,
    216 total
Grouser shoe..36 links; 13-in.
Gear/speed (mph) ....forward: 1/1.75,
    2/2.25, 3/3.25, 4/4.00;
    reverse: 1/2.25

McCormick-Deering T-40 TracTracTor

Manufacturer..International Harvester
    Co., Chicago, IL
Nebraska test number 280
Test date ....April 7–29, 1937
Test tractor serial number............................TKC 6655
Years produced 1934–1939

Serial number range .... 2501–9565 end
Serial number location .... metal plate on right seat side sheet
Number produced 7,065
Engine .... IHC vertical, I-head
Test engine serial number .... TKE 608
Cylinders 6
Bore and stroke (in.) .... 3.75 x 4.50
Rated rpm 1,750
Displacement (c.i.) 298.2
Fuel .... distillate/gasoline
Main tank capacity (gal.) 40
Auxiliary tank capacity (gal.) 1.25
Carburetor .... Zenith 50-AY12, 1.50-in.
Air cleaner .... IHC
Ignition .... IHC F-6 magneto
Cooling capacity (gal.) 12

Maximum brake horsepower tests
    PTO/belt horsepower 49.34
    Crankshaft rpm 1,753
    Fuel use (gal./hr.) 5.46
Maximum drawbar horsepower tests
    Gear 3rd
    Drawbar horsepower 42.63
    Pull weight (lb.) 5,758
    Speed (mph) 2.78
    Percent slippage 1.59
SAE drawbar horsepower 34.01
SAE belt/PTO horsepower 44.00
Type .... tracklayer
Length (in.) 140
Rear width (in.) 63.75
Weight (lb.) 12,000
Track length (in.) .... 70 on ground, 229 total
Grouser shoe .... 38 links; 16-in.
Gear/speed (mph) .... forward: 1/1.75, 2/2.25, 3/2.75, 4/3.25, 5/4.00; reverse: 1/2.25

McCormick-Deering T-40 TracTracTor

Manufacturer .... International Harvester Co., Chicago, IL
Nebraska test number 281
Test date .... May 4–14, 1937
Test tractor serial number .... TKC 6655
Years produced 1934–1939
Serial number range .... 2501–9565 end
Serial number location .... metal plate on right seat side sheet
Number produced 7,065
Engine .... IHC vertical I-head
Test engine serial number .... TKE 608
Cylinders 6
Bore and stroke (in.) .... 3.75 x 4.50
Rated rpm 1,750
Displacement (c.i.) 298.2
Fuel .... gasoline
Fuel tank capacity (gal.) 40
Carburetor .... Zenith 50-AY12, 1.50-in.
Air cleaner .... IHC
Ignition .... IHC magneto F-6
Cooling capacity (gal.) 12

Maximum brake horsepower tests
    PTO/belt horsepower 51.67
    Crankshaft rpm 1,749
    Fuel use (gal./hr.) 6.17
Maximum drawbar horsepower tests
    Gear 3rd
    Drawbar horsepower 44.28
    Pull weight (lb.) 6,051
    Speed (mph) 2.74
    Percent slippage 2.57
SAE drawbar horsepower 35.00
SAE belt/PTO horsepower 45.94
Type .... tracklayer
Length (in.) 140
Rear width (in.) 63.75
Weight (lb.) 12,000
Track length (in.) .... 70 on ground, 229 total
Grouser shoe .... 38 links; 16-in.
Gear/speed (mph) .... forward: 1/1.75, 2/2.25, 3/2.75, 4/3.25, 5/4.00; reverse: 1/2.25

Farmall F-14, McCormick-Deering

Manufacturer .... International Harvester Co., Chicago, IL
Nebraska test number 297
Test date .... April 19–27, 1938
Test tractor serial number .... FS 125509
Years produced 1938–1939
Serial number range .... 124000–155902 end
Serial number location .... plate on front fuel tank bracket
Number produced 27,401
Engine .... IHC vertical I-head
Test engine serial number .... FS 125509
Cylinders 4
Bore and stroke (in.) .... 3.00 x 4.00
Rated rpm 1,650
Displacement (c.i.) 113.1
Fuel .... distillate/gasoline
Main tank capacity (gal.) 13
Auxiliary tank capacity (gal.) 1
Carburetor .... IHC A-10, 1.00-in.
Air cleaner .... IHC
Ignition .... IHC F-4 magneto
Cooling capacity (gal.) 3.50

Maximum brake horsepower tests
    PTO/belt horsepower 17.44
    Crankshaft rpm 1,649
    Fuel use (gal./hr.) 1.67
Maximum drawbar horsepower tests
    Gear 2nd
    Drawbar horsepower 14.84
    Pull weight (lb.) 1,920
    Speed (mph) 2.90
    Percent slippage 8.16
SAE drawbar horsepower 11.52
SAE belt/PTO horsepower 15.48
Type .... tricycle
Front wheel (in.) .... steel: 22.50 x 4; (rubber: 5.00 x 15)
Rear wheel (in.) .... steel: 54 x 6; (rubber: 9.00 x 40)

Length (in.) 124.50
Height (in.) 70.38
Rear width (in.) 44–74.25
Tread width (in.) 44.50–79
Weight (lb.) ....steel: 2,700;
(rubber: 4,725)
Gear/speed (mph) ....forward: 1/2.38,
2/3.13, 3/4.00; reverse:
1/2.38

McCormick-Deering TD-40 Diesel TracTracTor

Manufacturer....................................International Harvester
Co., Chicago, IL
Nebraska test number 298
Test date ....April 20–30, 1938
Test tractor serial number ....TDC 5405
Years produced 1934–1939
Serial number range.......................2501–9565 end
Serial number location ....metal plate on right
seat side sheet
Number produced ....na, interspersed with
T-40
Engine ....IHC vertical I-head
Test engine serial number...............TDC 5405
Cylinders 4
Bore and stroke (in.) ....4.75 x 6.50
Rated rpm 1,200
Displacement (c.i.) 460.7
Fuel ....diesel/gasoline
Main tank capacity (gal.) 40
Auxiliary tank capacity (gal.) 1.25
Carburetor ....starting engine;
IHC C-12, 1.25-in.
Air cleaner ....Donaldson
Ignition..start; IHC F-4 magneto
Cooling capacity (gal.) 14
Maximum brake horsepower tests
PTO/belt horsepower.............53.46
Crankshaft rpm 1,200
Fuel use (gal./hr.) 3.73
Maximum drawbar horsepower tests
Gear......................................3rd
Drawbar horsepower.............48.25
Pull weight (lb.).....................6,552
Speed (mph) 2.76
Percent slippage...................1.48
SAE drawbar horsepower................37.16
SAE belt/PTO horsepower 48.21
Type ....tracklayer
Length (in.) 140
Rear width (in.) 63.75
Weight (lb.) 12,400
Track length (in.) ....70 on ground,
228 total
Grouser shoe...................................38 links; 16-in.
Gear/speed (mph) ....forward: 1/1.75,
2/2.25, 3/2.75, 4/3.25,
5/4.00; reverse: 1/2.25

International TD-18 Diesel TracTracTor

Manufacturer....................................International Harvester
Co., Chicago, IL
Nebraska test number 315
Test date ....March 27 to April 14,
1939

Test tractor serial number...............TDR 530
Years produced 1939–1949
Serial number range.......................520–22535 end
Serial number location ....metal plate on upper
left corner of dash
Number produced 22,016
Engine ....IHC vertical I-head
Test engine serial number...............TDRM 522
Cylinders 6
Bore and stroke (in.) ....4.75 x 6.50
Rated rpm 1,200
Displacement (c.i.) 691.1
Fuel ....diesel/gasoline
Main tank capacity (gal.) 60
Auxiliary tank capacity (gal.) 1.33
Carburetor ....starting engine; IHC C-
12, 1.25-in.
Air cleaner ....Donaldson
Ignition..start; IHC F-6 magneto
Cooling capacity (gal.) 26
Maximum brake horsepower tests
PTO/belt horsepower.............80.32
Crankshaft rpm 1,199
Fuel use (gal./hr.) 5.22
Maximum drawbar horsepower tests
Gear......................................3rd
Drawbar horsepower.............70.66
Pull weight (lb.).....................10,561
Speed (mph) 2.51
Percent slippage...................1.38
SAE drawbar horsepower................52.94
SAE belt/PTO horsepower 71.96
Type ....tracklayer
Length (in.) 158.25
Height (in.) 92
Rear width (in.) ....82.25 or 94.25
Tread width (in.)..............................62 or 74
Weight (lb.) 21,500
Track length (in.) ....84.63 on ground, 278
total
Grouser shoe...................................37 links; 18, (22)-in.
Gear/speed (mph) ....forward: 1/1.50,
2/2.00, 3/2.50, 4/3.25,
5/4.63, 6/5.75; reverse:
1/1.50, 2/3.25

Farmall M, McCormick-Deering

Manufacturer....................................International Harvester
Co., Chicago, IL
Nebraska test number 327
Test date ....September 5–17, 1939
Test tractor serial number ....FBK 742
Years produced 1939–1952
Serial number range.......................501–298218 end
Serial number location ....plate on left side of
clutch housing
Number produced 270,140
Engine ....IHC C-248 vertical
I-head, valve-in-head
Test engine serial number...............FBK-ME 544
Cylinders 4
Bore and stroke (in.) ....3.875 x 5.25
Rated rpm 1,450
Displacement (c.i.) 247.7
Fuel ....distillate/gasoline

Main tank capacity (gal.) 21
Auxiliary tank capacity (gal.) 1
Carburetor ....IHC E-12, 1.25-in.
Air cleaner ....Donaldson
Ignition ....IHC H-4 magneto
Cooling capacity (gal.) 6
Maximum brake horsepower tests
    PTO/belt horsepower 34.82
    Crankshaft rpm 1,447
    Fuel use (gal./hr.) 2.80
Maximum drawbar horsepower tests
    Gear 2nd
    Drawbar horsepower 30.62
    Pull weight (lb.) 3,653
    Speed (mph) 3.14
    Percent slippage 7.87
SAE drawbar horsepower 24.65
SAE belt/PTO horsepower 31.20
Type ....tricycle
Front wheel (in.) ....steel: 22.50 x 4;
    (rubber: 6.00 x 16)
Rear wheel (in.) ....steel: 51 x 8;
    (rubber: 11.25 x 36)
Length (in.) 133.13
Height (in.) 78.25
Rear width (in.) 84–100
Tread width (in.) 52–88
Weight (lb.) 4,910
Gear/speed (mph) ....forward: 1/2.63,
    2/3.50, 3/4.25, 4/5.13,
    5/16.38 rubber only;
    reverse: 1/3.13

Farmall M, McCormick-Deering
Manufacturer..International Harvester
    Co., Chicago, IL
Nebraska test number 328
Test date ....September 11–21,
    1939
Test tractor serial number...........................FBK ME 533
Years produced...1939–1952
Serial number range.....................................501–298218 end
Serial number location ....plate on left side of
    clutch housing
Number produced 270,140
Engine ....IHC C-248 vertical
    I-head, valve-in-head
Test engine serial number ....FBK-ME 533
Cylinders 4
Bore and stroke (in.) ....3.875 x 5.25
Rated rpm 1,450
Compression ratio..5.65:1
Displacement (c.i.) 247.7
Fuel ....gasoline
Fuel tank capacity (gal.) 21
Carburetor...IHC E-12, 1.25-in.
Air cleaner ....Donaldson
Ignition...IHC H-4 magneto
Cooling capacity (gal.) 6
Maximum brake horsepower tests
    PTO/belt horsepower 36.66
    Crankshaft rpm 1,451
    Fuel use (gal./hr.) 3.00

Maximum drawbar horsepower tests
    Gear 2nd
    Drawbar horsepower 33.05
    Pull weight (lb.) 4,060
    Speed (mph) 3.05
    Percent slippage 10.46
SAE drawbar horsepower 25.83
SAE belt/PTO horsepower 33.35
Type ....tricycle
Front wheel (in.) ....steel: 22.50 x 4;
    rubber: 6.00 x 16
Rear wheel (in.) ....steel: 51 x 8;
    rubber: 11.25 x 36
Length (in.) 133.13
Height (in.) 78.25
Rear width (in.) 84–100
Tread width (in.) 52–88
Weight (lb.) 4,910
Gear/speed (mph) ....forward: 1/2.63,
    2/3.50, 3/4.25, 4/5.13,
    5/16.38 rubber only;
    reverse: 1/3.13

Farmall A, McCormick-Deering
Manufacturer..International Harvester
    Co., Chicago, IL
Nebraska test number 329
Test date ....September 28 to
    October 6, 1939
Test tractor serial number...........................FAA 1051
Years produced...1939–1948
Serial number range.....................................501–220829 end
Serial number location ....plate on left seat
    support
Number produced ....117,552, A and B
    interspersed
Engine ....IHC C-113 vertical
    I-head, valve-in-head
Test engine serial number ....FAA 1051
Cylinders 4
Bore and stroke (in.) ....3.00 x 4.00
Rated rpm 1,400
Compression ratio..5.33:1
Displacement (c.i.) 113.1
Fuel ....gasoline
Fuel tank capacity (gal.) 10
Carburetor...Zenith 61AX7, 0.875-
    in.
Air cleaner ....Donaldson
Ignition...IHC H-4 magneto
Cooling capacity (gal.) 3.38
Maximum brake horsepower tests
    PTO/belt horsepower 18.34
    Crankshaft rpm 1,400
    Fuel use (gal./hr.) 1.57
Maximum drawbar horsepower tests
    Gear 2nd
    Drawbar horsepower 16.32
    Pull weight (lb.) 1,827
    Speed (mph) 3.35
    Percent slippage 8.98
SAE drawbar horsepower 13.01
SAE belt/PTO horsepower 16.20

Type ....standard
Front tire (in.).............................4.00 x 15
Rear tire (in.)..............................9.00 x 24
Length (in.) 106.25
Height (in.) 63.25
Rear width (in.) 76.75
Tread width (in.)..........................40–68
Weight (lb.) ....(3,395); 1,870
Gear/speed (mph) ....forward: 1/2.25,
2/3.63, 3/4.75,
4/10.00; reverse:
1/2.88

Farmall A, McCormick-Deering

Manufacturer................................International Harvester
Co., Chicago, IL
Nebraska test number 330
Test date ....October 9–16, 1939
Test tractor serial number..............FAA 1058
Years produced 1939–1948
Serial number range......................501–220829 end
Serial number location ....plate on left seat
support
Number produced ....117,552, A and B
interspersed
Engine ....IHC C-113 vertical
I-head, valve-in-head
Test engine serial number...............FAA 1058
Cylinders 4
Bore and stroke (in.) ....3.00 x 4.00
Rated rpm 1,400
Displacement (c.i.) 113.1
Fuel ....distillate/gasoline
Main tank capacity (gal.) 10
Auxiliary tank capacity (gal.) 1
Carburetor ....Zenith 61AX7, 0.875-
in.
Air cleaner ....Donaldson
Ignition..IHC H-4 magneto
Cooling capacity (gal.) 3.38
Maximum brake horsepower tests
PTO/belt horsepower................16.51
Crankshaft rpm 1,400
Fuel use (gal./hr.)....................1.40
Maximum drawbar horsepower tests
Gear.......................................2nd
Drawbar horsepower................15.17
Pull weight (lb.).......................1,648
Speed (mph)...........................3.45
Percent slippage.....................7.73
SAE drawbar horsepower...............11.65
SAE belt/PTO horsepower 14.55
Type ....standard
Front tire (in.)...............................4.00 x 15
Rear tire (in.)................................9.00 x 24
Length (in.) 106.25
Height (in.) 63.25
Rear width (in.) 76.75
Tread width (in.)............................40–68
Weight (lb.) ....(3,395)
Gear/speed (mph) ....forward: 1/2.25,
2/3.63, 3/4.75,
4/10.00; reverse:
1/2.88

Farmall B, McCormick-Deering

Manufacturer................................International Harvester
Co., Chicago, IL
Nebraska test number 331
Test date ....September 25–29,
1939
Test tractor serial number..............FAB 4239
Years produced 1940–1948
Serial number range......................501–220829 end
Serial number location ....plate on left seat
support
Number produced ....75,241, A and B
interspersed
Engine ....IHC C-113 vertical
I-head, valve-in-head
Test engine serial number...............FAB 4239
Cylinders 4
Bore and stroke (in.) ....3.00 x 4.00
Rated rpm 1,400
Compression ratio.........................5.33:1
Displacement (c.i.) 113.1
Fuel ....gasoline
Fuel tank capacity (gal.) 10
Carburetor ....Zenith 61AX7, 0.875-in.
Air cleaner ....Donaldson
Ignition..IHC H-4 magneto
Cooling capacity (gal.) 3.38
Maximum brake horsepower tests
PTO/belt horsepower................18.39
Crankshaft rpm 1,400
Fuel use (gal./hr.)....................1.58
Maximum drawbar horsepower tests
Gear.......................................2nd
Drawbar horsepower................16.21
Pull weight (lb.).......................1,794
Speed (mph)...........................3.39
Percent slippage.....................8.99
SAE drawbar horsepower...............12.98
SAE belt/PTO horsepower 16.34
Type ....tricycle
Front tire (in.)...............................6.00 x 12
Rear tire (in.)................................9.00 x 24
Length (in.) 107.88
Height (in.) 65
Rear width (in.) 100.50
Tread width (in.)............................64–92
Weight (lb.) ....(3,565); 1,830
Gear/speed (mph) ....forward: 1/2.25,
2/3.63, 3/4.75,
4/10.00; reverse:
1/2.88

Farmall B, McCormick-Deering

Manufacturer................................International Harvester
Co., Chicago, IL
Nebraska test number 332
Test date ....October 9–13, 1939
Test tractor serial number..............FAB 4560
Years produced 1940–1948
Serial number range......................501–220829 end
Serial number location ....plate on left seat
support
Number produced ....75,241, A and B
interspersed

Engine ....IHC C-113 vertical
I-head, valve-in-head
Test engine serial number ....FAB 4560
Cylinders 4
Bore and stroke (in.) ....3.00 x 4.00
Rated rpm 1,400
Displacement (c.i.) 113.1
Fuel ....distillate/gasoline
Main tank capacity (gal.) 10
Auxiliary tank capacity (gal.) 1
Carburetor ....Zenith 61AX7, 0.875-
in.
Air cleaner ....Donaldson
Ignition ....IHC H-4 magneto
Cooling capacity (gal.) 3.38
Maximum brake horsepower tests
    PTO/belt horsepower 16.00
    Crankshaft rpm 1,400
    Fuel use (gal./hr.) 1.36
Maximum drawbar horsepower tests
    Gear 2nd
    Drawbar horsepower 14.73
    Pull weight (lb.) 1,598
    Speed (mph) 3.46
    Percent slippage 6.91
SAE drawbar horsepower 11.47
SAE belt/PTO horsepower 14.20
Type ....tricycle
Front tire (in.) ....6.00 x 12
Rear tire (in.) ....9.00 x 24
Length (in.) 107.88
Height (in.) 65
Rear width (in.) 100.50
Tread width (in.) 64–92
Weight (lb.) ....(3,565); 1,830
Gear/speed (mph) ....forward: 1/2.25,
2/3.63, 3/4.75,
4/10.00; reverse:
1/2.88

Farmall H, McCormick-Deering
Manufacturer ....International Harvester
Co., Chicago, IL
Nebraska test number 333
Test date ....October 5–11, 1939
Test tractor serial number ....FBH 602
Years produced 1939–1953
Serial number range ....501–391730 end
Serial number location ....plate on left side of
clutch housing
Number produced 390,317
Engine ....IHC C-152
vertical I-head
Test engine serial number ....FBH 602
Cylinders 4
Bore and stroke (in.) ....3.375 x 4.25
Rated rpm 1,650
Compression ratio 5.9:1
Displacement (c.i.) 152.1
Fuel ....gasoline
Fuel tank capacity (gal.) 17
Carburetor ....IHC D-10, 1.00-in.
Air cleaner ....Donaldson
Ignition ....IHC H-4 magneto
Cooling capacity (gal.) 4.25

Maximum brake horsepower tests
    PTO/belt horsepower 26.20
    Crankshaft rpm 1,652
    Fuel use (gal./hr.) 2.26
Maximum drawbar horsepower tests
    Gear 2nd
    Drawbar horsepower 24.17
    Pull weight (lb.) 28.41
    Speed (mph) 3.19
    Percent slippage 6.09
SAE drawbar horsepower 19.13
SAE belt/PTO horsepower 23.72
Type ....tricycle
Front wheel (in.) ....steel: 22.50 x 3.50;
(rubber: 5.50 x 16)
Rear wheel (in.) ....steel: 51 x 6; (rubber:
10.00 x 36)
Length (in.) 125.25
Height (in.) 74
Rear width (in.) 75–90.75
Tread width (in.) 44–80
Weight (lb.) 5,375
Gear/speed (mph) ....forward: 1/2.63,
2/3.50, 3/4.25, 4/5.13,
5/16.38 rubber only;
reverse: 1/2.75

Farmall H, McCormick-Deering
Manufacturer ....International Harvester
Co., Chicago, IL
Nebraska test number 334
Test date ....November 6–11, 1939
Test tractor serial number ....FBH 744
Years produced 1939–1953
Serial number range ....501–391730 end
Serial number location ....plate on left side of
clutch housing
Number produced 390,317
Engine ....IHC C-152
vertical I-head
Test engine serial number ....FBH 744
Cylinders 4
Bore and stroke (in.) ....3.375 x 4.25
Rated rpm 1,650
Displacement (c.i.) 152.1
Fuel ....distillate/gasoline
Main tank capacity (gal.) 17
Auxiliary tank capacity (gal.) 1
Carburetor ....IHC D-10, 1.00-in.
Air cleaner ....Donaldson
Ignition ....IHC H-4 magneto
Cooling capacity (gal.) 4.25
Maximum brake horsepower tests
    PTO/belt horsepower 23.31
    Crankshaft rpm 1,650
    Fuel use (gal./hr.) 2.04
Maximum drawbar horsepower tests
    Gear 2nd
    Drawbar horsepower 21.37
    Pull weight (lb.) 2,484
    Speed (mph) 3.23
    Percent slippage 4.83
SAE drawbar horsepower 16.99
SAE belt/PTO horsepower 20.69
Type ....tricycle

Front wheel (in.) ....steel: 22.50 x 3.50;
(rubber: 5.50 x 16)
Rear wheel (in.) ....steel: 51 x 6;
(rubber: 10.00 x 36)
Length (in.) 125.25
Height (in.) 74
Rear width (in.) 75–90.75
Tread width (in.) 44–80
Weight (lb.) ....(5,375)
Gear/speed (mph) ....forward: 1/2.63,
2/3.50, 3/4.25, 4/5.13,
5/16.38 rubber only;
reverse: 1/2.75

McCormick-Deering W-4

Manufacturer ....International Harvester
Co., Chicago, IL
Nebraska test number 342
Test date ....May 9–25, 1940
Test tractor serial number ....WBH 502
Years produced 1940–1954
Serial number range ....501–34176 end,
through 1953; no data
available for 1954
Serial number location ....plate on left side of
clutch housing
Number produced ....24,377 through 1954
Engine ....IHC C-152
vertical I-head
Test engine serial number ....WBH 502
Cylinders 4
Bore and stroke (in.) ....3.375 x 4.25
Rated rpm 1,650
Displacement (c.i.) 152.1
Fuel ....distillate/gasoline
Main tank capacity (gal.) 17.50
Auxiliary tank capacity (gal.) 0.88
Carburetor ....IHC D-10, 1.00-in.
Air cleaner ....Donaldson
Ignition ....IHC H-4 magneto
Cooling capacity (gal.) 4.25
Maximum brake horsepower tests
PTO/belt horsepower 23.11
Crankshaft rpm 1,651
Fuel use (gal./hr.) 2.01
Maximum drawbar horsepower tests
Gear 2nd
Drawbar horsepower 21.38
Pull weight (lb.) 2,573
Speed (mph) 3.11
Percent slippage 6.40
SAE drawbar horsepower 16.87
SAE belt/PTO horsepower 21.14
Type ....standard
Front wheel (in.) ....steel: 22.50 x 3.50;
(rubber: 6.00 x 16)
Rear wheel (in.) ....steel: 40 x 8;
(rubber: 12.75 x 24)
Length (in.) 113.13
Height (in.) 80
Rear width (in.) 58.50
Tread width (in.) 50.50
Weight (lb.) ....(5,515)
Gear/speed (mph) ....forward: 1/2.38,
2/3.25, 3/4.00, 4/5.13,

5/14.75; reverse:
1/2.75

International TD-14 Diesel TracTracTor

Manufacturer ....International Harvester
Co., Chicago, IL
Nebraska test number 343
Test date ....May 6–31, 1940
Test tractor serial number 743
Years produced 1939–1949
Serial number range ....501–26759 end
Serial number location ....metal plate on upper
left corner of dash
Number produced 26,259
Engine ....IHC vertical I-head
Test engine serial number ....TDFM 517
Cylinders 4
Bore and stroke (in.) ....4.75 x 6.50
Rated rpm 1,350
Displacement (c.i.) 460.7
Fuel ....diesel/gasoline
Main tank capacity (gal.) 45
Auxiliary tank capacity (gal.) 1.33
Carburetor ....starting engine; IHC F,
0.75-in.
Air cleaner ....Donaldson
Ignition ....start; IHC H-4
magneto/Delco-Remy
with 6-v battery
Cooling capacity (gal.) 19
Maximum brake horsepower tests
PTO/belt horsepower 61.56
Crankshaft rpm 1,350
Fuel use (gal./hr.) 3.92
Maximum drawbar horsepower tests
Gear 3rd
Drawbar horsepower 51.71
Pull weight (lb.) 7,919
Speed (mph) 2.45
Percent slippage 6.07
SAE drawbar horsepower 40.53
SAE belt/PTO horsepower 54.42
Type ....tracklayer
Length (in.) 134.13
Height (in.) 77.50
Rear width (in.) ....74.13 or 92.13
Tread width (in.) ....56 or (74)
Weight (lb.) ....(17,420)
Track length (in.) ....78.63 on ground,
252 total
Grouser shoe ....36 links; 16, (20)-in.
Gear/speed (mph) ....forward: 1/1.50,
2/2.00, 3/2.50, 4/3.38,
5/4.75, 6/5.75; reverse:
1/1.50, 2/3.38

International TD-9 Diesel TracTracTor

Manufacturer ....International Harvester
Co., Chicago, IL
Nebraska test number 344
Test date ....June 10–12, 1940
Test tractor serial number 522
Years produced 1940–1956
Serial number range ....501–60300 end,
interspersed with T-9

Serial number location ....metal plate on upper left corner of dash
Number produced ....approximately 59,800, all types
Engine ....IHC vertical I-head
Test engine serial number ....TDCBM 532
Cylinders 4
Bore and stroke (in.) ....4.40 x 5.50
Rated rpm 1,400
Displacement (c.i.) 334.5
Fuel ....diesel/gasoline
Main tank capacity (gal.) 31
Auxiliary tank capacity (gal.) 0.66
Carburetor ....starting engine; IHC F, 0.75-in.
Air cleaner ....Donaldson
Ignition ....start; IHC H-4 magneto/Delco-Remy 12-v; with 2, 6-v battery
Cooling capacity (gal.) 13
Maximum brake horsepower tests
    PTO/belt horsepower 43.93
    Crankshaft rpm 1,399
    Fuel use (gal./hr.) 2.97
Maximum drawbar horsepower tests
    Gear...............................2nd
    Drawbar horsepower 37.21
    Pull weight (lb.) 6,637
    Speed (mph) 2.10
    Percent slippage 4.60
SAE drawbar horsepower...............................29.16
SAE belt/PTO horsepower...............................39.02
Type ....tracklayer
Length (in.) 114
Height (in.) 63.75
Rear width (in.) ....59.13 or 75.13
Tread width (in.) ....44 or (60)
Weight (lb.) ....(10,780)
Track length (in.) ....63.44 on ground, 213 total
Grouser shoe...............................33 links; 13, (18)-in.
Gear/speed (mph) ....forward: 1/1.50, 2/2.20, 3/3.20, 4/3.90, 5/5.30; reverse: 1/1.70

International TD-6 Diesel TracTracTor

Manufacturer...............................International Harvester Co., Chicago, IL
Nebraska test number 345
Test date ....May 6 to June 1, 1940
Test tractor serial number...............................507
Years produced 1940–1956
Serial number range...............................501–38950 end, interspersed with T-6
Serial number location ....metal plate on center right dash
Number produced ....approximately 38,450, all types
Engine ....IHC vertical I-head
Test engine serial number...............................TBKM 671
Cylinders 4
Bore and stroke (in.) ....3.875 x 5.25
Rated rpm 1,450

Displacement (c.i.) 247.7
Fuel ....diesel/gasoline
Main tank capacity (gal.)...............................20
Auxiliary tank capacity (gal.) 0.66
Carburetor ....starting engine; IHC F, 0.75-in.
Air cleaner ....Donaldson
Ignition...............................start; IHC H-4 magneto/Delco-Remy 12-v; with 2, 6-v battery
Cooling capacity (gal.) 10.50
Maximum brake horsepower tests
    PTO/belt horsepower...............................34.54
    Crankshaft rpm 1,448
    Fuel use (gal./hr.) 2.43
Maximum drawbar horsepower tests
    Gear...............................2nd
    Drawbar horsepower...............................28.14
    Pull weight (lb.)...............................4,929
    Speed (mph)...............................2.14
    Percent slippage...............................3.27
SAE drawbar horsepower...............................22.12
SAE belt/PTO horsepower...............................30.80
Type ....tracklayer
Length (in.) 104
Height (in.) 72.32
Rear width (in.) ....53 or 63
Tread width (in.) ....(40) or 50
Weight (lb.) ....(7,775)
Track length (in.) ....58.63 on ground, 192 total
Grouser shoe...............................32 links; 10, (16)-in.
Gear/speed (mph) ....forward: 1/1.50, 2/2.20, 3/3.10, 4/3.80, 5/5.40; reverse: 1/1.70

International T-6 TracTracTor

Manufacturer...............................International Harvester Co., Chicago, IL
Nebraska test number 346
Test date ....May 14 to June 6, 1940
Test tractor serial number...............................679
Years produced 1940–1956
Serial number range...............................501–38950 end, interspersed with TD-6
Serial number location ....metal plate on lower left dash
Number produced ....approximately 38,450, all types
Engine ....IHC vertical I-head
Test engine serial number...............................TBKM 581
Cylinders 4
Bore and stroke (in.) ....3.875 x 5.25
Rated rpm 1,450
Displacement (c.i.) 247.7
Fuel ....gasoline
Fuel tank capacity (gal.) 20
Carburetor ....IHC E-12, 1.25-in.
Air cleaner ....Donaldson
Ignition...............................IHC H-4 magneto or Delco-Remy with 6-v battery

Cooling capacity (gal.) 9.50
Maximum brake horsepower tests
    PTO/belt horsepower..........................36.96
    Crankshaft rpm 1,446
    Fuel use (gal./hr.).................................3.04
Maximum drawbar horsepower tests
    Gear..2nd
    Drawbar horsepower............................30.85
    Pull weight (lb.)...................................5,400
    Speed (mph)..2.14
    Percent slippage.................................3.74
SAE drawbar horsepower............................24.69
SAE belt/PTO horsepower 33.12
Type ....tracklayer
Length (in.) 104
Height (in.) 57.50
Rear width (in.) ....53 or 63
Tread width (in.)...40 or 50
Weight (lb.)..(7,505)
Track length (in.)..58.63 on ground,
    192 total
Grouser shoe...32 links; 10, (18)-in.
Gear/speed (mph) ....forward: 1/1.50,
    2/2.20, 3/3.10, 4/3.80,
    5/5.40; reverse: 1/1.70

International T-6 TracTracTor

Manufacturer...International Harvester
    Co., Chicago, IL
Nebraska test number 347
Test date ....May 22 to June 10,
    1940
Test tractor serial number..........................634
Years produced 1940–1956
Serial number range...................................501–38950 end,
    interspersed with TD-6
Serial number location ....metal plate on lower
    left dash
Number produced ....approximately 38,450,
    all types
Engine ....IHC vertical I-head
Test engine serial number..........................WBKME 501
Cylinders 4
Bore and stroke (in.) ....3.875 x 5.25
Rated rpm 1,450
Displacement (c.i.) 247.7
Fuel ....distillate/gasoline
Main tank capacity (gal.)............................20
Auxiliary tank capacity (gal.) 0.66
Carburetor...IHC E-12, 1.25-in.
Air cleaner ....Donaldson
Ignition..IHC H-4 magneto
Cooling capacity (gal.) 9.50
Maximum brake horsepower tests
    PTO/belt horsepower..........................34.54
    Crankshaft rpm 1,448
    Fuel use (gal./hr.).................................2.82
Maximum drawbar horsepower tests
    Gear..2nd
    Drawbar horsepower............................29.53
    Pull weight (lb.)...................................5,146
    Speed (mph)..2.15
    Percent slippage.................................3.49
SAE drawbar horsepower............................23.72
SAE belt/PTO horsepower 31.18

Type ....tracklayer
Length (in.) 104
Height (in.) 57.50
Rear width (in.) ....53 or 63
Tread width (in.)...40 or 50
Weight (lb.)..(7,505)
Track length (in.)..58.63 on ground,
    192 total
Grouser shoe...32 links; 10, (18)-in.
Gear/speed (mph) ....forward: 1/1.50,
    2/2.20, 3/3.10, 4/3.80,
    5/5.40; reverse: 1/1.70

McCormick-Deering W-4

Manufacturer...International Harvester
    Co., Chicago, IL
Nebraska test number 353
Test date ....September 16–20,
    1940
Test tractor serial number..........................WBH 627 x I
Years produced 1940–1954
Serial number range...................................501–34176 end,
    through 1953
Serial number location ....plate on left side of
    clutch housing
Number produced ....24,377 through 1954
Engine ....IHC C-152 vertical I-head
Test engine serial number..........................WBH 627 x I
Cylinders 4
Bore and stroke (in.) ....3.375 x 4.25
Rated rpm 1,650
Compression ratio.....................................5.9:1
Displacement (c.i.) 152.1
Fuel ....gasoline
Fuel tank capacity (gal.).............................17.50
Carburetor...IHC D-10, 1.00-in.
Air cleaner ....Donaldson
Ignition..IHC H-4 magneto
Cooling capacity (gal.) 4.25
Maximum brake horsepower tests
    PTO/belt horsepower..........................26.21
    Crankshaft rpm 1,650
    Fuel use (gal./hr.).................................2.25
Maximum drawbar horsepower tests
    Gear..2nd
    Drawbar horsepower............................23.97
    Pull weight (lb.)...................................2,957
    Speed (mph)..3.04
    Percent slippage.................................7.24
SAE drawbar horsepower............................19.25
SAE belt/PTO horsepower 23.71
Type ....standard
Front wheel (in.)..steel: 22.50 x 3.50;
    (rubber: 6.00 x 16)
Rear wheel (in.)...steel: 40 x 8;
    (rubber: 12.75 x 24)
Length (in.) 113.13
Height (in.) 80
Rear width (in.) 58.50
Tread width (in.)...50.50
Weight (lb.)..(5,675)
Gear/speed (mph) ....forward: 1/2.38, 2/3.25,
    3/4.00, 4/5.13, 5/14.75
    rubber only; reverse:
    1/2.75

McCormick-Deering W-6

Manufacturer	International Harvester Co., Chicago, IL
Nebraska test number	354
Test date	September 16–23, 1940
Test tractor serial number	WBK 512
Years produced	1940–1953
Serial number range	501–46011 end
Serial number location	plate on left side of clutch housing
Number produced	28,378
Engine	IHC C-248 vertical I-head
Test engine serial number	WBK ME 501
Cylinders	4
Bore and stroke (in.)	3.875 x 5.25
Rated rpm	1,450
Displacement (c.i.)	247.7
Fuel	distillate/gasoline
Main tank capacity (gal.)	21
Auxiliary tank capacity (gal.)	88
Carburetor	IHC E-12, 1.25-in.
Air cleaner	Donaldson
Ignition	IHC H-4 magneto
Cooling capacity (gal.)	6.25

Maximum brake horsepower tests

PTO/belt horsepower	34.23
Crankshaft rpm	1,450
Fuel use (gal./hr.)	2.81

Maximum drawbar horsepower tests

Gear	2nd
Drawbar horsepower	30.74
Pull weight (lb.)	3,963
Speed (mph)	2.91
Percent slippage	8.71
SAE drawbar horsepower	24.60
SAE belt/PTO horsepower	31.19
Type	standard
Front wheel (in.)	steel: 22.50 x 4; (rubber: 6.50 x 16)
Rear wheel (in.)	steel: 42 x 10; (rubber: 13.50 x 24)
Length (in.)	124.38
Height (in.)	90.75
Rear width (in.)	63
Tread width (in.)	53
Weight (lb.)	(7,569)
Gear/speed (mph)	forward: 1/2.38, 2/3.13, 3/4.00, 4/4.88, 5/14.50 rubber only; reverse: 1/2.88

McCormick-Deering W-6

Manufacturer	International Harvester Co., Chicago, IL
Nebraska test number	355
Test date	September 16–27, 1940
Test tractor serial number	WBK 511 x I
Years produced	1940–1953
Serial number range	501–46011 end
Serial number location	plate on left side of clutch housing
Number produced	28,378
Engine	IHC C-248 vertical I-head
Test engine serial number	WBK 511 x I
Cylinders	4
Bore and stroke (in.)	3.875 x 5.25
Rated rpm	1,450
Compression ratio	5.65:1
Displacement (c.i.)	247.7
Fuel	gasoline
Fuel tank capacity (gal.)	21
Carburetor	IHC E-12, 1.25-in.
Air cleaner	Donaldson
Ignition	IHC H-4 magneto
Cooling capacity (gal.)	6.25

Maximum brake horsepower tests

PTO/belt horsepower	36.97
Crankshaft rpm	1,450
Fuel use (gal./hr.)	2.96

Maximum drawbar horsepower tests

Gear	2nd
Drawbar horsepower	32.48
Pull weight (lb.)	4,282
Speed (mph)	2.84
Percent slippage	10.84
SAE drawbar horsepower	25.36
SAE belt/PTO horsepower	32.93
Type	standard
Front wheel (in.)	steel: 22.50 x 4; (rubber: 6.50 x 16)
Rear wheel (in.)	steel: 42 x 10; (rubber: 13.50 x 24)
Length (in.)	124.38
Height (in.)	90.75
Rear width (in.)	63
Tread width (in.)	53
Weight (lb.)	(7,435)
Gear/speed (mph)	forward: 1/2.38, 2/3.13, 3/4.00, 4/4.88, 5/14.50 rubber only; reverse: 1/2.88

McCormick-Deering WD-6 Diesel

Manufacturer	International Harvester Co., Chicago, IL
Nebraska test number	356
Test date	September 20–27, 1940
Test tractor serial number	WD6 WDBK655
Years produced	1940–1953
Serial number range	501–46011 end, interspersed with W-6
Serial number location	plate on left side of clutch housing
Number produced	28,378 total W-6; na WD-6
Engine	IHC D-248 vertical I-head
Test engine serial number	WDBKM 699
Cylinders	4
Bore and stroke (in.)	3.875 x 5.25
Rated rpm	1,450
Compression ratio	14.2:1
Displacement (c.i.)	247.7
Fuel	diesel/gasoline
Main tank capacity (gal.)	21

Auxiliary tank capacity (gal.) 88
Carburetor ....start; IHC F, 0.75-in.
Air cleaner ....Donaldson
Ignition ....start; IHC H-4 magneto
Cooling capacity (gal.) 6.75
Maximum brake horsepower tests
    PTO/belt horsepower........................34.75
    Crankshaft rpm 1,450
    Fuel use (gal./hr.) 2.34
Maximum drawbar horsepower tests
    Gear...2nd
    Drawbar horsepower..........................30.58
    Pull weight (lb.)...............................3,997
    Speed (mph)....................................2.87
    Percent slippage..............................9.78
SAE drawbar horsepower 23.54
SAE belt/PTO horsepower 30.92
Type ....standard
Front wheel (in.) ....steel: 22.50 x 4;
    (rubber: 6.50 x 16)
Rear wheel (in.) ....steel: 42 x 10;
    (rubber: 13.50 x 24)
Length (in.) 124.38
Height (in.) 89.25
Rear width (in.) 63
Tread width (in.)..53
Weight (lb.) ....(7,820)
Gear/speed (mph) ....forward: 1/2.38,
    2/3.13, 3/4.00, 4/4.88,
    5/14.50 rubber only;
    reverse: 1/2.88

Farmall MD Diesel, McCormick-Deering

Manufacturer...International Harvester
    Co., Chicago, IL
Nebraska test number 368
Test date ....May 21 to June 18,
    1941
Test tractor serial number...........................FDBK 29832
Years produced..1939–1952
Serial number range....................................501–298218 end
Serial number location ....plate on left side of
    clutch housing
Number produced ....18,253, interspersed
    with M
Engine...IHC D-248
    vertical I-head
Test engine serial number............................FDBKM 726
Cylinders 4
Bore and stroke (in.) ....3.875 x 5.25
Rated rpm 1,450
Compression ratio......................................14.2:1
Displacement (c.i.) 247.7
Fuel ....diesel/gasoline
Main tank capacity (gal.).............................21
Auxiliary tank capacity (gal.) 1
Carburetor ....starting engine; IHC F,
    0.75-in.
Air cleaner ....Donaldson
Ignition...start; IHC H-4 magneto
Cooling capacity (gal.) 7.50
Maximum brake horsepower tests
    PTO/belt horsepower........................35.02
    Crankshaft rpm 1,451
    Fuel use (gal./hr.) 2.40

Maximum drawbar horsepower tests
    Gear...2nd
    Drawbar horsepower..........................31.05
    Pull weight (lb.)...............................3,566
    Speed (mph)....................................3.26
    Percent slippage..............................7.82
SAE drawbar horsepower 24.78
SAE belt/PTO horsepower 31.08
Type ....tricycle
Front wheel (in.) ....steel: 22.50 x 4;
    (rubber: 6.50 x 16)
Rear wheel (in.) ....steel: 51 x 8;
    (rubber: 12.00 x 38)
Length (in.) 126.75
Height (in.) 78.25
Rear width (in.) 84.50–100
Tread width (in.)..52–88
Weight (lb.) 5,125
Gear/speed (mph) ....forward: 1/2.63,
    2/3.50, 3/4.25, 4/5.13,
    5/16.38; reverse:
    1/3.13

McCormick-Deering W-9

Manufacturer...International Harvester
    Co., Chicago, IL
Nebraska test number 369
Test date ....May 21 to June 17,
    1941
Test tractor serial number...........................WCB 546
Years produced..1940–1954
Serial number range....................................501–67969 no end
Serial number location ....plate on right side fuel
    tank support
Number produced 71,715
Engine...IHC C-335
    vertical I-head
Test engine serial number............................WCBM 517-W1
Cylinders 4
Bore and stroke (in.) ....4.40 x 5.50
Rated rpm 1,500
Compression ratio......................................5.4:1
Displacement (c.i.) 334.5
Fuel ....gasoline
Fuel tank capacity (gal.) 36
Carburetor ....IHC E-13, 1.375-in.
Air cleaner ....Donaldson
Ignition...IHC H-4 magneto
Cooling capacity (gal.) 10
Maximum brake horsepower tests
PTO/belt horsepower...................................49.40
Crankshaft rpm 1,500
Fuel use (gal./hr.) 4.22
Maximum drawbar horsepower tests
Gear..rubber: 3rd
Drawbar horsepower...................................44.15
Pull weight (lb.)..3,994
Speed (mph)..4.15
Percent slippage..6.68
SAE drawbar horsepower 35.30
SAE belt/PTO horsepower 44.51
Type ....standard
Front wheel (in.) ....steel: 30 x 6; (rubber:
    7.50 x 18)

Rear wheel (in.)..steel: 48 x 12;
(rubber: 14.00 x 32)
Length (in.) 133.50
Height (in.) 66
Rear width (in.) 68.13
Tread width (in.)..50–56.13
Weight (lb.) 6,175
Gear/speed (mph) ....forward: 1/2.38, 2/3.13,
3/4.38, 4/5.38, 5/15.38
rubber only; reverse:
1/2.88

McCormick-Deering WD-9 Diesel

Manufacturer...International Harvester
Co., Chicago, IL
Nebraska test number 370
Test date ....May 21 to June 18,
1941
Test tractor serial number............................WDCB 735
Years produced 1940–1954
Serial number range.......................................501–67969 no end,
interspersed with W-9
Serial number location ....plate on fuel tank
support
Number produced ....
Engine ....IHC D-335 vertical I-head
Test engine serial number............................WDCBM 739
Cylinders 4
Bore and stroke (in.) ....4.40 x 5.50
Rated rpm...1,500
Compression ratio..15.7:1
Displacement (c.i.)..334.5
Fuel ....diesel/gasoline
Main tank capacity (gal.)...............................36
Auxiliary tank capacity (gal.) 0.88
Carburetor ....starting engine; IHC F,
0.75-in.
Air cleaner ....Donaldson
Ignition..start; IHC H-4 magneto
Cooling capacity (gal.) 11
Maximum brake horsepower tests
    PTO/belt horsepower..........................46.43
    Crankshaft rpm 1,500
    Fuel use (gal./hr.) 3.16
Maximum drawbar horsepower tests
    Gear..rubber: 3rd
    Drawbar horsepower............................42.57
    Pull weight (lb.) 3,853
    Speed (mph) 4.14
    Percent slippage...................................6.54
SAE drawbar horsepower...............................33.59
SAE belt/PTO horsepower..............................41.79
Type ....standard
Front wheel (in.)..steel: 30 x 6;
(rubber: 7.50 x 18)
Rear wheel (in.)...steel: 48 x 12;
(rubber: 14.00 x 32)
Length (in.) 133.50
Height (in.) 66
Rear width (in.) 68.13
Tread width (in.)..50–56.13
Weight (lb.) 6,475
Gear/speed (mph) ....forward: 1/2.38,
2/3.13, 3/4.38, 4/5.38,
5/15.38 rubber only;
reverse: 1/4.38

McCormick-Deering W-9

Manufacturer...International Harvester
Co., Chicago, IL
Nebraska test number 371
Test date ....June 4–17, 1941
Test tractor serial number............................WCB 747
Years produced 1940–1954
Serial number range.......................................501–67969 no end
Serial number location ....plate on right side fuel
tank support
Number produced 71,715
Engine ....IHC C-335
vertical I-head
Test engine serial number............................WCBM 680
Cylinders 4
Bore and stroke (in.) ....4.40 x 5.50
Rated rpm...1,500
Displacement (c.i.)..334.5
Fuel ....distillate/gasoline
Main tank capacity (gal.)...............................35
Auxiliary tank capacity (gal.) 0.88
Carburetor ....IHC E-13, 1.125-in.
Air cleaner ....Donaldson
Ignition..IHC H-4 magneto
Cooling capacity (gal.) 11
Maximum brake horsepower tests
    PTO/belt horsepower..........................46.36
    Crankshaft rpm 1,500
    Fuel use (gal./hr.) 4.26
Maximum drawbar horsepower tests
    Gear..rubber: 3rd
    Drawbar horsepower............................42.67
    Pull weight (lb.) 3,832
    Speed (mph) 4.18
    Percent slippage...................................5.73
SAE drawbar horsepower...............................33.44
SAE belt/PTO horsepower..............................41.65
Type ....standard
Front wheel (in.)..steel: 30 x 6;
(rubber: 7.50 x 18)
Rear wheel (in.)...steel: 48 x 12;
(rubber: 14.00 x 32)
Length (in.) 133.50
Height (in.) 66
Rear width (in.) 68.13
Tread width (in.)..50–56.13
Weight (lb.) 6,215
Gear/speed (mph) ....forward: 1/2.38,
2/3.13, 3/4.38, 4/5.38,
5/15.38 rubber only;
reverse: 1/2.88

International T-9 TracTracTor

Manufacturer...International Harvester
Co., Chicago, IL
Nebraska test number 372
Test date ....May 27 to June 18,
1941
Test tractor serial number............................2413 T7
Years produced 1940–1956
Serial number range.......................................501–60300 end,
interspersed with TD-9
Serial number location ....metal plate on upper
left corner of dash
Number produced ....approximately 59,800,
all types

Engine .... IHC vertical I-head
Test engine serial number .... TCBM 517-T1
Cylinders 4
Bore and stroke (in.) .... 4.40 x 5.50
Rated rpm 1,400
Displacement (c.i.) 334.5
Fuel .... gasoline
Fuel tank capacity (gal.) 31
Carburetor .... IHC E-13, 1.375-in.
Air cleaner .... Donaldson
Ignition .... IHC H-4 magneto or
                                                  Delco-Remy with 6-v
                                                  battery
Cooling capacity (gal.) 12
Maximum brake horsepower tests
    PTO/belt horsepower 46.46
    Crankshaft rpm 1,400
    Fuel use (gal./hr.) 3.92
Maximum drawbar horsepower tests
    Gear 2nd
    Drawbar horsepower 40.59
    Pull weight (lb.) 7,091
    Speed (mph) 2.15
    Percent slippage 2.69
SAE drawbar horsepower 32.24
SAE belt/PTO horsepower 41.39
Type .... tracklayer
Length (in.) 114
Height (in.) 63.75
Rear width (in.) .... 59.13 or (75.13)
Tread width (in.) .... 44 or (60)
Weight (lb.) .... (10,655)
Track length (in.) .... 63.44 on ground,
                                                  213 total
Grouser shoe .... 33 links; 13, (20)-in.
Gear/speed (mph) .... forward: 1/1.50,
                                                  2/2.25, 3/3.25, 4/3.88,
                                                  5/5.25; reverse: 1/1.75

Farmall CUB, McCormick

Manufacturer .... International Harvester
                                                  Co., Chicago, IL
Nebraska test number 386
Test date .... September 29 to
                                                  October 9, 1947
Test tractor serial number 3202
Years produced 1947–1964
Serial number range .... 501–224703 end
Serial number location .... plate on right side of
                                                  steering gear housing
Number produced .... 203,814 through 1958
Engine .... IHC C-60
                                                  vertical L-head
Test engine serial number 3777
Cylinders 4
Bore and stroke (in.) .... 2.625 x 2.75
Rated rpm 1,600
Compression ratio 6.5:1
Displacement (c.i.) 59.50
Fuel .... gasoline
Fuel tank capacity (gal.) 7.50
Carburetor .... IHC, 0.75-in.
Air cleaner .... Donaldson
Ignition .... IHC J-4 magneto or
                                                  Delco-Remy with 6-v
                                                  battery

Cooling capacity (gal.) 1.50
Maximum brake horsepower tests
    PTO/belt horsepower 9.23
    Crankshaft rpm 1,601
    Fuel use (gal./hr.) 0.84
Maximum drawbar horsepower tests
    Gear 2nd
    Drawbar horsepower 8.47
    Pull weight (lb.) 1,063
    Speed (mph) 2.99
    Percent slippage 6.76
SAE drawbar horsepower 6.67
SAE belt/PTO horsepower 8.30
Type .... standard
Front tire (in.) .... 4.00 x 12
Rear tire (in.) .... 8.00 x 24
Length (in.) 98.50
Height (in.) 62.50
Rear width (in.) 47.25–63.38
Tread width (in.) 40–56
Weight (lb.) 1,364
Gear/speed (mph) .... forward: 1/2.14,
                                                  2/3.12, 3/6.42; reverse:
                                                  1/2.39

Farmall C, McCormick-Deering

Manufacturer .... The International
                                                  Harvester Co., Chicago,
                                                  IL
Nebraska test number 395
Test date .... June 7–17, 1948
Test tractor serial number .... FC 2127
Years produced 1948–1951
Serial number range .... 501–80432 end
Serial number location .... plate on toolbox and
                                                  seat support
Number produced .... approximately 103,816
Engine .... IHC C-113
                                                  vertical I-head
Test engine serial number .... FC 4431G
Cylinders 4
Bore and stroke (in.) .... 3.00 x 4.00
Rated rpm 1,650
Compression ratio 6.0:1
Displacement (c.i.) 113
Fuel .... gasoline
Fuel tank capacity (gal.) 11
Carburetor .... Zenith 161 x 6, 0.875-
                                                  in.
Air cleaner .... Donaldson
Ignition .... IHC magneto
Cooling capacity (gal.) 3.25
Maximum brake horsepower tests
    PTO/belt horsepower 21.12
    Crankshaft rpm 1,651
    Fuel use (gal./hr.) 1.90
Maximum drawbar horsepower tests
    Gear 2nd
    Drawbar horsepower 18.57
    Pull weight (lb.) 1,982
    Speed (mph) 3.51
    Percent slippage 6.26
SAE drawbar horsepower 14.72
SAE belt/PTO horsepower 18.85
Type .... tricycle
Front tire (in.) .... 4.00 x 15

Rear tire (in.) ....9.00 x 36
Length (in.) 120.38
Height (in.) 70.38
Rear width (in.) 80
Tread width (in.) 47–100
Weight (lb.) 2,710
Gear/speed (mph) ....forward: 1/2.375,
2/3.75, 3/5.00,
4/10.25; reverse:
1/3.00

McCormick-Deering WD-9 Diesel

Manufacturer ....International Harvester
Co., Chicago, IL
Nebraska test number 441
Test date ....May 31 to June 7,
1950
Test tractor serial number ....WDCB 42216
Years produced 1940–1954
Serial number range ....501–67969 no end,
interspersed with W-9
Serial number location ....plate on fuel tank
support
Number produced ....71,715 total W-9; na
WD-9
Engine ....IHC D-335
vertical I-head
Test engine serial number ....WDCBM 18744
Cylinders 4
Bore and stroke (in.) ....4.40 x 5.50
Rated rpm 1,500
Compression ratio 15.7:1
Displacement (c.i.) 334.5
Fuel ....diesel
Fuel tank capacity (gal.) 35
Carburetor ....starting engine;
International F-8, 0.75-
in.
Air cleaner ....Donaldson
Ignition ....start; IHC H-4
magneto/12-v; with 2,
6-v battery
Cooling capacity (gal.) 9.50
Maximum brake horsepower tests
    PTO/belt horsepower 51.27
    Crankshaft rpm 1,500
    Fuel use (gal./hr.) 3.51
Maximum drawbar horsepower tests
    Gear 3rd
    Drawbar horsepower 46.02
    Pull weight (lb.) 4,018
    Speed (mph) 4.30
    Percent slippage 6.54
SAE drawbar horsepower 36.45
SAE belt/PTO horsepower 45.25
Type ....standard
Front tire (in.) ....7.50 x 18
Rear tire (in.) ....14.00 x 34
Length (in.) 134.25
Height (in.) 81.88
Rear width (in.) 75.75
Tread width (in.) 60
Weight (lb.) 6,810

Gear/speed (mph) ....forward: 1/2.38,
2/3.25, 3/4.63, 4/5.63,
5/16.25; reverse:
1/3.00

International TD-14A Diesel

Manufacturer ....International Harvester
Co., Chicago, IL
Nebraska test number 445
Test date ....June 26 to July 1,
1950
Test tractor serial number ....TDF 27443
Years produced 1949–1955
Serial number range ....26760–39300 end
Serial number location ....metal plate on upper
left corner of dash
Number produced 12,541
Engine ....IHC vertical I-head
Test engine serial number ....TDFM 27244
Cylinders 4
Bore and stroke (in.) ....4.75 x 6.50
Rated rpm 1,400
Compression ratio 15.5:1
Displacement (c.i.) 460.7
Fuel ....diesel/gasoline
Main tank capacity (gal.) 45
Auxiliary tank capacity (gal.) 1.33
Carburetor ....starting engine; IHC,
0.75-in.
Air cleaner ....Donaldson
Ignition ....start; IHC DH-4
magneto/12-v; with 2,
6-v battery
Cooling capacity (gal.) 19
Maximum brake horsepower tests
    PTO/belt horsepower 71.79
    Crankshaft rpm 1,400
    Fuel use (gal./hr.) 4.66
Maximum drawbar horsepower tests
    Gear 2nd
    Drawbar horsepower 62.68
    Pull weight (lb.) 11,772
    Speed (mph) 2.00
    Percent slippage 2.98
SAE drawbar horsepower 49.43
SAE belt/PTO horsepower 64.01
Type ....tracklayer
Length (in.) 134.13
Height (in.) 77.50
Rear width (in.) ....74.13 or 92.13
Tread width (in.) ....56 or (74)
Weight (lb.) 16,905
Track length (in.) ....78.63 on ground,
252 total
Grouser shoe ....36 links; 16, (20)-in.
Gear/speed (mph) ....forward: 1/1.60,
2/2.00, 3/2.60, 4/3.40,
5/4.40, 6/5.70; reverse:
1/1.60, 2/3.40

International TD-18A Diesel

Manufacturer ....International Harvester
Co., Chicago, IL
Nebraska test number 446

International

Test date .... June 27 to July 18, 1950
Test tractor serial number .... TDR 23465
Years produced 1949–1955
Serial number range .... 22536–33649 end
Serial number location .... metal plate on upper left corner of dash
Number produced 11,114
Engine .... IHC vertical I-head
Test engine serial number .... TDRM 23796
Cylinders 6
Bore and stroke (in.) .... 4.75 x 6.50
Rated rpm 1,350
Compression ratio 15.5:1
Displacement (c.i.) 691.1
Fuel .... diesel/gasoline
Main tank capacity (gal.) 60
Auxiliary tank capacity (gal.) 1.33
Carburetor .... start; IHC C-12, 0.75-in.
Air cleaner .... Donaldson
Ignition .... start; IHC F-6 magneto/12-v with 2, 6-v battery
Cooling capacity (gal.) 26
Maximum brake horsepower tests
    PTO/belt horsepower 97.83
    Crankshaft rpm 1,350
    Fuel use (gal./hr.) 6.65
Maximum drawbar horsepower tests
    Gear 2nd
    Drawbar horsepower 85.61
    Pull weight (lb.) 15,279
    Speed (mph) 2.10
    Percent slippage 3.95
SAE drawbar horsepower 66.97
SAE belt/PTO horsepower 86.68
Type .... tracklayer
Length (in.) 158.25
Height (in.) 92
Rear width (in.) .... 82.25 or 94.25
Tread width (in.) .... 62 or 74
Weight (lb.) 23,760
Track length (in.) .... 84.63 on ground, 277.50 total
Grouser shoe .... 37 links; 20, (22)-in.
Gear/speed (mph) .... forward: 1/1.70, 2/2.20, 3/2.70, 4/3.50, 5/4.60, 6/5.70; reverse: 1/1.60, 2/3.50

International TD-24 Diesel
Manufacturer .... International Harvester Co., Chicago, IL
Nebraska test number 447
Test date .... June 29 to July 18, 1950
Test tractor serial number .... TDE 2330
Years produced 1947–1955
Serial number range .... 501–8000 end
Serial number location .... metal plate on upper left corner of dash
Number produced .... approximately 7,500
Engine .... IHC vertical I-head
Test engine serial number .... TDEM 2169
Cylinders 6

Bore and stroke (in.) .... 5.75 x 7.00
Rated rpm 1,375
Compression ratio 15.22:1
Displacement (c.i.) 1,090.6
Fuel .... diesel/gasoline
Main tank capacity (gal.) 85
Auxiliary tank capacity (gal.) 2.13
Carburetor .... start; IHC C-12, 1.25-in.
Air cleaner .... Donaldson
Ignition .... start; 24-v with 4, 6-v battery
Cooling capacity (gal.) 37
Maximum drawbar horsepower tests
    Gear 3rd
    Drawbar horsepower 142.11
    Pull weight (lb.) 21,873
    Speed (mph) 2.44
    Percent slippage 0.92
SAE drawbar horsepower 111.32
Type .... tracklayer
Length (in.) 182.25
Height (in.) 95.25
Rear width (in.) 102
Tread width (in.) 80
Weight (lb.) 38,740
Track length (in.) .... 104.50 on ground, 331.50 total
Grouser shoe .... 39 links; 22, (24)-in.
Gear/speed (mph) .... forward: 1/1.60, 2/2.00, 3/2.40, 4/3.10, 5/4.00, 6/5.20, 7/6.10, 8/7.80; reverse: 1/1.60, 2/2.00, 3/2.40, 4/3.10, 5/4.00, 6/5.10, 7/6.00, 8/7.70

Farmall Super C, McCormick
Manufacturer .... International Harvester Co., Chicago, IL
Nebraska test number 458
Test date .... May 31 to June 9, 1951
Test tractor serial number 71669
Years produced 1951–1954
Serial number range .... 100001–198310 end
Serial number location .... plate on left side toolbox and seat support
Number produced 112,006
Engine .... IHC C-123 vertical I-head
Test engine serial number 71669
Cylinders 4
Bore and stroke (in.) .... 3.125 x 4.00
Rated rpm 1,650
Compression ratio 6.0:1
Displacement (c.i.) 122.7
Fuel .... gasoline
Fuel tank capacity (gal.) 11
Carburetor .... Carter, Marvel-Schebler, or Zenith, 0.875-in.
Air cleaner .... Donaldson
Ignition .... Delco-Remy with 6-v battery

Cooling capacity (gal.) 3.75
Maximum brake horsepower tests
    PTO/belt horsepower...........................23.67
    Crankshaft rpm....................................1,651
    Fuel use (gal./hr.)................................2.32
Maximum drawbar horsepower tests
    Gear..2nd
    Drawbar horsepower...........................20.72
    Pull weight (lb.)..................................2,108
    Speed (mph)..3.69
    Percent slippage.................................5.59
SAE drawbar horsepower............................16.25
SAE belt/PTO horsepower...........................20.78
Type ....tricycle
Front tire (in.) ....5.00 x 15
Rear tire (in.) ....10.00 x 36
Length (in.) 123
Height (in.) 85.50
Rear width (in.) 80–90.75
Tread width (in.).....................................48–71/57–80
Weight (lb.) 2,855
Gear/speed (mph) ....forward: 1/2.38, 2/3.75,
    3/5.00, 4/10.25;
    reverse: 1/3.00

McCormick WD-6 Diesel
Manufacturer...International Harvester
    Co., Chicago, IL
Nebraska test number 459
Test date ....June 1–14, 1951
Test tractor serial number..........................WDBK 39582
Years produced...1940–1953
Serial number range..................................501–46011 end
Serial number location ....plate on left side of
    clutch housing
Number produced ....28,378 total, diesels
    interspersed
Engine ....IHC D-248
    vertical I-head
Test engine serial number..........................FDBKM 18295
Cylinders 4
Bore and stroke (in.) ....3.875 x 5.25
Rated rpm 1,450
Compression ratio....................................16.8:1
Displacement (c.i.) 247.7
Fuel ....diesel/gasoline
Main tank capacity (gal.) 20.50
Auxiliary tank capacity (gal.) 1
Carburetor ....start; IHC F8, 0.75-in.
Air cleaner ....Donaldson
Ignition..start; IHC DH-4
    magneto/Delco-Remy
    12-v; with 2, 6-v
    battery
Cooling capacity (gal.) 7
Maximum brake horsepower tests
    PTO/belt horsepower...........................37.64
    Crankshaft rpm....................................1,451
    Fuel use (gal./hr.)................................2.71
Maximum drawbar horsepower tests
    Gear..3rd
    Drawbar horsepower...........................33.25
    Pull weight (lb.)..................................2,835
    Speed (mph)..4.40
    Percent slippage.................................5.03

SAE drawbar horsepower............................26.22
SAE belt/PTO horsepower...........................33.46
Type ....standard
Front tire (in.) ....6.00 x 16
Rear tire (in.) ....14.00 x 30
Length (in.) 125
Height (in.) 88.38
Rear width (in.) 63
Tread width (in.).....................................55
Weight (lb.) 5,410
Gear/speed (mph) ....forward: 1/2.38, 2/3.38,
    3/4.38, 4/5.25, 5/15.75;
    reverse: 1/2.88

Farmall MD Diesel, McCormick-Deering
Manufacturer...International Harvester
    Co., Chicago, IL
Nebraska test number 460
Test date ....June 1–16, 1951
Test tractor serial number..........................FDBK 261013
Years produced...1939–1952
Serial number range..................................501–298218 end
Serial number location ....plate on left side of
    clutch housing
Number produced ....18,253, interspersed
    with M
Engine ....IHC vertical I-head
Test engine serial number..........................FDBKM 18321
Cylinders 4
Bore and stroke (in.) ....3.875 x 5.25
Rated rpm 1,450
Compression ratio....................................16.8:1
Displacement (c.i.) 247.7
Fuel ....diesel/gasoline
Main tank capacity (gal.) 20.50
Auxiliary tank capacity (gal.) 1
Carburetor ....start; IHC F8 0.75-in.
Air cleaner ....Donaldson
Ignition..start; IHC DH-4
    magneto/Delco-Remy
    12-v; with 2, 6-v battery
Cooling capacity (gal.) 7
Maximum brake horsepower tests
    PTO/belt horsepower...........................38.21
    Crankshaft rpm....................................1,451
    Fuel use (gal./hr.)................................2.71
    Maximum drawbar horsepower tests
    Gear..3rd
    Drawbar horsepower...........................34.38
    Pull weight (lb.)..................................3,133
Speed (mph)...4.12
Percent slippage...6.18
SAE drawbar horsepower............................27.20
SAE belt/PTO horsepower...........................34.10
Type ....tricycle
Front tire (in.) ....6.00 x 16
Rear tire (in.) ....12.00 x 38
Length (in.) 136.13
Height (in.) 78.25
Tread width (in.).....................................52–88
Weight (lb.) 5,385
Gear/speed (mph) ....forward: 1/2.63,
    2/3.50, 3/4.25, 4/5.13,
    5/16.25; reverse:
    1/3.13

International TD-9 Diesel

Manufacturer	International Harvester Co., Chicago, IL
Nebraska test number	461
Test date	June 25 to July 10, 1951
Test tractor serial number	TDCB 42012
Years produced	1940–1956
Serial number range	501–60300 end, interspersed with T-9
Serial number location	metal plate on upper left corner of dash
Number produced	approximately 59,800, all types
Engine	IHC vertical I-head
Test engine serial number	T 33359
Cylinders	4
Bore and stroke (in.)	4.40 x 5.50
Rated rpm	1,400
Compression ratio	15.7:1
Displacement (c.i.)	334.5
Fuel	diesel/gasoline
Main tank capacity (gal.)	31
Auxiliary tank capacity (gal.)	1
Carburetor	start; IHC F-8, 0.75-in.
Air cleaner	Donaldson
Ignition	start; IHC DH-4 magneto/Delco-Remy 12-v; with 2, 6-v battery
Cooling capacity (gal.)	13

Maximum brake horsepower tests

PTO/belt horsepower	46.69
Crankshaft rpm	1,400
Fuel use (gal./hr.)	3.28

Maximum drawbar horsepower tests

Gear	2nd
Drawbar horsepower	39.50
Pull weight (lb.)	6,872
Speed (mph)	2.16
Percent slippage	2.67
SAE drawbar horsepower	30.98
SAE belt/PTO horsepower	41.57
Type	tracklayer
Length (in.)	114
Height (in.)	63.75
Rear width (in.)	59.13 or 75.13
Tread width (in.)	44 or (60)
Weight (lb.)	10,260
Track length (in.)	63.44 on ground, 213 total
Grouser shoe	33 links; 13, (20)-in.
Gear/speed (mph)	forward: 1/1.50, 2/2.20, 3/3.00, 4/3.90, 5/5.30; reverse: 1/1.70

International TD-6 Diesel

Manufacturer	International Harvester Co., Chicago, IL
Nebraska test number	462
Test date	June 25 to July 10, 1951
Test tractor serial number	TDBK 29165
Years produced	1940–1956
Serial number range	501–38950 end, interspersed with T-6

Number produced	approximately 38,450, all types
Engine	IHC vertical I-head
Test engine serial number	UBKM 13369
Cylinders	4
Bore and stroke (in.)	3.875 x 5.25
Rated rpm	1,450
Compression ratio	16.8:1
Displacement (c.i.)	247.7
Fuel	diesel/gasoline
Main tank capacity (gal.)	20
Auxiliary tank capacity (gal.)	1
Carburetor	start; IHC F-8, 0.75-in.
Air cleaner	Donaldson
Ignition	start; IHC F-8 magneto/Delco-Remy 12-v; with 2, 6-v battery
Cooling capacity (gal.)	10.50

Maximum brake horsepower tests

PTO/belt horsepower	38.20
Crankshaft rpm	1,450
Fuel use (gal./hr.)	2.68

Maximum drawbar horsepower tests

Gear	2nd
Drawbar horsepower	31.75
Pull weight (lb.)	5,514
Speed (mph)	2.16
Percent slippage	2.36
SAE drawbar horsepower	25.34
SAE belt/PTO horsepower	34.25
Type	tracklayer
Length (in.)	104
Height (in.)	59.50
Tread width (in.)	40 or (50)
Weight (lb.)	7,560
Track length (in.)	58.63 on ground
Grouser shoe	32 links; 12, (18)-in.
Gear/speed (mph)	forward: 1/1.50, 2/2.20, 3/3.10, 4/3.80, 5/5.40; reverse: 1/1.70

Farmall Super M, McCormick

Manufacturer	International Harvester Co., Chicago, IL
Nebraska test number	475
Test date	June 25 to July 2, 1952
Test tractor serial number	F 1947 J
Years produced	1952–1954
Serial number range	501–52627 end; 500001–512541 no end, includes Super MD, MDV, MV
Serial number location	plate on left side of clutch housing
Number produced	44,551 Super Models interspersed
Engine	IHC C-264 vertical I-head
Test engine serial number	2029
Cylinders	4
Bore and stroke (in.)	4.00 x 5.25
Rated rpm	1,450
Compression ratio	5.9:1
Displacement (c.i.)	264
Fuel	gasoline

Fuel tank capacity (gal.) 21
Carburetor ....IHC E-12, 1.25-in.
Air cleaner ....Donaldson
Ignition ....Delco-Remy with 6-v
                     battery
Cooling capacity (gal.) 6.25
Maximum brake horsepower tests
   PTO/belt horsepower.......................46.26
   Crankshaft rpm 1,451
   Fuel use (gal./hr.) 3.91
Maximum drawbar horsepower tests
   Gear...3rd
   Drawbar horsepower.........................41.79
   Pull weight (lb.)............................3,192
   Speed (mph)................................4.91
   Percent slippage...........................5.53
SAE drawbar horsepower.........................33.18
SAE belt/PTO horsepower........................41.28
Type ....tricycle
Front wheel (in.).....................................6.00 x 16
Rear wheel (in.)......................................13.00 x 38
Length (in.) 134.63
Height (in.) 94.25
Rear width (in.)......................................84–101.25
Tread width (in.).....................................52–88
Weight (lb.) 5,725
Gear/speed (mph) ....forward: 1/2.63, 2/3.75,
                     3/5.00, 4/6.75, 5/16.75;
                     reverse: 1/3.63

McCormick Super W-6

Manufacturer...International Harvester
                     Co., Chicago, IL
Nebraska test number 476
Test date ....June 25 to July 7,
                     1952
Test tractor serial number......................6071
Years produced 1952–1954
Serial number range...............................501–9084 end, all
                     types interspersed
Serial number location ....plate on left side of
                     clutch housing
Number produced 6,891
Engine ....IHC C-264 vertical I-head
Test engine serial number 1296
Cylinders 4
Bore and stroke (in.) ....4.00 x 5.25
Rated rpm 1,450
Compression ratio..................................5.9:1
Displacement (c.i.) 264
Fuel ....gasoline
Fuel tank capacity (gal.) 21
Carburetor...IHC E-12, 1.25-in.
Air cleaner ....Donaldson
Ignition ....Delco-Remy with 6-v
                     battery
Cooling capacity (gal.) 5
Maximum brake horsepower tests
   PTO/belt horsepower.......................46.25
   Crankshaft rpm 1,450
   Fuel use (gal./hr.) 4.00
Maximum drawbar horsepower tests
   Gear...3rd
   Drawbar horsepower.........................41.57
   Pull weight (lb.)............................3,141

Speed (mph) 4.96
   Percent slippage...........................5.53
SAE drawbar horsepower.........................32.78
SAE belt/PTO horsepower........................41.45
Type ....standard
Front wheel (in.).....................................6.00 x 16
Rear wheel (in.)......................................15.00 x 30
Length (in.) 125
Height (in.) 90.88
Rear width (in.)......................................70
Tread width (in.).....................................55
Weight (lb.) 5,490
Gear/speed (mph) ....forward: 1/2.63, 2/3.63,
                     3/4.75, 4/6.63, 5/16.13;
                     reverse: 1/3.50

Farmall Super MD Diesel, McCormick

Manufacturer...International Harvester
                     Co., Chicago, IL
Nebraska test number 477
Test date ....July 7–11, 1952
Test tractor serial number......................F 1570 J
Years produced 1952–1954
Serial number range...............................501–52627 end;
                     500001–512541 no
                     end, includes Super M,
                     MDV, MV
Serial number location ....plate on left side of
                     clutch housing
Number produced ....5,199, interspersed
                     with Super M
Engine ....IHC D-264
                     vertical I-head
Test engine serial number ....D 264759
Cylinders 4
Bore and stroke (in.) ....4.00 x 5.25
Rated rpm 1,450
Compression ratio..................................16.5:1
Displacement (c.i.) 264
Fuel ....diesel/gasoline
Fuel tank capacity (gal.) 20.50
Carburetor...start; IHC F-8, 0.75-in.
Air cleaner ....Donaldson
Ignition ....start; IHC DH-4
                     magneto/12-v with 2,
                     6-v battery
Cooling capacity (gal.) 7
Maximum brake horsepower tests
   PTO/belt horsepower.......................46.73
   Crankshaft rpm 1,450
   Fuel use (gal./hr.) 3.35
Maximum drawbar horsepower tests
   Gear...3rd
   Drawbar horsepower.........................42.19
   Pull weight (lb.)............................3,213
   Speed (mph)................................4.92
   Percent slippage...........................5.30
SAE drawbar horsepower.........................32.93
SAE belt/PTO horsepower........................41.07
Type ....tricycle
Front wheel (in.).....................................6.00 x 16
Rear wheel (in.)......................................13.00 x 38
Length (in.) 136.13
Height (in.) 93

Rear width (in.) 84–101.25
Tread width (in.) 52–88
Weight (lb.) 5,725
Gear/speed (mph) .... forward: 1/2.63, 2/3.75, 3/5.00, 4/6.75, 5/16.75; reverse: 1/3.63

McCormick Super WD-6 Diesel

Manufacturer .... International Harvester Co., Chicago, IL
Nebraska test number 478
Test date .... July 8–17, 1952
Test tractor serial number .... 2131 J
Years produced 1952–1954
Serial number range .... 501–9084 end, all types interspersed
Serial number location .... plate on left side of clutch housing
Number produced .... 1,691, interspersed with W6
Engine .... IHC D-264 vertical I-head
Test engine serial number .... D 264760
Cylinders 4
Bore and stroke (in.) .... 4.00 x 5.25
Rated rpm 1,450
Compression ratio 16.5:1
Displacement (c.i.) 264
Fuel .... diesel/gasoline
Main tank capacity (gal.) 20.50
Auxiliary tank capacity (gal.) 0.88
Carburetor .... start; IHC F-8, 0.75-in.
Air cleaner .... Donaldson
Ignition .... start; IHC DH-4 magneto/12-v; 2, 6-v battery
Cooling capacity (gal.) 7
Maximum brake horsepower tests
    PTO/belt horsepower 46.84
    Crankshaft rpm 1,450
    Fuel use (gal./hr.) 3.29
Maximum drawbar horsepower tests
    Gear 3rd
    Drawbar horsepower 41.77
    Pull weight (lb.) 3,167
    Speed (mph) 4.95
    Percent slippage 4.62
SAE drawbar horsepower 32.83
SAE belt/PTO horsepower 41.20
Type .... standard
Front wheel (in.) .... 6.00 x 16
Rear wheel (in.) .... 15.00 x 30
Length (in.) 125
Height (in.) 89.38
Rear width (in.) 70
Tread width (in.) 55
Weight (lb.) 5,490
Gear/speed (mph) .... forward: 1/2.63, 2/3.63, 3/4.75, 4/6.63, 5/16.13; reverse: 1/3.50

Farmall Super M LPG, McCormick

Manufacturer .... International Harvester Co., Chicago, IL

Nebraska test number 484
Test date .... October 1–10, 1952
Test tractor serial number .... F 1164 CJ
Years produced 1952–1954
Serial number range .... 501–52627 end; 500001–512541 no end, includes Super MD, MDV, MV
Serial number location .... plate on left side of clutch housing
Number produced .... 44,551 total, LPG and Super Models
Engine .... IHC C-264 vertical I-head
Test engine serial number .... 14647 C
Cylinders 4
Bore and stroke (in.) .... 4.00 x 5.25
Rated rpm 1,450
Compression ratio 6.75:1
Displacement (c.i.) 264
Fuel .... LPG
Fuel tank capacity (gal.) 30.50
Carburetor .... Ensign XG, 1.25-in.
Air cleaner .... Donaldson
Ignition .... Delco-Remy with 6-v battery
Cooling capacity (gal.) 6.25
Maximum brake horsepower tests
    PTO/belt horsepower 47.07
    Crankshaft rpm 1,451
    Fuel use (gal./hr.) 5.47
Maximum drawbar horsepower tests
    Gear 3rd
    Drawbar horsepower 44.23
    Pull weight (lb.) 3,355
    Speed (mph) 4.94
    Percent slippage 5.40
SAE drawbar horsepower 33.80
SAE belt/PTO horsepower 41.52
Type .... tricycle
Front wheel (in.) .... 6.00 x 16
Rear wheel (in.) .... 13.00 x 38
Length (in.) 134.63
Height (in.) 94.25
Rear width (in.) 84–101.25
Tread width (in.) 52–88
Weight (lb.) 5,725
Gear/speed (mph) .... forward: 1/2.63, 2/3.75, 3/5.00, 4/6.75, 5/16.75; reverse: 1/3.63

McCormick Super W-6 LPG

Manufacturer .... International Harvester Co., Chicago, IL
Nebraska test number 485
Test date .... October 1–13, 1952
Test tractor serial number .... 3800 CJ
Years produced 1952–1954
Serial number range .... 501–9084 end, all types interspersed
Serial number location .... plate on left side of clutch housing
Number produced .... 6,861 total, LPG interspersed

Engine ....IHC C-264
vertical I-head
Test engine serial number.......................14648 C
Cylinders 4
Bore and stroke (in.) ....4.00 x 5.25
Rated rpm 1,450
Compression ratio.................................6.75:1
Displacement (c.i.) 264
Fuel ....LPG
Fuel tank capacity (gal.) 30.50
Carburetor ....Ensign XG, 1.25-in.
Air cleaner ....Donaldson
Ignition ....Delco-Remy with 6-v
battery
Cooling capacity (gal.) 5

Maximum brake horsepower tests
    PTO/belt horsepower..........................47.53
    Crankshaft rpm 1,451
    Fuel use (gal./hr.).............................5.54
Maximum drawbar horsepower tests
    Gear...3rd
    Drawbar horsepower.........................42.64
    Pull weight (lb.)...............................3,181
    Speed (mph) 5.03
    Percent slippage.............................5.28
SAE drawbar horsepower.......................33.49
SAE belt/PTO horsepower.....................41.76
Type ....standard
Front wheel (in.) ....6.50 x 18
Rear wheel (in.) ....15.00 x 30
Length (in.) 125
Height (in.) 90.88
Rear width (in.) 70
Tread width (in.)....................................55
Weight (lb.) 5,490
Gear/speed (mph) ....forward: 1/2.63,
2/3.63, 3/4.75, 4/6.63,
5/16.13; reverse:
1/3.50

McCormick Super W-4
Manufacturer...International Harvester
Co., Chicago, IL
Nebraska test number 491
Test date ....April 27 to May 13,
1953
Test tractor serial number.....................649 J
Years produced 1953–1954
Serial number range..............................501–3292 end
Serial number location ....plate on left side of
clutch housing
Number produced 2,527
Engine ....IHC C-164 vertical I-head
Test engine serial number.....................C 164 1766
Cylinders 4
Bore and stroke (in.) ....3.50 x 4.25
Rated rpm 1,650
Compression ratio.................................6.1:1
Displacement (c.i.) 164
Fuel ....gasoline
Fuel tank capacity (gal.) 17.50
Carburetor ....IHC, 1.25-in.
Air cleaner ....Donaldson
Ignition ....Delco-Remy with 6-v
battery

Cooling capacity (gal.) 4.12
Maximum brake horsepower tests
    PTO/belt horsepower..........................33.85
    Crankshaft rpm 1,650
    Fuel use (gal./hr.).............................3.05
Maximum drawbar horsepower tests
    Gear...3rd
    Drawbar horsepower.........................29.31
    Pull weight (lb.).................................2,395
    Speed (mph) 4.59
    Percent slippage.............................4.95
SAE drawbar horsepower.......................22.86
SAE belt/PTO horsepower.....................29.50
Type ....standard
Front wheel (in.) ....5.50 x 16
Rear wheel (in.) ....13.00 x 26
Length (in.) 114
Height (in.) 80.50
Rear width (in.) 66.63
Tread width (in.)....................................52
Weight (lb.) 3,915
Gear/speed (mph) ....forward: 1/2.38,
2/3.50, 3/4.63, 4/6.25,
5/15.00; reverse:
1/3.00

Farmall Super H, McCormick
Manufacturer...International Harvester
Co., Chicago, IL
Nebraska test number 492
Test date ....April 27 to May 13,
1953
Test tractor serial number.....................1558 J
Years produced 1953–1954
Serial number range..............................501–29285 end,
includes Super HV
Serial number location ....plate on left side of
clutch housing
Number produced 28,691
Engine ....IHC C-164
vertical I-head
Test engine serial number.....................C 164 1763
Cylinders 4
Bore and stroke (in.) ....3.50 x 4.25
Rated rpm 1,650
Compression ratio.................................6.1:1
Displacement (c.i.) 164
Fuel ....gasoline
Fuel tank capacity (gal.) 17.50
Carburetor ....IHC 1.25-in.
Air cleaner ....Donaldson
Ignition ....Delco-Remy
with 6-v battery
Cooling capacity (gal.) 4.12
Maximum brake horsepower tests
    PTO/belt horsepower..........................33.40
    Crankshaft rpm 1,650
    Fuel use (gal./hr.).............................3.00
Maximum drawbar horsepower tests
    Gear...3rd
    Drawbar horsepower.........................30.69
    Pull weight (lb.).................................2,385
    Speed (mph) 4.83
    Percent slippage.............................4.78
SAE drawbar horsepower.......................22.38

International

SAE belt/PTO horsepower 29.42
Type ....tricycle
Front wheel (in.)....................................5.50 x 16
Rear wheel (in.).....................................11.00 x 38
Length (in.) 133
Height (in.) 85
Rear width (in.) 75
Tread width (in.)....................................48–88
Weight (lb.) 4,100
Gear/speed (mph) ....forward: 1/2.63, 2/3.75,
3/5.00, 4/6.63, 5/16.25;
reverse: 1/3.25

McCormick Super WD-9 Diesel
Manufacturer.......................................International Harvester
Co., Chicago, IL
Nebraska test number 518
Test date ....May 10–19, 1954
Test tractor serial number.......................722 J
Years produced 1953–1956
Serial number range...............................501–7232 end
Serial number location ....plate on fuel tank
support
Number produced 10,938
Engine ....IHC D-350
vertical I-head
Test engine serial number.......................928
Cylinders 4
Bore and stroke (in.) ....4.50 x 5.50
Rated rpm 1,500
Compression ratio.................................15.6:1
Displacement (c.i.) 350
Fuel ....diesel/gasoline
Fuel tank capacity (gal.) 35
Carburetor ....start; IHC E-13, 0.75-in.
Air cleaner ....Donaldson
Ignition..start; IHC H-4
magneto/Delco-Remy
12-v; with 2, 6-v battery
Cooling capacity (gal.) 9.50
Maximum brake horsepower tests
    PTO/belt horsepower...........................65.19
    Crankshaft rpm 1,500
    Fuel use (gal./hr.) 4.46
Maximum drawbar horsepower tests
    Gear...3rd
    Drawbar horsepower............................57.37
    Pull weight (lb.)..................................4,955
    Speed (mph)......................................4.34
    Percent slippage.................................6.57
SAE drawbar horsepower.........................44.55
SAE belt/PTO horsepower 57.15
Type ....standard
Front tire (in.)......................................7.50 x 18
Rear tire (in.).......................................18.00 x 26
Length (in.) 139.63
Height (in.) 82.75
Rear width (in.) 81
Tread width (in.)...................................60
Weight (lb.) 6,630
Gear/speed (mph) ....forward: 1/2.38,
2/3.13, 3/4.50, 4/5.50,
5/15.75; reverse:
1/3.00

International TD-24 Diesel
Manufacturer.......................................International Harvester
Co., Chicago, IL
Nebraska test number 529
Test date ....October 22–29, 1954
Test tractor serial number.......................TDE 6318
Years produced 1947–1955
Serial number range...............................501–8000 end
Serial number location ....metal plate on upper
left corner of dash
Number produced ....approximately 7,500
Engine ....IHC D1091
vertical I-head
Test engine serial number.......................TDEM 6623
Cylinders 6
Bore and stroke (in.) ....5.75 x 7.00
Rated rpm 1,400
Compression ratio.................................15.22:1
Displacement (c.i.) 1,090.6
Fuel ....diesel/gasoline
Main tank capacity (gal.) 85
Auxiliary tank capacity (gal.) 2.13
Carburetor ....start; IHC C-12, 1.25-
in.
Air cleaner ....Donaldson
Ignition..start; Delco-Remy 24-
v; with 4, 6-v battery
Cooling capacity (gal.) 37
Maximum drawbar horsepower tests
    Gear...3rd
    Drawbar horsepower............................154.05
    Pull weight (lb.)..................................23,416
    Speed (mph)......................................2.47
    Percent slippage.................................1.56
SAE drawbar horsepower.........................120.80
Type ....tracklayer
Length (in.) 182.25
Height (in.) 95.25
Rear width (in.) 102
Tread width (in.)...................................80
Weight (lb.) 40,524
Track length (in.) ....104.50 on ground,
331.50 total
Grouser shoe..39 links; 22, (24)-in.
Gear/speed (mph) ....forward: 1/1.60, 2/2.00,
3/2.50, 4/3.20, 5/4.10,
6/5.30, 7/6.30, 8/8.00;
reverse: 1/1.60, 2/2.00,
3/2.50, 4/3.10, 5/4.00,
6/5.10, 7/6.10, 8/7.80

Farmall 400, McCormick
Manufacturer.......................................International Harvester
Co., Chicago, IL
Nebraska test number 532
Test date ....March 28 to April 4,
1955
Test tractor serial number.......................4164 S
Years produced 1954–1956
Serial number range...............................501–41484 end
Serial number location ....plate on left side of
clutch housing
Number produced 31,806
Engine ....IHC C-264
vertical I-head

Test engine serial number 138509
Cylinders 4
Bore and stroke (in.) ....4.00 x 5.25
Rated rpm 1,450
Compression ratio 6.3:1
Displacement (c.i.) 264
Fuel ....gasoline
Fuel tank capacity (gal.) 18
Carburetor ....IHC E-12, 1.25-in.
Air cleaner ....Donaldson
Ignition ....IHC H-4 magneto or
Delco-Remy with 6-v
battery
Cooling capacity (gal.) 6.50
Maximum brake horsepower tests
　　PTO/belt horsepower 50.78
　　Crankshaft rpm 1,450
　　Fuel use (gal./hr.) 4.43
Maximum drawbar horsepower tests
　　Gear 3rd
　　Drawbar horsepower 45.34
　　Pull weight (lb.) 3,558
　　Speed (mph) 4.78
　　Percent slippage 5.98
SAE drawbar horsepower 35.51
SAE belt/PTO horsepower 44.80
Type ....tricycle
Front tire (in.) ....6.00 x 16
Rear tire (in.) ....13.00 x 38
Length (in.) 141.13
Height (in.) 95
Rear width (in.) 101.25
Tread width (in.) 50–94
Weight (lb.) 5,950
Gear/speed (mph) ....forward: 1/2.50, 1 Torque Amplifier/1.69, 2/3.85, 2 Torque Amplifier/2.60, 3/4.83, 3 Torque Amplifier/3.26, 4/6.71, 4 Torque Amplifier/4.53, 5/16.70, 5 Torque Amplifier/11.27; reverse: 1/3.33, 1 Torque Amplifier/2.27

International W-400

Manufacturer ....International Harvester
Co., Chicago, IL
Nebraska test number 533
Test date ....March 28 to April 8, 1955
Test tractor serial number ....668 S
Years produced 1954–1956
Serial number range ....501–3858 end, all
types interspersed
Serial number location ....plate on left side of
clutch housing
Number produced 2,070
Engine ....IHC C-264
vertical I-head
Test engine serial number 138511
Cylinders 4
Bore and stroke (in.) ....4.00 x 5.25
Rated rpm 1,450
Compression ratio 6.3:1
Displacement (c.i.) 264
Fuel ....gasoline
Fuel tank capacity (gal.) 18
Carburetor ....IHC E-12, 1.25-in.

Air cleaner ....Donaldson
Ignition ....IHC H-4 magneto or
Delco-Remy with
6-v battery
Cooling capacity (gal.) 6.75
Maximum brake horsepower tests
　　PTO/belt horsepower 51.94
　　Crankshaft rpm 1,450
　　Fuel use (gal./hr.) 4.41
Maximum drawbar horsepower tests
　　Gear 3rd
　　Drawbar horsepower 45.84
　　Pull weight (lb.) 3,565
　　Speed (mph) 4.82
　　Percent slippage 5.09
SAE drawbar horsepower 35.54
SAE belt/PTO horsepower 45.51
Type ....standard
Front wheel (in.) ....6.50 x 18
Rear wheel (in.) ....15.00 x 30
Length (in.) 130
Height (in.) 93.38
Rear width (in.) 75.75
Tread width (in.) 60.25
Weight (lb.) 5,940
Gear/speed (mph) ....forward: 1/2.42, 1 Torque Amplifier/1.63, 2/3.72, 2 Torque Amplifier/2.51, 3/4.67, 3 Torque Amplifier/3.15, 4/6.49, 4 Torque Amplifier/4.38, 5/16.15, 5 Torque Amplifier/10.90; reverse: 1/3.22, 1 Torque Amplifier/2.17

Farmall 400 Diesel, McCormick

Manufacturer ....International Harvester
Co., Chicago, IL
Nebraska test number 534
Test date ....April 8–16, 1955
Test tractor serial number ....4166 S
Years produced 1954–1956
Serial number range ....501–41484 end
Serial number location ....plate on left side of
clutch housing
Number produced ....31,806 total, diesels
interspersed
Engine ....IHC D-264
vertical I-head
Test engine serial number ....D 264 12423
Cylinders 4
Bore and stroke (in.) ....4.00 x 5.25
Rated rpm 1,450
Compression ratio 16.5:1
Displacement (c.i.) 264
Fuel ....diesel/gasoline
Fuel tank capacity (gal.) 18
Carburetor ....start; IHC F-8, 0.75-in.
Air cleaner ....Donaldson
Ignition ....start; IHC H-4 magneto
or Delco-Remy with
12-v battery
Cooling capacity (gal.) 7.25
Maximum brake horsepower tests
　　PTO/belt horsepower 46.73
　　Crankshaft rpm 1,450
　　Fuel use (gal./hr.) 3.36

Maximum drawbar horsepower tests

    Gear...3rd
    Drawbar horsepower............................42.69
    Pull weight (lb.).................................3,353
    Speed (mph).....................................4.78
    Percent slippage...............................5.48
SAE drawbar horsepower.................................33.54
SAE belt/PTO horsepower...............................41.11
Type...tricycle
Front wheel (in.)......................................6.00 x 16
Rear wheel (in.).......................................13.00 x 38
Length (in.)...141.13
Height (in.)...94
Rear width (in.).......................................101.25
Tread width (in.)......................................50–94
Weight (lb.)...6,390
Gear/speed (mph)............forward: 1/2.50, 1 Torque Amplifier/1.69, 2/3.85, 2 Torque Amplifier/2.60, 3/4.83, 3 Torque Amplifier/3.26, 4/6.71, 4 Torque Amplifier/4.53, 5/16.70, 5 Torque Amplifier/11.27; reverse: 1/3.33, 1 Torque Amplifier/2.25

International W-400 Diesel

Manufacturer..........................International Harvester Co., Chicago, IL
Nebraska test number.................535
Test date.............................April 8–20, 1955
Test tractor serial number............646 S
Years produced.......................1954–1956
Serial number range..................501–3858 end, all types interspersed
Serial number location...............plate on left side of clutch housing
Number produced......................1,118
Engine...............................IHC D-264 vertical I-head
Test engine serial number.............D 264 13392
Cylinders............................4
Bore and stroke (in.).................4.00 x 5.25
Rated rpm............................1,450
Compression ratio....................16.5:1
Displacement (c.i.)...................264
Fuel.................................diesel/gasoline
Fuel tank capacity (gal.).............18
Carburetor...........................start; IHC F-8, 0.75-in.
Air cleaner..........................Donaldson
Ignition.............................start; IHC H-4 magneto or Delco-Remy with 12-v battery
Cooling capacity (gal.)...............7.25
Maximum brake horsepower tests
    PTO/belt horsepower............................46.61
    Crankshaft rpm..................................1,452
    Fuel use (gal./hr.).............................3.42
Maximum drawbar horsepower tests
    Gear...3rd
    Drawbar horsepower............................42.85
    Pull weight (lb.).................................3,336
    Speed (mph).....................................4.82
    Percent slippage...............................4.37
SAE drawbar horsepower.................................33.93
SAE belt/PTO horsepower...............................41.28
Type...standard

Front wheel (in.)......................................6.50 x 18
Rear wheel (in.).......................................15.00 x 30
Length (in.)...130
Height (in.)...93.38
Rear width (in.).......................................75.75
Tread width (in.)......................................60.25
Weight (lb.)...6,260
Gear/speed (mph)............forward: 1/2.42, 1 Torque Amplifier/1.63, 2/3.72, 2 Torque Amplifier/2.51, 3/4.67, 3 Torque Amplifier/3.15, 4/6.49, 4 Torque Amplifier/4.38, 5/16.15, 5 Torque Amplifier/10.90; reverse: 1/3.22, 1 Torque Amplifier/2.17

Farmall 200, McCormick

Manufacturer..........................International Harvester Co., Chicago, IL
Nebraska test number.................536
Test date.............................April 18–29, 1955
Test tractor serial number............1907 J
Years produced.......................1954–1956
Serial number range..................501–15698 end
Serial number location...............plate on left side of clutch housing
Number produced......................13,726
Engine...............................IHC C-123 vertical I-head
Test engine serial number.............1892
Cylinders............................4
Bore and stroke (in.).................3.125 x 4.00
Rated rpm............................1,650
Compression ratio....................6.5:1
Displacement (c.i.)...................123
Fuel.................................gasoline
Fuel tank capacity (gal.).............11
Carburetor...........................Carter or Zenith 11340, 0.875-in.
Air cleaner..........................Donaldson
Ignition.............................IHC H-4 magneto or Delco-Remy with 6-v battery
Cooling capacity (gal.)...............3.75
Maximum brake horsepower tests
    PTO/belt horsepower............................24.11
    Crankshaft rpm..................................1,650
    Fuel use (gal./hr.).............................2.42
Maximum drawbar horsepower tests
    Gear...2nd
    Drawbar horsepower............................20.92
    Pull weight (lb.).................................2,112
    Speed (mph).....................................3.71
    Percent slippage...............................6.37
SAE drawbar horsepower.................................16.70
SAE belt/PTO horsepower...............................21.49
Type...tricycle
Front wheel (in.)......................................5.00 x 15
Rear wheel (in.).......................................10.00 x 36
Length (in.)...123
Height (in.)...85
Rear width (in.).......................................90.75
Tread width (in.)......................................48–80
Weight (lb.)...3,310
Gear/speed (mph)............forward: 1/2.50, 2/3.88, 3/5.13, 4/10.63; reverse: 1/3.13

Farmall 100, McCormick

Manufacturer	International Harvester Co., Chicago, IL
Nebraska test number	537
Test date	April 18– 29, 1955
Test tractor serial number	2643
Years produced	1954–1956
Serial number range	501–18940 end
Serial number location	plate on left side of clutch housing
Number produced	17,383
Engine	IHC C-123 vertical I-head
Test engine serial number	ECM 504711
Cylinders	4
Bore and stroke (in.)	3.125 x 4.00
Rated rpm	1,400
Compression ratio	6.5:1
Displacement (c.i.)	123
Fuel	gasoline
Fuel tank capacity (gal.)	11
Carburetor	Carter or Zenith 11340, 0.875-in.
Air cleaner	Donaldson or United
Ignition	IHC H-4 magneto or Delco Remy with 6-v battery
Cooling capacity (gal.)	3.75

Maximum brake horsepower tests

PTO/belt horsepower	20.13
Crankshaft rpm	1,401
Fuel use (gal./hr.)	2.06

Maximum drawbar horsepower tests

Gear	2nd
Drawbar horsepower	17.83
Pull weight (lb.)	1,719
Speed (mph)	3.89
Percent slippage	5.95
SAE drawbar horsepower	14.24
SAE belt/PTO horsepower	17.91
Type	standard
Front wheel (in.)	5.00 x 15
Rear wheel (in.)	11.00 x 24
Length (in.)	107
Height (in.)	82
Rear width (in.)	56
Tread width (in.)	40–68
Weight (lb.)	2,710
Gear/speed (mph)	forward: 1/2.32, 2/3.68, 3/4.84, 4/10.05; reverse: 1/2.90

Farmall 300, McCormick

Manufacturer	International Harvester Co., Chicago, IL
Nebraska test number	538
Test date	April 29 to May 2, 1955
Test tractor serial number	2910 SJ
Years produced	1954–1956
Serial number range	501–29578 end
Serial number location	plate on right side of clutch housing
Number produced	29,501

Engine	IHC C-169 vertical I-head
Test engine serial number	2913
Cylinders	4
Bore and stroke (in.)	3.5625 x 4.25
Rated rpm	1,750
Compression ratio	6.8:1
Displacement (c.i.)	169
Fuel	gasoline
Fuel tank capacity (gal.)	17
Carburetor	IHC E-12, 0.25-in.
Air cleaner	Donaldson
Ignition	IHC H-4 magneto or Delco-Remy with 6-v battery
Cooling capacity (gal.)	4.25

Maximum brake horsepower tests

PTO/belt horsepower	38.16
Crankshaft rpm	1,750
Fuel use (gal./hr.)	3.37

Maximum drawbar horsepower tests

Gear	3rd
Drawbar horsepower	33.73
Pull weight (lb.)	2,450
Speed (mph)	5.16
Percent slippage	4.73
SAE drawbar horsepower	26.90
SAE belt/PTO horsepower	33.86
Type	tricycle
Front wheel (in.)	5.50 x 16
Rear wheel (in.)	12.00 x 38
Length (in.)	136
Height (in.)	85
Rear width (in.)	100
Tread width (in.)	48–93
Weight (lb.)	4,840
Gear/speed (mph)	forward: 1/2.50, 1 Torque Amplifier/1.68, 2/3.82, 2 Torque Amplifier/2.58, 3/4.15, 3 Torque Amplifier/3.48, 4/6.60, 4 Torque Amplifier/4.46, 5/16.11, 5 Torque Amplifier/10.87; reverse: 1/3.12, 1 Torque Amplifier/2.10

300 Utility

Manufacturer	International Harvester Co., Chicago, IL
Nebraska test number	539
Test date	May 5–10, 1955
Test tractor serial number	2701 SJ
Years produced	1955–1956
Serial number range	501–33664 end
Serial number location	plate on right side of clutch housing
Number produced	33,176
Engine	IHC C-169 vertical I-head
Test engine serial number	13705
Cylinders	4
Bore and stroke (in.)	3.5625 x 4.25
Rated rpm	2,000
Compression ratio	6.8:1
Displacement (c.i.)	169
Fuel	gasoline
Fuel tank capacity (gal.)	17
Carburetor	IHC E-12, 1.25-in.

International

Air cleaner ....Donaldson
Ignition ....Delco-Remy
with 6-v battery
Cooling capacity (gal.) 4.25
Maximum brake horsepower tests
PTO/belt horsepower.........................41.26
Crankshaft rpm 2,000
Fuel use (gal./hr.) 3.98
Maximum drawbar horsepower tests
Gear 3rd
Drawbar horsepower........................37.36
Pull weight (lb.)................................2,769
Speed (mph)...................................5.06
Percent slippage...............................7.04
SAE drawbar horsepower..................29.61
SAE belt/PTO horsepower.................36.41
Type ....standard
Front wheel (in.)..............................5.50 x 16
Rear wheel (in.)...............................12.00 x 28
Length (in.) 118
Height (in.) 58
Rear width (in.) 65.25–89
Tread width (in.) 48–76
Weight (lb.) 4,140
Gear/speed (mph)............forward: 1/2.60, 1 Torque
Amplifier/1.75, 2/3.97, 2 Torque
Amplifier/2.68, 3/5.36, 3 Torque
Amplifier/3.61, 4/6.86, 4 Torque
Amplifier/4.63, 5/16.74, 5 Torque
Amplifier/11.30; reverse: 1/3.24, 1
Torque Amplifier/2.19

Farmall 400 LPG, McCormick
Manufacturer...................................International Harvester
Co., Chicago, IL
Nebraska test number 571
Test date ....May 7–28, 1956
Test tractor serial number...............25458 S
Years produced 1954–1956
Serial number range........................501–41484 end
Serial number location ....plate on left side of
clutch housing
Number produced ....31,806 total, LPG
interspersed
Engine ....IHC C264
vertical I-head
Test engine serial number................159094 E
Cylinders 4
Bore and stroke (in.) ....4.00 x 5.25
Rated rpm 1,450
Compression ratio..........................8.35:1
Displacement (c.i.) 264
Fuel ....LPG
Fuel tank capacity (gal.) 18
Carburetor......................................IHC E-12, 1.25-in.
Air cleaner......................................Donaldson
Ignition...IHC H-4 magneto or
Delco-Remy with 12-v
battery
Cooling capacity (gal.) 6.50
Maximum brake horsepower tests
PTO/belt horsepower........................52.36
Crankshaft rpm 1,450
Fuel use (gal./hr.) 5.82

Maximum drawbar horsepower tests
Gear 3rd
Drawbar horsepower........................48.12
Pull weight (lb.)................................3,813
Speed (mph)...................................4.73
Percent slippage...............................6.56
SAE drawbar horsepower..................37.16
SAE belt/PTO horsepower.................45.99
Type ....tricycle
Front wheel (in.)..............................6.50 x 16
Rear wheel (in.)...............................13.00 x 38
Length (in.) 141.13
Height (in.) 95
Rear width (in.) 101.25
Tread width (in.) 50–94
Weight (lb.) 5,980
Gear/speed (mph)............forward: 1/2.50, 1 Torque
Amplifier/1.69, 2/3.85, 2 Torque
Amplifier/2.60, 3/4.83, 3 Torque
Amplifier/3.26, 4/6.71, 4 Torque
Amplifier/4.53, 5/16.70, 5 Torque
Amplifier/11.27; reverse: 1/3.33, 1
Torque Amplifier/2.25

International W-400 LPG
Manufacturer...................................International Harvester
Co., Chicago, IL
Nebraska test number 572
Test date ....May 9–25, 1956
Test tractor serial number...............1971 S
Years produced 1954–1956
Serial number range........................501–3858 end, all
types interspersed
Serial number location ....plate on left side clutch
housing
Number produced ....2,070 total, LPG
interspersed
Engine ....IHC C-264 vertical I-head
Test engine serial number................159279 E
Cylinders 4
Bore and stroke (in.) ....4.00 x 5.25
Rated rpm 1,450
Compression ratio..........................8.33:1
Displacement (c.i.) 264
Fuel ....LPG
Fuel tank capacity (gal.) 31
Carburetor......................................IHC E-12, 1.25-in.
Air cleaner......................................Donaldson
Ignition...IHC H-4 magneto or
Delco-Remy with 12-v
battery
Cooling capacity (gal.) 6.75
Maximum brake horsepower tests
PTO/belt horsepower........................50.72
Crankshaft rpm 1,451
Fuel use (gal./hr.) 5.66
Maximum drawbar horsepower tests
Gear 3rd
Drawbar horsepower........................47.30
Pull weight (lb.)................................3,574
Speed (mph) 4.96
Percent slippage...............................4.89
SAE drawbar horsepower..................36.64
SAE belt/PTO horsepower 44.92

Type ....standard
Front wheel (in.)........................7.50 x 18
Rear wheel (in.).........................15.00 x 30
Length (in.) 130
Height (in.) 93.38
Rear width (in.) 75.75
Tread width (in.).........................60.25
Weight (lb.) 5,940
Gear/speed (mph)............forward: 1/2.42, 1 Torque
Amplifier/1.63, 2/3.72, 2 Torque
Amplifier/2.51, 3/4.67, 3 Torque
Amplifier/3.15, 4/6.49, 4 Torque
Amplifier/4.38, 5/16.15, 5 Torque
Amplifier/10.90; reverse: 1/3.22, 1
Torque Amplifier/2.17

Farmall 300 LPG, McCormick

Manufacturer...............................International Harvester
Co., Chicago, IL
Nebraska test number 573
Test date ....May 9 to June 4, 1956
Test tractor serial number.............24068 S J
Years produced 1954–1956
Serial number range.....................501–29578 end
Serial number location ....plate on right side of
clutch housing
Number produced ....29,501 total, LPG
interspersed
Engine.....................................IHC C-169
vertical I-head
Test engine serial number.............45300
Cylinders 4
Bore and stroke (in.) ....3.5625 x 4.25
Rated rpm 1,750
Compression ratio.......................8.75:1
Displacement (c.i.) 169
Fuel ....LPG
Carburetor.................................IHC E-12, 1.25-in.
Air cleaner ....Donaldson
Ignition.....................................IHC H-4 magneto or
Delco-Remy with
12-v battery
Cooling capacity (gal.) 4.25
Maximum brake horsepower tests
PTO/belt horsepower...................38.42
Crankshaft rpm 1,750
Fuel use (gal./hr.).......................4.36
Maximum drawbar horsepower tests
Gear..3rd
Drawbar horsepower..................35.43
Pull weight (lb.)..........................2,586
Speed (mph) 5.14
Percent slippage........................4.81
SAE drawbar horsepower.............27.41
SAE belt/PTO horsepower.............33.71
Type ....tricycle
Front wheel (in.).........................5.50 x 16
Rear wheel (in.)..........................12.00 x 38
Length (in.) 136
Height (in.) 85
Rear width (in.) 100
Tread width (in.)..........................48–93
Weight (lb.) 4,840

Gear/speed (mph) ...... forward: 1/2.50, 1 Torque
Amplifier/1.68, 2/3.82, 2 Torque
Amplifier/2.58, 3/5.15, 3 Torque
Amplifier/3.48, 4/6.60, 4 Torque
Amplifier/4.46, 5/16.11, 5 Torque
Amplifier/10.87; reverse: 1/3.12, 1
Torque Amplifier/2.10

International 300 Utility LPG

Manufacturer...............................International Harvester
Co., Chicago, IL
Nebraska test number 574
Test date ....May 16 to June 1,
1956
Test tractor serial number.............16154S J
Years produced 1955–1956
Serial number range.....................501–33664 end
Serial number location ....plate on right side of
clutch housing
Number produced ....33,176 total, LPG
interspersed
Engine.....................................IHC C-169
vertical I-head
Test engine serial number.............36443
Cylinders 4
Bore and stroke (in.) ....3.5625 x 4.25
Rated rpm 2,000
Compression ratio.......................8.75:1
Displacement (c.i.) 169
Fuel ....LPG
Carburetor.................................IHC E-12, 1.25-in.
Air cleaner ....Donaldson
Ignition.....................................IHC H-4 magneto or
Delco-Remy with
12-v battery
Cooling capacity (gal.) 4.50
Maximum brake horsepower tests
PTO/belt horsepower...................42.68
Crankshaft rpm 2,000
Fuel use (gal./hr.).......................4.70
Maximum drawbar horsepower tests
Gear..3rd
Drawbar horsepower..................38.32
Pull weight (lb.)..........................2,803
Speed (mph) 5.13
Percent slippage........................6.52
SAE drawbar horsepower.............30.07
SAE belt/PTO horsepower.............37.74
Type ....standard
Front wheel (in.).........................5.50 x 16
Rear wheel (in.)..........................12.00 x 28
Length (in.) 123
Height (in.) 58
Tread width (in.)..........................48–76
Weight (lb.) 4,140
Gear/speed (mph) ...... forward: 1/2.60, 1 Torque
Amplifier/1.80, 2/4.00, 2 Torque
Amplifier/2.70, 3/5.40, 3 Torque
Amplifier/3.60, 4/6.90, 4 Torque
Amplifier/4.60, 5/16.70, 5 Torque
Amplifier/11.30; reverse: 1/3.20, 1
Torque Amplifier/2.20

Farmall CUB, McCormick

Manufacturer	International Harvester Co., Chicago, IL
Nebraska test number	575
Test date	May 18 to June 3, 1956
Test tractor serial number	192845
Years produced	1947–1964
Serial number range	501–224703 end
Serial number location	plate on right side of steering gear housing
Number produced	203,814 through 1958
Engine	IHC C-60 vertical L-head
Test engine serial number	192845
Cylinders	4
Bore and stroke (in.)	2.625 x 2.75
Rated rpm	1,800
Compression ratio	6.5:1
Displacement (c.i.)	59.5
Fuel	gasoline
Fuel tank capacity (gal.)	7.50
Carburetor	IHC, 0.75-in.
Air cleaner	Donaldson
Ignition	IHC J-4 magneto or Delco-Remy with 6-v battery
Cooling capacity (gal.)	2.50

Maximum brake horsepower tests

PTO/belt horsepower	10.39
Crankshaft rpm	1,800
Fuel use (gal./hr.)	1.11

Maximum drawbar horsepower tests

Gear	2nd
Drawbar horsepower	9.87
Pull weight (lb.)	1,211
Speed (mph)	3.06
Percent slippage	5.13
SAE drawbar horsepower	7.56
SAE belt/PTO horsepower	9.14
Type	standard
Front wheel (in.)	4.00 x 12
Rear wheel (in.)	8.00 x 24
Length (in.)	99.38
Height (in.)	76
Rear width (in.)	48–64.25
Tread width (in.)	40–56
Weight (lb.)	1,590
Gear/speed (mph)	forward: 1/2.44, 2/3.25, 3/7.30; reverse: 1/2.71

International TD-14 Diesel, 142 Series

Manufacturer	International Harvester Co., Melrose Park, IL
Nebraska test number	585
Test date	August 11–17, 1956
Test tractor serial number	TD-14242394
Years produced	1956–1958
Serial number range	41551–45558 end
Serial number location	metal plate on lower right side of dash
Number produced	4,008
Engine	IHC D461 vertical I-head
Test engine serial number	UDFM 39513
Cylinders	4
Bore and stroke (in.)	4.75 x 6.50
Rated rpm	1,650
Compression ratio	15.04:1
Displacement (c.i.)	460.7
Fuel	diesel/gasoline
Main tank capacity (gal.)	61
Auxiliary tank capacity (gal.)	1.33
Carburetor	start; IHC F-8, 0.75-in.
Air cleaner	Donaldson or United
Ignition	start; IHC H-4 magneto/ 12-v with 2, 6-v battery
Cooling capacity (gal.)	19

Maximum brake horsepower tests

PTO/belt horsepower	91.33
Crankshaft rpm	1,650
Fuel use (gal./hr.)	6.71

Maximum drawbar horsepower tests

Gear	2nd
Drawbar horsepower	76.92
Pull weight (lb.)	13,893
Speed (mph)	2.08
Percent slippage	2.16
SAE drawbar horsepower	60.78
SAE belt/PTO horsepower	82.32
Type	tracklayer
Length (in.)	134.13
Height (in.)	78.88
Rear width (in.)	74.13 or 92.13
Tread width (in.)	56 or (74)
Weight (lb.)	20,340
Track length (in.)	78.50 on ground, 273 total
Grouser shoe	39 links; 16, (20)-in.
Gear/speed (mph)	forward: 1/1.60, 2/2.10, 3/2.70, 4/3.50, 5/4.50, 6/5.80; reverse: 1/1.60, 2/3.50

International TD-9 Diesel, 91 Series

Manufacturer	International Harvester Co., Melrose Park, IL
Nebraska test number	586
Test date	August 16–21, 1956
Test tractor serial number	TD-91 61220
Years produced	1956–1959
Serial number range	60301–67290 no end
Serial number location	metal plate on lower left corner of dash
Number produced	approximately 7,000
Engine	IHC D350 vertical, I-head
Test engine serial number	TD91 M1705
Cylinders	4
Bore and stroke (in.)	4.50 x 5.50
Rated rpm	1,550
Compression ratio	15.64:1
Displacement (c.i.)	350
Fuel	diesel/gasoline
Main tank capacity (gal.)	31.50
Auxiliary tank capacity (gal.)	0.66
Carburetor	IHC F-8, 0.75-in.
Air cleaner	Donaldson
Ignition	IHC H-4 magneto/Delco-Remy, 12-v with 2-6-v battery

Cooling capacity (gal.) 9
Maximum brake horsepower tests
    PTO/belt horsepower............................62.69
    Crankshaft rpm 1,550
    Fuel use (gal./hr.)..................................4.31
Maximum drawbar horsepower tests
    Gear...2nd
    Drawbar horsepower...........................52.79
    Pull weight (lb.)...................................8,404
    Speed (mph)..2.36
    Percent slippage.................................4.76
SAE drawbar horsepower.........................41.83
SAE belt/PTO horsepower.........................54.79
Type ....tracklayer
Length (in.) 114
Height (in.)...66.33
Rear width (in.) ....59 or 75
Tread width (in.)..44 or (60)
Weight (lb.) 11,670
Track length (in.) ....63.44 on ground,
                                     214.50 total
Grouser shoe...33 links; 13, (18)-in.
Gear/speed (mph) ....forward: 1/1.70,
                                     2/2.50, 3/3.40, 4/4.30,
                                     5/5.90; reverse: 1/1.90

International TD-6 Diesel, 61 Series
Manufacturer...International Harvester
                                     Co., Melrose Park, IL
Nebraska test number 587
Test date ....August 17–22, 1956
Test tractor serial number.........................TD-61 39037
Years produced...1956–1959
Serial number range..................................38951–41448 no end,
                                     interspersed with T-6
Serial number location ....metal plate on center
                                     right dash
Number produced ....approximately 2,500
Engine ....IHC D248 vertical I-head
Test engine serial number.........................TD61 M631
Cylinders 4
Bore and stroke (in.) ....4.00 x 5.25
Rated rpm 1,550
Compression ratio.....................................16.76:1
Displacement (c.i.) 264
Fuel ....diesel/gasoline
Main tank capacity (gal.)............................20
Auxiliary tank capacity (gal.) 0.66
Carburetor ....IHC F-8, 0.75-in.
Air cleaner ....Donaldson
Ignition...IHC H-4
                                     magneto/Delco-Remy,
                                     12-v with 2, 6-v battery
Cooling capacity (gal.) 10.50
Maximum brake horsepower tests
    PTO/belt horsepower............................48.99
    Crankshaft rpm 1,550
    Fuel use (gal./hr.)..................................3.63
Maximum drawbar horsepower tests
    Gear...2nd
    Drawbar horsepower...........................39.63
    Pull weight (lb.)...................................6,635
    Speed (mph)..2.24
    Percent slippage.................................4.60
SAE drawbar horsepower.........................31.77

SAE belt/PTO horsepower.........................43.77
Type ....tracklayer
Length (in.) 104
Height (in.)...72.32
Rear width (in.) ....53 or (63)
Tread width (in.)..40 or (50)
Weight (lb.) 8,515
Track length (in.) ....58.63 on ground, 192
                                     total
Grouser shoe...32 links; 12, (15.75)-in.
Gear/speed (mph) ....forward: 1/1.60,
                                     2/2.30, 3/3.30, 4/4.10,
                                     5/5.70; reverse: 1/1.80

International TD-18 Diesel, 182 Series
Manufacturer...International Harvester
                                      Co., Melrose Park, IL
Nebraska test number 588
Test date ....August 10–15, 1956
Test tractor serial number.........................TD-182 36807
Years produced...1956–1958
Serial number range..................................36101–38861 end
Serial number location ....metal plate on lower
                                     right side of dash
Number produced 2,761
Engine ....IHC D691 vertical I-head
Test engine serial number.........................TD-182M 1367
Cylinders 6
Bore and stroke (in.) ....4.75 x 6.50
Rated rpm 1,450
Compression ratio.....................................15.04:1
Displacement (c.i.) 691
Fuel ....diesel/gasoline
Main tank capacity (gal.)............................75
Auxiliary tank capacity (gal.) 1.33
Carburetor ....IHC C-12, 0.75-in.
Air cleaner ....Donaldson or United
Ignition...IHC F-6
                                     magneto/Delco-Remy,
                                     12-v with 2, 6-v battery
Cooling capacity (gal.) 18
Maximum brake horsepower tests
    PTO/belt horsepower............................121.62
    Crankshaft rpm 1,450
    Fuel use (gal./hr.)..................................9.01
Maximum drawbar horsepower tests
    Gear...2nd
    Drawbar horsepower...........................100.14
    Pull weight (lb.)...................................18,318
    Speed (mph)..2.05
    Percent slippage.................................2.89
SAE drawbar horsepower.........................79.41
SAE belt/PTO horsepower.........................109.06
Type ....tracklayer
Length (in.) 166
Height (in.)...106
Rear width (in.) 94
Tread width (in.)..74
Weight (lb.) 28,050
Track length (in.)......................................96 on ground, 300 total
Grouser shoe...40 links; 20, (22)-in.
Gear/speed (mph) ....forward: 1/1.60,
                                     2/2.10, 3/2.60, 4/3.40,
                                     5/4.50, 6/5.50; reverse:
                                     1/1.60, 2/3.40

International

International T-6, 61 Series

Manufacturer .... International Harvester
Co., Melrose Park, IL
Nebraska test number 589
Test date .... August 21–23, 1956
Test tractor serial number T-61 39038
Years produced 1956–1959
Serial number range .... 38951–41448 no end,
interspersed with TD-6
Serial number location .... metal plate on lower
left dash
Number produced .... approximately 2,500
Engine .... IHC 264 vertical I-head
Test engine serial number C-264 168046
Cylinders 4
Bore and stroke (in.) .... 4.00 x 5.25
Rated rpm 1,550
Compression ratio 6.3:1
Displacement (c.i.) 264
Fuel .... gasoline
Fuel tank capacity (gal.) 32
Carburetor .... IHC E-12, 1.25-in.
Air cleaner .... Donaldson
Ignition .... IHC H-4 magneto
or Delco-Remy with
6-v battery
Cooling capacity (gal.) 10

Maximum brake horsepower tests
    PTO/belt horsepower 48.11
    Crankshaft rpm 1,550
    Fuel use (gal./hr.) 4.14

Maximum drawbar horsepower tests
    Gear 2nd
    Drawbar horsepower 39.91
    Pull weight (lb.) 6,618
    Speed (mph) 2.26
    Percent slippage 3.85
SAE drawbar horsepower 31.14
SAE belt/PTO horsepower 43.04
Type .... tracklayer
Length (in.) 104
Height (in.) 61
Rear width (in.) .... 53 or 63
Tread width (in.) .... 40 or 50
Weight (lb.) 8,515
Track length (in.) .... 58.63 on ground,
192 total
Grouser shoe .... 32 links; 12, (18)
Gear/speed (mph) .... forward: 1/1.60,
2/2.30, 3/3.30, 4/4.00,
5/5.70; reverse: 1/1.80

Farmall 450 Diesel, McCormick

Manufacturer .... International Harvester
Co., Chicago, IL
Nebraska test number 608
Test date .... March 18 to April 1,
1957
Test tractor serial number .... 655 S
Years produced 1956–1958
Serial number range .... 501–26067 end
Serial number location .... plate on left side of
clutch housing
Number produced .... 6,961 interspersed

Engine .... IHC D-281 vertical I-head
Test engine serial number D281 505
Cylinders 4
Bore and stroke (in.) .... 4.125 x 5.25
Rated rpm 1,450
Compression ratio 17.45:1
Displacement (c.i.) 281
Fuel .... diesel
Fuel tank capacity (gal.) 18
Carburetor .... IHC F-8, 0.75-in.
Air cleaner .... Donaldson
Ignition .... IHC H-4
magneto/Delco-Remy
with 12-v battery
Cooling capacity (gal.) 7

Maximum brake horsepower tests
    PTO/belt horsepower 48.78
    Crankshaft rpm 1,450
    Fuel use (gal./hr.) 3.59

Maximum drawbar horsepower tests
    Gear 3rd
    Drawbar horsepower 45.17
    Pull weight (lb.) 3,623
    Speed (mph) 4.68
    Percent slippage 5.76
SAE drawbar horsepower 34.64
SAE belt/PTO horsepower 43.15
Type .... tricycle
Front wheel (in.) .... 6.00 x 16
Rear wheel (in.) .... 15.50 x 38
Length (in.) 143
Height (in.) 92
Rear width (in.) 84
Tread width (in.) 50–94
Weight (lb.) 6,260
Gear/speed (mph) .... forward: 1/2.50, 1 Torque
Amplifier/1.70, 2/3.80, 2 Torque
Amplifier/2.60, 3/4.80, 3 Torque
Amplifier/3.20, 4/6.70, 4 Torque
Amplifier/4.50, 5/16.60, 5 Torque
Amplifier/11.20; reverse: 1/3.30, 1
Torque Amplifier/2.20

Farmall 350 Diesel, McCormick

Manufacturer .... International Harvester
Co., Chicago, IL
Nebraska test number 609
Test date .... March 18 to April 5,
1957
Test tractor serial number .... 1003 S
Years produced 1956–1958
Serial number range .... 501–17215 end
Serial number location .... plate on right side of
clutch housing
Number produced .... 4,191 interspersed
Engine .... Continental D193
vertical I-head
Test engine serial number D193 980
Cylinders 4
Bore and stroke (in.) .... 3.75 x 4.375
Rated rpm 1,750
Compression ratio 16.87:1
Displacement (c.i.) 193
Fuel .... diesel
Fuel tank capacity (gal.) 17

Air cleaner ....Donaldson
Ignition ....Delco-Remy with 12-v
battery
Cooling capacity (gal.) 4.50
Maximum brake horsepower tests
    PTO/belt horsepower...........................38.65
    Crankshaft rpm 1,750
    Fuel use (gal./hr.) 2.61
Maximum drawbar horsepower tests
    Gear..3rd
    Drawbar horsepower............................36.26
    Pull weight (lb.)...................................2,648
    Speed (mph) 5.14
    Percent slippage.................................4.80
SAE drawbar horsepower.............................27.57
SAE belt/PTO horsepower 34.20
Type ....tricycle
Front wheel (in.)...5.50 x 16
Rear wheel (in.)..13.60 x 38
Length (in.) 136
Height (in.) 85
Rear width (in.) 83
Tread width (in.)...48–93
Weight (lb.) 4,720
Gear/speed (mph)..............forward: 1/2.50, 1 Torque
Amplifier/1.70, 2/3.80, 2 Torque
Amplifier/2.60, 3/5.20, 3 Torque
Amplifier/3.50, 4/6.60, 4 Torque
Amplifier/4.50, 5/16.10, 5 Torque
Amplifier/10.90; reverse: 1/3.10, 1
Torque Amplifier/2.10

International 350 Utility Diesel
Manufacturer..International Harvester
Co., Chicago, IL
Nebraska test number 610
Test date ....March 26 to April 15,
1957
Test tractor serial number............................1983
Years produced 1956–1958
Serial number range.....................................501–18346 end, all
types interspersed
Serial number location ....plate on right side of
clutch housing
Number produced 3,033
Engine ....Continental D–193
vertical I-head
Test engine serial number............................D193 822
Cylinders 4
Bore and stroke (in.) ....3.75 x 4.375
Rated rpm 2,000
Compression ratio..16.87:1
Displacement (c.i.) 193
Fuel ....diesel
Fuel tank capacity (gal.) 18
Air cleaner ....Donaldson
Ignition ....Delco-Remy with
12-v battery
Cooling capacity (gal.) 7.50
Maximum brake horsepower tests
    PTO/belt horsepower...........................42.89
    Crankshaft rpm 2,000
    Fuel use (gal./hr.) 3.06

Maximum drawbar horsepower tests
    Gear..3rd
    Drawbar horsepower............................40.42
    Pull weight (lb.)...................................2,813
    Speed (mph) 5.39
    Percent slippage.................................4.34
SAE drawbar horsepower.............................30.74
SAE belt/PTO horsepower 37.49
Type ....standard
Front wheel (in.)...5.50 x 16
Rear wheel (in.)..13.00 x 28
Length (in.) 119
Height (in.) 59
Rear width (in.) 64–89
Tread width (in.)...48–76
Weight (lb.) 4,180
Gear/speed (mph)..............forward: 1/2.60, 1 Torque Amplifier/1.80,
2/4.00, 2 Torque Amplifier/2.70, 3/5.40, 3
Torque Amplifier/3.60, 4/6.90, 4 Torque
Amplifier/4.60, 5/16.70, 5 Torque
Amplifier/11.30; reverse: 1/3.20, 1
Torque Amplifier/2.20

Farmall 350, McCormick
Manufacturer..International Harvester
Co., Chicago, IL
Nebraska test number 611
Test date ....April 1–13, 1957
Test tractor serial number............................1006 S
Years produced 1956–1958
Serial number range.....................................501–17215 end
Serial number location ....plate on right side of
clutch housing
Number produced 12,291
Engine ....IHC C175 vertical I-head
Test engine serial number............................C-175 2362
Cylinders 4
Bore and stroke (in.) ....3.625 x 4.25
Rated rpm 1,750
Compression ratio..7.0:1
Displacement (c.i.) 175
Fuel ....gasoline
Fuel tank capacity (gal.) 17
Carburetor..IHC E-12, 1.25-in.
Air cleaner ....Donaldson
Ignition ....IHC H-4 magneto
or Delco-Remy with
6-v battery
Cooling capacity (gal.) 4.50
Maximum brake horsepower tests
    PTO/belt horsepower...........................40.71
    Crankshaft rpm 1,751
    Fuel use (gal./hr.) 3.49
Maximum drawbar horsepower tests
    Gear..3rd
    Drawbar horsepower............................37.54
    Pull weight (lb.)...................................2,745
    Speed (mph) 5.13
    Percent slippage.................................4.44
SAE drawbar horsepower.............................28.90
SAE belt/PTO horsepower 36.07
Type ....tricycle
Front wheel (in.)...5.50 x 16

Rear wheel (in.) ....13.60 x 38
Length (in.) 136
Height (in.) 85
Rear width (in.) 83
Tread width (in.) 48–93
Weight (lb.) 4,720
Gear/speed (mph)..............forward: 1/2.50, 1 Torque Amplifier/1.70, 2/3.80, 2 Torque Amplifier/2.60, 3/5.20, 3 Torque Amplifier/3.50, 4/6.60, 4 Torque Amplifier/4.50, 5/16.10, 5 Torque Amplifier/10.90; reverse: 1/3.10, 1 Torque Amplifier/2.10

Farmall 450, McCormick

Manufacturer ....International Harvester Co., Chicago, IL
Nebraska test number 612
Test date ....April 9–14, 1957
Test tractor serial number...........................1751 S
Years produced 1956–1958
Serial number range......................................501–26067 end
Serial number location ....plate on left side of clutch housing
Number produced 18,305
Engine ....IHC C-281 vertical I-head
Test engine serial number.............................1645
Cylinders 4
Bore and stroke (in.) ....4.125 x 5.25
Rated rpm 1,450
Compression ratio...6.6:1
Displacement (c.i.) 281
Fuel ....gasoline
Fuel tank capacity (gal.) 18
Carburetor...IHC E-12, 1.25-in.
Air cleaner ....Donaldson
Ignition..IHC H-4 magneto or Delco-Remy with 6-v battery
Cooling capacity (gal.) 7
Maximum brake horsepower tests
   PTO/belt horsepower...........................55.28
   Crankshaft rpm 1,450
   Fuel use (gal./hr.) 4.82
Maximum drawbar horsepower tests
   Gear..3rd
   Drawbar horsepower...........................51.25
   Pull weight (lb.) 4,142
   Speed (mph) 4.64
   Percent slippage.................................5.19
SAE drawbar horsepower...............................38.44
SAE belt/PTO horsepower 48.49
Type ....tricycle
Front wheel (in.)..6.00 x 16
Rear wheel (in.) ....15.50 x 38
Length (in.) 143
Height (in.) 95
Rear width (in.) 84
Tread width (in.)..50–94
Weight (lb.) 5,970
Gear/speed (mph)..............forward: 1/2.58, 1 Torque Amplifier/1.70, 2/3.80, 2 Torque Amplifier/2.60, 3/4.80, 3 Torque Amplifier/3.20, 4/6.70, 4 Torque Amplifier/4.50, 5/16.60, 5 Torque Amplifier/11.20; reverse: 1/3.30, 1 Torque Amplifier/2.20

International 350 Utility

Manufacturer...International Harvester Co., Chicago, IL
Nebraska test number 615
Test date ....April 24 to May 1, 1957
Test tractor serial number...........................1909 S
Years produced 1956–1958
Serial number range.....................................501–18346 end, all types interspersed
Serial number location ....plate on right side of clutch housing
Number produced 12,998
Engine ....IHC C-175 vertical I-head
Test engine serial number.............................C-175 513
Cylinders 4
Bore and stroke (in.) ....3.625 x 4.25
Rated rpm 2,000
Compression ratio...7.0:1
Displacement (c.i.) 175
Fuel ....gasoline
Fuel tank capacity (gal.) 11.25
Carburetor...IHC E-12, 1.25-in.
Air cleaner ....Donaldson
Ignition..IHC H-4 magneto or Delco-Remy with 6-v battery
Cooling capacity (gal.) 4.50
Maximum brake horsepower tests
   PTO/belt horsepower...........................43.32
   Crankshaft rpm 2,000
   Fuel use (gal./hr.) 3.88
Maximum drawbar horsepower tests
   Gear..3rd
   Drawbar horsepower...........................39.53
   Pull weight (lb.) 2,771
   Speed (mph) 5.35
   Percent slippage.................................4.50
SAE drawbar horsepower...............................30.43
SAE belt/PTO horsepower 38.20
Type ....standard
Front wheel (in.)..5.50 x 16
Rear wheel (in.) ....13.00 x 28
Length (in.) 119
Height (in.) 59
Rear width (in.) 64–90
Tread width (in.)..48–76
Weight (lb.) 4,180
Gear/speed (mph)..............forward: 1/2.60, 1 Torque Amplifier/1.80, 2/4.00, 2 Torque Amplifier/2.70, 3/5.40, 3 Torque Amplifier/3.60, 4/6.90, 4 Torque Amplifier/4.60, 5/16.70, 5 Torque Amplifier/11.30; reverse: 1/3.20, 1 Torque Amplifier/2.20

Farmall 230, McCormick

Manufacturer...International Harvester Co., Chicago, IL
Nebraska test number 616
Test date ....April 25 to May 7, 1957
Test tractor serial number...........................813 J
Years produced 1956–1958
Serial number range.....................................501–7671 end

Serial number location ....plate on left side of clutch housing
Number produced 7,462
Engine ....IHC C-123 vertical I-head
Test engine serial number......................C-123 36826
Cylinders 4
Bore and stroke (in.) ....3.125 x 4.00
Rated rpm 1,800
Compression ratio..........................6.8:1
Displacement (c.i.) 123
Fuel ....gasoline
Fuel tank capacity (gal.) 11
Carburetor..........................Zenith 11340, 0.875-in.
Air cleaner..........................Donaldson
Ignition..........................IHC H-4 magneto or Delco-Remy with 6-v battery
Cooling capacity (gal.) 3.75
Maximum brake horsepower tests
   PTO/belt horsepower..........................28.06
   Crankshaft rpm 1,800
   Fuel use (gal./hr.) 2.35
Maximum drawbar horsepower tests
   Gear..........................2nd
   Drawbar horsepower..........................25.00
   Pull weight (lb.) 2,319
   Speed (mph) 4.04
   Percent slippage..........................5.77
SAE drawbar horsepower..........................19.40
SAE belt/PTO horsepower 24.84
Type ....tricycle
Front wheel (in.)..........................5.00 x 15
Rear wheel (in.)..........................11.20 x 36
Length (in.) 123
Height (in.) 85
Rear width (in.) 90.75
Tread width (in.)..........................48–80
Weight (lb.) 3,100
Gear/speed (mph) ....forward: 1/2.70, 2/4.30, 3/5.60, 4/11.70; reverse: 1/3.40

Farmall 130, McCormick
Manufacturer..........................International Harvester Co., Chicago, IL
Nebraska test number 617
Test date ....April 25 to May 7, 1957
Test tractor serial number..........................1120J
Years produced..........................1956–1958
Serial number range..........................501–10209 end
Serial number location ....plate on left side of clutch housing
Number produced 9,197
Engine ....IHC C123 vertical I-head
Test engine serial number..........................C-123 76788
Cylinders 4
Bore and stroke (in.) ....3.125 x 4.00
Rated rpm 1,400
Compression ratio..........................6.8:1
Displacement (c.i.) 122.7
Fuel ....gasoline

Fuel tank capacity (gal.) 11
Carburetor..........................Zenith 11340, 0.875-in.
Air cleaner..........................Donaldson
Ignition..........................IHC H-4 magneto or Delco-Remy with 6-v battery
Cooling capacity (gal.) 3.75
Maximum brake horsepower tests
   PTO/belt horsepower..........................22.23
   Crankshaft rpm 1,400
   Fuel use (gal./hr.) 1.82
Maximum drawbar horsepower tests
   Gear..........................2nd
   Drawbar horsepower..........................19.91
   Pull weight (lb.) 1,925
   Speed (mph) 3.88
   Percent slippage..........................5.11
SAE drawbar horsepower..........................15.82
SAE belt/PTO horsepower 19.64
Type ....standard
Front wheel (in.)..........................5.00 x 15
Rear wheel (in.)..........................11.00 x 24
Length (in.) 107
Height (in.) 82
Rear width (in.) 56–78
Tread width (in.)..........................40–68
Weight (lb.) 2,710
Gear/speed (mph) ....forward: 1/2.30, 2/3.70, 3/4.80, 4/10.00; reverse: 1/2.90

International 650
Manufacturer..........................International Harvester Co., Chicago, IL
Nebraska test number 618
Test date ....May 3–21, 1957
Test tractor serial number..........................1062 J
Years produced..........................1956–1958
Serial number range..........................501–5433 end, all types interspersed
Serial number location ....plate on right side fuel tank support
Number produced 4,933
Engine ....IHC C-350 vertical I-head
Test engine serial number..........................C-350 540
Cylinders 4
Bore and stroke (in.) ....4.50 x 5.50
Rated rpm 1,500
Compression ratio..........................6.12:1
Displacement (c.i.) 350
Fuel ....gasoline
Fuel tank capacity (gal.) 35
Carburetor..........................IHC F-8, 1.375-in.
Air cleaner..........................Donaldson
Ignition..........................IHC H-4 magneto or Delco-Remy 12-v; with 2, 6-v battery
Cooling capacity (gal.) 8.50
Maximum brake horsepower tests
   PTO/belt horsepower..........................62.11
   Crankshaft rpm 1,500
   Fuel use (gal./hr.) 6.01

International

Maximum drawbar horsepower tests

Gear	3rd
Drawbar horsepower	56.17
Pull weight (lb.)	4,708
Speed (mph)	4.47
Percent slippage	4.65

SAE drawbar horsepower ... 43.40
SAE belt/PTO horsepower ... 55.39
Type ... standard
Front wheel (in.) ... 7.50 x 18
Rear wheel (in.) ... 18.00 x 26
Length (in.) ... 135
Height (in.) ... 88
Rear width (in.) ... 76
Tread width (in.) ... 60
Weight (lb.) ... 6,650
Gear/speed (mph) ... forward: 1/2.40, 2/3.20, 3/4.50, 4/5.50, 5/15.70; reverse: 1/2.90

International 350 Utility LPG

Manufacturer ... International Harvester Co., Chicago, IL
Nebraska test number ... 619
Test date ... May 7–28, 1957
Test tractor serial number ... 615 CS
Years produced ... 1956–1958
Serial number range ... 501–18346 end, all types interspersed
Serial number location ... plate on right side of clutch housing
Number produced ... 12,998 total, LPG interspersed
Engine ... IHC C–175 vertical I-head
Test engine serial number ... C 175 654C
Cylinders ... 4
Bore and stroke (in.) ... 3.625 x 4.25
Rated rpm ... 2,000
Compression ratio ... 9.0:1
Displacement (c.i.) ... 175
Fuel ... LPG
Fuel tank capacity (gal.) ... 18.40
Carburetor ... Ensign, 1.25-in.
Air cleaner ... Donaldson
Ignition ... IHC H-4 magneto or Delco-Remy with 12-v battery
Cooling capacity (gal.) ... 4.50

Maximum brake horsepower tests

PTO/belt horsepower	45.24
Crankshaft rpm	2,000
Fuel use (gal./hr.)	5.04

Maximum drawbar horsepower tests

Gear	3rd
Drawbar horsepower	41.55
Pull weight (lb.)	2,900
Speed (mph)	5.37
Percent slippage	4.37

SAE drawbar horsepower ... 32.15
SAE belt/PTO horsepower ... 39.68
Type ... standard
Front wheel (in.) ... 6.00 x 16
Rear wheel (in.) ... 13.00 x 28
Length (in.) ... 119
Height (in.) ... 59
Rear width (in.) ... 64–89
Tread width (in.) ... 48–76
Weight (lb.) ... 4,180
Gear/speed (mph) ... forward: 1/2.60, 1 Torque Amplifier/1.80, 2/4.00, 2 Torque Amplifier/2.70, 3/5.40, 3 Torque Amplifier/3.60, 4/6.90, 4 Torque Amplifier/4.60, 5/16.70, 5 Torque Amplifier/11.30; reverse: 1/3.20, 1 Torque Amplifier/2.20

Farmall 450 LPG, McCormick

Manufacturer ... International Harvester Co., Chicago, IL
Nebraska test number ... 620
Test date ... May 7–29, 1957
Test tractor serial number ... 942 CS
Years produced ... 1956–1958
Serial number range ... 501–26067 end
Serial number location ... plate on left side of clutch housing
Number produced ... 18,305 total, LPG interspersed
Engine ... IHC C281 vertical I-head
Test engine serial number ... C281 1646C
Cylinders ... 4
Bore and stroke (in.) ... 4.125 x 5.25
Rated rpm ... 1,450
Compression ratio ... 8.35:1
Displacement (c.i.) ... 281
Fuel ... LPG
Carburetor ... IHC E-12, 1.25-in.
Air cleaner ... Donaldson
Ignition ... IHC H-4 magneto or Delco-Remy with 12-v battery
Cooling capacity (gal.) ... 7

Maximum brake horsepower tests

PTO/belt horsepower	54.12
Crankshaft rpm	1,450
Fuel use (gal./hr.)	5.77

Maximum drawbar horsepower tests

Gear	3rd
Drawbar horsepower	49.94
Pull weight (lb.)	4,039
Speed (mph)	4.64
Percent slippage	5.17

SAE drawbar horsepower ... 38.86
SAE belt/PTO horsepower ... 48.20
Type ... tricycle
Front wheel (in.) ... 6.00 x 16
Rear wheel (in.) ... 15.50 x 38
Length (in.) ... 143
Height (in.) ... 96
Rear width (in.) ... 84
Tread width (in.) ... 50–94
Weight (lb.) ... 5,970
Gear/speed (mph) ... forward: 1/2.50, 1 Torque Amplifier/1.70, 2/3.80, 2 Torque Amplifier/2.60, 3/4.80, 3 Torque Amplifier/3.20, 4/6.70, 4 Torque Amplifier/4.50, 5/16.60, 5 Torque Amplifier/11.20; reverse: 1/3.30, 1 Torque Amplifier/2.20

International 650 LPG

Manufacturer	International Harvester Co., Chicago, IL
Nebraska test number	621
Test date	May 21–27, 1957
Test tractor serial number	1275 L
Years produced	1956–1958
Serial number range	501–5433 end, all types interspersed
Serial number location	plate on right side fuel tank support
Number produced	4,933 total, LPG interspersed
Engine	IHC C-350 vertical I-head
Test engine serial number	C 350 579
Cylinders	4
Bore and stroke (in.)	4.50 x 5.50
Rated rpm	1,500
Compression ratio	8.25:1
Displacement (c.i.)	350
Fuel	LPG
Fuel tank capacity (gal.)	42
Carburetor	Ensign, 1.375-in.
Air cleaner	Donaldson
Ignition	IHC H-4 magneto or Delco-Remy 12-v; with 2, 6-v battery
Cooling capacity (gal.)	4.90

Maximum brake horsepower tests

PTO/belt horsepower	63.91
Crankshaft rpm	1,500
Fuel use (gal./hr.)	7.28

Maximum drawbar horsepower tests

Gear	3rd
Drawbar horsepower	58.22
Pull weight (lb.)	4,880
Speed (mph)	4.47
Percent slippage	4.52
SAE drawbar horsepower	45.53
SAE belt/PTO horsepower	56.97
Type	standard
Front wheel (in.)	7.50 x 18
Rear wheel (in.)	18.00 x 26
Length (in.)	135
Height (in.)	88
Rear width (in.)	76
Tread width (in.)	60
Weight (lb.)	6,650
Gear/speed (mph)	forward: 1/2.40, 2/3.20, 3/4.50, 4/5.50, 5/15.70; reverse: 1/2.90

Farmall 350 LPG, McCormick

Manufacturer	International Harvester Co., Chicago, IL
Nebraska test number	622
Test date	May 22–29, 1957
Test tractor serial number	565 CS
Years produced	1956–1958
Serial number range	501–17215 end
Serial number location	plate on right side of clutch housing
Number produced	12,291 total, LPG interspersed

Engine	IHC C-175 vertical I-head
Test engine serial number	C-175 753C
Cylinders	4
Bore and stroke (in.)	3.625 x 4.25
Rated rpm	1,750
Compression ratio	9.0:1
Displacement (c.i.)	175
Fuel	LPG
Fuel tank capacity (gal.)	18.40
Carburetor	Ensign, 1.25-in.
Air cleaner	Donaldson
Ignition	IHC H-4 magneto or Delco-Remy with 12-v battery
Cooling capacity (gal.)	4.90

Maximum brake horsepower tests

PTO/belt horsepower	41.53
Crankshaft rpm	1,750
Fuel use (gal./hr.)	4.44

Maximum drawbar horsepower tests

Gear	3rd
Drawbar horsepower	38.30
Pull weight (lb.)	2,781
Speed (mph)	5.16
Percent slippage	4.12
SAE drawbar horsepower	30.02
SAE belt/PTO horsepower	36.32
Type	tricycle
Front wheel (in.)	6.00 x 16
Rear wheel (in.)	13.60 x 38
Length (in.)	136
Height (in.)	85
Rear width (in.)	83
Tread width (in.)	48–93
Weight (lb.)	4,720
Gear/speed (mph)	forward: 1/2.50, 1 Torque Amplifier/1.70, 2/3.80, 2 Torque Amplifier/2.60, 3/5.20, 3 Torque Amplifier/3.50, 4/6.60, 4 Torque Amplifier/4.50, 5/16.10, 5 Torque Amplifier/10.90; reverse: 1/3.10, 1 Torque Amplifier/2.10

International TD-18 Diesel, 182 Series

Manufacturer	International Harvester Co., Chicago, IL
Nebraska test number	629
Test date	September 3–14, 1957
Test tractor serial number	TD-182 38655
Years produced	1956–1958
Serial number range	36101–38861
Serial number location	metal plate on lower right side of dash
Number produced	2,761
Engine	IHC D691 vertical I-head
Test engine serial number	TD-182M 3063
Cylinders	6
Bore and stroke (in.)	4.75 x 6.50
Rated rpm	1,550
Compression ratio	15.04:1
Displacement (c.i.)	691
Fuel	diesel/gasoline
Main tank capacity (gal.)	75
Auxiliary tank capacity (gal.)	1.33
Carburetor	IHC C-12, 1.25-in.
Air cleaner	Donaldson or United

Ignition ....IHC F-6 magneto or
           Delco-Remy 12-v; with
           2, 6-v battery
Cooling capacity (gal.) 18

Maximum drawbar horsepower tests
    Gear...2nd
    Drawbar horsepower.........................106.66
    Pull weight (lb.)...............................19,490
    Speed (mph) 2.05
    Percent slippage............................2.34
SAE drawbar horsepower....................83.73
Type ....tracklayer
Length (in.) 166
Height (in.)....................................106
Rear width (in.)..............................94
Tread width (in.)............................74
Weight (lb.)...................................28,250
Track length (in.)...........................96 on ground, 300
           total
Grouser shoe.................................40 links; 20, (22)-in.
Gear/speed (mph) ....forward: 1/1.60,
           2/2.10, 3/2.60, 4/3.40,
           5/4.40, 6/5.50; reverse:
           1/1.60, 2/3.40

International TD-24 Diesel, 241 Series

Manufacturer.................................International Harvester
           Co., Chicago, IL
Nebraska test number 630
Test date ....September 3–14, 1957
Test tractor serial number..............TD-241 10125
Years produced.............................1955–1959
Serial number range.......................8001–10631 no end
Serial number location ....metal plate on upper
           left corner of dash
Number produced ....approximately 2,700
Engine ....IHC D1091
           vertical I-head
Test engine serial number...............TDEM 10164
Cylinders 6
Bore and stroke (in.) ....5.75 x 7.00
Rated rpm 1,500
Compression ratio.........................14.87:1
Displacement (c.i.) 1,091
Fuel ....diesel/gasoline
Main tank capacity (gal.)................85
Auxiliary tank capacity (gal.) 2.13
Carburetor.....................................IHC C-12, 1.25-in. and
           injector pump
Air cleaner.....................................Donaldson
Ignition...Delco-Remy, 24-v with
           4, 6-v battery
Cooling capacity (gal.) 37

Maximum drawbar horsepower tests
    Gear...3rd
    Drawbar horsepower.........................168.06
    Pull weight (lb.)...............................26,600
    Speed (mph) 2.37
    Percent slippage............................1.56
SAE drawbar horsepower....................131.30
Type ....tracklayer
Length (in.) 182.25
Height (in.)....................................95.25
Rear width (in.) 102

Tread width (in.)............................80
Weight (lb.) 41,920
Track length (in.)...........................104.50 on ground, 357
           total
Grouser shoe.................................42 links; 22, (24)-in.
Gear/speed (mph)...........forward: 1/1.50, 2/2.00, 3/2.40, 4/3.00,
           5/4.10, 6/5.20, 7/6.00, 8/7.70; reverse:
           1/1.50, 2/2.00, 3/2.40, 4/3.00, 5/4.10,
           6/5.20, 7/6.00, 8/7.70

International 330 Utility

Manufacturer......................................International Harvester
           Co., Chicago, IL
Nebraska test number 634
Test date ....November 5–14, 1957
Test tractor serial number................501
Years produced................................1957–1958
Serial number range.........................501–4763 end
Serial number location ....plate on right side
           clutch housing
Number produced 4,261
Engine ....IHC C-135
           vertical I-head
Test engine serial number................701
Cylinders 4
Bore and stroke (in.) ....3.25 x 4.0625
Rated rpm 2,000
Compression ratio...........................7.38:1
Displacement (c.i.) 134.8
Fuel ....gasoline
Fuel tank capacity (gal.) 11.25
Carburetor.......................................Zenith 67 x 7, 0.875-in.
Air cleaner ....Donaldson
Ignition...IHC H-4 magneto or
           Delco-Remy with 6-v
           battery
Cooling capacity (gal.) 3.50

Maximum brake horsepower tests
    PTO/belt horsepower..........................34.24
    Crankshaft rpm 2,000
    Fuel use (gal./hr.) 2.95
Maximum drawbar horsepower tests
    Gear...3rd
    Drawbar horsepower.........................31.77
    Pull weight (lb.)...............................2,301
    Speed (mph) 5.18
    Percent slippage............................4.64
SAE drawbar horsepower....................24.31
SAE belt/PTO horsepower 29.95
Type ....standard
Front wheel (in.).............................5.50 x 16
Rear wheel (in.)..............................12.00 x 28
Length (in.) 117
Height (in.) 60
Rear width (in.)...............................64–88
Tread width (in.).............................48–76 or 52–78
Weight (lb.) 4,250
Gear/speed (mph) . . . . . . forward: 1/2.50, 1 Torque
           Amplifier/1.70, 2/3.80, 2 Torque
           Amplifier/2.60, 3/5.20, 3 Torque
           Amplifier/3.50, 4/6.60, 4 Torque
           Amplifier/4.50, 5/16.10, 5 Torque
           Amplifier/10.90; reverse: 1/3.10, 1
           Torque Amplifier/2.10

Farmall 340, McCormick

Manufacturer	International Harvester Co., Chicago, IL
Nebraska test number	665
Test date	September 3–25, 1958
Test tractor serial number	850 S
Years produced	1958–1963
Serial number range	501–7711 end
Serial number location	plate on left side of clutch housing
Number produced	approximately 7,500
Engine	IHC C-135 vertical I-head
Test engine serial number	6356
Cylinders	4
Bore and stroke (in.)	3.25 x 4.0625
Rated rpm	2,000
Compression ratio	7.52:1
Displacement (c.i.)	135
Fuel	gasoline
Fuel tank capacity (gal.)	15.30
Carburetor	Marvel-Schebler TSX or Zenith 67 x 7, 0.875-in.
Air cleaner	Donaldson
Ignition	IHC H-4 magneto or Delco-Remy with 6-v battery
Cooling capacity (gal.)	3.80

Maximum brake horsepower tests

PTO/belt horsepower	34.74
Crankshaft rpm	2,000
Fuel use (gal./hr.)	2.89

Maximum drawbar horsepower tests

Gear	3rd
Drawbar horsepower	31.76
Pull weight (lb.)	2,320
Speed (mph)	5.13
Percent slippage	4.52
SAE drawbar horsepower	24.51
SAE belt/PTO horsepower	30.70
Type	tricycle
Front wheel (in.)	5.00 x 15
Rear wheel (in.)	13.90 x 36
Height (in.)	91
Tread width (in.)	48–92
Weight (lb.)	4,250
Gear/speed (mph)	forward: 1/1.80, 1 Torque Amplifier/1.20, 2/3.90, 2 Torque Amplifier/2.70, 3/5.30, 3 Torque Amplifier/3.60, 4/7.50, 4 Torque Amplifier/5.10, 5/16.60, 5 Torque Amplifier/11.20; reverse: 1/2.30, 1 Torque Amplifier/1.50

Farmall 140, McCormick

Manufacturer	International Harvester Co., Chicago, IL
Nebraska test number	666
Test date	September 3–18, 1958
Test tractor serial number	504 J
Years produced	1958–1979
Serial number range	501–66790 end
Serial number location	plate on left side transmission housing
Number produced	approximately 66,290
Engine	IHC C-123 vertical I-head
Test engine serial number	65044
Cylinders	4
Bore and stroke (in.)	3.125 x 4.00
Rated rpm	1,400
Compression ratio	6.94:1
Displacement (c.i.)	122.7
Fuel	gasoline
Fuel tank capacity (gal.)	11
Carburetor	Marvel-Schebler TSX or Zenith 67 x 7, 0.875-in.
Air cleaner	Donaldson or United
Ignition	IHC H-4 magneto or Delco-Remy with 6-v battery
Cooling capacity (gal.)	3.80

Maximum brake horsepower tests

PTO/belt horsepower	23.02
Crankshaft rpm	1,400
Fuel use (gal./hr.)	2.02

Maximum drawbar horsepower tests

Gear	2nd
Drawbar horsepower	21.25
Pull weight (lb.)	2,083
Speed (mph)	3.83
Percent slippage	5.39
SAE drawbar horsepower	16.64
SAE belt/PTO horsepower	20.63
Type	standard
Front wheel (in.)	5.00 x 15
Rear wheel (in.)	11.00 x 24
Height (in.)	83
Tread width (in.)	40–68
Weight (lb.)	2,870
Gear/speed (mph)	forward: 1/1.90, 2/3.70, 3/4.80, 4/12.80; reverse: 1/3.10

Farmall 240, McCormick

Manufacturer	International Harvester Co., Chicago, IL
Nebraska test number	667
Test date	September 5–20, 1958
Test tractor serial number	505 J
Years produced	1958–1961
Serial number range	501–4124 end
Serial number location	plate on left side of clutch housing
Number produced	approximately 3,624
Engine	IHC C-123 vertical I-head
Test engine serial number	C 123
Cylinders	4
Bore and stroke (in.)	3.125 x 4.00
Rated rpm	2,000
Compression ratio	6.94:1
Displacement (c.i.)	122.7
Fuel	gasoline
Fuel tank capacity (gal.)	16.2
Carburetor	Marvel-Schebler TSX or Zenith 67 x 7, 0.875-in.
Air cleaner	Donaldson or United

International

Ignition..................................IHC H-4 magneto or Delco-Remy with 6-v battery
Cooling capacity (gal.) 3.80
Maximum brake horsepower tests
    PTO/belt horsepower.........................30.99
    Crankshaft rpm 2,000
    Fuel use (gal./hr.) 2.69
Maximum drawbar horsepower tests
    Gear..2nd
    Drawbar horsepower........................27.62
    Pull weight (lb.)................................2,513
    Speed (mph) 4.12
    Percent slippage..............................6.17
SAE drawbar horsepower.....................21.65
SAE belt/PTO horsepower 27.39
Type ....tricycle
Front wheel (in.).........................5.00 x 15
Rear wheel (in.).........................12.40 x 36
Height (in.).........................88
Tread width (in.).........................48–80
Weight (lb.).........................3,340
Gear/speed (mph) ....forward: 1/2.20, 2/4.20, 3/5.60, 4/14.70; reverse: 1/3.50

International 240 Utility
Manufacturer.........................International Harvester Co., Chicago, IL
Nebraska test number......................668
Test date ....September 6–20, 1958
Test tractor serial number.................528 J
Years produced.........................1958–1962
Serial number range.........................501–10788 end
Serial number location ....plate on right side of clutch housing
Number produced ....approximately 10,288
Engine ....IHC C-123 vertical I-head
Test engine serial number..................65157
Cylinders 4
Bore and stroke (in.) ....3.125 x 4.00
Rated rpm 2,000
Compression ratio..........................6.94:1
Displacement (c.i.) 122.7
Fuel ....gasoline
Fuel tank capacity (gal.) 16.2
Carburetor..........................Marvel-Schebler TSX or Zenith 67 x 7, 0.875-in.
Air cleaner ....Donaldson or United
Ignition..........................IHC H-4 magneto or Delco-Remy with 6-v battery
Cooling capacity (gal.) 3.80
Maximum brake horsepower tests
    PTO/belt horsepower.........................30.82
    Crankshaft rpm 2,000
    Fuel use (gal./hr.) 2.65
Maximum drawbar horsepower tests
    Gear..3rd
    Drawbar horsepower........................28.07
    Pull weight (lb.)................................2,340
    Speed (mph) 4.50
    Percent slippage..............................5.71

SAE drawbar horsepower.....................21.68
SAE belt/PTO horsepower 27.40
Type ....standard
Front wheel (in.).........................5.50 x 16
Rear wheel (in.).........................12.00 x 24
Height (in.).........................58
Tread width (in.).........................48–76
Weight (lb.).........................3,340
Gear/speed (mph) ....forward: 1/1.80, 2/3.40, 3/4.50, 4/11.80; reverse: 1/2.80

Farmall 560 Diesel, McCormick
Manufacturer.........................International Harvester Co., Chicago, IL
Nebraska test number......................669
Test date ....September 18–25, 1958
Test tractor serial number.................734 S
Years produced.........................1958–1963
Serial number range.........................501–66032 end
Serial number location ....plate on left side of clutch housing
Number produced ....approximately 65,982 total, diesels interspersed
Engine ....IHC D-282 vertical I-head
Test engine serial number..................D 282678
Cylinders 6
Bore and stroke (in.) ....3.6875 x 4.3906
Rated rpm 1,800
Compression ratio..........................18.2:1
Displacement (c.i.) 281
Fuel ....diesel
Fuel tank capacity (gal.) 33
Carburetor..........................Roosa injector pump
Air cleaner ....Donaldson or United
Ignition..........................Delco-Remy, 12-v; with 2, 6-v battery
Cooling capacity (gal.) 5.10
Maximum brake horsepower tests
    PTO/belt horsepower.........................59.48
    Crankshaft rpm 1,800
    Fuel use (gal./hr.) 4.11
Maximum drawbar horsepower tests
    Gear..3rd
    Drawbar horsepower........................54.86
    Pull weight (lb.)................................3,967
    Speed (mph) 5.19
    Percent slippage..............................5.44
SAE drawbar horsepower.....................44.00
SAE belt/PTO horsepower 53.21
Type ....tricycle
Front wheel (in.).........................6.50 x 16
Rear wheel (in.).........................15.50 x 38
Height (in.).........................99.50
Tread width (in.).........................50–94
Weight (lb.).........................6,710
Gear/speed (mph)............forward: 1/2.20, 1 Torque Amplifier/1.50, 2/3.80, 2 Torque Amplifier/2.60, 3/5.40, 3 Torque Amplifier/3.60, 4/7.50, 4 Torque Amplifier/5.00, 5/16.60, 5 Torque Amplifier/11.20; reverse: 1/2.80, 1 Torque Amplifier/1.90

Farmall 460, McCormick

Manufacturer ....International Harvester Co., Chicago, IL
Nebraska test number 670
Test date ....September 22 to October 3, 1958
Test tractor serial number ....502 S
Years produced 1958–1963
Serial number range.....................................501–33028 end
Serial number location ....plate on left side of clutch housing
Number produced ....approximately 32,528
Engine ....IHC C-221 vertical I-head
Test engine serial number............................C221 1131
Cylinders 6
Bore and stroke (in.) ....3.5625 x 3.6875
Rated rpm 1,800
Compression ratio...7.2:1
Displacement (c.i.) 221
Fuel ....gasoline
Fuel tank capacity (gal.) 33
Carburetor..Marvel-Schebler TSX or Zenith 67 x 7, 1.25-in.
Air cleaner ....Donaldson
Ignition...Wico XVE-6 magneto or Delco-Remy with 12-v battery
Cooling capacity (gal.) 4.10
Maximum brake horsepower tests
    PTO/belt horsepower............................49.47
    Crankshaft rpm 1,800
    Fuel use (gal./hr.) 4.24
Maximum drawbar horsepower tests
    Gear..3rd
    Drawbar horsepower.............................45.38
    Pull weight (lb.) 3,253
    Speed (mph) 5.23
    Percent slippage...................................4.02
SAE drawbar horsepower..............................35.43
SAE belt/PTO horsepower.............................43.89
Type ....tricycle
Front wheel (in.)..6.00 x 16
Rear wheel (in.)...13.60 x 38
Height (in.) 95
Tread width (in.)..48–93
Weight (lb.) 5,820
Gear/speed (mph).............forward: 1/2.60, 1 Torque Amplifier/1.70, 2/3.90, 2 Torque Amplifier/2.70, 3/5.30, 3 Torque Amplifier/3.60, 4/7.50, 4 Torque Amplifier/5.10, 5/16.60, 5 Torque Amplifier/11.20; reverse: 1/3.20, 1 Torque Amplifier/2.20

Farmall 560, McCormick

Manufacturer ....International Harvester Co., Chicago, IL
Nebraska test number 671
Test date ....September 24 to October 6, 1958
Test tractor serial number ....502 S
Years produced 1958–1963
Serial number range.....................................501–66032 end
Serial number location ....plate on left side of clutch housing
Number produced ....approximately 65,982
Engine ....IHC C-263 vertical I-head
Test engine serial number............................C 263 1165
Cylinders 6
Bore and stroke (in.) ....3.5625 x 4.3906
Rated rpm 1,800
Compression ratio...7.2:1
Displacement (c.i.) 263
Fuel ....gasoline
Fuel tank capacity (gal.) 33
Carburetor..IHC, 1.25-in.
Air cleaner ....Donaldson
Ignition...Wico XVE-6 magneto or Delco-Remy with 12-v battery
Cooling capacity (gal.) 4
Maximum brake horsepower tests
    PTO/belt horsepower............................63.03
    Crankshaft rpm 1,800
    Fuel use (gal./hr.) 5.17
Maximum drawbar horsepower tests
    Gear..3rd
    Drawbar horsepower.............................58.36
    Pull weight (lb.) 4,204
    Speed (mph) 5.21
    Percent slippage...................................4.22
SAE drawbar horsepower..............................44.60
SAE belt/PTO horsepower.............................55.46
Type ....tricycle
Front wheel (in.)..6.50 x 16
Rear wheel (in.)...15.50 x 38
Height (in.) 99.50
Tread width (in.)..50–94
Weight (lb.) 6,020
Gear/speed (mph).............forward: 1/2.20, 1 Torque Amplifier/1.50, 2/3.80, 2 Torque Amplifier/2.60, 3/5.40, 3 Torque Amplifier/3.60, 4/7.50, 4 Torque Amplifier/5.00, 5/16.60, 5 Torque Amplifier/11.20; reverse: 1/2.80, 1 Torque Amplifier/1.90

Farmall 460 Diesel, McCormick

Manufacturer ....International Harvester Co., Chicago, IL
Nebraska test number 672
Test date ....September 30 to October 11, 1958
Test tractor serial number ....720 S
Years produced 1958–1963
Serial number range.....................................501–33028 end
Serial number location ....plate on left side of clutch housing
Number produced ....approximately 32,528 total, diesels interspersed
Engine ....IHC D-236 vertical I-head
Test engine serial number............................D236 779
Cylinders 6
Bore and stroke (in.) ....3.6875 x 3.6875
Rated rpm 1,800
Compression ratio...17.6:1
Displacement (c.i.) 236
Fuel ....diesel

Fuel tank capacity (gal.) 33
Carburetor ....Roosa injector pump
Air cleaner ....Donaldson or United
Ignition ....Delco-Remy, 12-v with 2, 6-v battery
Cooling capacity (gal.) 5.25

Maximum brake horsepower tests
    PTO/belt horsepower............................50.10
    Crankshaft rpm 1,800
    Fuel use (gal./hr.) 3.57

Maximum drawbar horsepower tests
    Gear..4th
    Drawbar horsepower.............................46.43
    Pull weight (lb.)...................................2,321
    Speed (mph)..7.50
    Percent slippage..................................4.17
SAE drawbar horsepower.............................35.99
SAE belt/PTO horsepower.............................44.36
Type ....tricycle
Front wheel (in.)...6.00 x 16
Rear wheel (in.)..13.60 x 38
Height (in.)..95
Tread width (in.)...48–93
Weight (lb.) 5,820
Gear/speed (mph)..............forward: 1/2.60, 1 Torque Amplifier/1.70, 2/3.90, 2 Torque Amplifier/2.70, 3/5.30, 3 Torque Amplifier/3.60, 4/7.50, 4 Torque Amplifier/5.10, 5/16.60, 5 Torque Amplifier/11.20; reverse: 1/3.20, 1 Torque Amplifier/2.20

International 460 Utility Diesel
Manufacturer...International Harvester Co., Chicago, IL
Nebraska test number 673
Test date ....October 2–9, 1958
Test tractor serial number...........................695 S
Years produced..1958–1963
Serial number range....................................501–11898 no end, all types interspersed
Serial number location ....plate on right side of clutch housing
Number produced ....approximately 11,411 total, diesels interspersed
Engine ....IHC D-236 vertical I-head
Test engine serial number.............................D236 941
Cylinders 6
Bore and stroke (in.) ....3.6875 x 3.6875
Rated rpm 1,800
Compression ratio.......................................17.6:1
Displacement (c.i.) 236
Fuel ....diesel
Fuel tank capacity (gal.) 33
Carburetor ....Roosa injector pump
Air cleaner ....Donaldson or United
Ignition ....Delco-Remy, 12-v with 2, 6-v battery
Cooling capacity (gal.) 5.25

Maximum brake horsepower tests
    PTO/belt horsepower............................50.01
    Crankshaft rpm 1,800
    Fuel use (gal./hr.) 3.64

Maximum drawbar horsepower tests
    Gear..3rd
    Drawbar horsepower.............................45.52
    Pull weight (lb.)...................................3,192
    Speed (mph)..5.35
    Percent slippage..................................4.86
SAE drawbar horsepower.............................36.12
SAE belt/PTO horsepower.............................44.57
Type ....standard
Front wheel (in.)...6.00 x 16
Rear wheel (in.)..14.70 x 28
Height (in.)..61
Tread width (in.)...48–76
Weight (lb.) 5,800
Gear/speed (mph)..............forward: 1/1.80, 1 Torque Amplifier/1.20, 2/3.90, 2 Torque Amplifier/2.60, 3/5.30, 3 Torque Amplifier/3.60, 4/7.50, 4 Torque Amplifier/5.00, 5/16.50, 5 Torque Amplifier/11.10; reverse: 1/2.30, 1 Torque Amplifier/1.50

International 460 Utility
Manufacturer...International Harvester Co., Chicago, IL
Nebraska test number 674
Test date ....October 6–18, 1958
Test tractor serial number...........................524 S
Years produced..1958–1963
Serial number range....................................501–11911 end, all types interspersed
Serial number location ....plate on right side of clutch housing
Number produced ....approximately 11,411
Engine ....IHC C-221 vertical I-head
Test engine serial number.............................C 221 875
Cylinders 6
Bore and stroke (in.) ....3.5625 x 3.6875
Rated rpm 1,800
Compression ratio.......................................7.2:1
Displacement (c.i.) 221
Fuel ....gasoline
Fuel tank capacity (gal.) 33
Carburetor ....IHC 1.25-in.
Air cleaner ....Donaldson or United
Ignition ....Wico XVE-6 magneto or Delco-Remy with 12-v battery
Cooling capacity (gal.) 4.10

Maximum brake horsepower tests
    PTO/belt horsepower............................49.79
    Crankshaft rpm 1,800
    Fuel use (gal./hr.) 4.26

Maximum drawbar horsepower tests
    Gear..3rd
    Drawbar horsepower.............................45.91
    Pull weight (lb.)...................................3,197
    Speed (mph)..5.39
    Percent slippage..................................3.33
SAE drawbar horsepower.............................36.11
SAE belt/PTO horsepower.............................43.89
Type ....standard
Front wheel (in.)...6.00 x 16
Rear wheel (in.)..14.90 x 28
Height (in.)..61

Tread width (in.)............................48–76
Weight (lb.) 5,820
Gear/speed (mph)............forward: 1/1.80, 1 Torque
 Amplifier/1.20, 2/3.90, 2 Torque
 Amplifier/2.60, 3/5.30, 3 Torque
 Amplifier/3.60, 4/7.50, 4 Torque
 Amplifier/5.00, 5/16.50, 5 Torque
 Amplifier/11.10; reverse: 1/2.30, 1
 Torque Amplifier/1.50

Farmall 560 LPG, McCormick

Manufacturer...................................International Harvester
 Co., Chicago, IL
Nebraska test number 675
Test date ....October 8–20, 1958
Test tractor serial number ....1065 S
Years produced 1958–1963
Serial number range......................501–66032 end
Serial number location ....plate on left side of
 clutch housing
Number produced ....approximately 65,982
 total, LPG interspersed
Engine ....IHC C-263
 vertical I-head
Test engine serial number ....C 263 1144
Cylinders 6
Bore and stroke (in.) ....3.5625 x 4.3906
Rated rpm 1,800
Compression ratio..........................8.75:1
Displacement (c.i.) 263
Fuel ....LPG
Fuel tank capacity (gal.) 37
Carburetor......................................Ensign Xg, 1.25-in.
Air cleaner......................................Donaldson
Ignition...Wico XVE-6 magneto
 or Delco-Remy 12-v;
 with 2, 6-v battery
Cooling capacity (gal.) 4.25
Maximum brake horsepower tests
 PTO/belt horsepower.....................60.11
 Crankshaft rpm 1,800
 Fuel use (gal./hr.)...........................6.48
Maximum drawbar horsepower tests
 Gear..3rd
 Drawbar horsepower........................55.02
 Pull weight (lb.)...............................3,958
 Speed (mph).....................................5.21
 Percent slippage................................4.92
SAE drawbar horsepower.................43.53
SAE belt/PTO horsepower 53.17
Type ....tricycle
Front wheel (in.)..............................6.50 x 16
Rear wheel (in.)...............................15.50 x 38
Height (in.) 99.50
Tread width (in.)..............................50–94
Weight (lb.) 6,020
Gear/speed (mph)............forward: 1/2.20, 1 Torque
 Amplifier/1.50, 2/3.80, 2 Torque
 Amplifier/2.60, 3/5.40, 3 Torque
 Amplifier/3.60, 4/7.50, 4 Torque
 Amplifier/5.00, 5/16.60, 5 Torque
 Amplifier/11.20; reverse: 1/2.80, 1
 Torque Amplifier/1.90

International Farmall 460 LPG, McCormick

Manufacturer...................................International Harvester
 Co., Chicago, IL
Nebraska test number 676
Test date ....October 20–25, 1958
Test tractor serial number ....1075 S
Years produced 1958–1963
Serial number range......................501–33028 end
Serial number location ....plate on left side of
 clutch housing
Number produced ....approximately 32,528
 total, LPG interspersed
Engine ....IHC C-221
 vertical I-head
Test engine serial number C221 1613
Cylinders 6
Bore and stroke (in.) ....3.5625 x 3.6875
Rated rpm 1,800
Compression ratio..........................8.75:1
Displacement (c.i.) 221
Fuel ....LPG
Fuel tank capacity (gal.) 29
Carburetor......................................Ensign Xg, 1.25-in.
Air cleaner......................................Donaldson
Ignition...Wico XVE-6 magneto
 or Delco-Remy with
 12-v battery
Cooling capacity (gal.) 4.40
Maximum brake horsepower tests
 PTO/belt horsepower.....................49.85
 Crankshaft rpm 1,800
 Fuel use (gal./hr.)...........................5.61
Maximum drawbar horsepower tests
 Gear..3rd
 Drawbar horsepower........................46.11
 Pull weight (lb.)...............................3,290
 Speed (mph).....................................5.26
 Percent slippage................................3.84
SAE drawbar horsepower.................36.12
SAE belt/PTO horsepower 44.17
Type ....tricycle
Front wheel (in.)..............................6.00 x 16
Rear wheel (in.)...............................13.60 x 38
Height (in.) 95
Tread width (in.)..............................48–93
Weight (lb.) 5,820
Gear/speed (mph)............forward: 1/2.60, 1 Torque Amplifier/1.70,
 2/3.90, 2 Torque Amplifier/2.70, 3/5.30, 3
 Torque Amplifier/3.60, 4/7.50, 4 Torque
 Amplifier/5.10, 5/16.60, 5 Torque
 Amplifier/11.20; reverse: 1/3.20, 1
 Torque Amplifier/2.20

International 460 Utility LPG

Manufacturer...................................International Harvester
 Co., Chicago, IL
Nebraska test number 677
Test date ....October 17–25, 1958
Test tractor serial number ....715 S
Years produced 1958–1963
Serial number range......................501–11911 end, all
 types interspersed
Serial number location ....plate on right side of
 clutch housing

International

Number produced ....approximately 11,411
total, LPG interspersed
Engine ....IHC C-221
vertical I-head
Test engine serial number...................C221 959
Cylinders 6
Bore and stroke (in.)............................3.5625 x 3.6875
Rated rpm 1,800
Compression ratio.................................8.75:1
Displacement (c.i.) 221
Fuel ....LPG
Fuel tank capacity (gal.) 29
Carburetor ....Ensign Xg, 1.25-in.
Air cleaner ....Donaldson or United
Ignition..Wico XVE-6 magneto
or Delco-Remy with
12-v battery
Cooling capacity (gal.) 4.40
Maximum brake horsepower tests
PTO/belt horsepower...........................48.15
Crankshaft rpm 1,800
Fuel use (gal./hr.)..................................5.52
Maximum drawbar horsepower tests
Gear..3rd
Drawbar horsepower.............................45.35
Pull weight (lb.)....................................3,180
Speed (mph) 5.35
Percent slippage..................................4.21
SAE drawbar horsepower.....................35.18
SAE belt/PTO horsepower....................43.10
Type ....standard
Front wheel (in.)....................................6.00 x 16
Rear wheel (in.).....................................14.90 x 28
Height (in.) 95.50
Tread width (in.).....................................48–76
Weight (lb.) 5,820
Gear/speed (mph).............forward: 1/1.80, 1 Torque
Amplifier/1.20, 2/3.90, 2 Torque
Amplifier/2.60, 3/5.30, 3 Torque
Amplifier/3.60, 4/7.50, 4 Torque
Amplifier/5.00, 5/16.50, 5 Torque
Amplifier/11.10; reverse: 1/2.30, 1
Torque Amplifier/1.50

International 660 Diesel
Manufacturer..International Harvester
Co., Chicago, IL
Nebraska test number 715
Test date ....August 31 to
September 5, 1959
Test tractor serial number.......................1042
Years produced 1959–1963
Serial number range.................................501–7445 end, all
types interspersed
Serial number location ....plate on right side of
clutch housing
Number produced ....approximately 6,945
total, diesel
interspersed
Engine ....IHC D282
vertical L-head
Test engine serial number.........................13577
Cylinders 6
Bore and stroke (in.) ....3.6875 x 4.3906
Rated rpm 2,400

Compression ratio...................................18.2:1
Displacement (c.i.) 281
Fuel ....diesel
Fuel tank capacity (gal.) 33
Carburetor ....Roosa injector pump
Air cleaner ....Donaldson
Ignition..Delco-Remy 12-v; with
2, 6-v battery
Cooling capacity (gal.) 5
Maximum brake horsepower tests
PTO/belt horsepower.............................78.78
Crankshaft rpm 2,400
Fuel use (gal./hr.)...................................5.53
Maximum drawbar horsepower tests
Gear..3rd
Drawbar horsepower..............................69.43
Pull weight (lb.).....................................5,254
Speed (mph) 4.96
Percent slippage....................................4.52
SAE drawbar horsepower.........................71.38
SAE belt/PTO horsepower.......................78.78
Type ....standard
Front wheel (in.)......................................7.50 x 18
Rear wheel (in.).......................................18.00 x 26
Height (in.) 100.50
Tread width (in.).......................................60–80
Weight (lb.) 7,980
Gear/speed (mph)............forward: 1/2.01, 1 Torque Amplifier/1.35,
2/3.55, 2 Torque Amplifier/2.39, 3/4.97, 3
Torque Amplifier/3.35, 4/6.91, 4 Torque
Amplifier/4.66, 5/15.39, 5 Torque
Amplifier/10.39; reverse: 1/2.61, 1
Torque Amplifier/1.76

International 660
Manufacturer..International Harvester
Co., Chicago, IL
Nebraska test number 721
Test date ....October 1–12, 1959
Test tractor serial number.......................1060
Years produced 1959–1963
Serial number range.................................501–7445 end, all
types interspersed
Serial number location ....plate on right side of
clutch housing
Number produced ....approximately 6,945
Engine ....IHC C-263
vertical L-head
Test engine serial number.........................9686
Cylinders 6
Bore and stroke (in.) ....3.5625 x 4.3906
Rated rpm 2,400
Compression ratio.....................................7.2:1
Displacement (c.i.) 263
Fuel ....gasoline
Fuel tank capacity (gal.) 33
Carburetor ....IHC 1.375-in.
Air cleaner ....Donaldson
Ignition..Delco-Remy with
12-v battery
Cooling capacity (gal.) 4
Maximum brake horsepower tests
PTO/belt horsepower.............................81.39
Crankshaft rpm 2,400
Fuel use (gal./hr.)...................................6.38

Maximum drawbar horsepower tests

Gear	3rd
Drawbar horsepower	70.21
Pull weight (lb.)	5,262
Speed (mph)	5.00
Percent slippage	3.88
SAE drawbar horsepower	71.60
SAE belt/PTO horsepower	81.39
Type	standard
Front wheel (in.)	7.50 x 18
Rear wheel (in.)	18.00 x 26
Height (in.)	100.75
Tread width (in.)	60–80
Weight (lb.)	7,800
Gear/speed (mph)	forward: 1/2.01, 1 Torque Amplifier/1.35, 2/3.55, 2 Torque Amplifier/2.39, 3/4.97, 3 Torque Amplifier/3.35, 4/6.91, 4 Torque Amplifier/4.66, 5/15.39, 5 Torque Amplifier/10.39; reverse: 1/2.61, 1 Torque Amplifier/1.76

International 660 LPG

Manufacturer	International Harvester Co., Chicago, IL
Nebraska test number	722
Test date	October 3–12, 1959
Test tractor serial number	1045
Years produced	1959–1963
Serial number range	501–7445 end, all types interspersed
Serial number location	plate on right side of clutch housing
Number produced	approximately 6,945 total, LPG interspersed
Engine	IHC C-263 vertical L-head
Test engine serial number	9687 C
Cylinders	6
Bore and stroke (in.)	3.5625 x 4.3906
Rated rpm	2,400
Compression ratio	8.75:1
Displacement (c.i.)	263
Fuel	LPG
Fuel tank capacity (gal.)	37
Carburetor	Ensign Xg, 1.50-in.
Air cleaner	Donaldson
Ignition	Delco-Remy with 12-v battery
Cooling capacity (gal.)	4.25

Maximum brake horsepower tests

PTO/belt horsepower	80.63
Crankshaft rpm	2,400
Fuel use (gal./hr.)	8.95

Maximum drawbar horsepower tests

Gear	3rd
Drawbar horsepower	69.66
Pull weight (lb.)	4,933
Speed (mph)	5.30
Percent slippage	5.20
SAE drawbar horsepower	70.76
SAE belt/PTO horsepower	80.63
Type	standard
Front wheel (in.)	7.50 x 18
Rear wheel (in.)	15.00 x 34

Height (in.)	100.75
Tread width (in.)	60–80
Weight (lb.)	7,800
Gear/speed (mph)	forward: 1/2.15, 1 Torque Amplifier/1.45, 2/3.81, 2 Torque Amplifier/2.57, 3/5.33, 3 Torque Amplifier/3.60, 4/7.41, 4 Torque Amplifier/5.00, 5/16.52, 5 Torque Amplifier/11.14; reverse: 1/2.80, 1 Torque Amplifier/1.89

International T-340

Manufacturer	International Harvester Co., Chicago, IL
Nebraska test number	725
Test date	October 21–29, 1959
Test tractor serial number	T-340 946
Years produced	1959–1965
Serial number range	501–8525 no end, interspersed with TD-340
Serial number location	metal plate on dash
Number produced	approximately 8,025
Engine	IHC C-135 vertical L-head
Test engine serial number	16459 V
Cylinders	4
Bore and stroke (in.)	3.25 x 4.0625
Rated rpm	2,000
Compression ratio	7.38:1
Displacement (c.i.)	135
Fuel	gasoline
Fuel tank capacity (gal.)	15
Carburetor	IHC, 0.875-in.
Air cleaner	United
Ignition	IHC H-4 magneto or Delco-Remy with 6-v battery
Cooling capacity (gal.)	17

Maximum brake horsepower tests

PTO/belt horsepower	36.49
Crankshaft rpm	2,000
Fuel use (gal./hr.)	3.13

Maximum drawbar horsepower tests

Gear	2nd
Drawbar horsepower	28.33
Pull weight (lb.)	4,913
Speed (mph)	2.16
Percent slippage	3.07
SAE drawbar horsepower	31.04
SAE belt/PTO horsepower	36.49
Type	tracklayer
Length (in.)	124.75
Height (in.)	57.75
Rear width (in.)	58
Tread width (in.)	48
Weight (lb.)	5,750
Track length (in.)	67.2 on ground, 209 total
Grouser shoe	35 links; 10, 12, (14)
Gear/speed (mph)	forward: 1/1.5, 2/2.2, 3/3.0, 4/4.3, 5/5.8; reverse: 1/1.80

International

International B-275 Diesel, McCormick

Manufacturer...International Harvester Co., London, England
Nebraska test number...............................733
Test date..March 3–23, 1960
Test tractor serial number.........................15219
Years produced...1958–1968
Serial number range..................................501–55546 end
Number produced......................................approximately 52,432
Engine...IHC BD-144-A vertical L-head
Test engine serial number.........................15217 A
Cylinders...4
Bore and stroke (in.).................................3.375 x 4.00
Rated rpm...1,875
Compression ratio.....................................19.3:1
Displacement (c.i.)....................................143
Fuel...diesel
Carburetor...C.A.V. injector pump
Air cleaner...AC/Delco or Burgess
Ignition..Lucas 12-v; with 2, 6-v battery

Maximum brake horsepower tests
PTO/belt horsepower...........................32.88
Crankshaft rpm....................................1,875
Fuel use (gal./hr.)................................2.29
Maximum drawbar horsepower tests
Gear..4th, low range
Drawbar horsepower............................30.23
Pull weight (lb.)...................................2,293
Speed (mph)..4.94
Percent slippage.................................5.14
SAE drawbar horsepower...........................30.76
SAE belt/PTO horsepower.........................32.88
Type..standard
Front wheel (in.)..5.50 x 16
Rear wheel (in.)...11.00 x 28
Height (in.)..59.25
Tread width (in.)..48–76
Weight (lb.)..3,600
Gear/speed (mph)..............forward: 1 high range/4.20, 1 low range/1.60, 2 high range/6.60, 2 low range/2.50, 3 high range/9.40, 3 low range/3.50, 4 high range/14.00, 4 low range/5.30; reverse: 1 high range/6.30, 1 low range/2.30

International TD-15 Diesel, 150 Series

Manufacturer...International Harvester Co., Chicago, IL
Nebraska test number...............................750
Test date..July 30 to August 17, 1960
Test tractor serial number.........................TD-150 2989
Years produced...1958–1961
Serial number range..................................501–4000 end
Serial number location..............................metal plate on lower right side of dash
Number produced......................................3,500
Engine...IHC D-554 vertical L-head
Test engine serial number.........................TD150 M3132
Cylinders...6
Bore and stroke (in.).................................4.625 x 5.50
Rated rpm...1,650

Compression ratio.....................................15.95:1
Displacement (c.i.)....................................554
Fuel...diesel/gasoline
Main tank capacity (gal.)...........................61
Auxiliary tank capacity (gal.).....................1.33
Air cleaner...United
Ignition..Delco-Remy 12-v; with 2, 6-v battery
Cooling capacity (gal.)..............................19
Maximum drawbar horsepower tests
Gear..2nd
Drawbar horsepower............................76.97
Pull weight (lb.)...................................15,431
Speed (mph)..1.87
Percent slippage.................................2.18
SAE drawbar horsepower...........................84.22
SAE belt/PTO horsepower.........................76.97
Type..tracklayer
Height (in.)..93.50
Tread width (in.).......................................56 or (74)
Weight (lb.)..21,950
Track length (in.)......................................271.50
Grouser shoe..39 links; 16, (20), 22-in.
Gear/speed (mph)..............forward: 1/1.50, 2/1.90, 3/2.60, 4/3.30, 5/4.30, 6/5.80; reverse: 1/1.80, 2/2.30, 3/3.20, 4/4.10, 5/5.30, 6/7.10

International TD-9 Diesel, 92 Series

Manufacturer...International Harvester Co., Chicago, IL
Nebraska test number...............................751
Test date..August 2–17, 1960
Test tractor serial number.........................TD-92 3033
Years produced...1956–1959
Serial number range..................................501–6501 end
Serial number location..............................metal plate on lower left dash
Number produced......................................approximately 6,000
Engine...IHC DT-282 vertical L-head
Test engine serial number.........................TD92M 3241
Cylinders...6
Bore and stroke (in.).................................3.6875 x 4.39
Rated rpm...1,700
Compression ratio.....................................18.05:1
Displacement (c.i.)....................................282
Fuel...diesel
Main tank capacity (gal.)...........................31.50
Auxiliary tank capacity (gal.).....................0.66
Carburetor...Roosa injector pump
Air cleaner...Donaldson
Ignition..Delco-Remy 12-v; with 2, 6-v battery
Cooling capacity (gal.)..............................9
Maximum brake horsepower tests
PTO/belt horsepower...........................69.11
Crankshaft rpm....................................1,699
Fuel use (gal./hr.)................................4.66
Maximum drawbar horsepower tests
Gear..2nd
Drawbar horsepower............................56.26
Pull weight (lb.)...................................8,647
Speed (mph)..2.44
Percent slippage.................................1.78
SAE drawbar horsepower...........................57.63

SAE belt/PTO horsepower 69.11
Type ....tracklayer
Length (in.) 114
Height (in.) 66.32
Rear width (in.) ....59 or 75
Tread width (in.) ....44 or (60)
Weight (lb.) 11,589
Track length (in.)......................................63.44 on ground,
233 total
Grouser shoe..36 links; 13, (18), 22
Gear/speed (mph) ....forward: 1/1.70,
2/2.50, 3/3.40, 4/4.40,
5/6.00; reverse: 1/2.00

International TD-25 Diesel
Manufacturer..International Harvester
Co., Chicago, IL
Nebraska test number 752
Test date ....August 6–17, 1960
Test tractor serial number..........................TD-250 956
Years produced 1959–1960
Serial number range...................................501–1029 end
Serial number location ....metal plate on upper
left corner of dash
Number produced 529
Engine ....IHC DT-187
vertical L-head
Test engine serial number..........................TD250 M977
Cylinders 6
Bore and stroke (in.) ....5.375 x 6.00
Rated rpm 1,500
Compression ratio......................................15.35:1
Displacement (c.i.) 817
Fuel ....diesel
Fuel tank capacity (gal.) 85
Carburetor...IHC injector pump
Air cleaner ....Donaldson
Ignition ....Delco-Remy 24-v; with
4, 6-v battery

Maximum drawbar horsepower tests
Gear..3rd
Drawbar horsepower............................186.85
Pull weight (lb.)...................................30,049
Speed (mph)......................................2.33
Percent slippage................................2.52
SAE drawbar horsepower 188.58
Type ....tracklayer
Length (in.) 182.25
Height (in.) 96.75
Rear width (in.) 102
Tread width (in.) 80
Weight (lb.) 44,850
Track length (in.)......................................102.50 on ground,
355.50 total
Grouser shoe...42 links; (24), 26-in.
Gear/speed (mph)..............forward: 1/1.50, 2/2.00, 3/2.40, 4/3.00,
5/4.10, 6/5.20, 7/6.00, 8/7.70; reverse:
1/1.50, 2/2.00, 3/2.40, 4/3.00, 5/4.00,
6/5.10, 7/5.90, 8/7.50

International T-5
Manufacturer..International Harvester
Co., Ontario, Canada
Nebraska test number 753

Test date ....August 18 to
September 3, 1960
Test tractor serial number..........................2328 ADT
Years produced 1959–1960
Engine ....IHC C-135
vertical L-head
Test engine serial number..........................21288
Cylinders 4
Bore and stroke (in.) ....3.25 x 4.0625
Rated rpm 2,000
Compression ratio......................................7.5:1
Displacement (c.i.) 134.8
Fuel ....gasoline
Carburetor...0.875-in.
Ignition ....6-v battery
Maximum brake horsepower tests
PTO/belt horsepower...........................36.01
Crankshaft rpm 2,000
Fuel use (gal./hr.) 2.93
Maximum drawbar horsepower tests
Gear..2nd
Drawbar horsepower............................28.59
Pull weight (lb.)...................................4,858
Speed (mph)......................................2.21
Percent slippage................................2.80
SAE drawbar horsepower 29.80
SAE belt/PTO horsepower 36.01
Type ....tracklayer
Tread width (in.) 48
Weight (lb.) 6,355
Track length (in.)......................................210
Grouser shoe..35 links; 12-in.
Gear/speed (mph) ....forward: 1/1.48,
2/2.26, 3/3.58, 4/4.79,
5/6.54; reverse: 1/2.12

International T-4
Manufacturer..International Harvester
Co., Ontario, Canada
Nebraska test number 754
Test date ....August 18 to
September 3, 1960
Test tractor serial number..........................2329 ADT
Years produced 1959–1960
Engine ....IHC C-123
vertical L-head
Test engine serial number..........................84722
Cylinders 4
Bore and stroke (in.) ....3.125 x 4.00
Rated rpm 2,000
Compression ratio......................................7.3:1
Displacement (c.i.) 122.7
Fuel ....gasoline
Carburetor...0.875-in.
Ignition ....6-v battery
Maximum brake horsepower tests
PTO/belt horsepower...........................32.54
Crankshaft rpm 2,000
Fuel use (gal./hr.) 2.65
Maximum drawbar horsepower tests
Gear..2nd
Drawbar horsepower............................26.99
Pull weight (lb.)...................................4,559
Speed (mph)......................................2.22
Percent slippage................................2.20

SAE drawbar horsepower.............................27.10
SAE belt/PTO horsepower.............................32.54
Type ....tracklayer
Tread width (in.) 48
Weight (lb.) 6,345
Track length (in.) 210
Grouser shoe.......................................35 links; 12-in.
Gear/speed (mph) ....forward: 1/1.48,
2/2.26, 3/3.58, 4/4.79,
5/6.54; reverse: 1/2.12

International TD-5 Diesel
Manufacturer.......................................International Harvester
Co., Ontario, Canada
Nebraska test number 755
Test date ....August 24 to
September 3, 1960
Test tractor serial number.........................2344 ADT
Years produced 1959–1960
Engine ....IHC BD-144
vertical L-head
Test engine serial number..........................1988 C
Cylinders 4
Bore and stroke (in.) ....3.375 x 4.00
Rated rpm 2,000
Compression ratio..................................21.1:1
Displacement (c.i.) 144
Fuel ....diesel
Ignition...12-v battery
Maximum brake horsepower tests
    PTO/belt horsepower...........................35.25
    Crankshaft rpm 2,000
    Fuel use (gal./hr.)...........................2.51
Maximum drawbar horsepower tests
    Gear..2nd
    Drawbar horsepower............................29.61
    Pull weight (lb.).............................5,006
    Speed (mph)...................................2.22
    Percent slippage..............................1.45
SAE drawbar horsepower.............................30.21
SAE belt/PTO horsepower.............................35.25
Type ....tracklayer
Tread width (in.)..................................48
Weight (lb.) 6,505
Track length (in.).................................210
Grouser shoe.......................................35 links; 12-in.
Gear/speed (mph) ....forward: 1/1.48,
2/2.26, 3/3.58, 4/4.79,
5/6.54; reverse: 1/2.12

International Farmall 340 Diesel, McCormick
Manufacturer.......................................International Harvester
Co., Chicago, IL
Nebraska test number 775
Test date ....October 26 to
November 3, 1960
Test tractor serial number.........................5957 S Y
Years produced 1958–1963
Serial number range................................501–7711 end
Serial number location ....plate on left side of
clutch housing
Number produced ....na, interspersed
Engine ....IHC D166
vertical L-head
Test engine serial number..........................D166 516

Cylinders 4
Bore and stroke (in.) ....3.6875 x 3.875
Rated rpm 2,000
Compression ratio..................................19.7:1
Displacement (c.i.) 166
Fuel ....diesel
Carburetor...Roosa injector pump
Air cleaner..Donaldson or United
Ignition...Delco-Remy,
12-v battery
Maximum brake horsepower tests
    PTO/belt horsepower...........................38.93
    Crankshaft rpm 2,000
    Fuel use (gal./hr.)...........................2.82
Maximum drawbar horsepower tests
    Gear..3rd
    Drawbar horsepower............................36.14
    Pull weight (lb.).............................2,666
    Speed (mph)...................................5.08
    Percent slippage..............................4.79
SAE drawbar horsepower.............................35.48
SAE belt/PTO horsepower.............................38.93
Type ....standard
Front wheel (in.)..................................5.50 x 16
Rear wheel (in.)...................................13.90 x 36
Height (in.).......................................60
Tread width (in.)..................................48–92
Weight (lb.) 4,390
Gear/speed (mph).............forward: 1/1.20, 2/1.80, 3/2.70, 4/3.60,
5/3.90, 6/5.10, 7/5.30, 8/7.50, 9/11.20,
10/16.60; reverse: 1/1.50, 2/2.30

International TD-340 Diesel
Manufacturer.......................................International Harvester
Co., Chicago, IL
Nebraska test number 776
Test date ....October 29 to
November 2, 1960
Test tractor serial number.........................TD-340 4328
Years produced 1959–1965
Serial number range................................501–8525 no end,
interspersed with
T-340
Serial number location ....metal plate on dash
Number produced ....approximately 8,025
Engine ....IHC D166
vertical L-head
Test engine serial number..........................D166 911
Cylinders 4
Bore and stroke (in.) ....3.6875 x 3.875
Rated rpm 2,000
Compression ratio..................................19.7:1
Displacement (c.i.) 166
Fuel ....diesel
Fuel tank capacity (gal.) 15
Carburetor...Roosa injector pump
Air cleaner..United
Ignition...Delco-Remy 12-v;
with 2, 6-v battery
Cooling capacity (gal.) 17
Maximum brake horsepower tests
    PTO/belt horsepower...........................39.80
    Crankshaft rpm 2,000
    Fuel use (gal./hr.)...........................3.04

Maximum drawbar horsepower tests
Gear	2nd
Drawbar horsepower	31.64
Pull weight (lb.)	5,592
Speed (mph)	2.12
Percent slippage	4.97
SAE drawbar horsepower	32.72
SAE belt/PTO horsepower	39.80
Type	tracklayer
Length (in.)	124.75
Height (in.)	60.25

Rear width (in.)	58
Tread width (in.)	38 or 48
Weight (lb.)	5,800
Track length (in.)	67.2 on ground, 210 total
Grouser shoe	35 links; 10, 12, (14)-in.
Gear/speed (mph)	forward: 1/1.46, 2/2.23, 3/3.00, 4/4.26, 5/5.83; reverse: 1/1.82

Chapter 47

JOHN DEERE

John Deere D, 15-27
Manufacturer	Waterloo Gasoline Engine Co., Waterloo, IA
Nebraska test number	102
Test date	April 11–17, 1924
Test tractor serial number	30504
Years produced	1923–1927
Serial number range	30401–53387 end
Serial number location	brass plate under gear shift lever
Number produced	22,987
Engine	John Deere horizontal, valve-in-head
Test engine serial number	30504
Cylinders	2
Bore and stroke (in.)	6.50 x 7.00
Rated rpm	800
Displacement (c.i.)	465
Fuel	kerosene/gasoline
Main tank capacity (gal.)	18
Auxiliary tank capacity (gal.)	2.5
Carburetor	Schebler WD, DX-298, 1.50-in.
Air cleaner	Donaldson
Ignition	Dixie Aero, No. 32433 magneto
Cooling capacity (gal.)	13

Maximum brake horsepower tests
PTO/belt horsepower	30.40
Crankshaft rpm	801
Fuel use (gal./hr.)	3.88

Maximum drawbar horsepower tests
Gear	low
Drawbar horsepower	22.53
Pull weight (lb.)	3,277
Speed (mph)	2.58
Percent slippage	11.68
SAE drawbar horsepower	15
SAE belt/PTO horsepower	27
Type	4 wheel

Front wheel (in.)	steel: 28 x 5
Rear wheel (in.)	steel: 46 x 12
Length (in.)	109
Height (in.)	56
Rear width (in.)	63
Weight (lb.)	4,403
Gear/speed (mph)	forward: 1/2.45, 2/3.27; reverse: 1/2.00

John Deere D; 15-27
Manufacturer	John Deere Tractor Co., Waterloo, IA
Nebraska test number	146
Test date	October 24–29, 1927
Test tractor serial number	60250
Years produced	1927–1953
Serial number range	53388–191670 end
Serial number location	plate on rear transmission case below gear shift
Number produced	138,283
Engine	John Deere horizontal, valve-in-head
Test engine serial number	60250
Cylinders	2
Bore and stroke (in.)	6.75 x 7.00
Rated rpm	800
Compression ratio	3.90:1
Displacement (c.i.)	501
Fuel	kerosene/gasoline
Main tank capacity (gal.)	18
Auxiliary tank capacity (gal.)	2.75
Carburetor	Schebler DLT, 1.50-in.
Air cleaner	Donaldson-Simplex
Ignition	Splitdorf 246 C magneto
Cooling capacity (gal.)	11

Maximum brake horsepower tests
PTO/belt horsepower	36.98
Crankshaft rpm	801
Fuel use (gal./hr.)	3.98

Maximum drawbar horsepower tests
Gear	low
Drawbar horsepower	28.53
Pull weight (lb.)	4,463
Speed (mph)	2.40
Percent slippage	17.88
SAE drawbar horsepower	15
SAE belt/PTO horsepower	25
Type	4 wheel
Front wheel (in.)	steel: 28 x 5
Rear wheel (in.)	steel: 46 x 12
Length (in.)	109
Height (in.)	56
Rear width (in.)	63
Weight (lb.)	4,164
Gear/speed (mph)	forward: 1/2.50, 2/3.25

John Deere C/GP, General Purpose

Manufacturer	John Deere Tractor Co., Waterloo, IA
Nebraska test number	153
Test date	October 22–29, 1928
Test tractor serial number	200112
Years produced	1927–1935
Serial number range	200211–223802 end; 400000–402039 end
Serial number location	brass plate under gear shift lever
Number produced	30,534, all types
Engine	John Deere horizontal L-head
Test engine serial number	200112
Cylinders	2
Bore and stroke (in.)	5.75 x 6.00
Rated rpm	950
Displacement (c.i.)	312
Fuel	kerosene/gasoline
Main tank capacity (gal.)	16
Auxiliary tank capacity (gal.)	2
Carburetor	Ensign BJ, 1.50-in.
Air cleaner	Donaldson-Simplex
Ignition	Fairbanks-Morse R2 magneto
Cooling capacity (gal.)	9

Maximum brake horsepower tests
PTO/belt horsepower	24.97
Crankshaft rpm	948
Fuel use (gal./hr.)	2.72

Maximum drawbar horsepower tests
Gear	2nd
Drawbar horsepower	17.24
Pull weight (lb.)	2,489
Speed (mph)	2.60
Percent slippage	7.30
SAE drawbar horsepower	10
SAE belt/PTO horsepower	20
Type	4 wheel
Front wheel (in.)	steel: 24 x 6
Rear wheel (in.)	steel: 42.75 x 10
Length (in.)	114
Height (in.)	55.50
Rear width (in.)	60.50
Weight (lb.)	3,600
Gear/speed (mph)	forward: 1/2.33, 2/3.12, 3/4.33; reverse: 1/2.00

John Deere GP, General Purpose WT

Manufacturer	John Deere Tractor Co., Waterloo, IA
Nebraska test number	190
Test date	May 4–15, 1931
Test tractor serial number	404400
Years produced	1928–1935
Serial number range	223803–230745 end; 402040–404809 end
Serial number location	brass plate under gear shift lever
Number produced	30,534, all types
Engine	John Deere horizontal L-head
Test engine serial number	404400
Cylinders	2
Bore and stroke (in.)	6.00 x 6.00
Rated rpm	950
Displacement (c.i.)	339
Fuel	distillate/gasoline
Main tank capacity (gal.)	16
Auxiliary tank capacity (gal.)	2
Carburetor	(Schebler DLTX-5) Ensign K, 1.1875-in.
Air cleaner	Donaldson
Ignition	John Deere (Fairbanks Morse R2) magneto
Cooling capacity (gal.)	9

Maximum brake horsepower tests
PTO/belt horsepower	25.36
Crankshaft rpm	949
Fuel use (gal./hr.)	2.67

Maximum drawbar horsepower tests
Gear	low
Drawbar horsepower	18.86
Pull weight (lb.)	2,853
Speed (mph)	2.48
Percent slippage	5.32
SAE drawbar horsepower	15.53
SAE belt/PTO horsepower	24.30
Type	tricycle
Front wheel (in.)	steel: 24 x 6
Rear wheel (in.)	steel: 43 x 10
Length (in.)	112
Height (in.)	57.50
Rear width (in.)	60
Weight (lb.)	4,141
Gear/speed (mph)	forward: 1/2.25, 2/3.00, 3/4.13; reverse: 1/1.75

John Deere A Unstyled

Manufacturer	John Deere Tractor Co., Waterloo, IA
Nebraska test number	222
Test date	April 19–27, 1934
Test tractor serial number	410009
Years produced	1934–1938
Serial number range	410008–476999 end
Serial number location	upper left front corner of main case
Number produced	approximately 66,992
Engine	John Deere A horizontal I-head
Test engine serial number	410009
Cylinders	2

Bore and stroke (in.) ....5.50 x 6.50
Rated rpm 975
Compression ratio...3.96:1
Displacement (c.i.) 309
Fuel ....distillate/gasoline
Main tank capacity (gal.)...............................14
Auxiliary tank capacity (gal.) 1
Carburetor ....Schebler DLTX18,
1.50-in.
Air cleaner..Vortox, 2071 D
Ignition...Fairbanks-Morse DRV-
2A magneto
Cooling capacity (gal.) 9.50
Maximum brake horsepower tests
    PTO/belt horsepower..........................24.71
    Crankshaft rpm 974
    Fuel use (gal./hr.)...............................2.45
Maximum drawbar horsepower tests
    Gear..1st
    Drawbar horsepower...........................18.72
    Pull weight (lb.)...................................2,923
    Speed (mph) 2.40
    Percent slippage.................................9.29
SAE drawbar horsepower...........................16.22
SAE belt/PTO horsepower 23.52
Type ....4 wheel, tricycle
Front wheel (in.) ....steel: 24 x 4
Rear wheel (in.) ....steel: 50 x 6
Length (in.) 124
Height (in.) 60
Rear width (in.) 86
Weight (lb.) 4,059
Gear/speed (mph) ....forward: 1/2.33,
2/3.00, 3/4.75, 4/6.25;
reverse: 1/3.50

John Deere B Unstyled
Manufacturer...John Deere Tractor
Co., Waterloo, IA
Nebraska test number 232
Test date ....November 15, 1934 to
April 19, 1935
Test tractor serial number.............................1005
Years produced...1935–1937
Serial number range......................................1000–42133 end
Serial number location ....plate on left side top
front main case
Number produced 41,134
Engine ....John Deere B
horizontal I-head
Test engine serial number.............................1005
Cylinders 2
Bore and stroke (in.) ....4.25 x 5.25
Rated rpm 1,150
Displacement (c.i.) 149
Fuel ....distillate/gasoline
Main tank capacity (gal.)...............................12
Auxiliary tank capacity (gal.) 1
Carburetor ....Wheeler-Schebler
DLTX-10, 1.125-in.
Air cleaner ....Donaldson
Ignition..Fairbanks Morse
DRV-2 B magneto
Cooling capacity (gal.) 5.50

Maximum brake horsepower tests
    PTO/belt horsepower..........................16.01
    Crankshaft rpm 1,150
    Fuel use (gal./hr.) 2.07
Maximum drawbar horsepower tests
    Gear..2nd
    Drawbar horsepower...........................11.80
    Pull weight (lb.)...................................1,297
    Speed (mph) 3.41
    Percent slippage.................................1.88
SAE drawbar horsepower...........................9.28
SAE belt/PTO horsepower 14.25
Type ....4 wheel, tricycle
Front wheel (in.)..(steel: 22 x 3.25);
rubber: 5.50 x 15
Rear wheel (in.) ....(steel: 48 x 5.25);
rubber: 7.50 x 36
Length (in.) 120.50
Height (in.) 56
Rear width (in.) 85
Weight (lb.) 2,763
Gear/speed (mph) ....forward: 1/2.25,
2/3.33, 3/4.75, 4/6.75;
reverse: 1/3.75

John Deere D
Manufacturer..John Deere Tractor
Co., Waterloo, IA
Nebraska test number 236
Test date ....June 26 to July 2,
1935
Test tractor serial number.............................121132
Years produced...1927–1953
Serial number range......................................53388–191670 end
Serial number location ....plate rear transmission
case below gear shift
Number produced 138,283
Engine ....John Deere
horizontal I-head
Test engine serial number.............................121132
Cylinders 2
Bore and stroke (in.) ....6.75 x 7.00
Rated rpm 900
Compression ratio...3.91:1
Displacement (c.i.) 501
Fuel ....distillate/gasoline
Main tank capacity (gal.)...............................21
Auxiliary tank capacity (gal.) 2.75
Carburetor ....Schebler DLTX-63,
1.50-in.
Air cleaner ....Donaldson
Ignition..Splitdorf 246 T
magneto
Cooling capacity (gal.) 10–14
Maximum brake horsepower tests
    PTO/belt horsepower..........................41.59
    Crankshaft rpm 900
    Fuel use (gal./hr.) 4.33
Maximum drawbar horsepower tests
    Gear..2nd
    Drawbar horsepower...........................29.90
    Pull weight (lb.)...................................2,899
    Speed (mph) 3.87
    Percent slippage.................................4.21

SAE drawbar horsepower....................24.02
SAE belt/PTO horsepower..........................37.37
Type ....4 wheel
Front wheel (in.)...............................(steel: 28 x 6);
rubber: 7.50 x 18
Rear wheel (in.).................................(steel: 46 x 11.125);
rubber: 12.75 x 28
Length (in.) 109
Height (in.) 56
Rear width (in.) 63
Weight (lb.) 4,917
Gear/speed (mph) ....forward: 1/2.50, 2/3.50,
3/5.00; reverse: 1/2.00

John Deere G Unstyled,
Manufacturer.................................John Deere Tractor
Co., Waterloo, IA
Nebraska test number 295
Test date ....November 15–19,
1937
Test tractor serial number..........................G 1081
Years produced..............................1938–1941
Serial number range..............................1000–12192 end
Serial number location ....plate on left side top
front main case;
(1939) right side top
front main case under
magneto
Number produced 11,193
Engine ....John Deere
horizontal I-head
Test engine serial number..........................G 1081
Cylinders 2
Bore and stroke (in.) ....6.125 x 7.00
Rated rpm 975
Compression ratio....................................4.20:1
Displacement (c.i.) 412.5
Fuel ....distillate/gasoline
Main tank capacity (gal.).........................17
Auxiliary tank capacity (gal.) 1.5
Carburetor ....Schebler DLTX-24,
1.625-in.
Air cleaner ....Donaldson
Ignition..Edison-Splitdorf CD-2
magneto
Cooling capacity (gal.) 11
Maximum brake horsepower tests
PTO/belt horsepower.........................35.91
Crankshaft rpm 975
Fuel use (gal./hr.).............................3.92
Maximum drawbar horsepower tests
Gear...2nd
Drawbar horsepower.........................27.63
Pull weight (lb.)...............................3,079
Speed (mph) 3.36
Percent slippage..............................6.40
SAE drawbar horsepower......................20.70
SAE belt/PTO horsepower.....................31.44
Type ....tricycle
Front wheel (in.)................................steel: 24 x 5
Rear wheel (in.)................................steel: 51.5 x 7
Length (in.) 135
Height (in.) 61.50
Rear width (in.) 84
Weight (lb.) 4,488

Gear/speed (mph) ....forward: 1/2.25,
2/3.25, 3/4.25, 4/6.00;
reverse: 1/3.00

John Deere B Styled
Manufacturer.................................John Deere Tractor
Co., Waterloo, IA
Nebraska test number 305
Test date ....September 6–16, 1938
Test tractor serial number..........................B 60003
Years produced..............................1938–1940
Serial number range..............................60000–95201 end
Serial number location ....plate on right top front
main case under
magneto
Number produced 35,202
Engine ....John Deere B
horizontal I-head
Test engine serial number..........................B 60003
Cylinders 2
Bore and stroke (in.) ....4.50 x 5.50
Rated rpm 1,150
Compression ratio....................................4.45:1
Displacement (c.i.) 174.9
Fuel ....distillate/gasoline
Main tank capacity (gal.).........................13.50
Auxiliary tank capacity (gal.) 1
Carburetor ....Schebler DLTX-10,
1.125-in.
Air cleaner ....Donaldson
Ignition..Wico AP-477-B
magneto
Cooling capacity (gal.) 6
Maximum brake horsepower tests
PTO/belt horsepower.........................18.53
Crankshaft rpm 1,150
Fuel use (gal./hr.).............................1.87
Maximum drawbar horsepower tests
Gear...2nd
Drawbar horsepower.........................13.41
Pull weight (lb.)...............................1,508
Speed (mph) 3.34
Percent slippage..............................2.44
SAE drawbar horsepower......................10.76
SAE belt/PTO horsepower.....................16.86
Type ....tricycle
Front wheel (in.)................................(steel: 22 x 3.25);
rubber: 5.00 x 15
Rear wheel (in.)................................(steel: 48 x 5.25);
rubber: 9.00 x 36
Length (in.) 125.50
Height (in.) 57
Rear width (in.) 83.50
Weight (lb.) ....steel: 2,731;
(rubber: 4,185)
Gear/speed (mph) ....forward: 1/2.33,
2/3.00, 3/4.00, 4/5.25;
reverse: 1/3.75

John Deere H
Manufacturer.................................John Deere Tractor
Co., Waterloo, IA
Nebraska test number 312
Test date ....October 31 to
November 10, 1938

Test tractor serial number............................H-1000
Years produced 1939–1947
Serial number range....................................1000–61116 end
Serial number location ....plate on right side under magneto on main case
Number produced 58,263
Engine ....John Deere horizontal I-head
Test engine serial number..........................H 1000
Cylinders 2
Bore and stroke (in.) ....3.5625 x 5.00
Rated rpm 1,400
Compression ratio......................................4.75:1
Displacement (c.i.) 99.68
Fuel ....distillate/gasoline
Main tank capacity (gal.) 7.50
Auxiliary tank capacity (gal.) 0.875
Carburetor ....Marvel-Schebler DLTX-26, 1.00-in.
Air cleaner ....United
Ignition ....(Edison-Splitdorf RM-2) Wico magneto
Cooling capacity (gal.) 5.50
Maximum brake horsepower tests
    PTO/belt horsepower...........................14.84
    Crankshaft rpm 1,399
    Fuel use (gal./hr.) 1.31
Maximum drawbar horsepower tests
    Gear..2nd
    Drawbar horsepower............................12.48
    Pull weight (lb.)...................................1,386
    Speed (mph) 3.38
    Percent slippage.................................6.72
SAE drawbar horsepower.............................9.68
SAE belt/PTO horsepower............................12.97
Type ....tricycle
Front tire (in.) ....4.00 x 15
Rear tire (in.)..7.50 x 32
Length (in.) 111.25
Height (in.) 52
Rear width (in.) 79
Weight (lb.) 2,100
Gear/speed (mph) ....forward: 1/2.50, 2/3.50, 3/5.75; reverse: 1/1.75

John Deere L Styled
Manufacturer..John Deere Wagon Works, Moline, IL
Nebraska test number 313
Test date ....November 14–16, 1938
Test tractor serial number............................625030
Years produced 1938–1941
Serial number range....................................625000–634840 end
Serial number location ....plate on right rear axle housing
Number produced 9,841
Engine ....John Deere/Hercules NXB vertical L-head
Test engine serial number..........................422811
Cylinders 2

Bore and stroke (in.) ....3.25 x 4.00
Rated rpm 1,550
Compression ratio......................................5.50:1
Displacement (c.i.) 66
Fuel ....gasoline
Fuel tank capacity (gal.) 6
Carburetor ....Marvel-Schebler TSX-13, 0.875-in.
Air cleaner ....United
Ignition ....Edison Splitdorf RM-03509 magneto
Cooling capacity (gal.) 2.50
Maximum brake horsepower tests
    PTO/belt horsepower...........................10.42
    Crankshaft rpm 1,549
    Fuel use (gal./hr.) 1.06
Maximum drawbar horsepower tests
    Gear..2nd
    Drawbar horsepower............................9.06
    Pull weight (lb.)...................................908
    Speed (mph) 3.74
    Percent slippage.................................7.65
SAE drawbar horsepower.............................7.01
SAE belt/PTO horsepower............................9.27
Type ....standard
Front tire (in.) ....4.00 x 15
Rear tire (in.)..6.00 x 22
Length (in.) 91
Height (in.) 50
Rear width (in.) 49
Weight (lb.) 1,570
Gear/speed (mph) ....forward: 1/2.50, 2/3.75, 3/6.00; reverse: 1/3.75

John Deere A Styled,
Manufacturer..John Deere Tractor Co., Waterloo, IA
Nebraska test number 335
Test date ....November 13–16, 1939
Test tractor serial number............................488005
Years produced 1938–1940
Serial number range....................................477000–498999 end
Serial number location ....upper left front corner of main case; (1938) right top front main case under magneto
Number produced ....approximately 22,000
Engine ....John Deere A horizontal I-head
Test engine serial number..........................488005
Cylinders 2
Bore and stroke (in.) ....5.50 x 6.75
Rated rpm 975
Compression ratio......................................3.96:1
Displacement (c.i.) 309
Fuel ....distillate/gasoline
Main tank capacity (gal.) 15
Auxiliary tank capacity (gal.) 1
Carburetor ....Schebler DLTX-24, 1.50-in.
Air cleaner ....United
Ignition ....Wico C-1042 magneto
Cooling capacity (gal.) 9.25

Maximum brake horsepower tests
- PTO/belt horsepower............................29.59
- Crankshaft rpm 975
- Fuel use (gal./hr.).............................2.81

Maximum drawbar horsepower tests
- Gear...3rd
- Drawbar horsepower............................26.20
- Pull weight (lb.)................................2,339
- Speed (mph).....................................4.20
- Percent slippage................................4.96

SAE drawbar horsepower.............................20.12
SAE belt/PTO horsepower............................26.33
Type ....tricycle
Front wheel (in.)..................................steel: 24 x 4;
(rubber: 5.50 x 16)
Rear wheel (in.)...................................steel: 50 x 6;
(rubber: 11.00 x 38)
Length (in.) 124
Height (in.) 60
Rear width (in.) 86
Weight (lb.) 4,059
Gear/speed (mph) ....forward: 1/2.33,
2/3.00, 3/4.00, 4/5.25;
reverse: 1/3.75

John Deere D

Manufacturer.......................................John Deere Tractor
Co., Waterloo, IA
Nebraska test number 350
Test date ....July 22–26, 1940
Test tractor serial number.........................147824
Years produced 1927–1953
Serial number range................................53388–191670 end
Serial number location ....plate rear transmission
case below gear shift
Number produced 138,283
Engine ....John Deere
horizontal I-head
Test engine serial number..........................147824
Cylinders 2
Bore and stroke (in.) ....6.75 x 7.00
Rated rpm 900
Compression ratio..................................3.91:1
Displacement (c.i.) 501
Fuel ....distillate/gasoline
Main tank capacity (gal.)..........................21
Auxiliary tank capacity (gal.) 2.75
Carburetor...Marvel-Schebler
DLTX-16, 1.50-in.
Air cleaner..Donaldson
Ignition...Edison-Splitdorf
CD-2 magneto
Cooling capacity (gal.) 10

Maximum brake horsepower tests
- PTO/belt horsepower............................42.05
- Crankshaft rpm 900
- Fuel use (gal./hr.).............................4.76

Maximum drawbar horsepower tests
- Gear...2nd
- Drawbar horsepower............................38.02
- Pull weight (lb.)................................3,641
- Speed (mph).....................................3.92
- Percent slippage................................8.61

SAE drawbar horsepower.............................30.46
SAE belt/PTO horsepower............................38.11

Front tire (in.)...................................7.50 x 18
Rear tire (in.)....................................13.50 x 28
Length (in.) 130
Height (in.) 56
Rear width (in.) 68.75
Tread width (in.) 55.25
Weight (lb.) ....(4,917)
Gear/speed (mph) ....forward: 1/3.00, 2/4.00,
3/5.25; reverse: 1/2.00

John Deere B Styled

Manufacturer.......................................John Deere Tractor
Co., Waterloo, IA
Nebraska test number 366
Test date ....November 7, 1940 to
April 25, 1941
Test tractor serial number.........................B 96502
Years produced 1941–1947
Serial number range................................96000–200999 end
Serial number location ....plate on front main
case under magneto
Number produced 105,000
Engine ....John Deere B
horizontal I-head
Test engine serial number..........................B 96502
Cylinders 2
Bore and stroke (in.) ....4.50 x 5.50
Rated rpm 1,150
Compression ratio..................................4.45:1
Displacement (c.i.) 174.9
Fuel ....distillate/gasoline
Main tank capacity (gal.)..........................13.50
Auxiliary tank capacity (gal.) 1
Carburetor...Schebler DLTX-34,
1.50-in.
Air cleaner..Donaldson
Ignition...Wico C-1042 magneto
Cooling capacity (gal.) 6

Maximum brake horsepower tests
- PTO/belt horsepower............................20.52
- Crankshaft rpm 1,150
- Fuel use (gal./hr.).............................2.05

Maximum drawbar horsepower tests
- Gear...2nd
- Drawbar horsepower............................18.26
- Pull weight (lb.)................................2,174
- Speed (mph).....................................3.15
- Percent slippage................................6.56

SAE drawbar horsepower.............................14.08
SAE belt/PTO horsepower............................17.46
Type ....tricycle
Front tire (in.)...................................5.00 x 15
Rear tire (in.)....................................10.00 x 38
Length (in.) 125.50
Height (in.) 57
Rear width (in.) 83.50
Tread width (in.) 56–84
Weight (lb.) 3,725
Gear/speed (mph) ....forward: 1/2.33, 2/3.25,
3/4.00, 4/5.33, 5/7.25,
6/12.25; reverse: 1/4.00

John Deere LA

Manufacturer.......................................John Deere Wagon
Works, Moline, IL

Nebraska test number 373
Test date ....June 20–28, 1941
Test tractor serial number.....................LA 1229
Years produced 1940–1946
Serial number range............................1001–13475 end
Serial number location ....plate on right rear axle
                                                housing
Number produced 12,475
Engine ....John Deere
                                                vertical   L-head
Test engine serial number...................LA 1229
Cylinders 2
Bore and stroke (in.) ....3.50 x 4.00
Rated rpm 1,850
Compression ratio..............................6.00:1
Displacement (c.i.) 77
Fuel ....gasoline
Fuel tank capacity (gal.) 8
Carburetor..Marvel-Schebler
                                                TSX-60, 0.875-in.
Air cleaner ....United
Ignition..Edison-Splitdorf
                                                RM-03761 magneto
Cooling capacity (gal.) 2.50
Maximum brake horsepower tests
    PTO/belt horsepower............................14.34
    Crankshaft rpm 1,849
    Fuel use (gal./hr.)...........................1.37
Maximum drawbar horsepower tests
    Gear...2nd
    Drawbar horsepower.......................13.10
    Pull weight (lb.)............................1,351
    Speed (mph)...................................3.64
    Percent slippage..............................5.64
SAE drawbar horsepower............................10.46
SAE belt/PTO horsepower.......................12.93
Type ....standard
Front tire (in.).....................................5.00 x 15
Rear tire (in.).......................................9.00 x 24
Length (in.) 93
Height (in.) 60
Rear width (in.) 47
Weight (lb.) 2,285
Gear/speed (mph) ....forward: 1/2.50, 2/3.50,
                                                3/9.00;   reverse: 1/2.50

John Deere AR Unstyled,
Manufacturer.......................................John Deere Tractor
                                                Co., Waterloo, IA
Nebraska test number 378
Test date ....October 27 to
                                                November 3, 1941
Test tractor serial number.....................260725
Years produced 1941–1949
Serial number range............................260001–271593 end
Serial number location ....upper left front corner
                                                of main case
Number produced 11,593
Engine ....John Deere A
                                                horizontal I-head
Test engine serial number...................260725
Cylinders 2
Bore and stroke (in.) ....5.50 x 6.75
Rated rpm 975
Compression ratio..............................5.60:1

Displacement (c.i.) 321.2
Fuel ....distillate/gasoline
Main tank capacity (gal.)......................14
Auxiliary tank capacity (gal.) 1
Carburetor..Marvel-Schebler
                                                DLTX-41, 1.50-in.
Air cleaner ....Vortox
Ignition..Wico C-1042 magneto
Cooling capacity (gal.) 8.75
Maximum brake horsepower tests
    PTO/belt horsepower............................30.33
    Crankshaft rpm 975
    Fuel use (gal./hr.)...........................3.12
Maximum drawbar horsepower tests
    Gear...3rd
    Drawbar horsepower.......................26.52
    Pull weight (lb.)............................2,417
    Speed (mph)...................................4.11
    Percent slippage..............................5.84
SAE drawbar horsepower............................20.35
SAE belt/PTO horsepower.......................26.30
Type ....standard
Front tire (in.).....................................6.00 x 16
Rear tire (in.).......................................12.00 x 26
Length (in.) 134
Height (in.) 63.87
Rear width (in.) 86.37
Weight (lb.) 4,640
Gear/speed (mph) ....forward: 1/2.00,
                                                2/3.00, 3/4.00, 4/6.50;
                                                reverse: 1/3.00

John Deere B Late Styled
Manufacturer.......................................John Deere Tractor
                                                Co., Waterloo, IA
Nebraska test number 380
Test date ....April 28 to
                                                May 14, 1947
Test tractor serial number.....................B 201369
Years produced 1947–1952
Serial number range............................201000–310775 end
Serial number location ....plate on right top front
                                                main case under
                                                magneto
Number produced 109,776
Engine ....John Deere B
                                                horizontal I-head
Test engine serial number...................B 201369
Cylinders 2
Bore and stroke (in.) ....4.6875 x 5.50
Rated rpm 1,250
Compression ratio..............................4.65:1
Displacement (c.i.) 190.4
Fuel ....gasoline
Fuel tank capacity (gal.) 14
Carburetor..Marvel-Schebler
                                                DLTX-67, 1.50-in.
Air cleaner ....Donaldson
Ignition..Wico C-1042B
                                                magneto
Cooling capacity (gal.) 6.75
Maximum brake horsepower tests
    PTO/belt horsepower............................27.58
    Crankshaft rpm 1,249
    Fuel use (gal./hr.)...........................2.55

Maximum drawbar horsepower tests
- Gear............4th
- Drawbar horsepower............24.62
- Pull weight (lb.)............2,187
- Speed (mph)............4.22
- Percent slippage............6.42

SAE drawbar horsepower............19.13
SAE belt/PTO horsepower............24.39
Type............tricycle
Front tire (in.)............5.50 x 16
Rear tire (in.)............10.00 x 38
Length (in.)............132.25
Height (in.)............59.62
Rear width (in.)............87
Tread width (in.)............56–88
Weight (lb.)............4,225
Gear/speed (mph)............forward: 1/1.50, 2/2.50, 3/3.50, 4/4.50, 5/5.75, 6/10.00; reverse: 1/2.50

John Deere B Late Styled

Manufacturer............John Deere Tractor Co., Waterloo, IA
Nebraska test number............381
Test date............May 9–15, 1947
Test tractor serial number............B 201320
Years produced............1947–1952
Serial number range............201000–310775 end
Serial number location............plate on right top front main case under magneto
Number produced............109,776
Engine............John Deere B horizontal I-head
Test engine serial number............B 201320
Cylinders............2
Bore and stroke (in.)............4.6875 x 5.50
Rated rpm............1,250
Compression ratio............4.65:1
Displacement (c.i.)............190.4
Fuel............all-fuel/gasoline
Main tank capacity (gal.)............14
Auxiliary tank capacity (gal.)............1
Carburetor............Marvel-Schebler DLTX-73, 1.50-in.
Air cleaner............Donaldson
Ignition............Wico C-1042B magneto
Cooling capacity (gal.)............6.75

Maximum brake horsepower tests
- PTO/belt horsepower............23.53
- Crankshaft rpm............1,251
- Fuel use (gal./hr.)............2.33

Maximum drawbar horsepower tests
- Gear............3rd
- Drawbar horsepower............21.14
- Pull weight (lb.)............2,467
- Speed (mph)............3.21
- Percent slippage............8.37

SAE drawbar horsepower............16.64
SAE belt/PTO horsepower............20.68
Type............tricycle
Front tire (in.)............5.50 x 16
Rear tire (in.)............10.00 x 38

Length (in.)............132.25
Height (in.)............59.62
Rear width (in.)............87
Tread width (in.)............56–88
Weight (lb.)............4,240
Gear/speed (mph)............forward: 1/1.50, 2/2.50, 3/3.50, 4/4.50, 5/5.75, 6/10.00; reverse: 1/2.50

John Deere G Styled,

Manufacturer............John Deere Tractor Co., Waterloo, IA
Nebraska test number............383
Test date............June 5–16, 1947
Test tractor serial number............21945
Years produced............1941–1953
Serial number range............13000–64530 end
Serial number location............plate on right side top front main case under magneto
Number produced............51,531
Engine............John Deere horizontal I-head
Test engine serial number............21945
Cylinders............2
Bore and stroke (in.)............6.125 x 7.00
Rated rpm............975
Compression ratio............4.20:1
Displacement (c.i.)............412.5
Fuel............all-fuel/gasoline
Main tank capacity (gal.)............17
Auxiliary tank capacity (gal.)............1.50
Carburetor............Marvel-Schebler DLTX-51, 1.50-in.
Air cleaner............Donaldson
Ignition............Wico C-1042 magneto
Cooling capacity (gal.)............13

Maximum brake horsepower tests
- PTO/belt horsepower............38.10
- Crankshaft rpm............976
- Fuel use (gal./hr.)............3.93

Maximum drawbar horsepower tests
- Gear............3rd
- Drawbar horsepower............34.49
- Pull weight (lb.)............2,985
- Speed (mph)............4.33
- Percent slippage............6.54

SAE drawbar horsepower............27.01
SAE belt/PTO horsepower............33.83
Type............tricycle
Front tire (in.)............6.00 x 16
Rear tire (in.)............12.00 x 38
Length (in.)............137.43
Height (in.)............65.87
Rear width (in.)............84.75
Tread width (in.)............60–84
Weight (lb.)............5,624
Gear/speed (mph)............forward: 1/2.50, 2/3.50, 3/4.50, 4/6.50, 5/8.75, 6/12.50; reverse: 1/3.25

John Deere A Late Styled

Manufacturer............John Deere Tractor Co., Waterloo, IA
Nebraska test number............384
Test date............June 7–16, 1947

Test tractor serial number 584043
Years produced 1947–1952
Serial number range ....584000–703384 end
Serial number location ....right top front main
case under magneto
Number produced 119,385
Engine ....John Deere A
horizontal I-head
Test engine serial number 584043
Cylinders 2
Bore and stroke (in.) ....5.50 x 6.75
Rated rpm 975
Compression ratio 5.60:1
Displacement (c.i.) 321.2
Fuel ....gasoline
Fuel tank capacity (gal.) 14
Carburetor ....Marvel-Schebler
DLTX-71, 1.50-in.
Air cleaner ....Donaldson
Ignition ....Wico C-1042-B
magneto
Cooling capacity (gal.) 8.75
Maximum brake horsepower tests
PTO/belt horsepower 38.02
Crankshaft rpm 976
Fuel use (gal./hr.) 3.71
Maximum drawbar horsepower tests
Gear 3rd
Drawbar horsepower 34.14
Pull weight (lb.) 3,158
Speed (mph) 4.06
Percent slippage 6.92
SAE drawbar horsepower 26.48
SAE belt/PTO horsepower 33.53
Type ....tricycle
Front tire (in.) ....5.50 x 16
Rear tire (in.) ....11.00 x 38
Length (in.) 134
Height (in.) 63.87
Rear width (in.) 86.37
Tread width (in.) 56–88
Weight (lb.) 4,909
Gear/speed (mph) ....forward: 1/2.50,
2/3.50, 3/4.50, 4/5.75,
5/7.75, 6/13.00;
reverse: 1/4.50

John Deere M
Manufacturer ....John Deere Dubuque
Tractor Works,
Dubuque, IA
Nebraska test number 387
Test date ....October 6–16, 1947
Test tractor serial number 10271
Years produced 1947–1952
Serial number range ....10001–55799 end
Serial number location ....plate at base of
instrument panel
Number produced 45,799
Engine ....John Deere,
M vertical L-head
Test engine serial number 1,290
Cylinders 2
Bore and stroke (in.) ....4.00 x 4.00

Rated rpm 1,650
Compression ratio 6.0:1
Displacement (c.i.) 101
Fuel ....gasoline
Fuel tank capacity (gal.) 10
Carburetor ....Marvel-Schebler
TSX-245, 1.00-in.
Air cleaner ....Donaldson
Ignition ....Delco-Remy with
6-v battery
Cooling capacity (gal.) 3.50
Maximum brake horsepower tests
PTO/belt horsepower 20.45
Crankshaft rpm 1,651
Fuel use (gal./hr.) 1.97
Maximum drawbar horsepower tests
Gear 3rd
Drawbar horsepower 18.15
Pull weight (lb.) 1,581
Speed (mph) 4.30
Percent slippage 6.91
SAE drawbar horsepower 14.39
SAE belt/PTO horsepower 18.21
Type ....standard
Front tire (in.) ....5.00 x 15
Rear tire (in.) ....9.00 x 24
Length (in.) 110
Height (in.) 56
Rear width (in.) 51
Weight (lb.) 2,520
Gear/speed (mph) ....forward: 1/1.62,
2/3.12, 3/4.25,
4/10.00–12.00;
reverse: 1/1.62

John Deere R Diesel
Manufacturer ....John Deere Waterloo
Tractor Works,
Waterloo, IA
Nebraska test number 406
Test date ....April 19–28, 1949
Test tractor serial number ....R 1358
Years produced 1949–1954
Serial number range ....1000–22293 end
Serial number location ....plate on right side
above belt pulley
Number produced 21,294
Engine ....John Deere horizontal
I-head
Test engine serial number ....R 1358
Cylinders 2
Bore and stroke (in.) ....5.75 x 8.00
Rated rpm 1,000
Compression ratio 16.0:1
Displacement (c.i.) 416
Fuel ....diesel/gasoline
Main tank capacity (gal.) 22
Auxiliary tank capacity (gal.) 0.25
Carburetor ....start engine: Marvel-
Schebler SL- 2
Air cleaner ....Donaldson
Ignition ....Wico XH
magneto/Delco-Remy
with 6-v battery

Cooling capacity (gal.) 13.62
Maximum brake horsepower tests
    PTO/belt horsepower...........................48.58
    Crankshaft rpm 1,000
    Fuel use (gal./hr.) 2.80
Maximum drawbar horsepower tests
    Gear...3rd
    Drawbar horsepower..........................43.15
    Pull weight (lb.).............................4,000
    Speed (mph) 4.05
    Percent slippage.............................6.55
SAE drawbar horsepower 34.27
SAE belt/PTO horsepower 43.32
Type ....standard
Front tire (in.).................................7.50 x 18
Rear tire (in.).................................14.00 x 34
Length (in.) 147
Height (in.) 78.12
Rear width (in.) 79.50
Tread width (in.)..............................62.50
Weight (lb.) 7,400
Gear/speed (mph) ....forward: 1/2.12,
    2/3.33, 3/4.25, 4/5.33,
    5/11.50; reverse: 1/2.50

John Deere MT

Manufacturer.................................John Deere Dubuque
    Tractor Works,
    Dubuque, IA
Nebraska test number 423
Test date ....September 7–16, 1949
Test tractor serial number...................MT 10825
Years produced 1949–1952
Serial number range..........................10001–40472 end
Serial number location ....plate at base of
    instrument panel
Number produced 30,472
Engine ....John Deere M
    vertical L-head
Test engine serial number...................2,157
Cylinders 2
Bore and stroke (in.) ....4.00 x 4.00
Rated rpm 1,650
Compression ratio...........................6.0:1
Displacement (c.i.) 101
Fuel ....gasoline
Fuel tank capacity (gal.) 10
Carburetor...................................Marvel-Schebler
    TSX-245, 1.00-in.
Air cleaner ....Donaldson
Ignition......................................Delco-Remy with
    6-v battery
Cooling capacity (gal.) 3.50
Maximum brake horsepower tests
    PTO/belt horsepower...........................20.78
    Crankshaft rpm 1,651
    Fuel use (gal./hr.) 2.07
Maximum drawbar horsepower tests
    Gear...3rd
    Drawbar horsepower..........................18.27
    Pull weight (lb.).............................1,455
    Speed (mph) 4.71
    Percent slippage.............................4.46
SAE drawbar horsepower 14.08
SAE belt/PTO horsepower 18.33

Type ....tricycle
Front tire (in.)................................5.00 x 15
Rear tire (in.)................................9.00 x 34
Length (in.) 125.38
Height (in.) 73.75
Rear width (in.) 51
Tread width (in.)..............................48–96
Weight (lb.) 3,200
Gear/speed (mph) ....forward: 1/1.75, 2/3.25,
    3/4.50, 4/11.00–12.00;
    reverse: 1/1.75

John Deere AR Styled

Manufacturer.................................John Deere Waterloo
    Tractor Works,
    Waterloo, IA
Nebraska test number 429
Test date ....October 11–15, 1949
Test tractor serial number...................272197
Years produced 1949–1953
Serial number range..........................272000–284074 end
Serial number location ....upper left front corner
    of main case
Number produced 12,075
Engine ....John Deere A
    horizontal I-head
Test engine serial number...................272197
Cylinders 2
Bore and stroke (in.) ....5.50 x 6.75
Rated rpm 975
Compression ratio...........................5.57:1
Displacement (c.i.) 321.2
Fuel ....gasoline
Fuel tank capacity (gal.) 14
Carburetor...................................Marvel-Schebler
    DLTX 71, 1.50-in.
Air cleaner ....Donaldson
Ignition......................................Wico X magneto or
    Delco-Remy 12-v; with
    2, 6-v battery
Cooling capacity (gal.) 8.75
Maximum brake horsepower tests
    PTO/belt horsepower...........................37.87
    Crankshaft rpm 975
    Fuel use (gal./hr.) 3.55
Maximum drawbar horsepower tests
    Gear...4th
    Drawbar horsepower..........................34.03
    Pull weight (lb.).............................2,999
    Speed (mph) 4.26
Percent slippage.............................6.08
SAE drawbar horsepower 26.16
SAE belt/PTO horsepower 33.24
Type ....standard
Front tire (in.)................................6.00 x 16
Rear tire (in.)................................13.00 x 26
Length (in.) 125.50
Height (in.) 70.75
Rear width (in.) 86.37
Tread width (in.)..............................54.44–58.44
Weight (lb.) 5,244
Gear/speed (mph) ....forward: 1/1.25,
    2/2.50, 3/3.25, 4/4.37,
    5/6.25, 6/11.00;
    reverse: 1/2.75

John Deere MC

Manufacturer	John Deere Dubuque Tractor Works, Dubuque, IA
Nebraska test number	448
Test date	July 20–26, 1950
Test tractor serial number	MC 11444
Years produced	1949–1952
Serial number range	10001–20509 end
Serial number location	plate at base of instrument panel
Number produced	10,509
Engine	John Deere M vertical L-head
Test engine serial number	26365
Cylinders	2
Bore and stroke (in.)	4.00 x 4.00
Rated rpm	1,650
Compression ratio	6.0:1
Displacement (c.i.)	101
Fuel	gasoline
Fuel tank capacity (gal.)	10
Carburetor	Marvel-Schebler TSX-245, 1.00-in.
Air cleaner	Donaldson
Ignition	Delco-Remy with 6-v battery
Cooling capacity (gal.)	3.50

Maximum brake horsepower tests

PTO/belt horsepower	21.24
Crankshaft rpm	1,651
Fuel use (gal./hr.)	2.06

Maximum drawbar horsepower tests

Gear	3rd
Drawbar horsepower	17.49
Pull weight (lb.)	2,309
Speed (mph)	2.84
Percent slippage	1.93
SAE drawbar horsepower	13.70
SAE belt/PTO horsepower	18.89
Type	tracklayer
Length (in.)	102
Height (in.)	50.5
Rear width (in.)	67
Tread width (in.)	36 and 46 or 38.50 and 44.50
Weight (lb.)	3,875
Track length (in.)	192
Grouser shoe	28 links; 10, (12), 14
Gear/speed (mph)	forward: 1/0.90, 2/2.20, 3/2.90, 4/4.70; reverse: 1/1.00

John Deere 60

Manufacturer	John Deere Waterloo Tractor Works, Waterloo, IA
Nebraska test number	472
Test date	May 26 to June 2, 1952
Test tractor serial number	6000003
Years produced	1952–1957
Serial number range	6000001–6064096 end
Serial number location	plate on right side main case
Number produced	approximately 61,000
Engine	John Deere 60 horizontal I-head
Test engine serial number	6000003
Cylinders	2
Bore and stroke (in.)	5.50 x 6.75
Rated rpm	975
Compression ratio	6.00:1
Displacement (c.i.)	321
Fuel	gasoline
Fuel tank capacity (gal.)	20.50
Carburetor	Marvel-Schebler DLTX-81, 1.50-in.
Air cleaner	Donaldson
Ignition	Delco-Remy, 12-v with 2, 6-v battery
Cooling capacity (gal.)	8.25

Maximum brake horsepower tests

PTO/belt horsepower	40.24
Crankshaft rpm	976
Fuel use (gal./hr.)	3.84

Maximum drawbar horsepower tests

Gear	4th
Drawbar horsepower	35.18
Pull weight (lb.)	3,057
Speed (mph)	4.32
Percent slippage	7.03
SAE drawbar horsepower	27.71
SAE belt/PTO horsepower	35.33
Type	tricycle
Front tire (in.)	6.00 x 16
Rear tire (in.)	12.00 x 38
Length (in.)	139
Height (in.)	65.56
Rear width (in.)	86.62
Tread width (in.)	56–88
Weight (lb.)	5,300
Gear/speed (mph)	forward: 1/1.50, 2/2.50, 3/3.50, 4/4.50, 5/6.25, 6/11.00; reverse: 1/3.00

John Deere 50

Manufacturer	John Deere Waterloo Tractor Works, Waterloo, IA
Nebraska test number	486
Test date	October 15–22, 1952
Test tractor serial number	5000003
Years produced	1952–1956
Serial number range	5000001–5033751 end
Serial number location	plate on right side main case
Number produced	32,574
Engine	John Deere 50 horizontal I-head
Test engine serial number	5000003
Cylinders	2
Bore and stroke (in.)	4.6875 x 5.50
Rated rpm	1,250
Compression ratio	6.10:1
Displacement (c.i.)	190.4
Fuel	gasoline
Fuel tank capacity (gal.)	15.50

Carburetor ....Marvel-Schebler
DLTX-75, 1.50-in.
Air cleaner ....Donaldson
Ignition ....Wico XB4023, 12-v
with 2, 6-v battery
Cooling capacity (gal.) 7

Maximum brake horsepower tests
    PTO/belt horsepower............................30.35
    Crankshaft rpm 1,250
    Fuel use (gal./hr.) 2.85

Maximum drawbar horsepower tests
    Gear...4th
    Drawbar horsepower............................27.07
    Pull weight (lb.)..................................2,286
    Speed (mph) 4.44
    Percent slippage................................6.55
SAE drawbar horsepower............................20.62
SAE belt/PTO horsepower..........................26.32
Type ....tricycle
Front tire (in.)...5.50 x 16
Rear tire (in.)..11.00 x 38
Length (in.) 132.75
Height (in.) 59.87
Rear width (in.) 86.62
Tread width (in.)......................................56–88
Weight (lb.) 4,435
Gear/speed (mph) ....forward: 1/1.50,
2/2.50, 3/3.50, 4/4.50,
5/5.75, 6/10.00;
reverse: 1/2.50

John Deere 60

Manufacturer...John Deere Waterloo
Tractor Works,
Waterloo, IA
Nebraska test number 490
Test date ....April 15–21, 1953
Test tractor serial number 6015516
Years produced 1952–1957
Serial number range.................................6000001–6064096 end
Serial number location ....plate on right side of
main case
Number produced ....approximately 61,000
Engine ....John Deere 60
horizontal I-head
Test engine serial number.........................6015516
Cylinders 2
Bore and stroke (in.) ....5.50 x 6.75
Rated rpm 975
Compression ratio....................................4.70:1
Displacement (c.i.) 321
Fuel ....all-fuel/gasoline
Main tank capacity (gal.) 20.50
Auxiliary tank capacity (gal.) 1
Carburetor ....Marvel-Schebler
DLTX-84, 1.50-in.
Air cleaner ....Donaldson
Ignition ....Delco-Remy 12-v;
with 2, 6-v battery
Cooling capacity (gal.) 8.25

Maximum brake horsepower tests
    PTO/belt horsepower............................32.48
    Crankshaft rpm 975
    Fuel use (gal./hr.)...............................3.15

Maximum drawbar horsepower tests
    Gear...4th
    Drawbar horsepower............................29.17
    Pull weight (lb.)..................................2,491
    Speed (mph) 4.39
    Percent slippage................................5.47
SAE drawbar horsepower............................22.57
SAE belt/PTO horsepower..........................28.27
Type ....tricycle
Front tire (in.)...6.00 x 16
Rear tire (in.)..12.00 x 38
Length (in.) 139
Height (in.) 65.56
Rear width (in.) 86.62
Tread width (in.) 56–88
Weight (lb.) 5,300
Gear/speed (mph) ....forward: 1/1.50,
2/2.50, 3/3.50, 4/4.50,
5/6.25, 6/11.00;
reverse: 1/3.00

John Deere 70

Manufacturer...John Deere Waterloo
Tractor Works,
Waterloo, IA
Nebraska test number 493
Test date ....May 15–20, 1953
Test tractor serial number 7000003
Years produced 1953–1956
Serial number range.................................7000001–7043757 end
Serial number location ....plate on right side
main case
Number produced ....17,043 interspersed
Engine ....John Deere 70
horizontal I-head
Test engine serial number..........................7000003
Cylinders 2
Bore and stroke (in.) ....5.875 x 7.00
Rated rpm 975
Compression ratio....................................6.15:1
Displacement (c.i.) 379.5
Fuel ....gasoline
Fuel tank capacity (gal.) 24.50
Carburetor ....Marvel-Schebler
DLTX-82, 1.50-in.
Air cleaner ....Donaldson
Ignition ....Delco-Remy, 12-v
with 2, 6-v battery
Cooling capacity (gal.) 8.50

Maximum brake horsepower tests
    PTO/belt horsepower............................48.29
    Crankshaft rpm 975
    Fuel use (gal./hr.)...............................4.50

Maximum drawbar horsepower tests
    Gear...3rd
    Drawbar horsepower............................42.24
    Pull weight (lb.)..................................3,539
    Speed (mph) 4.48
    Percent slippage................................6.72
SAE drawbar horsepower............................33.16
SAE belt/PTO horsepower 42.80
Type ....tricycle
Front tire (in.)...6.00 x 16
Rear tire (in.)..13.00 x 38

Length (in.) 136.25
Height (in.) 65.56
Rear width (in.) 86.62
Tread width (in.) 60–88
Weight (lb.) 6,035
Gear/speed (mph) ....forward: 1/2.50, 2/3.50,
3/4.50, 4/6.50, 5/8.75,
6/12.50; reverse: 1/3.25

John Deere 40

Manufacturer...John Deere Dubuque
Tractor Works,
Dubuque, IA
Nebraska test number 503
Test date ....September 9–17, 1953
Test tractor serial number 67273
Years produced.....................................1953–1955
Serial number range..............................60001–77906 end
Serial number location ....stamped left side of
center frame
Number produced 17,906
Engine ....John Deere M
vertical I-head
Test engine serial number.......................79421
Cylinders 2
Bore and stroke (in.) ....4.00 x 4.00
Rated rpm 1,850
Compression ratio................................6.50:1
Displacement (c.i.) 100
Fuel ....gasoline
Fuel tank capacity (gal.) 10.5
Carburetor...Marvel-Schebler
TSX-530, 1.00-in.
Air cleaner ....Donaldson
Ignition...Delco-Remy with
6-v battery
Cooling capacity (gal.) 3.50
Maximum brake horsepower tests
PTO/belt horsepower...........................24.25
Crankshaft rpm 1,850
Fuel use (gal./hr.) 2.32
Maximum drawbar horsepower tests
Gear...3rd
Drawbar horsepower...........................21.71
Pull weight (lb.)..................................1,879
Speed (mph) 4.33
Percent slippage................................7.57
SAE drawbar horsepower........................17.16
SAE belt/PTO horsepower 21.45
Type ....tricycle
Front tire (in.)..5.00 x 15
Rear tire (in.)..9.00 x 34
Length (in.) 130.63
Height (in.) 56
Rear width (in.) 55.50
Tread width (in.) 48–96
Weight (lb.) 3,000
Gear/speed (mph) ....forward: 1/1.62, 2/3.12,
3/4.25, 4/12.00;
reverse: 1/2.50

John Deere 40 Standard

Manufacturer...John Deere Dubuque
Tractor Works,
Dubuque, IA

Nebraska test number 504
Test date ....September 9–23, 1953
Test tractor serial number 64727
Years produced.....................................1953–1955
Serial number range..............................60001–71814 end
Serial number location ....stamped on left side of
center frame
Number produced 11,814
Engine ....John Deere M
vertical I-head
Test engine serial number.......................64727
Cylinders 2
Bore and stroke (in.) ....4.00 x 4.00
Rated rpm 1,850
Compression ratio................................6.50:1
Displacement (c.i.) 101
Fuel ....gasoline
Fuel tank capacity (gal.) 10.5
Carburetor...Marvel-Schebler
TSX-530, 1.00-in.
Air cleaner ....Donaldson
Ignition...Delco-Remy with
6-v battery
Cooling capacity (gal.) 3.50
Maximum brake horsepower tests
PTO/belt horsepower...........................23.61
Crankshaft rpm 1,851
Fuel use (gal./hr.) 2.34
Maximum drawbar horsepower tests
Gear...3rd
Drawbar horsepower...........................21.01
Pull weight (lb.)..................................1,690
Speed (mph) 4.66
Percent slippage................................6.70
SAE drawbar horsepower........................16.77
SAE belt/PTO horsepower 21.13
Type ....standard
Front tire (in.)..5.00 x 15
Rear tire (in.)..10.00 x 24
Length (in.) 114.75
Height (in.) 54
Rear width (in.) 55.50
Tread width (in.) 38.50–54
Weight (lb.) 2,750
Gear/speed (mph) ....forward: 1/1.62, 2/3.12,
3/4.25, 4/12.00;
reverse: 1/2.50

John Deere 40 Crawler

Manufacturer...John Deere Dubuque
Tractor Works,
Dubuque, IA
Nebraska test number 505
Test date ....September 9–23, 1953
Test tractor serial number 84362
Years produced.....................................1953–1955
Serial number range..............................60001–71689 end
Serial number location ....stamped on left side of
center frame
Number produced 11,689
Engine ....John Deere, M
vertical I-head
Test engine serial number.......................62310
Cylinders 2
Bore and stroke (in.) ....4.00 x 4.00

Rated rpm 1,850
Compression ratio..6.50:1
Displacement (c.i.) 101
Fuel ....gasoline
Fuel tank capacity (gal.) 10.5
Carburetor ....Marvel-Schebler
TSX-530, 1.00-in.
Air cleaner ....Donaldson
Ignition...Delco-Remy with
6-v battery
Cooling capacity (gal.) 3.50

Maximum brake horsepower tests
    PTO/belt horsepower............................24.09
    Crankshaft rpm 1,850
    Fuel use (gal./hr.)................................2.27

Maximum drawbar horsepower tests
    Gear...3rd
    Drawbar horsepower..........................19.63
    Pull weight (lb.)..................................2,504
    Speed (mph).......................................2.94
    Percent slippage...............................1.06
SAE drawbar horsepower...............................15.11
SAE belt/PTO horsepower...............................21.24
Type ....tracklayer
Length (in.) 102
Height (in.)..50.50
Tread width (in.)...36 and 46 or 38 and
44
Weight (lb.) 3,875
Track length (in.)..178
Grouser shoe...31 links; (10), 12-in.
Gear/speed (mph) ....forward: 1/0.82,
2/2.21, 3/2.95, 4/5.31;
reverse: 1/1.64

John Deere 70 All-Fuel

Manufacturer..John Deere Waterloo
Tractor Works,
Waterloo, IA
Nebraska test number 506
Test date ....September 25 to
October 1, 1953
Test tractor serial number..............................7001448
Years produced..1953–1956
Serial number range......................................7000001–7043757 end
Serial number location ....plate on right side of
main case
Number produced ....2,964 interspersed
Engine ....John Deere 70
horizontal I-head
Test engine serial number..............................7001448
Cylinders 2
Bore and stroke (in.) ....6.125 x 7.00
Rated rpm 975
Compression ratio..4.60:1
Displacement (c.i.) 412.5
Fuel ....all-fuel/gasoline
Main tank capacity (gal.)................................24.50
Auxiliary tank capacity (gal.) 1.75
Carburetor ....Marvel-Schebler
DLTX-85, 1.50-in.
Air cleaner ....Donaldson
Ignition..Delco-Remy, 12-v
with 2, 6-v battery
Cooling capacity (gal.) 8.50

Maximum brake horsepower tests
    PTO/belt horsepower............................43.15
    Crankshaft rpm 975
    Fuel use (gal./hr.)................................4.23

Maximum drawbar horsepower tests
    Gear...3rd
    Drawbar horsepower..........................39.58
    Pull weight (lb.)..................................3,292
    Speed (mph).......................................4.51
    Percent slippage...............................5.71
SAE drawbar horsepower...............................30.75
SAE belt/PTO horsepower...............................38.22
Type ....tricycle
Front tire (in.)...6.00 x 16
Rear tire (in.)..13.00 x 38
Length (in.) 136.25
Height (in.)..65.56
Rear width (in.)..86.62
Tread width (in.)...60–88
Weight (lb.) 6,035
Gear/speed (mph) ....forward: 1/2.50,
2/3.50, 3/4.50, 4/6.50,
5/8.75, 6/12.50;
reverse: 1/3.25

John Deere 50

Manufacturer..John Deere Waterloo
Tractor Works,
Waterloo, IA
Nebraska test number 507
Test date ....September 25 to
October 2, 1953
Test tractor serial number..............................5014452
Years produced..1952–1956
Serial number range......................................5000001–5033751 end
Serial number location ....plate on right side of
main case
Number produced ....2,097 interspersed
Engine ....John Deere 50
horizontal I-head
Test engine serial number..............................5014452
Cylinders 2
Bore and stroke (in.) ....4.6875 x 5.50
Rated rpm 1,250
Compression ratio..5.35:1
Displacement (c.i.) 190.4
Fuel ....all-fuel/gasoline
Main tank capacity (gal.)................................15.50
Auxiliary tank capacity (gal.) 2
Carburetor ....Marvel-Schebler
DLTX-73, 1.50-in.
Air cleaner ....Donaldson
Ignition..Wico XB4023, 12-v
with 2, 6-v battery
Cooling capacity (gal.) 7

Maximum brake horsepower tests
    PTO/belt horsepower............................24.83
    Crankshaft rpm 1,250
    Fuel use (gal./hr.)................................2.46

Maximum drawbar horsepower tests
    Gear...3rd
    Drawbar horsepower..........................22.45
    Pull weight (lb.)..................................2,447
    Speed (mph).......................................3.44
    Percent slippage...............................5.86

SAE drawbar horsepower................................17.42
SAE belt/PTO horsepower 21.89
Type ....tricycle
Front tire (in.)..5.50 x 16
Rear tire (in.)..11.00 x 38
Length (in.) 132.75
Height (in.) 59.87
Rear width (in.) 86.62
Tread width (in.)...56–88
Weight (lb.) 4,435
Gear/speed (mph) ....forward: 1/1.50, 2/2.50,
3/3.50, 4/4.50, 5/5.75,
6/10.00; reverse: 1/2.50

John Deere 60 LPG

Manufacturer....................................John Deere Waterloo
Tractor Works,
Waterloo, IA
Nebraska test number 513
Test date ....November 6–12, 1953
Test tractor serial number.........................6026347
Years produced...................................1952–1957
Serial number range..............................6000001–6064096 end
Serial number location ....plate on right side
main case
Number produced ....approximately 61,000
Engine ....John Deere 60
horizontal I-head
Test engine serial number..........................6026347
Cylinders 2
Bore and stroke (in.) ....5.50 x 6.75
Rated rpm 975
Compression ratio....................................7.3:1
Displacement (c.i.) 321
Fuel ....LPG
Fuel tank capacity (gal.) 33
Carburetor ....John Deere AA6084R,
1.50-in.
Air cleaner ....Donaldson
Ignition...Delco-Remy, 12-v
with 2, 6-v battery
Cooling capacity (gal.) 8.25
Maximum brake horsepower tests
  PTO/belt horsepower.................................41.18
  Crankshaft rpm 975
  Fuel use (gal./hr.)................................4.71
Maximum drawbar horsepower tests
  Gear...3rd
  Drawbar horsepower.................................37.68
  Pull weight (lb.)..................................3,258
  Speed (mph) 4.34
  Percent slippage...................................6.40
SAE drawbar horsepower................................28.59
SAE belt/PTO horsepower 35.90
Type ....tricycle
Front tire (in.)..6.00 x 16
Rear tire (in.)...12.00 x 38
Length (in.) 134.44
Height (in.) 65.56
Rear width (in.) 86.62
Tread width (in.)...56–88
Weight (lb.) 5,300
Gear/speed (mph) ....forward: 1/1.50,
2/2.50, 3/3.50, 4/4.50,
5/6.25, 6/11.00;
reverse: 1/3.00

John Deere 70 LPG

Manufacturer....................................John Deere Waterloo
Tractor Works,
Waterloo, IA
Nebraska test number 514
Test date ....November 6–12, 1953
Test tractor serial number.........................7003465
Years produced...................................1953–1956
Serial number range..............................7000001–7043757 end
Serial number location ....plate on right side of
main case
Number produced ....6,618 interspersed
Engine ....John Deere 70
horizontal I-head
Test engine serial number..........................7003465
Cylinders 2
Bore and stroke (in.) ....5.875 x 7.00
Rated rpm 975
Compression ratio....................................7.3:1
Displacement (c.i.) 379.5
Fuel ....LPG
Fuel tank capacity (gal.) 33
Carburetor ....John Deere AA6084R,
1.50-in.
Air cleaner ....Donaldson
Ignition...Delco-Remy 12-v;
with 2, 6-v battery
Cooling capacity (gal.) 8.50
Maximum brake horsepower tests
  PTO/belt horsepower.................................50.86
  Crankshaft rpm 975
  Fuel use (gal./hr.)................................5.76
Maximum drawbar horsepower tests
  Gear...3rd
  Drawbar horsepower.................................45.60
  Pull weight (lb.)..................................3,819
  Speed (mph) 4.48
  Percent slippage...................................6.57
SAE drawbar horsepower................................34.58
SAE belt/PTO horsepower 44.17
Type ....tricycle
Front tire (in.)..6.00 x 16
Rear tire (in.)...13.00 x 38
Length (in.) 136.25
Height (in.) 65.56
Rear width (in.) 86.62
Tread width (in.)...60–88
Weight (lb.) 6,035
Gear/speed (mph) ....forward: 1/2.50, 2/3.50,
3/4.50, 4/6.50, 5/8.75,
6/12.50; reverse: 1/3.25

John Deere 70 Diesel, Row Crop

Manufacturer....................................John Deere Waterloo
Tractor Works,
Waterloo, IA
Nebraska test number 528
Test date ....October 19–22, 1954
Test tractor serial number.........................7017500
Years produced...................................1954–1956
Serial number range..............................7017500–7043757 end
Serial number location ....plate on right side
main case
Number produced ....14,397 interspersed
Engine ....John Deere 70
horizontal, I-head

Test engine serial number 7017500
Cylinders 2
Bore and stroke (in.) ....6.125 x 6.375
Rated rpm 1,125
Compression ratio 16:1
Displacement (c.i.) 376
Fuel ....diesel/gasoline
Main tank capacity (gal.) 20
Auxiliary tank capacity (gal.) 0.25
Carburetor ....start engine: Zenith
TU3-1/2 x 1C
Air cleaner ....Donaldson
Ignition ....start; Wico B4027
magneto/Delco-Remy,
6-v battery

Cooling capacity (gal.) 7
Maximum brake horsepower tests
    PTO/belt horsepower 50.40
    Crankshaft rpm 1,125
    Fuel use (gal./hr.) 2.84
Maximum drawbar horsepower tests
    Gear...4th
    Drawbar horsepower..........................45.09
    Pull weight (lb.).............................2,589
    Speed (mph) 6.53
    Percent slippage..............................4.30
SAE drawbar horsepower.............................34.25
SAE belt/PTO horsepower..............................43.77
Type ....tricycle
Front tire (in.)...6.00 x 16
Rear tire (in.)..13.00 x 38
Length (in.) 136.25
Height (in.) 65.56
Rear width (in.)..86.62
Tread width (in.).......................................60–88
Weight (lb.) 6,510
Gear/speed (mph) ....forward: 1/2.50,
2/3.50, 3/4.50, 4/6.50,
5/8.75, 6/12.50;
reverse: 1/3.25

John Deere 50 LPG
Manufacturer...John Deere Waterloo
Tractor Works,
Waterloo, IA
Nebraska test number 540
Test date ....May 9–13, 1955
Test tractor serial number..........................5024461
Years produced 1955–1956
Serial number range..................................5021977–5033751 end
Serial number location ....plate on right side of
main case
Number produced ....731, interspersed
Engine ....John Deere 50
horizontal I-head
Test engine serial number...........................5024461
Cylinders 2
Bore and stroke (in.) ....4.6875 x 5.50
Rated rpm 1,250
Compression ratio....................................8.0:1
Displacement (c.i.) 190.4
Fuel ....LPG
Fuel tank capacity (gal.) 33
Carburetor ....John Deere AB4872R,
1.375-in.

Air cleaner ....Donaldson
Ignition ....Delco-Remy 12-v;
with 2, 6-v battery
Cooling capacity (gal.) 4.75
Maximum brake horsepower tests
    PTO/belt horsepower..........................31.20
    Crankshaft rpm 1,250
    Fuel use (gal./hr.) 3.62
Maximum drawbar horsepower tests
    Gear..4th
    Drawbar horsepower..........................28.11
    Pull weight (lb.).............................2,389
    Speed (mph) 4.41
    Percent slippage..............................6.07
SAE drawbar horsepower.............................21.90
SAE belt/PTO horsepower...........................27.45
Type ....tricycle
Front tire (in.)..5.50 x 16
Rear tire (in.)..11.00 x 38
Length (in.) 132.75
Height (in.) 59.87
Rear width (in.)..86.62
Tread width (in.).......................................56–88
Weight (lb.) 4,435
Gear/speed (mph) ....forward: 1/1.50,
2/2.50, 3/3.50, 4/4.50,
5/5.75, 6/10.00;
reverse: 1/2.50

John Deere 40 Standard
Manufacturer...John Deere Dubuque
Tractor Works,
Dubuque, IA
Nebraska test number 546
Test date ....June 3–10, 1955
Test tractor serial number...........................40S 69114
Years produced 1953–1955
Serial number range..................................60001–71814 end
Serial number location ....stamped left side of
center frame
Number produced 11,814
Engine ....John Deere M
vertical I-head
Test engine serial number...........................69114
Cylinders 2
Bore and stroke (in.) ....4.00 x 4.00
Rated rpm 1,850
Compression ratio....................................5.20:1
Displacement (c.i.) 101
Fuel ....all-fuel/gasoline
Main tank capacity (gal.) 10.5
Auxiliary tank capacity (gal.) 0.9
Carburetor ....Marvel-Schebler
TSX-562
Air cleaner ....Donaldson
Ignition ....Delco-Remy with
6-v battery
Cooling capacity (gal.) 3.50
Maximum brake horsepower tests
    PTO/belt horsepower..........................20.04
    Crankshaft rpm 1,850
    Fuel use (gal./hr.) 2.00
Maximum drawbar horsepower tests
    Gear..3rd
    Drawbar horsepower..........................18.12

Pull weight (lb.) 1,707
Speed (mph) 3.98
Percent slippage 7.72
SAE drawbar horsepower 14.25
SAE belt/PTO horsepower 17.76
Type ....standard
Front tire (in.) ....5.00 x 15
Rear tire (in.) ....9.00 x 24
Length (in.) 114.75
Height (in.) 56
Rear width (in.) 55.50
Weight (lb.) 2,750
Gear/speed (mph) ....forward: 1/1.625,
2/3.125, 3/4.25,
4/12.00; reverse: 1/2.50

John Deere 80 Diesel
Manufacturer ....John Deere Waterloo
Tractor Works,
Waterloo, IA
Nebraska test number 567
Test date ....October 27 to
November 1, 1955
Test tractor serial number 8000002
Years produced 1955–1956
Serial number range.......................8000001–8003500 end
Serial number location ....plate on right side
main case
Number produced ....approximately 3,500
Engine ....John Deere 80
horizontal I-head
Test engine serial number 8000002
Cylinders 2
Bore and stroke (in.) ....6.125 x 8.00
Rated rpm 1,125
Compression ratio.........................16:1
Displacement (c.i.) 471.5
Fuel ....diesel/gasoline
Main tank capacity (gal.) 32.50
Auxiliary tank capacity (gal.) 0.25
Carburetor ....start engine; Zenith
TU3-1/2 x 1C
Air cleaner ....Donaldson
Ignition......................................Delco-Remy with
6-v battery
Cooling capacity (gal.) 8.75
Maximum brake horsepower tests
PTO/belt horsepower 65.33
Crankshaft rpm 1,125
Fuel use (gal./hr.) 3.72
Maximum drawbar horsepower tests
Gear...................................3rd
Drawbar horsepower 60.04
Pull weight (lb.) 5,161
Speed (mph) 4.36
Percent slippage 7.60
SAE drawbar horsepower 46.32
SAE belt/PTO horsepower 57.49
Type ....standard
Front tire (in.) ....7.50 x 18
Rear tire (in.) ....15.00 x 34
Length (in.) 137.63
Height (in.) 82
Rear width (in.) 79.50
Tread width (in.) 64–68

Weight (lb.) 8,028
Gear/speed (mph) ....forward: 1/2.50,
2/3.50, 3/4.50, 4/5.33,
5/6.75, 6/12.25;
reverse: 1/2.70

John Deere 520 LPG
Manufacturer ....John Deere Waterloo
Tractor Works,
Waterloo, IA
Nebraska test number 590
Test date ....September 5–11, 1956
Test tractor serial number 5200017
Years produced 1956–1958
Serial number range.......................5200000–5213189 end
Serial number location ....plate on right side of
main case
Number produced ....764 interspersed
Engine ....John Deere 520
horizontal I-head
Test engine serial number 5200017
Cylinders 2
Bore and stroke (in.) ....4.6875 x 5.50
Rated rpm 1,325
Compression ratio.........................8.75:1
Displacement (c.i.) 189.8
Fuel ....LPG
Fuel tank capacity (gal.) 24
Carburetor ....John Deere AB5285R
Air cleaner ....Donaldson
Ignition......................................Delco-Remy, 12-v with
2, 6-v battery
Cooling capacity (gal.) 4.50
Maximum brake horsepower tests
PTO/belt horsepower 37.24
Crankshaft rpm 1,325
Fuel use (gal./hr.) 3.88
Maximum drawbar horsepower tests
Gear...................................4th
Drawbar horsepower 33.30
Pull weight (lb.) 2,891
Speed (mph) 4.32
Percent slippage 5.42
SAE drawbar horsepower 25.63
SAE belt/PTO horsepower 32.38
Type ....tricycle
Front tire (in.) ....5.50 x 16
Rear tire (in.) ....13.90 x 36
Length (in.) 132.75
Height (in.) 59.75
Rear width (in.) 86.62
Tread width (in.) 56–88
Weight (lb.) 5,110
Gear/speed (mph) ....forward: 1/1.50,
2/2.50, 3/3.50, 4/4.50,
5/5.75, 6/10.00;
reverse: 1/2.50

John Deere 620 LPG
Manufacturer ....John Deere Waterloo
Tractor Works,
Waterloo, IA
Nebraska test number 591
Test date ....September 6–11, 1956
Test tractor serial number 6200017

Years produced 1956–1960
Serial number range...........................6200000–6223247 end
Serial number location ....plate on right side main case
Number produced 22,532
Engine ....John Deere 620 horizontal I-head
Test engine serial number...................6200017
Cylinders 2
Bore and stroke (in.) ....5.50 x 6.375
Rated rpm 1,125
Compression ratio 8.1:1
Displacement (c.i.) 302.9
Fuel ....LPG
Fuel tank capacity (gal.) 33
Carburetor ....John Deere AA6821R, 0.875-in.
Air cleaner ....Donaldson
Ignition...Delco-Remy, 12-v with 2, 6-v battery
Cooling capacity (gal.) 6.50

Maximum brake horsepower tests
    PTO/belt horsepower.....................49.19
    Crankshaft rpm 1,125
    Fuel use (gal./hr.) 5.17

Maximum drawbar horsepower tests
    Gear...4th
    Drawbar horsepower.......................44.81
    Pull weight (lb.).............................3,881
    Speed (mph) 4.33
    Percent slippage............................7.16
SAE drawbar horsepower.....................34.34
SAE belt/PTO horsepower 42.79
Type ....tricycle
Front tire (in.).....................................6.00 x 16
Rear tire (in.)......................................13.60 x 38
Length (in.) 135.25
Height (in.) 66
Rear width (in.) 86.62
Tread width (in.)..................................56–88
Weight (lb.) 6,150
Gear/speed (mph) ....forward: 1/1.50, 2/2.50, 3/3.50, 4/4.50, 5/6.50, 6/11.50; reverse: 1/3.00

John Deere 520

Manufacturer.......................................John Deere Waterloo Tractor Works, Waterloo, IA
Nebraska test number 592
Test date ....September 13–17, 1956
Test tractor serial number...................5200891
Years produced 1956–1958
Serial number range...........................5200000–5213189 end
Serial number location ....plate on right side main case
Number produced ....240, interspersed
Engine ....John Deere 520 horizontal I-head
Test engine serial number...................5200891
Cylinders 2
Bore and stroke (in.) ....4.6875 x 5.50

Rated rpm 1,325
Compression ratio...............................4.90:1
Displacement (c.i.) 189.8
Fuel ....all-fuel/gasoline
Main tank capacity (gal.) 18
Auxiliary tank capacity (gal.) 1
Carburetor ....Marvel-Schebler DLTX-96, 1.50-in.
Air cleaner ....Donaldson
Ignition...Delco-Remy 12-v; with 2, 6-v battery
Cooling capacity (gal.) 4.50

Maximum brake horsepower tests
    PTO/belt horsepower.....................25.41
    Crankshaft rpm 1,325
    Fuel use (gal./hr.) 2.52

Maximum drawbar horsepower tests
    Gear...3rd
    Drawbar horsepower.......................23.98
    Pull weight (lb.).............................2,674
    Speed (mph) 3.36
    Percent slippage............................4.67
SAE drawbar horsepower.....................18.58
SAE belt/PTO horsepower 22.62
Type ....tricycle
Front tire (in.).....................................5.50 x 16
Rear tire (in.)......................................13.90 x 36
Length (in.) 132.75
Height (in.) 59.75
Rear width (in.) 86.62
Tread width (in.)..................................56–88
Weight (lb.) 5,110
Gear/speed (mph) ....forward: 1/1.50, 2/2.50, 3/3.50, 4/4.50, 5/5.75, 6/10.00; reverse: 1/2.50

John Deere 720 LPG

Manufacturer.......................................John Deere Waterloo Tractor Works, Waterloo, IA
Nebraska test number 593
Test date ....September 17–19, 1956
Test tractor serial number...................7200017
Years produced 1956–1958
Serial number range...........................7200000–7229002 end
Serial number location ....plate on right side main case
Number produced ....4,037 interspersed
Engine ....John Deere 720 horizontal I-head
Test engine serial number...................7200017
Cylinders 2
Bore and stroke (in.) ....6.00 x 6.375
Rated rpm 1,125
Compression ratio...............................7.94:1
Displacement (c.i.) 360.5
Fuel ....LPG
Fuel tank capacity (gal.) 33
Carburetor ....John Deere AF2828R
Air cleaner ....Donaldson
Ignition...Delco-Remy 12-v; with 2, 6-v battery
Cooling capacity (gal.) 7.12

Maximum brake horsepower tests
>PTO/belt horsepower............................57.33
>Crankshaft rpm 1,125
>Fuel use (gal./hr.)................................6.29

Maximum drawbar horsepower tests
>Gear...4th
>Drawbar horsepower............................52.38
>Pull weight (lb.)...................................4,664
>Speed (mph) 4.21
>Percent slippage.................................6.65

SAE drawbar horsepower............................40.63
SAE belt/PTO horsepower............................50.67
Type ....tricycle
Front tire (in.) ....6.00 x 16
Rear tire (in.) ....15.50 x 38
Length (in.) 135.25
Height (in.) 88.25
Rear width (in.) 86.62
Tread width (in.) 60–88
Weight (lb.) 7,405
Gear/speed (mph) ....forward: 1/1.50, 2/2.25, 3/3.50, 4/4.50, 5/5.75, 6/11.50; reverse: 1/3.50

John Deere 720 Diesel

Manufacturer...John Deere Waterloo Tractor Works, Waterloo, IA
Nebraska test number 594
Test date ....September 18–22, 1956
Test tractor serial number............................7200022
Years produced 1956–1958
Serial number range......................................7200000–7229002 end
Serial number location ....plate on right side main case
Number produced ....17,594 interspersed
Engine ....John Deere 720 horizontal I-head
Test engine serial number............................7200022
Cylinders 2
Bore and stroke (in.) ....6.125 x 6.375
Rated rpm 1,125
Compression ratio...16:1
Displacement (c.i.) 376
Fuel ....diesel/gasoline
Main tank capacity (gal.).............................20
Auxiliary tank capacity (gal.) 0.25
Carburetor...start engine; Zenith TU3-1/2 x 1C
Air cleaner ....Donaldson
Ignition...Delco-Remy with 6-v or 24, 12-v battery
Cooling capacity (gal.) 7

Maximum brake horsepower tests
>PTO/belt horsepower............................56.66
>Crankshaft rpm 1,125
>Fuel use (gal./hr.)................................3.15

Maximum drawbar horsepower tests
>Gear...4th
>Drawbar horsepower............................51.66
>Pull weight (lb.)...................................4,644
>Speed (mph) 4.17
>Percent slippage.................................7.85

SAE drawbar horsepower............................40.25

SAE belt/PTO horsepower............................50.01
Type ....tricycle
Front tire (in.) ....6.00 x 16
Rear tire (in.) ....15.50 x 38
Length (in.) 135.25
Height (in.) ....88.25 overall
Rear width (in.) 86.62
Tread width (in.) 60–88
Weight (lb.) 7,105
Gear/speed (mph) ....forward: 1/1.50, 2/2.25, 3/3.50, 4/4.50, 5/5.75, 6/11.50; reverse: 1/3.50

John Deere 520

Manufacturer...John Deere Waterloo Tractor Works, Waterloo, IA
Nebraska test number 597
Test date ....October 6–10, 1956
Test tractor serial number............................5200003
Years produced 1956–1958
Serial number range......................................5200000–5213189 end
Serial number location ....plate on right side of main case
Number produced ....12,040 interspersed
Engine ....John Deere 520 horizontal I-head
Test engine serial number............................5200003
Cylinders 2
Bore and stroke (in.) ....4.6875 x 5.50
Rated rpm 1,325
Compression ratio...7.1:1
Displacement (c.i.) 189.8
Fuel ....gasoline
Fuel tank capacity (gal.) 18
Carburetor...Marvel-Schebler DLTX-99, 1.50-in.
Air cleaner ....Donaldson
Ignition...Delco-Remy 12-v; with 2, 6-v battery
Cooling capacity (gal.) 4.50

Maximum brake horsepower tests
>PTO/belt horsepower............................37.52
>Crankshaft rpm 1,325
>Fuel use (gal./hr.)................................3.27

Maximum drawbar horsepower tests
>Gear...4th
>Drawbar horsepower............................33.27
>Pull weight (lb.)...................................2,898
>Speed (mph) 4.30
>Percent slippage.................................5.32

SAE drawbar horsepower............................25.73
SAE belt/PTO horsepower............................32.79
Type ....tricycle
Front tire (in.) ....5.50 x 16
Rear tire (in.) ....13.90 x 36
Length (in.) 132.75
Height (in.) 59.75
Rear width (in.) 86.62
Tread width (in.) 56–88
Weight (lb.) 5,110
Gear/speed (mph) ....forward: 1/1.50, 2/2.50, 3/3.50, 4/4.50, 5/5.75, 6/10.00; reverse: 1/2.50

John Deere 620

Manufacturer...John Deere Waterloo Tractor Works, Waterloo, IA
Nebraska test number.................................598
Test date ....October 10–15, 1956
Test tractor serial number........................6200000
Years produced 1956–1960
Serial number range...................................6200000–6223247 end
Serial number location ....plate on right side of main case
Number produced 22,532
Engine ....John Deere 620 horizontal I-head
Test engine serial number.........................6200000
Cylinders 2
Bore and stroke (in.) ....5.50 x 6.375
Rated rpm..1,125
Compression ratio......................................6.38:1
Displacement (c.i.) 302.9
Fuel ....gasoline
Fuel tank capacity (gal.) 22.25
Carburetor...Marvel-Schebler DLTX-94, 1.6875-in.
Air cleaner ....Donaldson
Ignition..Delco-Remy 12-v; with 2, 6-v battery
Cooling capacity (gal.) 6.50
Maximum brake horsepower tests
    PTO/belt horsepower...........................46.75
    Crankshaft rpm....................................1,125
    Fuel use (gal./hr.) 4.22
Maximum drawbar horsepower tests
    Gear..4th
    Drawbar horsepower.............................42.40
    Pull weight (lb.).....................................3,639
    Speed (mph) 4.37
    Percent slippage..................................5.87
SAE drawbar horsepower...........................33.12
SAE belt/PTO horsepower 41.38
Type ....tricycle
Front tire (in.)...6.00 x 16
Rear tire (in.)..13.60 x 38
Length (in.) 135.25
Height (in.) 66
Rear width (in.) 86.62
Tread width (in.)..56–88
Weight (lb.) 6,150
Gear/speed (mph) ....forward: 1/1.50, 2/2.50, 3/3.50, 4/4.50, 5/6.50, 6/11.50; reverse: 1/3.00

John Deere 420 W; Two-Row Utility

Manufacturer...John Deere Dubuque Tractor Works, Dubuque, IA
Nebraska test number.................................599
Test date ....October 13–25, 1956
Test tractor serial number........................420W 91466
Years produced 1956–1958
Serial number range...................................80001–136866 end
Serial number location ....stamped left side of center frame
Number produced ....11,197 interspersed

Engine ....John Deere 420 vertical I-head
Test engine serial number.........................B 1582
Cylinders 2
Bore and stroke (in.) ....4.25 x 4.00
Rated rpm..1,850
Compression ratio......................................7.2:1
Displacement (c.i.) 113
Fuel ....gasoline
Fuel tank capacity (gal.) 10.5
Carburetor...Marvel-Schebler TSX-641, 1.00-in.
Air cleaner ....Donaldson
Ignition..Delco-Remy with 6-v battery
Cooling capacity (gal.) 2.75
Maximum brake horsepower tests
    PTO/belt horsepower...........................28.31
    Crankshaft rpm....................................1,850
    Fuel use (gal./hr.) 2.56
Maximum drawbar horsepower tests
    Gear..3rd
    Drawbar horsepower.............................26.15
    Pull weight (lb.).....................................2,162
    Speed (mph) 4.54
    Percent slippage..................................6.25
SAE drawbar horsepower...........................20.31
SAE belt/PTO horsepower 24.83
Type ....standard
Front tire (in.)...6.00 x 16
Rear tire (in.)..12.00 x 28
Length (in.) 114.75
Height (in.) 55.50
Rear width (in.) 55.50
Tread width (in.)..40.88–56.31
Weight (lb.) 2,850
Gear/speed (mph) ....forward: 1/1.62, 2/3.12, 3/4.25, 4/12.00, 5/optional; reverse: 1/2.50

John Deere 420 S, Standard

Manufacturer...John Deere Dubuque Tractor Works, Dubuque, IA
Nebraska test number.................................600
Test date ....October 13–25, 1956
Test tractor serial number........................420S 88206
Years produced 1956–1958
Serial number range...................................80001–136866 end
Serial number location ....stamped left side of center frame
Number produced ....3,908 interspersed
Engine ....John Deere 420 vertical I-head
Test engine serial number.........................A 8270
Cylinders 2
Bore and stroke (in.) ....4.25 x 4.00
Rated rpm..1,850
Compression ratio......................................5.1:1
Displacement (c.i.) 113
Fuel ....all-fuel/gasoline
Main tank capacity (gal.) 10.50
Auxiliary tank capacity (gal.) 0.9
Carburetor...Marvel-Schebler TSX-678, 1.00-in.

Air cleaner ....Donaldson
Ignition ....Delco-Remy with
6-v battery
Cooling capacity (gal.) 2.75
Maximum brake horsepower tests
PTO/belt horsepower............................22.73
Crankshaft rpm 1,850
Fuel use (gal./hr.)................................2.28
Maximum drawbar horsepower tests
Gear..3rd
Drawbar horsepower.............................21.29
Pull weight (lb.)....................................1,891
Speed (mph) 4.22
Percent slippage..................................7.32
SAE drawbar horsepower................................16.42
SAE belt/PTO horsepower...............................19.95
Type ....standard
Front tire (in.) ....5.00 x 15
Rear tire (in.) ....10.00 x 24
Length (in.) 114.75
Height (in.) 55.50
Rear width (in.) 55.50
Tread width (in.) 38.75–54.25
Weight (lb.) 2,750
Gear/speed (mph) ....forward: 1/1.62, 2/3.12,
3/4.25, 4/12.00;
reverse: 1/2.50

John Deere 420 Crawler
Manufacturer...John Deere Dubuque
Tractor Works,
Dubuque, IA
Nebraska test number 601
Test date ....October 15–25, 1956
Test tractor serial number 420C 88443
Years produced 1956–1958
Serial number range......................................80001–136866 end
Serial number location ....stamped left side of
center frame
Number produced ....17,882 interspersed
Engine...John Deere 420
horizontal I-head
Test engine serial number ....A 8476
Cylinders 2
Bore and stroke (in.) ....4.25 x 4.00
Rated rpm 1,850
Compression ratio...7.2:1
Displacement (c.i.) 113
Fuel ....gasoline
Fuel tank capacity (gal.) 10.5
Carburetor...Marvel-Schebler
TSX-641, 1.00-in.
Air cleaner ....Donaldson
Ignition ....Delco-Remy with
6-v battery
Cooling capacity (gal.) 2.75
Maximum brake horsepower tests
PTO/belt horsepower............................28.76
Crankshaft rpm 1,850
Fuel use (gal./hr.)................................2.59
Maximum drawbar horsepower tests
Gear..3rd
Drawbar horsepower.............................23.53
Pull weight (lb.)....................................3,039
Speed (mph) 2.90
Percent slippage..................................2.34

SAE drawbar horsepower................................18.09
SAE belt/PTO horsepower...............................25.26
Type ....tracklayer
Length (in.) 102
Height (in.) 51.87
Rear width (in.) 67.25
Tread width (in.) 36–46
Weight (lb.) 4,825
Track length (in.)..176.50
Grouser shoe..31 links; 10-in.
Gear/speed (mph) ....forward: 1/0.87,
2/2.25, 3/3.00, 4/5.25;
reverse: 1/1.75

John Deere 620
Manufacturer...John Deere Waterloo
Tractor Works,
Waterloo, IA
Nebraska test number 604
Test date ....November 1–8, 1956
Test tractor serial number 6200287
Years produced 1956–1960
Serial number range......................................6200000–6223247 end
Serial number location ....plate on right side of
main case
Number produced 22,532
Engine...John Deere 620
horizontal I-head
Test engine serial number 6200287
Cylinders 2
Bore and stroke (in.) ....5.50 x 6.375
Rated rpm 1,125
Compression ratio...4.78:1
Displacement (c.i.) 302.9
Fuel ....all-fuel/gasoline
Main tank capacity (gal.) 22.25
Auxiliary tank capacity (gal.) 1
Carburetor...Marvel-Schebler DLTX-
97, 1.6875-in.
Air cleaner ....Donaldson
Ignition ....Delco-Remy 12-v; with
2, 6-v battery
Cooling capacity (gal.) 6.50
Maximum brake horsepower tests
PTO/belt horsepower............................34.57
Crankshaft rpm 1,125
Fuel use (gal./hr.)................................3.39
Maximum drawbar horsepower tests
Gear..4th
Drawbar horsepower.............................32.37
Pull weight (lb.)....................................2,731
Speed (mph) 4.45
Percent slippage..................................3.94
SAE drawbar horsepower................................24.50
SAE belt/PTO horsepower...............................30.33
Type ....tricycle
Front tire (in.) ....6.00 x 16
Rear tire (in.) ....13.60 x 38
Length (in.) 135.25
Height (in.) 66
Rear width (in.) 86.62
Tread width (in.) 56–88
Weight (lb.) 6,150
Gear/speed (mph) ....forward: 1/1.50, 2/2.50,
3/3.50, 4/4.50, 5/6.50,
6/11.50; reverse: 1/3.00

John Deere

John Deere 720

Manufacturer	John Deere Waterloo Tractor Works, Waterloo, IA
Nebraska test number	605
Test date	November 6–12, 1956
Test tractor serial number	7200000
Years produced	1956–1958
Serial number range	7200000–7229002 end
Serial number location	plate on right side main case
Number produced	5,442 interspersed
Engine	John Deere 720 horizontal I-head
Test engine serial number	7200000
Cylinders	2
Bore and stroke (in.)	6.00 x 6.375
Rated rpm	1,125
Compression ratio	6.14:1
Displacement (c.i.)	360.5
Fuel	gasoline
Fuel tank capacity (gal.)	26.50
Carburetor	Marvel-Schebler DLTX-95, 1.6875-in.
Air cleaner	Donaldson
Ignition	Delco-Remy 12-v; with 2, 6-v battery
Cooling capacity (gal.)	7.12

Maximum brake horsepower tests

PTO/belt horsepower	57.77
Crankshaft rpm	1,125
Fuel use (gal./hr.)	5.19

Maximum drawbar horsepower tests

Gear	4th
Drawbar horsepower	53.41
Pull weight (lb.)	4,718
Speed (mph)	4.25
Percent slippage	5.70
SAE drawbar horsepower	39.79
SAE belt/PTO horsepower	50.25
Type	tricycle
Front tire (in.)	6.00 x 16
Rear tire (in.)	15.50 x 38
Length (in.)	135.25
Height (in.)	88.25
Rear width (in.)	86.62
Tread width (in.)	60–88
Weight (lb.)	7,405
Gear/speed (mph)	forward: 1/1.50, 2/2.25, 3/3.50, 4/4.50, 5/5.75, 6/11.50; reverse: 1/3.50

John Deere 720

Manufacturer	John Deere Waterloo Tractor Works, Waterloo, IA
Nebraska test number	606
Test date	November 12–19, 1956
Test tractor serial number	7200003
Years produced	1956–1958
Serial number range	7200000–7229002 end
Serial number location	plate on right side main case
Number produced	500, interspersed
Engine	John Deere 720 horizontal I-head
Test engine serial number	7200003
Cylinders	2
Bore and stroke (in.)	6.00 x 6.375
Rated rpm	1,125
Compression ratio	4.91:1
Displacement (c.i.)	360.5
Fuel	all-fuel/gasoline
Main tank capacity (gal.)	26
Auxiliary tank capacity (gal.)	1
Carburetor	Marvel-Schebler DLTX-98, 1.6875-in.
Air cleaner	Donaldson
Ignition	Delco-Remy 12-v; with 2, 6-v battery
Cooling capacity (gal.)	7.12

Maximum brake horsepower tests

PTO/belt horsepower	44.13
Crankshaft rpm	1,125
Fuel use (gal./hr.)	4.35

Maximum drawbar horsepower tests

Gear	4th
Drawbar horsepower	40.78
Pull weight (lb.)	3,538
Speed (mph)	4.32
Percent slippage	4.22
SAE drawbar horsepower	30.97
SAE belt/PTO horsepower	38.53
Type	tricycle
Front tire (in.)	6.00 x 16
Rear tire (in.)	15.50 x 38
Length (in.)	135.25
Height (in.)	88.25
Rear width (in.)	86.62
Tread width (in.)	60–88
Weight (lb.)	7,405
Gear/speed (mph)	forward: 1/1.50, 2/2.25, 3/3.50, 4/4.50, 5/5.75, 6/11.50; reverse: 1/3.50

John Deere 820 Diesel

Manufacturer	John Deere Waterloo Tractor Works, Waterloo, IA
Nebraska test number	632
Test date	October 14–18, 1957
Test tractor serial number	8203452
Years produced	1956–1958
Serial number range	8200000–8207078 end
Serial number location	plate on right side main case
Number produced	6,864
Engine	John Deere 820 horizontal I-head
Test engine serial number	8203452
Cylinders	2
Bore and stroke (in.)	6.125 x 8.00
Rated rpm	1,125
Compression ratio	16:1
Displacement (c.i.)	471.5
Fuel	diesel/gasoline
Main tank capacity (gal.)	32.50
Auxiliary tank capacity (gal.)	0.25

Carburetor ....start engine: Zenith TU3-1/2 x 1C
Air cleaner ....Donaldson
Ignition ....start engine; Delco-Remy with 6-v battery
Cooling capacity (gal.) 8.75

Maximum brake horsepower tests
    PTO/belt horsepower............................72.82
    Crankshaft rpm 1,125
    Fuel use (gal./hr.)................................4.21

Maximum drawbar horsepower tests
    Gear...3rd
    Drawbar horsepower..............................67.15
    Pull weight (lb.)...................................5,898
    Speed (mph).......................................4.27
    Percent slippage...................................8.06
SAE drawbar horsepower..........................52.25
SAE belt/PTO horsepower..........................64.26
Type ....standard
Front tire (in.) ....7.50 x 18
Rear tire (in.) ....15.00 x 34
Length (in.) 142.75
Height (in.) 81
Rear width (in.) 79.50
Tread width (in.).......................................64.50–68.50
Weight (lb.) 8,745
Gear/speed (mph) ....forward: 1/2.50, 2/3.50, 3/4.50, 4/5.33, 5/6.75, 6/12.25; reverse: 1/2.70

John Deere 435 Diesel
Manufacturer...John Deere Dubuque Tractor Works, Dubuque, IA
Nebraska test number 716
Test date ....September 8–18, 1959
Test tractor serial number 435532
Years produced 1959–1960
Serial number range..................................435001–439626 end
Serial number location ....plate at base of instrument panel
Number produced 4,625
Engine ....GM 2-53 Two Cycle vertical
Test engine serial number..........................2D 3363
Cylinders 2
Bore and stroke (in.) ....3.875 x 4.50
Rated rpm 1,850
Compression ratio....................................17.0:1
Displacement (c.i.) 106.1
Fuel ....diesel
Fuel tank capacity (gal.) 10.5
Carburetor..GM injector pump
Air cleaner ....Donaldson
Ignition..Delco-Remy with 12-v battery
Cooling capacity (gal.) 2.50

Maximum brake horsepower tests
    PTO/belt horsepower............................32.91
    Crankshaft rpm 1,850
    Fuel use (gal./hr.)................................2.29

Maximum drawbar horsepower tests
    Gear...3rd
    Drawbar horsepower............................27.59

    Pull weight (lb.)...................................2,044
    Speed (mph) 5.06
    Percent slippage..................................4.63
SAE drawbar horsepower..........................28.41
SAE belt/PTO horsepower.........................32.91
Type ....standard
Front tire (in.) ....6.00 x 16
Rear tire (in.) ....13.60 x 28
Length (in.) 136.12
Height (in.) 54.50
Rear width (in.) 85.75
Tread width (in.).......................................48–90
Weight (lb.) 3,750
Gear/speed (mph) ....forward: 1/1.87, 2/3.50, 3/4.75, 4/13.50; reverse: 1/2.87

John Deere 440 ID; Diesel
Manufacturer...John Deere Dubuque Tractor Works, Dubuque, IA
Nebraska test number 717
Test date ....September 9–19, 1959
Test tractor serial number 453282
Years produced 1958–1960
Serial number range..................................440001–461929 end
Serial number location ....stamped left side of center frame and bell housing
Number produced ....21,928, all models
Engine ....GM 2-53 Two Cycle vertical
Test engine serial number..........................2D 3353
Cylinders 2
Bore and stroke (in.) ....3.875 x 4.50
Rated rpm 1,850
Compression ratio....................................17.0:1
Displacement (c.i.) 106.2
Fuel ....diesel
Fuel tank capacity (gal.) 10.50
Carburetor..GM injector pump
Air cleaner ....Donaldson
Ignition..Delco-Remy with 12-v battery
Cooling capacity (gal.) 2.50

Maximum brake horsepower tests
    PTO/belt horsepower............................32.70
    Crankshaft rpm 1,850
    Fuel use (gal./hr.)................................2.27

Maximum drawbar horsepower tests
    Gear...3rd
    Drawbar horsepower............................26.68
    Pull weight (lb.)...................................1,976
    Speed (mph).......................................5.06
    Percent slippage...................................4.47
SAE drawbar horsepower..........................27.51
SAE belt/PTO horsepower 32.70
Type ....standard
Front tire (in.) ....6.00 x 16
Rear tire (in.) ....13.60 x 28
Length (in.) 125.63
Height (in.) 53.86
Rear width (in.) 74.50
Tread width (in.).......................................60

Weight (lb.) 4,200
Gear/speed (mph) ....forward: 1/2.00, 2/3.93, 3/5.25, 4/6.82, 5/12.93; reverse: 1/2.91

John Deere 440 I

Manufacturer..John Deere Dubuque Tractor Works, Dubuque, IA
Nebraska test number 718
Test date ....September 10–21, 1959
Test tractor serial number.......................449401
Years produced 1958–1960
Serial number range................................440001–461929 end
Serial number location ....stamped left side center frame and bell housing
Number produced ....21,928, all models
Engine ....John Deere 440 vertical
Test engine serial number.......................G 4071
Cylinders 2
Bore and stroke (in.) ....4.25 x 4.00
Rated rpm 2,000
Compression ratio..................................7.5:1
Displacement (c.i.) 113
Fuel ....gasoline
Fuel tank capacity (gal.) 10.5
Carburetor ....Marvel Schebler TSX-777, 1.00-in.
Air cleaner ....Donaldson
Ignition..Delco-Remy with 12-v battery
Cooling capacity (gal.) 2.75
Maximum brake horsepower tests
    PTO/belt horsepower...........................31.06
    Crankshaft rpm 2,000
    Fuel use (gal./hr.)................................2.75
Maximum drawbar horsepower tests
    Gear..3rd
    Drawbar horsepower............................26.17
    Pull weight (lb.)...................................1,793
    Speed (mph)...5.47
    Percent slippage..................................4.66
SAE drawbar horsepower.......................26.23
SAE belt/PTO horsepower......................31.06
Type ....standard
Front tire (in.) ....6.00 x 16
Rear tire (in.)..13.60 x 28
Length (in.) 126.00
Height (in.) 53.86
Rear width (in.) 74.50
Tread width (in.)......................................60
Weight (lb.) 3,830
Gear/speed (mph) ....forward: 1/2.17, 2/4.25, 3/5.68, 4/7.38, 5/13.98; reverse: 1/3.15

John Deere 440 ICD, Diesel

Manufacturer...John Deere Dubuque Tractor Works, Dubuque, IA
Nebraska test number 719
Test date ....September 10 to October 1, 1959

Test tractor serial number..........................449354
Years produced 1958–1960
Serial number range................................440001–461929 end
Serial number location ....stamped left side center frame and bell housing
Number produced ....21,928, all models
Engine ....GM 2-53 Two-cycle vertical
Test engine serial number 2D 463
Cylinders 2
Bore and stroke (in.) ....3.875 x 4.50
Rated rpm 1,850
Compression ratio..................................17.0:1
Displacement (c.i.) 106.2
Fuel ....diesel
Fuel tank capacity (gal.) 10.50
Carburetor ....GM injector pump
Air cleaner ....Donaldson
Ignition..Delco-Remy with 12-v battery
Cooling capacity (gal.) 2.50
Maximum brake horsepower tests
    PTO/belt horsepower...........................32.88
    Crankshaft rpm 1,850
    Fuel use (gal./hr.)................................2.25
Maximum drawbar horsepower tests
    Gear..3rd
    Drawbar horsepower............................26.15
    Pull weight (lb.)...................................3,377
    Speed (mph)...2.90
    Percent slippage..................................1.11
SAE drawbar horsepower.......................25.93
SAE belt/PTO horsepower......................32.88
Type ....tracklayer
Length (in.) 106.50
Height (in.) 50.50
Rear width (in.) 61.13
Tread width (in.)......................................48
Weight (lb.) 6,220
Track length (in.).....................................207
Grouser shoe..36 links; (10), 12, 14-in.
Gear/speed (mph) ....forward: 1/1.04, 2/1.66, 3/2.95, 4/3.83, 5/5.30; reverse: 1/1.76

John Deere 440 IC

Manufacturer...John Deere Dubuque Tractor Works, Dubuque, IA
Nebraska test number 720
Test date ....September 10 to October 1, 1959
Test tractor serial number.......................449370
Years produced 1958–1960
Serial number range................................440001–461929 end
Serial number location ....stamped left side center frame and bell housing
Number produced ....21,928, all models
Engine ....John Deere 440 vertical
Test engine serial number.......................G 161
Cylinders 2
Bore and stroke (in.) ....4.25 x 4.00
Rated rpm 2,000

Compression ratio 7.5:1
Displacement (c.i.) 113
Fuel ....gasoline
Fuel tank capacity (gal.) 10.5
Carburetor ....Marvel-Schebler
TSX-777, 1.00-in.
Air cleaner ....Donaldson
Ignition ....Delco-Remy with
6-v battery
Cooling capacity (gal.) 2.50
Maximum brake horsepower tests
PTO/belt horsepower...........................31.91
Crankshaft rpm 2,000
Fuel use (gal./hr.) 2.80
Maximum drawbar horsepower tests
Gear..3rd
Drawbar horsepower............................23.31
Pull weight (lb.)...................................3,092
Speed (mph) 2.83
Percent slippage..................................1.42
SAE drawbar horsepower.............................24.23
SAE belt/PTO horsepower 31.91
Type ....tracklayer
Length (in.) 106.50
Height (in.) 50.50
Rear width (in.) 61.86
Tread width (in.)...48
Weight (lb.) 5,850
Track length (in.) 207
Grouser shoe..36 links; (10), 12,
14-in.
Gear/speed (mph) ....forward: 1/1.02,
2/1.65, 3/2.91, 4/3.78,
5/5.23; reverse: 1/1.73

John Deere 4010 Row Crop
Manufacturer..John Deere Waterloo
Tractor Works,
Waterloo, IA
Nebraska test number 759
Test date ....September 12–23,
1960
Test tractor serial number...........................21T 1494
Years produced 1961–1963
Serial number range....................................1000–59431 end
Serial number location ....plate on rear of
transmission case
Number produced ....3,613 interspersed
Engine ....John Deere 4010
vertical L-head
Test engine serial number...........................21E 1391
Cylinders 6
Bore and stroke (in.) ....4.00 x 4.00
Rated rpm 2,200
Compression ratio......................................7.5:1
Displacement (c.i.).....................................302
Fuel ....gasoline
Fuel tank capacity (gal.) 34
Carburetor ....Marvel-Schebler USX
or Zenith, 1.6875-in.
Air cleaner ....Donaldson
Ignition ....Delco-Remy with
12-v battery
Cooling capacity (gal.) 6

Maximum brake horsepower tests
PTO/belt horsepower...........................80.96
Crankshaft rpm 2,200
Fuel use (gal./hr.) 7.19
Maximum drawbar horsepower tests
Gear..5th
Drawbar horsepower............................71.25
Pull weight (lb.)...................................4,699
Speed (mph) 5.69
Percent slippage..................................5.44
SAE drawbar horsepower.............................72.53
SAE belt/PTO horsepower 80.96
Type ....tricycle
Front wheel (in.) ....6.00 x 16
Rear wheel (in.) ....15.50 x 38
Length (in.) 150
Height (in.) 88.75
Rear width (in.) 86.63
Tread width (in.) 60–88
Weight (lb.) 6,525
Gear/speed (mph) ....forward: 1/1.50,
2/2.50, 3/3.25, 4/4.25,
5/5.25, 6/6.75, 7/8.75,
8/14.25; reverse:
1/3.25, 2/5.00, 3/8.25

John Deere 4010 LPG, Row Crop
Manufacturer..John Deere Waterloo
Tractor Works,
Waterloo, IA
Nebraska test number 760
Test date ....September
12–23, 1960
Test tractor serial number...........................21T 1530
Years produced 1961–1963
Serial number range....................................1000–59431 end
Serial number location ....plate on rear of
transmission case
Number produced ....4,459 interspersed
Engine ....John Deere 4010
vertical L-head
Test engine serial number...........................22E 1405
Cylinders 6
Bore and stroke (in.) ....4.00 x 4.00
Rated rpm 2,200
Compression ratio......................................9.0:1
Displacement (c.i.).....................................302
Fuel ....LPG
Fuel tank capacity (gal.) 39
Carburetor ....John Deere, 1.6875-in.
Air cleaner ....Donaldson
Ignition ....Delco-Remy with
12-v battery
Cooling capacity (gal.) 6
Maximum brake horsepower tests
PTO/belt horsepower...........................80.60
Crankshaft rpm 2,200
Fuel use (gal./hr.) 9.24
Maximum drawbar horsepower tests
Gear..5th
Drawbar horsepower............................71.77
Pull weight (lb.)...................................4,691
Speed (mph) 5.74
Percent slippage..................................5.55

SAE drawbar horsepower............................72.13
SAE belt/PTO horsepower..........................80.60
Type ....tricycle
Front wheel (in.)....................................6.00 x 16
Rear wheel (in.)....................................15.50 x 38
Length (in.) 150
Height (in.)...88.75
Rear width (in.).......................................86.63
Tread width (in.)......................................60–88
Weight (lb.) 6,525
Gear/speed (mph) ....forward: 1/1.50,
2/2.50, 3/3.25, 4/4.25,
5/5.25, 6/6.75, 7/7.75,
8/14.25; reverse:
1/3.25, 2/5.00, 3/8.50

John Deere 4010 Diesel, Row Crop
Manufacturer...............................John Deere Waterloo
Tractor Works,
Waterloo, IA
Nebraska test number 761
Test date ....September
19–23, 1960
Test tractor serial number......................1255
Years produced 1961–1963
Serial number range....................1000–59431 end
Serial number location ....plate on rear of
transmission case
Number produced ....36,736 interspersed
Engine ....John Deere 4010
vertical L-head
Test engine serial number.......................23E 1025
Cylinders 6
Bore and stroke (in.) ....4.125 x 4.75
Rated rpm 2,200
Compression ratio....................................16.4:1
Displacement (c.i.) 380
Fuel ....diesel
Fuel tank capacity (gal.) 34
Carburetor...Roosa Master
injector pump
Air cleaner ....Donaldson
Ignition...Delco-Remy 24-v;
with 2, 12-v battery
Cooling capacity (gal.) 6
Maximum brake horsepower tests
    PTO/belt horsepower.........................84.00
    Crankshaft rpm 2,200
    Fuel use (gal./hr.).............................5.61
Maximum drawbar horsepower tests
    Gear..5th
    Drawbar horsepower.........................71.93
    Pull weight (lb.)................................4,737
    Speed (mph) 5.69
    Percent slippage...............................5.80
SAE drawbar horsepower............................73.65
SAE belt/PTO horsepower..........................84.00
Type ....tricycle
Front wheel (in.)....................................6.00 x 16
Rear wheel (in.)....................................15.50 x 38
Length (in.) 150
Height (in.)...88.25
Rear width (in.).......................................86.63
Tread width (in.)......................................60–88
Weight (lb.) 6,525

Gear/speed (mph) ....forward: 1/1.50, 2/2.50,
3/3.25, 4/4.25, 5/5.25,
6/6.75, 7/8.75, 8/14.25;
reverse: 1/3.25, 2/5.00,
3/8.50

John Deere 3010 Diesel, Row Crop
Manufacturer...............................John Deere Waterloo
Tractor Works,
Waterloo, IA
Nebraska test number 762
Test date ....September 19–24,
1960
Test tractor serial number......................T 1259
Years produced 1961–1963
Serial number range....................1000–46952 end
Serial number location ....plate on rear of
transmission case
Number produced ....23,675 interspersed
Engine ....John Deere 3010
vertical L-head
Test engine serial number.......................13E 1145
Cylinders 4
Bore and stroke (in.) ....4.125 x 4.75
Rated rpm 2,200
Compression ratio....................................16.4:1
Displacement (c.i.) 254
Fuel ....diesel
Fuel tank capacity (gal.) 29
Carburetor...Roosa Master
injector pump
Air cleaner ....Donaldson
Ignition...Delco-Remy 24-v;
with 2, 12-v battery
Cooling capacity (gal.) 4.75
Maximum brake horsepower tests
    PTO/belt horsepower.........................59.44
    Crankshaft rpm 2,200
    Fuel use (gal./hr.).............................4.09
Maximum drawbar horsepower tests
    Gear..4th
    Drawbar horsepower.........................52.77
    Pull weight (lb.)................................4,256
    Speed (mph) 4.65
    Percent slippage...............................8.12
SAE drawbar horsepower............................54.36
SAE belt/PTO horsepower..........................59.44
Type ....tricycle
Front wheel (in.)....................................6.00 x 14
Rear wheel (in.)....................................13.90 x 36
Length (in.) 138.50
Height (in.)...86.63
Rear width (in.).......................................86.69
Tread width (in.)......................................57–88
Weight (lb.) 5,820
Gear/speed (mph) ....forward: 1/1.75, 2/2.50,
3/3.25, 4/4.25, 5/5.25,
6/7.00, 7/9.00, 8/14.50;
reverse: 1/3.25, 2/5.00,
3/8.50

John Deere 3010 Row Crop
Manufacturer...............................John Deere Waterloo
Tractor Works,
Waterloo, IA

Nebraska test number 763
Test date .... September 24–28, 1960
Test tractor serial number .... T 1136
Years produced 1961–1963
Serial number range .... 1000–46952 end
Serial number location .... plate on rear of transmission case
Number produced .... 12,525 interspersed
Engine .... John Deere 3010 vertical L-head
Test engine serial number 11E 1080
Cylinders 4
Bore and stroke (in.) .... 4.00 x 4.00
Rated rpm 2,200
Compression ratio 7.5:1
Displacement (c.i.) 201
Fuel .... gasoline
Fuel tank capacity (gal.) 29
Carburetor .... Marvel-Schebler USX or Zenith, 1.6875-in.
Air cleaner .... Donaldson
Ignition .... Delco-Remy with 12-v battery
Cooling capacity (gal.) 4.75
Maximum brake horsepower tests
    PTO/belt horsepower 55.09
    Crankshaft rpm 2,200
    Fuel use (gal./hr.) 5.15
Maximum drawbar horsepower tests
    Gear 4th
    Drawbar horsepower 50.98
    Pull weight (lb.) 4,040
    Speed (mph) 4.73
    Percent slippage 5.91
SAE drawbar horsepower 51.73
SAE belt/PTO horsepower 55.09
Type .... tricycle
Front wheel (in.) .... 6.00 x 14
Rear wheel (in.) .... 13.90 x 36
Length (in.) 138.50
Height (in.) 86.63
Rear width (in.) 86.69
Tread width (in.) 57–88
Weight (lb.) 5,820
Gear/speed (mph) .... forward: 1/1.75, 2/2.50, 3/3.25, 4/4.25, 5/5.25, 6/7.00, 7/9.00, 8/14.50; reverse: 1/3.75, 2/5.00, 3/8.80

John Deere 3010 LPG, Row Crop

Manufacturer .... John Deere Waterloo Tractor Works, Waterloo, IA
Nebraska test number 764
Test date .... September 24–29, 1960
Test tractor serial number 11T 1195
Years produced 1961–1963
Serial number range .... 1000–46952 end
Serial number location .... plate on rear of transmission case
Number produced .... 2,442, interspersed
Engine .... John Deere 3010 vertical L-head
Test engine serial number 12E 1090
Cylinders 4
Bore and stroke (in.) .... 4.00 x 4.00
Rated rpm 2,200
Compression ratio 9.0:1
Displacement (c.i.) 201
Fuel .... LPG
Fuel tank capacity (gal.) 25.10
Carburetor .... John Deere, 1.5625-in.
Air cleaner .... Donaldson
Ignition .... Delco-Remy with 12-v battery
Cooling capacity (gal.) 4.75
Maximum brake horsepower tests
    PTO/belt horsepower 55.39
    Crankshaft rpm 2,200
    Fuel use (gal./hr.) 6.55
Maximum drawbar horsepower tests
    Gear 4th
    Drawbar horsepower 49.22
    Pull weight (lb.) 3,897
    Speed (mph) 4.74
    Percent slippage 6.27
SAE drawbar horsepower 50.25
SAE belt/PTO horsepower 55.39
Type .... tricycle
Front wheel (in.) .... 6.00 x 14
Rear wheel (in.) .... 13.90 x 36
Length (in.) 138.50
Height (in.) 86.63
Rear width (in.) 86.69
Tread width (in.) 57–88
Weight (lb.) 5,820
Gear/speed (mph) .... forward: 1/1.75, 2/2.50, 3/3.25, 4/4.25, 5/5.25, 6/7.00, 7/9.00, 8/14.50; reverse: 1/3.25, 2/5.00, 3/8.50

Chapter 48
LA CROSSE

La Crosse G, 12-24

Manufacturer...La Crosse Tractor Co.,
La Crosse, WI
Nebraska test number 29
Test date..August 2–5, 1920
Test tractor serial number.........................18024
Years produced 1917–1920
Engine ....Lauson horizontal,
valve-in-head
Test engine serial number.........................18024
Cylinders...2
Bore and stroke (in.) ....6.00 x 7.00
Rated rpm 900
Displacement (c.i.) 395.8
Fuel ....kerosene/gasoline
Main tank capacity (gal.) 13
Auxiliary tank capacity (gal.) 2
Carburetor...Kingston (Stromberg
MB3), 1.50-in.
Air cleaner ....Bennett
Ignition..Atwater-Kent K-3
magneto and dry
battery

Cooling capacity (gal.) 9
Maximum brake horsepower tests
    PTO/belt horsepower...........................24.94
    Crankshaft rpm 902
    Fuel use (gal./hr.)...............................4.36
Maximum drawbar horsepower tests
    Drawbar horsepower............................17.83
    Pull weight (lb.)...................................2,155
    Speed (mph)..3.10
    Percent slippage..................................5.10
SAE drawbar horsepower...........................12
SAE belt/PTO horsepower 24
Type ....4 wheel
Front wheel (in.)...steel: 36 x 4
Rear wheel (in.)..steel: 56 x 10
Length (in.) ....wheelbase: 90;
total: 135
Height (in.) 62
Rear width (in.) 82.50
Weight (lb.) 3,800
Gear/speed (mph) ....forward: 1/2.50;
reverse: 1/2.50

Chapter 49
LAND-ROVER

Land-Rover 88

Manufacturer...The Rover Co. Ltd.,
Warwickshire, England
Nebraska test number 749
Test date ....July 25 to
August 2, 1960
Test tractor serial number.........................144901833
Engine ....Rover vertical L-head
Test engine serial number.........................151910995
Cylinders...4
Bore and stroke (in.) ....3.562 x 3.500
Rated rpm 2,000
Compression ratio....................................7:1
Displacement (c.i.) 139.5
Fuel ....gasoline
Carburetor...1.25-in.
Ignition..12-v battery
Maximum brake horsepower tests
    PTO/belt horsepower...........................30.90
    Crankshaft rpm 2,000
    Fuel use (gal./hr.)...............................3.23

Maximum drawbar horsepower tests
    Gear...2nd
    Drawbar horsepower............................28.05
    Pull weight (lb.)...................................1,891
    Speed (mph) 5.56
    Percent slippage..................................5.43
SAE drawbar horsepower...........................28.09
SAE belt/PTO horsepower 30.90
Type ....4 wheel drive
Front wheel (in.)...6.00 x 16
Rear wheel (in.)..6.00 x 16
Tread width (in.)...51.50
Weight (lb.) 3,274
Gear/speed (mph) ....forward: 1/4.00,
2/5.80, 3/8.60,
4/10.00, 5/12.00,
6/14.70, 7/21.60,
8/30.00; reverse:
1/4.80, 2/12.00

Chapter 50
LAUSON

Lauson 15-30

Manufacturer .... John Lauson Mfg. Co.,
New Holstein, WI
Nebraska test number 51
Test date .... August 13 to
September 6, 1920
Test tractor serial number 2232
Years produced 1920–1921
Engine .... Beaver vertical,
valve-in-head
Test engine serial number .... 45 B 110
Cylinders 4
Bore and stroke (in.) .... 4.75 x 6.00
Rated rpm 950
Displacement (c.i.) 425.3
Fuel .... kerosene/gasoline
Main tank capacity (gal.) 27
Auxiliary tank capacity (gal.) 5
Carburetor .... Kingston L, 1.375-in.
Air cleaner .... Lausen
Ignition .... Splitdorf, Dixie
46 magneto
Cooling capacity (gal.) 12
Maximum brake horsepower tests
    PTO/belt horsepower 32.46
    Crankshaft rpm 980
    Fuel use (gal./hr.) 4.49
Maximum drawbar horsepower tests
    Gear .... low
    Drawbar horsepower 26.51
    Pull weight (lb.) 5,191
    Speed (mph) 1.91
    Percent slippage 14.90
SAE drawbar horsepower 15
SAE belt/PTO horsepower 30
Type .... 4 wheel
Front wheel (in.) .... steel: 36 x 6
Rear wheel (in.) .... steel: 54 x 12
Length (in.) 136
Height (in.) 62
Rear width (in.) 74
Weight (lb.) 6,000
Gear/speed (mph) .... forward: 1/1.75,
2/2.50; reverse: 1/1.75

Lauson 12-25

Manufacturer .... John Lauson Mfg. Co.,
New Holstein, WI
Nebraska test number 75
Test date .... April 30 to May 6,
1921
Test tractor serial number 2503
Years produced 1921–1925
Engine .... Midwest HD 402
vertical, valve-in-head
Test engine serial number 10452
Cylinders 4
Bore and stroke (in.) .... 4.125 x 5.25
Rated rpm 1,200
Displacement (c.i.) 280.6

Fuel .... gasoline
Fuel tank capacity (gal.) 19
Carburetor .... Kingston L, 1.25-in.
Air cleaner .... Taco Siphon
Ignition .... Splitdorf, Dixie 46,
Number 732167
magneto
Cooling capacity (gal.) 8
Maximum brake horsepower tests
    PTO/belt horsepower 37.38
    Crankshaft rpm 1,219
    Fuel use (gal./hr.) 5.17
Maximum drawbar horsepower tests
    Gear .... high
    Drawbar horsepower 20.91
    Pull weight (lb.) 2,985
    Speed (mph) 2.63
    Percent slippage 17.80
SAE drawbar horsepower 12
SAE belt/PTO horsepower 25
Type .... 4 wheel
Front wheel (in.) .... steel: 32 x 6
Rear wheel (in.) .... steel: 48 x 12
Weight (lb.) 4,500
Gear/speed (mph) .... forward: 1/2.00,
2/3.00; reverse: 1/2.50

Lauson 16-32

Manufacturer .... John Lauson Mfg. Co.,
New Holstein, WI
Nebraska test number 131
Test date .... March 28 to
April 8, 1927
Test tractor serial number 3236
Years produced 1926–1927
Engine .... Beaver vertical,
valve-in-head
Test engine serial number 803-20
Cylinders 4
Bore and stroke (in.) .... 4.50 x 6.00
Rated rpm 1,100
Displacement (c.i.) 381.7
Fuel .... gasoline
Fuel tank capacity (gal.) 18.50
Carburetor .... Kingston L3, 1.25-in.
Air cleaner .... Taco Siphon
Ignition .... Splitdorf (American
Bosch ZR4 Ed26)
magneto
Cooling capacity (gal.) 8.50
Maximum brake horsepower tests
    PTO/belt horsepower 36.97
    Crankshaft rpm 1,097
    Fuel use (gal./hr.) 5.34
Maximum drawbar horsepower tests
    Gear .... low
    Drawbar horsepower 28.90
    Pull weight (lb.) 4,975
    Speed (mph) 2.18
    Percent slippage 11.50

SAE drawbar horsepower............................16
SAE belt/PTO horsepower........................32
Type ....4 wheel
Front wheel (in.)....................................steel: 32 x 6
Rear wheel (in.).....................................steel: 48 x 12
Length (in.) 140
Height (in.) 62
Rear width (in.) 72
Weight (lb.) 5,550
Gear/speed (mph) ....forward: 1/2.25, 2/3.25; reverse: 1/2.35

Lauson 20-40
Manufacturer...John Lauson Mfg. Co., New Holstein, WI
Nebraska test number 132
Test date ....March 28 to April 22, 1927
Test tractor serial number.......................3235
Years produced 1926–1929
Engine ....Beaver vertical, valve-in-head
Test engine serial number........................N80110
Cylinders 4
Bore and stroke (in.) ....4.75 x 6.00
Rated rpm 1,040
Displacement (c.i.) 425.3
Fuel ....gasoline
Fuel tank capacity (gal.) 33.50
Carburetor..Kingston L3, 1.50-in.
Air cleaner ....Taco Siphon
Ignition...Spiltdorf (American Bosch ZR4 Ed26) magneto
Cooling capacity (gal.) 8.25
Maximum brake horsepower tests
    PTO/belt horsepower...........................41.87
    Crankshaft rpm 1,040
    Fuel use (gal./hr.) 6.12
Maximum drawbar horsepower tests
    Gear..low
    Drawbar horsepower.............................32.82
    Pull weight (lb.)....................................5,050
    Speed (mph) 2.44
    Percent slippage..................................5.73
SAE drawbar horsepower............................20
SAE belt/PTO horsepower........................40
Type ....4 wheel
Front wheel (in.).....................................steel: 36 x 6
Rear wheel (in.)......................................steel: 54 x 16–20

Length (in.) 147
Height (in.) 68
Rear width (in.) 82
Weight (lb.) 7,580
Gear/speed (mph) ....forward: 1/2.25-2.50, 2/3.25-3.50; reverse: 1/2.00

Lauson S12, 20-35
Manufacturer...John Lauson Mfg. Co., New Holstein, WI
Nebraska test number 148
Test date ....April 2–16, 1928
Test tractor serial number.......................3800
Years produced 1926–1929
Engine ....Le Roi JA - I vertical I-head, valve-in-head
Test engine serial number........................901-19
Cylinders 4
Bore and stroke (in.) ....4.50 x 6.00
Rated rpm 1,100
Displacement (c.i.) 381.7
Fuel ....gasoline
Fuel tank capacity (gal.) 18.50
Carburetor..Tillotson R2, 1.25-in.
Air cleaner ....Taco Siphon
Ignition...Splitdorf (American Bosch ZR4) magneto
Cooling capacity (gal.) 8.50
Maximum brake horsepower tests
    PTO/belt horsepower...........................40.88
    Crankshaft rpm 1,113
    Fuel use (gal./hr.) 4.63
Maximum drawbar horsepower tests
    Gear..low
    Drawbar horsepower.............................29.63
    Pull weight (lb.)....................................3,259
    Speed (mph) 3.41
Percent slippage......................................5.48
SAE drawbar horsepower............................20
SAE belt/PTO horsepower........................35
Type ....4 wheel
Front wheel (in.).....................................steel: 32 x 6
Rear wheel (in.)......................................steel: 48 x 12
Length (in.) 140
Height (in.) 62
Rear width (in.) 72
Weight (lb.) 5,550
Gear/speed (mph) ....forward: 1/2.25-2.50, 2/3.25-3.50; reverse: 1/2.00

Chapter 51
LONG

Long A
Manufacturer...Long Mfg. Co., Inc., Tarboro, NC
Nebraska test number 410
Test date ....May 18–31, 1949

Test tractor serial number..........................4905275
Years produced 1949–1952
Engine ....Continental F162 vertical L-head
Test engine serial number..........................103446

Cylinders 4
Bore and stroke (in.) ....3.4375 x 4.375
Rated rpm 1,800
Compression ratio.............................6.1:1
Displacement (c.i.) 162.4
Fuel ....gasoline
Carburetor ....Marvel-Schebler
TSX-338; 0.875-in.
Air cleaner ....United
Ignition...Auto-Lite with
6-v battery

Maximum brake horsepower tests
PTO/belt horsepower.....................31.82
Crankshaft rpm 1,798
Fuel use (gal./hr.) 3.22

Maximum drawbar horsepower tests
Gear...2nd
Drawbar horsepower.....................28.58
Pull weight (lb.).............................2,560
Speed (mph) 4.19
Percent slippage..........................5.95
SAE drawbar horsepower.....................22.31
SAE belt/PTO horsepower 28.12
Type ....tricycle
Front tire (in.) ....5.50 x 16
Rear tire (in.).....................................11.00 x 38
Length (in.) 132
Height (in.)...73.50
Tread width (in.)................................56–84
Weight (lb.) 3,225
Gear/speed (mph) ....forward: 1/3.34, 2/4.82,
3/6.46, 4/13.27; reverse:
1/4.17

Chapter 52
MASSEY-FERGUSON

Massey-Ferguson MF 65 LPG
Manufacturer......................................Massey-Ferguson Inc.,
Detroit, MI
Nebraska test number 657
Test date ....June 16–27, 1958
Test tractor serial number..................SBM 650183
Years produced 1958–1964
Serial number range............................650001–701057
no end
Serial number location ....stamped on instrument
panel nameplate
Number produced ....na, types interspersed
Engine ....Continental G176
vertical I-head
Test engine serial number...................GB176 9891
Cylinders 4
Bore and stroke (in.) ....3.578 x 4.375
Rated rpm 2,000
Compression ratio.............................8.1:1
Displacement (c.i.) 176
Fuel ....LPG
Carburetor..Zenith GO12256, 1.25-in.
Air cleaner ....Donaldson
Ignition...Delco-Remy with
12-v battery
Cooling capacity (gal.) 2.60
Maximum brake horsepower tests
PTO/belt horsepower.....................42.60
Crankshaft rpm 2,000
Fuel use (gal./hr.) 5.17
Maximum drawbar horsepower tests
Gear...4th
Drawbar horsepower.....................38.54
Pull weight (lb.).............................2,870
Speed (mph) 5.04
Percent slippage..........................5.76

SAE drawbar horsepower.....................30.65
SAE belt/PTO horsepower 38.06
Type ....standard
Front wheel (in.) ....6.00 x 16
Rear wheel (in.).................................13.00 x 28
Height (in.)...65
Tread width (in.)................................52–88
Weight (lb.) 3,802
Gear/speed (mph) ....forward: 1/1.29, 2/1.94,
3/3.56, 4/5.18, 5/7.77,
6/14.23; reverse: 1/1.76

Massey-Ferguson MF 50 LPG
Manufacturer......................................Massey-Ferguson Inc.,
Detroit, MI
Nebraska test number 658
Test date ....June 16–27, 1958
Test tractor serial number..................SBM 518702
Years produced 1958–1964
Serial number range............................515708–536062 no end
Serial number location ....stamped on instrument
panel nameplate
Engine ....Continental Z134
vertical I-head
Test engine serial number...................ZB 134 667063
Cylinders 4
Bore and stroke (in.) ....3.3125 x 3.875
Rated rpm 2,000
Compression ratio.............................8.0:1
Displacement (c.i.) 134
Fuel ....LPG
Carburetor..Zenith GO12157,
0.875-in.
Air cleaner ....Donaldson
Ignition...Delco-Remy with
12-v battery

Cooling capacity (gal.) 2.25
Maximum brake horsepower tests
    PTO/belt horsepower...........................32.12
    Crankshaft rpm 2,000
    Fuel use (gal./hr.) 3.73
Maximum drawbar horsepower tests
    Gear 4th
    Drawbar horsepower.............................29.44
    Pull weight (lb.) 2,098
    Speed (mph) 5.26
    Percent slippage..................................4.00
SAE drawbar horsepower..............................23.06
SAE belt/PTO horsepower 28.45
Type ....standard
Front wheel (in.) ....6.00 x 16
Rear wheel (in.) ....13.00 x 24
Height (in.) 57
Tread width (in.) 48–76
Weight (lb.) 3,405
Gear/speed (mph) ....forward: 1/1.33,
    2/1.99, 3/3.65, 4/5.30,
    5/7.96, 6/14.59;
    reverse: 1/1.79, 2/7.19

Massey-Ferguson MF 65

Manufacturer...Massey-Ferguson Inc.,
    Detroit, MI
Nebraska test number 659
Test date ....June 16–27, 1958
Test tractor serial number.............................SGM 650215
Years produced 1958–1964
Serial number range......................................650001–701057 no end
Serial number location ....stamped on instrument
    panel nameplate
Number produced ....na, types interspersed
Engine...Continental G176
    vertical I-head
Test engine serial number.............................G176 1219
Cylinders 4
Bore and stroke (in.) ....3.578 x 4.375
Rated rpm 2,000
Compression ratio...7.1:1
Displacement (c.i.) 176
Fuel ....gasoline
Fuel tank capacity (gal.) 17
Carburetor..Zenith 8-4090, 1.25-in.
Air cleaner ....Donaldson
Ignition..Delco-Remy with
    12-v battery
Cooling capacity (gal.) 2.60
Maximum brake horsepower tests
    PTO/belt horsepower...........................46.05
    Crankshaft rpm 2,000
    Fuel use (gal./hr.) 4.37
Maximum drawbar horsepower tests
    Gear..4th
    Drawbar horsepower.............................41.64
    Pull weight (lb.)..................................3,066
    Speed (mph) 5.09
    Percent slippage..................................5.21
SAE drawbar horsepower..............................32.66
SAE belt/PTO horsepower 40.72
Type ....standard
Front wheel (in.) ....6.00 x 16
Rear wheel (in.) ....13.00 x 28

Height (in.) 59
Tread width (in.) 52–88
Weight (lb.) 3,802
Gear/speed (mph) ....forward: 1/1.29,
    2/4.94, 3/3.56, 4/5.18,
    5/7.76, 6/14.23;
    reverse: 1/1.76, 2/7.05

Massey-Ferguson MF 85

Manufacturer...Massey-Ferguson Inc.,
    Detroit, MI
Nebraska test number 726
Test date ....November 2–13, 1959
Test tractor serial number.............................CGM 802291
Years produced 1959–1962
Serial number range......................................800001–808564
    no end
Serial number location ....stamped on instrument
    panel nameplate
Number produced ....na, types interspersed
Engine...Continental E-242
    vertical L-head
Test engine serial number.............................E242 1060
Cylinders 4
Bore and stroke (in.) ....3.875 x 5.125
Rated rpm 2,000
Compression ratio...7.35:1
Displacement (c.i.) 242
Fuel ....gasoline
Carburetor..Marvel-Schebler
    TSX-786, 1.25-in.
Air cleaner ....Donaldson
Ignition..Delco-Remy with
    12-v battery
Cooling capacity (gal.) 3.75
Maximum brake horsepower tests
    PTO/belt horsepower...........................61.23
    Crankshaft rpm 2,000
    Fuel use (gal./hr.) 5.26
Maximum drawbar horsepower tests
    Gear..3rd
    Drawbar horsepower.............................50.76
    Pull weight (lb.)..................................5,194
    Speed (mph) 3.66
    Percent slippage..................................7.55
SAE drawbar horsepower..............................51.34
SAE belt/PTO horsepower 61.23
Type ....standard
Front wheel (in.) ....7.50 x 16
Rear wheel (in.) ....15.00 x 30
Height (in.) 64.38
Tread width (in.) 56–92
Weight (lb.) 5,690
Gear/speed (mph) ....forward: 1/1.48, 2/2.09,
    3/3.41, 4/4.69, 5/5.92,
    6/8.36, 7/13.64, 8/18.76;
    reverse: 1/1.21, 2/4.84

Massey-Ferguson MF 85 LPG

Manufacturer...Massey-Ferguson Inc.,
    Detroit, MI
Nebraska test number 727
Test date ....November 2–13, 1959
Test tractor serial number.............................SBM 803559
Years produced 1959–1962

Serial number range....................................800001–808564 no end
Serial number location ....stamped on instrument
panel nameplate
Number produced ....na, types interspersed
Engine ....Continental E-242
vertical L-head
Test engine serial number.........................EB242 202
Cylinders 4
Bore and stroke (in.) ....3.875 x 5.125
Rated rpm 2,000
Compression ratio.....................................8.8:1
Displacement (c.i.) 242
Fuel ....LPG
Carburetor ....Zenith PC1J10,
1.25-in.
Air cleaner ....Donaldson
Ignition...Delco-Remy with
12-v battery
Cooling capacity (gal.) 3.75
Maximum brake horsepower tests
PTO/belt horsepower..........................62.21
Crankshaft rpm 2,000
Fuel use (gal./hr.) 6.55
Maximum drawbar horsepower tests
Gear..3rd
Drawbar horsepower...........................55.03
Pull weight (lb.)..................................5,101
Speed (mph) 4.05
Percent slippage.................................7.37
SAE drawbar horsepower............................56.47
SAE belt/PTO horsepower..........................62.21
Type ....standard
Front wheel (in.) ....7.50 x 16
Rear wheel (in.) ....15.00 x 30
Height (in.) 64.38
Tread width (in.)..52–88
Weight (lb.) 5,690
Gear/speed (mph) ....forward: 1/1.70,
2/2.36, 3/4.22, 4/5.35,
5/6.78, 6/9.46,
7/16.88, 8/21.45;
reverse: 1/1.37, 2/5.48

Massey-Ferguson MF 35 Diesel

Manufacturer..Massey-Ferguson Inc.,
Detroit, MI
Nebraska test number 744
Test date ....May 16–23, 1960
Test tractor serial number.........................SNM 204182
Years produced 1960–1963
Serial number range...................................204181–235123 no end
Serial number location ....stamped on instrument
panel nameplate
Engine ....Perkins 3A-152
vertical L-head
Test engine serial number.........................CL 1802819
Cylinders 3
Bore and stroke (in.) ....3.60 x 5.00
Rated rpm 2,000
Compression ratio.....................................17.4:1
Displacement (c.i.) 152.7
Fuel ....diesel
Carburetor ....C.A.V. injector pump
Air cleaner ....Donaldson
Ignition...Delco-Remy with
12-v battery

Cooling capacity (gal.) 2.25
Maximum brake horsepower tests
PTO/belt horsepower..........................37.04
Crankshaft rpm 2,000
Fuel use (gal./hr.) 2.36
Maximum drawbar horsepower tests
Gear..4th
Drawbar horsepower...........................32.13
Pull weight (lb.)..................................2,410
Speed (mph) 5.00
Percent slippage.................................6.52
SAE drawbar horsepower............................33.02
SAE belt/PTO horsepower..........................37.04
Type ....standard
Front wheel (in.) ....6.00 x 16
Rear wheel (in.) ....11.00 x 28
Height (in.) 57
Tread width (in.)..48–76
Weight (lb.) 3,200
Gear/speed (mph) ....forward: 1/1.33,
2/1.99, 3/3.64, 4/5.32,
5/7.96, 6/14.57;
reverse: 1/1.77, 2/7.09

Massey-Ferguson MF 65 Diesel

Manufacturer..Massey-Ferguson Inc.,
Detroit, MI
Nebraska test number 745
Test date ....May 16–24, 1960
Test tractor serial number.........................SNM 669513
Years produced 1958–1964
Serial number range...................................650001–701057 no end
Serial number location ....stamped on instrument
panel nameplate
Number produced ....na, types interspersed
Engine ....Perkins 4A-203
vertical L-head
Test engine serial number.........................2803843
Cylinders 4
Bore and stroke (in.) ....3.60 x 5.00
Rated rpm 2,000
Compression ratio.....................................17.4:1
Displacement (c.i.) 203.5
Fuel ....diesel
Carburetor ....C.A.V. injector pump
Air cleaner ....Donaldson
Ignition...Delco-Remy 12-v;
with 2, 6-v battery
Cooling capacity (gal.) 2.50
Maximum brake horsepower tests
PTO/belt horsepower..........................48.59
Crankshaft rpm 2,000
Fuel use (gal./hr.) 3.11
Maximum drawbar horsepower tests
Gear..4th
Drawbar horsepower...........................42.13
Pull weight (lb.)..................................3,077
Speed (mph) 5.13
Percent slippage.................................5.45
SAE drawbar horsepower............................42.96
SAE belt/PTO horsepower..........................48.59
Type ....standard
Front wheel (in.) ....6.00 x 16
Rear wheel (in.) ....13.00 x 28
Height (in.) 57
Tread width (in.)..52–88

Weight (lb.) 4,272
Gear/speed (mph) ....forward: 1/1.29,
2/1.94, 3/3.56, 4/5.18,
5/7.76, 6/14.23;
reverse: 1/1.76, 2/7.05

Massey-Ferguson MF 88 Diesel
Manufacturer ....Massey-Ferguson Inc.,
Detroit, MI
Nebraska test number 765
Test date ....September 29 to
October 4, 1960
Test tractor serial number ....D 881746
Years produced 1959–1962
Serial number range ....880001–882496 no end
Serial number location ....stamped on instrument
panel nameplate
Engine ....Continental HD277
vertical L-head
Test engine serial number 4694
Cylinders 4
Bore and stroke (in.) ....4.00 x 5.50
Rated rpm 2,000
Compression ratio 15.2:1
Displacement (c.i.) 276.5
Fuel ....diesel
Carburetor ....Roosa injector pump

Air cleaner ....Donaldson
Ignition ....Delco-Remy, 12-v with
2, 6-v battery
Cooling capacity (gal.) 5.50
Maximum brake horsepower tests
PTO/belt horsepower 63.31
Crankshaft rpm 2,000
Fuel use (gal./hr.) 4.50
Maximum drawbar horsepower tests
Gear 3rd
Drawbar horsepower 53.25
Pull weight (lb.) 4,921
Speed (mph) 4.06
Percent slippage 5.94
SAE drawbar horsepower 55.54
SAE belt/PTO horsepower 63.31
Type ....standard
Front wheel (in.) ....7.50 x 18
Rear wheel (in.) ....18.40 x 30
Height (in.) 62.50
Tread width (in.) 70
Weight (lb.) 6,600
Gear/speed (mph) ....forward: 1/1.70,
2/2.36, 3/4.22, 4/5.35,
5/6.78, 6/9.46,
7/16.88, 8/21.45;
reverse: 1/1.37, 2/5.48

Chapter 53
MASSEY-HARRIS

Massey-Harris General Purpose, 15-22
Manufacturer ....Massey-Harris Co.,
Racine, WI
Nebraska test number 177
Test date ....May 5–27, 1930
Test tractor serial number 300089
Years produced 1930–1938
Serial number range ....300001–303001 no end
Serial number location ....metal tag left rear
tractor frame forward
of transmission case
and stamped top left
front corner
Number produced ....3,000 through 1935
Engine ....Hercules OOC vertical
L-head
Test engine serial number 220622
Cylinders 4
Bore and stroke (in.) ....4.00 x 4.50
Rated rpm 1,200
Displacement (c.i.) 226.2
Fuel ....gasoline
Fuel tank capacity (gal.) 14

Carburetor ....Zenith 94TO, 1.00-in.
Air cleaner ....Massey-Harris
Ignition ....American Bosch U4
Ed2 magneto
Cooling capacity (gal.) 4
Maximum brake horsepower tests
PTO/belt horsepower 24.84
Crankshaft rpm 1,198
Fuel use (gal./hr.) 3.01
Maximum drawbar horsepower tests
Gear 3rd
Drawbar horsepower 19.91
Pull weight (lb.) 3,247
Speed (mph) 2.30
Percent slippage 8.26
SAE drawbar horsepower 15.47
SAE belt/PTO horsepower 22.20
Type ....4 wheel drive
Front wheel (in.) ....steel: 38 x 8
Rear wheel (in.) ....steel: 38 x 8
Length (in.) 119
Height (in.) 54.75
Rear width (in.) 59

Weight (lb.) 3,861
Gear/speed (mph) ....forward: 1/2.20,
2/3.20, 3/4.00;
reverse: 1/2.50

Massey-Harris General Purpose; 15-22
Manufacturer..................................Massey-Harris Co.,
Racine, WI
Nebraska test number 191
Test date ....May 22 to June 12, 1931
Test tractor serial number............302164
Years produced 1930–1938
Serial number range.......................300001–303001 no end
Serial number location ....metal tag left rear
tractor frame forward
of transmission case
and stamped top left
front corner
Number produced ....3,000 through 1935
Engine ....Hercules OOC vertical
L-head
Test engine serial number..............224033
Cylinders 4
Bore and stroke (in.) ....4.00 x 4.50
Rated rpm 1,200
Displacement (c.i.) 226.2
Fuel ....distillate/gasoline
Main tank capacity (gal.) 14
Auxiliary tank capacity (gal.) 1.6
Carburetor.....................................Zenith TO94E, 1.00-in.
Air cleaner.....................................Massey-Harris
Ignition..American Bosch U4
Ed2 magneto
Cooling capacity (gal.) 4
Maximum brake horsepower tests
PTO/belt horsepower.......................22.50
Crankshaft rpm 1,202
Fuel use (gal./hr.) 2.90
Maximum drawbar horsepower tests
Gear..3rd
Drawbar horsepower.......................16.79
Pull weight (lb.)...............................2,764
Speed (mph) 2.28
Percent slippage.............................9.06
SAE drawbar horsepower.................13.02
SAE belt/PTO horsepower 20.31
Type ....4 wheel drive
Front wheel (in.) ....steel: 38 x 8
Rear wheel (in.) ....steel: 38 x 8
Length (in.) 119
Height (in.) 55
Rear width (in.) 59
Weight (lb.) 3,861
Gear/speed (mph) ....forward: 1/2.20,
2/3.20, 3/4.00; reverse:
1/2.50

Massey-Harris 25, 3-4 Plow
Manufacturer.................................Massey-Harris Co.,
Racine, WI
Nebraska test number 219
Test date ....October 24 to
November 10, 1933
Test tractor serial number............69001
Years produced 1932–1937
Serial number range.......................69001–90200 end

Serial number location ....brass plate on frame
below radiator and
stamped above tag
on frame
Number produced ....approximately 21,200
Engine ....Massey-Harris vertical
I-head, valve-in-head
Test engine serial number..............68530
Cylinders 4
Bore and stroke (in.) ....4.375 x 5.75
Rated rpm 1,200
Displacement (c.i.) 345.8
Fuel ....distillate/gasoline
Main tank capacity (gal.) 24
Auxiliary tank capacity (gal.) 1.6
Carburetor.....................................Kingston L-3-L,
1.50-in.
Air cleaner.....................................Massey-Harris
Ignition..American Bosch U 4
ED 4 magneto
Cooling capacity (gal.) 6
Maximum brake horsepower tests
PTO/belt horsepower.......................44.24
Crankshaft rpm 1,201
Fuel use (gal./hr.) 4.65
Maximum drawbar horsepower tests
Gear..2nd
Drawbar horsepower.......................33.12
Pull weight (lb.)...............................3,534
Speed (mph) 3.51
Percent slippage.............................7.60
SAE drawbar horsepower.................26.44
SAE belt/PTO horsepower 41.01
Type ....4 wheel
Front wheel (in.) ....steel: 30 x 6
Rear wheel (in.) ....steel: 48 x 12
Length (in.) 135
Height (in.) 57
Rear width (in.) 65.50
Tread width (in.).............................53.50
Weight (lb.) 4,917
Gear/speed (mph) ....forward: 1/2.50,
2/3.25, 3/4.00;
reverse: 1/2.50

Massey-Harris Challenger
Manufacturer.................................Massey-Harris Co.,
Racine, WI
Nebraska test number 265
Test date ....August 10–18, 1936
Test tractor serial number............131127
Years produced 1936–1938
Serial number range.......................130001–144000 end,
all types
Serial number location ....metal tag left rear
tractor frame forward
of transmission case
and stamped top left
front corner
Number produced ....14,000, all types
Engine ....Massey-Harris vertical
I-head, valve-in-head
Test engine serial number..............130656
Cylinders 4
Bore and stroke (in.) ....3.875 x 5.25
Rated rpm 1,200

Displacement (c.i.) 247.7
Fuel ....distillate/gasoline
Main tank capacity (gal.) 18
Auxiliary tank capacity (gal.) 1.6
Carburetor ....Kingston, 1.25-in.
Air cleaner ....Massey-Harris
Ignition ....American Bosch
U4ED4V1 magneto
Cooling capacity (gal.) 5

Maximum brake horsepower tests
    PTO/belt horsepower 28.58
    Crankshaft rpm 1,199
    Fuel use (gal./hr.) 3.18
Maximum drawbar horsepower tests
    Gear...........................2nd
    Drawbar horsepower 20.03
    Pull weight (lb.) 2,049
    Speed (mph) 3.67
    Percent slippage...........................6.66
SAE drawbar horsepower 16.13
SAE belt/PTO horsepower 25.99
Type ....4 wheel, tricycle
Front wheel (in.) ....(steel: 24 x 4.50);
rubber: 5.50 x 16
Rear wheel (in.) ....(steel: 52 x 8);
rubber: 9.00 x 36
Length (in.) ....wheelbase: 78
Height (in.) 53.50
Rear width (in.) 56
Weight (lb.) 3,695
Gear/speed (mph) ....forward: 1/2.40,
2/3.30, 3/4.10, 4/8.50;
reverse: 1/3.00

Massey-Harris Pacemaker
Manufacturer...........................Massey-Harris Co.,
Racine, WI
Nebraska test number 266
Test date ....August 10–19, 1936
Test tractor serial number...........................107484
Years produced 1936–1938
Serial number range...........................107001–206000 end,
all types
Serial number location ....metal tag left rear
tractor frame forward
of transmission case
and stamped top left
front corner
Number produced ....26,557, all types
Engine...........................Massey-Harris vertical
I-head, valve-in-head
Test engine serial number...........................107012
Cylinders 4
Bore and stroke (in.) ....3.875 x 5.25
Rated rpm 1,200
Displacement (c.i.) 247.7
Fuel ....distillate/gasoline
Main tank capacity (gal.) 18
Auxiliary tank capacity (gal.) 1.6
Carburetor...........................Kingston, 1.25-in.
Air cleaner...........................Massey-Harris
Ignition...........................American Bosch
U4ED4V1 magneto
Cooling capacity (gal.) 5

Maximum brake horsepower tests
    PTO/belt horsepower...........................29.09
    Crankshaft rpm 1,200
    Fuel use (gal./hr.) 3.14
Maximum drawbar horsepower tests
    Gear...........................2nd
    Drawbar horsepower 19.76
    Pull weight (lb.) 2,051
    Speed (mph) 3.61
    Percent slippage...........................9.19
SAE drawbar horsepower 16.02
SAE belt/PTO horsepower 26.49
Type ....4 wheel
Front wheel (in.) ....(steel: 28 x 5);
rubber: 6.00 x 16
Rear wheel (in.) ....(steel: 44 x 10);
rubber: 11.25 x 24
Length (in.) ....wheelbase: 78
Height (in.) 53.50
Rear width (in.) 56
Weight (lb.) 3,695
Gear/speed (mph) ....forward: 1/2.40,
2/3.30, 3/4.10, 4/8.50;
reverse: 1/3.00

Massey-Harris Challenger Twin Power
Manufacturer...........................Massey-Harris Co.,
Racine, WI
Nebraska test number 293
Test date ....October 25 to
November 16, 1937
Test tractor serial number...........................132578
Years produced 1936–1938
Serial number range...........................130001–144000 end,
all types
Serial number location ....metal tag left rear
tractor frame forward
of transmission case
and stamped top left
front corner
Number produced ....14,000, all types
Engine...........................Massey-Harris vertical
I-head, valve-in-head
Test engine serial number...........................132107
Cylinders 4
Bore and stroke (in.) ....3.875 x 5.25
Rated rpm 1,200
Displacement (c.i.) 247.7
Fuel ....gasoline
Fuel tank capacity (gal.) 18
Carburetor...........................Zenith 62-AX9, 1.25-in.
Air cleaner...........................Donaldson
Ignition...........................American Bosch,
MJB4A-306
Cooling capacity (gal.) 5

Maximum brake horsepower tests
    PTO/belt horsepower...........................34.85
    Crankshaft rpm 1,200
    Fuel use (gal./hr.) 3.71
Maximum drawbar horsepower tests
    Gear...........................steel: 2nd; rubber: 3rd
    Drawbar horsepower ....steel: 25.52;
rubber: 29.83
    Pull weight (lb.)...........................steel: 2,672;
rubber: 2,691

Speed (mph) ....steel: 3.58; rubber: 4.16
Percent slippage ....steel: 8.17; rubber: 6.52
SAE drawbar horsepower...........................19.67
SAE belt/PTO horsepower 31.60
Type ....tricycle
Front wheel (in.)...............................(steel: 24 x 4.50;
rubber: 5.50 x 16)
Rear wheel (in.)................................(steel: 52 x 8.00;
rubber: 11.25 x 36)
Length (in.) 129.25
Height (in.) 57.63
Rear width (in.) 78–88
Weight (lb.) ....steel: 3,860;
(rubber: 5,725)
Gear/speed (mph) ....forward: 1/2.40,
2/3.30, 3/4.10, 4/8.50;
reverse: 1/3.00

Massey-Harris Pacemaker Twin Power

Manufacturer.......................................Massey-Harris Co.,
Racine, WI
Nebraska test number 294
Test date ....October 25 to
November 16, 1937
Test tractor serial number..........................109538
Years produced 1936–1938
Serial number range.................................107001–206000 end,
all types
Serial number location ....metal tag left rear
tractor frame forward
of transmission case
and stamped top left
front corner
Number produced ....26,557, all types
Engine ....Massey-Harris vertical
I-head, valve-in-head
Test engine serial number..........................109067
Cylinders 4
Bore and stroke (in.) ....3.875 x 5.25
Rated rpm 1,200 (1,400)
Displacement (c.i.) 247.7
Fuel ....gasoline
Fuel tank capacity (gal.) 18
Carburetor...Zenith 62-AX9, 1.25-in.
Air cleaner ....Donaldson
Ignition ....American Bosch
MJB4A-306
Cooling capacity (gal.) 5
Maximum brake horsepower tests
PTO/belt horsepower.........................42.13
Crankshaft rpm 1,401
Fuel use (gal./hr.) 4.15
Maximum drawbar horsepower tests
Gear.......................................steel: 2nd; rubber: 3rd
Drawbar horsepower.........................steel: 26.26;
rubber: 30.58
Pull weight (lb.)..........................steel: 2,720;
rubber: 2,864
Speed (mph) ....steel: 3.62; rubber: 4.00
Percent slippage...........................steel: 8.42; SAE drawbar
horsepower 20.30
SAE belt/PTO horsepower 36.78
Type ....standard
Front wheel (in.)..................................(steel: 28 x 5;
rubber: 6.00 x 16)

Rear wheel (in.) ....(steel: 44 x 10;
rubber: 12.75 x 24)
Length (in.) 122
Height (in.) 53
Rear width (in.) 56
Weight (lb.) ....steel: 3,755;
(rubber: 5,075)
Gear/speed (mph) ....forward: 1/2.40,
2/3.30, 3/4.10, 4/8.50;
reverse: 1/3.00

Massey-Harris 101 S Sr., Standard

Manufacturer.......................................Massey-Harris Co.,
Racine, WI
Nebraska test number 306
Test date ....September 8–30, 1938
Test tractor serial number.........................355064
Years produced 1938–1946
Serial number range................................355001–363647 end
Serial number location ....metal tag left rear
tractor frame forward
of transmission case
and stamped top left
corner
Number produced 8,647
Engine ....Chrysler Industrial
vertical L-head
Test engine serial number..........................293
Cylinders 6
Bore and stroke (in.) ....3.125 x 4.375
Rated rpm 1,500
Displacement (c.i.) 201.3
Fuel ....gasoline
Fuel tank capacity (gal.) 15
Carburetor...Schebler TRX-22,
1.00-in.
Air cleaner ....United
Ignition ....Auto-Lite with 6-v
battery
Cooling capacity (gal.) 4.50
Maximum brake horsepower tests
PTO/belt horsepower........................35.02 and 40.04
Crankshaft rpm ....1,500 and 1,800
Fuel use (gal./hr.) ....3.08 and 3.61
Maximum drawbar horsepower tests
Gear......................................steel: 3rd; rubber: 3rd
Drawbar horsepower.........................steel: 23.11;
rubber: 30.80
Pull weight (lb.)..........................steel: 1,703;
rubber: 2,612
Speed (mph) ....steel: 5.09; rubber: 4.42
Percent slippage...........................steel: 3.88; rubber: 7.15
SAE drawbar horsepower...........................23.84
SAE belt/PTO horsepower ....31.31 and 36.01
Type ....standard
Front wheel (in.)..................................(steel: 28 x 4.63;
rubber: 6.00 x 16)
Rear wheel (in.)...................................(steel: 44 x 10;
rubber: 12.75 x 24)
Weight (lb.) ....steel: 3,800;
(rubber: 5,600)
Gear/speed (mph) ....forward: 1/2.40,
2/3.36, 3/4.50,
4/16.10; reverse:
1/2.15

Massey-Harris

Massey-Harris 101 R Sr., Row Crop

Manufacturer	Massey-Harris Co., Racine, WI
Nebraska test number	307
Test date	September 9–30, 1938
Test tractor serial number	255257
Years produced	1938–1946
Serial number range	255001–272506 end
Serial number location	metal tag left rear tractor frame forward of transmission case and stamped top left front corner
Number produced	approximately 17,506
Engine	Chrysler Industrial 201.3 vertical L-head
Test engine serial number	453
Cylinders	6
Bore and stroke (in.)	3.125 x 4.375
Rated rpm	1,500
Displacement (c.i.)	201.3
Fuel	gasoline
Fuel tank capacity (gal.)	18
Carburetor	Schebler TRX-22, 1.00-in.
Air cleaner	United
Ignition	Auto-Lite with 6-v battery
Cooling capacity (gal.)	4.50

Maximum brake horsepower tests

PTO/belt horsepower	35.40 and 40.67
Crankshaft rpm	1,500 and 1,800
Fuel use (gal./hr.)	3.11 and 3.65

Maximum drawbar horsepower tests

Gear	steel: 2nd; rubber: 3rd
Drawbar horsepower	steel: 25.38; rubber: 31.50
Pull weight (lb.)	steel: 2,624; rubber: 2,487
Speed (mph)	steel: 3.63; rubber: 4.75
Percent slippage	steel: 5.30; rubber: 5.34
SAE drawbar horsepower	24.78
SAE belt/PTO horsepower	31.30 and 36.19
Type	tricycle
Front wheel (in.)	(steel: 22.50 x 4; rubber: 5.50 x 16)
Rear wheel (in.)	(steel: 49 x 8; rubber: 11.25 x 36)
Weight (lb.)	steel: 3,705; (rubber: 5,225)
Gear/speed (mph)	forward: 1/2.59, 2/3.63, 3/4.85, 4/17.35; reverse: 1/2.30

Massey-Harris 101 R Jr., Row Crop

Manufacturer	Massey-Harris Co., Racine, WI
Nebraska test number	318
Test date	May 22–26, 1939
Test tractor serial number	375186
Years produced	1939–1946
Serial number range	375001–505513 end
Serial number location	metal tag left rear tractor frame forward of transmission case and stamped top left front corner
Number produced	approximately 130,513
Engine	Continental 124; this engine used from 1939 to 1940; vertical L-head
Test engine serial number	MFA 1245190
Cylinders	4
Bore and stroke (in.)	3.00 x 4.375
Rated rpm	1,500
Compression ratio	6.7:1
Displacement (c.i.)	123.7
Fuel	gasoline
Fuel tank capacity (gal.)	10
Carburetor	Schebler TSX-28, 0.875-in.
Air cleaner	Donaldson
Ignition	Auto-Lite with 6-v battery
Cooling capacity (gal.)	2.75

Maximum brake horsepower tests

PTO/belt horsepower	26.27
Crankshaft rpm	1,800
Fuel use (gal./hr.)	2.41

Maximum drawbar horsepower tests

Gear	3rd
Drawbar horsepower	20.47
Pull weight (lb.)	1,738
Speed (mph)	4.42
Percent slippage	5.80
SAE drawbar horsepower	16.35
SAE belt/PTO horsepower	23.74
Type	tricycle
Front tire (in.)	5.00 x 15
Rear tire (in.)	10.00 x 36
Length (in.)	wheelbase: 83.50
Tread width (in.)	52–88
Weight (lb.)	3,230
Gear/speed (mph)	forward: 1/2.60, 2/3.60, 3/4.90, 4/17.40; reverse: 1/2.30

Massey-Harris 101 R Jr., Row Crop

Manufacturer	Massey-Harris Co., Racine, WI
Nebraska test number	359
Test date	October 7–12, 1940
Test tractor serial number	J 376998
Years produced	1939–1946
Serial number range	375001–505513 end
Serial number location	metal tag left rear tractor frame forward of transmission case and stamped top left front corner
Number produced	approximately 130,513
Engine	Continental 140; this engine used from 1940 to 1943; vertical, L-head
Test engine serial number	MFA-140G-5526
Cylinders	4
Bore and stroke (in.)	3.1875 x 4.375
Rated rpm	1,800
Compression ratio	6.5:1
Displacement (c.i.)	139.6
Fuel	gasoline

Fuel tank capacity (gal.) 10
Carburetor ....Schebler TSX-28,
0.875-in.
Air cleaner ....Donaldson
Ignition...Auto-Lite with
6-v battery
Cooling capacity (gal.) 2.75

Maximum brake horsepower tests
PTO/belt horsepower..........................30.56
Crankshaft rpm 1,800
Fuel use (gal./hr.)................................2.61

Maximum drawbar horsepower tests
Gear...3rd
Drawbar horsepower............................24.65
Pull weight (lb.)...................................2,118
Speed (mph) 4.36
Percent slippage..................................6.14
SAE drawbar horsepower...........................19.45
SAE belt/PTO horsepower 27.40
Type ....tricycle
Front tire (in.)..4.75 x 15
Rear tire (in.)...10.00 x 36
Length (in.) ....wheelbase: 83.50
Tread width (in.)...52–88
Weight (lb.) ....(4,650)
Gear/speed (mph) ....forward: 1/2.60, 2/3.60,
3/4.90, 4/17.40;
reverse: 1/2.30

Massey-Harris 81 R, Row Crop

Manufacturer...Massey-Harris Co.,
Racine, WI
Nebraska test number 376
Test date ....September 29 to
October 20, 1941
Test tractor serial number..........................400475
Years produced 1941–1948
Serial number range....................................400001–406601 end
Serial number location ....metal tag left rear
tractor frame forward
of transmission case
and stamped top left
front corner
Number produced 6,601
Engine ....Continental 124
vertical L-head
Test engine serial number..........................MFB 124G 9405
Cylinders 4
Bore and stroke (in.) ....3.00 x 4.375
Rated rpm 1,500
Displacement (c.i.) 123.7
Fuel ....gasoline
Fuel tank capacity (gal.) 12
Carburetor ....Marvel-Schebler
TSX-8, 0.875-in.
Air cleaner ....Donaldson
Ignition...Auto-Lite I.G.W.-
4139-A distributor
with 6-v battery
Cooling capacity (gal.) 2.75

Maximum brake horsepower tests
PTO/belt horsepower..........................27.07
Crankshaft rpm 1,799
Fuel use (gal./hr.)................................2.47

Maximum drawbar horsepower tests
Gear...3rd
Drawbar horsepower............................20.79
Pull weight (lb.)...................................1,699
Speed (mph) 4.59
Percent slippage..................................5.86
SAE drawbar horsepower...........................16.20
SAE belt/PTO horsepower 24.09
Type ....tricycle
Front tire (in.)..4.00 x 15
Rear tire (in.)...9.00 x 32
Length (in.) 119
Height (in.) 57.50
Rear width (in.)..81.50
Tread width (in.)...48–88
Weight (lb.) 2,720
Gear/speed (mph) ....forward: 1/2.50,
2/3.60, 3/4.70,
4/16.00; reverse:
1/2.50

Massey-Harris 101 R Sr., Row Crop

Manufacturer...Massey-Harris Co.,
Racine, WI
Nebraska test number 377
Test date ....September 30 to
October 20, 1941
Test tractor serial number..........................258390
Years produced 1938–1946
Serial number range....................................265001–272506 end
Serial number location ....metal tag left rear
tractor frame forward
of transmission case
and stamped top left
corner
Number produced ....approximately 17,506
Engine ....Chrysler 217
vertical L-head
Test engine serial number..........................T112 501 525
Cylinders 6
Bore and stroke (in.) ....3.25 x 4.375
Rated rpm 1,500
Displacement (c.i.) 217.8
Fuel ....gasoline
Fuel tank capacity (gal.) 18
Carburetor ....Marvel-Schebler
TRX-22, 1.00-in.
Air cleaner ....United
Ignition...Auto-Lite with
6-v battery
Cooling capacity (gal.) 3.50

Maximum brake horsepower tests
PTO/belt horsepower..........................46.97
Crankshaft rpm 1,802
Fuel use (gal./hr.)................................4.01

Maximum drawbar horsepower tests
Gear...rubber: 3rd
Drawbar horsepower............................34.63
Pull weight (lb.)...................................2,747
Speed (mph) 4.73
Percent slippage..................................6.51
SAE drawbar horsepower...........................27.50
SAE belt/PTO horsepower 40.72
Type ....tricycle

Front wheel (in.)................................steel: 24.50 x 4;
(rubber: 5.00 x 15)

Rear wheel (in.)................................steel: 50 x 8;
(rubber: 11.00 x 38)

Tread width (in.)................................52–90

Weight (lb.)................................3,690

Gear/speed (mph) ....forward: 1/2.68,
2/3.74, 3/5.00, 4/17.85
rubber only; reverse:
1/2.40

Massey-Harris 44 RT, Row Crop

Manufacturer................................Massey-Harris Co.,
Racine, WI

Nebraska test number 389

Test date ....October 29 to
November 12, 1947

Test tractor serial number................................44GR 1018

Years produced 1946–1953

Serial number range................................1001–33890;
40001–47060 end,
1952–1953, types
interspersed

Serial number location ....metal tag left rear
tractor frame forward
of transmission case
and stamped top left
front corner

Number produced ....32,890 into 1952; na
1952 –1953

Engine ....Massey-Harris H 260
vertical I-head

Test engine serial number................................MHA 260G2250

Cylinders 4

Bore and stroke (in.) ....3.875 x 5.50

Rated rpm 1,350

Compression ratio................................5.65:1

Displacement (c.i.) 260

Fuel ....gasoline

Fuel tank capacity (gal.) 25

Carburetor................................Zenith 62AJ10, 1.25-in.

Air cleaner................................Donaldson

Ignition................................Auto-Lite with
6-v battery

Cooling capacity (gal.) 5.75

Maximum brake horsepower tests

  PTO/belt horsepower................................45.64

  Crankshaft rpm 1,351

  Fuel use (gal./hr.) 3.97

Maximum drawbar horsepower tests

  Gear................................3rd

  Drawbar horsepower................................39.90

  Pull weight (lb.)................................3,197

  Speed (mph) 4.68

  Percent slippage................................6.32

SAE drawbar horsepower................................31.02

SAE belt/PTO horsepower................................39.98

Type ....tricycle

Front tire (in.)................................5.50 x 16

Rear tire (in.)................................12.00 x 38

Length (in.) 135.25

Height (in.) 80

Rear width (in.) 79

Tread width (in.)................................52–88

Weight (lb.) 4,100

Gear/speed (mph) ....forward: 1/2.48, 2/3.75,
3/4.98, 4/6.47, 5/13.80;
reverse: 1/2.89

Massey-Harris 55, Standard

Manufacturer................................Massey-Harris Co.,
Racine, WI

Nebraska test number 394

Test date ....May 18–27, 1948

Test tractor serial number................................55GS 1498

Years produced 1946–1955

Serial number range................................1001–7077;
10001–17888 end,
1952–1955, types
interspersed

Serial number location ....metal tag left rear
tractor frame forward
of transmission case
and stamped top left
front corner

Number produced ....6,077 into 1952; na
1952–1955

Engine ....Massey-Harris J382
vertical I-head

Test engine serial number................................2,651

Cylinders 4

Bore and stroke (in.) ....4.50 x 6.00

Rated rpm 1,350

Compression ratio................................5.65:1

Displacement (c.i.) 382

Fuel ....gasoline

Fuel tank capacity (gal.) 27.50

Carburetor................................Zenith 62AJ10, 1.25-in.

Air cleaner ....Donaldson

Ignition................................Auto-Lite with
6-v battery

Cooling capacity (gal.) 7

Maximum brake horsepower tests

  PTO/belt horsepower................................58.98

  Crankshaft rpm 1,349

  Fuel use (gal./hr.) 5.17

Maximum drawbar horsepower tests

  Gear................................3rd

  Drawbar horsepower................................52.47

  Pull weight (lb.)................................4,028

  Speed (mph) 4.89

  Percent slippage................................6.90

SAE drawbar horsepower................................40.65

SAE belt/PTO horsepower................................52.18

Type ....standard

Front tire (in.)................................7.50 x 18

Rear tire (in.)................................14.00 x 34

Length (in.) 141.50

Height (in.) 78

Tread width (in.)................................57

Weight (lb.) 7,150

Gear/speed (mph) ....forward: 1/2.96, 2/4.22,
3/5.22, 4/12.07;
reverse: 1/2.54

Massey-Harris Pony

Manufacturer................................Massey-Harris Co.,
Ltd., Toronto, Ontario,
Canada

Nebraska test number 401

Test date ....September 14–22, 1948
Test tractor serial number.....................PGS 3461
Years produced 1947–1954
Serial number range.............................PGS 1001 to PGS 1570; PGA 1571 to PGA 22669
Serial number location ....metal plate on right side front frame below radiator
Number produced 21,669
Engine ....Continental N62 vertical L-head
Test engine serial number........................N 624863
Cylinders 4
Bore and stroke (in.) ....2.375 x 3.50
Rated rpm 1,800
Compression ratio.................................6.5:1
Displacement (c.i.) 62
Fuel ....gasoline
Carburetor ....Marvel-Schebler TSV-24, 0.625-in.
Air cleaner ....Donaldson
Ignition...Auto-Lite with 6-v battery
Cooling capacity (gal.) 1.75
Maximum brake horsepower tests
 PTO/belt horsepower............................11.62
 Crankshaft rpm 1,801
 Fuel use (gal./hr.)................................1.16
Maximum drawbar horsepower tests
 Gear...2nd
 Drawbar horsepower.............................10.43
 Pull weight (lb.)...................................1,124
 Speed (mph) 3.48
 Percent slippage..................................6.30
SAE drawbar horsepower........................8.31
SAE belt/PTO horsepower.......................10.34
Type ....standard
Front tire (in.) ....4.00 x 15
Rear tire (in.).......................................8.00 x 24
Length (in.) 98
Height (in.) 62
Tread width (in.)...................................41–72
Weight (lb.) 1,520
Gear/speed (mph) ....forward: 1/2.74, 2/3.59, 3/7.00; reverse: 1/3.22

Massey-Harris 22 RT, Row Crop
Manufacturer...Massey-Harris Co., Racine, WI
Nebraska test number 403
Test date ....October 15–21, 1948
Test tractor serial number.......................22GR 1019
Years produced 1948–1953
Serial number range...............................1001–10783; 20001–20623 end
Serial number location ....metal tag left rear tractor frame forward of transmission case and stamped top left front corner
Number produced ....approximately 10,406
Engine ....Continental Red Seal F vertical L-head

Test engine serial number.......................MFC 140G14754
Cylinders 4
Bore and stroke (in.) ....3.1875 x 4.375
Rated rpm 1,800
Compression ratio.................................6.3:1
Displacement (c.i.) 139.6
Fuel ....gasoline
Fuel tank capacity (gal.) 13
Carburetor ....Marvel-Schebler TSX-34, 0.875-in.
Air cleaner ....Donaldson
Ignition...Auto-Lite with 6-v battery
Cooling capacity (gal.) 2.75
Maximum brake horsepower tests
 PTO/belt horsepower............................31.05
 Crankshaft rpm 1,799
 Fuel use (gal./hr.)................................2.82
Maximum drawbar horsepower tests
 Gear...3rd
 Drawbar horsepower.............................22.87
 Pull weight (lb.)...................................1,962
 Speed (mph) 4.37
 Percent slippage..................................5.94
SAE drawbar horsepower........................17.93
SAE belt/PTO horsepower.......................26.85
Type ....tricycle
Front tire (in.) ....4.00 x 15
Rear tire (in.).......................................10.00 x 28
Length (in.) 119.50
Height (in.) 76
Tread width (in.)...................................48–88
Weight (lb.) 2,560
Gear/speed (mph) ....forward: 1/2.45, 2/3.51, 3/4.62, 4/13.02; reverse: 1/2.45

Massey-Harris 30 RT, Row Crop
Manufacturer...Massey-Harris Co., Racine, WI
Nebraska test number 409
Test date ....May 12–26, 1949
Test tractor serial number.......................30GR 5172
Years produced 1946–1953
Serial number range...............................1001–19382; 30001–30600
Serial number location ....metal tag left rear tractor frame forward of transmission case and stamped top left front corner
Number produced ....approximately 18,982
Engine ....Continental F162 vertical L-head
Test engine serial number.......................MFB 162G98861
Cylinders 4
Bore and stroke (in.) ....3.4375 x 4.375
Rated rpm 1,800
Compression ratio.................................6.1:1
Displacement (c.i.) 162.4
Fuel ....gasoline
Fuel tank capacity (gal.) 20
Carburetor ....Marvel-Schebler TSX-308, 0.875-in.

Air cleaner .... Donaldson
Ignition .... Auto-Lite with
6-v battery
Cooling capacity (gal.) 3
Maximum brake horsepower tests
PTO/belt horsepower 34.18
Crankshaft rpm 1,800
Fuel use (gal./hr.) 3.26
Maximum drawbar horsepower tests
Gear 3rd
Drawbar horsepower 26.24
Pull weight (lb.) 2,333
Speed (mph) 4.22
Percent slippage 6.00
SAE drawbar horsepower 20.42
SAE belt/PTO horsepower 29.99
Type .... tricycle
Front tire (in.) .... 5.00 x 15
Rear tire (in.) .... 10.00 x 38
Length (in.) 128
Height (in.) 74.25
Tread width (in.) 52–88
Weight (lb.) 3,770
Gear/speed (mph) .... forward: 1/2.58, 2/3.61,
3/4.51, 4/6.31, 5/12.63;
reverse: 1/2.93

Massey-Harris 44D, Diesel, Standard
Manufacturer .... Massey-Harris Co.,
Racine, WI
Nebraska test number 426
Test date .... September 28 to
October 1, 1949
Test tractor serial number 44DS 1116
Years produced 1948–1953
Serial number range 1001–6396;
40001–47060 end,
1952–1953, types
interspersed
Serial number location .... metal tag left rear
tractor frame forward
of transmission case
and stamped top left
front corner
Number produced .... 5,396 into 1952; na
1952–1953
Engine .... Massey-Harris HD260
vertical I-head
Test engine serial number .... HD 2601535
Cylinders 4
Bore and stroke (in.) .... 3.875 x 5.50
Rated rpm 1,350
Compression ratio 15.0:1
Displacement (c.i.) 259.4
Fuel .... diesel
Main tank capacity (gal.) 19
Auxiliary tank capacity (gal.) 5.75
Carburetor .... Bosch injector pump
Air cleaner .... Donaldson
Ignition .... Auto-Lite 12-v; with 2,
6-v battery
Maximum brake horsepower tests
PTO/belt horsepower 41.82
Crankshaft rpm 1,350
Fuel use (gal./hr.) 2.63

Maximum drawbar horsepower tests
Gear 3rd
Drawbar horsepower 37.91
Pull weight (lb.) 3,380
Speed (mph) 4.21
Percent slippage 6.79
SAE drawbar horsepower 29.61
SAE belt/PTO horsepower 36.58
Type .... standard
Front tire (in.) .... 6.00 x 16
Rear tire (in.) .... 13.00 x 30
Length (in.) 129
Tread width (in.) 54.13
Weight (lb.) 4,565
Gear/speed (mph) .... forward: 1/2.21,
2/3.33, 3/4.43, 4/5.75,
5/12.28; reverse:
1/2.89

Massey-Harris 44K, Standard
Manufacturer .... Massey-Harris Co.,
Racine, WI
Nebraska test number 427
Test date .... September 29 to
October 14, 1949
Test tractor serial number 44KS 4370
Years produced 1946–1953
Serial number range 1001–6822;
40001–47060 end,
1952–1953, types
interspersed
Serial number location .... metal tag left rear
tractor frame forward
of transmission case
and stamped top left
front corner
Number produced .... 5,822 into 1952, na
1952–1953
Engine .... Massey-Harris H260
vertical I-head
Test engine serial number .... MHA 260K25
Cylinders 4
Bore and stroke (in.) .... 3.875 x 5.50
Rated rpm 1,350
Compression ratio 4.65:1
Displacement (c.i.) 259.4
Fuel .... tractor fuel
Fuel tank capacity (gal.) 19
Carburetor .... Zenith 62 AJ10,
1.25-in.
Air cleaner .... Donaldson
Ignition .... Auto-Lite with
6-v battery
Cooling capacity (gal.) 5.75
Maximum brake horsepower tests
PTO/belt horsepower 38.11
Crankshaft rpm 1,350
Fuel use (gal./hr.) 3.77
Maximum drawbar horsepower tests
Gear 3rd
Drawbar horsepower 35.28
Pull weight (lb.) 3,122
Speed (mph) 4.24
Percent slippage 5.81
SAE drawbar horsepower 27.64

SAE belt/PTO horsepower 33.53
Type ....standard
Front tire (in.)...6.00 x 16
Rear tire (in.)..13.00 x 30
Length (in.) 129
Tread width (in.)..54.13
Weight (lb.) 4,500
Gear/speed (mph) ....forward: 1/2.21,
2/3.33, 3/4.43, 4/5.75,
5/12.28; reverse:
1/2.89

Massey-Harris 55K, Standard

Manufacturer...Massey-Harris Co.,
Racine, WI
Nebraska test number 428
Test date ....October 3–14, 1949
Test tractor serial number.........................55KS 2451
Years produced 1946–1955
Serial number range..................................1001–5504;
10001–17888 end,
1952–1955, types
interspersed
Serial number location ....metal tag left rear
tractor frame forward
of transmission case
and stamped top left
front corner
Number produced ....4,504 into 1952; na
1952–1955
Engine ....Massey-Harris J382
vertical I-head
Test engine serial number.........................MJA 382K8711
Cylinders 4
Bore and stroke (in.) ....4.50 x 6.00
Rated rpm 1,350
Compression ratio.....................................4.5:1
Displacement (c.i.) 382
Fuel ....tractor fuel
Fuel tank capacity (gal.) 27.50
Carburetor...Zenith 62 AJ 10,
1.25-in.
Air cleaner ....Donaldson
Ignition..Auto-Lite with
6-v battery
Cooling capacity (gal.) 7
Maximum brake horsepower tests
PTO/belt horsepower..........................52.17
Crankshaft rpm 1,350
Fuel use (gal./hr.)...............................5.32
Maximum drawbar horsepower tests
Gear..3rd
Drawbar horsepower...........................47.64
Pull weight (lb.)...................................3,588
Speed (mph) 4.98
Percent slippage.................................5.91
SAE drawbar horsepower...........................37.12
SAE belt/PTO horsepower 46.32
Type ....standard
Front tire (in.)...7.50 x 18
Rear tire (in.)..14.00 x 34
Length (in.) 145
Height (in.) 83.25
Tread width (in.)..57.31
Weight (lb.) 7,150

Gear/speed (mph) ....forward: 1/2.96, 2/4.22,
3/5.22, 4/12.07;
reverse: 1/2.54

Massey-Harris 55D, Diesel, Standard

Manufacturer...Massey-Harris Co.,
Racine, WI
Nebraska test number 452
Test date ....October 17–26, 1950
Test tractor serial number.........................55DS 1827
Years produced 1949–1955
Serial number range..................................1001–2964;
10001–17888 end,
1952–1955, types
interspersed
Serial number location ....metal tag left rear
tractor frame forward
of transmission case
and stamped top left
front corner
Number produced ....1,964 into 1952; na
1952–1955
Engine ....Massey-Harris JD382
vertical I-head
Test engine serial number.........................JD 3821160
Cylinders 4
Bore and stroke (in.) ....4.50 x 6.00
Rated rpm 1,350
Compression ratio.....................................15:1
Displacement (c.i.) 382
Fuel ....diesel
Fuel tank capacity (gal.) 27.50
Carburetor...Bosch injector pump
PSB
Air cleaner ....Donaldson
Ignition..Auto-Lite 12-v; with 2,
6-v battery
Cooling capacity (gal.) 7
Maximum brake horsepower tests
PTO/belt horsepower..........................59.04
Crankshaft rpm 1,351
Fuel use (gal./hr.)...............................3.94
Maximum drawbar horsepower tests
Gear..3rd
Drawbar horsepower...........................52.49
Pull weight (lb.)...................................3,777
Speed (mph) 5.21
Percent slippage.................................5.78
SAE drawbar horsepower...........................40.87
SAE belt/PTO horsepower 51.23
Type ....standard
Front tire (in.)...7.50 x 18
Rear tire (in.)..15.00 x 34
Length (in.) 145.50
Height (in.) 83.25
Tread width (in.)..57.31
Weight (lb.) 6,930
Gear/speed (mph) ....forward: 1/2.96, 2/4.22,
3/5.22, 4/12.07;
reverse: 1/2.54

Massey-Harris 55, Standard

Manufacturer...Massey-Harris Co.,
Racine, WI
Nebraska test number 455

Test date ....April 16 to May 7, 1951
Test tractor serial number 55GS 6184
Years produced 1946–1955
Serial number range 1001–7077;
10001–17888 end,
1952–1955, types
interspersed
Serial number location ....metal tag left rear
tractor frame forward
of transmission case
and stamped top left
front corner
Number produced ....6,077 into 1952; na
1952–1955
Engine ....Massey-Harris J382
vertical I-head
Test engine serial number ....MJA 382G 8726
Cylinders 4
Bore and stroke (in.) ....4.50 x 6.00
Rated rpm 1,350
Compression ratio 5.82:1
Displacement (c.i.) 382
Fuel ....gasoline
Fuel tank capacity (gal.) 27.50
Carburetor ....Zenith 62AJ10, 1.25-in.
Air cleaner ....Donaldson
Ignition ....Auto-Lite with
6-v battery
Cooling capacity (gal.) 7

Maximum brake horsepower tests
PTO/belt horsepower 66.91
Crankshaft rpm 1,350
Fuel use (gal./hr.) 5.91

Maximum drawbar horsepower tests
Gear 3rd
Drawbar horsepower 57.55
Pull weight (lb.) 4,135
Speed (mph) 5.22
Percent slippage 5.39
SAE drawbar horsepower 45.34
SAE belt/PTO horsepower 57.97
Type ....standard
Front tire (in.) ....7.50 x 18
Rear tire (in.) ....15.00 x 34
Length (in.) 145.50
Height (in.) 83.25
Tread width (in.) 57.31
Weight (lb.) 6,725
Gear/speed (mph) ....forward: 1/2.96, 2/4.22,
3/5.22, 4/12.07;
reverse: 1/2.54

Massey-Harris 33 RT, Row Crop

Manufacturer ....Massey-Harris Co.,
Racine, WI
Nebraska test number 509
Test date ....October 10–24, 1953
Test tractor serial number 33GIRF 4690
Years produced 1952–1954
Serial number range 1001–9781
Serial number location ....metal tag left rear
tractor frame forward
of transmission case
and stamped top left
front corner

Number produced 8,781
Engine ....Massey-Harris E201
vertical I-head
Test engine serial number MEA201G 6248
Cylinders 4
Bore and stroke (in.) ....3.625 x 4.875
Rated rpm 1,500
Compression ratio 6.3:1
Displacement (c.i.) 201
Fuel ....gasoline
Fuel tank capacity (gal.) 19
Carburetor ....Marvel-Schebler
TSX-305, 1.00-in.
Air cleaner ....Donaldson
Ignition ....Auto-Lite with
6-v battery
Cooling capacity (gal.) 4.50

Maximum brake horsepower tests
PTO/belt horsepower 39.52
Crankshaft rpm 1,500
Fuel use (gal./hr.) 3.43

Maximum drawbar horsepower tests
Gear 3rd
Drawbar horsepower 35.54
Pull weight (lb.) 2,906
Speed (mph) 4.59
Percent slippage 5.87
SAE drawbar horsepower 27.98
SAE belt/PTO horsepower 34.37
Type ....tricycle
Front wheel (in.) ....5.50 x 16
Rear wheel (in.) ....12.00 x 38
Length (in.) 129
Height (in.) 80.75
Tread width (in.) 52.75–88.63
Weight (lb.) 4,030
Gear/speed (mph) ....forward: 1/2.75, 2/3.84,
3/4.80, 4/6.72, 5/13.46;
reverse: 1/3.11

Massey-Harris 44 Special

Manufacturer ....Massey-Harris Co.,
Racine, WI
Nebraska test number 510
Test date ....October 10–24, 1953
Test tractor serial number 44G1SF 50001
Years produced 1953–1955
Serial number range ....50001–60719 end
Serial number location ....metal tag left rear
tractor frame forward
of transmission case
and stamped top left
front corner
Number produced 10,719
Engine ....Massey-Harris H-277
vertical I-head
Test engine serial number ....MHL 277G
Cylinders 4
Bore and stroke (in.) ....4.00 x 5.50
Rated rpm 1,350
Compression ratio 6.25:1
Displacement (c.i.) 277
Fuel ....gasoline
Fuel tank capacity (gal.) 19
Carburetor ....Zenith 10279, 1.25-in.

Air cleaner ....Donaldson
Ignition ....Auto-Lite with 6-v battery
Cooling capacity (gal.) 5.50
Maximum brake horsepower tests
    PTO/belt horsepower............................48.95
    Crankshaft rpm 1,351
    Fuel use (gal./hr.) 4.30
Maximum drawbar horsepower tests
    Gear...3rd
    Drawbar horsepower..............................43.58
    Pull weight (lb.).....................................3,749
    Speed (mph) 4.36
    Percent slippage...................................6.86
SAE drawbar horsepower.............................34.39
SAE belt/PTO horsepower.............................42.75
Type ....standard
Front wheel (in.) ....7.50 x 16
Rear wheel (in.) ....14.00 x 30
Length (in.) 136.63
Height (in.) 75.50
Tread width (in.)...58–62
Weight (lb.) 5,185
Gear/speed (mph) ....forward: 1/2.24, 2/3.39, 3/4.50, 4/5.85, 5/12.50; reverse: 1/2.95

Massey-Harris No. 16, Pacer

Manufacturer...Massey-Harris-Ferguson Ltd., Toronto, Ontario, Canada
Nebraska test number 531
Test date ....November 10–15, 1954
Test tractor serial number...........................PGA 50891
Years produced...1954–1956
Serial number range....................................50001–52771 no end
Serial number location ....metal plate on right side front frame below radiator
Engine ....Continental Y-91 vertical I-head
Test engine serial number...........................F4 3664
Cylinders 4
Bore and stroke (in.) ....2.875 x 3.50
Rated rpm 1,800
Compression ratio.......................................6.1:1
Displacement (c.i.) 91
Fuel ....gasoline
Fuel tank capacity (gal.) 7.50
Carburetor..Marvel-Schebler TSX-541, 0.875-in.
Air cleaner ....Donaldson
Ignition..Auto-Lite with 6-v battery
Cooling capacity (gal.) 1.80
Maximum brake horsepower tests
    PTO/belt horsepower............................18.87
    Crankshaft rpm 1,800
    Fuel use (gal./hr.) 1.99
Maximum drawbar horsepower tests
    Gear...2nd
    Drawbar horsepower..............................17.05
    Pull weight (lb.).....................................1,686
    Speed (mph) 3.79
    Percent slippage...................................6.76

SAE drawbar horsepower.............................12.98
SAE belt/PTO horsepower.............................16.31
Type ....standard
Front tire (in.) ....4.00 x 15
Rear tire (in.) ....10.00 x 24
Length (in.) 103.63
Height (in.) 62.63
Tread width (in.)...41–69
Weight (lb.) 1,980
Gear/speed (mph) ....forward: 1/3.02, 2/3.98, 3/7.80; reverse: 1/3.57

Massey-Harris 444 Diesel

Manufacturer...Massey-Harris-Ferguson, Inc., Racine, WI
Nebraska test number 576
Test date ....June 2–14, 1956
Test tractor serial number...........................71402 P
Years produced...1956–1958
Serial number range....................................70001–77131 end
Serial number location ....metal tag left rear tractor frame forward of transmission case and stamped top left front corner
Number produced ....7,131, types interspersed
Engine ....Massey-Harris 277 vertical I-head
Test engine serial number...........................1132
Cylinders 4
Bore and stroke (in.) ....4.00 x 5.50
Rated rpm 1,500
Compression ratio.......................................15.9:1
Displacement (c.i.) 277
Fuel ....diesel
Fuel tank capacity (gal.) 27.20
Carburetor..Bosch injector pump
Air cleaner ....Donaldson
Ignition..Auto-Lite with 12-v battery
Cooling capacity (gal.) 5.50
Maximum brake horsepower tests
    PTO/belt horsepower............................48.21
    Crankshaft rpm 1,500
    Fuel use (gal./hr.) 3.20
Maximum drawbar horsepower tests
    Gear...3rd, high range
    Drawbar horsepower..............................43.84
    Pull weight (lb.).....................................3,285
    Speed (mph) 5.00
    Percent slippage...................................5.32
SAE drawbar horsepower.............................34.43
SAE belt/PTO horsepower.............................43.16
Type ....tricycle
Front wheel (in.) ....6.50 x 16
Rear wheel (in.) ....13.00 x 38
Weight (lb.) 6,324
Gear/speed (mph).............forward: 1 high range/2.59, 1 low range/1.52, 2 high range/3.91, 2 low range/2.29, 3 high range/5.19, 3 low range/3.05, 4 high range/6.75, 4 low range/3.96, 5 high range/14.40, 5 low range/8.46; reverse: 1 high range/3.40, 1 low range/1.99

Massey-Harris 333 Diesel

Manufacturer	Massey-Harris-Ferguson Inc., Racine, WI
Nebraska test number	577
Test date	June 8–13, 1956
Test tractor serial number	20848 P
Years produced	1956–1957
Serial number range	20001–22748 end
Serial number location	metal tag left rear tractor frame forward of transmission case and stamped top left front corner
Number produced	2,748, types interspersed
Engine	Massey-Harris 208 vertical I-head
Test engine serial number	1321
Cylinders	4
Bore and stroke (in.)	3.6875 x 4.875
Rated rpm	1,500
Compression ratio	16.0:1
Displacement (c.i.)	208
Fuel	diesel
Fuel tank capacity (gal.)	27
Carburetor	Bosch injector pump
Air cleaner	Donaldson
Ignition	Auto-Lite, 12-v with 2, 6-v battery
Cooling capacity (gal.)	4.33

Maximum brake horsepower tests

PTO/belt horsepower	37.15
Crankshaft rpm	1,500
Fuel use (gal./hr.)	2.64

Maximum drawbar horsepower tests

Gear	3rd, high range
Drawbar horsepower	33.34
Pull weight (lb.)	2,562
Speed (mph)	4.88
Percent slippage	4.68
SAE drawbar horsepower	26.13
SAE belt/PTO horsepower	32.78
Type	tricycle
Front wheel (in.)	6.50 x 16
Rear wheel (in.)	12.00 x 38
Weight (lb.)	5,830
Gear/speed (mph)	forward: 1 high range/2.51, 1 low range/1.47, 2 high range/3.79, 2 low range/2.22, 3 high range/5.03, 3 low range/2.95, 4 high range/6.55, 4 low range/3.84, 5 high range/14.00, 5 low range/8.21; reverse: 1 high range/3.30, 1 low range/1.93

Massey-Harris MH 50

Manufacturer	Massey-Harris-Ferguson, Inc., Detroit, MI
Nebraska test number	595
Test date	September 25 to October 4, 1956
Test tractor serial number	SGM 509603
Years produced	1955–1957
Serial number range	500001–515707 end
Serial number location	metal tag left rear tractor frame forward of transmission case and stamped top left front corner
Number produced	15,707
Engine	Continental Z-134 vertical I-head
Test engine serial number	Z134 626366
Cylinders	4
Bore and stroke (in.)	3.3125 x 3.875
Rated rpm	2,000
Compression ratio	6.6:1
Displacement (c.i.)	134
Fuel	gasoline
Fuel tank capacity (gal.)	17
Carburetor	Marvel-Schebler TSX-605, 0.875-in.
Air cleaner	Donaldson
Ignition	Delco-Remy with 12-v battery
Cooling capacity (gal.)	2.25

Maximum brake horsepower tests

PTO/belt horsepower	32.58
Crankshaft rpm	2,000
Fuel use (gal./hr.)	3.11

Maximum drawbar horsepower tests

Gear	4th
Drawbar horsepower	30.50
Pull weight (lb.)	2,267
Speed (mph)	5.05
Percent slippage	6.23
SAE drawbar horsepower	23.75
SAE belt/PTO horsepower	28.99
Type	standard
Front wheel (in.)	6.00 x 16
Rear wheel (in.)	11.00 x 28
Length (in.)	120
Height (in.)	57
Tread width (in.)	48–76
Weight (lb.)	3,082
Gear/speed (mph)	forward: 1/1.33, 2/1.99, 3/3.65, 4/5.30, 5/7.96, 6/14.59; reverse: 1/1.77, 2/7.09

Massey-Harris 444 LP, LPG

Manufacturer	Massey-Harris-Ferguson, Inc., Racine, WI
Nebraska test number	602
Test date	October 25 to November 3, 1956
Test tractor serial number	444BIRF 72917
Years produced	1956–1958
Serial number range	70001–77131 end
Serial number location	metal tag left rear tractor frame forward of transmission case and stamped top left front corner

Number produced ....7,131, types interspersed

Engine ....Massey-Harris 277 vertical I-head

Test engine serial number...........................MHA 277B 9870

Cylinders 4

Bore and stroke (in.) ....4.00 x 5.50

Rated rpm 1,500

Compression ratio.....................................8.98:1

Displacement (c.i.) 277

Fuel ....LPG

Carburetor...Ensign XG, 1.25-in.

Air cleaner ....Donaldson

Ignition ....Auto-Lite 12-v; with 1, 12-v or 2, 6-v battery

Cooling capacity (gal.) 5.75

Maximum brake horsepower tests

    PTO/belt horsepower...........................49.24

    Crankshaft rpm 1,500

    Fuel use (gal./hr.) 5.06

Maximum drawbar horsepower tests

    Gear..3rd, high range

    Drawbar horsepower.........................45.26

    Pull weight (lb.).............................3,372

    Speed (mph) 5.03

    Percent slippage............................4.77

SAE drawbar horsepower...........................35.15

SAE belt/PTO horsepower 43.80

Type ....tricycle

Front wheel (in.).......................................6.50 x 16

Rear wheel (in.).......................................13.00 x 38

Height (in.)..82.25

Tread width (in.).......................................56–88

Weight (lb.)...5,628

Gear/speed (mph) . . . . . . forward: 1 high range/2.59, 1 low range/1.52, 2 high range/3.91, 2 low range/2.29, 3 high range/5.19, 3 low range/3.05, 4 high range/6.75, 4 low range/3.96, 5 high range/14.40, 5 low range/8.46; reverse: 1 low range/1.99, 2 high range/3.40

Massey-Harris 333

Manufacturer..Massey-Harris-Ferguson, Inc., Racine, WI

Nebraska test number 603

Test date ....October 25 to November 3, 1956

Test tractor serial number...........................333GIRF 22173

Years produced 1956–1957

Serial number range...................................20001–22748 end

Serial number location ....metal tag left rear tractor frame forward of transmission case and stamped top left front corner

Number produced ....2,748, types interspersed

Engine ....Massey-Harris 208 vertical I-head

Test engine serial number..........................MEA 208G1842

Cylinders 4

Bore and stroke (in.) ....3.6875 x 4.875

Rated rpm 1,500

Compression ratio.....................................7.15:1

Displacement (c.i.) 208

Fuel ....gasoline

Fuel tank capacity (gal.) 27

Carburetor...Marvel-Schebler TSX-596, 1.00-in.

Air cleaner ....Donaldson

Ignition ....Auto-Lite, 12-v with 1, 12-v or 2, 6-v battery

Cooling capacity (gal.) 4.33

Maximum brake horsepower tests

    PTO/belt horsepower...........................41.89

    Crankshaft rpm 1,500

    Fuel use (gal./hr.)..............................3.57

Maximum drawbar horsepower tests

    Gear..3rd, high range

    Drawbar horsepower.........................37.26

    Pull weight (lb.).............................2,871

    Speed (mph) 4.87

    Percent slippage............................4.92

SAE drawbar horsepower...........................29.23

SAE belt/PTO horsepower 37.10

Type ....tricycle

Front wheel (in.).......................................6.50 x 16

Rear wheel (in.).......................................12.00 x 38

Height (in.)..83.50

Tread width (in.).......................................56–88

Weight (lb.)...4,668

Gear/speed (mph).............forward: 1 high range/2.51, 1 low range/1.47, 2 high range/3.79, 2 low range/2.22, 3 high range/5.03, 3 low range/2.95, 4 high range/6.55, 4 low range/3.84, 5 high range/14.00, 5 low range/8.21; reverse: 1 low range/1.93, 2 high range/3.30

Chapter 54
MINNEAPOLIS

Minneapolis 12-25

Manufacturer	Minneapolis Threshing Machine Co., Hopkins, MN
Nebraska test number	13
Test date	May 17 to June 3, 1920
Test tractor serial number	1604
Years produced	1920–1926
Serial number location	cast-iron plate on left frame behind front wheels
Number produced	na, all models interspersed
Engine	Minneapolis vertical L-head
Cylinders	4
Bore and stroke (in.)	4.50 x 7.00
Rated rpm	750
Displacement (c.i.)	445.3
Fuel	kerosene/gasoline
Main tank capacity (gal.)	18.50
Auxiliary tank capacity (gal.)	3
Carburetor	Kingston
Air cleaner	Bennett
Ignition	K-W, H magneto
Cooling capacity (gal.)	8.88

Maximum brake horsepower tests

PTO/belt horsepower	26.24
Crankshaft rpm	760
Fuel use (gal./hr.)	4.24

Maximum drawbar horsepower tests

Gear	low
Drawbar horsepower	16.26
Pull weight (lb.)	2,852
Speed (mph)	2.14
Percent slippage	10.18
SAE drawbar horsepower	12
SAE belt/PTO horsepower	25
Type	4 wheel
Front wheel (in.)	steel: 36 x 6
Rear wheel (in.)	steel: 56 x 12
Length (in.)	100 wheel, 166 total
Height (in.)	64
Rear width (in.)	86
Weight (lb.)	6,400
Gear/speed (mph)	forward: 1/2.21, 2/2.98; reverse: 1/2.21

Minneapolis 22-44

Manufacturer	Minneapolis Threshing Machine Co., Hopkins, MN
Nebraska test number	14
Test date	May 18 to June 3, 1920
Test tractor serial number	1754
Years produced	1921–1927
Serial number location	cast-iron plate on front frame
Number produced	na, all models interspersed
Engine	Minneapolis horizontal, valve-in-head
Cylinders	4
Bore and stroke (in.)	6.00 x 7.00
Rated rpm	700
Displacement (c.i.)	791.7
Fuel	kerosene/gasoline
Carburetor	Kingston E
Ignition	K-W, HT magneto

Maximum brake horsepower tests

PTO/belt horsepower	46.04
Crankshaft rpm	701
Fuel use (gal./hr.)	6.74

Maximum drawbar horsepower tests

Drawbar horsepower	33.21
Pull weight (lb.)	5,104
Speed (mph)	2.44
Percent slippage	12.36
SAE drawbar horsepower	22
SAE belt/PTO horsepower	44
Type	4 wheel
Front wheel (in.)	steel:
Rear wheel (in.)	steel: 66 x 20
Length (in.)	117 wheel, 167 total
Height (in.)	110
Rear width (in.)	96
Weight (lb.)	12,000
Gear/speed (mph)	forward: 1/2.70; reverse: 1/na

Minneapolis 35-70, 40-80

Manufacturer	Minneapolis Threshing Machine Co., Hopkins, MN
Nebraska test number	15
Test date	May 21 to June 4, 1920
Test tractor serial number	1647
Years produced	1912–1929
Serial number location	cast-iron plate on front frame
Number produced	na, all models interspersed
Engine	Minneapolis horizontal, valve-in-head
Cylinders	4
Bore and stroke (in.)	7.25 x 9.00
Rated rpm	550
Displacement (c.i.)	1486.2
Fuel	kerosene/gasoline
Main tank capacity (gal.)	80
Auxiliary tank capacity (gal.)	10
Carburetor	Kingston E
Ignition	K-W, HT magneto
Cooling capacity (gal.)	60

Maximum brake horsepower tests

PTO/belt horsepower	74.01
Crankshaft rpm	556
Fuel use (gal./hr.)	9.97

Maximum drawbar horsepower tests
- Drawbar horsepower 52.55
- Pull weight (lb.) 10,998
- Speed (mph) 1.79
- Percent slippage 18.30
- SAE drawbar horsepower 35
- SAE belt/PTO horsepower 70
- Type ....4 wheel
- Front wheel (in.) ....steel: 40 x 14
- Rear wheel (in.) ....steel: 85 x 30
- Length (in.) ....136 wheel, 206 total
- Height (in.) 136
- Rear width (in.) 108
- Weight (lb.) 22,500
- Gear/speed (mph) ....forward: 1/2.10; reverse: 1/2.10

Minneapolis 17-30, Type A

- Manufacturer ....Minneapolis Threshing Machine Co., Hopkins, MN
- Nebraska test number 70
- Test date ....March 28 to April 2,1921
- Test tractor serial number 2038
- Years produced 1922–1929
- Serial number location ....cast-iron plate on top of transmission
- Number produced ....na, all models interspersed
- Engine ....Minneapolis vertical, valve-in-head
- Test engine serial number 3745
- Cylinders 4
- Bore and stroke (in.) ....4.75 x 7.00
- Rated rpm 750
- Displacement (c.i.) 496.2
- Fuel ....kerosene/gasoline
- Main tank capacity (gal.) 17.90
- Auxiliary tank capacity (gal.) 6.30
- Carburetor ....Schebler (Kingston, Number 71797), 1.50-in.
- Air cleaner ....Donaldson
- Ignition ....Bosch (Dixie HT 46) magneto

Maximum brake horsepower tests
- PTO/belt horsepower 31.95
- Crankshaft rpm 782
- Fuel use (gal./hr.) 3.91

Maximum drawbar horsepower tests
- Gear ....low
- Drawbar horsepower 19.69
- Pull weight (lb.) 3,921
- Speed (mph) 1.88
- Percent slippage 12.40
- SAE drawbar horsepower 17
- SAE belt/PTO horsepower 30
- Type ....4 wheel
- Front wheel (in.) ....steel: 36 x 5
- Rear wheel (in.) ....steel: 54 x 12
- Length (in.) 132
- Height (in.) 70.50
- Rear width (in.) 75
- Weight (lb.) 6,400

- Gear/speed (mph) ....forward: 1/2.06, 2/2.70; reverse: 1/2.26

Minneapolis 17-30, Type B

- Manufacturer ....Minneapolis Threshing Machine Co., Hopkins, MN
- Nebraska test number 118
- Test date ....October 21 to November 12, 1925
- Test tractor serial number 3972
- Years produced 1926–1929
- Serial number location ....cast-iron plate on top of transmission
- Number produced ....na, all models interspersed
- Engine ....Minneapolis vertical, valve-in-head
- Test engine serial number 5073
- Cylinders 4
- Bore and stroke (in.) ....4.875 x 7.00
- Rated rpm 825
- Displacement (c.i.) 522.6
- Fuel ....kerosene/gasoline
- Main tank capacity (gal.) 17.90
- Auxiliary tank capacity (gal.) 6.3
- Carburetor ....Wheeler Schebler A, 1.50-in.
- Air cleaner ....Donaldson-Simplex
- Ignition ....American Bosch ED21TC magneto
- Cooling capacity (gal.) 10

Maximum brake horsepower tests
- PTO/belt horsepower 34.76
- Crankshaft rpm 824
- Fuel use (gal./hr.) 5.22

Maximum drawbar horsepower tests
- Gear ....high
- Drawbar horsepower 23.18
- Pull weight (lb.) 3,040
- Speed (mph) 2.86
- Percent slippage 8.57
- SAE drawbar horsepower 17
- SAE belt/PTO horsepower 30
- Type ....4 wheel
- Front wheel (in.) ....steel: 36 x 5
- Rear wheel (in.) ....steel: 54 x 12
- Length (in.) 142.50
- Height (in.) 72
- Rear width (in.) 76.50
- Tread width (in.) 58.50
- Weight (lb.) 7,300
- Gear/speed (mph) ....forward: 1/2.23, 2/2.84; reverse: 1/2.26

Minneapolis 27-42

- Manufacturer ....Minneapolis Threshing Machine Co., Hopkins, MN
- Nebraska test number 162
- Test date ....May 28 to June 11, 1929
- Test tractor serial number 9044
- Years produced 1926–1929
- Serial number location ....cast-iron plate on top of transmission

Number produced ....na, all models
  interspersed
Engine ....Minneapolis vertical I,
  valve-in-head
Test engine serial number....................10801
Cylinders 4
Bore and stroke (in.) ....4.875 x 7.00
Rated rpm 925
Displacement (c.i.) 522.6
Fuel ....gasoline
Fuel tank capacity (gal.) 18
Carburetor..Stromberg UTR, 1.50-in.
Air cleaner ....Donaldson-Simplex
Ignition..American Bosch ZR4
  Ed34 magneto
Cooling capacity (gal.) 12.60
Maximum brake horsepower tests
PTO/belt horsepower.............................48.42
Crankshaft rpm 925
Fuel use (gal./hr.) 5.13
Maximum drawbar horsepower tests
Gear..low
Drawbar horsepower.............................34.30
Pull weight (lb.) 3,694
Speed (mph) 3.48
Percent slippage....................................4.72
SAE drawbar horsepower......................27
SAE belt/PTO horsepower 42
Type ....4 wheel
Front wheel (in.)....................................steel: 36 x 5
Rear wheel (in.).....................................steel: 53 x 12
Length (in.) 143
Height (in.) 72
Rear width (in.) 76.50
Weight (lb.) 6,800
Gear/speed (mph) ....forward: 1/2.69,
  2/3.42; reverse: 1/2.52

Minneapolis 39-57, 30-50
Manufacturer..Minneapolis Threshing
  Machine Co., Hopkins, MN

Nebraska test number 163
Test date ....June 5–14, 1929
Test tractor serial number.....................9574
Years produced 1928–1929
Serial number range...............................9550-10681
Serial number location ....cast-iron plate on front
  frame
Number produced ....na, all models
  interspersed
Engine ....Stearns vertical I-head
Test engine serial number.....................282024
Cylinders 4
Bore and stroke (in.) ....5.50 x 6.50
Rated rpm 1,000
Displacement (c.i.) 617.7
Fuel ....gasoline
Carburetor..Stromberg M4, 1.75-
  in.
Air cleaner ....Donaldson-Simplex
Ignition..American Bosch ZR4
  Ed34 magneto
Maximum brake horsepower tests
PTO/belt horsepower.............................64.55
Crankshaft rpm 1,004
Fuel use (gal./hr.) 6.37
Maximum drawbar horsepower tests
Gear..high
Drawbar horsepower.............................47.77
Pull weight (lb.) 5,950
Speed (mph) 3.01
Percent slippage....................................6.67
SAE drawbar horsepower......................39
SAE belt/PTO horsepower 57
Type ....4 wheel
Front wheel (in.)....................................steel: na
Rear wheel (in.).....................................steel: 58 x 19.50
Weight (lb.) 9,545
Gear/speed (mph) ....forward: 1/3.00,
  2/3.90; reverse: 1/2.49

Chapter 55
MINNEAPOLIS-MOLINE

Minneapolis-Moline Twin City KT, 11-20, 14-23
Manufacturer...Minneapolis-Moline
  Power Implement,
  Minneapolis, MN
Nebraska test number 175
Test date ....March 24 to
  April 12, 1930
Test tractor serial number.....................300 221
Years produced 1929–1934
Serial number range...............................300 001–302 078 end
Serial number location ....metal plate on top right
  side of transmission case

Number produced 2,078
Engine ....Minneapolis-Moline
  vertical I-head,
  valve-in-head
Test engine serial number.....................375260
Cylinders 4
Bore and stroke (in.) ....4.25 x 5.00
Rated rpm 1,000
Displacement (c.i.) 283.7
Fuel ....kerosene/gasoline
Main tank capacity (gal.) 24
Auxiliary tank capacity (gal.) 3

Carburetor ....Stromberg UT1, 1.00-in.
Air cleaner ....Donaldson
Ignition ....American Bosch U4
Ed2V7 magneto
Cooling capacity (gal.) 6

Maximum brake horsepower tests
PTO/belt horsepower...........................25.83
Crankshaft rpm 1,000
Fuel use (gal./hr.) 2.59

Maximum drawbar horsepower tests
Gear..2nd
Drawbar horsepower............................18.89
Pull weight (lb.)....................................2,076
Speed (mph) 3.41
Percent slippage..................................4.99
SAE drawbar horsepower.............................14.70
SAE belt/PTO horsepower............................23.23
Type ....4 wheel
Front wheel (in.)..steel: 28 x 5
Rear wheel (in.)...steel: 42 x 10
Length (in.) 131
Height (in.) 60.50
Rear width (in.) 59
Weight (lb.) 4,300
Gear/speed (mph) ....forward: 1/2.10, 2/3.13,
3/4.15; reverse: 1/1.80

Minneapolis-Moline Universal MT, 13-25, Twin City

Manufacturer..Minneapolis-Moline
Power Implement,
Minneapolis, MN
Nebraska test number 197
Test date ....September 30 to
October 8, 1931
Test tractor serial number............................525 001
Years produced 1930–1934
Serial number range.....................................525 001–525 420
Serial number location ....metal plate on top right
side of transmission case
Number produced 420
Engine ....Minneapolis-Moline
vertical I-head,
valve-in-head
Test engine serial number............................376609
Cylinders 4
Bore and stroke (in.) ....4.25 x 5.00
Rated rpm 1,000
Displacement (c.i.) 283.7
Fuel ....kerosene/gasoline
Main tank capacity (gal.)..............................21
Auxiliary tank capacity (gal.) 2.50
Carburetor...Schebler TT, 1.00-in.
Air cleaner ....Donaldson
Ignition ....American Bosch U4
Ed4V2 magneto
Cooling capacity (gal.) 6

Maximum brake horsepower tests
PTO/belt horsepower...........................26.68
Crankshaft rpm 1,000
Fuel use (gal./hr.) 2.61

Maximum drawbar horsepower tests
Gear..low
Drawbar horsepower............................18.17
Pull weight (lb.)....................................2,889
Speed (mph) 2.36
Percent slippage..................................5.14

SAE drawbar horsepower.............................13.81
SAE belt/PTO horsepower............................25.17
Type ....4 wheel; tricycle
Front wheel (in.)..steel: 26 x 5.75
Rear wheel (in.)...steel: 42 x 10
Length (in.) 143
Height (in.) 64.50
Rear width (in.) 93
Weight (lb.) 4,860
Gear/speed (mph) ....forward: 1/2.10, 2/3.13,
3/4.15; reverse: 1/1.80

Minneapolis-Moline Twin City JT, Universal J

Manufacturer..Minneapolis-Moline
Power Implement,
Minneapolis, MN
Nebraska test number 233
Test date ....April 17–29, 1936
Test tractor serial number............................550 073 JT
Years produced 1934–1937
Serial number range.....................................550 001–556 244 end
Serial number location ....metal plate on top right
side of transmission
case
Number produced 6,244
Engine ....Minneapolis-Moline
JE vertical F,
valve-in-head
Test engine serial number............................361271 JE
Cylinders 4
Bore and stroke (in.) ....3.625 x 4.75
Rated rpm 1,275
Displacement (c.i.) 196.1
Fuel ....distillate/gasoline
Main tank capacity (gal.)..............................17
Auxiliary tank capacity (gal.) 2
Carburetor...Zenith, 124.5 T,
1.00-in.
Air cleaner ....Donaldson
Ignition ....Fairbanks-Morse,
RV-4 magneto
Cooling capacity (gal.) 5

Maximum brake horsepower tests
PTO/belt horsepower...........................24.22
Crankshaft rpm 1,278
Fuel use (gal./hr.) 2.42

Maximum drawbar horsepower tests
Gear..3rd
Drawbar horsepower............................17.98
Pull weight (lb.)....................................1,972
Speed (mph) 3.42
Percent slippage..................................2.80
SAE drawbar horsepower.............................14.31
SAE belt/PTO horsepower............................22.07
Type ....4 wheel; tricycle
Front wheel (in.)..(steel: 25 x 4.50)
rubber: 5.25 x 16
Rear wheel (in.)...(steel: 50 x 8) rubber:
9.00 x 36
Length (in.) 115.50
Height (in.) 56
Rear width (in.) 79
Weight (lb.) 3,450
Gear/speed (mph) ....forward: 1/2.20, 2/2.65,
3/3.13, 4/4.57, 5/12.10;
reverse: 1/1.19

Minneapolis-Moline Twin City KT-A

Manufacturer ....Minneapolis-Moline Power Implement, Minneapolis, MN
Nebraska test number 247
Test date ....October 2–9, 1935
Test tractor serial number 303 351
Years produced 1934–1938
Serial number range ....302 200–306 751 end
Serial number location ....metal plate on top right side of transmission case
Number produced 4,552
Engine ....Minneapolis-Moline KEA vertical I-head, valve-in-head
Test engine serial number 526720
Cylinders 4
Bore and stroke (in.) ....4.25 x 5.00
Rated rpm 1,150
Displacement (c.i.) 283.7
Fuel ....distillate/gasoline
Main tank capacity (gal.) 24
Auxiliary tank capacity (gal.) 3
Carburetor ....Schebler, TTX 15, 1.00-in.
Air cleaner ....Donaldson
Ignition..American Bosch, U 4 magneto
Cooling capacity (gal.) 6
Maximum brake horsepower tests
    PTO/belt horsepower..........................33.65
    Crankshaft rpm 1,150
    Fuel use (gal./hr.) 4.11
Maximum drawbar horsepower tests
    Gear..2nd
    Drawbar horsepower 24.80
    Pull weight (lb.)............................2,718
    Speed (mph) 3.42
    Percent slippage............................4.87
SAE drawbar horsepower.................19.38
SAE belt/PTO horsepower................30.03
Type ....4 wheel
Front wheel (in.) ....steel: 28 x 5
Rear wheel (in.) ....steel: 42 x 10
Length (in.) 131
Height (in.) 64.50
Rear width (in.) 59
Weight (lb.) 4,300
Gear/speed (mph) ....forward: 1/2.10, 2/3.10, 3/4.10; reverse: 1/1.80

Minneapolis-Moline Twin City MT-A, Universal M

Manufacturer..................................Minneapolis-Moline Power Implement, Minneapolis, MN
Nebraska test number 248
Test date ....October 2–17, 1935
Test tractor serial number 525 789
Years produced 1934–1938
Serial number range........................525 421–528 645 end
Serial number location ....metal plate on top right side of transmission case
Number produced 3,225

Engine ....Minneapolis-Moline KEA vertical I-head, valve-in-head
Test engine serial number 526653
Cylinders 4
Bore and stroke (in.) ....4.25 x 5.00
Rated rpm 1,150
Displacement (c.i.) 283.7
Fuel ....distillate/gasoline
Main tank capacity (gal.) 21
Auxiliary tank capacity (gal.) 2.50
Carburetor ....Schebler, TTX 15, 1.00-in.
Air cleaner ....Donaldson
Ignition..American Bosch, U 4 magneto
Cooling capacity (gal.) 6
Maximum brake horsepower tests
    PTO/belt horsepower..........................33.23
    Crankshaft rpm 1,148
    Fuel use (gal./hr.) 3.80
Maximum drawbar horsepower tests
    Gear 2nd
    Drawbar horsepower 24.50
    Pull weight (lb.)............................2,692
    Speed (mph) 3.41
    Percent slippage............................5.05
SAE drawbar horsepower.................19.37
SAE belt/PTO horsepower................29.63
Type ....4 wheel; tricycle
Front wheel (in.) ....(steel: 28 x 5) rubber: 5.50 x 16
Rear wheel (in.) ....(steel: 42 x 10) rubber: 9.00 x 36
Length (in.) 143
Height (in.) 64.50
Rear width (in.) 93
Weight (lb.) 4,860
Gear/speed (mph) ....forward: 1/2.10, 2/3.10, 3/4.10; reverse: 1/1.80

Minneapolis-Moline Twin City KT-A

Manufacturer...................................Minneapolis-Moline Power Implement, Minneapolis, MN
Nebraska test number 249
Test date ....March 30 to April 10, 1936
Test tractor serial number 304070
Years produced 1934–1938
Serial number range........................302 200–306 751 end
Serial number location ....metal plate on top right side of transmission case
Number produced 4,552
Engine ....Minneapolis-Moline KEA vertical I-head, valve-in-head
Test engine serial number 527875
Cylinders 4
Bore and stroke (in.) ....4.25 x 5.00
Rated rpm 1,150
Displacement (c.i.) 283.7
Fuel ....gasoline
Fuel tank capacity (gal.) 24
Carburetor ....Schebler, TTX 15, 1.00-in.
Air cleaner ....Donaldson

Ignition..American Bosch,
U 4 magneto
Cooling capacity (gal.) 6
Maximum brake horsepower tests
    PTO/belt horsepower...........................41.60
    Crankshaft rpm 1,150
    Fuel use (gal./hr.)...............................3.59
Maximum drawbar horsepower tests
    Gear..St 2nd, Ru 3rd
    Drawbar horsepower.........................St 30.07, Ru 25.97
    Pull weight (lb.)................................St 3,302, Ru 2,540
    Speed (mph)....................................St 3.41, Ru 3.83
    Percent slippage..............................St 5.06, Ru 17.06
SAE drawbar horsepower.........................22.96
SAE belt/PTO horsepower........................36.95
Type ....4 wheel
Front wheel (in.).....................................(steel: 28 x 5;
rubber: 6.00 x 16)
Rear wheel (in.)......................................(steel: 42 x 10;
rubber: 12.75 x 24)
Length (in.) 131
Height (in.) 64.50
Rear width (in.) 59
Weight (lb.) ....St 4,300
Gear/speed (mph) ....forward: 1/2.25, 2/3.25,
3/4.25; reverse: 1/1.90

Minneapolis-Moline Twin City FTA, 21-32

Manufacturer...Minneapolis-Moline
Power Implement,
Minneapolis, MN
Nebraska test number 270
Test date ....September 10–18, 1936
Test tractor serial number.......................155 297
Years produced 1935–1938
Serial number range...............................154 300–157 229 end
Serial number location ....metal plate on top right
side of transmission case
Number produced 2,930
Engine ....Minneapolis-Moline FE
vertical I-head,
valve-in-head
Test engine serial number.......................900961
Cylinders 4
Bore and stroke (in.) ....4.625 x 6.00
Rated rpm 1,075
Displacement (c.i.) 403.2
Fuel ....distillate/gasoline
Main tank capacity (gal.) 30
Auxiliary tank capacity (gal.) 3.50
Carburetor...Schebler, TTX-16,
1.25-in.
Air cleaner...Donaldson
Ignition...American Bosch,
MJB4A-102 magneto
Cooling capacity (gal.) 10
Maximum brake horsepower tests
    PTO/belt horsepower...........................44.72
    Crankshaft rpm 1,074
    Fuel use (gal./hr.)...............................4.36
Maximum drawbar horsepower tests
    Gear..2nd
    Drawbar horsepower.........................35.23
    Pull weight (lb.)................................3,691
    Speed (mph)....................................3.58
    Percent slippage..............................2.17

SAE drawbar horsepower.........................27.38
SAE belt/PTO horsepower........................41.13
Type ....4 wheel
Front wheel (in.).....................................(steel: 34 x 5.75) 7.50
x 18
Rear wheel (in.)......................................(steel: 50 x 12)
12.75 x 32
Length (in.) 137
Height (in.) 66
Rear width (in.) 66
Weight (lb.) 6,070
Gear/speed (mph) ....forward: 1/2.36, 2/3.17,
3/4.05; reverse: 1/1.74

Minneapolis-Moline Twin City ZT, ZTU, ZTN

Manufacturer...Minneapolis-Moline
Power Implement,
Minneapolis, MN
Nebraska test number 290
Test date ....October 4–12, 1937
Test tractor serial number.......................560228
Years produced 1936–1948
Serial number range...............................560001–585817 end
Serial number location ....metal plate on top
right side of
transmission case
Number produced 23,440
Engine ....Minneapolis-Moline
KEA vertical I-head,
valve-in-head
Test engine serial number.......................40973
Cylinders 4
Bore and stroke (in.) ....3.625 x 4.50
Rated rpm 1,500
Displacement (c.i.) 185.8
Fuel ....distillate/gasoline
Main tank capacity (gal.) 15.50
Auxiliary tank capacity (gal.) 1.25
Carburetor...Schebler, TRX 12,
1.00-in.
Air cleaner...Donaldson
Ignition...Fairbanks-Morse
magneto, RV-4
Cooling capacity (gal.) 3.50
Maximum brake horsepower tests
    PTO/belt horsepower...........................26.84
    Crankshaft rpm 1,498
    Fuel use (gal./hr.)...............................2.91
Maximum drawbar horsepower tests
    Gear..3rd
    Drawbar horsepower.........................20.53
    Pull weight (lb.)................................2,270
    Speed (mph)....................................3.39
    Percent slippage..............................4.51
SAE drawbar horsepower.........................15.91
SAE belt/PTO horsepower........................23.43
Type ....tricycle
Front wheel (in.).....................................(steel: 25 x 4.50)
rubber: 5.50 x 16
Rear wheel (in.)......................................(steel: 50 x 8)
rubber: 9.00 x 36
Length (in.) 132
Height (in.) 60
Rear width (in.) 79
Weight (lb.) 3,650

Gear/speed (mph) ....forward: 1/2.18,
2/2.62, 3/3.13, 4/4.57,
5/14.30 rubber;
reverse: 1/1.00

Minneapolis-Moline Twin City, UTS
Manufacturer ....Minneapolis-Moline
Power Implement,
Minneapolis, MN
Nebraska test number 310
Test date ....October 24 to
November 16, 1938
Test tractor serial number 310 305
Years produced 1938–1955
Serial number range 310 026–339 453,
0124800001–
01214125 end
Serial number location ....metal plate on top
right side of
transmission case
Number produced ....2,500 UT; 32,449 UTS
Engine ....Minneapolis-Moline
vertical I-head
Test engine serial number ....540560 C
Cylinders 4
Bore and stroke (in.) ....4.25 x 5.00
Rated rpm 1,275
Compression ratio.......................5.40:1
Displacement (c.i.) 283.7
Fuel ....gasoline
Fuel tank capacity (gal.) 21.50
Carburetor ....Schebler, TTX-17,
1.00-in.
Air cleaner ....Donaldson
Ignition......................................Fairbanks-Morse,
FM-4B magneto
Cooling capacity (gal.) 6
Maximum brake horsepower tests
    PTO/belt horsepower...............42.88
    Crankshaft rpm 1,274
    Fuel use (gal./hr.) 4.11
Maximum drawbar horsepower tests
    Gear..3rd
    Drawbar horsepower.................39.00
    Pull weight (lb.).......................3,285
    Speed (mph) 4.45
    Percent slippage......................6.63
SAE drawbar horsepower...............30.86
SAE belt/PTO horsepower 38.12
Type ....Standard
Front wheel (in.)..........................tire, 7.50 x 16
Rear wheel (in.)...........................tire, 12.75 x 32
Length (in.) 135
Height (in.) 70
Rear width (in.) 74.25
Weight (lb.) 5,250
Gear/speed (mph) ....forward: 1/2.70,
2/3.50, 3/4.70, 4/6.20,
5/20.20; reverse:
1/1.30

Minneapolis-Moline Twin City, UTS
Manufacturer...............................Minneapolis-Moline
Power Implement,
Minneapolis, MN

Nebraska test number 311
Test date ....November 21–25,
1938
Test tractor serial number............310 305
Years produced 1938–1948
Serial number range....................310 026–339 453,
0124800001–0121412
5 end
Serial number location ....metal plate on top
right side of
transmission case
Number produced ....2,500 UT; 32,449 UTS
Engine ....Minneapolis-Moline
vertical I-head
Test engine serial number ....540560 C
Cylinders 4
Bore and stroke (in.) ....4.25 x 5.00
Rated rpm 1,275
Compression ratio.......................5.40:1
Displacement (c.i.) 283.7
Fuel ....distillate/gasoline
Main tank capacity (gal.) 21.50
Auxiliary tank capacity (gal.) 1.50
Carburetor..................................Schebler, TTX-17,
1.00-in.
Air cleaner ....Donaldson
Ignition.......................................Fairbanks-Morse,
FM 4B magneto
Cooling capacity (gal.) 6
Maximum brake horsepower tests
    PTO/belt horsepower............36.48
    Crankshaft rpm 1,274
    Fuel use (gal./hr.) 3.87
Maximum drawbar horsepower tests
    Gear..3rd
    Drawbar horsepower.................33.29
    Pull weight (lb.).......................2,781
    Speed (mph) 4.49
    Percent slippage......................5.11
SAE drawbar horsepower...............24.54
SAE belt/PTO horsepower 31.54
Type ....Standard
Front wheel (in.)..........................tire, 7.50 x 16
Rear wheel (in.)...........................tire, 12.75 x 32
Length (in.) 134
Height (in.) 70
Rear width (in.) 74.25
Weight (lb.) 5,250
Gear/speed (mph) ....forward: 1/2.70, 2/3.50,
3/4.70, 4/6.20, 5/20.20;
reverse: 1/1.30

Minneapolis-Moline Twin City, GT
Manufacturer...............................Minneapolis-Moline
Power Implement,
Minneapolis, MN

Nebraska test number 317
Test date ....May 1–12, 1939
Test tractor serial number ....GT 160 329
Years produced 1938–1941
Serial number range.....................160 001–161 253 end
Serial number location ....metal plate on top right
side of transmission
case
Number produced 1,246

Engine ....Minneapolis-Moline
vertical I-head
Test engine serial number...........................GE 903416
Cylinders 4
Bore and stroke (in.) ....4.625 x 6.00
Rated rpm 1,075
Displacement (c.i.) 403.2
Fuel ....gasoline
Fuel tank capacity (gal.) 30
Carburetor..Schebler, TTX-23,
1.25-in.
Air cleaner ....Donaldson
Ignition...Fairbanks-Morse,
FM-4 magneto
Cooling capacity (gal.) 7

Maximum brake horsepower tests
    PTO/belt horsepower...........................55.08
    Crankshaft rpm 1,075
    Fuel use (gal./hr.) 4.81
Maximum drawbar horsepower tests
    Gear..2nd
    Drawbar horsepower............................44.99
    Pull weight (lb.)..............................4,964
    Speed (mph)...................................3.40
    Percent slippage..............................13.69
SAE drawbar horsepower...............................36.27
SAE belt/PTO horsepower..............................48.93
Type ....Standard
Front wheel (in.).....................................tire, 7.50 x 18
Rear wheel (in.)......................................tire, 13.50 x 32
Length (in.) 136.50
Height (in.) 76
Rear width (in.) 72
Weight (lb.) 6,220
Gear/speed (mph) ....forward: 1/2.70,
2/3.80, 3/5.80, 4/9.60;
reverse: 1/2.80

Minneapolis-Moline Twin City, UTU
Manufacturer..Minneapolis-Moline
Power Implement,
Minneapolis, MN
Nebraska test number 319
Test date ....June 13–17, 1939
Test tractor serial number...........................311 150
Years produced 1938–1955
Serial number range...................................310 026–338603,
0114800001–0111345
6 end
Serial number location ....metal plate on top right
side of transmission case
Number produced 33,268
Engine ....Minneapolis-Moline
vertical I-head
Test engine serial number...........................541034 C
Cylinders 4
Bore and stroke (in.) ....4.25 x 5.00
Rated rpm 1,275
Compression ratio.....................................5.40:1
Displacement (c.i.) 283.7
Fuel ....gasoline
Fuel tank capacity (gal.) 21.50
Carburetor..Schebler, TTX-17,
1.00-in.
Air cleaner ....United

Ignition..Fairbanks-Morse,
FM-4B magneto
Cooling capacity (gal.) 6
Maximum brake horsepower tests
    PTO/belt horsepower...........................42.71
    Crankshaft rpm 1,275
    Fuel use (gal./hr.) 4.11
Maximum drawbar horsepower tests
    Gear..3rd
    Drawbar horsepower............................35.16
    Pull weight (lb.)..............................3,582
    Speed (mph)...................................3.68
    Percent slippage..............................15.41
SAE drawbar horsepower...............................28.32
SAE belt/PTO horsepower..............................38.48
Type ....tricycle
Front wheel (in.).....................................tire, 6.00 x 16
Rear wheel (in.)......................................tire, 11.00 x 36
Length (in.) 138
Height (in.) 70.50
Rear width (in.) 92
Tread width (in.).....................................54–83
Weight (lb.) 5,500
Gear/speed (mph) ....forward: 1/2.50, 2/3.20,
3/4.30, 4/5.70, 5/18.50;
reverse: 1/1.20

Minneapolis-Moline Twin City, RTU
Manufacturer..Minneapolis-Moline
Power Implement,
Minneapolis, MN
Nebraska test number 341
Test date ....April 29 to
May 10, 1940
Test tractor serial number...........................402 393 U
Years produced 1939–1947
Serial number range...................................400 001–422 057 end
Serial number location ....metal plate on top right
side of transmission case
Number produced 22,057
Engine ....Minneapolis-Moline EE
vertical I-head
Test engine serial number...........................402514 EE
Cylinders 4
Bore and stroke (in.) ....3.625 x 4.00
Rated rpm 1,400
Compression ratio.....................................5.75:1
Displacement (c.i.) 165.1
Fuel ....gasoline
Fuel tank capacity (gal.) 14
Carburetor..Schebler, TSX-30,
1.00-in.
Air cleaner ....United
Ignition..Fairbanks-Morse,
F.M. K4B magneto
Cooling capacity (gal.) 3.50
Maximum brake horsepower tests
    PTO/belt horsepower...........................23.22
    Crankshaft rpm 1,400
    Fuel use (gal./hr.) 2.39
Maximum drawbar horsepower tests
    Gear..3rd
    Drawbar horsepower............................20.01
    Pull weight (lb.)..............................1,938
    Speed (mph)...................................3.87
    Percent slippage..............................7.58

SAE drawbar horsepower 15.58
SAE belt/PTO horsepower 20.49
Type .... tricycle
Front wheel (in.) .... tire, 4.00 x 15
Rear wheel (in.) .... tire, 8.00 x 36
Length (in.) 112
Height (in.) 64.50
Rear width (in.) 81.25
Tread width (in.) 52–84
Weight (lb.) .... (3,960)
Gear/speed (mph) .... forward: 1/2.30, 2/3.30, 3/4.20, 4/12.00; reverse: 1/2.60

Minneapolis-Moline Twin City, ZTU, Universal

Manufacturer .... Minneapolis-Moline Power Implement, Minneapolis, MN
Nebraska test number 352
Test date .... September 3–7, 1940
Test tractor serial number 567 884
Years produced 1936–1948
Serial number range .... 560 001–585 817 end
Serial number location .... metal plate on top right side of transmission case
Number produced 23,440
Engine .... Minneapolis-Moline vertical I-head
Test engine serial number 53543
Cylinders 4
Bore and stroke (in.) .... 3.625 x 4.50
Rated rpm 1,500
Compression ratio 5.75:1
Displacement (c.i.) 185.8
Fuel .... gasoline
Fuel tank capacity (gal.) 16.75
Carburetor .... Schebler, TRX-12, 1.00-in.
Air cleaner .... United
Ignition .... Fairbanks-Morse, FMK4B magneto
Cooling capacity (gal.) 3.50
Maximum brake horsepower tests
    PTO/belt horsepower 31.14
    Crankshaft rpm 1,500
    Fuel use (gal./hr.) 2.91
Maximum drawbar horsepower tests
    Gear 4th
    Drawbar horsepower 26.39
    Pull weight (lb.) 2,258
    Speed (mph) 4.38
    Percent slippage 8.94
SAE drawbar horsepower 20.98
SAE belt/PTO horsepower 27.95
Type .... tricycle
Front wheel (in.) .... tire, 5.50 x 16
Rear wheel (in.) .... tire, 9.00 x 38
Length (in.) 122
Height (in.) 87
Rear width (in.) 87.50
Tread width (in.) 54–84
Weight (lb.) .... (4,850)
Gear/speed (mph) .... forward: 1/2.20, 2/2.70, 3/3.70, 4/4.70, 5/14.60; reverse: 1/1.10

Minneapolis-Moline U Standard LPG, Type S, UTS

Manufacturer .... Minneapolis-Moline Co., Minneapolis, MN
Nebraska test number 411
Test date .... May 31 to June 8, 1949
Test tractor serial number 0124900417
Years produced 1938–1955
Serial number range .... 310026–339453, 0124800001–0121412 5 end
Serial number location .... metal plate on top right side of transmission case
Number produced .... 2,500 UT; 32,449 UTS
Engine .... Minneapolis-Moline 283 A vertical I-head
Test engine serial number 0194902397
Cylinders 4
Bore and stroke (in.) .... 4.25 x 5.00
Rated rpm 1,275
Compression ratio 6.8:1
Displacement (c.i.) 283
Fuel .... LPG
Carburetor .... Ensign, KGL, 1.00-in.
Air cleaner .... United
Ignition .... Delco-Remy, 6-v battery
Cooling capacity (gal.) 6
Maximum brake horsepower tests
    PTO/belt horsepower 46.87
    Crankshaft rpm 1,275
    Fuel use (gal./hr.) 5.38
Maximum drawbar horsepower tests
    Gear 3rd
    Drawbar horsepower 41.05
    Pull weight (lb.) 3,977
    Speed (mph) 3.87
    Percent slippage 8.64
SAE drawbar horsepower 32.27
SAE belt/PTO horsepower 41.45
Type .... Standard
Front wheel (in.) .... tire, 7.50 x 16
Rear wheel (in.) .... tire, 14.00 x 30
Length (in.) 130.75
Height (in.) 70
Tread width (in.) 57–62.50
Weight (lb.) 5,300
Gear/speed (mph) .... forward: 1/2.70, 2/3.80, 3/4.50, 4/6.40, 5/14.80; reverse: 1/2.10

Minneapolis-Moline G, GTB

Manufacturer .... Minneapolis-Moline Co., Minneapolis, MN
Nebraska test number 437
Test date .... April 21 to May 16, 1950
Test tractor serial number 016 490 0686
Years produced 1947–1954
Serial number range .... 164001–01606289 end, 5 number series
Serial number location .... metal plate on top right side of transmission case
Number produced 8,308

Engine ....Minneapolis-Moline
403A vertical I-head
Test engine serial number 0204000646
Cylinders 4
Bore and stroke (in.) ....4.625 x 6.00
Rated rpm 1,100
Compression ratio...................................5.38:1
Displacement (c.i.) 403.2
Fuel ....gasoline
Fuel tank capacity (gal.) 29
Carburetor ....Marvel-Schebler
TSX-68, 1.25-in.
Air cleaner ....Donaldson
Ignition ....Delco-Remy,
6-v battery
Cooling capacity (gal.) 12

Maximum brake horsepower tests
PTO/belt horsepower...........................58.03
Crankshaft rpm 1,100
Fuel use (gal./hr.) 5.28

Maximum drawbar horsepower tests
Gear...3rd
Drawbar horsepower 49.53
Pull weight (lb.) 4,769
Speed (mph) 3.89
Percent slippage...............................7.89
SAE drawbar horsepower 38.90
SAE belt/PTO horsepower 50.58
Type ....Standard
Front wheel (in.)....................................tire, 7.50 x 18
Rear wheel (in.).....................................tire, 14.00 x 34
Length (in.) 135.88
Height (in.) 71
Tread width (in.) 62
Weight (lb.) 6,400
Gear/speed (mph) ....forward: 1/2.50, 2/3.50,
3/4.10, 4/6.00, 5/13.80;
reverse: 1/2.00

Minneapolis-Moline Z, Type N or U, ZAU
Manufacturer...Minneapolis-Moline
Co., Minneapolis, MN
Nebraska test number 438
Test date ....May 6–15, 1950
Test tractor serial number 0064900842
Years produced 1949–1952
Serial number range 0064900001–00614658
end
Serial number location ....metal plate on top right
side of transmission case
Number produced 17,671
Engine ....Minneapolis-Moline
206B-4 vertical L-head
Test engine serial number 0184900956
Cylinders 4
Bore and stroke (in.) ....3.625 x 5.00
Rated rpm 1,500
Compression ratio...................................6.19:1
Displacement (c.i.) 206
Fuel ....gasoline
Fuel tank capacity (gal.) 19
Carburetor ....Marvel-Schebler
TSX-97, 1.00-in.
Air cleaner ....Donaldson
Ignition ....Delco-Remy,
6-v battery

Cooling capacity (gal.) 3.75
Maximum brake horsepower tests
PTO/belt horsepower...........................36.20
Crankshaft rpm 1,500
Fuel use (gal./hr.) 3.52
Maximum drawbar horsepower tests
Gear...3rd
Drawbar horsepower 32.07
Pull weight (lb.) 2,780
Speed (mph) 4.33
Percent slippage...............................7.04
SAE drawbar horsepower 25.02
SAE belt/PTO horsepower 31.86
Type ....tricycle
Front wheel (in.)....................................tire, 5.50 x 16
Rear wheel (in.).....................................tire, 11.00 x 38
Length (in.) 134.88
Height (in.) 78
Tread width (in.) 54–88
Weight (lb.) 3,750
Gear/speed (mph) ....forward: 1/2.40, 2/3.60,
3/4.60, 4/6.30, 5/13.10;
reverse: 1/2.20

Minneapolis-Moline R, Type U, RTU
Manufacturer...Minneapolis-Moline
Co., Minneapolis, MN
Nebraska test number 468
Test date ....October 20 to
November 1, 1951
Test tractor serial number 00103973
Years produced 1948–1954
Serial number range 0014800001–0015002155;
00102156–00104831 end
Serial number location ....metal plate on top right
side of transmission
case
Number produced 10,272
Engine ....Minneapolis-Moline EE
vertical I-head
Test engine serial number 01705445
Cylinders 4
Bore and stroke (in.) ....3.625 x 4.00
Rated rpm 1,500
Compression ratio...................................6.1:1
Displacement (c.i.) 165
Fuel ....gasoline
Fuel tank capacity (gal.) 14
Carburetor ....Marvel-Schebler
TSX-67, .875-in.
Air cleaner ....United
Ignition ....Delco-Remy,
6-v battery
Cooling capacity (gal.) 3.38
Maximum brake horsepower tests
PTO/belt horsepower...........................27.09
Crankshaft rpm 1,501
Fuel use (gal./hr.) 2.89
Maximum drawbar horsepower tests
Gear...3rd
Drawbar horsepower 23.90
Pull weight (lb.) 2,048
Speed (mph) 4.38
Percent slippage...............................6.65
SAE drawbar horsepower 18

SAE belt/PTO horsepower 23.71
Type ....tricycle
Front wheel (in.) ....tire, 5.00 x 15
Rear wheel (in.) ....tire, 10.00 x 34
Length (in.) 120.38
Height (in.) 68.50
Tread width (in.) 52–88
Weight (lb.) 3,050
Gear/speed (mph) ....forward: 1/2.60, 2/3.60, 3/4.70, 4/13.20; reverse: 1/2.90

Minneapolis-Moline BF, Avery

Manufacturer...Minneapolis-Moline Co., Minneapolis, MN
Nebraska test number 469
Test date ....October 22–27, 1951
Test tractor serial number ....R 3292
Years produced 1950–1953
Serial number range.......................................R500–R7571; 57700001–58000150 end
Serial number location ....metal plate on top right side of transmission case
Number produced 7,627
Engine ....Hercules IXB3SL vertical L-head
Test engine serial number.............................2453318
Cylinders 4
Bore and stroke (in.) ....3.25 x 4.00
Rated rpm 1,800
Compression ratio...6.8:1
Displacement (c.i.) 133
Fuel ....gasoline
Fuel tank capacity (gal.) 12
Carburetor..Marvel-Schebler TSX-400, .875-in.
Air cleaner ....Vortox
Ignition...Delco-Remy, 6-v battery
Cooling capacity (gal.) 2.75
Maximum brake horsepower tests
    PTO/belt horsepower.............................27.12
    Crankshaft rpm 1,800
    Fuel use (gal./hr.) 2.77
Maximum drawbar horsepower tests
    Gear..3rd
    Drawbar horsepower...............................24.12
    Pull weight (lb.).......................................1,807
    Speed (mph) 5.01
    Percent slippage.....................................5.99
SAE drawbar horsepower...............................18.83
SAE belt/PTO horsepower 23.49
Type ....tricycle
Front wheel (in.) ....tire, 5.50 x 15
Rear wheel (in.) ....tire, 10.00 x 28
Length (in.) 116.75
Height (in.) 76
Tread width (in.)...52–76
Weight (lb.) 2,735
Gear/speed (mph) ....forward: 1/2.42, 2/3.67, 3/5.23, 4/13.12; reverse: 1/2.81

Minneapolis-Moline UB, Type U, UBU

Manufacturer...Minneapolis-Moline Co., Minneapolis, MN
Nebraska test number 520
Test date ....May 25 to June 10, 1954
Test tractor serial number.............................05801904
Years produced 1953–1955
Serial number range.......................................05800001–25805077 end
Serial number location ....metal plate on top right side of transmission case
Number produced 5,077
Engine ....Minneapolis-Moline 283 B vertical I-head
Test engine serial number.............................16103778
Cylinders 4
Bore and stroke (in.) ....4.25 x 5.00
Rated rpm 1,300
Compression ratio...6.3:1
Displacement (c.i.) 283
Fuel ....gasoline
Fuel tank capacity (gal.) 12
Carburetor..Marvel-Schebler TSX-67, 1.25-in.
Air cleaner ....Donaldson or United
Ignition...Delco-Remy, 12-v battery
Cooling capacity (gal.) 2.75
Maximum brake horsepower tests
    PTO/belt horsepower.............................48.38
    Crankshaft rpm 1,300
    Fuel use (gal./hr.) 4.33
Maximum drawbar horsepower tests
    Gear..3rd
    Drawbar horsepower...............................42.90
    Pull weight (lb.).......................................3,591
    Speed (mph) 4.48
    Percent slippage.....................................5.95
SAE drawbar horsepower...............................34.07
SAE belt/PTO horsepower 42.82
Type ....tricycle
Front wheel (in.) ....tire, 6.00 x 16
Rear wheel (in.) ....tire, 13.00 x 38
Length (in.) 133
Height (in.) 78.50
Tread width (in.)...54.50–84.50
Weight (lb.) 5,700
Gear/speed (mph) ....forward: 1/2.80, 2/4.00, 3/4.60, 4/6.70, 5/15.60; reverse: 1/2.20

Minneapolis-Moline U, Type S, UTS

Manufacturer...Minneapolis-Moline Co., Minneapolis, MN
Nebraska test number 521
Test date ....May 27 to June 7, 1954
Test tractor serial number.............................01212648
Years produced 1938–1955
Serial number range.......................................310026–339453, 0124800001–0121412 5 end

Serial number location ....metal plate on top right side of transmission case
Number produced ....2,500 UT; 32,449 UTS
Engine ....Minneapolis-Moline, 283 B vertical I-head
Test engine serial number 06105961
Cylinders 4
Bore and stroke (in.) ....4.25 x 5.00
Rated rpm 1,300
Compression ratio.......................................4.41:1
Displacement (c.i.) 283.7
Fuel ....tractor fuel
Fuel tank capacity (gal.) 12
Carburetor ....Marvel-Schebler TSX67, 1.25-in.
Air cleaner ....Donaldson or United
Ignition ....Delco-Remy, 12-v battery
Cooling capacity (gal.) 2.75
Maximum brake horsepower tests
    PTO/belt horsepower...........................37.23
    Crankshaft rpm 1,300
    Fuel use (gal./hr.) 4.29
Maximum drawbar horsepower tests
    Gear..3rd
    Drawbar horsepower.............................33.51
    Pull weight (lb.).....................................3,099
    Speed (mph) 4.05
    Percent slippage...................................7.10
SAE drawbar horsepower.............................26.48
SAE belt/PTO horsepower 33.54
Type ....Standard
Front wheel (in.) ....tire, 7.50 x 16
Rear wheel (in.) ....tire, 14.00 x 30
Length (in.) 130.75
Height (in.) 72
Tread width (in.) 57–62.50
Weight (lb.) 5,500

Minneapolis-Moline UB LPG, Type U, UBU

Manufacturer...Minneapolis-Moline Co., Minneapolis, MN
Nebraska test number 522
Test date ....May 25 to June 14, 1954
Test tractor serial number 05802395
Years produced 1953–1955
Serial number range.....................................05800001–05805077 end
Serial number location ....metal plate on top right side of transmission case
Number produced 5,077
Engine ....Minneapolis-Moline 283 B vertical I-head
Test engine serial number 06104469
Cylinders 4
Bore and stroke (in.) ....4.25 x 5.00
Rated rpm 1,300
Compression ratio.......................................8.0:1
Displacement (c.i.) 283
Fuel ....LPG
Fuel tank capacity (gal.) 35
Carburetor ....Ensign, KG1, 1.00-in.

Air cleaner ....Donaldson or United
Ignition ....Delco-Remy, 12-v battery
Cooling capacity (gal.) 2.75
Maximum brake horsepower tests
    PTO/belt horsepower...........................51.27
    Crankshaft rpm 1,300
    Fuel use (gal./hr.) 5.62
Maximum drawbar horsepower tests
    Gear..3rd
    Drawbar horsepower.............................44.57
    Pull weight (lb.).....................................3,749
    Speed (mph) 4.46
    Percent slippage...................................6.80
SAE drawbar horsepower.............................35.30
SAE belt/PTO horsepower 45.25
Type ....tricycle
Front wheel (in.) ....tire, 6.00 x 16
Rear wheel (in.) ....tire, 13.00 x 38
Length (in.) 133
Height (in.) 78.50
Tread width (in.) 54.50–84.50
Weight (lb.) 5,700
Gear/speed (mph) ....forward: 1/2.80, 2/4.00, 3/4.60, 4/6.70, 5/15.60; reverse: 1/2.20

Minneapolis-Moline GB LPG

Manufacturer...Minneapolis-Moline Co., Minneapolis, MN
Nebraska test number 545
Test date ....May 31 to June 7, 1955
Test tractor serial number 08900527
Years produced 1955–1959
Serial number range.....................................08900001–08904492 end
Serial number location ....metal plate on top right side of transmission case
Number produced ....na, interspersed
Engine ....Minneapolis-Moline 403C vertical I-head
Test engine serial number 02006907
Cylinders 4
Bore and stroke (in.) ....4.625 x 6.00
Rated rpm 1,300
Compression ratio.......................................8.37:1
Displacement (c.i.) 403.2
Fuel ....LPG
Fuel tank capacity (gal.) 45
Carburetor ....Ensign KG1, 1.25-in.
Air cleaner ....Donaldson
Ignition ....Delco-Remy, 12-v battery
Cooling capacity (gal.) 12
Maximum brake horsepower tests
    PTO/belt horsepower...........................70.55
    Crankshaft rpm 1,300
    Fuel use (gal./hr.) 7.54
Maximum drawbar horsepower tests
    Gear..3rd
    Drawbar horsepower.............................62.14
    Pull weight (lb.).....................................5,557
    Speed (mph) 4.19
    Percent slippage...................................8.17

SAE drawbar horsepower 49.56
SAE belt/PTO horsepower 63.71
Type .... Standard
Front wheel (in.) .... 7.50 x 18
Rear wheel (in.) .... 15.00 x 34
Length (in.) 137.50
Height (in.) 72.50
Tread width (in.) 66
Weight (lb.) 6,600
Gear/speed (mph) .... forward: 1/2.70, 2/3.80,
3/4.40, 4/6.30, 5/14.70;
reverse: 1/2.10

Minneapolis-Moline GB

Manufacturer .... Minneapolis-Moline
Co., Minneapolis, MN
Nebraska test number 547
Test date .... June 8–15, 1955
Test tractor serial number 08900276
Years produced 1955–1959
Serial number range 08900001–08904492
end
Serial number location .... metal plate on top
right side of
transmission case
Number produced 4,491
Engine .... Minneapolis-Moline
403C vertical I-head
Test engine serial number 02006687
Cylinders 4
Bore and stroke (in.) .... 4.625 x 6.00
Rated rpm 1,300
Compression ratio 5.74:1
Displacement (c.i.) 403.2
Fuel .... gasoline
Fuel tank capacity (gal.) 29
Carburetor .... Marvel-Schebler
TSX-68, 1.25-in.
Air cleaner .... Donaldson
Ignition .... Delco-Remy,
12-v battery
Cooling capacity (gal.) 12
Maximum brake horsepower tests
    PTO/belt horsepower 65.64
    Crankshaft rpm 1,300
    Fuel use (gal./hr.) 6.03
Maximum drawbar horsepower tests
    Gear 3rd
    Drawbar horsepower 59.12
    Pull weight (lb.) 5,229
    Speed (mph) 4.24
    Percent slippage 7.57
SAE drawbar horsepower 46.09
SAE belt/PTO horsepower 58.23
Type .... Standard
Front wheel (in.) .... 7.50 x 18
Rear wheel (in.) .... 15.00 x 34
Length (in.) 137.50
Height (in.) 72.50
Tread width (in.) 66
Weight (lb.) 6,600
Gear/speed (mph) .... forward: 1/2.70, 2/3.80,
3/4.40, 4/6.30, 5/14.70;
reverse: 1/2.10

Minneapolis-Moline GBD Diesel

Manufacturer .... Minneapolis-Moline
Co., Minneapolis, MN
Nebraska test number 568
Test date .... November 1–7, 1955
Test tractor serial number G13 09000143
Years produced 1955–1959
Serial number range 09000001–09002790
end
Serial number location .... metal plate on top
right side of
transmission case
Number produced 2,790
Engine .... Minneapolis-Moline
D425-6A vertical
I-head
Test engine serial number 06701051
Cylinders 6
Bore and stroke (in.) .... 4.25 x 5.00
Rated rpm 1,300
Compression ratio 14.9:1
Displacement (c.i.) 425.5
Fuel .... diesel
Fuel tank capacity (gal.) 29
Carburetor .... Bosch injector pump
Air cleaner .... Donaldson
Ignition .... Delco-Remy, 12-v;
with 3, 12-v battery
Cooling capacity (gal.) 12
Maximum brake horsepower tests
    PTO/belt horsepower 62.78
    Crankshaft rpm 1,300
    Fuel use (gal./hr.) 4.08
Maximum drawbar horsepower tests
    Gear 3rd
    Drawbar horsepower 55.44
    Pull weight (lb.) 4,978
    Speed (mph) 4.18
    Percent slippage 7.00
SAE drawbar horsepower 43.61
SAE belt/PTO horsepower 55.46
Type .... Standard
Front wheel (in.) .... 7.50 x 18
Rear wheel (in.) .... 15.00 x 34
Length (in.) 151.38
Height (in.) 72.50
Tread width (in.) 66
Weight (lb.) 7,400
Gear/speed (mph) .... forward: 1/2.70, 2/3.80,
3/4.40, 4/6.30, 5/14.70;
reverse: 1/2.10

Minneapolis-Moline 445 Universal

Manufacturer .... Minneapolis-Moline
Co., Minneapolis, MN
Nebraska test number 578
Test date .... June 23–30, 1956
Test tractor serial number 10101395
Years produced 1956–1959
Serial number range 10100001–10104847
end
Serial number location .... metal plate on top
right side of
transmission case

Number produced 4,847
Engine ....Minneapolis-Moline
206H-4 vertical I-head
Test engine serial number............................10002109
Cylinders 4
Bore and stroke (in.) ....3.625 x 5.00
Rated rpm 1,550
Compression ratio..................................7.3:1
Displacement (c.i.) 206
Fuel ....gasoline
Fuel tank capacity (gal.) 17
Carburetor...Marvel-Schebler
TSX-97, 1.00-in.
Air cleaner ....Donaldson
Ignition..Delco-Remy,
12-v battery
Cooling capacity (gal.) 13.50
Maximum brake horsepower tests
   PTO/belt horsepower...........................41.95
   Crankshaft rpm 1,550
   Fuel use (gal./hr.)................................3.99
Maximum drawbar horsepower tests
   Gear..2nd
   Drawbar horsepower............................38.48
   Pull weight (lb.)...................................3,464
   Speed (mph)..4.17
   Percent slippage..................................6.51
SAE drawbar horsepower...........................30.61
SAE belt/PTO horsepower 37.56
Type ....Standard
Front wheel (in.)......................................5.50 x 16
Rear wheel (in.)..12.00 x 38
Length (in.) 140.50
Height (in.) 101
Tread width (in.).......................................56–88
Weight (lb.) 3,900
Gear/speed (mph)..............forward: 1/2.78, 1 Ampli-Torc/1.46,
2/4.26, 2 Ampli-Torc/2.28, 3/6.48, 3
Ampli-Torc/3.40, 4/10.05, 4 Ampli-
Torc/5.28, 5/15.40, 5 Ampli-Torc/8.09;
reverse: 1/4.26, 1 Ampli-Torc/2.23

Minneapolis-Moline 445 Utility
Manufacturer..Minneapolis-Moline
Co., Minneapolis, MN
Nebraska test number 579
Test date ....June 24 to July 2,
1956
Test tractor serial number.........................10200581
Years produced 1956–1959
Serial number range...................................10200001–10202249
end
Serial number location ....metal plate on top
right side of
transmission case
Number produced 2,249
Engine ....Minneapolis-Moline
206H-4 vertical I-head
Test engine serial number............................10002088
Cylinders 4
Bore and stroke (in.) ....3.625 x 5.00
Rated rpm 1,550
Compression ratio..................................7.3:1
Displacement (c.i.) 206
Fuel ....gasoline

Fuel tank capacity (gal.) 14
Carburetor...Marvel-Schebler
TSX-97, 1.00-in.
Air cleaner ....Donaldson
Ignition..Delco-Remy,
12-v battery
Cooling capacity (gal.) 13.50
Maximum brake horsepower tests
   PTO/belt horsepower...........................41.95
   Crankshaft rpm 1,550
   Fuel use (gal./hr.)................................4.03
Maximum drawbar horsepower tests
   Gear..2nd
   Drawbar horsepower............................38.85
   Pull weight (lb.)...................................3,751
   Speed (mph)..3.88
   Percent slippage..................................9.54
SAE drawbar horsepower...........................30.18
SAE belt/PTO horsepower 37.56
Type ....Standard
Front wheel (in.)......................................5.50 x 16
Rear wheel (in.)..12.00 x 28
Length (in.) 130.63
Height (in.) 93.88
Tread width (in.).......................................56–84
Weight (lb.) 3,750
Gear/speed (mph)..............forward: 1/2.61, 1 Ampli-Torc/1.37,
2/3.99, 2 Ampli-Torc/2.09, 3/6.08, 3
Ampli-Torc/3.19, 4/9.42, 4 Ampli-
Torc/4.95, 5/14.44, 5 Ampli-Torc/7.58;
reverse: 1/3.99, 1 Ampli-Torc/2.09

Minneapolis-Moline 335 Utility
Manufacturer..Minneapolis-Moline
Co., Minneapolis, MN
Nebraska test number 624
Test date ....June 7–17, 1957
Test tractor serial number.........................10401476
Years produced 1956–1961
Serial number range...................................10400001–10402539
end
Serial number location ....metal plate on top
right side of
transmission case
Number produced 2,539
Engine ....Minneapolis-Moline
165A vertical I-head
Test engine serial number............................10301623
Cylinders 4
Bore and stroke (in.) ....3.625 x 4.00
Rated rpm 1,600
Compression ratio..................................7.35:1
Displacement (c.i.) 165
Fuel ....gasoline
Fuel tank capacity (gal.) 14
Carburetor...Marvel-Schebler
TSX-714, 1.00-in.
Air cleaner ....Donaldson
Ignition..Delco-Remy,
6-v battery
Cooling capacity (gal.) 2.75
Maximum brake horsepower tests
   PTO/belt horsepower...........................33.50
   Crankshaft rpm 1,600
   Fuel use (gal./hr.)................................3.39

Maximum drawbar horsepower tests
    Gear..2nd
    Drawbar horsepower.............................29.84
    Pull weight (lb.)....................................2,601
    Speed (mph)..4.30
    Percent slippage.................................7.72
SAE drawbar horsepower.............................23.56
SAE belt/PTO horsepower............................29.81
Type ....Standard
Front wheel (in.)..5.50 x 16
Rear wheel (in.)..12.00 x 24
Height (in.)...58.50
Tread width (in.).......................................48–76
Weight (lb.)..3,070
Gear/speed (mph)..............forward: 1/2.72, 1 Ampli-Torc/1.44,
    2/4.17, 2 Ampli-Torc/2.19, 3/6.36, 3
    Ampli-Torc/3.34, 4/9.85, 4 Ampli-
    Torc/5.17, 5/15.09, 5 Ampli-Torc/7.94;
    reverse: 1/4.17, 1 Ampli-Torc/2.19

Minneapolis-Moline 5 Star Universal
Manufacturer...Minneapolis-Moline
    Co., Minneapolis, MN
Nebraska test number 651
Test date ....May 13–24, 1958
Test tractor serial number.........................11001464
Years produced 1957–1959
Serial number range..................................11000001–11002914
    end
Serial number location ....metal plate on top
    right side of
    transmission case
Number produced 2,914
Engine ....Minneapolis-Moline
    283E vertical I-head
Test engine serial number.........................10901472
Cylinders 4
Bore and stroke (in.) ....4.25 x 5.00
Rated rpm 1,500
Compression ratio....................................8.3:1
Displacement (c.i.) 283
Fuel ....LPG
Carburetor..Marvel-Schebler
    TSX-693, 1.25-in.
Air cleaner ....Donaldson
Ignition...Delco-Remy,
    12-v battery
Cooling capacity (gal.) 5.50
Maximum brake horsepower tests
    PTO/belt horsepower.........................54.96
    Crankshaft rpm 1,500
    Fuel use (gal./hr.) 6.25
Maximum drawbar horsepower tests
    Gear..2nd
    Drawbar horsepower.............................49.36
    Pull weight (lb.)....................................4,025
    Speed (mph)..4.60
    Percent slippage.................................5.21
SAE drawbar horsepower.............................39.05
SAE belt/PTO horsepower............................48.59
Type ....tricycle
Front wheel (in.)..6.00 x 16
Rear wheel (in.)..15.50 x 38
Height (in.)...70

Tread width (in.)..56–88
Weight (lb.) 6,070
Gear/speed (mph)..............forward: 1/3.14, 1 Ampli-Torc/1.65,
    2/4.80, 2 Ampli-Torc/2.52, 3/7.31, 3
    Ampli-Torc/3.84, 4/11.34, 4 Ampli-
    Torc/5.95, 5/17.37, 5 Ampli-Torc/9.12;
    reverse: 1/4.80, 1 Ampli-Torc/2.52

Minneapolis-Moline 5 Star Universal Diesel
Manufacturer...Minneapolis-Moline
    Co., Minneapolis, MN
Nebraska test number 652
Test date ....May 13–21, 1958
Test tractor serial number.........................14400287
Years produced 1957–1959
Serial number range..................................14400001–14401295
    end
Serial number location ....metal plate on top
    right side of
    transmission case
Number produced 1,295
Engine ....Minneapolis-Moline
    D336 vertical I-head
Test engine serial number.........................11400370
Cylinders 4
Bore and stroke (in.) ....4.625 x 5.00
Rated rpm 1,450
Compression ratio....................................15:1
Displacement (c.i.) 336
Fuel ....diesel
Fuel tank capacity (gal.) 22.50
Carburetor..Bosch injector pump
Air cleaner ....Donaldson
Ignition...Delco-Remy,
    12-v battery
Cooling capacity (gal.) 5.50
Maximum brake horsepower tests
    PTO/belt horsepower.........................54.68
    Crankshaft rpm 1,450
    Fuel use (gal./hr.) 3.74
Maximum drawbar horsepower tests
    Gear..2nd
    Drawbar horsepower.............................49.62
    Pull weight (lb.)....................................4,206
    Speed (mph)..4.42
    Percent slippage.................................5.05
SAE drawbar horsepower.............................38.85
SAE belt/PTO horsepower............................48.65
Type ....tricycle
Front wheel (in.)..6.00 x 16
Rear wheel (in.)..15.50 x 38
Height (in.)...70
Tread width (in.)..56–88
Weight (lb.) 6,070
Gear/speed (mph)..............forward: 1/3.04, 1 Ampli-Torc/1.60,
    2/4.64, 2 Ampli-Torc/2.43, 3/7.07, 3
    Ampli-Torc/3.71, 4/10.96, 4 Ampli-
    Torc/5.75, 5/16.79, 5 Ampli-Torc/8.81;
    reverse: 1/4.64, 1 Ampli-Torc/2.43

Minneapolis-Moline M5
Manufacturer...Minneapolis-Moline
    Co., Hopkins, MN
Nebraska test number 756

Test date ....August 31 to
September 10, 1960
Test tractor serial number 17100742
Years produced 1960–1963
Serial number range.................................17100001–17105157
end
Serial number location ....metal plate on top
right side of
transmission case
Number produced 5,157
Engine ....Minneapolis-Moline
336-4 vertical L-head
Test engine serial number..........................16900672
Cylinders 4
Bore and stroke (in.) ....4.625 x 5.00
Rated rpm 1,500
Compression ratio.....................................6.5:1
Displacement (c.i.) 336
Fuel ....gasoline
Carburetor ....Marvel-Schebler
TSX-795, 1.25-in.
Air cleaner ....Donaldson
Ignition..Auto-Lite, 12-v battery
Maximum brake horsepower tests
PTO/belt horsepower...........................61.01
Crankshaft rpm 1,500
Fuel use (gal./hr.) 5.33
Maximum drawbar horsepower tests
Gear...2nd
Drawbar horsepower............................52.51
Pull weight (lb.) 4,331
Speed (mph) 4.55
Percent slippage.................................6.41
SAE drawbar horsepower.............................53.07
SAE belt/PTO horsepower............................61.01
Type ....Standard
Front wheel (in.) ....6.00 x 16
Rear wheel (in.) ....15.50 x 38
Height (in.)...72
Tread width (in.).......................................60–88
Weight (lb.) 6,550
Gear/speed (mph) ....forward: 1/3.14, 2/4.80,
3/5.95, 4/7.31, 5/17.37;
reverse: 1/4.80

Minneapolis-Moline M5 LPG

Manufacturer...Minneapolis-Moline
Co., Hopkins, MN
Nebraska test number 757
Test date ....August 31 to
September 10, 1960
Test tractor serial number..........................17100746
Years produced 1960–1963
Serial number range.................................17100001–17105157
end
Serial number location ....metal plate on top
right side of
transmission case
Number produced ....na, interspersed
Engine ....Minneapolis-Moline
336-4 vertical L-head
Test engine serial number..........................16900704
Cylinders 4
Bore and stroke (in.) ....4.625 x 5.00
Rated rpm 1,500

Compression ratio.....................................7.9:1
Displacement (c.i.)....................................336
Fuel ....LPG
Carburetor ....Ensign 9152, 1.25-in.
Air cleaner ....Donaldson
Ignition..Auto-Lite, 12-v battery
Maximum brake horsepower tests
PTO/belt horsepower...........................61.26
Crankshaft rpm 1,500
Fuel use (gal./hr.) 6.81
Maximum drawbar horsepower tests
Gear...2nd
Drawbar horsepower............................54.47
Pull weight (lb.) 4,458
Speed (mph) 4.58
Percent slippage.................................6.94
SAE drawbar horsepower.............................54.00
SAE belt/PTO horsepower............................61.26
Type ....Standard
Front wheel (in.) ....6.00 x 16
Rear wheel (in.) ....15.50 x 38
Height (in.)...72
Tread width (in.).......................................60–88
Weight (lb.) 6,550
Gear/speed (mph) ....forward: 1/3.14, 2/4.80,
3/5.95, 4/7.31, 5/17.37;
reverse: 1/4.80

Minneapolis-Moline M5 Diesel

Manufacturer...Minneapolis-Moline
Co., Hopkins, MN
Nebraska test number 758
Test date ....September 6–10, 1960
Test tractor serial number..........................17200357
Years produced 1960–1963
Serial number range.................................17200001–17202656
end
Serial number location ....metal plate on top
right side of
transmission case
Number produced 2,656
Engine ....Minneapolis-Moline
D336-4 vertical L-head
Test engine serial number..........................11401899
Cylinders 4
Bore and stroke (in.) ....4.625 x 5.00
Rated rpm 1,500
Compression ratio.....................................14.8:1
Displacement (c.i.)....................................336
Fuel ....diesel
Carburetor ....Bosch injector pump
Air cleaner ....Donaldson
Ignition..Delco-Remy, 12-v;
with 2, 12-v battery
Maximum brake horsepower tests
PTO/belt horsepower...........................58.15
Crankshaft rpm 1,500
Fuel use (gal./hr.) 3.84
Maximum drawbar horsepower tests
Gear...2nd
Drawbar horsepower............................51.37
Pull weight (lb.) 4,235
Speed (mph) 4.55
Percent slippage.................................6.78
SAE drawbar horsepower.............................50.99

SAE belt/PTO horsepower 58.15
Type ....Standard
Front wheel (in.) ....6.00 x 16
Rear wheel (in.) ....15.50 x 38
Height (in.) 72

Tread width (in.) 60–88
Weight (lb.) 6,550
Gear/speed (mph) ....forward: 1/3.14, 2/4.80,
3/5.95, 4/7.31, 5/17.37;
reverse: 1/4.80

Chapter 56

MOLINE UNIVERSAL

Moline Universal D; 9-18
Manufacturer ....Moline Plow Co.,
Moline, IL
Nebraska test number 33
Test date ....July 14–17, 1920
Test tractor serial number 28268
Years produced 1918–1923
Engine ....Moline vertical,
valve-in-head
Test engine serial number ....OR 50554
Cylinders 4
Bore and stroke (in.) ....3.50 x 5.00
Rated rpm 1,800
Displacement (c.i.) 192.4
Fuel ....gasoline
Fuel tank capacity (gal.) 15
Carburetor ....Holley, 1.25-in.
Air cleaner ....Bennett
Ignition ....Remy starter/generator
Cooling capacity (gal.) 6

Maximum brake horsepower tests
PTO/belt horsepower 27.45
Crankshaft rpm 1,788
Fuel use (gal./hr.) 3.09
Maximum drawbar horsepower tests
Drawbar horsepower 17.40
Pull weight (lb.) 1,778
Speed (mph) 3.67
Percent slippage 6.10
SAE drawbar horsepower 9
SAE belt/PTO horsepower 18
Type ....2 drive wheels,
2 rear wheel trucks
Front wheel (in.) ....steel: 52 x 8
Rear wheel (in.) ....steel
Length (in.) ....wheelbase: 84; total:
131
Height (in.) 70
Rear width (in.) 54
Weight (lb.) 3,380
Gear/speed (mph) ....forward: 1/.75–3.58

Chapter 57

MONARCH

Monarch N, 18-30
Manufacturer ....General Tractors, Inc.,
Watertown, WI
Nebraska test number 56
Test date ....August 21–27, 1920
Test tractor serial number 3464
Year produced 1920
Engine ....Beaver vertical, valve-
in-head
Test engine serial number ....JB 208 108
Cylinders 4
Bore and stroke (in.) ....4.75 x 6.00
Rated rpm 950
Displacement (c.i.) 425.3
Fuel ....kerosene/gasoline

Main tank capacity (gal.) 20
Auxiliary tank capacity (gal.) 2
Carburetor ....Kingston L, 1.50-in.
Air cleaner ....Bennett
Ignition ....K-W, T magneto
Cooling capacity (gal.) 12
Maximum brake horsepower tests
PTO/belt horsepower 31.40
Crankshaft rpm 957
Fuel use (gal./hr.) 3.94
Maximum drawbar horsepower tests
Gear 2nd
Drawbar horsepower 21.03
Pull weight (lb.) 4,670
Speed (mph) 1.69
Percent slippage 4.80

SAE drawbar horsepower............................18
SAE belt/PTO horsepower..........................30
Type ....tracklayer
Length (in.) 126
Height (in.) 75
Rear width (in.) 65
Weight (lb.) 7,400
Track length (in.) ....66 on ground
Grouser shoe......................................12-in.
Gear/speed (mph) ....forward: 1/1.50, 2/2.25,
                                              3/3.50; reverse: 1/2.00

Monarch D, 6-60, 40-60
Manufacturer.....................................Monarch Tractors Inc.,
                                              Watertown, WI
Nebraska test number 108
Test date ....October 24 to
                                              November 1, 1924
Test tractor serial number.....................6044
Years produced 1923–1925
Engine ....Beaver vertical,
                                              valve-in-head
Test engine serial number.....................JD 525 - 4
Cylinders 6
Bore and stroke (in.) ....4.75 x 6.00
Rated rpm 1,200
Displacement (c.i.) 637.9
Fuel ....gasoline
Fuel tank capacity (gal.) 45
Carburetor ....Stromberg M4,
                                              1.75-in.
Air cleaner ....Bennett
Ignition...Bosch AT6 lc magneto
Cooling capacity (gal.) 15
Maximum brake horsepower tests
       PTO/belt horsepower.........................70.74
       Crankshaft rpm 1,202
       Fuel use (gal./hr.)..........................9.33
Maximum drawbar horsepower tests
       Gear..2nd
       Drawbar horsepower.........................53.25
       Pull weight (lb.)............................9,967
       Speed (mph)................................2.01
       Percent slippage...........................4.97
SAE drawbar horsepower 40
SAE belt/PTO horsepower 60
Type ....tracklayer
Length (in.) 140
Height (in.) 79
Rear width (in.) 88.38
Weight (lb.) 16,500
Track length (in.) ....89.25 on ground
Grouser shoe......................................12-in.
Gear/speed (mph) ....forward: 1/1.50, 2/2.50,
                                              3/3.50; reverse: 1/na

Monarch C, 25-35
Manufacturer.....................................Monarch Tractors Inc.,
                                              Watertown, WI
Nebraska test number 113
Test date ....April 16–24, 1925
Test tractor serial number.....................30 20
Engine ....Beaver vertical, valve-
                                              in-head
Test engine serial number.....................3833

Cylinders 4
Bore and stroke (in.) ....4.75 x 6.00
Rated rpm 1,200
Displacement (c.i.) 425.3
Fuel ....gasoline
Fuel tank capacity (gal.) 35
Carburetor ....Stromberg M4,
                                              1.75-in.
Air cleaner ....Bennett
Ignition...Bosch DU4 magneto
Cooling capacity (gal.) 12
Maximum brake horsepower tests
       PTO/belt horsepower.........................43.67
       Crankshaft rpm 1,200
       Fuel use (gal./hr.)..........................5.73
Maximum drawbar horsepower tests
       Gear..low
       Drawbar horsepower.........................37.59
       Pull weight (lb.)............................6,680
       Speed (mph)................................2.11
       Percent slippage...........................5.15
SAE drawbar horsepower 25
SAE belt/PTO horsepower 35
Type ....tracklayer
Length (in.) 126
Height (in.) 75
Rear width (in.) 66
Weight (lb.) 9,800
Track length (in.) ....67.25 on ground
Grouser shoe......................................12-in.
Gear/speed (mph) ....forward: 1/1.75,
                                              2/2.50, 3/3.25;
                                              reverse: 1/1.25

Monarch F, 10 Ton, 75
Manufacturer.....................................Monarch Tractors
                                              Corp., Springfield, IL
Nebraska test number 139
Test date ....August 15–26, 1927
Test tractor serial number.....................10191
Years produced 1926–1928;
                                              1928–1931
Serial number range.............................10001–10250;
                                              70001–71066 end
Number produced ....250, 10 ton; 1066, 75s
Engine ....Beaver-Le Roi vertical,
                                              valve-in-head
Test engine serial number.....................795 67
Cylinders 4
Bore and stroke (in.) ....6.50 x 7.00
Rated rpm 850
Displacement (c.i.) 929.1
Fuel ....gasoline
Fuel tank capacity (gal.) 60
Carburetor ....Zenith L7T, 1.75-in.
Air cleaner ....Pomona (United)
Ignition...American Bosch ZR4
                                              Ed26 magneto
Cooling capacity (gal.) 13
Maximum brake horsepower tests
       PTO/belt horsepower.........................None
Maximum drawbar horsepower tests
       Gear..2nd
       Drawbar horsepower.........................78.17
       Pull weight (lb.).............................11,960

Speed (mph) 2.45
Percent slippage 1.94
SAE drawbar horsepower ....None
SAE belt/PTO horsepower ....None
Type ....tracklayer
Length (in.) 150
Height (in.) 77
Rear width (in.) 96
Weight (lb.) 22,500
Track length (in.) ....61 on ground
Grouser shoe ....16-in.
Gear/speed (mph) ....forward: 1/1.50,
2/2.60, 3/3.30;
reverse: 1/2.50

Monarch H, 6 Ton
Manufacturer ....Monarch Tractors
Corp., Springfield, IL
Nebraska test number 147
Test date ....November 14–24,
1927
Test tractor serial number 60172
Years produced 1927–1928
Serial number range ....60001–60297 end
Number produced 297
Engine ....Stearns vertical, valve-
in-head
Test engine serial number 60172
Cylinders 4
Bore and stroke (in.) ....5.125 x 6.50
Rated rpm 1,000
Displacement (c.i.) 536.4
Fuel ....gasoline
Fuel tank capacity (gal.) 31
Carburetor ....Zenith 77, 1.75-in.
Air cleaner ....Pomona (United)
Ignition ....American Bosch ZR4
Ed26 magneto
Cooling capacity (gal.) 8
Maximum brake horsepower tests
PTO/belt horsepower ....None
Maximum drawbar horsepower tests
Gear ....low
Drawbar horsepower 50.55
Pull weight (lb.) 10,537
Speed (mph) 1.80
Percent slippage 3.89
Type ....tracklayer
Length (in.) 118
Height (in.) 63.75
Rear width (in.) 75.50
Weight (lb.) 14,500
Track length (in.) ....54.25 on ground
Grouser shoe ....13-in.
Gear/speed (mph) ....forward: 1/1.86, 2/2.82,
3/4.07; reverse: 1/3.26

Monarch 35, 30-35
Manufacturer ....Allis-Chalmers Mfg.
Co., Milwaukee, WI
Nebraska test number 171
Test date ....November 4–9, 1929
Test tractor serial number 39277
Engine ....Allis-Chalmers vertical
I-head, valve-in-head
Test engine serial number 39277

Cylinders 4
Bore and stroke (in.) ....4.75 x 6.50
Rated rpm 930
Displacement (c.i.) 460.7
Fuel ....gasoline
Fuel tank capacity (gal.) 33
Carburetor ....Zenith 6C, 1.50-in.
Air cleaner ....Allis-Chalmers
Ignition ....Eisemann G4 magneto
Cooling capacity (gal.) 11
Maximum brake horsepower tests
PTO/belt horsepower ....None
Maximum drawbar horsepower tests
Gear 2nd
Drawbar horsepower 40.99
Pull weight (lb.) 8,450
Speed (mph) 1.82
Percent slippage 4.17
SAE drawbar horsepower 30
SAE belt/PTO horsepower 35
Type ....tracklayer
Length (in.) 119
Height (in.) 66
Rear width (in.) 66
Weight (lb.) 10,500
Track length (in.) ....67 on ground, 235
total
Grouser shoe ....36 links; (11), 13-in.
Gear/speed (mph) ....forward: 1/1.84, 2/2.76,
3/4.01; reverse: 1/2.13

Monarch 50, 43-55
Manufacturer ....Allis-Chalmers Mfg.
Co., Springfield, IL
Nebraska test number 179
Test date ....June 27 to July 3,
1930
Test tractor serial number 61999
Years produced 1928–1931
Serial number range ....60298–62297 end
Serial number location ....front of main frame/on
instruction plate on
dash
Number produced 2,000
Engine ....Allis-Chalmers vertical
I-head, valve-in-head
Test engine serial number ....M 104
Cylinders 4
Bore and stroke (in.) ....5.25 x 6.50
Rated rpm 1,000
Displacement (c.i.) 562.8
Fuel ....gasoline
Fuel tank capacity (gal.) 35
Carburetor ....Zenith C-6, 1.50-in.
Air cleaner ....Allis-Chalmers
Ignition ....Eisemann GV-4
magneto
Cooling capacity (gal.) 8
Maximum brake horsepower tests
PTO/belt horsepower 62.18
Crankshaft rpm 1,002
Fuel use (gal./hr.) 6.69
Maximum drawbar horsepower tests
Gear ....low
Drawbar horsepower 53.28
Pull weight (lb.) 7,213

Speed (mph) 2.77
Percent slippage 1.04
SAE drawbar horsepower 43.04
SAE belt/PTO horsepower 55.81
Type ....tracklayer
Length (in.) 128
Height (in.) 85.25

Rear width (in.) 75.50
Weight (lb.) 14,000
Track length (in.) ....85 on ground,
 249 total
Grouser shoe ....32 links; 13-in.
Gear/speed (mph) ....forward: 1/1.82, 2/2.76,
 3/3.99; reverse: 1/2.06

Chapter 58

NUFFIELD UNIVERSAL

Nuffield Universal DM-4 Diesel
Manufacturer ....Morris Motors Ltd.,
 Birmingham, England
Nebraska test number 558
Test date ....August 27 to
 September 5, 1955
Test tractor serial number ....DE 4345
Engine ....Morris Motors vertical
 I-head
Test engine serial number ....OEA 1216236
Cylinders 4
Bore and stroke (in.) ....3.74 x 4.724
Rated rpm 2,000
Compression ratio 16.5:1
Displacement (c.i.) 208
Fuel ....diesel
Ignition ....12-v with 2, 6-v battery
Maximum brake horsepower tests
 PTO/belt horsepower 45.27
 Crankshaft rpm 2,002
 Fuel use (gal./hr.) 2.96
Maximum drawbar horsepower tests
 Gear 3rd
 Drawbar horsepower 41.30
 Pull weight (lb.) 3,210
 Speed (mph) 4.83
 Percent slippage 6.79
SAE drawbar horsepower 32.36
SAE belt/PTO horsepower 40.44
Type ....standard
Front wheel (in.) ....7.50 x 18
Rear wheel (in.) ....14.00 x 30
Weight (lb.) 5,385
Gear/speed (mph) ....forward: 1/2.26, 2/3.60,
 3/5.05, 4/7.45, 5/17.30;
 reverse: 1/3.96

Nuffield Universal PM-4
Manufacturer ....Morris Motors Ltd.,
 Birmingham, England
Nebraska test number 559
Test date ....August 29 to
 September 8, 1955
Test tractor serial number ....N 178310
Engine ....Morris Motors vertical
 L-head
Test engine serial number ....ETD 120388

Cylinders 4
Bore and stroke (in.) ....3.9375 x 4.724
Rated rpm 2,000
Compression ratio 6:1
Displacement (c.i.) 230
Fuel ....gasoline
Carburetor ....30- mm
Ignition ....12-v battery
Maximum brake horsepower tests
 PTO/belt horsepower 38.40
 Crankshaft rpm 2,000
 Fuel use (gal./hr.) 3.91
Maximum drawbar horsepower tests
 Gear 3rd
 Drawbar horsepower 34.34
 Pull weight (lb.) 2,623
 Speed (mph) 4.91
 Percent slippage 5.11
SAE drawbar horsepower 27.21
SAE belt/PTO horsepower 33.94
Type ....standard
Front wheel (in.) ....7.50 x 18
Rear wheel (in.) ....14.00 x 30
Weight (lb.) 5,132
Gear/speed (mph) ....forward: 1/2.26, 2/3.60,
 3/5.05, 4/7.45, 5/17.30;
 reverse: 1/3.96

Nuffield Universal Three Diesel
Manufacturer ....Morris Motors Ltd.,
 Birmingham, England
Nebraska test number 663
Test date ....August 15–20, 1958
Test tractor serial number 3DL 771 2771
Engine ....Morris Motors, Ltd.
 vertical I-head
Test engine serial number 2720
Cylinders 3
Bore and stroke (in.) ....3.74 x 4.724
Rated rpm 2,000
Compression ratio 16.5:1
Displacement (c.i.) 155.6
Fuel ....diesel
Ignition ....12-v battery
Maximum brake horsepower tests
 PTO/belt horsepower 34.21
 Crankshaft rpm 2,001
 Fuel use (gal./hr.) 2.43

Maximum drawbar horsepower tests
- Gear...3rd
- Drawbar horsepower.....................31.00
- Pull weight (lb.)..........................2,784
- Speed (mph)..............................4.18
- Percent slippage.........................5.62
- SAE drawbar horsepower.................24.55
- SAE belt/PTO horsepower...............30.46

Type ....standard
Front wheel (in.)................................6.00 x 16
Rear wheel (in.)................................13.00 x 24
Tread width (in.)...............................52–80
Weight (lb.)......................................4,640
Gear/speed (mph) ....forward: 1/1.96, 2/3.07, 3/4.35, 4/6.40, 5/14.90; reverse: 1/3.42

Chapter 59
OLIVER

Oliver Hart-Parr 18-27, Row Crop

Manufacturer................................Oliver Farm Equipment Co., Charles City, IA
Nebraska test number 176
Test date ....April 14–24, 1930
Test tractor serial number............100003
Years produced 1930–1937
Serial number range.....................100001–109151 end
Serial number location ....brass plate on right side next to oil filter
Number produced 9,151
Engine ....Oliver-Waukesha vertical I-head, valve-in-head
Test engine serial number..............100003
Cylinders 4
Bore and stroke (in.) ....4.125 x 5.25
Rated rpm...................................1,150
Displacement (c.i.) 280.6
Fuel ....kerosene/gasoline
Main tank capacity (gal.)...............13
Auxiliary tank capacity (gal.) 1
Carburetor..................................Ensign K, 1.25-in.
Air cleaner ....Oliver (Donaldson)
Ignition.......................................American Bosch U4 Ed2 magneto
Cooling capacity (gal.) 6

Maximum brake horsepower tests
- PTO/belt horsepower....................29.72
- Crankshaft rpm 1,148
- Fuel use (gal./hr.).........................3.06

Maximum drawbar horsepower tests
- Gear...2nd
- Drawbar horsepower.....................24.40
- Pull weight (lb.)...........................2,894
- Speed (mph)...............................3.16
- Percent slippage..........................10.31
- SAE drawbar horsepower...............18.29
- SAE belt/PTO horsepower..............27.60
- Type ....3 wheel, 2 drivers, tricycle
- Front wheel (in.)...........................1 steel: 29 x 8
- Rear wheel (in.).............................steel: 59.50 x .5625
- Length (in.) 125
- Height (in.) 64
- Rear width (in.) 80
- Weight (lb.) 3,500

Gear/speed (mph) ....forward: 1/2.60, 2/3.20, 3/4.15; reverse: 1/2.90

Oliver Hart-Parr 18-28; 2-3 Plow

Manufacturer................................Oliver Farm Equipment Co., Charles City, IA
Nebraska test number 180
Test date ....July 7–15, 1930
Test tractor serial number............101763
Years produced 1930–1937
Serial number range.....................800001–803928 end
Serial number location ....brass plate on right side next to oil filter
Number produced 3,928
Engine ....Oliver-Waukesha vertical I-head, valve-in-head
Test engine serial number..............248958
Cylinders 4
Bore and stroke (in.) ....4.125 x 5.25
Rated rpm...................................1,190
Displacement (c.i.) 280.6
Fuel ....kerosene/gasoline
Main tank capacity (gal.)...............13
Auxiliary tank capacity (gal.) 1
Carburetor..................................Ensign KZ, 1.50-in.
Air cleaner ....Oliver (Donaldson)
Ignition.......................................American Bosch U4D2 magneto
Cooling capacity (gal.) 6

Maximum brake horsepower tests
- PTO/belt horsepower....................30.29
- Crankshaft rpm 1,192
- Fuel use (gal./hr.).........................3.04

Maximum drawbar horsepower tests
- Gear...low
- Drawbar horsepower.....................23.56
- Pull weight (lb.)...........................3,241
- Speed (mph)...............................2.73
- Percent slippage..........................13.23
- SAE drawbar horsepower...............18.43
- SAE belt/PTO horsepower..............28.22
- Type ....4 wheel, 2 drivers; standard
- Front wheel (in.)...........................steel: 28 x 5
- Rear wheel (in.).............................steel: 44 x 10
- Length (in.) 112

Height (in.) 53.50
Rear width (in.) 61
Weight (lb.) 4,000
Gear/speed (mph) ....forward: 1/2.60, 2/3.20,
3/4.15; reverse: 1/2.90

Oliver Hart-Parr 28-44, 3-5 Plow

Manufacturer ....Oliver Farm Equipment
Co., Charles City, IA
Nebraska test number 183
Test date ....October 13–27, 1930
Test tractor serial number 500105
Years produced 1930–1937
Serial number range ....500001–508917 end
Serial number location ....brass plate on right
side next to oil filter
Number produced 8,917
Engine ....Oliver-Waukesha
vertical I-head,
valve-in-head
Test engine serial number 500105
Cylinders 4
Bore and stroke (in.) ....4.75 x 6.25
Rated rpm 1,125
Displacement (c.i.) 443
Fuel ....kerosene/gasoline
Main tank capacity (gal.) 34
Auxiliary tank capacity (gal.) 1
Carburetor ....Ensign K, 1.50-in.
Air cleaner ....Oliver (Donaldson)
Ignition ....American Bosch U4
magneto
Cooling capacity (gal.) 10.50
Maximum brake horsepower tests
PTO/belt horsepower 49.04
Crankshaft rpm 1,132
Fuel use (gal./hr.) 4.91
Maximum drawbar horsepower tests
Gear 2nd
Drawbar horsepower 34.21
Pull weight (lb.) 3,650
Speed (mph) 3.51
Percent slippage 11.35
SAE drawbar horsepower 28.54
SAE belt/PTO horsepower 44.63
Type ....4 wheel
Front wheel (in.) ....steel: 29 x 6
Rear wheel (in.) ....steel: 46 x 12
Length (in.) 125.75
Height (in.) 59.50
Rear width (in.) 65
Weight (lb.) 5,575
Gear/speed (mph) ....forward: 1/2.23, 2/3.30,
3/4.33; reverse: 1/2.63

Oliver Hart-Parr 70 Row Crop, 70 HC

Manufacturer ....Oliver Farm Equipment
Co., Charles City, IA
Nebraska test number 252
Test date ....April 13–24, 1936
Test tractor serial number 202845
Years produced 1935–1948
Serial number range ....200001–267866 end;
4- and 6-speed

Serial number location ....brass plate on left side
of center block
Number produced 4-speed: 45,040;
6-speed: 22,826
Engine ....Oliver-Continental
vertical I-head,
valve-in-head
Test engine serial number 1157
Cylinders 6
Bore and stroke (in.) ....3.125 x 4.375
Rated rpm 1,500
Displacement (c.i.) 201.3
Fuel ....gasoline
Fuel tank capacity (gal.) 15
Carburetor ....Zenith 124.5 EX,
1.25-in.
Air cleaner ....Donaldson
Ignition ....American Bosch
MJB6A-302 magneto
Cooling capacity (gal.) 4.50
Maximum brake horsepower tests
PTO/belt horsepower 28.40
Crankshaft rpm 1,501
Fuel use (gal./hr.) 2.67
Maximum drawbar horsepower tests
Gear 3rd
Drawbar horsepower 21.93
Pull weight (lb.) 1,878
Speed (mph) 4.38
Percent slippage 7.56
SAE drawbar horsepower 16.94
SAE belt/PTO horsepower 25.13
Type ....4 wheel, tricycle
Front wheel (in.) ....(steel: 24 x 4.50);
rubber: 5.50 x 16
Rear wheel (in.) ....(steel: 55 x .50);
rubber: 9.00 x 40
Length (in.) 133.75
Height (in.) 58
Rear width (in.) 80.50
Weight (lb.) 3,000
Gear/speed (mph) ....forward: 1/2.44,
2/3.32, 3/4.33, 4/5.88;
reverse: 1/2.44

Oliver Hart-Parr 70 Row Crop, 70 HC

Manufacturer ....Oliver Farm Equipment
Co., Charles City, IA
Nebraska test number 267
Test date ....August 20–31, 1936
Test tractor serial number ....202845 KD
Years produced 1935–1948
Serial number range ....200001–267866 end;
4- and 6-speed
Serial number location ....brass plate on left side
of center block
Number produced ....4 speed: 45,040;
6-speed: 22,826
Engine ....Oliver-Continental
vertical I-head,
valve-in-head
Test engine serial number 1157
Cylinders 6
Bore and stroke (in.) ....3.125 x 4.375

Rated rpm 1,500
Displacement (c.i.) 201.3
Fuel ....distillate/gasoline
Main tank capacity (gal.) 15
Auxiliary tank capacity (gal.) 1
Carburetor ....Zenith 124.50 EX,
1.25-in.
Air cleaner ....Donaldson
Ignition ....American Bosch
MJB6A-302 magneto
Cooling capacity (gal.) 4.50

Maximum brake horsepower tests
    PTO/belt horsepower............................27.15
    Crankshaft rpm 1,500
    Fuel use (gal./hr.)................................3.35
Maximum drawbar horsepower tests
    Gear 3rd
    Drawbar horsepower.............................20.48
    Pull weight (lb.) 1,778
    Speed (mph)..4.32
    Percent slippage..................................8.61
SAE drawbar horsepower.......................16.53
SAE belt/PTO horsepower 24.49
Type ....4 wheel, tricycle
Front wheel (in.) ....(steel: 24 x 4.50);
rubber: 5.50 x 16
Rear wheel (in.) ....(steel: 55 x .50);
rubber: 9.00 x 40
Length (in.) 133.75
Height (in.) 58
Rear width (in.) 80.50
Weight (lb.) 3,000
Gear/speed (mph) ....forward: 1/2.44,
2/3.32, 3/4.33,
4/5.88; reverse:
1/2.44

Oliver Hart-Parr Standard 70 HC

Manufacturer.....................................Oliver Farm Equipment
Co., Charles City, IA
Nebraska test number 283
Test date ....June 14–22, 1937
Test tractor serial number..................300940
Years produced 1936–1948
Serial number range...........................300001–315420 end
Serial number location ....metal plate on front
left of engine
Number produced 15,420
Engine ....Oliver-Continental
vertical I-head,
valve-in-head
Test engine serial number...................13477
Cylinders 6
Bore and stroke (in.) ....3.125 x 4.375
Rated rpm 1,500
Compression ratio.............................6.50:1
Displacement (c.i.) 201
Fuel ....gasoline
Fuel tank capacity (gal.) 15
Carburetor ....Zenith 124-1/2 EX,
1.25-in.
Air cleaner ....Donaldson
Ignition..American Bosch
magneto MJB6A-302
Cooling capacity (gal.) 4.50

Maximum brake horsepower tests
    PTO/belt horsepower............................27.79
    Crankshaft rpm 1,499
    Fuel use (gal./hr.)................................2.83
Maximum drawbar horsepower tests
    Gear 3rd
    Drawbar horsepower.............................19.84
    Pull weight (lb.) 1,529
    Speed (mph)..4.87
    Percent slippage..................................4.83
SAE drawbar horsepower.......................15.89
SAE belt/PTO horsepower 24.95
Type ....standard
Front wheel (in.)...............................(steel: 27 x 4.50);
rubber: 5.50 x 16
Rear wheel (in.) ....(steel: 42 x 10);
rubber: 9.00 x 24
Length (in.) 120.50
Height (in.) 51
Rear width (in.) 40–53.50; 48–61.50
Weight (lb.) ....steel: 3,100;
rubber: 3,340
Gear/speed (mph) ....forward: 1/2.44,
2/3.32, 3/4.33, 4/5.88;
reverse: 1/2.44

Oliver 70 KD, Standard

Manufacturer.....................................Oliver Farm Equipment
Co., Charles City, IA
Nebraska test number 284
Test date ....June 24–30, 1937
Test tractor serial number..................300940 KD
Years produced 1936–1948
Serial number range...........................300001–315420 end
Serial number location ....metal plate on front
left of engine
Number produced 15,420
Engine ....Oliver-Continental
vertical I-head,
valve-in-head
Test engine serial number...................0 13477
Cylinders 6
Bore and stroke (in.) ....3.125 x 4.375
Rated rpm 1,500
Compression ratio.............................4.50:1
Displacement (c.i.) 201
Fuel ....distillate/gasoline
Main tank capacity (gal.) 15
Auxiliary tank capacity (gal.) 1
Carburetor ....Zenith 124-1/2 EX, 1.25-in.
Air cleaner ....Donaldson
Ignition..American Bosch
MJB6A-301 magneto
Cooling capacity (gal.) 4.50

Maximum brake horsepower tests
    PTO/belt horsepower............................26.75
    Crankshaft rpm 1,500
    Fuel use (gal./hr.)................................3.38
Maximum drawbar horsepower tests
    Gear 3rd
    Drawbar horsepower.............................19.83
    Pull weight (lb.)...................................1,535
    Speed (mph) 4.85
    Percent slippage..................................5.71

SAE drawbar horsepower............................15.87
SAE belt/PTO horsepower 23.89
Type ....standard
Front wheel (in.)......................................(steel: 27 x 4.50);
    rubber: 5.50 x 16
Rear wheel (in.) ....(steel: 42 x 10);
    rubber: 9.00 x 24
Length (in.) 120.50
Height (in.) 51
Rear width (in.) 40–53.50; 48–61.50
Weight (lb.) ....steel: 3,120; rubber:
    3,360
Gear/speed (mph) ....forward: 1/2.44, 2/3.32,
    3/4.33, 4/5.88; reverse:
    1/2.44

Oliver 80 KD, Row Crop
Manufacturer..Oliver Farm Equipment
    Co., Charles City, IA
Nebraska test number 300
Test date ....May 16–26, 1938
Test tractor serial number ....109557 KD
Years produced 1937–1948
Serial number range.................................109152–115373 end
Serial number location ....metal plate on right
    rear of engine
Number produced 6,222
Engine ....Oliver-Waukesha
    vertical I-head,
    valve-in-head
Test engine serial number 0432865
Cylinders 4
Bore and stroke (in.) ....4.50 x 5.25
Rated rpm 1,200
Compression ratio....................................4.23:1
Displacement (c.i.) 334
Fuel ....distillate/gasoline
Main tank capacity (gal.)..........................17
Auxiliary tank capacity (gal.) 1
Carburetor...Schebler TTX-18,
    1.25-in.
Air cleaner ....Donaldson
Ignition...American Bosch
    MJB4A-308 magneto
Cooling capacity (gal.) 10
Maximum brake horsepower tests
    PTO/belt horsepower.........................38.78
    Crankshaft rpm 1,200
    Fuel use (gal./hr.) 4.98
Maximum drawbar horsepower tests
    Gear...steel: 2nd
    Drawbar horsepower..........................29.92
    Pull weight (lb.).................................3,300
    Speed (mph) 3.40
    Percent slippage................................5.91
SAE drawbar horsepower...........................23.27
SAE belt/PTO horsepower 35.14
Type ....tricycle
Front wheel (in.)......................................(steel: 24 x 4.50);
    rubber: 6.00 x 16
Rear wheel (in.) ....(steel: 59.50 x .5625);
    rubber: 11.25 x 40
Length (in.) 144
Height (in.) 64.50
Rear width (in.) 80
Tread width (in.) 60–72

Weight (lb.) 4,565
Gear/speed (mph) ....forward: 1/2.70,
    2/3.33, 3/4.33;
    reverse: 1/3.00

Oliver 80 KD, Standard
Manufacturer..Oliver Farm Equipment
    Co., Charles City, IA
Nebraska test number 301
Test date ....May 16–28, 1938
Test tractor serial number ....804479 KD
Years produced 1937–1948
Serial number range.................................803929–816241 end
Serial number location ....metal plate on right
    rear of engine
Number produced 12,313
Engine ....Oliver-Waukesha
    vertical I-head,
    valve-in-head
Test engine serial number 0425148
Cylinders 4
Bore and stroke (in.) ....4.50 x 5.25
Rated rpm 1,200
Compression ratio....................................4.23:1
Displacement (c.i.) 334
Fuel ....distillate/gasoline
Main tank capacity (gal.)..........................17
Auxiliary tank capacity (gal.) 1
Carburetor...Schebler TTX-18,
    1.25-in.
Air cleaner ....Donaldson
Ignition...American Bosch,
    MJB4A-308 magneto
Cooling capacity (gal.) 10
Maximum brake horsepower tests
    PTO/belt horsepower.........................39.32
    Crankshaft rpm 1,200
    Fuel use (gal./hr.) 4.75
Maximum drawbar horsepower tests
    Gear...steel: 2nd
    Drawbar horsepower..........................28.55
    Pull weight (lb.).................................2,911
    Speed (mph) 3.68
    Percent slippage................................4.83
SAE drawbar horsepower...........................22.16
SAE belt/PTO horsepower 35.16
Type ....standard
Front wheel (in.)......................................(steel: 28 x 5);
    rubber: 6.00 x 16
Rear wheel (in.) ....(steel: 44 x 10);
    rubber: 11.25 x 40
Length (in.) 112
Height (in.) 56.50
Rear width (in.) 61
Weight (lb.) 4,200
Gear/speed (mph) ....forward: 1/2.60,
    2/3.20, 3/4.14;
    reverse: 1/3.00

Oliver 70 HC, Row Crop
Manufacturer..Oliver Farm Equipment
    Co., Charles City, IA
Nebraska test number 351
Test date ....August 23–29, 1940
Test tractor serial number 233706
Years produced 1935–1948

Oliver

Serial number range................................200001–267866 end
Serial number location ....metal plate on front left of engine
Number produced 4-speed: 45,040; 6-speed: 22,826
Engine ....Oliver-Continental vertical I-head
Test engine serial number........................42120-G3
Cylinders 6
Bore and stroke (in.) ....3.125 x 4.375
Rated rpm 1,500
Compression ratio 6.50:1
Displacement (c.i.) 201
Fuel ....gasoline
Fuel tank capacity (gal.) 15
Carburetor ....Zenith 61AXJ7, 1.00-in.
Air cleaner ....Donaldson
Ignition..American Bosch MJC6C-312 magneto
Cooling capacity (gal.) 4.50
Maximum brake horsepower tests
    PTO/belt horsepower........................31.52
    Crankshaft rpm 1,500
    Fuel use (gal./hr.) 2.95
Maximum drawbar horsepower tests
    Gear...3rd
    Drawbar horsepower..........................28.63
    Pull weight (lb.)................................2,528
    Speed (mph) 4.25
    Percent slippage...............................5.82
SAE drawbar horsepower..........................22.64
SAE belt/PTO horsepower 28.37
Type ....tricycle
Front wheel (in.) ....steel: 24 x 4.50; (rubber: 5.50 x 16)
Rear wheel (in.)..steel: 55 x .50; (rubber: 11.00 x 40)
Length (in.) 133.75
Height (in.) 58
Rear width (in.) 80.50
Tread width (in.).......................................60–72
Weight (lb.) ....(6,595)
Gear/speed (mph) ....forward: 1/2.56, 2/3.47, 3/4.55, 4/6.17, 5/7.61, 6/13.44 rubber only; reverse: 1/2.56

Oliver 80 HC, Standard
Manufacturer..Oliver Farm Equipment Co., Charles City, IA
Nebraska test number 365
Test date ....November 4–8, 1940
Test tractor serial number.........................807839
Years produced 1937–1948
Serial number range.................................803929–816241 end
Serial number location ....metal plate on right rear of engine
Number produced 12,313
Engine ....Oliver-Waukesha vertical I-head
Test engine serial number.........................466790
Cylinders 4
Bore and stroke (in.) ....4.25 x 5.25
Rated rpm 1,200

Compression ratio 5.25:1
Displacement (c.i.) 298
Fuel ....gasoline
Fuel tank capacity (gal.) 17
Carburetor ....Schebler TTX, 1.25-in.
Air cleaner ....Donaldson
Ignition..American Bosch MJB4A-308 magneto
Cooling capacity (gal.) 8.50
Maximum brake horsepower tests
    PTO/belt horsepower........................41.27
    Crankshaft rpm 1,200
    Fuel use (gal./hr.) 3.85
Maximum drawbar horsepower tests
    Gear...2nd
    Drawbar horsepower..........................35.91
    Pull weight (lb.)................................3,982
    Speed (mph) 3.38
    Percent slippage...............................8.59
SAE drawbar horsepower..........................27.66
SAE belt/PTO horsepower 36.07
Type ....standard
Front wheel (in.) ....steel: 28 x 5; (rubber: 7.50 x 18)
Rear wheel (in.)..steel: 44 x 10; (rubber: 12.75 x 28)
Length (in.) 112
Height (in.) 56.50
Rear width (in.) 61
Tread width (in.).......................................50
Weight (lb.) ....(7,970)
Gear/speed (mph) ....forward: 1/2.78, 2/3.71, 3/4.79, 4/6.44; reverse: 1/3.44

Oliver 60 HC, Row Crop
Manufacturer..Oliver Farm Equipment Co., Charles City, IA
Nebraska test number 375
Test date ....September 10–23, 1941
Test tractor serial number.........................604216
Years produced 1940–1948
Serial number range.................................600001–625131 end
Serial number location ....metal plate on front left of engine
Number produced 25,130
Engine ....Oliver-Waukesha vertical I-head
Test engine serial number.........................485362 G1
Cylinders 4
Bore and stroke (in.) ....3.3125 x 3.50
Rated rpm 1,500
Compression ratio 6.00:1
Displacement (c.i.) 120.6
Fuel ....gasoline
Fuel tank capacity (gal.) 10
Carburetor ....Marvel-Schebler TSX-49, 1.00-in.
Air cleaner ....Donaldson
Ignition..Wico JEM-1348 magneto
Cooling capacity (gal.) 2.50
Maximum brake horsepower tests
    PTO/belt horsepower........................18.76
    Crankshaft rpm 1,499
    Fuel use (gal./hr.) 1.57

Maximum drawbar horsepower tests
- Gear.....................................rubber: 3rd
- Drawbar horsepower........................16.92
- Pull weight (lb.).............................1,490
- Speed (mph) 4.26
- Percent slippage............................6.73
- SAE drawbar horsepower......................13.39
- SAE belt/PTO horsepower.....................16.58
- Type......................................tricycle
- Front wheel (in.)............................steel: 23 x 4.50; (rubber: 5.00 x 15)
- Rear wheel (in.)............................steel: 46 x .50; (rubber: 9.00 x 32)
- Length (in.) 128
- Height (in.)................................56.75
- Rear width (in.) 79.25
- Tread width (in.)...........................60–72
- Weight (lb.)...............................2,275
- Gear/speed (mph) ....forward: 1/2.58, 2/3.45, 3/4.57, 4/6.10; reverse: 1/3.32

Oliver 88 HC, Row Crop, Streamline

- Manufacturer......................The Oliver Corp., Charles City, IA
- Nebraska test number 388
- Test date ....October 20–31, 1947
- Test tractor serial number..........120003
- Years produced 1947–1948
- Serial number range...............120001–121300 end
- Serial number location ....metal plate on right front of rear main frame
- Number produced 1,300
- Engine ....Oliver-Waukesha vertical I-head
- Test engine serial number..........707053
- Cylinders 6
- Bore and stroke (in.) ....3.50 x 4.00
- Rated rpm 1,600
- Compression ratio...............6.75:1
- Displacement (c.i.) 231
- Fuel ....gasoline
- Fuel tank capacity (gal.) 22
- Carburetor......................Marvel-Schebler TSX-181, 1.00-in.
- Air cleaner......................Donaldson
- Ignition.........................Delco-Remy, 6-v battery
- Cooling capacity (gal.) 4.50

Maximum brake horsepower tests
- PTO/belt horsepower...............41.99
- Crankshaft rpm 1,601
- Fuel use (gal./hr.)................3.71

Maximum drawbar horsepower tests
- Gear............................3rd
- Drawbar horsepower..............36.97
- Pull weight (lb.).................3,023
- Speed (mph) 4.59
- Percent slippage.................5.37
- SAE drawbar horsepower..........28.80
- SAE belt/PTO horsepower.........37.96
- Type...........................tricycle
- Front tire (in.)..................6.00 x 16
- Rear tire (in.)..................13.00 x 38
- Length (in.) 141.88
- Height (in.) 73.50
- Rear width (in.) 80.25
- Tread width (in.)...............60–92.50
- Weight (lb.)...................5,110
- Gear/speed (mph) ....forward: 1/2.62, 2/3.39, 3/4.50, 4/5.83, 5/7.17, 6/12.32; reverse: 1/2.68, 2/4.60

Oliver 88 HC, Standard, Streamline

- Manufacturer......................The Oliver Corp., Charles City, IA
- Nebraska test number 391
- Test date ....November 14–30, 1947
- Test tractor serial number..........820045
- Years produced ....1947–1948; style changed, 1948–1954
- Serial number range...............820001–820485, 820486–827966, 3501813–4505081 end
- Serial number location ....metal plate on right front of rear main frame; mid-1952: below instrument panel
- Number produced 485
- Engine ....Oliver-Waukesha vertical I-head
- Test engine serial number..........707088 G 1
- Cylinders 6
- Bore and stroke (in.) ....3.50 x 4.00
- Rated rpm 1,600
- Compression ratio...............6.75:1
- Displacement (c.i.) 231
- Fuel ....gasoline
- Fuel tank capacity (gal.) 22
- Carburetor......................Marvel-Schebler TSX-181, 1.00-in.
- Air cleaner......................Donaldson
- Ignition.........................Delco-Remy, 6-v battery
- Cooling capacity (gal.) 4.50

Maximum brake horsepower tests
- PTO/belt horsepower...............43.15
- Crankshaft rpm 1,600
- Fuel use (gal./hr.)................3.83

Maximum drawbar horsepower tests
- Gear............................3rd
- Drawbar horsepower..............37.27
- Pull weight (lb.).................3,162
- Speed (mph) 4.42
- Percent slippage.................5.14
- SAE drawbar horsepower..........28.92
- SAE belt/PTO horsepower.........38.22
- Type...........................standard
- Front tire (in.)..................6.00 x 16
- Rear tire (in.)..................14.00 x 26
- Length (in.) 171.88
- Height (in.) 68.50
- Rear width (in.) 68
- Tread width (in.)...............54–62
- Weight (lb.)...................4,688
- Gear/speed (mph) ....forward: 1/2.51, 2/3.25, 3/4.31, 4/5.58, 5/6.87, 6/11.80; reverse: 1/2.56, 2/4.41

Oliver

Oliver 77 HC Row Crop

Manufacturer ....The Oliver Corp., Charles City, IA
Nebraska test number 404
Test date ....October 21 to November 9, 1948
Test tractor serial number.........................320005
Years produced 1948–1954
Serial number range ....320001–354447; 3500001–3510830; 4501301–4504470 end
Serial number location ......metal plate on right front of rear main frame; mid-1952: below instrument panel
Number produced.............1948–1952: 34,447, all types interspersed; 1953-on. All models, wheel type numbered consecutively. 1953–1954, first two digits are year in reverse
Engine ....Oliver-Waukesha vertical I-head
Test engine serial number..........................721398
Cylinders 6
Bore and stroke (in.) ....3.3125 x 3.75
Rated rpm 1,600
Compression ratio.....................................6.75:1
Displacement (c.i.) 194
Fuel ....gasoline
Fuel tank capacity (gal.) 16.50
Carburetor ....Marvel-Schebler TSX-363, 0.875-in.
Air cleaner ....Donaldson
Ignition...Delco-Remy with 6-v battery
Cooling capacity (gal.) 3.38
Maximum brake horsepower tests
    PTO/belt horsepower...........................33.98
    Crankshaft rpm 1,600
    Fuel use (gal./hr.) 2.98
Maximum drawbar horsepower tests
    Gear...3rd
    Drawbar horsepower.............................28.68
    Pull weight (lb.)....................................2,300
    Speed (mph) 4.68
    Percent slippage..................................3.55
SAE drawbar horsepower...........................22.43
SAE belt/PTO horsepower..........................29.86
Type ....tricycle
Front tire (in.)...5.50 x 16
Rear tire (in.)..12.00 x 38
Length (in.) 139.25
Height (in.) 74
Tread width (in.)..60–92.50
Weight (lb.) 3,240
Gear/speed (mph) ....forward: 1/2.625, 2/3.50, 3/4.50, 4/6.00, 5/7.00, 6/12.25; reverse: 1/2.75, 2/4.75

Oliver 77 HC, Standard

Manufacturer ....The Oliver Corp., Charles City, IA
Nebraska test number 405
Test date ....October 21 to November 6, 1948
Test tractor serial number..........................269012
Years produced 1948–1952
Serial number range ....269001–274051 end

Serial number location ....metal plate on right front of rear main frame; mid-1952: below instrument panel
Number produced 5,051
Engine ....Oliver-Waukesha vertical I-head
Test engine serial number..........................721399
Cylinders 6
Bore and stroke (in.) ....3.3125 x 3.75
Rated rpm 1,600
Compression ratio.....................................6.75:1
Displacement (c.i.) 194
Fuel ....gasoline
Fuel tank capacity (gal.) 16.50
Carburetor ....Marvel-Schebler TSX-363, 0.875-in.
Air cleaner ....Donaldson
Ignition...Delco-Remy with 6-v battery
Cooling capacity (gal.) 3.38
Maximum brake horsepower tests
    PTO/belt horsepower...........................33.56
    Crankshaft rpm 1,601
    Fuel use (gal./hr.) 2.89
Maximum drawbar horsepower tests
    Gear...3rd
    Drawbar horsepower.............................28.48
    Pull weight (lb.)....................................2,247
    Speed (mph) 4.75
    Percent slippage..................................3.80
SAE drawbar horsepower...........................22.34
SAE belt/PTO horsepower..........................29.99
Type ....standard
Front tire (in.)...5.50 x 16
Rear tire (in.)..13.00 x 26
Length (in.) 129.50
Height (in.) 74
Tread width (in.)..52.50
Weight (lb.) 3,675
Gear/speed (mph) ....forward: 1/2.63, 2/3.50, 3/4.63, 4/6.00, 5/7.13, 6/12.33; reverse: 1/2.75, 2/4.88

Oliver 66 HC, Row Crop

Manufacturer ....The Oliver Corp., Charles City, IA
Nebraska test number 412
Test date ....June 6–24, 1949
Test tractor serial number..........................420006
Years produced 1949–1954
Serial number range ....420001–431472; 3503990-3510962; 4500309–4503563 end
Serial number location ......metal plate on right front of rear main frame; mid-1952-on: below instrument panel
Number produced.............1949–1952: 11,472, all types interspersed; 1953-on. All models, wheel type numbered consecutively. 1953–1954, first two digits are year in reverse
Engine ....Oliver-Waukesha vertical I-head
Test engine serial number..........................G2 771730
Cylinders 4

Bore and stroke (in.) ....3.3125 x 3.75
Rated rpm 1,600
Compression ratio......................................6.75:1
Displacement (c.i.) 129
Fuel ....gasoline
Fuel tank capacity (gal.) 10
Carburetor ....Marvel-Schebler
TSX-363, 0.875-in.
Air cleaner ....Donaldson
Ignition ....Delco-Remy with
6-v battery
Cooling capacity (gal.) 3.50

Maximum brake horsepower tests
    PTO/belt horsepower............................24.91
    Crankshaft rpm 1,600
    Fuel use (gal./hr.) 2.13

Maximum drawbar horsepower tests
    Gear..3rd
    Drawbar horsepower..............................21.03
    Pull weight (lb.) 1,914
    Speed (mph) 4.12
    Percent slippage...................................5.02
SAE drawbar horsepower............................16.73
SAE belt/PTO horsepower 22.14
Type ....tricycle
Front tire (in.) ....5.00 x 15
Rear tire (in.) ....10.00 x 38
Length (in.) 134.88
Height (in.) 85.25
Tread width (in.) 60–88
Weight (lb.) 2,600
Gear/speed (mph) ....forward: 1/2.50,
2/3.25, 3/4.25, 4/5.63,
5/6.63, 6/11.38;
reverse: 1/2.50, 2/4.38

Oliver 66 HC, Standard
Manufacturer...The Oliver Corp.,
Charles City, IA
Nebraska test number 413
Test date ....June 6–25, 1949
Test tractor serial number...........................47003
Years produced 1949–1954
Serial number range 470001–476408; 3504001-3511337;
4501624–4504476 end
Serial number location ......metal plate on right front of rear
main frame; mid-1952-on: below
instrument panel
Number produced..............1949–1952: 6,408; 1953-on. All
models, wheel type numbered
consecutively. 1953–1954, first two
digits are year in reverse
Engine ....Oliver-Waukesha
vertical I-head
Test engine serial number...........................G2 771681
Cylinders 4
Bore and stroke (in.) ....3.3125 x 3.75
Rated rpm 1,600
Compression ratio......................................6.75:1
Displacement (c.i.) 129
Fuel ....gasoline
Fuel tank capacity (gal.) 10
Carburetor ....Marvel-Schebler
TSX-363, 0.875-in.
Air cleaner ....Donaldson

Ignition ....Delco-Remy with
6-v battery
Cooling capacity (gal.) 3.50

Maximum brake horsepower tests
    PTO/belt horsepower............................24.90
    Crankshaft rpm 1,600
    Fuel use (gal./hr.) 2.09

Maximum drawbar horsepower tests
    Gear..3rd
    Drawbar horsepower..............................21.52
    Pull weight (lb.) 1,821
    Speed (mph) 4.43
    Percent slippage...................................6.12
SAE drawbar horsepower............................16.96
SAE belt/PTO horsepower 22.28
Type ....standard
Front tire (in.) ....5.00 x 15
Rear tire (in.) ....11.00 x 24
Length (in.) 123.88
Height (in.) 78.88
Tread width (in.) 50.75–59
Weight (lb.) 2,480
Gear/speed (mph) ....forward: 1/2.50,
2/3.25, 3/4.38, 4/5.75,
5/6.75, 6/11.63;
reverse: 1/2.63, 2/4.50

Oliver 77 HC, Row Crop
Manufacturer...The Oliver Corp.,
Charles City, IA
Nebraska test number 425
Test date ....September 23–29,
1949
Test tractor serial number...........................325494
Years produced 1948–1954
Serial number range 320001–354447; 3500001–3510830;
4501301–4504470 end
Serial number location ......metal plate on right front of rear
main frame; mid-1952-on: below
instrument panel
Number produced..............1948–1952: 34,447, all types
interspersed; 1953-on. All models,
wheel type numbered consecutively.
1953–1954, first two digits are year in
reverse
Engine ....Oliver-Waukesha
vertical I-head
Test engine serial number...........................G2 779367
Cylinders 6
Bore and stroke (in.) ....3.3125 x 3.75
Rated rpm 1,600
Compression ratio......................................6.75:1
Displacement (c.i.) 194
Fuel ....gasoline
Fuel tank capacity (gal.) 16.50
Carburetor ....Marvel-Schebler
TSX-363, 0.875-in.
Air cleaner ....Donaldson
Ignition ....Delco-Remy with
6-v battery
Cooling capacity (gal.) 4.38

Maximum brake horsepower tests
    PTO/belt horsepower............................34.34
    Crankshaft rpm 1,600
    Fuel use (gal./hr.) 2.93

Oliver

Maximum drawbar horsepower tests
- Gear...3rd
- Drawbar horsepower.........................30.19
- Pull weight (lb.)...............................2,652
- Speed (mph)...................................4.27
- Percent slippage............................4.23

SAE drawbar horsepower.........................25.65
SAE belt/PTO horsepower.........................33.00
Type...tricycle
Front tire (in.)....................................5.50 x 16
Rear tire (in.)....................................12.00 x 38
Length (in.)......................................139.25
Height (in.).......................................75
Tread width (in.)................................60–92.50
Weight (lb.)......................................4,032
Gear/speed (mph) ....forward: 1/2.50, 2/3.25, 3/4.25, 4/5.63, 5/6.63, 6/11.50; reverse: 1/2.63, 2/4.50

Oliver HG

Manufacturer....................................The Oliver Corp., Cleveland, OH
Nebraska test number 434
Test date ....November 11–21, 1949
Test tractor serial number....................52 GA 000
Years produced................................1939–1951
Serial number range...........................1GA000 to 59GA858 end, even numbers
Serial number location ....metal plate on right frame rail in front of axle and on right side of bell housing
Number produced ....approximately 29,930
Engine...Hercules IXB3 vertical L-head
Test engine serial number...................2428943
Cylinders 4
Bore and stroke (in.) ....3.25 x 4.00
Rated rpm 1,700
Compression ratio............................6.66:1
Displacement (c.i.) 133
Fuel ....gasoline
Fuel tank capacity (gal.) 12
Carburetor.....................................Marvel-Schebler TSX-403, 0.875
Air cleaner......................................Vortox
Ignition..Wico XH-1113 or Delco-Remy with 6-v battery
Cooling capacity (gal.) 2.75
Maximum brake horsepower tests
- PTO/belt horsepower........................25.30
- Crankshaft rpm 1,700
- Fuel use (gal./hr.)............................2.29

Maximum drawbar horsepower tests
- Gear..2nd
- Drawbar horsepower.........................21.30
- Pull weight (lb.)...............................2,604
- Speed (mph)...................................3.07
- Percent slippage............................4.42

SAE drawbar horsepower.........................16.39
SAE belt/PTO horsepower.........................22.41
Type...tracklayer

Length (in.) 100.13
Height (in.) 50
Tread width (in.)................................31, 42, 60, or 68
Weight (lb.) 3,163
Track length (in.)...............................176
Grouser shoe...................................30 links; 6, 8, 10, (12)-in.
Gear/speed (mph) ....forward: 1/2.01, 2/3.19, 3/5.24; reverse: 1/2.33

Oliver DG

Manufacturer....................................The Oliver Corp., Cleveland, OH
Nebraska test number 435
Test date ....November 8–21, 1949
Test tractor serial number....................3E 282
Years produced................................1936–1956
Serial number range..........1E00–3E516 no end, even numbers to 1953. 1953–1954, all models numbered consecutively. First two numbers are year in reverse
Serial number location ....metal plate on right front of firewall
Number produced ....approximately 1,715 through 1952
Engine...Hercules RXC vertical, L-head
Test engine serial number...................2015249
Cylinders 6
Bore and stroke (in.) ....4.625 x 5.25
Rated rpm 1,300
Compression ratio............................5.78:1
Displacement (c.i.) 529
Fuel ....gasoline
Fuel tank capacity (gal.) 30
Carburetor.....................................Marvel-Schebler TXS-399, 1.25-in.
Air cleaner......................................Vortox
Ignition..Delco-Remy with 12-v battery
Cooling capacity (gal.) 10.25
Maximum brake horsepower tests
- PTO/belt horsepower........................69.03
- Crankshaft rpm 1,300
- Fuel use (gal./hr.)............................6.72

Maximum drawbar horsepower tests
- Gear..3rd
- Drawbar horsepower.........................59.39
- Pull weight (lb.)...............................7,363
- Speed (mph)...................................3.03
- Percent slippage............................1.75

SAE drawbar horsepower.........................45.50
SAE belt/PTO horsepower.........................60.69
Type...tracklayer
Length (in.) 128
Height (in.) 67
Tread width (in.)................................48 or 61
Weight (lb.) 12,472
Track length (in.)...............................224
Grouser shoe...................................31 links; 14, 16, 18, (20), 24-in.
Gear/speed (mph) ....forward: 1/1.45, 2/2.28, 3/3.04, 4/4.85; reverse: 1/1.72, 2/3.62

Oliver DD, Diesel

Manufacturer ....The Oliver Corp.,
Cleveland, OH
Nebraska test number 436
Test date ....November 8–22, 1949
Test tractor serial number 2L 3368
Years produced 1936–1958
Serial number range ....10832–11580; 1L3000 to 3L596 no
end; even numbers to 1950.
1953–1954, all models numbered
consecutively. First two numbers are
year in reverse
Serial number location ....metal plate on left front
of firewall
Number produced ....approximately 5624
to 1950
Engine ....Hercules DRXB
vertical I-head
Test engine serial number 5389458
Cylinders 6
Bore and stroke (in.) ....4.375 x 5.25
Rated rpm 1,300
Compression ratio......................................15.0:1
Displacement (c.i.) 474
Fuel ....diesel
Fuel tank capacity (gal.) 30
Carburetor ....Bosch injector pump
Air cleaner ....Vortox
Ignition..Delco-Remy 24-v;
with 2, 12-v battery
Cooling capacity (gal.) 10.50
Maximum brake horsepower tests
PTO/belt horsepower............................73.30
Crankshaft rpm 1,300
Fuel use (gal./hr.) 4.73
Maximum drawbar horsepower tests
Gear..3rd
Drawbar horsepower............................58.81
Pull weight (lb.) 7,277
Speed (mph) 3.03
Percent slippage..................................1.28
SAE drawbar horsepower 45.35
SAE belt/PTO horsepower 63.27
Type ....tracklayer
Length (in.) 128
Height (in.) 67
Tread width (in.) ....48 or 61
Weight (lb.) 13,233
Track length (in.) 224
Grouser shoe..31 links; 14, 16, 18,
(20), 24-in.
Gear/speed (mph) ....forward: 1/1.45,
2/2.28, 3/3.04, 4/4.85;
reverse: 1/1.72, 2/3.62

Oliver 88, Diesel, Row Crop, Fleetline

Manufacturer..The Oliver Corp.,
Charles City, IA
Nebraska test number 450
Test date ....September 25 to
October 9, 1950
Test tractor serial number ....DSL 129431
Years produced 1948–1954
Serial number range 121301–143232; 3500977–3511566;
4500076–4505123 end

Serial number location ......metal plate on right front of rear
main frame; mid-1952-on: below
instrument panel
Number produced.............1948–1952: 21,932, all types interspersed;
1953-on. All models, wheel type numbered
consecutively. 1953–1954, first two digits
are year in reverse
Engine ....Oliver-Waukesha
vertical I-head
Test engine serial number D2 800823
Cylinders 6
Bore and stroke (in.) ....3.50 x 4.00
Rated rpm 1,600
Compression ratio......................................15.0:1
Displacement (c.i.) 231
Fuel ....diesel
Fuel tank capacity (gal.) 20
Carburetor ....Bosch injector pump
PSB
Air cleaner ....Donaldson
Ignition..Delco-Remy 12-v;
with 2, 6-v
Cooling capacity (gal.) 4.50
Maximum brake horsepower tests
PTO/belt horsepower............................43.53
Crankshaft rpm 1,600
Fuel use (gal./hr.) 2.93
Maximum drawbar horsepower tests
Gear..3rd
Drawbar horsepower............................38.30
Pull weight (lb.) 3,418
Speed (mph) 4.20
Percent slippage..................................6.32
SAE drawbar horsepower 29.30
SAE belt/PTO horsepower 38.38
Type ....tricycle
Front tire (in.) ....6.00 x 16
Rear tire (in.) ....13.00 x 38
Length (in.) 143.56
Height (in.) 75
Tread width (in.) 60–92.50
Weight (lb.) 5,025
Gear/speed (mph) ....forward: 1/2.50,
2/3.25, 3/4.25, 4/5.50,
5/6.75, 6/11.75;
reverse: 1/2.50, 2/4.38

Oliver 99, Standard, Unstyled

Manufacturer..The Oliver Corp.,
Charles City, IA
Nebraska test number 451
Test date ....September 29 to
October 9, 1950
Test tractor serial number 516060 C66
Years produced 1937–1952
Serial number range ....508918–518212 end
Serial number location ....metal plate on right
rear engine block
Number produced ....9,295, models 90 and
99 interspersed
Engine ....Oliver-Waukesha
vertical I-head
Test engine serial number 9864
Cylinders 4
Bore and stroke (in.) ....4.75 x 6.25

Oliver

Rated rpm 1,125
Compression ratio...........................5.50:1
Displacement (c.i.) 443
Fuel ....gasoline
Fuel tank capacity (gal.) 30
Carburetor ....Marvel-Schebler
TSX-394, 1.25-in.
Air cleaner ....Donaldson
Ignition ....Delco-Remy with
6-v battery
Cooling capacity (gal.) 5.25
Maximum brake horsepower tests
PTO/belt horsepower.....................62.28
Crankshaft rpm 1,125
Fuel use (gal./hr.) 6.25
Maximum drawbar horsepower tests
Gear...2nd
Drawbar horsepower.....................52.05
Pull weight (lb.) 5,293
Speed (mph) 3.69
Percent slippage.........................9.52
SAE drawbar horsepower...................40.93
SAE belt/PTO horsepower 54.29
Type ....standard
Front tire (in.)................................7.50 x 18
Rear tire (in.).................................15.00 x 30
Length (in.) 132.75
Height (in.) 70.34
Tread width (in.)..............................57.50
Weight (lb.) 6,966
Gear/speed (mph) ....forward: 1/2.50, 2/3.88,
3/5.00, 4/13.50;
reverse: 1/3.75

Oliver 77, Diesel, Row Crop

Manufacturer..................................The Oliver Corp.,
Charles City, IA
Nebraska test number 457
Test date ....May 21–28, 1951
Test tractor serial number.................DSL 337222
Years produced 1948–1954
Serial number range 320001–354447; 3500001–3510830;
4501301–4504470 end
Serial number location ......metal plate on right front of rear
main frame; mid-1952-on: below
instrument panel
Number produced.............1948–1952: 34,447, all types
interspersed; 1953-on. All models,
wheel type numbered consecutively.
1953–1954, first two digits are the year
in reverse
Engine ....Oliver-Waukesha 77D
vertical I-head
Test engine serial number.................D 1831128
Cylinders 6
Bore and stroke (in.) ....3.3125 x 3.75
Rated rpm 1,600
Compression ratio...........................15.75:1
Displacement (c.i.) 193.9
Fuel ....diesel
Fuel tank capacity (gal.) 16.50
Carburetor ....Bosch injector pump
PSB
Air cleaner ....Donaldson

Ignition..Delco-Remy 12-v;
with 2, 6-v battery
Cooling capacity (gal.) 4.50
Maximum brake horsepower tests
PTO/belt horsepower.....................35.79
Crankshaft rpm 1,601
Fuel use (gal./hr.) 2.47
Maximum drawbar horsepower tests
Gear...3rd
Drawbar horsepower.....................31.28
Pull weight (lb.) 2,795
Speed (mph) 4.20
Percent slippage.........................5.19
SAE drawbar horsepower...................24.82
SAE belt/PTO horsepower 31.59
Type ....tricycle
Front tire (in.)................................5.50 x 16
Rear tire (in.).................................12.00 x 38
Length (in.) 139.25
Height (in.) 75
Tread width (in.)..............................60–92.50
Weight (lb.) 3,775
Gear/speed (mph) ....forward: 1/2.50,
2/3.25, 3/4.25, 4/5.63,
5/6.63, 6/11.50;
reverse: 1/2.63, 2/4.50

Oliver 66 D, Diesel, Row Crop

Manufacturer..................................The Oliver Corp.,
Charles City, IA
Nebraska test number 467
Test date ....October 12–18, 1951
Test tractor serial number.................DSL 428467
Years produced 1949–1954
Serial number range 420001–431472; 3503990–3510962;
4500309–4503563 end
Serial number location ......metal plate on right front of rear
main frame; mid-1952-on: below
instrument panel
Number produced.............1949–1952: 11,472, all types
interspersed; 1953 on. All models,
wheel type numbered consecutively.
1953–1954, first two digits are the year
in reverse
Engine ....Oliver-Waukesha
vertical I-head
Test engine serial number.................D 1846622
Cylinders 4
Bore and stroke (in.) ....3.3125 x 3.75
Rated rpm 1,600
Compression ratio...........................15.5:1
Displacement (c.i.) 129.3
Fuel ....diesel
Fuel tank capacity (gal.) 10
Carburetor ....Bosch injector pump
PSB
Air cleaner ....Donaldson
Ignition..Delco-Remy 12-v;
with 2, 6-v battery
Cooling capacity (gal.) 3.50
Maximum brake horsepower tests
PTO/belt horsepower.....................25.03
Crankshaft rpm 1,602
Fuel use (gal./hr.) 1.76

Maximum drawbar horsepower tests
Gear	3rd
Drawbar horsepower	22.05
Pull weight (lb.)	2,011
Speed (mph)	4.11
Percent slippage	6.64
SAE drawbar horsepower	17.36
SAE belt/PTO horsepower	22.43
Type	tricycle
Front tire (in.)	5.00 x 15
Rear tire (in.)	10.00 x 38
Length (in.)	134.88
Height (in.)	85.25
Tread width (in.)	60–88
Weight (lb.)	2,600
Gear/speed (mph)	forward: 1/2.50, 2/3.25, 3/4.25, 4/5.63, 5/6.63, 6/11.38; reverse: 1/2.50, 2/4.38

Oliver 77 LP, LPG, Row Crop
Manufacturer	The Oliver Corp., Charles City, IA
Nebraska test number	470
Test date	April 28–10, 1952
Test tractor serial number	347835 C77D
Years produced	1948–1954
Serial number range	320001–354423; 3500001–3510830; 4501301–4504470 end
Serial number location	metal plate on right front of rear main frame; mid-1952-on: below instrument panel
Number produced	1948–1952: 34,447, all types interspersed; 1953-on. All models, wheel type numbered consecutively. 1953–1954, first two digits are the year in reverse
Engine	Oliver-Waukesha vertical I-head
Test engine serial number	G 2373961
Cylinders	6
Bore and stroke (in.)	3.3125 x 3.75
Rated rpm	1,600
Compression ratio	6.75:1
Displacement (c.i.)	193.9
Fuel	LPG
Carburetor	Century, 1.25-in.
Air cleaner	Donaldson
Ignition	Delco-Remy with 6-v battery
Cooling capacity (gal.)	4.50

Maximum brake horsepower tests
PTO/belt horsepower	36.33
Crankshaft rpm	1,601
Fuel use (gal./hr.)	4.57

Maximum drawbar horsepower tests
Gear	3rd
Drawbar horsepower	32.26
Pull weight (lb.)	2,846
Speed (mph)	4.25
Percent slippage	6.16
SAE drawbar horsepower	25.46
SAE belt/PTO horsepower	32.39
Type	tricycle
Front tire (in.)	6.00 x 16
Rear tire (in.)	12.00 x 38
Length (in.)	139.25

Height (in.)	75
Tread width (in.)	47–52.50
Weight (lb.)	4,545
Gear/speed (mph)	forward: 1/2.50, 2/3.25, 3/4.33, 4/5.75, 5/6.63, 6/11.63; reverse: 1/2.63, 2/4.50

Oliver OC-18, Diesel
Manufacturer	The Oliver Corp., Cleveland, OH
Nebraska test number	489
Test date	November 10–24, 1952
Test tractor serial number	1KS022
Years produced	1952–1960
Serial number range	1KS002 to 1KS758 no end, consecutive numbers
Serial number location	metal plate front center of instrument panel
Number produced	1952 and 1955–1960: about 697; 1953 and 1954. 1953–1954, all models numbered consecutively. First two digits are year in reverse
Engine	Hercules DFXE vertical I-head
Test engine serial number	DFXE 376524
Cylinders	6
Bore and stroke (in.)	5.625 x 6.00
Rated rpm	1,500
Compression ratio	14.8:1
Displacement (c.i.)	895
Fuel	diesel
Fuel tank capacity (gal.)	66
Carburetor	injector pump
Air cleaner	Vortox
Ignition	Delco-Remy 24-v; with 2, 12-v battery
Cooling capacity (gal.)	15.50

Maximum drawbar horsepower tests
Gear	2nd
Drawbar horsepower	128.08
Pull weight (lb.)	18,513
Speed (mph)	2.59
Percent slippage	1.29
SAE drawbar horsepower	99.77
Type	tracklayer
Length (in.)	167.25
Height (in.)	82.75
Tread width (in.)	78
Weight (lb.)	31,915
Track length (in.)	294.25
Grouser shoe	35 links; 20, 22, 24, (26)
Gear/speed (mph)	forward: 1/1.50, 2/2.61, 3/3.76, 4/5.45; reverse: 1/1.83, 2/3.53

Oliver OC-6
Manufacturer	The Oliver Corp., Cleveland, OH
Nebraska test number	516
Test date	April 15–28, 1954
Test tractor serial number	4501134
Years produced	1953–1960
Serial number range	3501258 to 2RM126 no end, consecutive numbers

Oliver

Serial number location ......metal plate front center below instrument panel
Number produced.............1953–1954. 1953–1954, all models numbered consecutively. First two digits are year in reverse; 1955–1959: about 1,124
Engine ....Oliver-Waukesha vertical I-head
Test engine serial number..........................932009
Cylinders 6
Bore and stroke (in.) ....3.3125 x 3.75
Rated rpm 1,600
Compression ratio.................................6.75:1
Displacement (c.i.) 193.9
Fuel ....gasoline
Fuel tank capacity (gal.) 16.50
Carburetor ....Marvel-Schebler TSX-405, 0.875-in.
Air cleaner..........................Vortox
Ignition................................Delco-Remy with 6-v battery
Cooling capacity (gal.) 4.25
Maximum drawbar horsepower tests
    Gear.................................2nd
    Drawbar horsepower.........................31.92
    Pull weight (lb.)...................4,962
    Speed (mph) 2.41
    Percent slippage................1.54
SAE drawbar horsepower.........................24.74
Type ....tracklayer
Length (in.) 121.50
Height (in.) 56.25
Tread width (in.) ....32, 42, 60, or (68)
Weight (lb.) 5,430
Track length (in.)................196
Grouser shoe.......................33 links; 8, 10, (12), 14
Gear/speed (mph) ....forward: 1/1.88, 2/2.44, 3/3.23, 4/4.19, 5/5.15, 6/8.86; reverse: 1/1.92, 2/3.31

Oliver OC-6D, Diesel

Manufacturer.......................The Oliver Corp., Cleveland, OH
Nebraska test number 517
Test date ....April 17 to May 7, 1954
Test tractor serial number.........................4501134
Years produced 1953–1960
Serial number range ....3502776 to 2RC458 no end, consecutive numbers
Serial number location ......metal plate front center below instrument panel
Number produced.............1953–1954. 1953–1954, all models numbered consecutively. First two digits are year in reverse; 1954–1959: about 1,456
Engine ....Oliver-Waukesha vertical I-head
Test engine serial number..........................D1 922054
Cylinders 6
Bore and stroke (in.) ....3.3125 x 3.75
Rated rpm 1,600
Compression ratio.................................15.75:1
Displacement (c.i.) 193.9

Fuel ....diesel
Fuel tank capacity (gal.) 16.50
Carburetor ....Bosch injector pump
Air cleaner ....Vortox
Ignition................................Delco-Remy 12-v; with 2, 6-v battery
Cooling capacity (gal.) 4.25
Maximum drawbar horsepower tests
    Gear.................................2nd
    Drawbar horsepower.........................33.46
    Pull weight (lb.)...................5,204
    Speed (mph) 2.41
    Percent slippage................1.67
SAE drawbar horsepower.........................26.06
Type ....tracklayer
Length (in.) 121.50
Height (in.) 56.25
Tread width (in.) ....32, 42, 60, or (68)
Weight (lb.) 5,575
Track length (in.)................196
Grouser shoe.......................33 links; 8, 10, (12), 14
Gear/speed (mph) ....forward: 1/1.88, 2/2.44, 3/3.23, 4/4.19, 5/5.15, 6/8.86; reverse: 1/1.92, 2/3.31

Oliver Super 55 HC

Manufacturer.......................The Oliver Corp., Charles City, IA
Nebraska test number 524
Test date ....September 27 to October 12, 1954
Test tractor serial number.........................6252 500
Years produced 1954–1958
Serial number range..............6001–59033 end, all models numbered consecutively
Serial number location ....metal plate below instrument panel
Number produced ....na, interspersed
Engine ....Oliver-Waukesha vertical I-head
Test engine serial number..........................951492
Cylinders 4
Bore and stroke (in.) ....3.50 x 3.75
Rated rpm 2,000
Compression ratio.................................7.0:1
Displacement (c.i.) 144
Fuel ....gasoline
Fuel tank capacity (gal.) 13
Carburetor ....Marvel Schebler TSX-603, 0.875-in.
Air cleaner ....Donaldson
Ignition................................Delco-Remy with 6-v battery
Cooling capacity (gal.) 3.50
Maximum brake horsepower tests
    PTO/belt horsepower.........................34.39
    Crankshaft rpm 2,000
    Fuel use (gal./hr.) 3.13
Maximum drawbar horsepower tests
    Gear.................................4th
    Drawbar horsepower.........................29.60
    Pull weight (lb.)...................2,190

Speed (mph) 5.07
Percent slippage.................................7.23
SAE drawbar horsepower............................23.06
SAE belt/PTO horsepower...........................30.50
Type ....standard
Front tire (in.)...................................6.00 x 16
Rear tire (in.)....................................11.00 x 28
Length (in.) 120
Height (in.).......................................70.38
Tread width (in.)..................................48–76
Weight (lb.) 2,833
Gear/speed (mph) ....forward: 1/1.69,
2/2.58, 3/3.46, 4/5.33,
5/6.39, 6/13.18;
reverse: 1/1.89, 2/3.90

Oliver Super 88 HC, Row Crop

Manufacturer......................................The Oliver Corp.,
Charles City, IA
Nebraska test number 525
Test date ....September 27 to
October 16, 1954
Test tractor serial number........................6619 800
Years produced 1954–1958
Serial number range...............................6503–59001 end, all
models numbered
consecutively
Serial number location ....metal plate below
instrument panel
Number produced ....na, interspersed
Engine ....Oliver-Waukesha
vertical I-head
Test engine serial number.........................949637
Cylinders 6
Bore and stroke (in.) ....3.75 x 4.00
Rated rpm 1,600
Compression ratio.................................7.0:1
Displacement (c.i.) 265
Fuel ....gasoline
Fuel tank capacity (gal.) 20
Carburetor..Marvel-Schebler
TSX-610, 1.00-in.
Air cleaner.......................................Donaldson
Ignition..Delco-Remy with
6-v battery
Cooling capacity (gal.) 4.50
Maximum brake horsepower tests
PTO/belt horsepower...........................55.77
Crankshaft rpm 1,601
Fuel use (gal./hr.) 4.51
Maximum drawbar horsepower tests
Gear..3rd
Drawbar horsepower............................47.08
Pull weight (lb.).............................4,166
Speed (mph)...................................4.24
Percent slippage..............................6.99
SAE drawbar horsepower............................37.36
SAE belt/PTO horsepower...........................49.37
Type ....tricycle
Front tire (in.)..................................6.00 x 16
Rear tire (in.)...................................13.00 x 38
Length (in.) 143.63
Height (in.)......................................75
Tread width (in.).................................60–92.50
Weight (lb.) 4,597

Gear/speed (mph) ....forward: 1/2.49,
2/3.22, 3/4.28, 4/5.55,
5/6.82, 6/11.75;
reverse: 1/2.55, 2/4.38

Oliver Super 55, Diesel

Manufacturer......................................The Oliver Corp.,
Charles City, IA
Nebraska test number 526
Test date ....September 27 to
October 14, 1954
Test tractor serial number........................6274 500
Years produced 1954–1958
Serial number range...............................6001–59033 end, all
models numbered
consecutively
Serial number location ....metal plate below
instrument panel
Number produced ....na, interspersed
Engine ....Oliver-Waukesha
vertical I-head
Test engine serial number.........................950473
Cylinders 4
Bore and stroke (in.) ....3.50 x 3.75
Rated rpm 2,000
Compression ratio.................................15.75:1
Displacement (c.i.) 144
Fuel ....diesel
Fuel tank capacity (gal.) 13
Carburetor..Bosch injector pump
Air cleaner.......................................Donaldson
Ignition..Delco-Remy 12-v;
with 2, 6-v battery
Cooling capacity (gal.) 3.50
Maximum brake horsepower tests
PTO/belt horsepower...........................33.71
Crankshaft rpm 2,000
Fuel use (gal./hr.) 2.39
Maximum drawbar horsepower tests
Gear..4th
Drawbar horsepower............................27.45
Pull weight (lb.).............................2,067
Speed (mph)...................................4.98
Percent slippage..............................6.78
SAE drawbar horsepower............................21.73
SAE belt/PTO horsepower...........................28.98
Type ....standard
Front tire (in.)..................................6.00 x 16
Rear tire (in.)...................................11.00 x 28
Length (in.) 120
Height (in.)......................................70.38
Tread width (in.).................................48–76
Weight (lb.) 2,933
Gear/speed (mph) ....forward: 1/1.69,
2/2.58, 3/3.46, 4/5.33,
5/6.39, 6/13.18;
reverse: 1/1.89, 2/3.90

Oliver Super 88, Diesel, Row Crop

Manufacturer......................................The Oliver Corp.,
Charles City, IA
Nebraska test number 527
Test date ....October 4–13, 1954
Test tractor serial number........................6671 800
Years produced 1954–1958

Oliver

Serial number range....................................6503–59001 end, all models numbered consecutively
Serial number location ....metal plate below instrument panel
Number produced ....na, interspersed
Engine ....Oliver-Waukesha vertical I-head
Test engine serial number...........................949310
Cylinders 6
Bore and stroke (in.) ....3.75 x 4.00
Rated rpm 1,600
Compression ratio 15.5:1
Displacement (c.i.) 265
Fuel ....diesel
Fuel tank capacity (gal.) 20
Carburetor ....Bosch injector pump
Air cleaner ....Donaldson
Ignition...Delco-Remy 12-v; with 2, 6-v battery
Cooling capacity (gal.) 4.50

Maximum brake horsepower tests
    PTO/belt horsepower............................54.88
    Crankshaft rpm 1,600
    Fuel use (gal./hr.) 3.60

Maximum drawbar horsepower tests
    Gear..3rd
    Drawbar horsepower.............................47.20
    Pull weight (lb.)....................................4,220
    Speed (mph) 4.19
    Percent slippage..................................7.22
    SAE drawbar horsepower.......................37.19
SAE belt/PTO horsepower 47.29
Type ....tricycle
Front tire (in.)...6.00 x 16
Rear tire (in.)..13.00 x 38
Length (in.) 143.63
Height (in.) 75
Tread width (in.)..60–92.50
Weight (lb.) 4,812
Gear/speed (mph) ....forward: 1/2.49, 2/3.22, 3/4.28, 4/5.55, 5/6.82, 6/11.75; reverse: 1/2.55, 2/4.38

Oliver Super 66 HC, Row Crop

Manufacturer...The Oliver Corp., Charles City, IA
Nebraska test number 541
Test date ....May 16–19, 1955
Test tractor serial number...........................7212 606
Years produced 1954–1958
Serial number range....................................7085–72824 end, all models numbered consecutively
Serial number location ....metal plate below instrument panel
Number produced ....na, interspersed
Engine ....Oliver-Waukesha vertical I-head
Test engine serial number...........................934675
Cylinders 4
Bore and stroke (in.) ....3.50 x 3.75
Rated rpm 2,000
Compression ratio 7.0:1

Displacement (c.i.) 144
Fuel ....gasoline
Fuel tank capacity (gal.) 13
Carburetor ....(Marvel-Schebler TSX-603) Carter 2257S
Air cleaner ....Donaldson
Ignition...Delco-Remy, 6-v battery
Cooling capacity (gal.) 3.50

Maximum brake horsepower tests
    PTO/belt horsepower............................33.62
    Crankshaft rpm 2,001
    Fuel use (gal./hr.) 3.09

Maximum drawbar horsepower tests
    Gear..4th
    Drawbar horsepower.............................27.99
    Pull weight (lb.)....................................2,037
    Speed (mph) 5.15
    Percent slippage..................................4.88
SAE drawbar horsepower 22.20
SAE belt/PTO horsepower 30.21
Type ....tricycle
Front wheel (in.)...5.00 x 15
Rear wheel (in.)..10.00 x 38
Length (in.) 134.44
Height (in.) 87.44
Tread width (in.)..50–88
Weight (lb.) 2,945
Gear/speed (mph) ....forward: 1/2.14, 2/3.08, 3/3.68, 4/5.31, 5/6.27, 6/10.81; reverse: 1/2.43, 2/4.19

Oliver Super 77 HC, Row Crop

Manufacturer...The Oliver Corp., Charles City, IA
Nebraska test number 542
Test date ....May 18–24, 1955
Test tractor serial number...........................8871 702
Years produced 1954–1958
Serial number range....................................8303–59008 end, all models numbered consecutively
Serial number location ....metal plate below instrument panel
Number produced ....na, interspersed
Engine ....Oliver-Waukesha vertical I-head
Test engine serial number...........................957685
Cylinders 6
Bore and stroke (in.) ....3.50 x 3.75
Rated rpm 1,600
Compression ratio 7.0:1
Displacement (c.i.) 216
Fuel ....gasoline
Fuel tank capacity (gal.) 16.75
Carburetor ....(Marvel-Schebler TSX-374) Zenith 11580
Air cleaner ....Donaldson
Ignition...Delco-Remy, 6-v battery
Cooling capacity (gal.) 4.50

Maximum brake horsepower tests
    PTO/belt horsepower............................43.98
    Crankshaft rpm 1,600
    Fuel use (gal./hr.) 4.06

Maximum drawbar horsepower tests
```
    Gear.........................................4th
    Drawbar horsepower..........................37.61
    Pull weight (lb.)...........................2,516
    Speed (mph) ................................5.61
    Percent slippage............................5.35
SAE drawbar horsepower..........................30.12
SAE belt/PTO horsepower ........................39.25
Type ...........................................tricycle
Front wheel (in.)...............................6.00 x 16
Rear wheel (in.)................................12.00 x 38
Length (in.) ...................................139.25
Height (in.) ...................................75
Tread width (in.)...............................60–92.50
Weight (lb.) ...................................4,508
Gear/speed (mph) ...............................forward: 1/2.50,
                                                2/3.25, 3/4.25, 4/5.63,
                                                5/6.63, 6/11.50;
                                                reverse: 1/2.63, 2/4.50
```

Oliver Super 77 Diesel, Row Crop
```
Manufacturer....................................The Oliver Corp.,
                                                Charles City, IA
Nebraska test number ...........................543
Test date ......................................May 16–26, 1955
Test tractor serial number......................15361 702
Years produced .................................1954–1958
Serial number range.............................8303–59008 end, all
                                                models numbered
                                                consecutively
Serial number location .........................metal plate below
                                                instrument panel
Number produced ................................na, interspersed
Engine .........................................Oliver-Waukesha
                                                vertical I-head
Test engine serial number.......................965948
Cylinders ......................................6
Bore and stroke (in.) ..........................3.50 x 3.75
Rated rpm ......................................1,600
Compression ratio...............................16.0:1
Displacement (c.i.) ............................216
Fuel ...........................................diesel
Fuel tank capacity (gal.) ......................16.75
Carburetor......................................Bosch injector pump
Air cleaner ....................................Donaldson
Ignition........................................Delco-Remy 12-v;
                                                with 2, 6-v battery
Cooling capacity (gal.) ........................4.50
```
Maximum brake horsepower tests
```
    PTO/belt horsepower.........................44.05
    Crankshaft rpm .............................1,600
    Fuel use (gal./hr.).........................2.98
```
Maximum drawbar horsepower tests
```
    Gear........................................4th
    Drawbar horsepower..........................38.13
    Pull weight (lb.)...........................2,562
    Speed (mph).................................5.58
    Percent slippage............................5.26
SAE drawbar horsepower..........................30.03
SAE belt/PTO horsepower ........................39.05
Type ...........................................tricycle
Front wheel (in.)...............................5.50 x 16
Rear wheel (in.)................................12.00 x 38
Length (in.) ...................................139.25
Height (in.) ...................................75
```

```
Tread width (in.)...............................60–92.50
Weight (lb.) ...................................4,628
Gear/speed (mph) ...............................forward: 1/2.50,
                                                2/3.25, 3/4.25, 4/5.63,
                                                5/6.63, 6/11.50;
                                                reverse: 1/2.63, 2/4.50
```

Oliver Super 66 Diesel, Row Crop
```
Manufacturer....................................The Oliver Corp.,
                                                Charles City, IA
Nebraska test number ...........................544
Test date ......................................May 19–26, 1955
Test tractor serial number......................7204 606
Years produced .................................1954–1958
Serial number range.............................7085–72824 end, all
                                                models numbered
                                                consecutively
Serial number location .........................metal plate below
                                                instrument panel
Number produced ................................na, interspersed
Engine .........................................Oliver-Waukesha
                                                vertical I-head
Test engine serial number.......................947405
Cylinders ......................................4
Bore and stroke (in.) ..........................3.50 x 3.75
Rated rpm ......................................2,000
Compression ratio...............................16.0:1
Displacement (c.i.) ............................144
Fuel ...........................................diesel
Fuel tank capacity (gal.) ......................13
Carburetor......................................Bosch injector pump
Air cleaner ....................................Donaldson
Ignition........................................Delco-Remy 12-v;
                                                with 2, 6-v battery
Cooling capacity (gal.) ........................3.50
```
Maximum brake horsepower tests
```
    PTO/belt horsepower.........................33.69
    Crankshaft rpm .............................2,000
    Fuel use (gal./hr.).........................2.38
```
Maximum drawbar horsepower tests
```
    Gear........................................4th
    Drawbar horsepower..........................27.48
    Pull weight (lb.)...........................1,995
    Speed (mph).................................5.16
    Percent slippage............................4.55
SAE drawbar horsepower..........................21.82
SAE belt/PTO horsepower ........................30.12
Type ...........................................tricycle
Front wheel (in.)...............................5.00 x 15
Rear wheel (in.)................................10.00 x 38
Length (in.) ...................................134.44
Height (in.) ...................................87.44
Tread width (in.)...............................50–88
Weight (lb.) ...................................3,061
Gear/speed (mph) ...............................forward: 1/2.25,
                                                2/3.08, 3/3.68, 4/5.31,
                                                5/6.27, 6/10.81;
                                                reverse: 1/2.43, 2/4.19
```

Oliver OC-12
```
Manufacturer....................................The Oliver Corp.,
                                                Cleveland, OH
Nebraska test number ...........................548
Test date ......................................June 15–28, 1955
Test tractor serial number......................1JR000
```

Oliver

Years produced	1955–1960
Serial number range	1JR000–1JR228 no end, consecutive numbers
Serial number location	metal plate front center of instrument panel
Number produced	1955–1959: about 226; 1966: na
Engine	Hercules JXLD vertical L-head
Test engine serial number	1739198
Cylinders	6
Bore and stroke (in.)	4.00 x 4.50
Rated rpm	1,750
Compression ratio	6.25:1
Displacement (c.i.)	339
Fuel	gasoline
Fuel tank capacity (gal.)	35
Carburetor	Marvel-Schebler TSX-399, 1.4375-in.
Air cleaner	Vortox
Ignition	Delco-Remy with 6-v battery
Cooling capacity (gal.)	6

Maximum brake horsepower tests

PTO/belt horsepower	57.93
Crankshaft rpm	1,750
Fuel use (gal./hr.)	5.97

Maximum drawbar horsepower tests

Gear	2nd
Drawbar horsepower	50.83
Pull weight (lb.)	8,403
Speed (mph)	2.27
Percent slippage	3.40
SAE drawbar horsepower	39.86
SAE belt/PTO horsepower	51.23
Type	tracklayer
Length (in.)	109.88
Height (in.)	77
Tread width (in.)	(44) and 60
Weight (lb.)	9,800
Track length (in.)	219
Grouser shoe	33 links; 14, (16), 18, 20-in.
Gear/speed (mph)	forward: 1/1.60, 2/2.34, 3/3.34, 4/5.27; reverse: 1/1.72, 2/3.60

Oliver OC-12, Diesel

Manufacturer	The Oliver Corp., Cleveland, OH
Nebraska test number	549
Test date	June 15–28, 1955
Test tractor serial number	IJX244
Years produced	1954–1961
Serial number range	1JX000 to 5JX828 no end, consecutive numbers
Serial number location	metal plate front center of instrument panel
Number produced	1954–1960: 4,828; 1960: na
Engine	Hercules DJXC vertical I-head
Test engine serial number	RS 823102

Cylinders	6
Bore and stroke (in.)	3.75 x 4.50
Rated rpm	1,750
Compression ratio	15.5:1
Displacement (c.i.)	298
Fuel	diesel
Fuel tank capacity (gal.)	35
Carburetor	Roosa injector pump
Air cleaner	(Vortox); Donaldson
Ignition	Delco-Remy with 12-v battery
Cooling capacity (gal.)	5

Maximum brake horsepower tests

PTO/belt horsepower	56.55
Crankshaft rpm	1,750
Fuel use (gal./hr.)	4.83

Maximum drawbar horsepower tests

Gear	2nd
Drawbar horsepower	50.54
Pull weight (lb.)	8,310
Speed (mph)	2.28
Percent slippage	2.80
SAE drawbar horsepower	39.79
SAE belt/PTO horsepower	50.13
Type	tracklayer
Length (in.)	109.88
Height (in.)	77
Tread width (in.)	(44) and 60
Weight (lb.)	10,140
Track length (in.)	219
Grouser shoe	33 links; 14, (16), 18, 20-in.
Gear/speed (mph)	forward: 1/1.60, 2/2.34, 3/3.34, 4/5.27; reverse: 1/1.72, 2/3.60

Oliver Super 99 GM, Diesel

Manufacturer	The Oliver Corp., South Bend, IN
Nebraska test number	556
Test date	August 22–27, 1955
Test tractor serial number	520197 C
Years produced	1954–1958
Serial number range	519300–521635 end
Serial number location	steel plate on right rear of engine block
Number produced	2,336, interspersed
Engine	GM 3-71, 2-cycle vertical I-head
Test engine serial number	3A 22194 RB
Cylinders	3
Bore and stroke (in.)	4.25 x 5.00
Rated rpm	1,675
Compression ratio	17:1
Displacement (c.i.)	213
Fuel	diesel
Fuel tank capacity (gal.)	30
Carburetor	GM injector pump
Air cleaner	Donaldson
Ignition	Delco-Remy 12-v; with 2, 6-v battery
Cooling capacity (gal.)	5.50

Maximum brake horsepower tests

PTO/belt horsepower	78.74
Crankshaft rpm	1,675

Fuel use (gal./hr.) 5.93
Maximum drawbar horsepower tests
    Gear 3rd
    Drawbar horsepower 73.31
    Pull weight (lb.) 6,661
    Speed (mph) 4.13
    Percent slippage 6.92
SAE drawbar horsepower 58.08
SAE belt/PTO horsepower 70.94
Type ....standard
Front wheel (in.) ....7.50 x 18
Rear wheel (in.) ....18.00 x 26
Length (in.) 136.88
Height (in.) 90
Tread width (in.) 62
Weight (lb.) 7,800
Gear/speed (mph) ....forward: 1/2.63,
    2/3.45, 3/4.66, 4/6.13,
    5/7.70, 6/13.68;
    reverse: 1/2.88, 2/5.11

Oliver Super 99 D, Diesel
Manufacturer ....The Oliver Corp.,
    South Bend, IN
Nebraska test number 557
Test date ....August 29 to
    September 3, 1955
Test tractor serial number 520198
Years produced 1954–1958
Serial number range ....519300–521635 end
Serial number location ....steel plate on right
    rear of engine block
Number produced ....2,336, interspersed
Engine ....Oliver-Waukesha
    vertical I-head
Test engine serial number 952681
Cylinders 6
Bore and stroke (in.) ....4.00 x 4.00
Rated rpm 1,675
Compression ratio 15.5:1
Displacement (c.i.) 302
Fuel ....diesel
Fuel tank capacity (gal.) 30
Carburetor ....Bosch injector pump
Air cleaner ....Donaldson
Ignition ....Delco-Remy 12-v;
    with 2, 6-v battery
Cooling capacity (gal.) 5.50
Maximum brake horsepower tests
    PTO/belt horsepower 62.39
    Crankshaft rpm 1,675
    Fuel use (gal./hr.) 4.44
Maximum drawbar horsepower tests
    Gear 3rd
    Drawbar horsepower 58.27
    Pull weight (lb.) 5,290
    Speed (mph) 4.13
    Percent slippage 5.17
SAE drawbar horsepower 45.68
SAE belt/PTO horsepower 55.26
Type ....standard
Front wheel (in.) ....7.50 x 18
Rear wheel (in.) ....18.00 x 26
Length (in.) 136.88
Height (in.) 90

Tread width (in.) 62
Weight (lb.) 7,000
Gear/speed (mph) ....forward: 1/2.46,
    2/3.23, 3/4.37, 4/5.74,
    5/7.22, 6/12.81;
    reverse: 1/2.69, 2/4.78

Oliver OC-15, Diesel
Manufacturer ....The Oliver Corp.,
    Cleveland, OH
Nebraska test number 633
Test date ....November 4–9, 1957
Test tractor serial number IVL104
Years produced 1956–1961
Serial number range ....1VL000–1VL640 no
    end, consecutive
    numbers
Serial number location ....metal plate front center
    of instrument panel
Number produced ....1956–1960: about 585;
    1960: na
Engine ....Hercules DRXC
    vertical I-head
Test engine serial number ....R 394113
Cylinders 6
Bore and stroke (in.) ....4.625 x 5.25
Rated rpm 1,500
Compression ratio 15:1
Displacement (c.i.) 529
Fuel ....diesel
Fuel tank capacity (gal.) 46
Carburetor ....Roosa injector pump
Air cleaner ....Donaldson
Ignition ....Delco-Remy 24-v;
    with 2, 12-v battery
Cooling capacity (gal.) 10.50
Maximum brake horsepower tests
    PTO/belt horsepower 101.97
    Crankshaft rpm 1,500
    Fuel use (gal./hr.) 7.50
Maximum drawbar horsepower tests
    Gear 2nd
    Drawbar horsepower 91.07
    Pull weight (lb.) 13,135
    Speed (mph) 2.60
    Percent slippage 1.98
SAE drawbar horsepower 70.63
SAE belt/PTO horsepower 88.94
Type ....tracklayer
Tread width (in.) 74
Weight (lb.) 14,470
Track length (in.) 254
Grouser shoe ....35 links; 16, 18, (20)-in.
Gear/speed (mph) ....forward: 1/1.67,
    2/2.64, 3/3.76, 4/5.60;
    reverse: 1/1.99, 2/4.48

Oliver 880
Manufacturer ....The Oliver Corp.,
    Charles City, IA
Nebraska test number 647
Test date ....April 21 to May 1,
    1958
Test tractor serial number 60852 824
Years produced 1958–1963

Oliver

Serial number range ....60505–135054 end, all models numbered consecutively
Serial number location ....metal plate lower left rear panel assembly
Number produced ....na, interspersed
Engine ....Oliver-Waukesha vertical I-head
Test engine serial number 1054145
Cylinders 6
Bore and stroke (in.) ....3.75 x 4.00
Rated rpm 1,750
Compression ratio 7.3:1
Displacement (c.i.) 265.1
Fuel ....gasoline
Fuel tank capacity (gal.) 20.30
Carburetor ....Zenith 62AJ10, 1.25-in.
Air cleaner ....Donaldson
Ignition ....Delco-Remy with 12-v battery
Cooling capacity (gal.) 4.50

Maximum brake horsepower tests
    PTO/belt horsepower 61.86
    Crankshaft rpm 1,750
    Fuel use (gal./hr.) 5.39

Maximum drawbar horsepower tests
    Gear 4th
    Drawbar horsepower 54.92
    Pull weight (lb.) 4,279
    Speed (mph) 4.79
    Percent slippage 5.62
SAE drawbar horsepower 42.22
SAE belt/PTO horsepower 54.58
Type ....tricycle
Front wheel (in.) ....6.50 x 16
Rear wheel (in.) ....14.00 x 34
Height (in.) 91.75
Tread width (in.) 46–92.50
Weight (lb.) 5,350
Gear/speed (mph) ....forward: 1/2.07, 2/2.94, 3/3.57, 4/5.06, 5/6.22, 6/10.70; reverse: 1/2.32, 2/4.00

Oliver 770

Manufacturer ....The Oliver Corp., Charles City, IA
Nebraska test number 648
Test date ....April 21 to May 7, 1958
Test tractor serial number 61956 721
Years produced 1958–1967
Serial number range ....60504–193365 end, all models numbered consecutively
Serial number location ....metal plate lower left rear panel assembly
Number produced ....na, interspersed
Engine ....Oliver-Waukesha vertical I-head
Test engine serial number 1055057
Cylinders 6
Bore and stroke (in.) ....3.50 x 3.75
Rated rpm 1,750
Compression ratio 7.3:1
Displacement (c.i.) 216.5

Fuel ....gasoline
Fuel tank capacity (gal.) 20.30
Carburetor ....Marvel-Schebler TSX-755, 1.00-in.
Air cleaner ....Donaldson
Ignition ....Delco-Remy with 12-v battery
Cooling capacity (gal.) 4.50

Maximum brake horsepower tests
    PTO/belt horsepower 50.04
    Crankshaft rpm 1,750
    Fuel use (gal./hr.) 4.34

Maximum drawbar horsepower tests
    Gear 4th
    Drawbar horsepower 42.75
    Pull weight (lb.) 3,063
    Speed (mph) 5.23
    Percent slippage 4.33
SAE drawbar horsepower 33.79
SAE belt/PTO horsepower 43.89
Type ....tricycle
Front wheel (in.) ....6.00 x 16
Rear wheel (in.) ....15.50 x 38
Height (in.) 94.62
Tread width (in.) 46–92.50
Weight (lb.) 4,947
Gear/speed (mph) ....forward: 1/2.11, 2/3.01, 3/3.68, 4/5.25, 5/6.18, 6/10.80; reverse: 1/2.44, 2/4.21

Oliver 770 Diesel

Manufacturer ....The Oliver Corp., Charles City, IA
Nebraska test number 649
Test date ....April 23 to May 7, 1958
Test tractor serial number 61957 721
Years produced 1958–1967
Serial number range ....60504–193365 end, all models numbered consecutively
Serial number location ....metal plate lower left rear panel assembly
Number produced ....na, interspersed
Engine ....Oliver-Waukesha vertical I-head
Test engine serial number 1055620
Cylinders 6
Bore and stroke (in.) ....3.50 x 3.75
Rated rpm 1,750
Compression ratio 16.0:1
Displacement (c.i.) 216
Fuel ....diesel
Fuel tank capacity (gal.) 18.20
Carburetor ....Bosch injector pump
Air cleaner ....Donaldson
Ignition ....Delco-Remy, 12-v battery
Cooling capacity (gal.) 4.50

Maximum brake horsepower tests
    PTO/belt horsepower 48.80
    Crankshaft rpm 1,750
    Fuel use (gal./hr.) 3.41

Maximum drawbar horsepower tests
    Gear 4th
    Drawbar horsepower 44.38

Pull weight (lb.)................................3,163
Speed (mph) 5.26
Percent slippage.............................3.57
SAE drawbar horsepower.......................34.53
SAE belt/PTO horsepower......................43.10
Type ....tricycle
Front wheel (in.)............................6.00 x 16
Rear wheel (in.).............................15.50 x 38
Height (in.).................................94.62
Tread width (in.)...........................46–92.50
Weight (lb.)................................4,947
Gear/speed (mph) ....forward: 1/2.11, 2/3.01,
3/3.68, 4/5.25, 5/6.18,
6/10.80; reverse:
1/2.44, 2/4.21

Oliver 880 Diesel
Manufacturer................................The Oliver Corp.,
Charles City, IA
Nebraska test number 650
Test date ....April 23 to May 7, 1958
Test tractor serial number 62475 822
Years produced..............................1958–1963
Serial number range.........................60505–135054 end,
all models numbered
consecutively
Serial number location ....metal plate lower left
rear panel assembly
Number produced ....na, interspersed
Engine ....Oliver-Waukesha
vertical I-head
Test engine serial number...................1051012
Cylinders 6
Bore and stroke (in.) ....3.75 x 4.00
Rated rpm 1,750
Compression ratio...........................16:1
Displacement (c.i.) 265.1
Fuel ....diesel
Fuel tank capacity (gal.) 18.20
Carburetor..................................Bosch injector pump
Air cleaner.................................Donaldson
Ignition....................................Delco-Remy with
12-v battery
Cooling capacity (gal.) 4.50
Maximum brake horsepower tests
PTO/belt horsepower..........................59.48
Crankshaft rpm 1,750
Fuel use (gal./hr.)..........................4.03
Maximum drawbar horsepower tests
Gear..4th
Drawbar horsepower..........................52.64
Pull weight (lb.)...........................4,124
Speed (mph).................................4.79
Percent slippage............................4.79
SAE drawbar horsepower......................41.23
SAE belt/PTO horsepower.....................52.57
Type ....tricycle
Front wheel (in.)...........................6.50 x 16
Rear wheel (in.)............................14.00 x 34
Height (in.)................................95.81
Tread width (in.)...........................46–92.50
Weight (lb.)................................5,350
Gear/speed (mph) ....forward: 1/2.07,
2/2.94, 3/3.57, 4/5.06,
5/6.22, 6/10.70;
reverse: 1/2.32, 2/4.00

Oliver OC-4 Diesel
Manufacturer................................The Oliver Corp.,
Cleveland, OH
Nebraska test number 655
Test date ....June 5–16, 1958
Test tractor serial number..................1WD446
Years produced..............................1957–1965
Serial number range.........................1WD002 to 3WD594
no end;
800001–801795 no
end, consecutive
numbers
Serial number location ....metal plate on left side
of dash assembly
Number produced ....1957–1961: about
5,593; 1962–1964:
about 1,794; 1965: na
Engine ....Hercules DD130
vertical I-head
Test engine serial number...................3600202
Cylinders 3
Bore and stroke (in.) ....3.50 x 4.50
Rated rpm 1,700
Compression ratio...........................15:1
Displacement (c.i.) 130
Fuel ....diesel
Fuel tank capacity (gal.) 11
Carburetor..................................Roosa injector pump
Air cleaner.................................Donaldson
Ignition....................................Delco-Remy 12-v;
with 2, 6-v battery
Cooling capacity (gal.) 3
Maximum brake horsepower tests
PTO/belt horsepower..........................26.08
Crankshaft rpm 1,700
Fuel use (gal./hr.)..........................2.25
Maximum drawbar horsepower tests
Gear..2nd
Drawbar horsepower..........................24.15
Pull weight (lb.)...........................3,951
Speed (mph).................................2.29
Percent slippage............................4.25
SAE drawbar horsepower......................18.56
SAE belt/PTO horsepower.....................23.21
Type ....tracklayer
Height (in.)................................69
Tread width (in.)...........................31, 42, (46), 60, 68
Weight (lb.)................................4,090
Track length (in.)..........................186.75
Grouser shoe................................32 links; 6, 8, 10, (12)-in.
Gear/speed (mph) ....forward: 1/1.56,
2/2.37, 3/3.33, 4/5.28;
reverse: 1/1.81

Oliver OC-4
Manufacturer................................The Oliver Corp.,
Cleveland, OH
Nebraska test number 656
Test date ....June 5–16, 1958
Test tractor serial number..................1WR376
Years produced..............................1958–1965
Serial number range.........................1WR002 to 6WR746 no
end, 800001–801794 no
end, consecutive numbers
Serial number location ....metal plate on left side
of dash assembly

Number produced ....1958–1961: about 5,745; 1962–1965: about 1,794
Engine ....Hercules GO130 vertical I-head
Test engine serial number 3750320
Cylinders 3
Bore and stroke (in.) ....3.50 x 4.50
Rated rpm 1,700
Compression ratio....................................6.5:1
Displacement (c.i.) 130
Fuel ....gasoline
Fuel tank capacity (gal.) 11
Carburetor...Marvel-Schebler TSX-738, 1.00-in.
Air cleaner..Donaldson
Ignition..Delco-Remy with 6-v battery
Cooling capacity (gal.) 3
Maximum brake horsepower tests
    PTO/belt horsepower..........................25.34
    Crankshaft rpm 1,700
    Fuel use (gal./hr.) 2.50
Maximum drawbar horsepower tests
    Gear..2nd
    Drawbar horsepower............................23.14
    Pull weight (lb.)..................................3,809
    Speed (mph) 2.28
    Percent slippage..................................4.48
SAE drawbar horsepower.............................18.05
SAE belt/PTO horsepower 22.52
Type ....tracklayer
Height (in.) 69
Tread width (in.)......................................31, 42, (46), 60, 68
Weight (lb.) 4,090
Track length (in.).......................................186.75
Grouser shoe...32 links; 6, 8, 10, (12)-in.
Gear/speed (mph) ....forward: 1/1.56, 2/2.39, 3/3.36, 4/5.27; reverse: 1/1.81

Oliver 950 Diesel
Manufacturer..The Oliver Corp., Charles City, IA
Nebraska test number 660
Test date ....July 7–17, 1958
Test tractor serial number 530272
Years produced 1958–1961
Serial number range..................................530001–530387, 67828–95350, 110064–115469 end, all models numbered consecutively
Serial number location ....metal plate on left side of clutch dust cover
Number produced ....na, 950, 990, and 995, interspersed
Engine ....Oliver-Waukesha vertical I-head
Test engine serial number 1063693
Cylinders 6
Bore and stroke (in.) ....4.00 x 4.00
Rated rpm 1,800
Compression ratio....................................16.0:1
Displacement (c.i.) 302

Fuel ....diesel
Fuel tank capacity (gal.) 30
Carburetor...Bosch injector pump
Air cleaner..Donaldson
Ignition..Delco-Remy 12-v; with 2, 6-v battery
Cooling capacity (gal.) 5.50
Maximum brake horsepower tests
    PTO/belt horsepower..........................67.23
    Crankshaft rpm 1,800
    Fuel use (gal./hr.) 4.80
Maximum drawbar horsepower tests
    Gear..3rd
    Drawbar horsepower............................61.53
    Pull weight (lb.)..................................5,563
    Speed (mph) 4.15
    Percent slippage..................................4.66
SAE drawbar horsepower.............................48.51
SAE belt/PTO horsepower 59.77
Type ....standard
Front wheel (in.) ....7.50 x 18
Rear wheel (in.)..18.00 x 26
Height (in.) 91.75
Tread width (in.)......................................62
Weight (lb.) 4,947
Gear/speed (mph) ....forward: 1/2.43, 2/3.20, 3/4.32, 4/5.68, 5/7.14, 6/12.68; reverse: 1/2.67, 2/4.74

Oliver 990 GM Diesel
Manufacturer..The Oliver Corp., Charles City, IA
Nebraska test number 661
Test date ....July 7–18, 1958
Test tractor serial number 530199
Years produced 1958–1961
Serial number range..................................530001–530387, 67828–95359, 110064–115469 end, all models numbered consecutively
Serial number location ....metal plate on left side of clutch dust cover
Number produced ....na, 950, 990, and 995, interspersed
Engine ....GM 3-71, 2-cycle vertical I-head
Test engine serial number 3A 34592
Cylinders 3
Bore and stroke (in.) ....4.25 x 5.00
Rated rpm 1,800
Compression ratio....................................17:1
Displacement (c.i.) 213
Fuel ....diesel
Fuel tank capacity (gal.) 30
Carburetor...GM injector pump
Air cleaner..Donaldson
Ignition..Delco-Remy 12-v; with 2, 6-v battery
Cooling capacity (gal.) 5.50
Maximum brake horsepower tests
    PTO/belt horsepower..........................84.10
    Crankshaft rpm 1,800
    Fuel use (gal./hr.) 6.29

Maximum drawbar horsepower tests
Gear..3rd
Drawbar horsepower......................77.41
Pull weight (lb.)............................7,068
Speed (mph)..................................4.11
Percent slippage............................5.44
SAE drawbar horsepower........................60.90
SAE belt/PTO horsepower 75.19
Type ....standard
Front wheel (in.)................................7.50 x 18
Rear wheel (in.)................................18.00 x 26
Height (in.).....................................91.75
Tread width (in.)..............................66
Weight (lb.)....................................8,155
Gear/speed (mph) ....forward: 1/2.33,
2/3.07, 3/4.15, 4/5.46,
5/6.85, 6/12.19;
reverse: 1/2.55, 2/4.55

Oliver 995 GM Lugmatic, Diesel
Manufacturer.....................................The Oliver Corp.,
Charles City, IA
Nebraska test number 662
Test date ....July 7–23, 1958
Test tractor serial number 530273
Years produced 1958–1961
Serial number range...........................530001–530387.
67828–95350,
110064–115469 end,
all models numbered
consecutively
Serial number location ....metal plate on left side
of clutch dust cover
Number produced ....na, 950, 990, and 995,
interspersed
Engine ....GM 3-71, 2-cycle
vertical I-head
Test engine serial number.....................3A 34591
Cylinders 3
Bore and stroke (in.) ....4.25 x 5.00
Rated rpm 2,000
Compression ratio..............................17:1
Displacement (c.i.) 213
Fuel ....diesel
Fuel tank capacity (gal.) 30
Carburetor......................................GM injector pump
Air cleaner ....Donaldson
Ignition...Delco-Remy 12-v;
with 2, 6-v battery
Cooling capacity (gal.) 5.50
Maximum brake horsepower tests
PTO/belt horsepower..........................85.37
Crankshaft rpm 2,000
Fuel use (gal./hr.).............................6.78
Maximum drawbar horsepower tests
Gear..3rd
Drawbar horsepower......................71.44
Pull weight (lb.)............................6,523
Speed (mph)..................................4.11
Percent slippage............................4.32
SAE drawbar horsepower........................71.44
SAE belt/PTO horsepower 85.37
Type ....standard
Front wheel (in.)................................7.50 x 18
Rear wheel (in.)................................18.00 x 26

Height (in.)......................................91.75
Tread width (in.)..............................66
Weight (lb.)....................................8,185
Gear/speed (mph)............forward: 1/0.9–2.60, 2/1.2–3.50, 3/1.6–4.70,
4/2.1–6.20, 5/2.7–7.80, 6/4.7–13.80;
reverse: 1/1.00–2.90, 2/1.80–5.20

Oliver 550
Manufacturer.....................................The Oliver Corp.,
Charles City, IA
Nebraska test number 697
Test date ....May 11–26, 1959
Test tractor serial number 73456 519
Years produced 1958–1975
Serial number range...........................60501–259491 end,
all types numbered
consecutively
Serial number location ....metal plate on left of
center frame
Number produced ....na, all types
interspersed
Engine ....Oliver-Waukesha
vertical L-head
Test engine serial number.....................1082115
Cylinders 4
Bore and stroke (in.) ....3.625 x 3.75
Rated rpm 2,000
Compression ratio..............................7.75:1
Displacement (c.i.) 155
Fuel ....gasoline
Fuel tank capacity (gal.) 13
Carburetor......................................Marvel-Schebler
TSX-755, 1.125-in.
Air cleaner ....Donaldson
Ignition...Delco-Remy with
12-v battery
Cooling capacity (gal.) 3.50
Maximum brake horsepower tests
PTO/belt horsepower..........................41.39
Crankshaft rpm 2,000
Fuel use (gal./hr.).............................3.30
Maximum drawbar horsepower tests
Gear..4th
Drawbar horsepower......................35.36
Pull weight (lb.)............................2,632
Speed (mph)..................................5.04
Percent slippage............................5.55
SAE drawbar horsepower........................35.45
SAE belt/PTO horsepower 41.39
Type ....standard
Front wheel (in.)................................6.00 x 16
Rear wheel (in.)................................12.00 x 26
Length (in.) 119.85
Height (in.)......................................73.43
Tread width (in.)..............................48–76
Weight (lb.)....................................3,100
Gear/speed (mph) ....forward: 1/1.92,
2/2.55, 3/3.95, 4/5.27,
5/7.21, 6/14.88;
reverse: 1/2.00, 2/4.12

Oliver 550 Diesel
Manufacturer.....................................The Oliver Corp.,
Charles City, IA
Nebraska test number 698

Oliver

Test date .... May 13–26, 1959
Test tractor serial number 73458 519
Years produced 1958–1975
Serial number range .... 60501–259491 end, all types numbered consecutively
Serial number location .... metal plate on left of center frame
Number produced .... na, all types interspersed
Engine .... Oliver-Waukesha vertical L-head
Test engine serial number 1081794
Cylinders 4
Bore and stroke (in.) .... 3.625 x 3.75
Rated rpm 2,000
Compression ratio 16:1
Displacement (c.i.) 155
Fuel .... diesel
Carburetor .... Bosch injector pump
Air cleaner .... Donaldson
Ignition .... Delco-Remy with 12-v battery
Cooling capacity (gal.) 3.50

Maximum brake horsepower tests
    PTO/belt horsepower 39.21
    Crankshaft rpm 2,000
    Fuel use (gal./hr.) 2.81

Maximum drawbar horsepower tests
    Gear 4th
    Drawbar horsepower 35.09
    Pull weight (lb.) 2,643
    Speed (mph) 4.98
    Percent slippage 6.25
SAE drawbar horsepower 35.36
SAE belt/PTO horsepower 39.21
Type .... standard
Front wheel (in.) .... 6.00 x 16
Rear wheel (in.) .... 12.00 x 26
Height (in.) 73.43
Tread width (in.) 48–76
Weight (lb.) 3,100
Gear/speed (mph) .... forward: 1/1.92, 2/2.55, 3/3.95, 4/5.27, 5/7.21, 6/14.88; reverse: 1/2.00, 2/4.12

Oliver 1800

Manufacturer .... The Oliver Corp., Charles City, IA
Nebraska test number 766
Test date .... October 3–11, 1960
Test tractor serial number 90526 886
Years produced 1960–1964
Serial number range .... 90525–149818 end, all models numbered consecutively
Serial number location .... metal plate on base of instrument panel
Number produced .... na, interspersed
Engine .... Oliver-Waukesha 1800 vertical L-head
Test engine serial number 115662
Cylinders 6
Bore and stroke (in.) .... 3.75 x 4.00
Rated rpm 2,000

Compression ratio 8.5:1
Displacement (c.i.) 265
Fuel .... gasoline
Fuel tank capacity (gal.) 36.50
Carburetor .... Marvel-Schebler TSX-807, 1.25-in.
Air cleaner .... Donaldson
Ignition .... Delco-Remy with 12-v battery
Cooling capacity (gal.) 5

Maximum brake horsepower tests
    PTO/belt horsepower 73.92
    Crankshaft rpm 2,000
    Fuel use (gal./hr.) 5.61

Maximum drawbar horsepower tests
    Gear 4th
    Drawbar horsepower 61.66
    Pull weight (lb.) 4,427
    Speed (mph) 5.22
    Percent slippage 4.33
SAE drawbar horsepower 63.71
SAE belt/PTO horsepower 73.92
Type .... tricycle
Front wheel (in.) .... 7.50 x 15
Rear wheel (in.) .... 18.40 x 34
Height (in.) 99.63
Tread width (in.) 68–89.50
Weight (lb.) 10,400
Gear/speed (mph) .... forward: 1/1.59, 2/3.07, 3/4.29, 4/5.31, 5/8.27, 6/14.30; reverse: 1/1.80, 2/4.84

Oliver 1800 Diesel

Manufacturer .... The Oliver Corp., Charles City, IA
Nebraska test number 767
Test date .... October 4–12, 1960
Test tractor serial number 90528 886
Years produced 1960–1964
Serial number range .... 90525–149818 end, all models numbered consecutively
Serial number location .... metal plate on base of instrument panel
Number produced .... na, interspersed
Engine .... Oliver-Waukesha 1800 vertical L-head
Test engine serial number 111582
Cylinders 6
Bore and stroke (in.) .... 3.875 x 4.00
Rated rpm 2,000
Compression ratio 16.0:1
Displacement (c.i.) 283
Fuel .... diesel
Fuel tank capacity (gal.) 31.50
Carburetor .... Roosa Master injector pump
Air cleaner .... Donaldson
Ignition .... Delco-Remy 12-v; with 2, 6-v battery
Cooling capacity (gal.) 5

Maximum brake horsepower tests
    PTO/belt horsepower 70.15
    Crankshaft rpm 2,000
    Fuel use (gal./hr.) 4.95

Maximum drawbar horsepower tests
- Gear...4th
- Drawbar horsepower...........................62.55
- Pull weight (lb.)...............................4,472
- Speed (mph) 5.25
- Percent slippage..............................4.33
SAE drawbar horsepower.........................61.80
SAE belt/PTO horsepower 70.15
Type ....tricycle
Front wheel (in.)..............................7.50 x 15
Rear wheel (in.)...............................18.40 x 34
Height (in.)....................................99.63
Tread width (in.)..............................68–89.50
Weight (lb.) 10,400
Gear/speed (mph) ....forward: 1/1.59, 2/3.07, 3/4.29, 4/5.31, 5/8.27, 6/14.30; reverse: 1/1.80, 2/4.84

Oliver 1900 Diesel
Manufacturer.................................The Oliver Corp., Charles City, IA
Nebraska test number.......................768
Test date ....October 3–8, 1960
Test tractor serial number...................90533 986
Years produced 1960–1964
Serial number range.........................90532–148651 end, all models numbered consecutively
Serial number location ....metal plate on base of instrument panel
Number produced ....na, interspersed
Engine.......................................GM 4-53, 2-cycle vertical L-head

Test engine serial number..................4D 1344
Cylinders 4
Bore and stroke (in.) ....3.875 x 4.50
Rated rpm 2,000
Compression ratio..........................17:1
Displacement (c.i.) 212.4
Fuel ....diesel
Fuel tank capacity (gal.) 31.50
Carburetor..................................GM injector pump
Air cleaner ....Donaldson
Ignition.....................................Delco-Remy 12-v; with 2, 6-v battery
Cooling capacity (gal.) 5.25
Maximum brake horsepower tests
PTO/belt horsepower.........................89.35
Crankshaft rpm 2,000
Fuel use (gal./hr.) 6.20
Maximum drawbar horsepower tests
- Gear...4th
- Drawbar horsepower..........................82.85
- Pull weight (lb.)............................6,282
- Speed (mph) 4.95
- Percent slippage............................3.77
SAE drawbar horsepower........................80.42
SAE belt/PTO horsepower 89.35
Type ....standard
Front wheel (in.)............................7.50 x 18
Rear wheel (in.)............................18.00 x 26
Height (in.) 101.25
Tread width (in.)............................74–82
Weight (lb.) 11,500
Gear/speed (mph) ....forward: 1/1.49, 2/2.86, 3/4.00, 4/4.95, 5/7.72, 6/13.35; reverse: 1/1.68, 2/4.51

Chapter 60
PARRETT

Parrett K, 15-30
Manufacturer.................................Parrett Tractor Co., Chicago Height (in.)s, IL
Nebraska test number.......................37
Test date ....July 19 to August 17, 1920
Test tractor serial number...................4,000
Years produced 1920–1921
Engine.......................................Parrett vertical, overhead-valve
Test engine serial number...................12
Cylinders 4
Bore and stroke (in.) ....4.50 x 6.00
Rated rpm 1,000
Displacement (c.i.) 381.7
Fuel ....kerosene/gasoline
Carburetor..................................Kingston (Stromberg M2)
Air cleaner ....Parrett

Ignition.....................................Eisemann G4 magneto
Maximum brake horsepower tests
- PTO/belt horsepower.........................31.79
- Crankshaft rpm 1,010
- Fuel use (gal./hr.) 3.96
Maximum drawbar horsepower tests
- Gear...low
- Drawbar horsepower..........................20.94
- Pull weight (lb.)............................2,988
- Speed (mph) 2.63
- Percent slippage............................9.70
SAE drawbar horsepower........................15
SAE belt/PTO horsepower 30
Type ....4 wheel
Front wheel (in.)............................steel
Rear wheel (in.)............................steel
Length (in.) ....wheelbase: 92
Weight (lb.) 5,250
Gear/speed (mph) ....forward: 1/2.75, 2/4.07

Chapter 61

PLANET JR.

Planet Jr. Garden Tractor

Manufacturer	S.L. Allen and Co., Inc., Philadelphia, PA
Nebraska test number	234
Test date	June 5–19, 1935
Test tractor serial number	1633
Engine	Toro O vertical L-head
Test engine serial number	0694
Cylinders	1
Bore and stroke (in.)	2.75 x 3.25
Rated rpm	1,800
Displacement (c.i.)	19.3
Fuel	gasoline
Fuel tank capacity (gal.)	1.50
Carburetor	Tillotson M-20-A, 0.75-in.
Air cleaner	Donaldson (Air-Maze)
Ignition	Eisemann 71-F magneto

Maximum brake horsepower tests
PTO/belt horsepower	2.31
Crankshaft rpm	1,799
Fuel use (gal./hr.)	0.37

Maximum drawbar horsepower tests
Gear	low
Drawbar horsepower	1.36
Pull weight (lb.)	292
Speed (mph)	1.74
Percent slippage	15.09
SAE drawbar horsepower	1.10
SAE belt/PTO horsepower	2.07
Type	garden, 2 wheel
Front wheel (in.)	steel: 20 x 3; traction wheels
Rear wheel (in.)	steel: 8.36 x 1.50
Length (in.)	75
Height (in.)	49
Rear width (in.)	27.50
Weight (lb.)	500
Gear/speed (mph)	forward: 1/.50–4.00

Chapter 62

PORSCHE

Porsche L108, Diesel Junior

Manufacturer	Porsche-Diesel, Friedrichshafen, Germany
Nebraska test number	699
Test date	May 21 to June 9, 1959
Test tractor serial number	L 546 H
Engine	Porsche F108 vertical L-head
Test engine serial number	12851 H
Cylinders	1
Bore and stroke (in.)	3.74 x 4.567
Rated rpm	2,250
Compression ratio	19:1
Displacement (c.i.)	50.2
Fuel	diesel
Fuel tank capacity (gal.)	5.9
Carburetor	Bosch injector pump
Ignition	Bosch with 12-v battery
Cooling	air

Maximum brake horsepower tests
PTO/belt horsepower	11.29
Crankshaft rpm	2,250
Fuel use (gal./hr.)	0.89

Maximum drawbar horsepower tests
Gear	4th
Drawbar horsepower	9.28
Pull weight (lb.)	772
Speed (mph)	4.51
Percent slippage	3.38
SAE drawbar horsepower	9.58
SAE belt/PTO horsepower	11.29
Type	standard
Front wheel (in.)	4.50 x 16
Rear wheel (in.)	9.00 x 24
Height (in.)	61
Tread width (in.)	49.25–68.94
Weight (lb.)	2,160
Gear/speed (mph)	forward: 1/1.2, 2/1.9, 3/3.3, 4/4.7, 5/8.4, 6/12.9; reverse: 1/0.80, 2/3.30

Porsche Super L 318 Diesel

Manufacturer	Porsche-Diesel, Friedrichshafen, Germany
Nebraska test number	728
Test date	November 14–21, 1959
Test tractor serial number	318 L 007
Engine	Porsche F318 vertical L-head
Test engine serial number	12755
Cylinders	3
Bore and stroke (in.)	3.74 x 4.567
Rated rpm	2,300
Compression ratio	19:1

Displacement (c.i.) 150.6
Fuel ....diesel
Carburetor ....Bosch injector pump
Ignition ....Bosch 12-v; with
                                          2-6-v battery
Cooling ....air
Maximum brake horsepower tests
    PTO/belt horsepower 37.21
    Crankshaft rpm 2,300
    Fuel use (gal./hr.) 2.87
Maximum drawbar horsepower tests
    Gear...6th
    Drawbar horsepower 32.37
    Pull weight (lb.) 2,848

Speed (mph) 4.26
Percent slippage...5.07
SAE drawbar horsepower.............................33.40
SAE belt/PTO horsepower 37.21
Type ....standard
Front wheel (in.)...6.00 x 20
Rear wheel (in.)..13.00 x 30
Height (in.)...86
Tread width (in.)..59–69
Weight (lb.) 4,445
Gear/speed (mph).............forward: 1/0.70, 2/1.30, 3/2.10, 4/2.70,
                  5/3.50, 6/4.70, 7/7.30, 8/12.30; reverse:
                  1/1.30, 2/2.30, 3/3.60, 4/6.00

Chapter 63
PORT HURON

Port Huron 12-25
Manufacturer...Port Huron Engine &
                                    Thresher Co., Port
                                    Huron, MI
Nebraska test number 69
Test date ....October 20–27, 1920
Test tractor serial number........................316
Years produced 1918–1921
Engine ....Chief vertical, valve-in-
                                    head
Test engine serial number.........................1258
Cylinders 4
Bore and stroke (in.) ....4.75 x 6.00
Rated rpm 900
Displacement (c.i.) 425.3
Fuel ....kerosene/gasoline
Main tank capacity (gal.) 25
Auxiliary tank capacity (gal.) 5
Carburetor...Kingston L, 1.25-in.
Air cleaner ....Bennett
Ignition..Eisemann GS4-11
                                    magneto

Cooling capacity (gal.) 12
Maximum brake horsepower tests
    PTO/belt horsepower 28.46
    Crankshaft rpm 895
    Fuel use (gal./hr.) 4.26
Maximum drawbar horsepower tests
    Gear...low
    Drawbar horsepower 20.42
    Pull weight (lb.) 4,144
    Speed (mph) 1.85
    Percent slippage...................................16.10
SAE drawbar horsepower.............................12
SAE belt/PTO horsepower 25
Type ....4 wheel
Front wheel (in.)...steel: 34 x 6
Rear wheel (in.)..steel: 56 x 10
Length (in.) 156
Height (in.)...105
Rear width (in.) 75
Weight (lb.) 6,300
Gear/speed (mph) ....forward: 1/1.88–4.00;
                                    reverse: 1/1.88–4.00

Chapter 64
ROCK ISLAND

Rock Island F, 18-35
Manufacturer...Rock Island Plow Co.,
                                    Rock Island, IL
Nebraska test number 144
Test date ....October 12–19, 1927
Test tractor serial number........................F270178

Years produced 1927–1936
Engine ....Buda vertical L-head
Test engine serial number.........................154949
Cylinders 4
Bore and stroke (in.) ....4.50 x 6.00
Rated rpm 1,100

Displacement (c.i.) 381.7
Fuel ....distillate/gasoline
Main tank capacity (gal.)..............................23.75
Auxiliary tank capacity (gal.) 3.50
Carburetor ....Stromberg M3,
1.50-in.
Air cleaner ....Pomona (United)
Ignition...Splitdorf Dixie 46C
magneto
Cooling capacity (gal.) 8.75

Maximum brake horsepower tests
    PTO/belt horsepower............................36.50
    Crankshaft rpm 1,094
    Fuel use (gal./hr.) 4.74

Maximum drawbar horsepower tests
    Gear..low
    Drawbar horsepower.............................30.42
    Pull weight (lb.).....................................3,190
    Speed (mph) 3.58
    Percent slippage...................................4.58
SAE drawbar horsepower..............................18
SAE belt/PTO horsepower.............................35
Type ....4 wheel
Front wheel (in.)...steel: 30 x 6
Rear wheel (in.)..steel: 48 x 12
Length (in.) 124
Height (in.) 65
Rear width (in.) 70
Weight (lb.) 4,700
Gear/speed (mph) ....forward: 1/3.00,
2/4.50; reverse: 1/2.00

Rock Island G-2, 15-25

Manufacturer...Rock Island Plow Co.,
Rock Island, IL
Nebraska test number 157
Test date ....April 24 to May 3,
1929
Test tractor serial number............................G-2 90001
Years produced 1929–1937
Engine ....Waukesha CSR
vertical L-head
Test engine serial number............................198846
Cylinders 4
Bore and stroke (in.) ....4.25 x 5.75
Rated rpm 1,100
Displacement (c.i.) 345.5
Fuel ....distillate/gasoline
Main tank capacity (gal.)..............................21
Auxiliary tank capacity (gal.) 3.50
Carburetor ....Stromberg M2,
1.25-in.
Air cleaner ....Pomona Vortox or
Donaldson
Ignition...Splitdorf 46T magneto
Cooling capacity (gal.) 7.75

Maximum brake horsepower tests
    PTO/belt horsepower............................29.00
    Crankshaft rpm 1,100
    Fuel use (gal./hr.) 3.62

Maximum drawbar horsepower tests
    Gear..low
    Drawbar horsepower.............................22.08
    Pull weight (lb.).....................................2,880
    Speed (mph) 2.88
    Percent slippage...................................9.19
SAE drawbar horsepower..............................18
SAE belt/PTO horsepower.............................30
Type ....4 wheel
Front wheel (in.)...steel: 28 x 5
Rear wheel (in.)..steel: 46 x 11
Length (in.) 118
Height (in.) 62
Rear width (in.) 66
Weight (lb.) 4,200
Gear/speed (mph) ....forward: 1/2.75,
2/4.00; reverse: 1/1.75

Rock Island G-2, 18-30

Manufacturer...Rock Island Plow Co.,
Rock Island, IL
Nebraska test number 158
Test date ....May 4–8, 1929
Test tractor serial number............................G-2 90001
Years produced 1929–1937
Engine ....Waukesha CSR
vertical L-head
Test engine serial number............................198846
Cylinders 4
Bore and stroke (in.) ....4.25 x 5.75
Rated rpm 1,100
Displacement (c.i.) 345.5
Fuel ....gasoline
Fuel tank capacity (gal.) 21
Carburetor ....Stromberg M2,
1.25-in.
Air cleaner ....Pomona Vortox or
Donaldson
Ignition...Splitdorf 46T magneto
Cooling capacity (gal.) 7.75

Maximum brake horsepower tests
    PTO/belt horsepower............................35.69
    Crankshaft rpm 1,102
    Fuel use (gal./hr.) 3.91

Maximum drawbar horsepower tests
    Gear..low
    Drawbar horsepower.............................25.50
    Pull weight (lb.).....................................3,549
    Speed (mph) 2.69
    Percent slippage...................................15.18
SAE drawbar horsepower..............................18
SAE belt/PTO horsepower.............................30
Type ....4 wheel
Front wheel (in.)...steel: 28 x 5
Rear wheel (in.)..steel: 46 x 11
Length (in.) 118
Height (in.) 62
Rear width (in.) 66
Weight (lb.) 4,200
Gear/speed (mph) ....forward: 1/2.75,
2/4.00; reverse: 1/1.75

Chapter 65

ROGERS

Rogers

Manufacturer...Rogers Tractor & Trailer Co., Albion, PA
Nebraska test number..............................84
Test date ....April 1 to May 10, 1922
Test tractor serial number.......................207
Years produced...1922–1923
Engine ....Buffalo vertical L-head
Test engine serial number.........................106
Cylinders 4
Bore and stroke (in.) ....6.75 x 9.00
Rated rpm 800
Displacement (c.i.) 1,288.3
Fuel ....gasoline
Carburetor ....Zenith L8, 2.00-in.
Ignition..Berling FL41 No. 172464 magneto

Maximum brake horsepower tests
    PTO/belt horsepower...........................63.04
    Crankshaft rpm 822
    Fuel use (gal./hr.).................................9.71
Maximum drawbar horsepower tests
    Gear..high
    Drawbar horsepower...........................38..99
    Pull weight (lb.)....................................4,215
    Speed (mph) 3.47
    Percent slippage..................................4.26
SAE drawbar horsepower.........................39
SAE belt/PTO horsepower 63
Type ....4 wheel drive
Weight (lb.) 19,500
Gear/speed (mph) ....forward: 1/1.60, 2/3.60; reverse: 1/1.60, 2/3.60

Chapter 66

RUMELY

Rumely Oil Pull E, 30-60

Manufacturer...Advance-Rumely Thresher Co., La Porte, IN
Nebraska test number..............................8
Test date ....April 23 to May 11, 1920
Test tractor serial number.......................11521
Years produced..1910–1923
Serial number range.................................101–1787, 1819–2100, 2997–8902, 11500–11596, 2252–2503 end
Serial number location ....Aluminum plate on inside right fender/ stamped on end of crankshaft, flywheel side
Number produced 8,224
Engine ....Advance-Rumley horizontal, valve-in-head
Cylinders 2
Bore and stroke (in.) ....10.00 x 12.00
Rated rpm 375
Displacement (c.i.) 1,885

Fuel ....kerosene/gasoline
Main tank capacity (gal.)..........................70
Auxiliary tank capacity (gal.) 3
Carburetor ....Secor-Higgins, 3.25-in.
Ignition...Bosch low tension magneto
Cooling capacity (gal.) 70
Maximum brake horsepower tests
    PTO/belt horsepower...........................75.60
    Crankshaft rpm 378
    Fuel use (gal./hr.)................................10.73
Maximum drawbar horsepower tests
    Drawbar horsepower...........................49.91
    Pull weight (lb.)....................................10,025
    Speed (mph) 1.87
    Percent slippage..................................10.28
SAE drawbar horsepower.........................30
SAE belt/PTO horsepower 60
Type ....4 wheel
Front wheel (in.)...steel: 44 x 16
Rear wheel (in.)..steel: 80 x 30
Length (in.) ....141 wheel, 228 total
Height (in.) 132
Rear width (in.) 116
Weight (lb.) 26,000

Gear/speed (mph) .... forward: 1/1.91;
reverse: 1/1.37

Rumely Oil Pull H, 16-30

Manufacturer .... Advance-Rumely
Thresher Co.,
La Porte, IN
Nebraska test number 9
Test date .... April 24 to
May 21, 1920
Test tractor serial number 4925
Years produced 1917–1924
Serial number range 8627–16284;
H3751–H9645 end
Serial number location .... Aluminum plate on
inside right
fender/stamped on
right front frame
Number produced 13,553
Engine .... Advance-Rumely
horizontal opposed,
valve-in-head
Cylinders 2
Bore and stroke (in.) .... 7.00 x 8.50
Rated rpm 530
Displacement (c.i.) 654.2
Fuel .... kerosene/gasoline
Main tank capacity (gal.) 34
Auxiliary tank capacity (gal.) 1
Carburetor .... Secor-Higgins, 2.50-in.
Air cleaner .... Donaldson
Ignition .... Bosch DU2 magneto
Cooling capacity (gal.) 15
Maximum brake horsepower tests
    PTO/belt horsepower 33.52
    Crankshaft rpm 537
    Fuel use (gal./hr.) 5.96
Maximum drawbar horsepower tests
    Gear .... low
    Drawbar horsepower 22.90
    Pull weight (lb.) 4,674
    Speed (mph) 1.84
    Percent slippage 16.29
SAE drawbar horsepower 16
SAE belt/PTO horsepower 30
Type .... 4 wheel
Front wheel (in.) .... steel: 40 x 7
Rear wheel (in.) .... steel: 56 x 18
Length (in.) .... 92.5 wheel, 158 total
Height (in.) 99
Rear width (in.) 80
Weight (lb.) 9,506
Gear/speed (mph) .... forward: 1/2.10,
2/3.00; reverse: 1/2.65

Rumely Oil Pull K, 12-20

Manufacturer .... Advance-Rumely
Thresher Co.,
La Porte, IN
Nebraska test number 10
Test date .... May 1–21, 1920
Test tractor serial number 13817
Years produced 1918–1924
Serial number range 12000–15100,
16836–21018 end

Serial number location .... Aluminum plate on
inside right
fender/stamped on
right front frame
Number produced 7,284
Engine .... Advance-Rumely
horizontal opposed,
valve-in-head
Cylinders 2
Bore and stroke (in.) .... 6.00 x 8.00
Rated rpm 560
Displacement (c.i.) 452.4
Fuel .... kerosene/gasoline
Main tank capacity (gal.) 23
Auxiliary tank capacity (gal.) 1
Carburetor .... Secor-Higgins
Air cleaner .... Donaldson
Ignition .... Bosch DU2 magneto
Cooling capacity (gal.) 10
Maximum brake horsepower tests
    PTO/belt horsepower 25.87
    Crankshaft rpm 566
    Fuel use (gal./hr.) 3.25
Maximum drawbar horsepower tests
    Gear .... low
    Drawbar horsepower 15.02
    Pull weight (lb.) 2,780
    Speed (mph) 2.02
    Percent slippage 8.42
SAE drawbar horsepower 12
SAE belt/PTO horsepower 20
Type .... 4 wheel
Front wheel (in.) .... steel: 34 x 6
Rear wheel (in.) .... steel: 51 x 12
Length (in.) .... 80.5 wheel, 132 total
Height (in.) 75
Rear width (in.) 64
Weight (lb.) 6,430
Gear/speed (mph) .... forward: 1/2.10,
2/3.26; reverse: 1/2.62

Rumely Oil Pull G, 20-40

Manufacturer .... Advance-Rumely
Thresher Co.,
La Porte, IN
Nebraska test number 11
Test date .... May 6–22, 1920
Test tractor serial number 10535
Years produced 1918–1924
Serial number range 10425–15221;
G741–G3894 end
Serial number location .... Aluminum plate on
inside right
fender/stamped on
right front frame
Number produced 7,951
Engine .... Advance-Rumely
horizontal opposed,
valve-in-head
Cylinders 2
Bore and stroke (in.) .... 8.00 x 10.00
Rated rpm 450
Displacement (c.i.) 1005.3
Fuel .... kerosene/gasoline
Main tank capacity (gal.) 41

Auxiliary tank capacity (gal.) 1
Carburetor ....Secor-Higgins, 2.75-in.
Air cleaner ....Donaldson
Ignition ....Bosch DU2 magneto
Cooling capacity (gal.) 17.50
Maximum brake horsepower tests
    PTO/belt horsepower..........................46.19
    Crankshaft rpm 465
    Fuel use (gal./hr.) 5.71
Maximum drawbar horsepower tests
    Gear...low
    Drawbar horsepower..........................30.07
    Pull weight (lb.)................................6,365
    Speed (mph) 1.77
    Percent slippage...............................16.60
SAE drawbar horsepower 20
SAE belt/PTO horsepower 40
Type ....4 wheel
Front wheel (in.) ....steel: 44 x 8
Rear wheel (in.) ....steel: 64 x 20
Length (in.) ....103 wheel, 175 total
Height (in.) 108
Rear width (in.) 89
Weight (lb.) 12,880
Gear/speed (mph) ....forward: 1/2.00,
    2/3.20; reverse: 1/2.53

Rumely Oil Pull S, 30-60

Manufacturer..Advance-Rumely
    Thresher Co. Inc.,
    La Porte, IN
Nebraska test number 103
Test date ....September 6–13, 1924
Test tractor serial number S-33
Years produced 1924–1928
Serial number range..................................1–514 end
Serial number location ....Aluminum plate on
    rocker arm
    cover/stamped on
    frame below radiator
    on boss/top of front
    axle
Number produced 514
Engine ....Rumely horizontal,
    valve-in-head
Test engine serial number S-34
Cylinders 2
Bore and stroke (in.) ....9.00 x 11.00
Rated rpm 470
Displacement (c.i.) 1,399.5
Fuel ....kerosene/gasoline
Main tank capacity (gal.) 52.50
Auxiliary tank capacity (gal.) 2
Carburetor ....Secor-Higgins fuel
    valve, 2.75-in.
Air cleaner ....Donaldson
Ignition...Bosch DU4, Number
    3641253 magneto
Cooling capacity (gal.) 38
Maximum brake horsepower tests
    PTO/belt horsepower..........................70.16
    Crankshaft rpm 474
    Fuel use (gal./hr.) 8.59

Maximum drawbar horsepower tests
    Gear...high
    Drawbar horsepower..........................40.58
    Pull weight (lb.)................................4,731
    Speed (mph) 3.22
    Percent slippage...............................7.04
SAE drawbar horsepower 30
SAE belt/PTO horsepower 60
Type ....4 wheel
Front wheel (in.) ....steel: 44 x 10
Rear wheel (in.) ....steel: 64 x 24
Length (in.) 191
Height (in.) 114.50
Rear width (in.) 100
Weight (lb.) 17,500
Gear/speed (mph) ....forward: 1/2.00, 2/2.50,
    3/3.00; reverse: 1/2.50

Rumely Oil Pull M, 20-35

Manufacturer..Advance-Rumely
    Thresher Co. Inc.,
    La Porte, IN
Nebraska test number 111
Test date ....March 29 to April 15,
    1925
Test tractor serial number 79
Years produced 1924–1927
Serial number range..................................1–3671 end
Serial number location ....Aluminum plate on
    rocker arm
    cover/stamped on
    frame below radiator on
    boss/top of front axle
Number produced 3,671
Engine ....Rumely horizontal,
    valve-in-head
Test engine serial number 79
Cylinders 2
Bore and stroke (in.) ....6.8125 x 8.25
Rated rpm 640
Displacement (c.i.) 601.4
Fuel ....kerosene/gasoline
Main tank capacity (gal.) 25.75
Auxiliary tank capacity (gal.) 1.25
Carburetor ....Secor-Higgins fuel
    valve, 2.125-in.
Air cleaner ....Donaldson-Simplex
Ignition...American Bosch DU
    4/2 Ed 22 magneto
Cooling capacity (gal.) 13
Maximum brake horsepower tests
    PTO/belt horsepower..........................43.07
    Crankshaft rpm 642
    Fuel use (gal./hr.) 5.11
Maximum drawbar horsepower tests
    Gear...low
    Drawbar horsepower..........................27.54
    Pull weight (lb.)................................4,850
    Speed (mph) 2.13
    Percent slippage...............................16.48
SAE drawbar horsepower 20
SAE belt/PTO horsepower 35
Type ....4 wheel
Front wheel (in.)......................................steel: 34 x 7

Rear wheel (in.) ....steel: 52 x 16
Length (in.) 151
Height (in.) 101
Rear width (in.) 71.50
Weight (lb.) 8,600
Gear/speed (mph) ....forward: 1/2.00, 2/2.50, 3/3.00; reverse: 1/2.50

Rumely Oil Pull L, 15-25

Manufacturer ....Advance-Rumely Thresher Co. Inc., La Porte, IN
Nebraska test number 112
Test date ....March 29 to April 16, 1925
Test tractor serial number 96
Years produced 1924–1927
Serial number range ....1–4855 end
Serial number location ....Aluminum plate on rocker arm cover/stamped on frame below radiator on boss/top of front axle
Number produced 4,855
Engine ....Rumely horizontal, valve-in-head
Test engine serial number 96
Cylinders 2
Bore and stroke (in.) ....5.8125 x 7.00
Rated rpm 755
Displacement (c.i.) 371.5
Fuel ....kerosene/gasoline
Main tank capacity (gal.) 18.25
Auxiliary tank capacity (gal.) 1.25
Carburetor ....Secor-Higgins fuel valve, 1.9375-in.
Air cleaner ....Donaldson-Simplex
Ignition ....American Bosch DU4/2Ed22 magneto
Cooling capacity (gal.) 10
Maximum brake horsepower tests
    PTO/belt horsepower 30.52
    Crankshaft rpm 754
    Fuel use (gal./hr.) 3.63
Maximum drawbar horsepower tests
    Gear 2nd
    Drawbar horsepower 19.34
    Pull weight (lb.) 2,816
    Speed (mph) 2.58
    Percent slippage 12.87
SAE drawbar horsepower 15
SAE belt/PTO horsepower 25
Type ....4 wheel
Front wheel (in.) ....steel: 30 x 6
Rear wheel (in.) ....steel: 44 x 12; (48 x 12)
Length (in.) 136
Height (in.) 90.50
Rear width (in.) 55.75
Weight (lb.) 5,900
Gear/speed (mph) ....forward: 1/2.00, 2/2.50, 3/3.00; reverse: 1/2.50

Rumely Oil Pull R, 25-45

Manufacturer ....Advance-Rumely Thresher Co. Inc., La Porte, IN

Nebraska test number 116
Test date ....July 7–14, 1925
Test tractor serial number R-20
Years produced 1924–1927
Serial number range ....1–761 end
Serial number location ....Aluminum plate on rocker arm cover/stamped on frame below radiator on boss/Top of front axle
Number produced 761
Engine ....Rumely horizontal, valve-in-head
Test engine serial number R-50
Cylinders 2
Bore and stroke (in.) ....7.8125 x 9.50
Rated rpm 540
Displacement (c.i.) 910.8
Fuel ....kerosene/gasoline
Main tank capacity (gal.) 31
Auxiliary tank capacity (gal.) 1.25
Carburetor ....Secor-Higgins fuel valve, 2.375-in.
Air cleaner ....Donaldson
Ignition ....American Bosch DU4/2 Ed22 magneto
Cooling capacity (gal.) 23
Maximum brake horsepower tests
    PTO/belt horsepower 50.57
    Crankshaft rpm 541
    Fuel use (gal./hr.) 5.37
Maximum drawbar horsepower tests
    Gear 2nd
    Drawbar horsepower 35.54
    Pull weight (lb.) 4,922
    Speed (mph) 2.71
    Percent slippage 7.82
SAE drawbar horsepower 25
SAE belt/PTO horsepower 45
Type ....4 wheel
Front wheel (in.) ....steel: 38.50 x 8
Rear wheel (in.) ....steel: 57.50 x 18
Length (in.) 167
Height (in.) 107
Rear width (in.) 82
Weight (lb.) 11,750
Gear/speed (mph) ....forward: 1/2.00, 2/2.50, 3/3.00; reverse: 1/2.50

Rumely W, 20-30

Manufacturer ....Advance-Rumely Co., La Porte, IN
Nebraska test number 141
Test date ....September 15–24, 1927
Test tractor serial number W1
Years produced 1928–1930
Serial number range ....1–3952 end
Serial number location ....Aluminum plate on rocker arm cover/stamped on frame below radiator on boss/top of front axle
Number produced 3,952
Engine ....Rumely horizontal, valve-in-head

Test engine serial number W1
Cylinders 2
Bore and stroke (in.) ....5.8125 x 7.00
Rated rpm 850
Displacement (c.i.) 371.5
Fuel ....kerosene/gasoline
Main tank capacity (gal.) 18.25
Auxiliary tank capacity (gal.) 1.25
Carburetor ....Rumely, 2.125-in.
Air cleaner ....Donaldson
Ignition ....American Bosch DU4
2Ed26 magneto
Cooling capacity (gal.) 10
Maximum brake horsepower tests
   PTO/belt horsepower 35.36
   Crankshaft rpm 850
   Fuel use (gal./hr.) 4.48
Maximum drawbar horsepower tests
   Gear 2nd
   Drawbar horsepower 26.10
   Pull weight (lb.) 3,008
   Speed (mph) 3.25
   Percent slippage 7.71
SAE drawbar horsepower 20
SAE belt/PTO horsepower 30
Type ....4 wheel
Front wheel (in.) ....steel: 30 x 5.50
Rear wheel (in.) ....steel: 46 x 12
Length (in.) 136
Height (in.) 90.50
Rear width (in.) 55.75
Weight (lb.) 6,626
Gear/speed (mph) ....forward: 1/2.20, 2/2.90,
3/3.50; reverse: 1/2.70

Rumely X, 25-40
Manufacturer ....Advance-Rumely Co.,
La Porte, IN
Nebraska test number 143
Test date ....October 6–13, 1927
Test tractor serial number X1
Years produced 1928–1930
Serial number range ....1–2400 end
Serial number location ....Aluminum plate on
rocker arm
cover/stamped on
frame below radiator
on boss/top of front
axle
Number produced 2,400
Engine ....Rumely horizontal,
valve-in-head
Test engine serial number X1
Cylinders 2
Bore and stroke (in.) ....6.8125 x 8.25
Rated rpm 725
Displacement (c.i.) 601.4
Fuel ....kerosene/gasoline
Main tank capacity (gal.) 25.75
Auxiliary tank capacity (gal.) 1.25
Carburetor ....Rumely, 2.25-in.
Air cleaner ....Donaldson
Ignition ....American Bosch DU4
2Ed26 magneto
Cooling capacity (gal.) 13

Maximum brake horsepower tests
   PTO/belt horsepower 50.26
   Crankshaft rpm 725
   Fuel use (gal./hr.) 5.77
Maximum drawbar horsepower tests
   Gear 2nd
   Drawbar horsepower 38.66
   Pull weight (lb.) 4,788
   Speed (mph) 3.02
Percent slippage 5.88
SAE drawbar horsepower 25
SAE belt/PTO horsepower 40
Type ....4 wheel
Front wheel (in.) ....steel: 34 x 7
Rear wheel (in.) ....steel: 52 x 16
Length (in.) 151
Height (in.) 101
Rear width (in.) 71.50
Weight (lb.) 9,290
Gear/speed (mph) ....forward: 1/2.30, 2/2.90,
3/3.50; reverse: 1/2.80

Rumely Y, 30-50
Manufacturer ....Advance-Rumely Co.,
La Porte, IN
Nebraska test number 145
Test date ....October 13–24, 1927
Test tractor serial number Y1
Years produced 1929
Serial number range ....1–245 end
Serial number location ....Aluminum plate on
rocker arm
cover/stamped on
frame below radiator
on boss/top of front
axle
Number produced 245
Engine ....Rumely horizontal,
valve-in-head
Test engine serial number Y1
Cylinders 2
Bore and stroke (in.) ....7.8125 x 9.50
Rated rpm 635
Displacement (c.i.) 910.8
Fuel ....kerosene/gasoline
Main tank capacity (gal.) 31
Auxiliary tank capacity (gal.) 1.25
Carburetor ....Rumely, 2.5625-in.
Air cleaner ....Donaldson
Ignition ....American Bosch DU4
2Ed26 magneto
Cooling capacity (gal.) 23
Maximum brake horsepower tests
   PTO/belt horsepower 63.32
   Crankshaft rpm 635
   Fuel use (gal./hr.) 7.16
Maximum drawbar horsepower tests
   Gear ....low
   Drawbar horsepower 47.18
   Pull weight (lb.) 6,965
   Speed (mph) 2.54
   Percent slippage 7.79
SAE drawbar horsepower 30
SAE belt/PTO horsepower 50
Type ....4 wheel

Front wheel (in.) ....steel: 38.50 x 8
Rear wheel (in.) ....steel: 57.50 x 18
Length (in.) 167
Height (in.) 107
Rear width (in.) 82
Weight (lb.) 13,055
Gear/speed (mph) ....forward: 1/2.30,
2/2.90, 3/3.50;
reverse: 1/2.90

Rumely Do-All, 10-20
Manufacturer ....Advance-Rumely
Thresher Co., La Porte,
IN
Nebraska test number 154
Test date ....October 29 to
November 24, 1928
Test tractor serial number ....D 674
Years produced 1928–1931
Serial number range ....501–3693 end
Number produced 3,193
Engine ....Waukesha X Special
vertical L-head
Test engine serial number 136821
Cylinders 4
Bore and stroke (in.) ....3.50 x 4.50
Rated rpm 1,400
Displacement (c.i.) 173.2
Fuel ....gasoline
Fuel tank capacity (gal.) 15
Carburetor ....Zenith (Stromberg MI)
1.00-in.
Air cleaner ....Donaldson-Simplex
Ignition ....Splitdorf (Eisemann
GV4) magneto
Cooling capacity (gal.) 5.50
Maximum brake horsepower tests
　　PTO/belt horsepower 21.61
　　Crankshaft rpm 1,400
　　Fuel use (gal./hr.) 2.37
Maximum drawbar horsepower tests
　　Gear ....low
　　Drawbar horsepower 16.32
　　Pull weight (lb.) 2,012
　　Speed (mph) 3.04
　　Percent slippage 6.39
SAE drawbar horsepower 10
SAE belt/PTO horsepower 20
Type ....4 wheel
Front wheel (in.) ....steel: 26 x 5
Rear wheel (in.) ....steel: 42 x 7
Length (in.) 110

Height (in.) 64
Rear width (in.) 82
Weight (lb.) 3,000
Gear/speed (mph) ....forward: 1/2.63,
2/3.75; reverse: 1/2.88

Rumely 6A, Rumely Six
Manufacturer ....Advance-Rumely
Thresher Co. Inc., La
Porte, IN
Nebraska test number 185
Test date ....October 28 to
November 19, 1930
Test tractor serial number 6A 502
Years produced 1930–1931
Serial number range ....501–1302 end
Number produced 802
Engine ....Waukesha Special
vertical L-head
Test engine serial number 6A 502
Cylinders 6
Bore and stroke (in.) ....4.25 x 4.75
Rated rpm 1,365
Displacement (c.i.) 404.3
Fuel ....gasoline
Fuel tank capacity (gal.) 25
Carburetor ....Zenith 156, 1.50-in.
Air cleaner ....Vortox & Donaldson
Ignition ....Splitdorf (American
Bosch U6) magneto
Cooling capacity (gal.) 9.50
Maximum brake horsepower tests
　　PTO/belt horsepower 48.37
　　Crankshaft rpm 1,362
　　Fuel use (gal./hr.) 5.50
Maximum drawbar horsepower tests
　　Gear ....low
　　Drawbar horsepower 33.57
　　Pull weight (lb.) 4,273
　　Speed (mph) 2.95
　　Percent slippage 9.96
SAE drawbar horsepower 27.65
SAE belt/PTO horsepower 43.20
Type ....4 wheel
Front wheel (in.) ....steel: 30 x 6
Rear wheel (in.) ....steel: 48 x 12
Length (in.) 163
Height (in.) 74
Rear width (in.) 70
Weight (lb.) 5,510
Gear/speed (mph) ....forward: 1/2.82, 2/3.66,
3/4.72; reverse: 1/3.44

Chapter 67

RUSSELL

Russell Giant, 30-60
Manufacturer..Russell & Co.,
     Massillon, OH
Nebraska test number...............................78
Test date ....June 6–25, 1921
Test tractor serial number........................X2146; owned by Dennis
     Powers, Ogden, IA
Years produced 1910–1924
Serial number range...................................X120–X2218
Serial number location ....Painted front left side
     lower frame
Number produced ....214 interspersed
Engine ....Russell vertical L-head
Test engine serial number.........................188
Cylinders 4
Bore and stroke (in.) ....8.00 x 10.00
Rated rpm 525
Displacement (c.i.) 2010.6
Fuel ....kerosene/gasoline
Main tank capacity (gal.)...........................88
Auxiliary tank capacity (gal.) 22
Carburetor..Kingston Dual E, 2.00-in.
Air cleaner ....Bennett
Ignition..Bosch DU4, Number
     3346611 magneto
Cooling capacity (gal.) 25
Maximum brake horsepower tests
    PTO/belt horsepower..........................66.13
    Crankshaft rpm 532
    Fuel use (gal./hr.) 16.18
Maximum drawbar horsepower tests
    Gear..low
    Drawbar horsepower...........................43.53
    Pull weight (lb.)..................................8,800
    Speed (mph)..1.85
    Percent slippage.................................7.71
SAE drawbar horsepower...........................30
SAE belt/PTO horsepower 60
Type ....4 wheel
Front wheel (in.)...steel: 42 x 10
Rear wheel (in.)..steel: 84 x 22
Length (in.) 234
Height (in.) 130
Rear width (in.) 115.25
Tread width (in.)..93.25
Weight (lb.)..24,000
Gear/speed (mph) ....forward: 1/2.00,
     2/3.20; reverse: 1/1.50

Russell C, 15-30, Little Boss
Manufacturer..Russell & Co.,
     Massillon, OH
Nebraska test number...............................93
Test date ....May 16–23, 1923
Test tractor serial number........................X2175
Years produced 1921–1924
Serial number range...................................X2124–X2234
Serial number location ....Painted top center side
     hood panels

Number produced ....40 interspersed
Engine ....Climax K vertical L-head
Test engine serial number.........................K 4092
Cylinders 4
Bore and stroke (in.) ....5.00 x 6.50
Rated rpm 950
Displacement (c.i.) 510.5
Fuel ....kerosene/gasoline
Main tank capacity (gal.) 21.50
Auxiliary tank capacity (gal.) 3.50
Carburetor..Kingston L, 1.50-in.
Air cleaner ....Bennett
Ignition..Splitdorf Aero 448
     magneto
Cooling capacity (gal.) 8
Maximum brake horsepower tests
    PTO/belt horsepower..........................33.57
    Crankshaft rpm 935
    Fuel use (gal./hr.) 6.07
Maximum drawbar horsepower tests
    Gear..low
    Drawbar horsepower...........................24.05
    Pull weight (lb.)..................................3,870
    Speed (mph)..2.33
    Percent slippage.................................11.09
SAE drawbar horsepower...........................15
SAE belt/PTO horsepower 30
Type ....4 wheel
Front wheel (in.)...steel: 34 x 5
Rear wheel (in.)..steel: 56 x 14
Length (in.) 147.50
Height (in.) 82
Rear width (in.) 60
Tread width (in.)..42.75
Weight (lb.)..5,800
Gear/speed (mph) ....forward: 1/2.40,
     2/3.70; reverse: 1/2.00

Russell C, 20-40, Big Boss
Manufacturer..Russell & Co.,
     Massillon, OH
Nebraska test number...............................94
Test date ....May 16–25, 1923
Test tractor serial number........................X2186
Years produced 1917–1924
Serial number range...................................X1373–X2236
Serial number location ....brass plate left center
     front frame/painted left
     side panel in front of
     wheel
Number produced ....162, interspersed
Engine ....Climax vertical L-head
Test engine serial number.........................3272
Cylinders 4
Bore and stroke (in.) ....5.50 x 7.00
Rated rpm 900
Displacement (c.i.) 665.2
Fuel ....kerosene/gasoline
Main tank capacity (gal.)...........................30

Auxiliary tank capacity (gal.) 5
Carburetor ....Kingston L, 1.50-in.
Air cleaner ....Bennett
Ignition ....Splitdorf Aero 448
                                            magneto
Cooling capacity (gal.) 9.50
Maximum brake horsepower tests
    PTO/belt horsepower............................43.00
    Crankshaft rpm 898
    Fuel use (gal./hr.) 6.48
Maximum drawbar horsepower tests
    Gear................................low
    Drawbar horsepower............................32.05
    Pull weight (lb.)................................5,070

Speed (mph) 2.37
    Percent slippage................................11.05
SAE drawbar horsepower................................20
SAE belt/PTO horsepower................................40
Type ....4 wheel
Front wheel (in.)................................steel: 38 x 6
Rear wheel (in.)................................steel: 60 x 16
Length (in.) 164
Height (in.) 87
Rear width (in.) 68
Tread width (in.)................................50.38
Weight (lb.) 7,740
Gear/speed (mph) ....forward: 1/2.40,
                                            2/3.70; reverse: 1/2.00

Chapter 68

SAMSON

Samson M
Manufacturer................................Samson Tractor Co.,
                                            Janesville, WI
Nebraska test number 27
Test date ....June 19–30, 1920
Test tractor serial number................................12784
Years produced................................1919–1922
Serial number range................................1000–27103 no end,
                                            last reported number
Serial number location ....base of gear shift lever
Engine ....Northway
                                            vertical L-head
Test engine serial number................................13490
Cylinders 4
Bore and stroke (in.) ....4.00 x 5.50
Rated rpm 1,100
Displacement (c.i.) 276.4
Fuel ....kerosene/gasoline
Main tank capacity (gal.)................................20
Auxiliary tank capacity (gal.) 3
Carburetor................................Kingston L2, 1.25-in.
Air cleaner ....Samson
Ignition................................Simms K4 magneto

Cooling capacity (gal.) 10
Maximum brake horsepower tests
    PTO/belt horsepower............................19.39
    Crankshaft rpm 1,111
    Fuel use (gal./hr.) 2.79
Maximum drawbar horsepower tests
    Gear................................high
    Drawbar horsepower............................11.60
    Pull weight (lb.)................................1,670
    Speed (mph) 2.60
    Percent slippage................................15.10
Type ....4 wheel
Front wheel (in.)................................steel: 4.50 x 27
Rear wheel (in.)................................steel: 12 x 45
Length (in.) ....wheelbase: 64.25;
                                            total: 114
Height (in.) 66
Rear width (in.) 59
Weight (lb.) 3,480
Gear/speed (mph) ....forward: 1/2.30,
                                            2/3.19; reverse: 1/1.06

Chapter 69

SHAW DU-ALL

Shaw Du-All T 25 Garden Tractor
Manufacturer................................Shaw Mfg. Co.,
                                            Galesburg, KS
Nebraska test number 136
Test date ....June 7–22, 1927
Test tractor serial number................................PB18407
Engine ....Briggs & Stratton
                                            vertical, F Head

Test engine serial number................................PB18407
Cylinders 1
Bore and stroke (in.) ....2.50 x 2.50
Rated rpm 2,200
Displacement (c.i.) 12.3
Fuel ....gasoline
Carburetor ....Tillotson MS6A
Ignition................................Briggs & Stratton
                                            magneto

Maximum brake horsepower tests
    PTO/belt horsepower.............................1.08
    Crankshaft rpm 2,213
    Fuel use (gal./hr.)................................0.29
Maximum drawbar horsepower tests
    Gear...high
    Drawbar horsepower...........................0.73
    Pull weight (lb.)..................................140.50
    Speed (mph) 1.94
    Percent slippage................................14.58
Type ....garden, 2 wheel
Weight (lb.) 400
Gear/speed (mph) ....forward: 1/.50–1.50,
    2/1.25–2.50

Shaw Du-All T 45 Garden Tractor

Manufacturer...Shaw Mfg. Co.,
    Galesburg, KS
Nebraska test number 137
Test date ....June 7–23, 1927
Test tractor serial number.........................795
Engine ....Briggs & Stratton
    vertical L-head

Test engine serial number..........................795
Cylinders 1
Bore and stroke (in.) ....2.75 x 3.00
Rated rpm 1,600
Displacement (c.i.) 17.8
Fuel ....gasoline
Carburetor..Tillotson MS7A
Ignition...Briggs & Stratton
    magneto

Maximum brake horsepower tests
    PTO/belt horsepower.............................1.68
    Crankshaft rpm 1,610
    Fuel use (gal./hr.)................................0.35
Maximum drawbar horsepower tests
    Gear...high
    Drawbar horsepower...........................0.71
    Pull weight (lb.)..................................159.50
    Speed (mph) 1.65
    Percent slippage................................21.88
Type ....garden, 2 wheel
Weight (lb.) 437
Gear/speed (mph) ....forward: 1/1.00, 2/1.68

Chapter 70
SHAWNEE THIRTY

Shawnee Thirty Road Maintainer

Manufacturer...Shaw-Enochs Tractor
    Co., Minneapolis, MN
Nebraska test number 115
Test date ....May 16–28, 1925
Test tractor serial number.........................950 1269
Engine ....Waukesha
    vertical L-head
Test engine serial number..........................72367
Cylinders 4
Bore and stroke (in.) ....3.75 x 5.75
Rated rpm 1,200
Displacement (c.i.) 254
Fuel ....gasoline

Carburetor..Zenith
Air cleaner ....United
Ignition...Eisemann GS4
    magneto
Maximum drawbar horsepower tests
    Gear...2nd
    Drawbar horsepower...........................13.19
    Pull weight (lb.)..................................1,969
    Speed (mph) 2.51
    Percent slippage................................8.61
Type ....4 wheel; 2 front
    drivers, 2 rear
Weight (lb.) 9,690
Gear/speed (mph) ....forward: 1/1.50, 2/3.00

Chapter 71
SILVER KING

Silver King 3 Wheel; S66 R66

Manufacturer...Fate-Root-Heath Co.,
    Plymouth, OH
Nebraska test number 250
Test date ....March 23 to April 20,
    1936
Test tractor serial number.........................996

Years produced 1936–1941
Serial number range....................................1001–5256 no end
Serial number location ....steel plate on left side
    of transmission
Number produced ....na, models
    interspersed
Engine ....Hercules IXB
    vertical L-head

Test engine serial number 406947
Cylinders 4
Bore and stroke (in.) ....3.25 x 4.00
Rated rpm 1,400
Displacement (c.i.) 132.7
Fuel ....gasoline
Fuel tank capacity (gal.) 9.50
Carburetor ....Zenith 193.5, 1.00-in.
Air cleaner ....Air-Maze
Ignition ....Fairbanks-Morse RV-4
magneto
Cooling capacity (gal.) 2.50
Maximum brake horsepower tests
    PTO/belt horsepower 19.74
    Crankshaft rpm 1,401
    Fuel use (gal./hr.) 2.35
Maximum drawbar horsepower tests
    Gear ....steel: 2nd; rubber: 3rd
    Drawbar horsepower ....steel: 13.04;
rubber: 16.44
    Pull weight (lb.) ....steel: 1,321; rubber: 990
    Speed (mph) ....steel: 3.70; rubber: 6.23
    Percent slippage ....steel: 8.86; rubber: 6.12
SAE drawbar horsepower.............................10.36
SAE belt/PTO horsepower 17.20
Type ....3 wheel, tricycle
Front wheel (in.) ....(steel: 28 x 6;
rubber: 6.00 x 16)
Rear wheel (in.) ....(steel: 42 x 9;
rubber: 9.00 x 24)
Length (in.) 128
Height (in.) 64
Rear width (in.) ....75–79 (in.) 60, 66, 72
Weight (lb.) ....steel: 2,400;
rubber: 3,440
Gear/speed (mph) ....forward: 1/2.25,
2/3.35, 3/5.50,
4/14.50; reverse:
1/1.50

Silver King 3 Wheel Row Crop, Model 349
Manufacturer...Fate-Root-Heath Co.,
Plymouth, OH
Nebraska test number 424
Test date ....September 19–22, 1949

Test tractor serial number...........................8309
Years produced 1949–1953
Serial number range....................................8246–8720 end
Serial number location ....steel plate on bell housing
below battery box
Number produced ....na, models
interspersed
Engine ....Continental F162
vertical L-head
Test engine serial number ....F 162111196
Cylinders 4
Bore and stroke (in.) ....3.4375 x 4.375
Rated rpm 1,800
Compression ratio.......................................6.23:1
Displacement (c.i.) 162.4
Fuel ....gasoline
Fuel tank capacity (gal.) 11.75
Carburetor ....Marvel-Schebler
TSX-112, 1.00-in.
Air cleaner ....Donaldson
Ignition ....Delco-Remy,
6-v battery
Cooling capacity (gal.) 3
Maximum brake horsepower tests
    PTO/belt horsepower 31.17
    Crankshaft rpm 1,800
    Fuel use (gal./hr.) 2.78
Maximum drawbar horsepower tests
    Gear 2nd
    Drawbar horsepower 28.03
    Pull weight (lb.) 2,698
    Speed (mph) 3.90
    Percent slippage 9.04
SAE drawbar horsepower.............................22.35
SAE belt/PTO horsepower 29.35
Type ....tricycle
Front tire (in.) ....7.50 x 16
Rear tire (in.)..10.00 x 38
Length (in.) 131
Height (in.) 78
Tread width (in.)...56–84
Weight (lb.) 3,550
Gear/speed (mph) ....forward: 1/2.67, 2/4.10,
3/5.93, 4/19.10;
reverse: 1/1.97

Chapter 72

SOMECA

Someca DA 50 Diesel
Manufacturer..Someca 47, BD.
Ornano, Saint-Denis
(Seine) France
Nebraska test number 495
Test date ....June 8–13, 1953
Test tractor serial number............................10045
Engine ....O.M. Milano (Italy)
vertical I-head

Test engine serial number 100088
Cylinders 4
Bore and stroke (in.) ....3.9375 x 4.724
Rated rpm 1,500
Compression ratio.......................................16.0:1
Displacement (c.i.) 230
Fuel ....diesel
Ignition ....12-v with 2, 6-v battery

Maximum brake horsepower tests
    PTO/belt horsepower...........................38.94
    Crankshaft rpm...................................1,500
    Fuel use (gal./hr.)................................2.49
Maximum drawbar horsepower tests
    Gear...4th
    Drawbar horsepower.........................33.37
    Pull weight (lb.).................................1,962
    Speed (mph).......................................6.38
    Percent slippage................................5.12
SAE drawbar horsepower.........................26.37
SAE belt/PTO horsepower.........................35.09
Type..standard
Front wheel (in.)..6.00 x 19
Rear wheel (in.)..12.00 x 75
Weight (lb.)..4,836
Gear/speed (mph).....................................forward: 1/2.34, 2/3.12, 3/4.08, 4/7.06, 5/13.30; reverse: 1/1.85

Someca Som 45 Diesel
Manufacturer..Someca 47, BD. Ornano, Ornano, Saint-Denis, France
Nebraska test number...............................625
Test date..June 14–19, 1957
Test tractor serial number........................30032
Engine..O.M. Milano vertical I-head
Test engine serial number........................117091

Cylinders..4
Bore and stroke (in.)..................................4.135 x 4.724
Rated rpm...1,600
Compression ratio.....................................15.5:1
Displacement (c.i.)....................................253.5
Fuel..diesel
Ignition..12-v with 2, 6-v battery
Maximum brake horsepower tests
    PTO/belt horsepower...........................40.43
    Crankshaft rpm...................................1,600
    Fuel use (gal./hr.)................................2.60
Maximum drawbar horsepower tests
    Gear...4th
    Drawbar horsepower.........................37.09
    Pull weight (lb.).................................3,449
    Speed (mph).......................................4.03
    Percent slippage................................6.29
SAE drawbar horsepower.........................29.09
SAE belt/PTO horsepower.........................36.18
Type..standard
Front wheel (in.)..6.00 x 19
Rear wheel (in.)..14.00 x 30
Tread width (in.)...51.25–78.75
Weight (lb.)..5,320
Gear/speed (mph).....................................forward: 1/1.19, 2/1.82, 3/2.81, 4/4.20, 5/6.40, 6/9.92, 7/13.16; reverse: 1/1.88, 2/6.65

Chapter 73
SQUARE TURN

Square Turn 18-35
Manufacturer..Square Turn Tractor Co., Norfolk, NE
Nebraska test number...............................66
Test date..September 27 to October 7, 1920
Test tractor serial number........................T 406 A
Years produced...1918–1921
Engine..Climax vertical L-head
Test engine serial number........................K 1733
Cylinders..4
Bore and stroke (in.)..................................5.00 x 6.50
Rated rpm...850
Displacement (c.i.)....................................510.5
Fuel..kerosene/gasoline
Fuel tank capacity (gal.)............................17
Auxiliary tank capacity (gal.)....................17
Carburetor..Stromberg M3, 1.50-in.
Air cleaner..Bennett
Ignition...Splitdorf Dixie 46 magneto
Cooling capacity (gal.)...............................10

Maximum brake horsepower tests
    PTO/belt horsepower...........................32.19
    Crankshaft rpm...................................848
    Fuel use (gal./hr.)................................5.35
Maximum drawbar horsepower tests
    Drawbar horsepower.........................23.45
    Pull weight (lb.).................................3,090
    Speed (mph).......................................2.85
    Percent slippage................................6.24
SAE drawbar horsepower.........................18
SAE belt/PTO horsepower.........................35
Type..3 wheel, tricycle
Front wheel (in.)...steel: 60 x 12 drive wheel
Rear wheel (in.)..1 steel: 28 x 8
Length (in.)...199
Height (in.)...81
Rear width (in.)..98
Weight (lb.)..7,400
Gear/speed (mph).....................................forward: 1/2.00–3.00; reverse: 1/2.00–3.00

Chapter 74

TERRATRAC

Terratrac GT 30

Manufacturer	American Tractor Corp., Churubusco, IN
Nebraska test number	471
Test date	May 19–27, 1952
Test tractor serial number	10671
Years produced	1951–1955
Engine	Continental Red Seal F-140 vertical L-head
Test engine serial number	22929
Cylinders	4
Bore and stroke (in.)	3.1875 x 4.375
Rated rpm	1,850
Compression ratio	6.5:1
Displacement (c.i.)	140
Fuel	gasoline
Fuel tank capacity (gal.)	10
Carburetor	Marvel-Schebler, 0.875-in.
Air cleaner	Donaldson
Ignition	Auto-Lite with 6-v battery
Cooling capacity (gal.)	3

Maximum brake horsepower tests

PTO/belt horsepower	30.41
Crankshaft rpm	1,851
Fuel use (gal./hr.)	2.82

Maximum drawbar horsepower tests

Gear	2nd
Drawbar horsepower	25.16
Pull weight (lb.)	3,448
Speed (mph)	2.74
Percent slippage	2.95
SAE drawbar horsepower	19.73
SAE belt/PTO horsepower	26.69
Type	tracklayer
Length (in.)	96
Height (in.)	51
Tread width (in.)	42–72
Weight (lb.)	3,400
Track length (in.)	181
Grouser shoe	30 links; 10, (12)-in.
Gear/speed (mph)	forward: 1/1.78, 2/2.81, 3/4.61; reverse: 1/2.05

Chapter 75

TORO

Toro 6-10, 12, 10

Manufacturer	Toro Tractor Co., Minneapolis, MN
Nebraska test number	65
Test date	September 23–29, 1920
Test tractor serial number	1547
Years produced	1920–1927
Engine	Le Roi vertical L-head
Test engine serial number	21902
Cylinders	4
Bore and stroke (in.)	3.125 x 4.50
Rated rpm	1,200
Displacement (c.i.)	138
Fuel	gasoline
Fuel tank capacity (gal.)	11
Carburetor	Kingston L, 0.875-in.
Air cleaner	Bennett
Ignition	Eisemann GS4 magneto
Cooling capacity (gal.)	3.50

Maximum brake horsepower tests

PTO/belt horsepower	13.31
Crankshaft rpm	1,219
Fuel use (gal./hr.)	1.73

Maximum drawbar horsepower tests

Gear	low
Drawbar horsepower	9.92
Pull weight (lb.)	1,310
Speed (mph)	2.84
Percent slippage	6.52
SAE drawbar horsepower	6
SAE belt/PTO horsepower	10
Type	4 wheel
Front wheel (in.)	steel: 26 x 4
Rear wheel (in.)	steel: 42 x 6
Length (in.)	105
Height (in.)	54
Rear width (in.)	44
Weight (lb.)	2,600
Gear/speed (mph)	forward: 1/2.60, 2/3.70; reverse: 1/3.00

Chapter 76

TOWNSEND

Townsend 15-30

Manufacturer..Townsend Mfg. Co.,
Janesville, WI
Nebraska test number..................................63
Test date...September 9–23, 1920
Test tractor serial number...........................1348
Years produced..1919–1924
Engine..Townsend horizontal,
valve-in-head
Test engine serial number...........................1348
Cylinders..2
Bore and stroke (in.)...................................7.00 x 8.00
Rated rpm...525
Displacement (c.i.).......................................615.8
Fuel...kerosene/gasoline
Fuel tank capacity (gal.)..............................18
Carburetor..Townsend
Ignition...Splitdorf Dixie 462 C
magneto
Cooling capacity (gal.).................................75

Maximum brake horsepower tests
   PTO/belt horsepower............................29.51
   Crankshaft rpm.....................................533
   Fuel use (gal./hr.)................................3.90
Maximum drawbar horsepower tests
   Drawbar horsepower............................17.85
   Pull weight (lb.)....................................2,681
   Speed (mph)...2.50
   Percent slippage...................................12.60
SAE drawbar horsepower.............................15
SAE belt/PTO horsepower...........................30
Type..4 wheel
Front wheel (in.)...steel: 30 x 8
Rear wheel (in.)..steel: 56 x 18
Length (in.)...140
Height (in.)..78
Rear width (in.)..78
Weight (lb.)...7,000
Gear/speed (mph).......................................forward: 1/2.30

Chapter 77

TWIN CITY

Twin City 12-20

Manufacturer..Minneapolis Steel &
Machinery Co.,
Minneapolis, MN
Nebraska test number..................................19
Test date...June 3 to June 12, 1920
Test tractor serial number...........................12278
Years produced..1919–1926
Serial number range.....................................10201–19903 end
Serial number location.................................brass plate left side
front of transmission
Number produced...approximately 9700
Engine..Minneapolis Steel
vertical, valve-in-head
Test engine serial number...........................12137
Cylinders..4
Bore and stroke (in.)...................................4.25 x 6.00
Rated rpm...1,000
Displacement (c.i.).......................................340.5
Fuel...kerosene/gasoline
Main tank capacity (gal.)..............................23
Auxiliary tank capacity (gal.).......................3
Carburetor..Holley, 1.25-in.
Air cleaner..Bennett
Ignition...Bosch DU4 magneto
Cooling capacity (gal.).................................7
Maximum brake horsepower tests
   PTO/belt horsepower............................27.93
   Crankshaft rpm.....................................1,017
   Fuel use (gal./hr.)................................3.18

Maximum drawbar horsepower tests
   Gear...low
   Drawbar horsepower............................18.43
   Pull weight (lb.)....................................3,476
   Speed (mph)...1.99
   Percent slippage...................................20.10
SAE drawbar horsepower.............................12
SAE belt/PTO horsepower...........................20
Type..4 wheel
Front wheel (in.)...steel: 34 x 5.75
Rear wheel (in.)..steel: 50 x 12
Length (in.)...84 wheel, 134 total
Height (in.)..63.50
Rear width (in.)..63
Weight (lb.)...4,000
Gear/speed (mph).......................................forward: 1/2.20,
2/2.93; reverse: 1/na

Twin City 40-65

Manufacturer..Minneapolis Steel &
Machinery Co.,
Minneapolis, MN
Nebraska test number..................................48
Test date...August 5–14, 1920
Test tractor serial number...........................1766
Years produced..1916–1925
Serial number range.....................................1001–1825 end
Serial number location.................................brass plate on front
frame

Twin City

Number produced 825
Engine ....Minneapolis Steel
vertical L-head
Test engine serial number.......................3009
Cylinders 4
Bore and stroke (in.) ....7.25 x 9.00
Rated rpm 535
Displacement (c.i.) 1,486.2
Fuel ....kerosene/gasoline
Main tank capacity (gal.) 95
Auxiliary tank capacity (gal.) 10
Carburetor ....Kingston (Holley 257),
2.50-in.
Ignition.................................K-W, HK magneto
Cooling capacity (gal.) 130
Maximum brake horsepower tests
PTO/belt horsepower.........................65.53
Crankshaft rpm 530
Fuel use (gal./hr.) 7.88
Maximum drawbar horsepower tests
Drawbar horsepower.........................49.71
Pull weight (lb.)...........................10,820
Speed (mph) 1.72
Percent slippage.........................13.75
SAE drawbar horsepower........................40
SAE belt/PTO horsepower 65
Type ....4 wheel
Front wheel (in.) ....steel: 42 x 12
Rear wheel (in.).............................steel: 84 x 24
Length (in.) 240
Height (in.) 122
Rear width (in.) 102
Weight (lb.) 23,700
Gear/speed (mph) ....forward: 1/1.90;
reverse: 1/1.90

Twin City 20-35, 27-44
Manufacturer................................Minneapolis Steel &
Machinery Co.,
Minneapolis, MN
Nebraska test number 67
Test date ....October 5–9, 1920
Test tractor serial number.......................3217
Years produced 1920–1927
Serial number range............................3201–4097 number
end
Serial number location ....brass plate left side
front of transmission
Engine ....Minneapolis Steel
vertical, valve-in-head
Test engine serial number.......................5110
Cylinders 4
Bore and stroke (in.) ....5.50 x 6.75
Rated rpm 900
Displacement (c.i.) 641.5
Fuel ....kerosene/gasoline
Main tank capacity (gal.) 40
Auxiliary tank capacity (gal.) 3
Carburetor.................................Holley 257, 2.00-in.
Air cleaner.................................Bennett
Ignition.................................Bosch DU magneto
Cooling capacity (gal.) 18
Maximum brake horsepower tests
PTO/belt horsepower.........................46.88
Crankshaft rpm 905
Fuel use (gal./hr.) 6.00

Maximum drawbar horsepower tests
Gear.................................low
Drawbar horsepower.........................34.12
Pull weight (lb.)...........................5,730
Speed (mph) 2.23
Percent slippage.........................7.60
SAE drawbar horsepower........................20
SAE belt/PTO horsepower 35
Type ....4 wheel
Front wheel (in.).............................steel: 36 x 8.50
Rear wheel (in.).............................steel: 60 x 20
Length (in.) 152
Height (in.) 73
Rear width (in.) 88
Weight (lb.) 8,100
Gear/speed (mph) ....forward: 1/2.20,
2/2.90; reverse: 1/1.85

Twin City 17-28
Manufacturer................................Minneapolis steel &
Machinery Co.,
Minneapolis, MN
Nebraska test number 121
Test date ....May 17–21, 1926
Test tractor serial number.......................19220
Years produced 1926–1935
Serial number range............................approximately
19000–30808 end
Serial number location ....brass plate left side
front of transmission
Number produced ....approximately 15,000
Engine ....Minneapolis vertical,
valve-in-head
Test engine serial number.......................19040
Cylinders 4
Bore and stroke (in.) ....4.25 x 6.00
Rated rpm 1,000
Displacement (c.i.) 340.5
Fuel ....kerosene/gasoline
Main tank capacity (gal.) 30
Auxiliary tank capacity (gal.) 1
Carburetor.................................Holley 257, 1.25-in.
Air cleaner.................................Donaldson (Bennett)
Ignition.................................American Bosch ZR4
Ed26 magneto
Cooling capacity (gal.) 10.50
Maximum brake horsepower tests
PTO/belt horsepower.........................30.91
Crankshaft rpm 1,005
Fuel use (gal./hr.) 3.16
Maximum drawbar horsepower tests
Gear.................................low
Drawbar horsepower.........................22.51
Pull weight (lb.)...........................3,778
Speed (mph) 2.24
Percent slippage.........................9.19
SAE drawbar horsepower........................17
SAE belt/PTO horsepower 28
Type ....4 wheel
Front wheel (in.).............................steel: 34 x 5.75
Rear wheel (in.).............................steel: 50 x 12
Length (in.) 134
Height (in.) 63.50
Rear width (in.) 63
Weight (lb.) 5,050
Gear/speed (mph) ....forward: 1/2.20,
2/2.90; reverse: 1/1.75

Twin City 27-44, AT

Manufacturer	Minneapolis Steel & Machinery Co., Minneapolis, MN
Nebraska test number	122
Test date	May 20–27, 1926
Test tractor serial number	250025
Years produced	1927–1935
Serial number range	250001–250839 end
Serial number location	brass plate left side front of transmission
Number produced	approximately 840
Engine	Minneapolis Steel vertical, valve-in-head
Test engine serial number	200006
Cylinders	4
Bore and stroke (in.)	5.50 x 6.75
Rated rpm	900
Displacement (c.i.)	641.5
Fuel	kerosene/gasoline
Main tank capacity (gal.)	40
Auxiliary tank capacity (gal.)	1.50
Carburetor	Wheeler Schebler A, 1.50-in.
Air cleaner	Donaldson Duplex
Ignition	American Bosch ZR4 Ed26 magneto
Cooling capacity (gal.)	18

Maximum brake horsepower tests

PTO/belt horsepower	49.05
Crankshaft rpm	899
Fuel use (gal./hr.)	5.53

Maximum drawbar horsepower tests

Gear	low
Drawbar horsepower	34.65
Pull weight (lb.)	5,640
Speed (mph)	2.31
Percent slippage	9.49
SAE drawbar horsepower	28
SAE belt/PTO horsepower	44
Type	4 wheel
Front wheel (in.)	steel: 36 x 8.50
Rear wheel (in.)	steel: 60 x 20
Length (in.)	152
Height (in.)	73
Rear width (in.)	88
Weight (lb.)	8,550
Gear/speed (mph)	forward: 1/2.20, 2/2.90; reverse: 1/1.87

Twin City FT, 21-32

Manufacturer	Minneapolis Steel & Machinery Co., Minneapolis, MN
Nebraska test number	127
Test date	October 7–13, 1926
Test tractor serial number	150026
Years produced	1928–1938
Serial number range	150001–157229 end
Serial number location	brass plate left side front of transmission
Number produced	approximately 7,229
Engine	Minneapolis Steel valve-in-head
Test engine serial number	100026

Cylinders	4
Bore and stroke (in.)	4.50 x 6.00
Rated rpm	1,000
Displacement (c.i.)	381.7
Fuel	kerosene/gasoline
Main tank capacity (gal.)	30
Auxiliary tank capacity (gal.)	4
Carburetor	Stromberg M3 (Zenith U6) 1.50-in.
Air cleaner	Donaldson (Bennett)
Ignition	American Bosch ZR4 Ed26 magneto
Cooling capacity (gal.)	9

Maximum brake horsepower tests

PTO/belt horsepower	35.88
Crankshaft rpm	999
Fuel use (gal./hr.)	4.32

Maximum drawbar horsepower tests

Gear	low
Drawbar horsepower	31.05
Pull weight (lb.)	5,093
Speed (mph)	2.28
Percent slippage	5.93
SAE drawbar horsepower	21
SAE belt/PTO horsepower	32
Type	4 wheel
Front wheel (in.)	steel: 34 x 5.75
Rear wheel (in.)	steel: 50 x 12
Length (in.)	137
Height (in.)	66
Rear width (in.)	66
Weight (lb.)	5,880
Gear/speed (mph)	forward: 1/2.20, 2/2.90; reverse: 1/1.75

Twin City FT, 21-32, FTA

Manufacturer	Minneapolis Steel & Machinery Co., Minneapolis, MN
Nebraska test number	152
Test date	October 1 to October 8, 1928
Test tractor serial number	X4; Owned by Sue Dougan, Ostrander, MN
Years produced	1928
Serial number range	X1–X6 Experimental
Serial number location	brass plate left side front of transmission
Number produced	6
Engine	Minneapolis Steel vertical I, valve-in-head
Test engine serial number	XII
Cylinders	4
Bore and stroke (in.)	4.50 x 6.00
Rated rpm	1,075
Displacement (c.i.)	381.7
Fuel	gasoline
Fuel tank capacity (gal.)	30
Carburetor	Stromberg M3, 1.50-in.
Air cleaner	Donaldson & Minn. steel
Ignition	Amer. Bosch (Robert Bosch FU4) magneto

Cooling capacity (gal.) 9
Maximum brake horsepower tests
    PTO/belt horsepower............................39.14
    Crankshaft rpm 1,075
    Fuel use (gal./hr.)................................3.98
Maximum drawbar horsepower tests
    Gear...low
    Drawbar horsepower............................30.20
    Pull weight (lb.)....................................3,335
    Speed (mph)..3.40
    Percent slippage.................................6.39

SAE drawbar horsepower............................21
SAE belt/PTO horsepower............................32
Type..4 wheel
Front wheel (in.)..................................steel: 34 x 5.75
Rear wheel (in.)...................................steel: 50 x 12
Length (in.) 137
Height (in.)..66
Rear width (in.) 66
Weight (lb.) 5,350
Gear/speed (mph) ....forward: 1/2.36, 2/3.17, 3/4.45; reverse: 1/1.74

Chapter 78

UNCLE SAM

Uncle Sam 20-30
Manufacturer..U.S. Tractor & Machine Co., Menasha, WI
Nebraska test number 64
Test date ....September 21–28, 1920
Test tractor serial number.......................1152
Years produced 1919–1922
Engine ....Beaver TB vertical, valve-in-head
Test engine serial number.......................226 2 JB
Cylinders 4
Bore and stroke (in.) ....4.75 x 6.00
Rated rpm 1,000
Displacement (c.i.) 425.3
Fuel ....kerosene/gasoline
Main tank capacity (gal.)...........................22
Auxiliary tank capacity (gal.) 3.50
Carburetor..Bennett, 1.50-in.
Air cleaner...Bennett
Ignition..Splitdorf Dixie 46C magneto
Cooling capacity (gal.) 10

Maximum brake horsepower tests
    PTO/belt horsepower............................32.20
    Crankshaft rpm 1,041
    Fuel use (gal./hr.)................................6.41
Maximum drawbar horsepower tests
    Gear...low
    Drawbar horsepower............................22.40
    Pull weight (lb.)....................................3,264
    Speed (mph)..2.57
    Percent slippage.................................18.00
SAE drawbar horsepower............................20
SAE belt/PTO horsepower............................30
Type..4 wheel
Front wheel (in.)..................................steel: 36 x 6
Rear wheel (in.)...................................steel: 50 x 12
Length (in.) 133
Height (in.)..72.50
Rear width (in.) 74
Weight (lb.) 4,500
Gear/speed (mph) ....forward: 1/2.50, 2/3.75; reverse: 1/1.75

Chapter 79

UNIMOG

Unimog 30 Diesel
Manufacturer..Daimler-Benz A.G., Stuttgart-Untertuerkheim
Nebraska test number 607
Test date ....March 5–13, 1957
Test tractor serial number.......................6500126

Engine ....Mercedes-Benz OM636 vertical I-head
Test engine serial number.......................6503289
Cylinders 4
Bore and stroke (in.) ....2.950 x 3.9375
Rated rpm 2,550
Compression ratio....................................19:1

Displacement (c.i.) 107.8
Fuel ....diesel
Fuel tank capacity (gal.) 10.88
Carburetor ....Bosch injector pump
Ignition ....12-v battery
Cooling capacity (gal.) 3.45
Maximum brake horsepower tests
    PTO/belt horsepower...........................28.43
    Crankshaft rpm 2,550
    Fuel use (gal./hr.) 2.28
Maximum drawbar horsepower tests
    Gear...4th
    Drawbar horsepower............................25.84
    Pull weight (lb.)......................................2,533

Speed (mph) 3.83
    Percent slippage................................5.02
SAE drawbar horsepower...........................19.93
SAE belt/PTO horsepower 24.76
Type ....4 wheel drive
Front wheel (in.)..7.50 x 18
Rear wheel (in.)...7.50 x 18
Height (in.)...80.75
Tread width (in.)..50.75 or 59
Weight (lb.)..4,024
Gear/speed (mph)............forward: 1/2.15, 1 creeper/0.72, 2/4.00,
        2 creeper/1.30, 3/7.40, 4/13.40, 5/21.80,
        6/33.00; reverse: 1/1.64, 2/3.00

Chapter 80

USTRAC

USTrac 10 A
Manufacturer...U.S. Tractor Corp.,
        Warren, OH
Nebraska test number 414
Test date ....June 22–30, 1949
Test tractor serial number.........................05636
Years produced 1948–1949
Engine ....Continental F124
        vertical L-head
Test engine serial number.........................F 1249614
Cylinders 4
Bore and stroke (in.) ....3.00 x 4.375
Rated rpm 1,900
Compression ratio.....................................6.3:1
Displacement (c.i.) 123.7
Fuel ....gasoline
Fuel tank capacity (gal.) 10
Carburetor ....Zenith 161-7, 1.00-in.
Air cleaner ....Donaldson
Ignition...Auto-Lite with 6-v
        battery
Cooling capacity (gal.) 3.50

Maximum brake horsepower tests
    PTO/belt horsepower...........................21.33
    Crankshaft rpm 1,899
    Fuel use (gal./hr.)................................2.49
Maximum drawbar horsepower tests
    Gear...3rd
    Drawbar horsepower............................15.26
    Pull weight (lb.)....................................1,747
    Speed (mph) 3.28
    Percent slippage...................................2.38
SAE drawbar horsepower...........................12.28
SAE belt/PTO horsepower 19.20
Type ....tracklayer
Length (in.) 92
Height (in.)..56
Tread width (in.)..29.50
Weight (lb.) 3,425
Track length (in.)...170
Grouser shoe..28 links; 7.50-in.
Gear/speed (mph) ....forward: 1/0.92,
        2/1.89, 3/3.45, 4/5.87;
        reverse: 1/1.06, 2/2.17,
        3/3.97, 4/6.75

Chapter 81

VOLVO

Volvo T425
Manufacturer..A-B Bolinder-Munktell,
        Eskilstuna, Sweden
Nebraska test number 637
Test date ....February 26 to March
        10, 1958
Test tractor serial number.........................2571
Years produced 1956-na
Serial number range...................................315-na

Engine ....Volvo B 16 C
        vertical I-head
Test engine serial number..........................995
Cylinders 4
Bore and stroke (in.) ....3.125 x 3.15
Rated rpm 2,000
Compression ratio......................................7.4:1
Displacement (c.i.) 97.6
Fuel ....gasoline

Fuel tank capacity (gal.) 10.6
Carburetor ....Zenith 26VME, 0.75-in.
Air cleaner ....AC
Ignition ....Bosch with 6-v battery
Cooling capacity (gal.) 2.10
Maximum brake horsepower tests
    PTO/belt horsepower...........................23.99
    Crankshaft rpm 2,000
    Fuel use (gal./hr.) 2.26
Maximum drawbar horsepower tests
    Gear..2nd
    Drawbar horsepower.............................22.01
    Pull weight (lb.)....................................2,367
    Speed (mph) 3.49
    Percent slippage...................................5.14
SAE drawbar horsepower...........................16.76
SAE belt/PTO horsepower...........................21.13
Type ....standard
Front wheel (in.) ....5.50 x 16
Rear wheel (in.)...10.00 x 28
Height (in.)..53
Tread width (in.)..52.75–76.38
Weight (lb.) 3,000
Gear/speed (mph) ....forward: 1/2.12, 2/3.65, 3/5.88, 4/14.2; reverse: 1/1.88

Volvo T55 Diesel
Manufacturer...A-B Bolinder-Munktell, Eskilstuna, Sweden
Nebraska test number 638
Test date ....February 27 to March 12, 1958
Test tractor serial number 1928
Years produced 1950–na
Serial number range..................................313-na

Engine ....Bolinder-Munktell 1054 vertical I-head
Test engine serial number 11800 4488
Cylinders 4
Bore and stroke (in.) ....4.125 x 5.125
Rated rpm 1,800
Compression ratio.....................................16.5:1
Displacement (c.i.) 273.6
Fuel ....diesel
Fuel tank capacity (gal.) 29
Carburetor ....Bosch injector pump
Air cleaner ....RNA
Ignition ....Bosch with 12-v battery
Cooling capacity (gal.) 4.75
Maximum brake horsepower tests
    PTO/belt horsepower...........................63.86
    Crankshaft rpm 1,800
    Fuel use (gal./hr.) 3.86
Maximum drawbar horsepower tests
    Gear..3rd
    Drawbar horsepower.............................59.35
    Pull weight (lb.)....................................4,661
    Speed (mph) 4.78
    Percent slippage...................................5.36
SAE drawbar horsepower...........................44.63
SAE belt/PTO horsepower...........................56.47
Type ....standard
Front wheel (in.) ....7.50 x 18
Rear wheel (in.)...14.00 x 34
Height (in.)..94.50
Tread width (in.)..59.44
Weight (lb.) 6,500
Gear/speed (mph) ....forward: 1/2.46, 2/3.96, 3/4.92, 4/9.02, 5/17.20; reverse: 1/2.98

Chapter 82

WAGNER

Wagner TR-9 Diesel
Manufacturer...Wagner Tractor, Inc., Portland, OR
Nebraska test number 631
Test date ....September 24 to October 3, 1957
Test tractor serial number 357
Engine ....Cummins Diesel NHC4BI vertical I-head
Test engine serial number 186757
Cylinders 4
Bore and stroke (in.) ....5.125 x 6.00
Rated rpm 1,800
Compression ratio.....................................15.5:1
Displacement (c.i.) 495
Fuel ....diesel
Fuel tank capacity (gal.) 75

Ignition ....24-v with 2, 12-v battery
Cooling capacity (gal.) 7.50
Maximum drawbar horsepower tests
    Gear..5th
    Drawbar horsepower.............................87.45
    Pull weight (lb.)....................................7,729
    Speed (mph) 4.24
    Percent slippage...................................3.85
SAE drawbar horsepower...........................67.88
Type ....4 wheel drive
Front wheel (in.) ....15.00 x 26
Rear wheel (in.)...15.00 x 26
Length (in.) 2,000
Height (in.)..87
Rear width (in.) 94
Tread width (in.)..74

Weight (lb.) 15,270
Gear/speed (mph) ....forward: 1/1.22,
2/1.61, 3/2.28, 4/3.08,
5/4.24, 6/5.64, 7/6.68,
8/8.84, 9/11.46,
10/14.99; reverse:
1/1.57, 2/2.07

Wagner TR-14A Diesel
Manufacturer ....Wagner Tractor Co.,
Portland, OR
Nebraska test number 700
Test date ....June 4–10, 1959
Test tractor serial number 1980
Engine ....Cummins NH-220-BI
vertical L-head
Test engine serial number 227570
Cylinders 6
Bore and stroke (in.) ....5.125 x 6.00
Rated rpm 2,100
Compression ratio................................15.5:1
Displacement (c.i.) 743
Fuel ....diesel

Fuel tank capacity (gal.) 95
Ignition..24-v with 2, 12-v
battery
Cooling capacity (gal.) 9.75
Maximum drawbar horsepower tests
Gear...5th
Drawbar horsepower........................148.56
Pull weight (lb.).........................10,749
Speed (mph) 5.18
Percent slippage.........................4.47
SAE drawbar horsepower...........................155.04
Type ....4 wheel drive
Front wheel (in.) ....18.00 x 26
Rear wheel (in.) ....18.00 x 26
Length (in.) 237
Height (in.) 111
Rear width (in.) 102
Tread width (in.) 79
Weight (lb.) 21,050
Gear/speed (mph).............forward: 1/2.10, 2/2.70, 3/3.50, 4/4.50,
5/5.80, 6/7.50, 7/9.80, 8/12.50, 9/16.30,
10/20.90; reverse: 1/1.80, 2/6.40

Chapter 83
WALLIS

Wallis K, 15-25
Manufacturer.....................................J.I. Case Plow Works
Co., Racine, WI
Nebraska test number 49
Test date ....August 7–16, 1920
Test tractor serial number 21166
Years produced 1918–1922
Serial number range................................14442–23156 end
Serial number location ....stamped and plate on
front frame below
radiator
Number produced ....approximately 8,715
Engine ....J.I. Case vertical,
valve-in-head
Test engine serial number 20695
Cylinders 4
Bore and stroke (in.) ....4.25 x 5.75
Rated rpm 900
Displacement (c.i.) 326.3
Fuel ....kerosene/gasoline
Main tank capacity (gal.) 20
Auxiliary tank capacity (gal.) 1.6
Carburetor.......................................Bennett H&J, 1.25-in.
Air cleaner......................................Bennett
Ignition...Berling EQ 41 magneto
Cooling capacity (gal.) 6
Maximum brake horsepower tests
PTO/belt horsepower..........................27.57
Crankshaft rpm 907
Fuel use (gal./hr.) 4.01
Maximum drawbar horsepower tests
Gear...low
Drawbar horsepower...........................18.58

Pull weight (lb.)................................2,782
Speed (mph) 2.50
Percent slippage.................................19.60
SAE drawbar horsepower...........................15
SAE belt/PTO horsepower 25
Type ....4 wheel
Front wheel (in.) ....steel: 30 x 8
Rear wheel (in.).................................steel: 48 x 12
Length (in.) 132
Height (in.) 65
Rear width (in.) 61
Weight (lb.) 2,560
Gear/speed (mph) ....forward: 1/2.50,
2/3.50; reverse: 1/2.50

Wallis OK, OKO, 15-27
Manufacturer.....................................J.I. Case Plow Works,
Racine, WI
Nebraska test number 92
Test date ....April 26 to May 5,
1923
Test tractor serial number 23273
Years produced 1922–1926
Serial number range................................23200–40000 end
Serial number location ....stamped and plate on
front frame below
radiator
Number produced ....approximately 16,801
Engine ....Case vertical,
valve-in-head
Test engine serial number 22802
Cylinders 4

Bore and stroke (in.) ....4.25 x 5.75
Rated rpm 1,000
Displacement (c.i.) 326.3
Fuel ....gasoline
Fuel tank capacity (gal.) 20
Carburetor ....Bennett WS, 1.25-in.
Air cleaner ....Case
Ignition...Bosch DU4-ED 19
No. 3440309 magneto
Cooling capacity (gal.) 5.25

Maximum brake horsepower tests
  PTO/belt horsepower.............................28.60
  Crankshaft rpm 998
  Fuel use (gal./hr.) 3.47
Maximum drawbar horsepower tests
  Gear...low
  Drawbar horsepower.............................18.15
  Pull weight (lb.).....................................2,590
  Speed (mph) 2.63
  Percent slippage...................................13.66
SAE drawbar horsepower.............................15
SAE belt/PTO horsepower.............................27
Type ....4 wheel
Front wheel (in.)..steel: 30 x 8
Rear wheel (in.)...steel: 48 x 12
Length (in.) 132
Height (in.) 65
Rear width (in.) 61
Weight (lb.) 3,630
Gear/speed (mph) ....forward: 1/2.50,
2/3.50; reverse: 1/2.50

Wallis Certified 20-30

Manufacturer...J.I. Case Plow Works,
Racine, WI
Nebraska test number 134
Test date ....April 29 to May 10, 1927
Test tractor serial number.............................50470
Years produced 1926–1932
Serial number range.....................................40001–69000 end
Serial number location ....stamped and plate on
front frame below
radiator
Number produced ....approximately 29,000
Engine ....Case vertical,
valve-in-head
Test engine serial number.............................49999
Cylinders 4
Bore and stroke (in.) ....4.375 x 5.75
Rated rpm 1,050
Displacement (c.i.) 345.8
Fuel ....distillate/gasoline
Main tank capacity (gal.) 20
Auxiliary tank capacity (gal.) 1.6
Carburetor ....Kingston L, 1.25-in.
Air cleaner ....Case
Ignition...American Bosch ZR4
Ed26 magneto
Cooling capacity (gal.) 6.75
Maximum brake horsepower tests
  PTO/belt horsepower.............................35.29
  Crankshaft rpm 1,050
  Fuel use (gal./hr.) 4.23
Maximum drawbar horsepower tests
  Gear...low

Drawbar horsepower...........................27.02
Pull weight (lb.)...................................3,409
Speed (mph) 2.98
Percent slippage.................................10.95
SAE drawbar horsepower.............................20
SAE belt/PTO horsepower.............................30
Type ....4 wheel
Front wheel (in.)..steel: 30 x 8
Rear wheel (in.)...steel: 48 x 12
Length (in.) 132
Height (in.) 55
Rear width (in.) 61
Weight (lb.) 4,096
Gear/speed (mph) ....forward: 1/2.88,
2/3.49; reverse: 1/2.88

Wallis Certified 12-20

Manufacturer...Massey-Harris Co.,
Racine, WI
Nebraska test number 164
Test date ....June 18–27, 1929
Test tractor serial number.............................100137
Years produced 1929–1935
Serial number range.....................................100000–107000 end
Serial number location ....stamped and plate on
front frame below
radiator
Number produced ....approximately 7,000
Engine ....Massey-Harris vertical
I-head, valve-in-head
Test engine serial number.............................148 99666
Cylinders 4
Bore and stroke (in.) ....3.875 x 5.25
Rated rpm 1,000
Displacement (c.i.) 247.6
Fuel ....distillate/gasoline
Main tank capacity (gal.) 15
Auxiliary tank capacity (gal.) 1.6
Carburetor ....Kingston L3V,
1.125-in.
Air cleaner ....Massey-Harris
Ignition...American Bosch U4
Ed2 magneto
Cooling capacity (gal.) 5
Maximum brake horsepower tests
  PTO/belt horsepower.............................24.16
  Crankshaft rpm 999
  Fuel use (gal./hr.) 2.47
Maximum drawbar horsepower tests
  Gear...3rd
  Drawbar horsepower.............................18.07
  Pull weight (lb.).....................................3,018
  Speed (mph) 2.24
  Percent slippage...................................18.73
SAE drawbar horsepower.............................12
SAE belt/PTO horsepower.............................20
Type ....4 wheel
Front wheel (in.)..steel: 28 x 5
Rear wheel (in.)...steel: 44 x 10
Length (in.) ....wheelbase: 78
Height (in.) 51
Rear width (in.) 55
Weight (lb.) 3,544
Gear/speed (mph) ....forward: 1/2.33, 2/3.33,
3/4.33; reverse: 1/2.33

Chapter 84
WATERLOO BOY

Waterloo Boy N, 12-25

Manufacturer...Waterloo Gasoline Engine Co., Waterloo, IA
Nebraska test number...............................1
Test date ....March 31 to April 9, 1920
Test tractor serial number.......................19851
Years produced...1917–1924
Serial number range.................................10020–31412 end
Serial number location.............................brass nameplate on left side of gear shift
Number produced 21,392
Engine ....Waterloo Boy horizontal, valve-in-head
Cylinders 2
Bore and stroke (in.) ....6.50 x 7.00
Rated rpm 750
Displacement (c.i.) 465
Fuel ....kerosene/gasoline
Main tank capacity (gal.)..........................20
Auxiliary tank capacity (gal.) 1
Carburetor..Schebler Model D, 1.50 inch

Ignition ....Splitdorf Dixie 246 magneto
Cooling capacity (gal.) 8.50
Maximum brake horsepower tests
    PTO/belt horsepower..........................25.97
    Crankshaft rpm 724
    Fuel use (gal./hr.)...............................3.80
Maximum drawbar horsepower tests
    Gear...low
    Drawbar horsepower...........................15.98
    Pull weight (lb.)...................................2,900
    Speed (mph) 2.07
    Percent slippage..................................17.00
SAE drawbar horsepower.........................12
SAE belt/PTO horsepower 25
Type ....4 wheel
Front wheel (in.)..steel: 28 x 6
Rear wheel (in.)..steel: 52 x 12
Length (in.) 132
Height (in.) 63
Rear width (in.) 72
Weight (lb.) 6,183
Gear/speed (mph) ....forward: 1/2.25, 2/3.00; reverse: 1/2.25

Chapter 85
WETMORE

Wetmore 12-25

Manufacturer...H.A. Wetmore, Sioux City, IA
Nebraska test number...............................73
Test date ....April 6–12, 1921
Test tractor serial number.......................400
Years produced...1919–1928
Engine ....Weidely M vertical, valve-in-head
Test engine serial number.......................MAU 99
Cylinders 4
Bore and stroke (in.) ....4.00 x 5.50
Rated rpm 1,265
Displacement (c.i.) 276.5
Fuel ....kerosene/gasoline
Main tank capacity (gal.)..........................15
Auxiliary tank capacity (gal.) 2
Carburetor..Schebler ATX 47, 1.25-in.
Ignition...Splitdorf No. 825175 magneto

Maximum brake horsepower tests
    PTO/belt horsepower..........................27.94
    Crankshaft rpm 1,264
    Fuel use (gal./hr.)...............................3.46
Maximum drawbar horsepower tests
    Gear...2nd
    Drawbar horsepower...........................16.10
    Pull weight (lb.)...................................2,260
    Speed (mph) 2.67
    Percent slippage..................................25.40
    SAE drawbar horsepower...................12
SAE belt/PTO horsepower 25
Type ....4 wheel
Front wheel (in.)..steel: 28 x 5
Rear wheel (in.)..steel: 46 x 10
Weight (lb.) 2,900
Gear/speed (mph) ....forward: 1/2.00, 2/3.50, 3/5.90

Willys Universal Jeep CJ 3A

Manufacturer	Willys-Overland Motors, Inc., Toledo, OH
Nebraska test number	432
Test date	October 25 to November 2, 1949
Test tractor serial number	108196
Years produced	1949–1951
Engine	Willys vertical L-head
Test engine serial number	J 226916
Cylinders	4
Bore and stroke (in.)	3.125 x 4.375
Rated rpm	2,000
Compression ratio	6.48:1
Displacement (c.i.)	134.2
Fuel	gasoline
Fuel tank capacity (gal.)	10.50
Carburetor	Carter W-O-6365-A, 1.00-in.
Air cleaner	Donaldson
Ignition	Auto-Lite with 6-v battery
Cooling capacity (gal.)	2.75

Maximum brake horsepower tests

PTO/belt horsepower	28.43
Crankshaft rpm	1,998
Fuel use (gal./hr.)	3.68

Maximum drawbar horsepower tests

Gear	1st
Drawbar horsepower	24.32
Pull weight (lb.)	2,148
Speed (mph)	4.25
Percent slippage	5.46
SAE drawbar horsepower	19.09
SAE belt/PTO horsepower	25.32
Type	4 wheel drive
Front tire (in.)	7.00 x 15
Rear tire (in.)	7.00 x 15
Length (in.)	130
Height (in.)	66.75
Tread width (in.)	48.25
Weight (lb.)	2,203
Gear/speed (mph)	forward: 1/4.60, 2/8.20, 3/11.20, 4/12.90, 5/20.20, 6/31.30; reverse: 1/3.40, 2/8.20

Willys Farm Jeep

Manufacturer	Willys Motors Inc., Toledo, OH
Nebraska test number	502
Test date	August 28 to September 4, 1953
Test tractor serial number	453GC2 10083
Years produced	1953–1954
Engine	Willys CJ3B vertical F-head
Test engine serial number	4J 29621
Cylinders	4
Bore and stroke (in.)	3.125 x 4.375
Rated rpm	2,400
Compression ratio	6.9:1
Displacement (c.i.)	134.2
Fuel	gasoline
Fuel tank capacity (gal.)	10.50
Carburetor	Carter YF938S, 1.25-in.
Air cleaner	Oakes
Ignition	Auto-Lite with 6-v battery
Cooling capacity (gal.)	2.75

Maximum brake horsepower tests

PTO/belt horsepower	35.23
Crankshaft rpm	2,401
Fuel use (gal./hr.)	3.39

Maximum drawbar horsepower tests

Gear	1st
Drawbar horsepower	25.40
Pull weight (lb.)	2,317
Speed (mph)	4.11
Percent slippage	8.32
SAE drawbar horsepower	20.42
SAE belt/PTO horsepower	31.61
Type	4 wheel drive
Front wheel (in.)	7.00 x 15
Rear wheel (in.)	7.00 x 15
Length (in.)	130
Height (in.)	66.75
Tread width (in.)	48.25
Weight (lb.)	2,160
Gear/speed (mph)	forward: 1/4.60, 2/8.20, 3/11.20, 4/12.90, 5/20.20, 6/31.30; reverse: 1/3.40, 2/8.20

Chapter 87

WISCONSIN

Wisconsin E, 16-30

Manufacturer	Wisconsin Farm Tractor Co., Sauk City, WI
Nebraska test number	21
Test date	June 9–18, 1920
Test tractor serial number	2450
Years produced	1920–1921
Engine	Climax vertical L-head
Test engine serial number	2669
Cylinders	4
Bore and stroke (in.)	5.00 x 6.50
Rated rpm	900
Displacement (c.i.)	510.5
Fuel	kerosene/gasoline
Main tank capacity (gal.)	18
Auxiliary tank capacity (gal.)	6
Carburetor	Stromberg M3 (Schebler A), 1.50-in.
Air cleaner	Bennett
Ignition	Eisemann G4 magneto
Cooling capacity (gal.)	11

Maximum brake horsepower tests

PTO/belt horsepower	31.50
Crankshaft rpm	914
Fuel use (gal./hr.)	5.64

Maximum drawbar horsepower tests

Gear	low
Drawbar horsepower	22.22
Pull weight (lb.)	3,426
Speed (mph)	2.43
Percent slippage	15.30
SAE drawbar horsepower	16
SAE belt/PTO horsepower	30
Type	4 wheel
Front wheel (in.)	steel: 34 x 6
Rear wheel (in.)	steel: 52 x 12
Length (in.)	wheelbase: 92; total: 130
Height (in.)	65
Rear width (in.)	66
Weight (lb.)	5,440
Gear/speed (mph)	forward: 1/2.53, 2/3.66; reverse: 1/2.00

Chapter 88

ZETOR

Zetor 50 Super Diesel

Manufacturer	Zavody Jana Svermy, Brno, Czechoslovakia
Nebraska test number	748
Test date	July 5–16, 1960
Test tractor serial number	0 105 02188
Engine	Zetor vertical L-head
Test engine serial number	0 105 01917
Cylinders	4
Bore and stroke (in.)	4.134 x 4.724
Rated rpm	1,650
Compression ratio	15.6:1
Displacement (c.i.)	254
Fuel	diesel
Ignition	12-v battery

Maximum brake horsepower tests

PTO/belt horsepower	49.47
Crankshaft rpm	1,650
Fuel use (gal./hr.)	3.15

Maximum drawbar horsepower tests

Gear	5th
Drawbar horsepower	43.98
Pull weight (lb.)	4,361
Speed (mph)	3.78
Percent slippage	7.60
SAE drawbar horsepower	44.25
SAE belt/PTO horsepower	49..47
Type	standard
Front wheel (in.)	6.50 x 20
Rear wheel (in.)	14.00 x 28
Tread width (in.)	54.37–71.63
Weight (lb.)	6,246
Gear/speed (mph)	forward: 1/0.73, 2/1.40, 3/2.44, 4/2.90, 5/4.18, 6/5.54, 7/9.63, 8/16.50; reverse: 1/0.73, 2/2.90

Appendix
BIBLIOGRAPHY

Agrimotor. Chicago, 1917–1922.

The American Thresherman. Madison, WI, 1908–1920.

Barger, E. L., W. M. Carleton, E. G. McKibben, and R. Bainer. *Tractors and Their Power Units*. New York: John Wiley & Sons, Inc., 1952.

The Book of Knowledge. New York: The Grolier Society Inc., 1947.

California Cultivator. Los Angeles: G. H. A. Goodwin, Cultivator Publishing Co., 1909–1916.

Cooper, M. R., G. I. Barton, and A. P. Brodell. *Progress of Farm Mechanization*. U.S.D.A. Misc. Pub. 630, October 1947.

Department of Agriculture. *Yearbook*. Statistics. U.S.D.A., 1918–1923.

The Encyclopedia Americana. New York: Americana Corporation, 1945.

Erb, David, and E. Brumbaugh. *Full Steam Ahead*. St. Joseph, MI: American Society of Agricultural Engineers, 1993.

Farm Implement News. Chicago, 1909, 1911, 1915.

Farm Power. Madison, WI, 1908–1920.

Fay, Guy. *International Harvester Tractor Data Book*. Osceola, WI: MBI Publishing Company, 1997.

Gray, R. B. *The Agricultural Tractor, 1855–1950*. St. Joseph, MI: American Society of Agricultural Engineers, 1954.

Hurst, W. M., and L. M. Church. *Power and Machinery in Agriculture*. U.S.D.A. Misc. Pub. 157, April 1933.

Hurt, R. Douglas. *American Farm Tools*. Manhattan, KS: Sunflower University Press, 1982.

Larsen, L. F., and L. I. Leviticus. *Thirty Years of Nebraska Tractor Testing*. ASAE Paper No. 76-1045.

Nebraska Tractor Test Reports. No. 1–No. 782. Department of Agricultural Engineering, University of Nebraska, 1920–1960.

Pacific Rural Press. San Francisco: Dewey & Co., 1914.

Red Tractor Book. Kansas City, MO: Implement & Tractor, 1920–1964.

Rose, Philip S. *Analysis and Report of Tractor Industry*. Unpublished report, University of California Library, Special Collections, 1915.

Seyfarth, Arthur C. *Tractor History*. Unpublished manuscript, International Harvester, 1932

Svensson, Karl-Ake. *Volatile Tractor Fuels and Their Effect on Tractor Engine Performance*. Unpublished thesis, Iowa State College, Library, 1948.

Wendel, C. H. *The Allis-Chalmers Story*. Osceola, WI: MBI Publishing Company, 1988.

INDEX